VOLUME TWO

Britain and the War for the Union

Britain
&the War
for the Union

Volume Two

Brian Jenkins

McGill-Queen's
University Press

Montreal

This book has been published with the
help of a grant from the Social Science
Federation of Canada, using funds
provided by the Social Sciences and
Humanities Research Council of
Canada.

Design by Ronald Caplan
Printed in Canada by
Imprimerie Gagné Ltée

FOR
William Davies

AND
William MacVean

CONTENTS

PREFACE

THIS VOLUME CONCLUDES MY STUDY of Britain and the American Civil War. I did not set out to supplant the classic study written by E. D. Adams a half-century ago nor can I claim to have provided a novel interpretation of this phase of Anglo-American relations. I have benefited greatly from the work of others, although in my research I have concentrated on primary resources. The result is, I hope, a synthesis which contains at least a small measure of originality. This is diplomatic history but not narrowly focused on the exchange of correspondence. I have attempted through narrative and analysis (not incompatible elements) to describe the broad range of factors which influenced Britain's course. At a later date I plan to examine the postwar settlement, in the belief that the consequences of Britain's conduct and her people's attitudes during the war merit further investigation.

Readers familiar with the first volume will note two changes of form in the second. Summaries have been provided for all except three chapters; in the case of chapters 9, 10, and 14 the course of the narrative rendered a summary unnecessary. Some readers of the first volume found the notes less detailed and thus less helpful than they would have wished. In the present volume, therefore, instead of indicating only the sources of direct quotations and providing a general bibliographical essay as on the previous occasion, I have incorporated in the notes references to all the material I found particularly useful. Individual references for direct quotations have been retained whenever the source is not clear in the omnibus note. I have resorted to the old designation "Pickett Papers" merely to distinguish those diplomatic records of the Confederacy which are to be found in the Library of Congress but not in the published collections.

I wish to repeat here the acknowledgments I first made five years ago. The debts of gratitude owed to my wife and to my friends William and Margaret MacVean are too large ever to be repaid. For their financial support I thank the Canada Council and my University, which has also been generous in granting me the time in which to research and write. His Grace the Duke of Norfolk, and His Grace's Archivist and Librarian, Francis W. Steer, granted me permission to quote from the Lyons Papers; the Editor of *The Times* allowed me to use the Printing House Square Papers and I profited from the advice and friendly guidance of the newspaper's archivist, Gordon Phillips. I wish to thank H. C. Erwin for permission to quote from the Cobb Papers. Quotations from the Adams Papers are from microfilm edition, by permission of the Massachusetts Historical Society. Those from the Palmerston and the Shaftesbury Papers are by permission of the Trustees of the Broadlands Archives, and the National Trust granted permission to use and to quote from the Disraeli Collection at Hughenden. I wish to thank the Trustees of the British Museum, the Library of University College, London, University of Nottingham Library, Sheffield Public Library, Manchester Central Reference Library, the Manuscript Division of the Library of Congress, the University of Rochester Library, the University of North Carolina Library, and Duke University Library for permission to use manuscripts in their possession. Finally, I would be remiss if I failed to express my appreciation of the kindness of Major Richard Gregory in permitting me to make use of his grandfather's papers, or overlooked the hospitality of Mrs. Hilda Kirkwood of St. Andrews, Scotland, who as custodian of the W. S. Lindsay Papers (which she is preparing for publication) ensured that the brief time I spent in St. Andrews was both profitable and enjoyable.

BRIAN JENKINS
BISHOP'S UNIVERSITY
LENNOXVILLE, QUEBEC

Introduction

FROM THE OUTSET, Britain had seemed to have it within her power to decide the outcome of the American Civil War. Had she been so inclined she could have facilitated the North's suppression of the rebellion. An avowed policy of benevolent neutrality towards the Union would have done much to deflate a Southern cause puffed up with the expectation of foreign, but specifically British, assistance. However, few observers at the time, European or American, expected Britain to follow that course, and even those favoured with the advantages of hindsight ought to be able to understand why she did not side with the North. Britain's relations with the Union had not been of a kind that would spur her to come to its aid. Two wars and a succession of crises within a lifetime (Prime Minister Palmerston, born only a year after the revolutionary conflict, had been a junior minister during that of 1812–14), and a series of diplomatic settlements in which the United States seemed to have fared the better, were not the foundations for a relationship of mutual friendship and understanding. Moreover, the British had reason to look with particular coldness upon the Northern states. It was there that talk of the inevitable annexation of British North America had always been loudest, culminating in the irritating calls during the secession crisis for the taking of the British provinces as compensation for the loss of the Gulf states. There also the United States had developed an industrial system second only to Britain's, and the Americans' challenge for the control of trade had already spread from Latin America to the west coast of Africa. These conflicting economic interests had long been only dimly perceived, but the passage of the protective Morrill Tariff by a Congress from which most Southerners had withdrawn did much to sharpen the focus. Was it surprising, therefore, that the division of such an arrogant and burgeoning economic, commercial, and political rival, whose citizens had readily identified Britain as the great obstacle impeding their nation's rise to full greatness, excited so little dismay? Then there was the welcome thought that the Union's troubles would finally still an agitation for domestic political reforms which had drawn so much inspiration from the success of the United States. As one American wrote, after studying a selection of British journals, "Our democracy is disliked by their aristocracy; our manufactures rival theirs; our commerce threatens at many points to supplant theirs. We are in dangerous proximity to some of their best colonies." Dread of American power and its future growth, he concluded, controlled "the words and policy of many of England's greatest and best men."[1]

Dislike and distrust of the Republic may have swayed the opinions of more Englishmen than did fear in 1861, but the undeniable absence of widespread sympathy for the Union had not encouraged serious discussion of a policy favourable to the North. An alternative course, that of embracing the Confederacy in order to make permanent the Republic's division, failed to arouse much enthusiasm within the government. After all, the South's behaviour had not been entirely free of irritants. Her resort to export taxes on staples was considered almost as objectionable as the Union's imposition of duties on imported British manufactures, while the subsequent organization of a cotton embargo gave rise to the natural concern neither to be seen nor even to be thought to be responding to the economic pressure exerted by the Confederacy. Instead, Britain had quickly opted for a policy of neutrality which was ultimately to win for her only the enmity of both belligerents.

If neutrality may seem to be the relatively safe middle ground on which so many politicians instinctively seek shelter, the path when there is never quite as straight and narrow as it first appeared. Leading members of the government harboured as active a dislike of Americans and their institutions as did influential segments of popular opinion. Not a few of them wished the Union to fail and even more were alarmed lest its death throes bring economic dislocation and social misery to the textile districts of Lancashire and Cheshire. It was this very danger that the South had confidently expected to be able to exploit, yet Britain persisted with her neutrality throughout the first year of war. Why? The answer is to be found in the initial success of the American secretary of state, William Seward, in convincing the Palmerston government of the North's determination to resist by force any further step towards intervention. Seward's behaviour was carefully calculated to play upon British concern for the safety of their all too vulnerable empire in North America and their preoccupation with the balance of power in Europe. Difficulties with the Americans would give the untrustworthy and opportunistic French emperor too much room for manoeuvre on the Continent, or so Palmerston and Lord Russell, his foreign secretary, feared. A policy of neutrality, or inaction, could be rationalized not merely as the safest course but as

2

one that would ultimately enable Britain to gain all the benefits of intervention. British policy was shaped by the comforting conviction that the American war could not last long and that its outcome was certain. The Confederacy was simply too vast in size and too numerous in population to be conquered and subdued. Even Northerners would not be able to hide from this fact indefinitely.

The upshot was that the closest Britain came to involvement in the war, during its first year, was over the *Trent* episode. The stopping of this British mail packet on the high seas and the removal of two Confederate emissaries to Europe, James Murray Mason and John Slidell, made the Union captain responsible, Charles Wilkes, a hero in the North. However, it also brought the two nations to the edge of the precipice. Britain's demands for a disavowal of this act and the return of the captives were accompanied by preparations for the worst. The export of saltpetre was banned, the naval squadron on the North American Station was strengthened, and the military garrison in Canada was substantially increased. In the face of such resolute behaviour prudence triumphed over pride in the Union, and complete humiliation was skilfully avoided by Seward. He had kept open an escape hatch, by preventing the administration from formally endorsing Wilkes's conduct, and his despatch announcing the surrender of the captives was a masterpiece. By this act, he reassured his countrymen, the United States was not only remaining true to itself as a defender of neutral rights but had at last brought the British to accept the American position.

By the spring of 1862, however, it had become all too clear to Englishmen that the American war was going to drag on for many more months, if not years. Neither South nor North showed any sign of giving up the fight easily or early. No less evident was the deteriorating condition of the Lancashire textile industry and its operatives. Meanwhile the Confederacy's abandonment of the experiment with a cotton embargo focused attention upon the increasingly efficient Union blockade of the Southern ports as the primary reason for the shortage of inexpensive fibre which in turn silenced so many mill towns. Consequently, as hopes for an end to the fighting faded and the shadows of economic distress lengthened, the cries for intervention grew more strident, and during the course of the following year the British government wrestled with this problem. As for the two belligerents, they each struggled to influence the decision.

The year 1862 was to see the Confederacy's role in the international drama reduced to that of membership in the supporting cast. Two ambitious and frustrated men had already resigned from the post of secretary of state when Jefferson Davis appointed Judah Benjamin to the position in the spring of 1862. Although the new secretary brought an agile mind and a successful gambler's guile to his task, these attributes could not long disguise the weakness of the hand he was asked to play. The first year had revealed that cotton's foreign rule was by no means as absolute as Southerners had supposed, while the second year of fighting disclosed that victorious as were its armies the Confederacy lacked the power to inflict upon the Union defeats so crippling that Britain would act decisively. Desperately, Benjamin attempted to convince the French that their interests in America were far from identical with those of the British. From this it followed that they should separate their American policy from that of Britain. He was to achieve little.

Seward had his own set of problems. The Union's fluctuating military fortunes frequently obliged him to act smartly in order to adapt policies conceived in the flush of victory to the very different situation created by defeat. Moreover, he had to contend with persistent challenges to his authority over foreign affairs, even to his seat in the cabinet, and a popular mood of bitterness against Britain. Yet in his dealings with her he sought to follow for the most part a conciliatory course. Charles Sumner, chairman of the Foreign Relations Committee and the secretary of state's persistent critic, had advocated such a policy in 1861 and the spring of 1863 was to find him boasting that he had triumphed at last. But Seward's rejection of this diplomatic strategy during the early months of the conflict had been wise. Ironically, his grip on foreign policy was to be loosened at the very moment of triumph, when Britain finally turned her back on intervention.

ONE

The Belligerents

JEFFERSON DAVIS TOOK HIS OATH of office as president of the Confederate States of America on February 22, 1862. A plain black suit which accentuated the pallor of his complexion, and cheerless weather, added to the sombreness of the occasion. The South's future seemed no brighter than the murky skies, and the irony of now inaugurating a "permanent" Confederacy must have struck some of those who witnessed the ceremony. In the west Forts Henry and Donelson had been lost and with them command of the strategically important Tennessee and Cumberland rivers. In the east historic Roanoke Island, symbol as well as strong point, had been taken by a Federal fleet and 12,000 men. Albemarle Sound had thus been opened to the enemy, making possible a far more effective blockade of the North Carolina coastline. Bad as this was, worse soon followed. Early in March the Federals exploited their control of Pamlico Sound to seize the town of New Bern. Its fall exposed the Weldon Railroad, one of the few spokes in that unreliable wheel of communication upon which the Confederate armies in Virginia and the greatly swollen population of Richmond depended for supplies. By the middle of the month the troops at Manassas had pulled back to the south bank of the Rappahannock.

To the residents of the Confederate capital it was painfully clear that the war was rapidly closing in on them. "It must be acknowledged that the Yankees are gathering fast around us, and that we are getting into what might be called a very tight place," the *Richmond Dispatch* conceded. "They are at all points of the compass and like the anaconda, to which they take a peculiar delight in likening their army, are preparing to draw in their folds and crush us to death, if they can." The newspaper attempted to rally its readers' spirits by showing how favourable their position was when compared with that of the Romans after Cannae, or of the Spanish after the first Napoleon's invasion of the Iberian peninsula, but confused and frustrated at the apparent

5

frittering away of the strategic advantage won at Bull Run the previous year, the inhabitants of Richmond were becoming demoralized.[1]

Drooping spirits in Richmond and elsewhere were not revived by later reports from the west. The loss of the forts had been followed by that of Island no. 10 on the Mississippi and then in April came news of the bloody repulse at Shiloh. While the South was still mourning the death of Gen. Albert Sidney Johnston in that battle it suffered yet another "stunning blow" with the fall of New Orleans. The manner of this defeat was almost as unnerving as its consequences, for the attacking force had swept past the forts and brushed aside the Confederate naval squadron protecting the city. Another of those strong points which in a well-intentioned effort to bolster sagging public morale the authorities had boasted was virtually impregnable had gone. The reverse was doubly damaging, for no one could dispute the city's importance. Even though the port had been blockaded, New Orleans had remained a vital manufacturing and industrial centre. The Confederacy possessed so few of these that the loss of one was a very serious setback. It had been equally important as a communications centre. Through it had come the herds of Texas cattle and from it had been distributed sugar and molasses. No wonder " 'a thick darkness that could be felt' brooded over the land."[2]

As this chronicle of defeats began to unfold and public confidence to waver, the president's opponents in Congress found the courage to attack both the policies and the personalities of his administration. Long before New Orleans fell the House rang with the call for a policy of "Audacity, audacity, audacity," echoing Danton's immortal cry in revolutionary France seventy years earlier in a demand for the abandonment of Davis's defensive military strategy.[3]

The target of many critics was Judah Benjamin, whom Davis had moved from the wings to the centre of the stage when he transferred him from the Attorney-General's Department to that of War in September 1861. Benjamin had applied himself with characteristic diligence to the welter of problems and the mountain of administrative detail in his new department, leaving to a president vastly more experienced in these matters the actual direction of military affairs. Nevertheless, as acting-secretary he was held responsible for the reverses in February, especially the loss of Roanoke Island. Nor did he strengthen his position by quarrelling with several of the public's heroes. Like many a civilian he failed to allow for the acute sensitivity and punctilio of soldiers, with the result that he soon ran afoul of

6

several generals, among them the commander of the military district that included the Confederate capital, Joseph Johnston, a man whose undoubted ability was frequently obscured by a tiresomely difficult personality. Johnston's denunciation of the secretary at a dinner party attended by several congressmen, an attack which one of them repeated in the House, made Benjamin's position untenable. The assaults upon his competence increased in vigour while those upon him personally redoubled in vulgarity. He was vilified as "Judas Iscariot Benjamin," and "Mr. Davis's pet Jew."[4]

"The clamor compelled him [the president] to change his cabinet," Gen. Howell Cobb wrote to his wife, "and you know him well enough to know that he must have winced awfully under the infliction." Although Davis was obliged to try to broaden the appeal of his administration and disarm at least some of its critics, he was not a man to surrender unconditionally to his enemies or cast aside a valued adviser and loyal colleague. While the resignation of Thomas Bragg as attorney-general permitted him to appoint Thomas Watts of Alabama to that position, thereby satisfying the demands of former Union Whigs for cabinet representation, and Gen. George Randolph was summoned from the field to serve as secretary of war, stilling temporarily the criticism of that department, Davis refused to dismiss the unpopular Benjamin. The State Department was vacant once more. The ambitious Robert Hunter, who hoped to be the Confederacy's second president, had resigned in order to avoid sharing the responsibility for failures that might tarnish his presidential lustre. The president's nomination of Benjamin was approved by the Senate, but only after a fierce wrangle and the price Davis paid for this "ungracious and reckless defiance to popular sentiment" was unabated criticism of the government. Moreover, it now began to focus increasingly upon him. "Mr. Davis has sacrificed to popular clamor without yielding to public opinion," an angry *Richmond Examiner* protested. "The representation of the Synagogue is not diminished; it remains full. The administration has now an opportunity of making some reputation," the newspaper continued sarcastically, "for nothing being expected of it, of course every success will be clear gain." Predictable as this was, for the *Examiner* along with the *Charleston Mercury* had already won notoriety as unrelenting and unjust critics of the president, the ranks of the opposition were growing. The *Southern Confederacy*, having surveyed the current difficulties, asked in a leading article "Who is to blame?" and replied: Jefferson Davis.[5]

7

The beginning of May brought no relief from the demoralizing string of defeats. Yorktown fell and a huge Union army under the command of George B. McClellan began a slow but disconcertingly deliberate march up the peninsula towards Richmond. Then the Confederate ironclad *Virginia*, "the iron diadem of the South," the visible proof of the South's capacity to match through ingenuity its far more powerful enemy, was beached and burned by her commander. Although self-destruction was the only alternative to the vessel's capture by the advancing Federals, a bitterly disappointed Stephen Mallory, still smarting from the ignominious failure of the Confederate flotilla at New Orleans, complained privately that it had been premature and he looked now only for divine assistance. "May God protect us and cure us of weakness and folly," he commented. But if Lincoln could joke that while he hoped to have God on his side he must have Kentucky, Southerners might well have said the same of the European powers, especially Britain. Proud boasts of being able to fight on alone to victory now had a notably hollow ring to them. The truth was, as some Southerners frankly admitted, that they had small chance of escaping from the anaconda's tightening coils without foreign assistance. This realization helped to fan a long-smoldering antagonism toward Britain.[6]

The conduct of the British, and to a lesser extent of the French, in persistently refusing to recognize the existence of a *de facto* Confederate government, even though it had governed the South for more than a year, was assailed as contrary to precedent and to the general practice of nations, and repugnant to reason and justice. That "superannuated old humbug" Russell was singled out for particular criticism. He had revealed a perfect incomprehension of his nation's true interest: namely, the promotion of Southern independence. He was accused both of hostility to the Confederacy and a "base compliance" with the demands of the enemy. Lurking behind these verbal assaults, and occasionally spurring them on, was the nagging fear that Britain had resolved to allow the two American belligerents to fight themselves into a condition of mutual exhaustion. Were the British going to stand aside until the South had been destroyed as a large-scale producer of cotton, thereby opening the way for their Indian empire to establish a world-wide monopoly of its production? Others found a far less sinister explanation for the English paralysis in the conduct of William Seward. Grudgingly, they conceded that he had simply outfoxed the British, that by his return of Mason and Slidell and with his promise to throw open captured cotton ports he had lulled them to sleep. "England and France find themselves fairly, or if not fairly, at least fully deceived, outwitted, and ready to be defied," the *Wilmington Daily Journal* concluded.[7]

Nevertheless, some Southerners continued to take heart from reports that the cotton shortage was at last beginning to pinch hard in Britain and France, and that the unemployed there were growing restive. Their task was obvious. The Union proclamation lifting the blockade from the ports of New Orleans, Beaufort, and Port Royal must be shown to be worthless. The British and the French had to be taught the hard lesson that Northern victories were more to be feared than welcomed, because they would be followed by the destruction not just the withholding of cotton. "It is all burned or to be burned," the *Richmond Dispatch* defiantly declared, "and there will be no crop next year."[8] Southerners, by demonstrating their determination to fight on despite the recent reverses, burning their cotton if necessary, would at last convince foreign nations that the division of the Union was final, that they were in fact as well as name a separate people, and that the "protraction of an unavailing war for conquest is only a barbarism unworthy of the spirit of the age."[9]

The Confederacy's failure to obtain international recognition and support was naturally a recurring topic of debate in Congress. Its members were concerned to emphasize the South's grim resolve to soldier on. April 16 saw the passage of a Conscription Act which embraced all white males between the ages of eighteen and thirty-five, although its military effectiveness and its popularity were not enhanced by the liberal exemptions enacted five days later. However, there was no clearcut solution to the problem of foreign recognition. Congressmen were unequally divided between advocates of a suppliant policy and those who favoured a posture, if not a policy, of defiance. Among the former were the free traders who, having failed twice already to secure the repeal of the tariff laws, now struggled to resuscitate their moribund proposal. They called for the admission of all "imports duty free, except such as may be imported from the United States of America." They pointed to the free trade resolutions passed by both the Georgia and South Carolina legislatures, and those by the Commercial and Planters Convention and the Charleston Chamber of Commerce, as evidence of widespread public support. They cited the secretary of the treasury's own report to prove that the revenue raised by the tariff barely covered the costs of its collection.

9

Clearly the South would sacrifice little financially by committing itself to free trade. Just exactly what it would gain diplomatically remained in dispute, however. "England and France cannot be purchased by any propositions which we may submit," one realist warned, "and our action in this case will bring about a feeling of contempt for us on the part of those two Governments." Although the proposal sailed through the House it foundered in the Senate. What emerged from the upper chamber was a resolution authorizing the administration to offer European nations trading privileges in return for their raising of the blockade.[10]

More representative than the free traders of the bewildered and irritated mood of the Southern people were those members of Congress who called for retaliation against the aloof Europeans. There was some talk of recalling the commissioners to Britain and France, though what useful purpose this would serve was never made clear, and there was much discussion of the anomalous position of the foreign consuls in the Confederacy. For more than a year British and French consuls accredited to the Government of the United States had been permitted to exercise their functions in Confederate ports. The persistent refusal of the two nations to recognize the Confederacy now excited demands for the expulsion of these officials. Popular as this act would have been, Congress held its hand. This hesitation was understandable, for it was becoming ever more difficult to ignore an unpalatable and restraining fact—the South simply did not have the means of compelling the European powers to act. The Confederacy was condemned to play the role of a supplicant, to appeal for rather than demand or extort foreign recognition, and this truth was plain for all to see in the way Congress dealt with that commodity once thought to be diplomatically omnipotent, cotton.

Those who had always disputed the international sovereignty of cotton had been vindicated by events, and they were joined by others who had not only abandoned the notion that cotton was king but with it all hope of foreign intervention in the conflict. In the words of one congressman, "Sooner than England would employ her operatives at the expense of war with the United States, she would convert herself into a great eleemosynary institution for the purpose of providing for them by charity."[11] If such candour, born of pessimism or prescience, was unusual, there was nevertheless a discernible weakening of faith in the efficacy of a policy founded upon the restriction of cotton supplies. Although there was no lack of evidence that Britain's cotton shortage was daily growing more serious, efforts to extend the embargo organized the previous summer were strenuously opposed. The new proposal was for a virtual halt in cotton cultivation and a requirement that planters raise provisions, cattle, hogs, and sheep instead. No one questioned the necessity of stepping up the production of foodstuffs, needed both by the armies and the population, but the majority of congressmen still considered the production of the "great staple" essential to the welfare and prosperity of the Confederacy. Only if the South continued to accumulate vast surpluses of cotton would it have the capacity at the war's end to destroy the competition of India, by dumping them upon the international market and driving down the price. The fear that any prohibition of cotton cultivation and the continued prevention of its export would, far from compelling Britain's intervention, simply "build up the English East India cotton interest, and at length transfer altogether the power of King Cotton to her own throne," was beginning to grip many influential Confederates.[12]

The Davis administration, which had discreetly encouraged the embargo movement initially, had also begun to worry about the present and future consequences of the restrictive policy. Some of its members shared the growing apprehension that Britain would ultimately reap the benefit of the cotton shortage. "Her efforts to raise this staple in India, Egypt and Africa indicates her determination to look elsewhere than to us for it," Stephen Mallory concluded. "She would have nearly the monopoly of the cotton of the Earth in such case, and other countries would receive it in the shape of manufactured products only from her artisans."[13] The former secretary of state, Robert Hunter, who often served as an administration spokesman in the Senate, had made much the same point in opposing the call for an embargo on the cultivation of cotton. But there was an even more pressing reason to moderate the policy of restricting exports, as C. G. Memminger explained to his fellow South Carolinians when they forbade the shipment of cotton from their ports except by permission of the Confederate and state authorities.

By the spring of 1862 the South's financial illness, always chronic, had become critical. As baldly summarized by Thomas Bragg, Secretary Memminger "has nearly exhausted his means—large treasury notes will not circulate—small ones cannot be issued fast enough, and the am[oun]t issued is so great now that he fears he can no farther go." Yet another measure of the Confederacy's plight was the 70 per cent premium commanded by sterling bills. As a specie-poor country, but one rich in agricultural commodities, the Confederacy had quickly resorted to produce loans, often accompanied by an issue of Treasury notes, as a principal means of financing the war. Of course, of all the produce Southerners raised and were willing to exchange for government bonds cotton was the easiest to dispose of overseas. Therefore not only its continued cultivation but also its exportation were essential if Confederate finances were to avoid total collapse.[14]

Cotton was the one commodity which could serve as a basis for establishing the South's international credit, and the administration had taken the first step in that direction as early as January. At the very least, every shipment abroad earned the precious bills of exchange needed to make the purchases of military supplies without which the Confederacy, as an almost exclusively agricultural state, could not hope to survive the war. "Any obstruction to these shipments is, therefore, serious hindrance," Memminger warned the South Carolinians. "It cuts off the supply of funds." His warning was heeded, and what this suggested, as did the government's decision to purchase a blockade-runner, load her with cotton, and then run her through the blockade off Charleston, was that the need "to get means abroad" had become so desperate that the cabinet had been compelled to abandon the policy of attempting to coerce foreign intervention by withholding cotton. The force of necessity had driven it back to offering "the inducement which the free exportation of cotton holds out to all the world to break the blockade" of the South's ports. This was a far cry from the boastful self-assurance which had characterized Confederate policy only a few months earlier.[15]

The unenviable but crucial task of directing a renewed search for foreign recognition and support fell to the unpopular Benjamin. Physically, he was short, fat, and unimpressive. His "Jewish" features rarely escaped comment by his contemporaries, who noted the "keen black eye, marked nose and heavy mouth,"[16] the broad forehead, and the short black beard. His full, olive-coloured, and deceptively youthful face wore a perpetual smile or smirk. To some a source of reassurance, suggesting as it did "that he had just heard good news, which would be immediately promulgated for public delectation,"[17] to others it was "one of those serpent-like smiles which seems to assume that whoever opposes him is destined to come to grief."[18] One of his undoubted physical assets was a voice which an enemy conceded was "as dulcet and mellifluous as that of a nightingale,"[19] and he exploited it to good effect in conversation and debate. In private life he was a charming and gregarious man, one who was fond of gambling, "loved a good dinner," a glass of good wine, "and revelled in the delights of fine Havana cigars."[20] His keg-like build was a tribute to the excellence of his personal chef, who had developed his skills while tempting Cunard passengers crossing the stormy Atlantic. Yet this "Seal-sleak, black-eyed lawyer and epicure" was an intimate of the austere, prickly president. What attracted Davis to this man? He certainly admired his immense capacity for work and respected his intelligence. Benjamin willingly toiled away all day and every day, Sundays and holidays, giving unstintingly of his time and bringing to each problem a subtle and sophisticated mind. Almost as remarkable as his intellect was his disposition, for in him "hope and humor" seemed as inexhaustible as energy. He was a constant source of cheer to a president already worrying himself into chronically poor health. Moreover, he was unpretentious, unassuming, and deferential. Ever available, ever prepared to do what he could to lighten the president's burdens, to listen, to offer sensible advice whenever it was sought, and to executive faithfully his instructions, he was the friend, adviser, and subordinate Davis required.[21]

Benjamin freely admitted during the war and after that at its beginning he was one of those who had placed too much faith in the power of cotton. To him as to other Southerners, it had been unthinkable that the British government would allow a mighty industry to be closed down, throwing out of work thousands of operatives, for want of cotton. And if they did, it was inconceivable that the British people would long tolerate such a policy. This confidence underlay his predictions to William Howard Russell of *The Times*, to whom he had granted an interview in the spring of 1861, that Britain would lose her coyness about acknowledging a slave state, and would disregard any blockade the Union sought to mount at Confederate ports, once the traditional cotton shipping season opened. But October passed without the expected move by the British, and Benjamin's response, or so Robert Bunch reported from his consular post in Charleston, had been to assume the leadership of "the party which is disposed to risk everything upon the alleged necessity to Europe of Cotton and Tobacco, and to force recognition by withholding these productions." It was, in short, a gambler's policy. In any event, Bunch viewed Benjamin's appointment as secretary of state as "an unfortunate one," likely to lead to "disagreeable consequences."[22]

Identified by the British as an inflexible opponent of "the slightest concession in favour of Foreign Nations," the new secretary eagerly strengthened this impression. During a very long conversation with the British consul at Richmond in May he conceded that the loss of New Orleans was a serious blow to the South, but he warned that this Union victory had not brought any nearer the solution of Britain's problems of cotton supply. Little had fallen into Federal hands there and little would—Southerners would destroy it first—and there was no prospect of the staple being forwarded from the Confederate interior to any port under Union control. The implication was clear enough: to obtain cotton Englishmen must deal with Southerners. Nor had they any time to lose, for Benjamin warned that unless the planters saw some hope soon of being able to export it they would simply cease to cultivate the staple. Already the crop planted in the current year was but a fraction of that of earlier ones. The British consul at Savannah had given his government much the same news, forwarding the estimate that no more than one-tenth of the 1861 crop was in the ground in Georgia. The reason, he believed, was not so much the planters' inability to export what they grew but their need for cereals, cut off as they had been by the war from traditional suppliers in Kentucky and Tennessee.[23] Whatever the reason, the prospects were not rosy. The longer the war dragged on the greater the inevitable disruption of cotton production.

If the future was uncertain, what could not be denied in 1862 was that there were large stocks of cotton being held in the South. The surplus, together with the very favourable exchange rate offered for sterling bills, had tempted a number of wealthy Lancashire spinners to speculate. They made large purchases at the bargain price of the equivalent of two cents a pound. Their cotton had been stored in warehouses in the interior, but even there it was liable to be burned by the Confederate military whenever Union troops came near. Seeking protection for the property of neutrals, agents for the spinners approached Benjamin. He replied that the South, learning from experience, could only conclude that whenever cotton belonging to neutrals fell into the hands of the enemy it would be confiscated. Disregarding neutral rights and unhindered by neutral powers, the Union appropriated the cotton for its own use. Consequently, the staple would continue to be put to the torch whenever threatened with capture unless neutral nations provided the Confederacy with an assurance, "officially communicated," that their nationals' property would be effectually protected from seizure and appropriation by the Union. If this was another "endeavour to enlist the active interference of European Powers," Benjamin knew that there was little likelihood of the British government meeting his condition. No doubt the most he hoped to obtain from his sedulous opposition to concession was agitation by the spinners for a change in their government's American policy. Certainly it did not represent the main thrust of his policy. His willingness to exploit any opportunity of exerting additional pressure upon the British ministry is less significant than the fact that Benjamin's appointment as secretary of state led to an attempt to banish Britain to the periphery of Confederate foreign relations. In truth, the publication of Russell's observations on the blockade had left the Confederacy with little choice but to look elsewhere for help.[24]

The new secretary's interest in the law of blockade long predated the Civil War. Sixteen years earlier, during the conflict with Mexico, he had published an article on the subject in *DeBow's Review*. It was evident from his response to Russell's remarks that he had continued to follow the subject with interest, and had "a memory like Macaulay's." Thus the British government's decision to accept as effective a blockade which merely stationed sufficient ships off a port to create an "evident danger" to vessels seeking to use it was immediately identified by Benjamin as an addition to the Declaration of Paris (1856), even a reversion to the wording of a far less satisfactory convention, that of 1801. "It can not but be obvious that any blockade may be demonstrated to be effective by this mode of reasoning," he complained. At one stroke the British had dismissed the Confederates' evidence of the blockade's ineffectiveness, so carefully amassed and in which they had placed so much hope. Beyond this, the British decision was resented because it was peculiarly disadvantageous to the South. The Confederacy possessed no commercial marine of its own in which to carry on trade, so it was completely dependent upon the vessels of other nations. Now the world's principal carrying nation had agreed to respect the blockade "pretensions" of the United States. Inevitably this further heightened the already well-developed sense of injustice in the South and added another to a lengthening list of grievances against Britain.[25]

The deepening animosity towards Britain was rooted, however, in the conviction that she was responsible for the prolongation of the bloody conflict. Southerners might disagree over what determined British policy, whether it was a desire to corner the cotton production of the world, or inept, even senile political leadership, but few would have challenged Benjamin's claim that "The continuance of the desolating warfare which is now ravaging this country is attributable in no small degree to the attitude of neutral nations in abstaining from the acknowledgment of our independent existence as a nation of the earth." National pride, hatred of the South, "the exasperation of defeat" had combined to dissuade the Lincoln administration from recognizing the "accomplished fact" of Confederate independence, but British recognition would compel the Union to confront this political reality. Perhaps it would inspire the organization of a large and influential Northern party committed to peace. At the very least, as "the verdict of an impartial jury" it would finally dash all Union hopes of reducing the South to submission. In short, just "a few words emanating from her Britannic Majesty" would end the struggle.[26] Believing this, many Southerners found it difficult either to understand or to forgive Britain's silence.

Could the French be coaxed into offering what the British withheld? Their predicament was generally believed to be even more serious than that of the British, who were obtaining some cotton at considerable expense from Egypt, Brazil, and India. Then again, the French could not be suspected of wishing to see the war prolonged for commercial reasons, for they did not have colonial resources of the fibre to develop. Benjamin found it difficult to believe that they were a party to Russell's apparent modification of the rules of blockade agreed to in Paris in 1856. Not having heard from Mason, because of poor communications with Europe, he was unaware of the commissioner's suspicion that the change had been discussed with and approved by the French prior to the announcement. Benjamin did write to Slidell instructing him to find out whether Russell's letter to Lyons met with "the sanction and concurrence of the French Government," but confident that it did not, he began to outline a new diplomatic strategy. He affirmed that the shortage of cotton in Europe was due to the neutrals' respect for Lincoln's blockade; he denied that it was being withheld by the Confederate government in an effort to extort European help; and he invited the neutral powers, "and France in particular, to come for our cotton, and it will be gladly furnished in exchange for her manufactures. If she prefers buying it with gold, the choice is hers."[27]

Although an almost identical despatch was sent to Mason in London, naming Britain, France was the focal point of Benjamin's policy. Thus in a supplementary instruction to Slidell four days later he proposed a convention with the French, one that would grant them the right to land all their products in the Confederacy duty-free in return for their raising of the blockade. As a further inducement he offered the emperor, whose finances were reputed to be shaky, a huge trading profit. The Confederacy was willing to deliver to the French at Southern ports a subsidy of 100,000 bales of cotton, which would be worth $12.5 million in Europe. Such a sum would be more than enough to "maintain afloat a considerable fleet for a length of time quite sufficient to open the Atlantic and Gulf ports to the commerce of France." Indeed, this windfall profit might easily be doubled, for the French goods carried out to the Confederacy would command very high prices there. Here then was a policy well calculated to appeal to the French, whose concern was not simply with the grave shortage of cotton but also the damage wrought by the war and the blockade to their traditional North American trade in luxury goods. If Benjamin was hopeful that the French would bite upon this bait and raise the blockade, he was no less willing to hook them for recognition instead. "If you find, then," he wrote to Slidell, "that it would be more feasible to use the discretion vested in you to procure a recognition than to raise the blockade, you are to consider yourself authorized to *use the same means* as are placed at your disposal for raising the blockade."[28]

The wisdom of plotting a new course overseas was confirmed by one of the earliest reports from Henry Hotze, the Confederacy's commercial agent in London (the title was little more than a euphemism for propagandist). Writing at the end of February, he admitted "that most of us here have been too rapid in our conclusions and too sanguine in our expectations as regards the policy of Europe, and especially England." He had found British opinion "cold and indifferent" to the Southern cause, concerned less with the principles at stake than the "vexatious interruption to its wonted routine of thought and pursuits." He fancied he detected what amounted to a "cowardly dread of war" with the Union, while the countervailing effects of the cotton shortage had not been all that the South had expected. Some manufacturers had even welcomed the disruption of supplies, because it allowed them to dispose, at unexpectedly high prices, of large stocks of cloth accumulated during the bumper crop years immediately before the war. As for the unemployed operatives, their sufferings had been eased by an unusually mild winter. Not to

17

be ignored either was the existence of "a large and influential class" which appeared to be deluding itself with "vague hopes" that a prolonged American war would finally liberate Lancashire from its dependence upon Southern cotton by artificially stimulating its cultivation in India.[29]

Rumours of a scheme to entice the French into intervening in the war had begun to swirl around the South from the moment of Benjamin's appointment. Then in April came not only the Senate resolution authorizing the president to offer trade concessions in exchange for the raising of the blockade, but also Henri Mercier's visit to Richmond. Naturally the Frenchman's arrival encouraged much excited speculation, and a fresh bloom of false optimism. "His friendly sentiments to the Southern Confederacy, and his contempt for Lincolnism and Sewardism are well known," the *Mobile Advertiser and Register* remarked. "We venture to predict that some morning, not long hence, a telegram will flash over the wires with the news that Emperor Napoleon has become tired of waiting on the dilatory policy of Great Britain and has recognized the independence of the Confederate States." After all, was not French industry suffering terribly as a result of the war, would not French ambitions in Mexico be furthered by Confederate friendship? The emperor, unlike Lord Russell, was not in his "dotage." Thus reports originating in Havana and Baltimore, that Napoleon had indeed "granted the boon we so much crave," were readily believed.[30] As so often in the past they proved to be nothing more than rumour, but far from succumbing to discouragement the public was determined to cling to the notion that the reports had merely been premature not false.

Even the eternally cheerful Benjamin must have drooped briefly, however, with the arrival in mid-May of a despatch from Slidell. Written almost two months earlier, it contained the depressing judgment "that in all that concerns us the initiative must be taken by England; that the Emperor sets such value on her good will that he will make any sacrifice of his own opinions and policy to retain it." By way of illustration, Slidell pointed to the remarks of an imperial spokesman in the Corps Législatif endorsing Russell's controversial views on the efficiency of the blockade. No doubt Benjamin hoped that Napoleon would find the Confederacy's new proposals too attractive to resist, but Slidell's comments suggested just how difficult the reducing of Britain to a peripheral role was likely to be. Pierre Rost, who had travelled to Madrid in search of recognition, had already discovered as much. He emerged from a meeting with the Spanish foreign minister fully satisfied that Spain would not act separately from Britain and France.[31]

Ominous as these reports from Europe seemed for Benjamin's policy, the secretary soon had every reason to exhibit his inextinguishable optimism. In subsequent despatches Slidell had begun to sing a refrain made familiar by his predecessors—everything depended upon victories in the field. "Decided success of our arms would insure early recognition," he wrote from Paris. Even the enemy's failure "to make any serious impression" on the Confederate forces in Virginia, Tennessee, and on the Mississippi would lead to the same result. Those decided successes now came. Thomas Jackson launched a daring and brilliantly successful campaign in the Shenandoah Valley; a Federal assault upon Southern positions in Charleston harbour was repulsed, and McClellan's army was first halted, then defeated, and finally driven back from the Confederate capital. These victories raised to a new and lofty peak public expectations of foreign intervention. As always British newspapers were studied avidly for hints of the Palmerston government's intentions, and none more carefully than *The Times*. Its protests against the continuance of this "horrible war," its calls for the British people to give their "whole moral weight to the South," its demand that the Confederacy be permitted to withdraw from the Union peacefully, were joyfully reprinted and accorded a special significance. In the words of the *Richmond Daily Enquirer*, "The sentiment of Europe, as expressed through the great organs of public opinion, for some time past, indicates that McClellan's defeat, at this stage of the war, would be embraced as the occasion for Confederate recognition."[32]

The *Enquirer* was an administration organ, and its confidence accurately reflected that of Davis and Benjamin. "There is reason to believe that the Yankees have gained from England and France as the last extension, this month, and expect foreign intervention if we hold them at bay on the first of August," the president hopefully confided to an intimate at the beginning of July.[33] He knew also that the South was better prepared than ever before to capitalize upon these victories in Europe, at least to the extent of reinforcing public sympathy for the Confederacy. In April he and Benjamin had set a propaganda campaign on foot, to be financed out of secret service funds. The secretary had planned to provide the crafty Slidell with the means to enlighten "public opinion in Europe through the press."

However, this task went instead to Edwin DeLeon, a former American consul general in Egypt and a close friend of the president, who had journeyed widely across Europe and throughout Britain.

An experienced diplomat and journalist, DeLeon seemed an ideal choice. He had returned to the South from France earlier in the year for the express purpose of urging the president to give more attention to moulding foreign opinion and countering the activities of Union agents, such as Seward's familiar Thurlow Weed. In mid-April he had been sent off with $25,000. Henry Hotze, already busy at work in London but inadequately funded, was given an increase in salary and an annual contingency fund of $3,000. There was every reason to hope, therefore, that the military victories in Virginia would be followed by a triumph in the propaganda struggle in Europe. No doubt Benjamin found good grounds here for confidence that Napoleon would overcome his reluctance to act without Britain, if she persisted in her "dilatory" policy. It was a buoyant secretary who wrote to Slidell, "Our sky is at least bright, and is daily becoming more resplendent. We expect (we can scarcely suppose the contrary possible) that this series of triumphs will at last have satisfied the most skeptical of foreign Cabinets that we are an independent nation, and have the right to be so considered and treated."[34]

The winds of war that dispersed the dark clouds gathering over the South necessarily blew them northwards. The stunning Confederate victories in Virginia, which so transformed the mood of Richmond, threw the Union into the depths of despair. It was a cruel reversal of fortune for Northerners, even the most cautious of whom had thought they detected in the blossoming triumphs of the spring the beginning of the end for the Confederacy. What else were they to make of the War Department's closing of the recruiting offices, but that their government believed it had more than enough men already to finish the job? They were not to know that administrative confusion as much as over-confidence prompted the action, which had in fact merely suspended recruiting. Shortly afterwards Lincoln proclaimed April 13, the first anniversary of the surrender of Fort Sumter, a day of National Thanksgiving. As the influential *New York Times* observed, "This year closes brightly around us. Victory is ours; defeat is the portion of our enemies. We are confident in ourselves; we are conquering the approval of those who bear us none too much good will."[35]

Before the month of April was out New Orleans had been taken, and however indifferent foreign powers might have been to the Union's earlier military achievements it was safe to assume that they would have to take full notice of this remarkable success. The fresh surge of confidence these victories produced at home was reflected in the "spirited advance" of government securities and the quickening of an economy stagnant all winter. It responded well to the twin stimulants of the first issue of greenbacks and the cheering news from the front. By May 12 Seward could advise the nation's representatives overseas that the "progress of the national armies continues auspiciously." Richmond was "practically held in siege" by McClellan. Norfolk, with all the coasts and tributaries of Hampton Roads, had been "cleared of insurrectionary land forces and naval forces." A week later he was announcing the recovery "of the important port and town of Pensacola."[36] There was only one conclusion to be drawn, the writing was on the wall for the Confederacy.

Yet Northern anticipations of imminent triumph offered Seward no immediate respite either from his labours or his difficulties. Like the president, whose face bore the marks not just of worry and responsibility but of grief, for his young son Willie had died in February, Seward was showing signs both of age and strain. His hair was now "snow white," his clear, grey eyes "deep sunk," his skin colourless, "of a sort of parchment texture." Yet friends found him fresh, despite the passing of his sixty-first year on May 16, and he seemed just as vigorous as ever. He remained good company, still fond of a good cigar, a glass of good wine, and a good story. Of course, his renowned conviviality provided his many enemies with ammunition which they did not scruple to use, and false as they were the stories of his "drunkenness" had been "very extensively spread." One sniper, an important one from the congressional flank, was the chairman of the Senate Foreign Relations Committee, Charles Sumner. He believed that the only way to keep the Union's foreign relations, and especially those with Britain, on an even keel was to proclaim the war as one on slavery.

Abolitionists like Sumner held Seward responsible for their failure to persuade Lincoln to proclaim emancipation. In truth, the pragmatic secretary had little time for what he considered the "waste of talk on abstractions," or for inflammatory speeches in Congress. He could boast, and with some cause, that the administration had succeeded in carrying "practical measures of lasting importance" which challenged "the sympathies of mankind." Proudly he listed these "practical measures"—passports were now granted "without inquiry as to caste"; slavery had been abolished in the District of Columbia; the African slave trade was on the path to extinction, thanks to the treaty with Britain; Haiti and Liberia had been recognized; national aid to state emancipation had been sanctioned and the principle established that "slave holders to be secure must be loyal." Nevertheless, when Lincoln annulled Gen. David Hunter's order for the liberation of slaves, many disappointed abolitionists thought they detected the conservative influence of Seward at work once more. Not surprisingly, in an effort to strengthen his Congressional defences he was careful to remain on good terms with at least one of the important Democrats on the House Foreign Affairs Committee. Subsequently "Sunset" Cox was full of praise for the secretary's "spirit of moderation and patriotism," as well as for his ability, which had not been "surpassed in the diplomacy of any time."[37]

The agitation of the "rancorous set" of "extreme Abolitionists" was only one of the domestic problems with which Seward had to contend. Another was the deepening public antipathy towards Britain. Unpopular in the South for what they had not done, the British were despised in the North for what they had. Nor was the accounting of their wrongs confined to the pages of the notoriously hostile *New York Herald*. Greeley's *Tribune* could not boast the largest daily circulation of the New York journals (that distinction continued to be the *Herald*'s) but was in its several editions the most widely read and respected. Significantly, it was the *Tribune* which laid out before the American people with undisguised bitterness the "proof" of Britain's "one-sided and unfriendly" neutrality. The "indecent haste" of the recognition of Confederate belligerency a year earlier still infuriated Americans, and the *Tribune* continued to describe this step unfairly and inaccurately as "a studied insult" to the Union and as "a violation of the comity of nations." Russell's speech at Newcastle the previous October, in which he had depicted the Union as struggling merely for power, was only one of a number of speeches by prominent Englishmen which Unionists now viewed as part of a massive conspiracy to discourage them and encourage the rebels.[38]

Gladstone's Manchester address in April, during which he prudently voiced more concern for the welfare of the unemployed operatives than for the future of the American Union, had attracted particular attention in the North. After all, the chancellor of the exchequer was a highly regarded moderate, "not of the privileged orders." Yet he had spoken of the impossibility of subduing the South even though it might be conquered, had denied that the war was a struggle between slavery and freedom, and had protested that freedom could not be imposed anyway at the point of a sword. In some American circles Gladstone's apparent lack of sympathy for the North was greeted as "conclusive proof of the hostile policy of England." This harsh judgment revealed much about the public mood. England "has sunk fathoms deep in American opinion," one Unionist confided to a British correspondent. Nor were Northerners at a loss to explain the British attitude, which they thought evident not simply in speeches within Parliament and outside but also in the unpleasant leaders published by *The Times.* The governing classes of Britain stood unmasked, anxious to stunt the growth of a society founded upon the principles enshrined in the Declaration of Independence, in particular, the equality of man. In such a check, the popular refrain went, they saw some hope of perpetuating their own benighted social system which rested upon inherited privilege.[39]

Whatever lay at its heart, Americans seethed with anger at the varied manifestations of British hostility. Some of them had still not recovered from the *Trent* affair, for it had "left an arrow with poisoned barb festering in our flesh, and irritating our nerves." Britain was hated not so much for what she then did as for the manner in which she had done it. She stood condemned of having taken advantage of the North's preoccupation with the South, and "the erring judgment or impulsive zeal of a naval commander," to make it choose between a galling act of national humiliation and the abandonment of all hopes of restoring the Union. She had prepared for a war which the Republic was in no position to fight. Seward's clever despatch surrendering Mason and Slidell had closed the wound for a short time, but it reopened all too easily. Thurlow Weed, who returned home in June, was dismayed by the depth of anti-British sentiment he encountered in New York. "We shall in all probability be out of one war to plunge into another," he concluded gloomily. Manfully, he sought to check the spread of this infection. In an open letter to the New York Common Council which received considerable publicity, he explained that Britain's warlike response to the *Trent* episode had sprung from the conviction that the United States was planning a rupture with her. He assured his fellow countrymen that the Union "has many ardent, well-wishing friends in England, and can have many more if we act justly ourselves, and labour to correct impressions grossly erroneous." When it came to estimating the degree and value of this British sympathy, he urged Americans to recollect that Queen and Commons had modified harsh despatches and resisted proposed unfriendly legislation. His former companion in Britain, Bishop McIlvaine, lauded this attempt "to abate the excessive and perilous exasperation of the American mind toward Great Britain," yet Weed was crying into the wind. He could not deny, after all, that the British were vitiating the effects of the Union blockade of the Confederacy.[40]

Those who accused the British of actively supporting the rebellion had only to point to the fleets of blockade-runners plying their profitable trade with the South via the British West Indies. Especially galling to Northerners was the knowledge that because so many of these enterprises were successful insurers demanded no more than a 15 per cent premium to cover the "risks." As one confused and indignant correspondent pointed out to Seward, this "most impudent" rate was so much below the Morrill Tariff that Southerners would be able to import British goods more cheaply than Unionists could. It was not long before the public outcry against this trade found an American as well as a British target. The Navy Department's failure to stem let alone halt the traffic led to petitions in the port cities of Boston, New York, and Philadelphia for the removal of Gideon Welles, and this embarrassment did nothing to diminish the secretary's personal animosity toward the British. His enmity was fully shared by his deputy, Gustavus Fox, and by several of his commanders at sea. Samuel DuPont, among whose duties was the difficult one of blockading Charleston, wrote to his wife, "I never thought I should care to live my life over again, nor to have it much prolonged except to be with you and to look upon your face daily—but I am so roused by the course of England toward us, getting worse every day, that I can hardly contain myself."[41] Britain's boasted neutrality, the *Tribune* savagely concluded, amounted to her having resisted the temptation to cut the Union's throat now that she was encountering that nation with hands trussed behind its back. Or as a British North American newspaper summed up the situation somewhat less graphically, Britain's "neutrality has been of the cold, calculating type that commands little respect from either party, and certainly wins no love. It has been the neutrality of indecision and mercantile profit; and the consequence is that neither North nor South esteem it as generous or just."[42]

In this envenomed atmosphere Seward had to devise and execute policy. Fortunately there was little likelihood of his taking a deep breath. The dangers were all too apparent. Charles Francis Adams in London warned that to indulge this popular antipathy for Britain "would scarcely be wise." The news from France also dictated caution. From Dayton and Bigelow in Paris, from Weed, from Sanford, who regularly visited the French capital, from August Belmont, in France on business, and from Moses Grinnell, who forwarded translations of letters from French correspondents, Seward received similar messages—all the European nations were desperately short of cotton but none more so than France. Lacking England's capacity to make up some of the lost American supplies, she along with Belgium and Prussia was facing a grave crisis. The pressure in France and Prussia, especially, was "getting intolerable to the governments."[43]

These, then, were some of the pressures, domestic and foreign, which Seward had either to absorb or resist during the spring of 1862. Yet in urging caution Adams was preaching not merely to the faithful but to a congregant who was brimming with the zeal of the recent convert. On April 1, 1862, a year to the day after he had forwarded his "Thoughts" to the president, Seward was writing to Adams of the need for patience and understanding in the Union's relations with Britain. There was not a hint here of the old bellicosity, no remnant of the foreign war panacea, no trace even of a world view which saw the United States pitted against Britain in a struggle for global commercial supremacy and hemispheric dominance. "Let it be our endeavor," he wrote, "to extirpate the seeds of animosity and cultivate relations of friendship with a nation, that however perversely it may seem to act for a time, can really have no interest or ambition permanently conflicting with our own."[44] This spirit of cooperation and compromise was fittingly celebrated shortly afterwards with the signing of the treaty to suppress the slave trade. Seward continued to protest the activities of "a sordid class of persons" who gave aid and sympathy to the rebels, and he warned that the discontent of the American people on this matter was "fast ripening into an alienation which would perplex and embarrass the two nations for an indefinite period." The interception of a report from Caleb Huse, one of the Confederate agents in Britain, in which he detailed his purchases of arms and ammunition, provided Seward with an opportunity to return to this subject and to urge the British to stem this flow of supplies and thereby conciliate American opinion before the war came to an end.[45] However, the main thrust of his policy was to win from Britain and France a declaration that the Confederates would not receive any support from them.

Seward could be forgiven for believing that such a statement, coming after the demoralizing string of military setbacks, would finally extinguish the Southern will to fight on. Southerners had long conceded that European intervention was vital to the success of their cause. But their confidence that the blockade would be raised by the cotton-famished Europeans had been shaken by Russell's comments in February. The hope that remained was of foreign recognition of their independence, a hope that had shone brightly since the recognition of their belligerency in the previous year. If Seward could persuade Britain and France to retrace this step, he would be dealing the Confederacy a final, shattering blow. In words somewhat reminiscent of those used by Benjamin in seeking full recognition from the European powers, he claimed that "G.B. & France could arrest the whole thing, by rescinding those unfortunate belligerent decrees."[46] So he persisted, even though the British and French had already rejected the request.

Seward forwarded a map to Adams and Dayton to illustrate the North's latest striking successes in the field; he alluded to the War Department's closing of the recruiting offices and described the activities of a massive army of 711,000 men that was inexorably squeezing the South into submission. He also wrote of the need to convince the Europeans that their interests would be best served by withdrawing the "decrees," thereby speeding the inevitable end of the conflict. Freed from the necessity to blockade the Southern ports, the United States would be able to detach part of its navy for service with the French and British in China, helping them to quell the turmoil there and thus aid in preserving "a commerce of vast importance to them as well as to ourselves." For Britain there was the promise of a revival of the "legitimate" and profitable commerce with the United States.[47] Although these benefits were prospective only, the secretary was willing to offer one immediate concession. He would reopen some of the cotton ports the Union had retaken.

On April 25 Seward received a private letter from Henry Shelton Sanford, the peripatetic minister to Belgium, which described the deepening concern in French government circles over that nation's rapidly depleting cotton stocks. Thouvenel had told the minister that some of the communications coming in from the Chambers of Commerce "were even menacing in their language"—a disturbing turn of events for an emperor whose majesty rested upon the shaky foundation of popular opinion. Sanford denied that he was alarmed by these developments but he did press Seward to "find some means to give at least a partial satisfaction to the desires of the European Powers on this subject." More specifically, he suggested that the secretary "respond to this wide-spread anxiety by opening one at least of our Southern ports to cotton export—if it will come out—leaving it to the rebel authorities to refuse to permit their people to send it forward." If it achieved nothing else, such a decision would encourage the Europeans to hold the South responsible for their inability to obtain the cotton they so desperately needed. For this reason if for no other, Thurlow Weed, then still in Europe, made the same recommendation.[48]

Seward was receptive. He fancied that a number of ports could be safely opened, so long as there were restrictions to prevent the South deriving any benefit. Not that he expected France to obtain much cotton, but as he explained to Salmon Chase at the Treasury Department, "If we should open three or four ports, we should be able to save all the great ones, and make it a ground on which France might rescind her decree conceding belligerent rights."[49] However, later news from Europe would not admit of such a leisurely and artful form of proceeding. Before the end of the month Seward had heard again from Weed, and it was a far from reassuring letter. He reported that the Count de Morny, the emperor's influential half-brother, had sent for him in order to renew personally the pressure for the opening of some of the Southern ports that had recently fallen to the Union. The subsequent correspondence of Weed, Sanford, and Bigelow did not ease the tension. Quite the reverse, it suggested that some important step was afoot "which bodes our government no particular good."[50]

Seward needed to act promptly if he was to head off the danger of the Confederacy's spirit being bolstered by the sudden prospect of foreign intervention. He was assisted by the timely capture of New Orleans, for as the *New York Times* was quick to observe, a little optimistically, "All that Europe wants to set the wheels of its industry in renewed motion it can obtain here." By May 1 Seward was able to divulge to Lord Lyons that the cabinet was "maturing a plan for reopening New Orleans to American and Foreign Commerce."[51] On the following day the House of Representatives hurriedly enacted a bill, which the Senate was also expected to pass without delay, giving the Treasury Department the necessary powers to control the trade with the Southern ports. Finally, on May 12, Lincoln proclaimed the opening of the ports of Beaufort, Port Royal, and New Orleans from June 1, while Seward privately assured the British and French ministers that others would be opened in a short while. "It is believed here," he replied to the worried Bigelow, "that the virtual opening of New Orleans and other ports to trade will either allay the discontent existing in Europe, or at least render it necessary for those who are managing it for sinister purposes to change their plans of operation."[52]

Although he had been obliged to throw open the ports without securing the compensation he had sought, Seward strove to turn the concession to good account. He paraded this act as conclusive proof of the North's capacity to restore the Union both speedily and completely. Of course, peace and reunion would follow in one month, he added, "if either the Emperor or the Queen should speak the word and say, If the life of this unnatural insurrection hangs on an expectation of our favor, let it die." William Dayton in Paris was informed that his "present urgent duty" was to bring Napoleon to this self-same conviction.[53] Meanwhile Adams was reminded that this commercial concession had coincided with the American ratification of the slave trade treaty, and Seward suggested to the minister that he discreetly capitalize upon this conjunction by reviving the subject of a withdrawal of belligerent recognition. But for the British the secretary soon developed a special argument, although he disclaimed it was such.

On May 28, in the wake of the controversy over Hunter's proclamation, Seward at last untied a gag he had put on Adams early in the conflict when he instructed him to avoid discussing with Russell the probable consequences of the war for the institution of slavery. The secretary now wished to initiate discussion of the dislocating effects of the war, as fugitive slaves fled behind Union lines whenever the Federal armies advanced into the South. The time had come to remind Europeans, and especially the British, of the importance of slave labour to the production of the staples so essential to their economy. The longer the war lasted the greater the number of blacks who would flee to the North, and the more the South would be compelled to press slaves into war service as labourers, thereby further disorganizing its "industrial system" and subverting the "social system." In fact, the longer the war dragged on the greater would be the terrifying risk of a servile insurrection in the South. But the United States, "animated by a just regard for the general welfare, including that of the insurrectionary States," had adopted a policy designed "to save the Union and rescue society from that fearful catastrophe" while it considered "the ultimate peaceful relief of the nation from slavery." Baldly put, this resolute if cautious foe of slavery, committed to eventual rather than immediate emancipation and sure that gradualism was also in the interest of the British, was informing them that the only guarantee of the survival of the institution in the Cotton States for some considerable time, and therefore of the continued cultivation of that vital commodity, was to be found in an early Union victory. There was no alternative, for European intervention "by force to oblige the United States to accept a compromise of their sovereignty" would merely "render inevitable, and even hurry on, that servile war, so completely destructive of all European interests in this country," which the Union government was studiously striving to avoid. In the words of that classically educated State Department clerk, Adam Gurowski, immediate emancipation was held before the eyes of the English statesmen "rather as a Medusa head."[54] Whether or not they would dare look upon the gorgon remained to be seen.

The news he received from Lyons a few days later, that the minister was going home for a summer's leave, was welcomed by Seward. Personally he was reluctant to see the Englishman go. However, Lyons had done much good for Anglo-American relations by his "just and friendly" conduct, and the secretary had hopes that he could "do some good just now at home." He would be able to explain in person to the members of the British government the true state of affairs in America, correcting some of the misconceptions shared by such men as Russell and Gladstone. Perhaps he would urge them to revoke the recognition of Confederate belligerency.[55]

Lyons had not sought leave out of any sense of duty. Rather, he was tired of Washington and not a little afraid of spending yet another uncomfortable summer there. Exhibiting that fastidious concern for his health not uncommon among bachelors, he complained to his ever solicitous sister that the arrival of the warmer weather in May had led to a recurrence of complaints in his throat and chest "which had been so much less troublesome all the winter." Nor was there any prospect of finding relief in America. It took a full twenty-four hours' travel from Washington just to reach somewhere cool, and an entire day on an American train was "enough to knock one up for a month." The onset of severe headaches at the beginning of June convinced him that it was time to be off, for Russell had granted him a full three months' leave. So, after an affectionate parting from the president on June 13, during which Lincoln encouraged the minister to explain to the people of England that he meant them no harm, Lyons set out for New York and home.[56]

At a meeting with the Englishman six days earlier Seward had forecast plain sailing for Anglo-American relations over the summer. It was a confidence Lyons fully shared. He believed that before long the Union would be in control of almost all the Southern ports, thereby ending the irritants and other problems arising out of the blockade. Furthermore, the American government had recently shown him a "conciliatory" face. Yet the war in Virginia had taken an ominous turn before Lyons set out for home. Jackson's daring campaign up the Shenandoah Valley, inflicting defeat after defeat on the Union forces and even feinting an attack on Washington, had thrown the national capital into a panic. Along with the president Seward sought to act as a steadying force, proclaiming his belief that General McClellan would enable the Union to celebrate July 4 in Richmond. For a time this seemed tantalizingly possible, as elements of the Union army advanced to within sight of the Confederate capital. Then, at the end of June, came the succession of battles that obliged McClellan to withdraw. This sudden crumbling of all their high expectations soon worked its demoralizing effect upon the sorely disappointed Northerners. Wall Street responded predictably; there was a sharp depreciation in the government's paper currency; recruiting at offices reopened on June 6 fell off, while discharges and desertions from the armies increased. To make matters worse, there was the "usual paroxysm of the foreign intervention fever."[57] Even Seward seems temporarily to have fallen victim to it. He confided to a New York friend that Napoleon was tempted to intervene in the conflict "because he wants his son recognized as his successor by European powers and thinks he will secure recognition of his dynasty by active hostility to free institutions."[58] But Seward soon recovered his determination "to meet and repel new discouragements; to endure and surmount new difficulties." "In this confusion of nations and men," he wrote to his daughter, "I must be calm, undisturbed, hopeful of all things, and gracious in every way. Well, I try." In this spirit he encouraged Weed to cheer up others, for even strong men were becoming disturbed. He took comfort himself from the widespread public fear of foreign intervention. "Their apprehensions of danger from abroad," he wrote of the American people, "will serve to steady their actions."[59]

In an effort both to steady the people and to check any foreign inclination to intervene, Seward played the central role in ensuring that the reports to Europe of the setback before Richmond were immediately followed by the news that Lincoln, responding to a request from the loyal governors, had called upon their states to strengthen the Union armies to the number of 300,000 men. It was Seward who persuaded several congressmen to leave Washington for their districts before the end of the session, so as to be on hand to encourage recruiting. It was Seward also who prompted Stanton to offer recruits an immediate bounty of $25 as soon as their regiments were mustered into service, with more to follow. After a week of frantic activity he was able, in the review of the military situation which he had composed with difficulty and sent to the ministers overseas at the beginning of July, to pass on the news not merely of the call but of its meaning. "The delusion that the soldiers of the Union would not fight for it, with as much courage and resolution as its enemies will fight against it, has been one of the chief elements of the insurrection. It has now been effectually dispelled." Here was a dramatic demonstration of the Union's determination to prosecute the war "with greater vigor and certainty of success than before."[60]

Seward tried to do more. He went up to Capitol Hill to urge Congress to provide for a draft, only to be met with complaints about past mistakes, arguments about who was to blame, and demands for a more radical policy towards slavery, including the use of blacks to fight and work. But the messages he received from the governors convinced him that such a policy would dry up the stream of recruits. Nor was he in any doubt that it would damage the Union cause abroad, where he had depicted the Lincoln administration as an instrument of restraint, one that had prevented the dislocating effect of the war being further complicated by a slave upheaval. Consequently, his irritation with the radicals on the slavery issue found a release in his correspondence with Adams. "It seems as if the extreme advocates of African slavery and its most vehement opponents were acting in concert together to precipitate a servile war," he complained, "the former by making the most desperate attempts to overthrow the federal Union, the latter by demanding an edict of universal emancipation as a lawful and necessary, if not, as they say, the only legitimate, way of saving the Union."[61] It was an imprudent comparison which later returned to haunt him, for he was to compound the mistake by publishing the despatch. However, for the time being he, like Americans everywhere, South and North, could do little more than wait for the European reaction to the dramatic reversal of military fortunes.

Confronted by difficulties that were in some respects remarkably alike, for they both faced vocal domestic opponents seeking to undermine their authority and mounting public hostility towards Britain, Benjamin and Seward had each attempted to work a significant change in diplomatic policy during the spring of 1862. Their conduct naturally reflected the changing fortunes of war. There was more than a hint of desperation in the Confederates' abandonment of the cotton embargo and Benjamin's effort to free the South of its international dependence upon Britain. Yet even with the welcome military victories in May and June it was impossible to disguise the fundamental weakness of the Confederacy's diplomatic position. Lacking the power to compel foreign assistance, it would have to wait for the Europeans to decide that the time was right to extend recognition or mediate the conflict. Hence the modestly financed propaganda campaign to influence European public opinion. Meanwhile Seward had embarked upon a policy of conciliation, hoping to exploit the favourable turn the war had taken for the Union to break the spirit of the South by securing a withdrawal of British and French recognition of Confederate belligerency. But news of the dangerous impatience of the Europeans for cotton, and then a succession of disastrous setbacks in the field, prevented him from developing this policy. Instead, desperation infected his behaviour as he strove to convince the British that the North intended to press on with the struggle and that only a Union victory could guarantee the social stability so necessary for the production of cotton in the South.

T W O

The Neutral

"THE PEOPLE OF THIS PLACE if not the entire Kingdom seem to be becoming every day more and more enlisted" in behalf of the Confederacy. That was the considered opinion of Thomas Dudley, the American consul at Liverpool, in May 1862.[1] From his vantage point at the American legation in London, the youthful Henry Adams was more certain and certainly no less pessimistic about the outlook. "As for this country," he wrote to his brother Charles, serving in the Union army, "the simple fact is that it is unanimously against us and becomes more fairly set every day. From hesitation and neutrality, people here are now fairly decided. It is acknowledged that our army is magnificent and that we have been successful and may be still more so, but the feeling is universal against us."[2]

Opinion in Britain was not unanimously hostile to the Union cause. The radical *Morning Star* and the liberal *Daily News* even won praise from the *New York Tribune* for their "steadfast friendship," while the *Spectator*, *Macmillan's*, and several important provincial newspapers were sympathetic to the Union, although that did not make them uncritically pro-Northern. Well-wishers and supporters of varying degrees of warmth were to be found in all classes of society, some of them persons of both influence and station. The Duke of Argyll, who sympathized with the Union's struggle for national sovereignty, and whose attitudes to slavery had been greatly influenced by admiration for Harriet Beecher Stowe and friendship with Charles Sumner, was a member of the Palmerston cabinet. Another highly placed friend of the Union was the president of the Board of Trade, Thomas Milner Gibson. That witty, "genial chatty man," Monckton Milnes, was prominent in the fashionable world and by no means inconspicuous in the Commons. A gourmand as well as a gourmet, he predicted that his exit would be "the result of too many entrées." W. E. Forster was a most effective parliamentary debater and strategist for the Union cause, and John Bright was evidently doing what he could to galvanize working class support at public meetings. Richard Cobden's support was more qualified and less overt, but it was slowly strengthening. John Stuart Mill, Thomas Hughes, and Elizabeth Gaskell were just three of the North's partisans in the world of letters, although Northerners were puzzled and dismayed by the seeming indifference to their struggle of the great bulk of the literary and intellectual world in Britain. It was a silence one thoughtful American visitor attributed to hatred of war and a conviction that the conflict in the United States would not benefit anyone.[3]

In the forefront of the pro-Union literary activists were Harriet Martineau and Edward Dicey. Doggedly, they attempted to rouse their countrymen to the moral and practical issues at stake in the war, and thereby induce them to cheer lustily for a Union victory from the sidelines. The didactic Miss Martineau, who had long regarded the problems of America as a vital part of the wider struggle between despotism and liberty, made much, too much, of the abolition of slavery in the District of Columbia. The Union did seem to be slowly turning away from compromise with slavery, but she extolled this particular step as the "closing of a period of guilt and danger, and the entrance upon one of genuine republicanism." This act had dramatically transformed the American nation into one ready to "at once join company with other Christian peoples, free to reprobate and extinguish a barbarism and a curse."[4] The regeneration of the Republic, for which she had long called, was occurring. Yet as Dicey demonstrated with less hyperbole, abolition in the national capital, when taken together with the Slave Trade Treaty and Lincoln's recognition of the Black Republic of Haiti, proved that the war was "working directly for the overthrow of slavery." So also was the increasing popularity in the North of the once despised abolitionists. Clearly, Dicey concluded, "If the war continues it must become, ere long, a war for emancipation."[5]

Writing from the United States, to which he had journeyed early in 1862 as a special correspondent of *Macmillan's* and the *Spectator*, Dicey constantly sought to sharpen the focus of the conflict for his readers by contrasting the ennobling transformation of the Union cause with the sordid constancy of that of the South. Far from fighting for independence, as some of its foreign sympathizers chose to believe, the Confederacy was in reality struggling for empire, for the right to extend slavery across the American continent, Dicey insisted, and in his mind this fact demanded opposition to the South from everyone who believed slavery to be a sin. He dwelt upon the grave implications of a Confederate victory. Britain's dependence upon slave-grown cotton would be revived, a dependence he considered both immoral and dangerous. If the immorality was obvious, what was the danger? Simply that Britain would be drawn into the South's inevitable post-war troubles with the Union, and from these she might not escape short of a war with the remaining United States. Burning with a sense of shame at the loss of so much of their former nation, yet still prosperous and powerful, Northerners might very well seek to bind themselves together and gratify their national pride through a war with the hated British. Nor should Britain delude herself with the notion that she could rely on the South in such an emergency. The Union would purchase the Confederacy's neutrality by acquiescing in the slave republic's designs on Cuba and Mexico. "Those who wish for peace, then," Dicey warned, "must desire the success of the North."[6]

Efforts to awaken greater numbers of Englishmen to the profound moral questions posed by the American war were a response not merely to the developments there but to the disturbingly popular success in Britain of very different interpretations of the struggle. One of the most influential of these was a book by James Spence, *The American Union*, which although not published until late in 1861 had gone through four editions by the spring of 1862. Forty-five years old, once a successful iron merchant, and important enough to be asked to play a minor role in the negotiation of the Cobden Treaty with France, Spence had recently fallen upon leaner times. The American panic of 1857 and then the disruption of business activity caused by the outbreak of the Civil War had brought about the failure of several Northern firms heavily indebted to him, and his losses had been substantial. Perhaps this influenced his attitude towards the Union, which had committed the "deplorable mistake" of fighting rather than accept the loss of the South. Whatever the reason, he offered the Confederacy the services of an intelligent zealot, "fertile in expedients, vigorous in action, of wide mercantile experience; one accustomed to deal with large and difficult things, able to influence public opinion through the press, and not afraid of any encounter as a speaker."[7] His book was to be only the first of many such contrib-utions to the Southern cause in Britain.

As a glowing review in the April issue of *Blackwood's* suggested, Spence's popularity was a measure of his success in salving the conscience of his audience by reassuring them that slavery did not lie at the root of the conflict across the Atlantic. Moreover, he reinforced a notion which many of his contemporaries already found persuasive; namely, that the dissolution of the Union had been the inevitable outcome of a foredoomed attempt to unite an enormous, complex, diverse territory. As even the sympathetic Mrs. Gaskell observed to an American friend, "You included (by your annexations) people of different breeds, and consequently different opinions and habits of thought; the time was sure to come when you could not act together as a nation; the only wonder to me is that you cohered so long."[8] The differences between North and South were, in short, essentially sectional and geographical rather than moral. They were differences of feeling, interests, manners, origins, occupations, society, soil, and climate. Some of them had caused the South to develop as an almost exclusively agricultural section while in the North manufacturing had not only predominated but had then sought to impose its demands, in the form of a protective tariff, upon the South. It was in this conflict of interests and in an accompanying "extinction of Southern influence" in the Union that so many Englishmen increasingly and not unreasonably discovered the "real motive" for secession. As for slavery, the Confederacy would be obliged to accept its gradual abolition in order to win international acceptance. No wonder the *Saturday Review* had predicted success for a book which allowed for Britain's hostility to the abominable institution yet "dealt with the subject in a 'thoroughly English way'."

To contradict Spence something more substantial than Harriet Martineau's thrice-weekly leaders in the *Daily News* and occasional pieces in *Macmillan's*, or even Dicey's first-hand observations, was required. It was provided by John Elliott Cairnes, a young professor of political economy at Queen's College, Galway, who had begun to lecture on American slavery following the outbreak of the war. Cairnes was "mortified" by the unedifying spectacle of Britons openly sympathizing with slaveholding insurgents, and the outlines of a book soon took shape in his mind. By August 1861 he had obtained the endorsement and encouragement of his intellectual mentor, John Stuart Mill. Urged on by Mill, this "admirable man," "thoroughly instructed in American affairs,"[9] published early in the summer of 1862 his counterblast, *The Slave Power: Its Character, Career and Public Design: Being an Attempt to Explain the Real Issues Involved in the American Contest.*

Cairnes made short work of the popular idea that the tariff was in some way the immediate cause of secession. The break-up of the Union, he pointed out, had been "hatched, matured," and implemented while the liberal tariff of 1857 was still in force. He then challenged those Englishmen who claimed to support the Confederacy out of sympathy for all struggles for national independence. The right to independent political existence must justify itself with reference to the ends for which it was employed, Cairnes declared in professorial tones. In the case of the South there could be no doubt that the means were bloody and the end reprehensible—the extension of slavery. The author depicted American history since 1819 as a succession of aggressions by the slave power. The annexations of Florida, Texas, and half of Mexico, as well as the filibustering raids into Central America and against Cuba, were all laid at the door of Southern slaveowners. It was to their control of the national government, rather than to democracy, that Cairnes attributed the generally accepted and widely deplored deterioration of American institutions and character during the half-century preceding the outbreak of the war. As for Britain's response to the conflict, he urged that it be governed by concern for a settlement that would merit her moral support. Personally he was appalled by the thought of a Southern victory but by no means convinced of the desirability of the Union's complete restoration. The explanation was his fear lest anxiety to reunify the entire nation induced the North to make concessions to slavery. Far better in his eyes if the Confederacy was confined to the territory bordered by the Mississippi, the Gulf, the Atlantic, and the states of the Upper South. Such a political settlement would be doubly advantageous to the cause of emancipation. Relieved of so much of the incubus, the Union could remove the stigma of slavery patiently and without fear of social dislocation. Its eradication in the North, together with the confining of the South in a territorial straitjacket, would eventually lead to the painless extinction of the hated institution in that shrivelled state as well. This conclusion was not unlike Spence's.

Mill, who had done so much to encourage Cairnes to write his book, was well pleased with the result. This was a "splendid" piece of work, "impressively and popularly written," but if it was to tell it had to be read, and he suggested the author send a copy to that aged abolitionist Lord Brougham who "would probably talk about it, and help to get it read." He confidently predicted that *Macmillan's*, the

Daily News, and the *National Review* would give it good publicity, and it was not long before the *Review* published an article "with large extracts and in an excellent tone." Meanwhile the *News* had been no less generous, printing three leaders by Harriet Martineau long in length and praise. The judgment of the *Anti-Slavery Reporter*, that Cairnes had provided "a perfect antithesis to the pro-slavery lucubrations of Mr. Spence," may have attracted little attention and caused not a ripple of surprise, but the same could not be said of the nearly identical reaction of the *Economist*. It also praised this "powerful book" for wisely exposing the "plausible sophistries" of Spence. However, it was from Mill that the weightiest support for Cairnes's interpretation of the conflict came.[10]

Britain's pre-eminent political economist had outlined his view of the war in a short article published by *Fraser's Magazine* in February. On that occasion he had expressed relief that his nation had emerged from the *Trent* incident without finding itself obliged to make common cause with a group of slaveholders aspiring to nationhood. Such an association would have been a "disgrace" for Britain and a "calamity" for the world. Now, having intended for some time to submit a piece to the *Westminster*, he forwarded a brief but powerful discussion of *The Slave Power*. He lavished praise upon his disciple —Cairnes was not merely a "first-rate political economist" but a "moral and political philosopher," while his book was "an invaluable exposition" both of the principles and the facts of the case, certain to convince minds not already closed. Success in their present struggle, Mill warned, would merely encourage the Southern "conspirators" to seek the expansion of the empire of slavery. First it would be Mexico, next South America, and finally, their ambition whetted by success, they might be tempted to conquer and annex the West Indies. Inevitably, the slave trade would be reopened. "Such are the issues to humanity which are at stake in the present contest between free and slaveholding America," Mill claimed, "and such is the cause to which a majority of English writers, and of Englishmen who have the ear of the public, have given the support of their sympathies." It was an astute appeal to the pride Englishmen had taken in the twin examples of their antislavery philanthropy—the abolition of slavery in the West Indian colonies and the war on the slave trade.

No less striking was Mill's willingness to meet head on the oft-repeated assertion that the Northerners were not fighting against slavery but for the Union. What if that was the case, he replied, "is there anything so very unjustifiable in resisting, even by arms, the dismemberment of their country?" Did public morality require that the United States abdicate the character of a nation, "and be ready at the first summons to allow any discontented section to dissever itself from the rest by a single vote of a local majority, fictitious or real, taken without any established form, or public guarantee for its genuineness and deliberateness?" The conditions under which an established government was duty-bound to honour the wishes of a portion of its citizens to break up the state still remained to be defined. And until some rule had evolved to govern this problem, no government could be expected to yield to a rebellion before a "fair" trial of strength in the field. Indeed, were it not for the certainty of opposition, and the knowledge that the price of failure was severe punishment, revolts would be the resort of all disaffected minorities. Would England, he asked pointedly, tamely acquiesce in the separation of Scotland and Ireland? This said, however, Mill refused to concede that the cause of the Union could be distinguished from that of freedom. "The North fights for the Union," he admitted, but for the Union under conditions "which deprive the Slave Power of its pernicious ascendancy." Like Martineau and Dicey before him, he pointed to the abolition of slavery in the District of Columbia, its exclusion from the territories, and the slave trade treaty with Britain as proof of the Union's sincerity. The United States was making war on slavery within the confines of the Constitution.[11]

These labours were not without their reward. *The Slave Power* proved sufficiently popular to go into a second edition the following year, while the several copies purchased by Mudie's, then the greatest circulating library in the world, were in constant demand. The book made, in Mill's words, "a great and useful impression" upon a number of influential individuals, convincing them that the war did originate in slavery. They included Mill's friend Dr. John Chapman, who was the proprietor-editor of the *Westminster*, Charles Darwin, and the young intellectual, Leslie Stephen. Nevertheless, in the battle with Spence, if publication figures were a guide, Cairnes finished a distant second. As he conceded privately, he had only half succeeded. He believed that he had proved his case against the South but had failed to convince his countrymen that the aims of the North were any less dangerous to civilization. "A very general apprehension prevails here that the ruling motive of the North in the war is ambition purely," he confided to a new American friend, "and that slavery abolition is only regarded as an effectual expedient for crushing its antagonist in the last resort."[12]

In truth, hard as the band of Union sympathizers worked to establish that slavery was the pivotal issue in the American war, their success seemed slight. Feeling for the South remained strong in polite society, but Americans at the legation had fully expected that. What began to break their hearts, however, as Henry Adams recalled many years later, was the unexpected hostility to the Union they now detected among the middle classes. The *Daily News* paid dearly for its sympathies in advertising revenue, as large auctioneers and publishers cancelled their advertisements. The American consul at Southampton shunned social activities, for he could not abide the inevitable discussion of his nation's troubles. To one visitor from home he complained that the "masses of laborers" and "the trading and commercial classes" sympathized "altogether with the secessionists." Of course, the war's dislocation of trade and the working-class suffering this caused provided him with a rational explanation of the desire of both these classes for an early peace, something they believed could be achieved through British recognition of the Confederacy. What aroused the consul's dismay, however, was the discovery that the educated classes "who had no personal interest at stake, were for the rebels, or nearly so."[13] Thus did Unionists tend to rank as hostile not merely those in Britain who supported the South or disliked both sides in the conflict, but also the ever-increasing number in all classes and parties who deplored any prolongation of the war.

The growing unity of opinion was founded upon a broad base of interests and emotions, theories and speculations, which had been moulding British attitudes since the opening shot at Fort Sumter. The undeniable fact that the leaders of the Union had earlier refused to declare war on slavery, and in words if not in deeds had persistently denied that this was their purpose, discouraged many British abolitionists and led them to conclude that the struggle could not be justified. It was a position they were slow to abandon, despite the recent antislavery measures. How could the war be a "bonafide" one against slavery when gains made by the slaves were evidently accidental and unpopular even in the North? Certainly the Garrisonian *Anti-Slavery Advocate* did not make haste to help Cairnes, Dicey, and Martineau. The British and Foreign Anti-Slavery Society was somewhat more positive in its response. A committee was appointed to call upon Charles Francis Adams "to express sympathy with those

who represent constitutional government in the United States," and
the society's organ, the *Anti-Slavery Reporter*, did greet Lincoln's
proposal for compensated emancipation as evidence that slavery had
at last been officially recognized as the cause of the rebellion and its
abolition "a substantial means of ending it." Nevertheless the *Reporter*
continued to dispute whether the recovery of the South was a cause
worth a war and the attendant suffering.[14]

If abolitionists were less than enthusiastic in their support of the
North's struggle, perhaps it was not surprising that so many Englishmen agreed with Spence that the Union had outgrown its strength
and had become too diverse to remain whole. Political separation
seemed to them both natural and inevitable. Having surveyed the
religious and quarterly journals, one American was moved to complain that "with the single exception of the *London Review*, published
by the Wesleyans, these periodicals are unanimous against the cause
of the North, echoing the partial and perverted theories" of James
Spence. Ignoring Cairnes's qualification, some in Britain continued
to identify the Confederacy with the highly respectable cause of
national sovereignty. Still others professed to see in States Rights, of
which secession was the ultimate expression, "the only availing check
upon the absolutism of the sovereign will." As a result, they associated
the Southern cause with the advance not the retreat of democracy.
Orthodox liberals, moreover, were outraged by the tariff policies of
the Union, for in June 1862 the Congress committed another act of
economic heresy by increasing yet again the duties on imports. But
for the great majority of Britons their mounting opposition to the
continuation of the war was surely stirred by less ideological considerations.

The ever-worsening situation in Lancashire, where disaster was
popularly believed to be threatening the homes of thousands of
operatives, naturally continued to do much to shape working-class
opinion, and not only in the mill towns. It certainly prompted the
repeated calls by *Reynolds's* for recognition of the South and mediation of the conflict, and played a large part in determining the
editorial policy of the *Bee-Hive*, a weekly controlled by members of the
working class and with a better claim than most to speak for them. Its
editor, George Troup, had long been an enemy of the trade and
tariff policies of the United States and his dislike of the North had
been accentuated by an obscure religious quarrel involving the Free
Church of Scotland, to which he belonged. By 1862 he was preaching

41

the doctrine of peaceful separation as the only solution for the conflict. And when a delegation of workingmen called upon Spence, to discuss the operatives' predicament, he advised them to organize meetings in the cotton districts and draw up petitions to Parliament requesting recognition of the Confederacy as the best way of speedily ending the war. As well as advice, he gave them money to cover some of their expenses, promised them more, and offered to help them draft their petitions.[15]

The suffering in the textile regions also made a deep impression upon the members of other classes, who felt compassion for the victims and feared that if their misery was prolonged it would erupt in social strife. Clearly there was a danger to the delicate equipoise and much treasured calm of mid-Victorian society. No less important was the widespread if passive dislike of the United States, compounded of contempt for American materialism (not unmixed with envy), resentment of their boastfulness, jealousy if not fear of the Union's power, and anger at the "obnoxious" behaviour of the North.

In one combination or another these concerns and emotions provided a bond strong enough to unite a few Radicals, some Liberals, and a great many Tories in the call for an end to the war and the peaceful coexistence of two American republics. Meanwhile Whigs and Tories continued to see in the failure of the Union a flail with which to beat back those advanced Liberals and Radicals agitating for political reform in Britain. "Philanthropists and Christians," of whatever party or class, were horrified by the appalling casualties each side was now inflicting upon the other, and to what end? *Punch* portrayed two contestants, one clinging precariously to the broken branch of unionism, locked in a death struggle over the abyss of bankruptcy. Certainly the South, despite its setbacks, betrayed not a hint of a weakening resolve. Even if the Union succeeded in conquering the Confederacy, which few Englishmen thought possible, given both the extent of the territory involved and the size of its population, would it not be obliged to resort to a form of government for this hostile region which would sacrifice essential freedoms and thus jeopardize constitutional government everywhere within the Republic? Finally, to the pull of humanitarianism was added the tug of admiration. By the summer of 1862 more and more Englishmen were coming to admire the pluck and skill with which the heavily outnumbered Southerners were fighting. Monckton Milnes privately conceded that in America "the lower civilization, as represented by the South, is so much braver & cunninger & daringer than the cultivated shopkeepers of the North." Even the *Spectator* admitted that evil though the Confederates' cause was, "it is wholly impossible to suppress an immoral admiration for the energy they have displayed."[16]

Well placed to capitalize upon English sentiment was Henry Hotze, the Confederacy's young propaganda agent in London. He had arrived in England at the end of January and had found Union agents already busy at work, yet he quickly perceived the advantages that lay with the South. The reverses suffered by the Confederacy during the spring of 1862 had at last awakened the British to the likelihood of "a protracted war," a frightening prospect which paradoxically prompted many of them "to do something to strengthen us who but a few days ago professed themselves indifferent spectators of the contest." Even more encouraging, the spectre of a cotton famine was at last haunting the land. Quick to see his opportunities, Hotze was vigorous and imaginative in his exploitation of them.[17]

A Swiss by birth, in whom a short residence in the United States had not eradicated "European manners and tastes," a man of some diplomatic experience and considerable journalistic training, Hotze promptly embarked upon an ambitious campaign to shape the attitudes of the shapers of British public opinion. With the assistance of James Murray Mason he gained an entrée to society, especially the gentlemen's clubs. There he distributed gifts of fine Havana cigars and bottles of American whiskey, in this and other ways seeking to convey an impression of the Southerner's closer affinity with English gentlemen than with the "mongrel" population of the Northern states. More importantly, he struck up friendships and cooperated closely with members of the Confederate lobby. It was Hotze who wrote Lord Campbell's speech of March 10, 1862, denouncing the Union blockade. However, as a trained journalist who had been taught his trade by the eminent John Forsyth of the *Mobile Register*, Hotze had always expected to work to greatest effect through the press.[18]

Initially he used his contacts, his knowledge, and his skill to secure access to the columns of some of the leading British newspapers. At the request of those friends of the South who were planning to press the issue in Parliament, Hotze wrote a series of letters advocating British recognition of the Confederacy which were published in the *Morning Post*, Palmerston's mouthpiece. These contributions were soon followed by others to the two most important Tory dailies, the *Morning Herald* and the *Standard*. Hotze also willingly accepted an an offer to write pieces for the *Money Market Review*, which he described as "a weekly of small circulation but great authority among capitalists." Impressive as these early successes were, they did not satisfy the energetic young propagandist, who had planned to devote himself "almost exclusively to the ministerial press," in the belief that "the initiative must come from that quarter" and that the Tory organs would of their own accord keep pace with "any movement in the desired direction." Before the end of April he had concluded that what was needed in Britain was a weekly newspaper "wholly devoted" to Confederate interests and "exclusively" under his control. It would disseminate information about the South as well as the war, "bringing before the public with proper comments the vast amount of important information" which was received in Europe through private channels. It would provide an avenue for unofficial communication between the South and Europe when more direct routes were not available. Finally, it would enable Hotze to influence discreetly other British newspapers, by quietly employing many of their contributors. "This is in my opinion," he advised Benjamin, "the cheapest, the only honorable, and the most effective mode of subsidizing the foreign press."[19]

With the approval and support of Mason and Slidell, and aided initially by Spence, who wrote some of the "best leaders" in the early numbers, that is until the two men found each other less than congenial collaborators, Hotze delivered his brain-child in May. The *Index*'s small circulation, and the fact that the news of his increased allowance took so long to reach him from Richmond, condemned the newspaper to a hand-to-mouth existence, although by rigid economies he managed to keep it going. He also kept up the pretence that it was an English newspaper, but this transparent fiction deceived few of his contemporaries. The English press watched with some amusement the outbreak of the American war on Fleet Street, for a Northern propaganda organ, the *London American*, soon established itself one door away from the office of the *Index*. Somehow it seemed appropriate that they were separated by a tobacconist's shop.[20]

Through the *Index* Hotze laboured to excite in Britain support for the recognition of the Confederacy. He dwelt upon the close ethnic ties of the two peoples. "The South, for generations back, has proved its closer affinity of blood to the British parent stock, than the North, with its mongrel compound of the surplus population of all the world, could boast of." He emphasized their greater sense of political solidarity. "The political institutions of Great Britain always had their warmest and most sincere admirers among the people of the South." It was in the North that "Old World governments" had been denounced "as 'rotten monarchies' and 'petrified corpses'." The North was responsible for all those political innovations of which English Radicals were so enamoured. But the theme to which the *Index* always returned was that of the two societies' commercial compatibility. "The people of the South are conscious that they have not an interest in conflict with any interest of England. They produce all that England consumes, they consume all that England produces." Of course what the South produced and what Britain so desperately needed was cheap cotton, and Hotze exploited to the full the mounting public concern over the distress in Lancashire. Public benevolence, the *Index* warned, was futile when the destitute were numbered in the tens of thousands. "Until the cotton famine is at an end, Lancashire must suffer partial starvation, and very general privation." Nor was any hope to be placed in Northern promises of opening Southern ports. "Some of the ports have been occupied by the Federals," the *Index* reminded its readers in July, "but where is the promised cotton?" And the longer the famine dragged on the shorter the odds on social upheaval. Cautiously Hotze attempted to tap the uneasiness. "We trust that when the laboring people of England discover how they have been duped by the agents of the United States they will continue to exhibit the excellent and orderly bearing that has already won for them universal admiration and respect."[21]

The answer to Lancashire's grave problems was peace in America, and the only sure way of bringing it quickly, the *Index* claimed, was recognition of the Confederacy. To those who held back from this step for fear that it would goad the Union into a declaration of war, Hotze spoke reassuringly. Britain would not be acting alone, but in association with other European nations, perhaps France, Spain, and Belgium, a grouping the Union could neither ignore nor afford to antagonize. European recognition would also liberate those many Northerners who had long realized that the hopes of subjugating the South were "chimerical" and could only end in national bankruptcy, by freeing them from the fear of repression if they spoke their minds. For this action by the Great Powers would "sober down" excitement "into reason and the great majority of the community would wake as

45

from a distempered dream." Thus through the columns of the *Index* Hotze, no doubt at the suggestion of Mason, presented to the British people the case Benjamin was seeking to make to their government, that "recognition is a peacemaker, and nothing else."[22]

If the *Index* provided the Confederate cause with a well-managed and skilfully directed propaganda organ in Britain, its influence paled before that of the mighty *Times*. Having successfully beaten back the strong challenge of the inexpensive *Standard* and the *Telegraph* by cutting its price, achieving a circulation of 65,000, and giving a lead to much of the provincial press, *The Times* seemed more firmly established than ever as the authentic voice of British public opinion. Moreover, it was an opinion the newspaper was usually content to reflect rather than attempt to shape. Nor was its authority diminished by its intimate and "universally known" connection with the Palmerston government.[23]

From the outbreak of the American war the newspaper's editorials had been marked by hostility to the Union. They were frequently the work of Robert Lowe, a friend and former tutor of Delane, an anti-democrat, and at this stage of his political career a minor member of the Palmerston government. Lowe's travels in North America during the summer of 1856 had confirmed him in his political élitism and awakened him to the accelerating pace of disunity in the United States. Sharing the conviction that the federal system was fundamentally unsound and could never be satisfactorily patched up, Lowe and his editor quickly concluded that the Lincoln administration's determination "to restore the Union by force was irrational and its perseverance in that impossible attempt was perverse."[24] Hitherto the newspaper's prejudiced leaders had been balanced to some extent by the critical but fair reports of its distinguished special correspondent in the United States, William H. Russell. However, the spring and summer of 1862 saw important changes among *The Times*'s personnel in America.

The newspaper had been searching for a new American correspondent for some time. The post was offered to Lewis Filmore, the former political editor of the *Illustrated London News* and a former special correspondent of *The Times* in the United States. Although he declined, he did recommend Charles Mackay. In the spring Mackay went out and at about the same time Russell withdrew. He had long been unhappy there, acutely sensitive to the unpopularity his reports had earned him, and when he was denied permission to accompany the Union army on another campaign against Richmond he saw an excuse to return home and seized it. He was replaced by Frank Lawley, and neither he nor Mackay struggled to be objective in their reporting. As the *New York Herald* soon concluded, "writing stocks up or writing stocks down, as may suit their employers, and doing this country all the damage they can through their letters and through the editorials and speeches based upon their letters, are the honorable, gentlemenly and moral occupations of this pair of noble brothers."[25]

Forty-eight years old when he took up his post, Mackay brought with him a reputation as something of a literary dilettante. He was a poet of "small celebrity but of large popularity," an author, and a journalist who claimed knowledge of the United States and friendship with prominent Americans. He had toured the Republic in the winter of 1857–58, giving a series of lectures, and later published his observations, first in the *Illustrated Evening News*, of which he was then managing editor, and subsequently in two volumes entitled *Life and Liberty in America*. Like so many of his contemporaries he had concluded that the United States had grown too large to be successfully governed. It was his opinion that the Republic was fated to break up into as many as four federations. The secession of the South had done nothing to prick the bubble of vanity which enveloped his judgments, nor did his association with leading Unionists such as Seward, for whom he had acted as a guide during the New Yorker's visit to London in 1859, dissuade him from publicly supporting the Southern cause. Before leaving for Boston in February he chaired a public lecture by a rabid secessionist who, predictably enough, called upon the Union to halt the senseless war and permit the Southern states to separate. Although this indiscretion cost Mackay his Union friends, and earned him a frosty reception in Boston, it did not damage his position at Printing House Square.[26]

The newspaper's manager, Mowbrey Morris, who identified the North with the abolitionists he hated—he was convinced that emancipation had cost his family its fortune in the West Indies—offered the experienced Mackay some gratuitous advice on the general duties of a correspondent. He was "to supply information, and next to amuse by illustration and reflection." More to the point was Morris's careful explanation of what was first expected of the new correspondent. "The financial position of the [Union] government and the imminent risk of repudiation and bankruptcy are objects that ought not to be unnoticed in *The Times*, or if noticed, discussed with a few generalities. There *are* writers in America who maintain that the money market is sound and the finances flourishing and these persons find believers in England—Why not take their statements and contradict them and demolish their arguments?"[27] Not surprisingly Mackay saw this as encouragement to give free rein to his anti-Union sentiments. Occasionally thereafter Morris would hint that his criticisms of the Union and its leadership were too strong, but *The Times* continued to print them, ignoring the bitter Northern attacks on Mackay as a "wretched and double-tongued poetaster," who had "invented and perverted with inexhaustible ingenuity and impudence." Only with the collapse of the Confederacy was he to be dismissed and belatedly accused of a "blind and unreasonable condemnation of all public men and measures on the Federal side." The unfortunate Mackay was charged with the responsibility for much of the exasperation "in the American mind against the English," and for the newspaper's loss of reputation.[28]

In any just apportionment of blame, however, a larger measure clearly belongs to Morris and editor Delane, "the London *Times* establishment." For they not only selected Mackay to go out to the Union but replaced Russell with Frank Lawley. A gentleman by birth, well educated and well connected politically, Lawley had appeared set for a bright career when as a very young man he entered Parliament and was appointed private secretary to Gladstone, then chancellor of the exchequer in the Aberdeen coalition. Two years later, although still not thirty, he was named by another friend of the family, Newcastle, to fill the vacant post of governor of South Australia. But his fair prospects suddenly became bleak when the suspicion grew that he had abused his confidential position close to Gladstone to speculate on the stock market, for it was well known that his addiction to the turf had left him saddled with debts. The upshot, as Charles Greville recorded, was that Lawley "contrived at once to lose his place as private secretary, his government [South Australia], his seat in Parliament, and his money." And within two years of this humiliation he was obliged to flee Britain to escape his creditors. He went to the United States determined to labour as a journalist, in order to accumulate sufficient funds to settle his debts and perhaps retrieve something of his reputation in England. By 1861 he had done well enough to return home briefly if secretly, for some of his creditors remained on his trail, and it was while he was on a second *sub rosa* visit the following year that he met Morris and accepted his offer of the position of war correspondent.[29]

Lawley's view of the United States underwent a radical transformation in the six years that elapsed between his arrival as a refugee debtor and his return as a correspondent of the most famous of newspapers. As an advanced Liberal in English politics, he had worshipped the Republic from afar but closer inspection "wonderfully modified" his enthusiasm. Nevertheless, his conviction that the future lay with the United States weathered well, hence his advice to his close friend William Gregory to visit North America and read Tocqueville as part of a program of study that would equip him as a parliamentary expert on American affairs. Then came secession, to which he initially responded like "a great Northerner," and the war. Living in the United States throughout the first year of the conflict, Lawley was profoundly impressed by the depth of Northern animosity toward his native land. He began to fear that if the Union ever subdued the South domestic victory would be followed by a settling of scores with Britain for such humiliations as the *Trent* affair. From this it followed that the true policy of British statesmen was to place the Union in such a predicament that for a century to come it "should be of no more account in European affairs than the Sandwich Islands." The best way to guarantee this, Lawley believed, was to emasculate its military capacity and political influence by fostering an independent Confederacy. At the very least, it was "almost necessary" for England to recognize the South. Preferably she should do all that could be done for the Southern states and thus assist "as a man midwife" at the new nation's birth.[30] His appointment to the staff of *The Times* gave him the opportunity to recommend this policy to his countrymen.

Subsequently, in reports well calculated to nourish British humanitarian dismay, Lawley repeatedly emphasized the bloodshed and horror of this "hopeless" struggle by the North. Nor did he stop short of a call for British intervention to halt it. After a few months he made his way into the Confederacy bearing introductions "to the authorities, and to the Society at Richmond," furnished by Mason at the urging of the friend they had in common, Gregory. Lawley promptly enlisted as an unofficial propagandist of the Southern cause. His accounts of the South's "easy" military position and its population's wonderful spirit made "a most profound impression," and not only in Britain. They provided further evidence of "the impossibility of subduing such a people."[31]

49

Charles Francis Adams later remarked in London that Lawley had "evidently been a willing instrument to subserve a purpose here." Certainly his letters brought few protests from Printing House Square. Morris did express his personal disagreement with the correspondent's advocacy of British recognition of the Confederacy, arguing that the Federals' determination to have a quarrel with Britain was reason enough to keep "aloof from them as long as possible." Occasionally the newspaper's manager questioned the wisdom of Lawley wearing his sympathies on his sleeve. "Certainly you cannot accuse the newspaper of Northern proclivities," he wrote, "so when I complain of your Southerness, it is not as an enemy but a friend that I speak. We will believe, since you say so, that the Confederate Generals from Lee downwards are possessed of all the virtues that should adorn a soldier but we cannot believe that all Southerners are faultless and that they can be truly described only in terms of unqualified praise." But if they questioned the effectiveness of some of his despatches, the newspaper's management never exercised their option to terminate Lawley's handsome contract. On the contrary, when he returned home for a well-deserved rest in 1864 Morris's only worry was that Lawley would decline to go back to America. In truth, both he and Mackay reported what *The Times*'s "establishment" wanted to print and many of its subscribers to read. "Your views are entirely in accordance with those of the paper and I believe of the majority in this country," Morris wrote to Mackay in 1863, commending him for his "art of expressing them" in a way that ensured they would be read.[32]

Sadly beleaguered already, British sympathizers with the Union's struggle could well have done without the assistance Benjamin Butler provided to their opponents. A former lawyer and always a politician, Butler had embarked upon a military career with the opening of the war. A man of ample energy but scant military skill, he owed his command of the Union troops at New Orleans no less than his original commission to his political weight. "This old spoilsman, whose cross-eyes could never see beyond his paunch," was in appearance a heavy, forbidding figure, and his approach to the difficult and sensitive task of administering the captured Southern city proved equally stern. Commanding a force of no more than 2,500 men with which to control a hostile population of 160,000 he chose to cow the sullen citizenry into submission. Revelling in the almost unlimited power of his command, for it took a full month if not longer to communicate with Washington, he summarily imprisoned contractors who declined to work for the occupying force, seized and auctioned off the merchandise of shopkeepers who refused to sell to Union troops, and eventually hanged one resident for tearing down the flag of the United States. However, when he turned his attention to the foreign consuls in this important commercial centre, his roughshod tactics evoked an international outcry of protest.[33]

Before entering the city Butler had convinced himself that the members of foreign communities there, including the consuls, were Confederate sympathizers if not supporters. Soon after his arrival he was informed that the British Guard, a section of the company of foreigners organized to police the city during the brief period between the withdrawal of the Southern troops and the arrival of the Northern, had voted to turn their arms over to the Confederates. Indeed, it was rumoured that some weapons had already been forwarded. Butler's response was to order out of the city all those members of the Guard unable to produce their full equipment, a decision which precipitated an unpleasant correspondence with the British consul. But this was merely one in a series of collisions with foreign representatives. Within a few weeks Butler had affronted the dignity and violated the privileges of the French, Dutch, and Spanish consuls. Naturally they turned for help in restraining the general to their nations' ministers in Washington, and Seward was soon being pestered with complaints about Butler's cavalier disregard of the diplomatic proprieties.[34]

Committed already to his policy of conciliation, Seward responded to these protests in the same spirit. He saw to it that Butler was relieved of the civil administration of the city and he despatched a special State Department agent to investigate the charges of wholesale violations of consular rights and privileges. He also persuaded Edwin Stanton at the War Department to order the general "to refrain from any severities or strictures of doubtful right" upon any foreign consul or subject. In Butler's opinion, as he later recalled, Seward "was in distress whenever I did anything that caused a little whipper-snapper emissary from some government in Europe to complain of my just treatment of a man who claimed to be a consul, and this caused perpetual interference and annoyance."[35] In this way the excitement over the rough treatment of the consuls was quickly calmed, but Seward found himself helpless to limit the international consequences of Butler's other indiscretion. On May 15 he issued his "infamous" General Order—"As the officers and soldiers of the United States have been subject to repeated insults from women (calling themselves ladies) of New Orleans, in return for the most scrupulous non-interference and courtesy on our part, it is ordered that hereafter when any female shall, by word, gesture or movement, insult or show contempt for any officer or soldier of the United States, she shall be regarded and held liable to be treated as a woman of the town plying her avocation."[36]

As the order suggested, provocation had not been lacking. The citizens of New Orleans, and the women in particular, had subjected the occupying force to a campaign of insults, sly and bold, verbal and physical. "The spirit of impotent but impertinent hate in this population is astonishing," one soldier from New England wrote home.[37] Women who met Union troops in the carriage ways ostentatiously held their skirts aside as if they "feared they might be contaminated if they touched the soldier," and this act was accompanied "with every possible gesture of contempt and abhorrence."[38] Butler suffered a similar indignity himself, while his naval counterpart, David Farragut, had the even more distasteful experience of being showered with what appears to have been the contents of a bucket of slops. In an effort to revive his men's spirits the general issued the order, although he no doubt relished the controversy it was certain to stir. Unfortunately, in addition to amusing the Northern public and exciting the Confederates to impotent fury, it attracted international attention and became a source of acute embarrassment to Union sympathizers abroad, especially those in Britain.

British friends of the Union expected the capture of New Orleans to have a great effect upon public opinion, both as an illustration of the growing strength of the Union and as a revelation of the vulnerability of the Confederacy. Although the inveterately hostile *Punch* depicted "Big Lincoln Horner" holding the plum of New Orleans and sitting in front of a list of expenses that totalled $250,000,000— was it worth the price?—the initial response in Britain was generally more favourable to the Union. The city's fall was seen as a damaging defeat for the South, "the heaviest blow" it had yet sustained, "as injurious from the manner of capture as from the value of the city itself." But the more the British thought about it the less important this Confederate reverse seemed. Instead, the unflagging hostility of the citizenry to the Union troops, and then Butler's order, emerged as the truly significant events. They finally disproved the North's contention that the Confederacy was populated by loyal Unionists simply awaiting an opportunity to demonstrate their true sentiments, and vindicated those Englishmen who warned that the Union would only be able to subdue the South through a reign of terror which would eventually jeopardize liberty everywhere in the Republic.[39] However, the outcry in Britain against Butler and his order was also one of genuine Victorian indignation and outrage.

Victorians accepted that the legitimate object of war was to reduce the enemy to submission, and they conceded that this might be done "both directly by defeating his fleet and armies, and indirectly, by laying waste his territory, harassing his commerce, and, by those or other means, so weakening or distressing him, as to render the continuance of war unsupportable." What distinguished civilized from savage societies was the way in which these tasks were performed. The latter pursued them with "unmitigated ferocity" whereas the former sought to do no more injury to the enemy than was necessary, and certainly refrained from useless aggravations of the horrors of warfare. Yet this was exactly what Butler had done, at least in British eyes, for his order had not advanced by a single day the triumph of the North. He was guilty of transgressing the boundaries of civilized warfare, and his conduct further strengthened the convictions of those who ever since the Stone Fleet controversy had deplored the mounting ferocity of the American war and were now calling for its end on the only "sensible" terms—the separation of North and South.[40]

If Butler stood convicted of contravening the conventions of civilized behaviour, what made his crime so heinous in Victorian eyes was that his victims were women. Although the cult of true womanhood, with its emphasis upon the virtues of purity, piety, submissiveness, and domesticity, was already under attack by some early feminists, Victorian males continued to regard the opposite sex in terms of the stereotype. In Palmerston's words, at a Guildhall banquet in 1857, "In the ordinary course of life the functions of women are to cheer the days of adversity, to soothe the hours of suffering, and to give additional brilliancy to the sunshine of prosperity." They were "angelic creatures" whom men worshipped in return for such domestic bliss. A woman's fulfilment lay in marriage, and her role there was a subordinate one, but it was the duty of the male to provide care, support, and protection. Butler had not only disregarded this duty but had further compounded his offence by threatening his victims with treatment as "fallen women." The good women of New Orleans, it seemed, were to be deliberately exposed to those sordid aspects of life from which they had always been sheltered. Thus Butler's order could not have been more successfully composed had his intention been to excite the fury and scorn of Victorian England. The *Saturday Review* expressed the general contempt for men who sought "to protect themselves from the tongues of a handful of women by official and authoritative threats of rape. The bloodiest savages could do nothing crueller—the most loathsome Yahoo of fiction could do nothing filthier."[41]

Pilloried in the press, the general was further excoriated in Parliament, and in both forums his "gross, unmanly and brutal insult to every woman in New Orleans" was spoken of in the same breath as possible European mediation of the American war.[42] There could be no escaping the damage Butler had done to the Union cause in Britain nor the aid he had given to the Confederate. Conspicuous among his indignant assailers was William Gregory, member for Galway. Few British politicians were so intimately identified with the Southern cause as this former Peelite who had found a political home in the Whig-Liberal coalition. A loyal friend and political dependent of the scandalous Earl of Clanricarde, whose entrance into the first Palmerston cabinet had done much to weaken its standing in Parliament, Gregory had not been damaged by the association. He was held in high esteem on both sides of the Commons and was to refuse offers of minor office from the Liberals in 1865 and Conservatives in 1866. Early in the war he had emerged as the leader of the Confederate lobby in the Commons. It had taken the combined efforts of Palmerston and Russell to dissuade him in May 1861 from pressing ahead with a precipitous motion calling for British recognition of the Confederacy; he had played a prominent role in the blockade debate and had become both a friend and an adviser to Mason, as he had also been to the earlier Confederate commissioners.

The roots of Gregory's full-hearted commitment to the South lay in his journey to North America in 1859. He had undertaken it in that spirit of enquiry and exploration recommended by his friend Lawley, and in order to place himself physically beyond the reach of his many creditors, thereby encouraging them to settle his debts on more favourable terms. (Like Lawley, he was another unsuccessful enthusiast of the turf.) In the Republic this Anglo-Irish gentleman had found the company of Southerners especially congenial, and during his visit to the national capital he had stayed in a Southern "mess," establishing a number of close and lasting friendships.

William Porcher Miles, in particular, had served as his "guide, philosopher and friend," and the South Carolinian had succeeded in filling Gregory's head as full of rebellion as his own. Such personal attachments merely strengthened a sense of social affinity with Southerners. To Gregory's mind, and perhaps to his surprise, they really were "agreeable, polished, highly educated gentlemen in the fullest sense of the word." Here were the American gentry of Thackeray's *The Virginians*, and once the war started and Virginia became the principal battleground and thus the focus of British attention, the temptation to liken them to the Cavaliers in England's own civil war proved irresistible. It was fostered by Lawley's romantic descriptions of Robert E. Lee, James Longstreet, and J. E. B. Stuart, the South's Prince Rupert, although the stern Thomas "Stonewall" Jackson could be likened only to the great Cromwell and his "foot cavalry" to the New Model Army. As for James Murray Mason, the Confederate commissioner in London, his family had fled to America following the Royalist defeat at Worcester. He was living proof that "There still remains among them the ancestral and hereditary recollections of England."[43]

Transplanted Englishmen they might be, but the Southern gentry were unquestionably slave-owners. Having seen the institution at first hand, Gregory deplored its inherent brutality and the violence it committed upon the intellects of otherwise rational people. He had discovered that no proposition was too preposterous for his Southern friends to accept "in order to secure the stability of what they call their peculiar institution, no theory too monstrous by which they do not seek to justify it." From theology to physiology they sought and naturally they found evidence that slavery was justifiable, expedient, and necessary. Clearly, as he had recognized, the disruption of the Union would see Britain pulled in opposite directions. Her commercial interests would attract her to the South, which produced cotton and espoused free trade, whereas her "social and moral instincts would be with the North or the antagonistic element to slavery." He resolved this dilemma for himself by giving precedence to racial and material considerations rather than moral, although much later in his life he was sufficiently embarrassed by this decision to seek to obscure it. At the time, however, he was impressed by the warnings of his friends that emancipation meant not merely "absolute hopeless ruin, and the loss of enormous capital sunk in sugar, rice, cotton and tobacco plantations," but even the extirpation of either the black or the white race in the South. Freed blacks would inevitably demand the full rights of citizenship which if granted would place them in many parts of the South in a position to "override" whites, and few of that race would ever accept such a prospect peacefully.[44]

Unthinkable as this situation would be for white men of any nationality, Gregory and some of his countrymen found its likelihood doubly disturbing. For if white supremacy was one article of racial faith, a second was black indolence whenever the compulsion to work was lifted, and a third was the inability of whites to labour in the subtropical regions of the American South. Yet the cotton of this region was vital to the prosperity of Lancashire's industrial cities, and their prosperity was in turn essential for the profitability of British agriculture, especially that of Ireland. As an Irish landowner William Gregory comprehended the interest Britain had in the maintenance of a reliable labour force in the cotton states, and what other means was there of ensuring black dependability than slavery? As Lord Lyons once explained to his Russian counterpart in Washington, Englishmen sought cheap cotton and believed that only by the toil of slaves would they obtain it.[45] Seward's diplomacy had been founded upon the same belief and a similar perception of British interests.

Moved, then, by the ties of friendship, by a sense of social affinity with Southern gentlemen, by a belief in the validity of the Southern right to secede, convinced of the strength of the independence sentiment, anxious to protect the South's capacity to supply Britain with cotton, and like any good Palmerstonian keen to see an increasingly significant political and economic rival to Britain weakened, Gregory had emerged as the Confederacy's parliamentary champion. As such he exploited to the full the news from New Orleans. Even when the most generous construction was placed upon Butler's words, he charged, they constituted a threat to imprison ladies "in the calaboose with drunken negroes and all the rascality" of the city. In short, a punishment "too horrible to contemplate." It was certainly too horrible for Palmerston, whom Gregory had little difficulty drawing publicly into the controversy. In the House of Lords Russell had gone to some lengths in an effort to quell the excitement. The purport of Butler's "indefensible" order, he explained, was to make those women of New Orleans who showed contempt for the Union forces liable to punishment under a local ordinance which provided that women of the town caught plying their trade might be imprisoned for disturbing the peace. As Gregory pointed out this was repugnant enough to

British sensibilities, but it was a great deal less sensational than the image of the offending women being treated as common prostitutes by the Union soldiery. Palmerston, replying to a question from Gregory, was far less temperate—he added his to the voices of outrage. "It is a proclamation to which I do not scruple to attach the epithet infamous," he angrily announced. "Sir, an Englishman must blush to think that such an act has been committed by one belonging to the Anglo-Saxon race."[46] But the true measure of the prime minister's indignation was his private squabble with the American minister, for one other unforeseen consequence of Butler's order was a lamentable deterioration in Palmerston's relations with Adams.

Palmerston's remarkable political success in his later years and his immense personal popularity were attributable in no small measure to his ability both to perceive and reflect the mood of his countrymen. As Adams remarked, and he intended no compliment, "His mind is typical of John Bull."[47] In a series of personal notes to Adams on the Butler affair, the prime minister did no more than express privately what many Englishmen were saying publicly. Nevertheless, he was the prime minister and his criticism extended to the Lincoln administration. "If the Federal Government chooses to be served by men capable of such revolting outrages," he informed Adams, "they must submit to abide by the deserved opinion which mankind will form of their conduct."[48]

The self-restraint in which the American minister had clothed himself since his arrival in Britain was by now more than a little threadbare. He was acutely conscious of his "lonely position of prominence among a people selfish, jealous, and at heart hostile" to the Union, and was tiring of the "distasteful" and "fatiguing" if not hopeless task of modifying the attitude of the British in general and their government in particular to his nation's terrible difficulties. He resented the government's refusal to ease his position by offering even "the smallest manifestation of good will in act."[49] The British rejection of his request for the return of the *Emily St. Pierre*, seized by the blockading squadron off Charleston only to be recaptured from the prize crew and brought triumphantly into Liverpool, was but the latest example. Adams could only fume privately as the English made heroes of the captain, the cook, and the steward, the three men who had retaken the vessel, even though they were a Scot, a German, and an Irishman respectively. Praise and presents were showered upon them by grateful merchants and the Mercantile Marine Association.[50]

Almost inevitably the American's anger was drawn to Palmerston like lightning to a conductor. He was the highest point in the administration and he, rather than Russell, appeared to devise British policy towards America. Adams considered Palmerston a "relic of the prejudices and passions which brought on the War of 1812," and a representative of those privileged classes whose anxiety to see the Union fail was "remarkable." He attributed to Palmerston's malign influence the lack of sympathy for the Union cause exhibited by Lord Shaftesbury ("the nominal chief of the philanthropy of Great Britain"). It was the premier whom he held responsible for the "obvious ill will" to the United States shown by *The Times*, the *Post*, and the *Globe*. In short, Adams had a score or two to settle with the prime minister and through him the people of Britain. The American's behaviour was a measure also of his fear that a far-reaching change of British policy was in the offing. Indeed, he had been uneasy for some time, as he watched the pressures on the government increasing.[51]

It had not escaped Adams's attention that the two newspapers most closely identified with Palmerston, *The Times* and the *Morning Post*, were "becoming more and more distinct in favor of some form of interference or other." On June 13 London was buzzing with the rumour that Britain and France were planning a joint intervention, and the arrival of one of the emperor's ministers had done nothing to break the tension. To the unhappy and agitated Adams, convinced that a hostile Palmerston had only been held in check earlier by his cabinet, it did not seem at all improbable that the prime minister's private note about Butler was an "irregular method of precipitating us all into a misunderstanding." He responded vigorously, and for a few days the American legation "considered things so serious as to strongly anticipate a sudden rupture of all intercourse."[52]

Having first briefly replied to Palmerston, asking for some clarification of the capacity in which he had written, as private gentleman or prime minister, Adams next visited the Foreign Office. According to Russell the American was in "a dreadful state" and gave vent to his anger and resentment. For his part the foreign secretary sought to calm the uncharacteristically emotional Adams, and after his departure wrote to the prime minister suggesting that he withdraw the note or at least make it clear that he did not hold the United States government responsible for Butler's order. Unfortunately, in a second note to Adams, Palmerston merely expressed the hope that Lincoln had immediately "given peremptory orders for withdrawing and cancelling the Proclamation." Even then he could not resist the temptation to read Adams another lecture on the behaviour of the Union troops. Not surprisingly these gratuitous observations did little to cool the American, who angrily repeated his earlier request that Palmerston define his role.[53]

Palmerston's Victorian outrage over Butler's conduct in New Orleans was now transformed into testiness with Adams. However, he did indicate a desire to let the matter drop, and Adams might well have done so. From a second interview with Russell, "the most kindly" to date, he had emerged somewhat more confident that the British were not planning any sudden change of policy. Nevertheless, the pleasure of rebuking the prime minister was one the American was in no mood to forgo.[54] The infuriated Palmerston responded by ignoring Adams whenever he could. He declined to acknowledge him when they met at the International Exhibition, the names of the members of the American legation were stricken from Lady Palmerston's guest list, and when the Adamses left their card at the Palmerstons it remained unanswered. Petty as this all was, it indicated the depth of Palmerston's personal animosity toward the American, an attitude other important figures, such as Edmund Hammond, the permanent under-secretary at the Foreign Office, rushed to share. And this rupture in personal relations came at a particularly dangerous moment for the Union cause in Britain.

Adams ought to have been at his anodyne best in the summer of 1862, soothing abrasions and lessening tensions, especially in his dealings with the popular prime minister. Support for the Union in the press, Parliament, government, society, and among intellectuals, if not entirely absent, was far from overwhelming. The efforts of friends to identify the Union cause with that of freedom had made little appreciable headway. Spence's was the most popular interpretation of the conflict's origins, and there was no escaping the evidence of a growing public belief that the war had already gone on long enough and that reunion was impossible. Butler's conduct at New Orleans had served to strengthen both these convictions. Unable to find any moral justification for the struggle, a great many

59

Englishmen had good reason to wish for its early termination. Worry about the economic and social consequences for the textile districts and the nation of protracted strife was mixed with admiration for the plucky and outnumbered Southerners and humanitarian dismay at the high toll in casualties suffered by both sides. And if their commitment to the Confederate cause was more positive and active than that of most of their countrymen, the sentiments and calculations that moved William Gregory and Frank Lawley were by no means peculiar to them. It was the fear that the Palmerston government would adjust its course to catch this freshening breeze of public opinion that led Adams into the needless and personal dispute over the Butler episode.

THREE

A Policy of Postponement

DAILY LEADERS IN THE PRINCIPAL NEWSPAPERS, frequent reports by special correspondents, lengthy articles in the periodicals, all testified to the Englishman's continuing interest in the American war. After more than a year the fighting and suffering across the Atlantic still gripped his attention, while some of the participants were beginning to capture his imagination. The fascination was discoloured by horror, however, and any tendency to complacency born of Britain's peace and prosperity was tempered by the fear that the effects of the conflict would soon be felt in England. How long would it be before the British economy was so disrupted that national prosperity and social stability became imperilled? After all, the cotton trade was the "great fly-wheel" of a thriving economy and once it was broken would not the rest of the nation's industrial machinery be thrown out of gear?[1] Confronted by the difficulties and dangers as well as the opportunities inherent in the Civil War, the Palmerston cabinet had at its outset taken refuge in a policy of neutrality. As a response more to the urgings of expediency than any summons to principle, such a policy was scarcely fixed and unalterable. Yet neither the changing character of the war nor its threatened economic and social implications for Britain prompted any thoroughgoing reappraisal of policy within the government. If left to themselves, Palmerston and his colleagues intended to go along much as they had been and for much the same reasons.

France remained the principal preoccupation, if not fixation, of "le vieux Pam" and "le vénérable John." Although Napoleon was slowly being drawn deeper into the morass of Mexico, an adventure from which the British prime minister was by no means keen to discourage him, his capacity for mischief in Europe still seemed considerable to these two veterans. Recently installed as lord warden of the Cinque Ports, Palmerston had stayed briefly at Walmer Castle, the traditional residence of the warden. Beautiful weather and the magnificent view of the Channel must have reminded him of the proximity of "a people who, say what they may, hate us as a nation from the bottom of their hearts, and would make any sacrifice to inflict a deep humiliation upon England." Able to recall clearly the great victories of the Napoleonic Wars half a century earlier, he was quite sure that the "eminently vain" French, with their passion for "glory in war," had neither forgotten nor forgiven these defeats. Consumed by a dangerous desire for revenge, Britain's neighbours were ruled by another Bonaparte, "an able, active, wary, counsel keeping, but ever planning sovereign." And not content with an army which dwarfed that of the British, he was "labouring hard to create a navy equal to, if not superior" to theirs.[2]

Palmerston's suspicions, occasionally exaggerated for effect, were echoed by Russell. He believed that the emperor of the French was busily at work undermining all governments already in trouble, thereby creating pretexts for interference. The foreign secretary was watching with particular concern the developing contest between Austria and Prussia for supremacy in Germany, not because of any immediate threat to British interests, but out of fear that one of the two contestants might be "induced to yield German interests to France for the sake of French support." The appointment of that well-known "partisan of Russia and of France," Bismarck, to the Prussian embassy in Paris, was seen in some British circles as an indication of Prussia's willingness to purchase Napoleon's favour.[3]

For these reasons, if no other, the spring of 1862 seemed as inopportune a time as any during the past year to follow a course which might end with embroilment in the American war. This was not the moment to offer Napoleon too much freedom of action in Europe. Far better to persevere with the joint policy of neutrality. Consequently, when the arrival in London of the French minister of the interior, Persigny, hard on the heels of speculative leaders in semi-official Paris newspapers, excited talk of mediation and prompted questions in Parliament, Palmerston and Russell brushed them aside. There had been no official French intimation of a change of policy, and writing from the French capital a few days later, on June 20, Cowley reassured them that although there "is a feeling in the Emperor's mind that it was a mistake to recognize the blockade originally," an opinion with which the British ambassador tended to agree, yet that "does not prompt him to a desire to quit the neutrality which we have both adopted now."[4]

United in a common distrust of France, Palmerston and Russell were also troubled about their nation's future relations with the United States. The fear that the Union might in a fit of madness add a foreign war to the domestic one had long since receded, but the disquieting thought was never far from their minds that at the end of the Civil War the North, triumphant or not, would turn on Britain. The responses to this disagreeable prospect were varied. Certainly it was one more weapon in an arsenal of arguments used by Palmerston in his running battle with Gladstone over the chancellor's proposals to cut defence appropriations. For Russell it was another reason to accelerate the already expensive program of iron ship construction. "The French have been long before us," he reminded the prime minister, "and in six months more the United States will be far ahead of us unless our builders in the Navy Department exert themselves." To allow this to happen was to run the risk of a repetition of some of the least illustrious events of a half-century earlier. "Only think," he wrote, "of our position if in the case of the Yankees turning upon us they should by means of iron ships renew the triumphs they achieved in 1812–1813 by means of superior size and weight of metal."[5]

Disturbing memories of the War of 1812 served also to remind the government that Canada remained as vulnerable as ever to attack. At the Colonial Office Newcastle had long feared that an assault on the colony would be the epilogue to the American drama. Clearly there could be no lessening of the number of imperial troops stationed there. In this atmosphere it was not surprising that some Englishmen thought that the best guarantee against difficulties with the Americans, at least for the time being, was in a continuation of the war. Of these the Earl of Clarendon was one of the most highly placed. He was not a member of the government, but he had served as foreign secretary in Palmerston's previous cabinet. Although he had declined to join the present one at its formation, his brother, C. P. Villiers, did sit in it as did his brother-in-law, Lewis, and he was to join it before long. He remained on close terms with Palmerston. In short, he was an influential figure who moved in cabinet circles, and he probably reflected a more general opinion than his own when he wrote to Edmund Hammond, "I hate the Confederates almost as much as the Federals but I hope for success and the consequent prolongation of the war because it is only the complete exhaustion of both parties that will prevent their uniting against us."[6]

Further strengthening the disinclination to meddle in America at this time was the fact that the members of the cabinet were not of a common mind about the issues at stake in the war. Thus Argyll rebuked Gladstone, although privately and mildly, for his remarks in Manchester. "That this war is having a powerful,—a daily increasing effect on the hold of slavery over opinion in America" was a fact so evident and natural, the lord privy seal asserted, that he could not understand how anyone questioned it. His colleague Thomas Milner Gibson was of a like mind and so it seems was Villiers. And while Argyll conceded that the war was not being fought for this purpose, he did not think it was required as a justification. All governments should ponder long on the fact that "The doctrine of secession is simply the doctrine of anarchy." In this frame of mind, and with these sympathies, he also expressed his dissent from Russell's concept of the duties of a neutral. It was "a very loose doctrine," he complained to Gladstone, which permitted Britain to inform the Federals that she was under no obligation to prevent her merchant vessels carrying arms to the South. "If a neutral government is not bound to prevent,—so far as it can such a trade," he went on, "all government neutrality is a farce and there w[oul]d be constant danger of our neutrality being compromised." This concern even goaded him into sounding out Gladstone on the possibility of their approaching independently the solicitor general, Roundell Palmer, for an opinion on Russell's response to the Union complaints. The chancellor quickly scotched that suggestion, pointing out that "the Law Officers are for these purposes the right hand men of the Foreign Office and must be presumed to have been consulted." Nor was Gladstone willing to retreat far from the position he had taken at Manchester, that freedom could not be established at the point of a sword. He did not deny that "the continuance of the horrible struggle" was "faintly favourable to emancipation," but he could not welcome such "very moderate amounts of advantage at so frightful a cost."[7]

Gladstone's conviction that the war was not worth the cost could only have been strengthened by one of his correspondents, a Liberian diplomat who had been a victim of racial discrimination in the United States. Writing in June, he reported that the war "has not yet assumed a moral aspect; it is purely political—the leading men —excepting such noble spirits as Mr. Sumner—having no idea of freeing the slaves."[8] In brief, the Union had a poor claim to any genuine moral superiority in the struggle. It was a view Russell shared. At Newcastle, several months earlier, the foreign secretary had voiced the opinion that the Northern states were fighting for "empire," for political rather than moral ends, and nothing that had taken place since then had caused him to change his mind. Thus he had no hesitation in expressing the belief at the beginning of May, in a despatch to Lyons intended for publication, that "separation would be best for the North as well as for the South, for America and for Europe, for the future welfare of the free, and for the future emancipation of the slave." If only the North could be made to see that by letting the South depart and then applying Lincoln's scheme of compensated emancipation to the border states it might create a great nation of free men, "there might be some hope of an end to the struggle." Left independent but surrounded by free territory, no longer able to require the assistance of the free states to recover fugitive slaves, Southerners would gradually have to yield to the prevailing opinion of civilized and Christian nations in favour of personal freedom. Popular as this notion was in Britain, the foreign secretary also shared the wish of some of his countrymen that any abolition of slavery be both practical and peaceful. For obvious reasons the British had no desire to see Southern society pushed into a convulsion which would leave its "rich and fertile lands" a prey to anarchy.[9]

Palmerston had little time for "guesses as to future events," and he ridiculed this effort to place them on record. He observed that "the course of events between the Federals & Confederates has realized but few of the guesses which the best informed people have from time to time made upon those matters." Russell's remarks were well enough written and might be read with interest if published in the *Edinburgh Review*, he noted condescendingly, but they had little place in a diplomatic despatch. Anyway, these "speculations" as to "the probable Future of the North American Republic" might be concurred in by some members of the cabinet but not by others. However, it was neither the need to preserve cabinet solidarity nor any preoccupation with the institution of slavery that confirmed the prime minister in his adherence to the policy of nonintervention. Although Villiers had reassured John Bright at the beginning of the year that Palmerston's detestation of slavery made him more reluctant than some of their colleagues in the cabinet to establish diplomatic relations with the Confederacy, far less elevated considerations were in the forefront of the prime minister's mind now, five months later, as he resisted suggestions that Britain mediate the war or recognize the Confederacy.[10]

The news reaching England in May, of the string of Federal successes culminating in the captures of New Orleans and Yorktown, did seem "to portend the conquest of the South." The prime minister was shown an official Union map which marked the disposition and numbers of Federal troops. Graphically, it detailed the desperate Southern position. Believing as always only what he wished, perhaps influenced by the ardent supporters of the South in his own household (both his private secretary, Evelyn Ashley, who may also have been his grandson, and Ashley's father, Shaftesbury, fell into this category), Palmerston accepted that the Confederates "were in great straits" but fancied he saw two or three ways in which they might yet win more battles. Certainly it was time to find out whether the Southern population shared the undying enmity for the North expressed so freely to Mercier by the political leaders of the Confederacy during his trip to Richmond in April. Palmerston rejected any notion of mediation, which in the context of the times meant the establishment of an independent South. Resorting to one of his colourful analogies, he likened it to "offering to make it up between Sayers and Heenan [warriors in the epic bare-knuckle contest at Farnborough, Kent, in 1860] after the Third Round." It was a waste of time, for there was no likelihood of both sides welcoming the good offices of a third party.[11]

The proposal that Britain recognize the Confederacy, which William Lindsay had given notice of his intention to move in the Commons, was not one the prime minister considered timely. Although he clung to the belief that despite their recent setbacks the Southerners "may and probably will maintain the contest," Britain "ought to know that their separate independence is a truth and a fact" before she declared it to be so. Nor did he see how British recognition would materially advance the Confederate cause. They would not be "a bit the more independent for our saying so unless we followed up our Declaration by taking Part with them in the war," he commented to Russell's deputy, Henry Layard, and no one in Britain was seriously proposing that. Therefore acknowledgment of their independence would add nothing to the "Rights" the Southerners already enjoyed as belligerents.[12] Convinced that as things stood it would be foolish to offer mediation, and pointless to recognize the South, uneasy about relations with the Union once the war was over, anxious above all to keep a weather-eye on the French in Europe, Palmerston and Russell made no move to initiate any change of policy in a cabinet whose members did not agree on the American war anyway. The advantages of holding to the policy of nonintervention were evident, but the question that remained to be answered was for how long would this be possible?

Everyone agreed that a cotton famine would be a social calamity, perhaps a national economic disaster, likely to curtail seriously if it did not cripple altogether the government's freedom of action with respect to America. As a result, the problems of the textile districts were never far from the minds of Palmerston and his ministers. During his visit to Manchester Gladstone had addressed the Association of Lancashire and Cheshire Mechanics' Institutes. Naturally he spoke of the problem confronting everyone in that area and he made no bones of the fact that the outlook was not promising. "On the contrary, if the present be dark, the signs of the immediate future seem darker still." He sought to console the working people with the thought that all are born to suffer no matter what their station in life, even the Queen, who had recently been bereaved. While Gladstone held up for emulation this example of royal stoicism, the prime minister sought from Sir Charles Wood the reassurance that India would forward as much cotton as it could to Britain. But there could be no hiding from the unpleasant fact, as Wood pointed out, that all the subcontinent "can send will not suffice for the consumption of Lancashire."[13] Thus the "most urgent matter" of the moment for the foreign secretary, at least on May 23, was to find out how much cotton could be "expected from the South in consequence of the military and naval successes of the Federal Forces." Russell was pessimistic. He gloomily predicted that Southerners, their spirit apparently unbroken by the recent reverses, would burn their stocks rather than permit them to be exported though Union-controlled ports. Nor was he unmindful of the danger of their sowing fields with corn and wheat instead of cotton. The analysis of the Board of Trade was still more chilling. Responding to a request from the Foreign Office for an opinion as to the effects of the Union's throwing open the ports of Beaufort, Port Royal, and New Orleans, the board drafted a report based upon the despatches of the British consuls in the South and a number of unofficial sources. It echoed Russell's dire prediction that all the evidence pointed to the destruction of cotton by the Confederates rather than to its exportation by the Union forces, and forecast that the longer the fighting dragged on the bleaker the future became. The war's impact upon the Southern labour system of slavery, the disruption of the traditional relationship between Northern capitalists and Southern planters, the inevitable neglect of farm buildings and agricultural machinery, the ravages wrought upon the communications of the South, as bridges, roads, steamships, and railroads were damaged or destroyed, all these factors led to the frightening conclusion that the cultivation of cotton in the United States was certain to be "paralysed for a long time to come, if not for ever."[14]

If Britain was to secure cotton in any quantity from the South it seemed obvious that some scheme would have to be devised whereby Confederates could export the fibre without fear that their enemies would profit. Consequently, although he had been antagonized by the earlier Southern policy of preventing its export in an effort to coerce British and French recognition of their independence, Russell now urged Seward to demonstrate that the Federal government was genuinely seeking to make it possible for the Europeans to obtain cotton. What he proposed was that the Union guarantee that every planter willing to sell would receive all the money any buyer paid. In short, that the transaction be made independent of political allegiance and Southerners have the assurance that none of the proceeds from the sale of cotton would be "applied to the purchase of arms to be used against themselves."[15] In this way the motive for burning cotton might have been removed. Yet it was a poorly considered proposal. The Union could scarcely be expected to help the Confederates fill up their empty coffers and thereby prop up their rebellion by permitting them export cotton freely to Europe. That Russell could seriously advance such a suggestion was a measure of the British government's anxiety about the consequences of a cotton shortage.

Within the cabinet, the first minister to feel the pressures building up in the mill towns of Lancashire was Charles Pelham Villiers, the president of the Poor Law Board. At sixty he was one of the younger members of a government of old men. His background was interesting. Born into the aristocracy, albeit as a younger son, he had always been attracted by radical causes. A Benthamite and a leading figure in the Anti-Corn Law campaign, he came to be regarded as an extreme free trader. The price he paid for this independence of political thought and behaviour was a long exclusion from high office. It was not until Palmerston went searching for Radical support for his coalition, when called upon to form a second administration in 1859, that Villiers gained belated recognition. And if, as one of his colleagues observed, he grew a little fat and pompous on the strength of his new eminence, he was nonetheless well-equipped for his new post. He had a first-hand knowledge of the workings of the Poor Law, gained during his service years before as an assistant commissioner, had participated in the great enquiry of 1832–34, and had been a fixture on subsequent committees. Clearly he was concerned with the welfare of working people. From 1835 until the end of a political career which extended almost to the eve of the next century, he sat for the unfashionable industrial borough of Wolverhampton, and his opposition to the Corn Laws had been sparked in part by a desire to raise the standard of living of the working poor by lowering the price they had to pay for their bread.[16]

As the crisis in Lancashire worsened, Villiers moved to prevent panic. He urged members for the county to keep a grip upon themselves and thus serve as a calming influence upon their constituents. Bad as the situation was, and it seemed certain to deteriorate, the last thing the government needed was for it to be exaggerated. To his aid he summoned Delane and *The Times*, which disabused Lancashire MPs of any notion that they would be able to obtain public money to relieve the distress. This was one of the points Villiers emphasized during the Commons debate on the distress in the manufacturing districts on May 9. Speaking so quietly that he could be heard only with difficulty, he had reassured the House and the country that the Poor Law authorities were equal to the emergency. His comparison of the Lancashire poor rate with that in other parts of the kingdom must have satisfied many of those listening that there was a very long way to go before this wealthy county exhausted its means. Villiers was supported by John Bright, who on this subject spoke with the added authority of a Lancashire resident and millowner. Great as the suffering was, Bright remarked, it was not as uniform as some people imagined and it did not as yet rival that of the miserable years of 1840 and 1841. He urged that the efforts of the local Poor Law authorities, the Boards of Guardians, be supplemented by local relief committees to which the wealthy ought to contribute, and he predicted that even "if this state of things should go on for many months longer, the county will find itself quite competent to take care of its own affairs, without sending the hat around to other parts of the country."[17]

Successfully resisted by Villiers, the point of pressure soon shifted to Charles Wood at the India Office. Accompanied by Col. Wilson Patten, who had led the Lancashire members to the Poor Law Office earlier, a delegation of workingmen called on June 18 at the India Board, which the *Morning Star* claimed was now being besieged by deputations of distressed operatives. They came to request, as had their masters in the past, a program of public works in the colony. The aim was to reduce the cost of Indian cotton and thus make it more competitive with American. J. B. "Corn Law" Smith, the Radical member for the mill town of Stockport, pressed the argument in the Commons the following day. Speaking in the same debate, Patten urged a further reduction in the duties levied on British cloth shipped to India, in part a protection for the small native industry. Presumably this would have the double advantage of increasing British exports and reducing the domestic Indian consumption of cotton, developments which could be expected to lessen unemployment in Lancashire.[18]

Wood deflected proposals that amounted to little more than shifting some of Lancashire's misery to India. In the Commons he patiently explained that the Indian government was doing all that it thought could properly be done to promote cotton cultivation. But saddled with enormous debts run up during the Mutiny, it was in no position to borrow heavily in order to undertake costly public works projects, such as making the Godavery river navigable. To Wood's credit, this extreme caution reflected not merely his concern with Indian finances, or the strength of his personal commitment to laissez-faire—and he remained not a little scornful of the Manchester men now demanding government interference—but also his suspicion that Lancashire had little genuine interest in the development of India as a permanent source of cotton. He feared that any resumption of American supplies would see an abandonment of India, without a thought to the consequences for its economy or its population. At the Foreign Office, meanwhile, the clamour for government action evoked a no more sympathetic response. Hammond suggested that Russell's letter of the previous year, offering the help of consuls, to which the "Manchester People" had made no reply, be dug out and held in readiness so that if they became troublesome it could be thrown "in their teeth."[19]

The government had weathered the first squall over conditions in Lancashire but the storm signals remained. On the eve of the Commons debate on the distress, during which Villiers cited Preston as an example of one of the hardest-hit towns where the poor rate remained far less than the charge on other regions of the country, *The Times* had published a letter from a person involved in the administration of relief in that hapless community. His had been a far more discouraging picture, one not only of rising unemployment but also of diminishing means to meet it. A special relief fund of the kind Bright was recommending had long been in existence but it was now almost exhausted, while the poor rates were crushing a host of small traders. Nor was there any doubt that the operatives themselves were growing restless. The six thousand who had gathered on April 30 at Ashton-under-Lyne, a town represented in Parliament by one of the staunchest Union sympathizers in the cabinet, Thomas Milner Gibson, had passed a resolution calling for the recognition of the Confederacy as the solution for their misery. Another three thousand had assembled that same day in Stevenson Square, Manchester. They sought some relaxation of the obnoxious labour test for relief, and an increase in the amount already being provided. As one speaker explained, a young man receiving two shillings and sixpence a week still had to pay a shilling for his lodging, unless he went to live in "Billy Brown's wheel-house"—the street. That left him threepence a day for food, except on the Sabbath, when he was obliged to give his jaws a rest. The plight of the married couple receiving a single additional shilling a week was no easier. Thus to some, including the relief committee of Blackburn, where fully one-seventh of the population had been on relief as early as the middle of April, and the numbers were growing, the only solution seemed to be some form of national help.[20] All of which the Radical, pro-Unionist *Morning Star* considered very sinister. It complained that the open-air meetings being got up to petition for the relaxation of the Poor Law Code were really being called to excite popular feeling against the North and against continued recognition of the blockade. The newspaper regarded the occasional calls for a parliamentary subsidy to meet the crisis as an even more devious ploy of the Confederacy's friends. "By bringing home to the whole body of English taxpayers the effect of the civil war upon our manufacturing population," the *Star* warned, "they no doubt hope to provoke an irresistible hostility against the immediate cause of the distress."[21]

However suspicious the *Star* was of the unrest, the grievances of the operatives were real enough. In those parts of the nation where wages were traditionally low, such as the agricultural areas, two shillings and sixpence might be welcomed as adequate but in Lancashire the textile workers had somewhat higher expectations. It was not that they had all lived in well-paid comfort. On the contrary, great numbers were all too familiar with or conscious of the manifold miseries of poverty. The rapid urbanization of the county (it was by 1851 the most highly urbanized in Britain with over half its population living in towns of a substantial size) had brought all the attendant evils of overcrowding. Poor housing and poor sanitation bred epidemics of disease. The low wages paid to some of the factory workers and most of the labourers subjected families to strains with which they were often unable to cope. Fathers sought the companionship of beer shops rather than sit in homes left empty when wives and even children were obliged to work in the mills in order to keep poverty at a distance. The census-takers in 1851 had found that fifteen adult women in every hundred were employed in the cotton industry. They worked all day long for ten shillings a week. Lucky were the few who were sent down to London in 1862 to work in the Machinery Annexe of the great International Exhibition, oiling the machines and minding the bobbins as at home, but paid twenty-four shillings for their week's labour. Yet long and hard though millwork was, the operatives were better paid than most other industrial labourers, and with the exception of a few major slumps, the last coming in the mid-1850s, employment had been steady for those with skill and experience. As a result, perhaps one-seventh of all the working families had managed to live in lasting freedom from the ravages of poverty.[22]

Although they had grown accustomed to employment and adequate family incomes, for young children could earn six shillings a week and adolescents as much as thirteen, the distressed operatives had too much pride to turn immediately to the Poor Law guardians. The workhouse was popularly known as the "Bastille," while the term "pauper" was an epithet to be avoided almost at any cost. They tended to try all alternatives before applying for relief, and this was one reason why the county's poor rates were far lower than elsewhere. For months following the onset of the depression in 1861 many operatives had lived off their own resources or on those of kith and kin. They resorted to "huddling," two families occupying a single house and sharing the cost of rent and fuel. But it was not long before the crisis ground away the means of all. Furniture and clothing pawned, savings exhausted, there was nowhere to go except to the guardians or the special relief committees.[23]

The knowledge that "the popular dread of the union-house, and the shame of eating workhouse bread" had kept the suffering of many thousands out of sight caused some Englishmen to question the need to extract from these unfortunate victims of the cotton famine the further humiliation of the labour test as a condition of out-relief. The Outdoor Relief Regulation Order of 1852, drafted specifically with the manufacturing districts in mind, had provided that such relief to the able-bodied should be given only in return for work, hence the labour test. To sympathetic onlookers it seemed inappropriate to test the rising poverty in Lancashire by "the most severe and revolting labour."[24] However, speaking for the government during the Commons debate on May 9, Villiers had denied that the test and the underlying principle, that the able-bodied should not receive money without working for it, were unreasonable. Perhaps he had been encouraged by the evidence given before the Select Committee on the Poor Law, which he had chaired one month earlier. On that occasion the clerk to the guardians of the Macclesfield Union had granted that there had been some problems initially in imposing the test upon operatives, "but when the Guardians are firm, and the people are spoken to they fall into it without difficulty, and without much trouble."[25] And when the special inspector, H. B. Farnall, despatched by the government to Lancashire, visited the unfortunate towns of Preston and Blackburn and spoke of the test, he denied that it was a mode of distinguishing between the idle and the deserving. Rather, it was a preservative against "melancholy and demoralisation." Nonetheless, he also made a plea to the guardians to apply it with discretion and with respect for the operatives.[26]

If the government's calm and cautious response to the crisis in Lancashire was a reflection of its determination to quell any sign of panic, and its natural conservatism, there was also the reassuring knowledge that the distress was confined not just to that county but to certain areas within it. Granville, one of the cabinet members sitting in the Lords, pointed to this encouraging fact. The privation "was not quite so general as had at first been imagined." He echoed the remarks made by Bright three days earlier in the Commons, for in Rochdale at least there was a worsted, wool, and silk industry as well as cotton mills and times were not as hard there as they were in towns such as Preston, Ashton, and Blackburn where the industry was less diversified. Another millowner with first-hand experience of the economic anomalies in Lancashire was a close friend of Cobden and Bright, Henry Ashworth, who along with his sons was the majority owner of the New Eagley Factory. Before the war it had returned a princely profit on invested capital, one that was three or four times the rate paid by securities. More than a year after the fighting had begun, the mill continued to operate profitably. The explanation was to be found in the fact that the Ashworths like many of their competitors had had a good stock of cotton on hand when the war broke out. Moreover, they were relatively free of large debts and thus of regular payments of interest. They continued to buy cotton, even at the grossly inflated prices it now commanded, though the Federal successes in May did bring the Manchester cotton market to a virtual standstill. No one wished to be caught with a large quantity of expensive cotton if the war was about to end and the market was thereby flooded with the stocks at present trapped in the South. It was not until the last few days of May that the market picked up again, the hard-headed men in the cotton business having concluded that the Union's victories did not signal a quick return to peace and the lifting of the blockade.[27]

While the Ashworths continued to buy, as did other millowners such as James Garnett of Low Moor, out of a sense of responsibility to their operatives and also because they believed the war would be a very long one, some owners were both less responsible and less discerning. Convinced that the struggle would be relatively short, they succumbed without resistance to the temptation to sell off their stocks at high prices while the going was good. They expected to be able eventually to replenish them with low-priced cotton. The knowledge that some owners were shutting down their mills out of greed not want, even selling their cotton on the New York market where it commanded a higher price than at Manchester, embittered the operatives. Such behaviour also excited the wrath of the members of a government under constant pressure to do something for the unemployed. Indeed, there was some suspicion that a minority of Manchester cotton merchants favoured the Union cause and the continuation of the war and the blockade for no other reason than to force cotton prices still higher and thereby make possible even greater profits from speculation.[28]

The situation was further clouded by evidence that what the American war had taken away with one hand from the textile regions of Lancashire it was returning with the other to the neighbouring districts of Yorkshire. The worsted industry was well placed to seize its opportunity as a result of the conversion from domestic to factory production which had been completed in 1860. The interruption in cotton supplies and the resulting leap in prices brought boom times to parts of the West Riding, especially to the Bradford constituency of that prominent Union sympathizer, W. E. Forster. Its cotton warp mixtures, in which wool was now the cheapening factor, were in such demand that "Piles of goods that had grown venerable in the hands of manufacturers have been laid low, even to the ground, and many a dark corner has seen daylight, not, as has been customary, at great sacrifice, but honourably, with profit." Inevitably wool prices also rose, dragged up by those for cotton, but far less steeply. All the while the demand for worsteds, particularly in the United States, spurred the industry to grow and at an unprecedented pace. 1862 witnessed the peak of this expansion.[29]

Even in the port of Liverpool, which along with the mill towns of Lancashire had always seemed doomed to be cast as a victim of the American war, the effects of the conflict were far from uniformly ill. By the middle of the nineteenth century, although the port maintained extensive connections with such traditional areas as the Mediterranean and the Baltic, and a great many ships cleared for African destinations, for the Cape of Good Hope, and for Australia, the greatest activity and the principal source of profits remained the transatlantic trade, especially that with the United States. It was far and away the single most important area to Liverpool. Raw cotton was the most important commodity imported and cotton yarn, piece-goods, and other textiles were the chief exports. Inevitably the war damaged this trade severely, not only disrupting the vital cotton trade but also disturbing others, such as that in tea. Wealthy Southern planters had been the consumers of the finest quality teas. As for the continuing trade with the Northern states, even that became far riskier. Exchange rates fluctuated wildly as the fortunes of war ebbed and flowed and the danger of a break with Britain rose and fell. It became difficult even for those British houses most knowledgeable about the Northern market to assess the credit-worthiness of their American customers, because the violent fluctuations in the rate and the periodic currency problems unexpectedly bankrupted the strongest of companies. Nevertheless, the more enterprising houses, such as the well-established and well-managed Rathbones, were able to turn handsome profits from the expanding and as it proved compensating trade in breadstuffs.[30]

Merchants less scrupulous than the Rathbones, who abandoned all trading in cotton in April 1862, for reasons of morality and expediency (they disliked slavery and the unpredictability of cotton prices) soon compensated themselves for the loss of the traditional trade. Immense profits could be turned from blockade-running. The ability to convert pennies into pounds, to obtain a colossal 700 per cent return on an investment, attracted small merchants and syndicates of large entrepreneurs as blood does sharks. They built or bought vessels, loaded them up and sent them off, sometimes under the command of British naval officers who had taken leave in order not to miss their chance to share in the rich prize. It was an activity with which the British government declined to interfere, despite the repeated protests of the Union, whose efforts to suppress it were carefully watched. Yet the Foreign Office was embarrassed by the trade, especially that in arms and ammunition. When a number of Liverpool merchants, with the help of their local member of Parliament, Thomas Horsfall, presented a memorial to Russell, protesting the fact that Union ships waited outside the port of Nassau in the Bahamas to detain suspected blockade-runners, and claiming that this was costing them an additional 10 per cent on their insurance premiums, they were roughly brushed aside. The Foreign Office saw nothing improper in the Americans sitting outside Nassau—so long as they did not encroach on British territorial waters—in order to stop vessels which their consul at Liverpool could have had no difficulty in identifying as blockade-runners. In his reply, upon which both he and the under-secretary, Layard, worked, Russell lectured the merchants on the impropriety of their conduct. "It exposes innocent commerce to vexatious detention and search by American cruisers; it produces irritation and ill will on the part of the population of the Northern States of America; it is contrary to the spirit of Her Majesty's Proclamation; and it exposes the British name to suspicions of bad faith," he charged. The duty of all British subjects was to conform to the proclamation and to abstain from furnishing either belligerent with the means of war. In short, the solution to the difficulties of these Liverpool merchants was to halt their notorious trade.[31] But this was not the kind of admonition to which they were inclined to pay much attention. They continued to profit royally from the American war, so it was not really surprising that the Bank of Liverpool, despite its close connection with the cotton trade, continued to prosper. Adequate compensation was found for the revenues lost as a result of the dramatic fall in raw cotton imports. Shipments of grains and jute provided a ready if partial substitute and increased activity in India and the Mediterranean took up some of the remaining slack in the North American trade. There were also the profits of the American war to be calculated— the transfer of American vessels to Liverpool registry, the boom in cotton broking, and the organization of blockade-running ventures. As one visitor to the port discovered, "the establishment of 400 new carriages since the outbreak of the war is cited as proof of the pervading ease."[32]

The truth was, as a justifiably proud Gladstone had emphasized during his budget speech on April 3, 1862, that with the important exception of the singular troubles of the textile industry, the economic condition of the country was "healthy." British exports to the United States had plummeted from a value of £21.5 million in 1860–61 to barely £9 million in the following year, yet there were indications that a recovery was already under way. The monthly returns for these exports, from September 1861 until February 1862, had revealed a threefold increase. In fact, despite the loss of some American markets, the need to import corn to supplement a British crop which had been of high quality but low yield, and the relinquishment of three sources of revenue, the government's income had not fallen significantly. The explanation for the economy's remarkable buoyancy, its capacity to withstand the buffeting it received from the transatlantic tempest, was to be found, the chancellor suggested, in the industry and energy of the people and the unexpectedly great benefits of the commercial treaty with France. Over a six months' period, trade with that nation had increased by the striking sum of £5.7 million. All in all he was able to predict that revenues for the coming year would exceed expenditures, if only slightly, a statement which produced a sensation in the House. Briefly he toyed with his listeners before reassuring them that through the simple device of entering the new financial year without a surplus on hand he expected to see it through without any increase in taxation. It was a forecast Disraeli, replying for the opposition, could only greet with disbelief.[33]

What Gladstone's budget had indicated, and any careful examination of the situation in Lancashire confirmed, was that there was as yet no compelling economic reason for British intervention in the American conflict. If this was the reality, equally important, if not more so, was the public's perception of the cost of the war to their nation in terms of economic dislocation and human misery. Hence the government's determination to act cautiously and sanely. Yet its success in controlling the widespread unease depended largely upon the way in which the press presented the suffering in the cotton districts.

At the very heart of the distressed area were the newspapers in the spinning towns. The editors and thus the politics of such journals tended to be Radical, which normally might have made them sympathetic to the Union, but their overriding concern now was for the welfare of the operatives and the prosperity of the communities they served. To them, mediation had become increasingly attractive as the course most likely to bring quickly the abundant supplies of low-priced cotton needed to put people back to work. Some, such as the *Bury Guardian* and the *Ashton and Stalybridge Reporter*, were willing, in desperation, to endorse British recognition of Confederate independence if that was what was necessary to obtain cotton. Much the same cry had long been heard from the national Radical weekly, *Reynolds's*. Knowing there was scant hope of any imminent easing of the supply problems, it urged that the Americans be informed that unless peace was rapidly restored Britain and France, "in the interests of the highest humanity, as well as in obedience to the requirements of the law of self-preservation," would be compelled to intervene "to stay the effusion of blood, arrest the destruction of property, and to procure for their now perishing operatives the raw material of their industry essential to their existence."[34]

Although local papers were familiar with conditions in the towns, and the plight of the unemployed and those operatives on short time, they were of narrow appeal and limited circulation, therefore of slight national significance. Somewhat more influential and dispassionate was the *Manchester Guardian*, for though in the midst of the distress Manchester was not being victimized to the same degree. The fact that the city was ceasing to be a manufacturing centre, and instead had become the hub of the area's commercial and credit organization, explains its better fortune. By June the *Guardian*'s hostility to the Union cause was growing daily. The paper moaned that the North had seemingly left no stone unturned in an attempt to alienate the respect and sympathy of "genuine" liberals—it had censored the press, arbitrarily imprisoned suspected dissidents, terrorized the women of New Orleans, and seized neutral vessels on the high seas merely on the suspicion that they intended to run the blockade. This sorry record brought the *Guardian* to the conclusion that in foreign intervention lay the best if not the only hope for America itself as well as for the cotton districts of England and France. But it did not think this was the time for British interference; moreover, it doubted whether such a time would ever come. Defining mediation as no more than a synonym for "interposition," it believed that France should always take the lead. She was not embarrassed by an earlier imperial relationship with America or recollections of recent rivalries. What France might legitimately expect to receive from Britain was an assurance of sympathy and approval for any steps she took to halt "the most crying scandal the Nineteenth Century has witnessed."[35]

Further removed still from Lancashire and its special difficulties were the *Daily News* and the *Morning Star*, both of which were in politics more Radical than the *Guardian* and in sympathies far more friendly to the Union. The *Star*, edited by Bright's brother-in-law, Samuel Lucas, sought to focus English resentment at the consequences of the disruption in cotton supplies upon the Confederacy. It drew a sharp distinction between the Southern decision to destroy cotton at New Orleans, rather than allow the staple to fall into Union hands, and the "honourable" policy of "desperate patriotism" pursued by the Russians during the French invasion in 1812. The difference was that by their scorched earth policy Confederates were impoverishing themselves "without in the least injuring the victors." Even more deplorably, they were doing so at the expense of the British and the French. "They must be mad, indeed, to reckon that England and France will come to the help of men who are wantonly injuring themselves and the subjects of those Powers," the newspaper remarked. And speaking to those in England contemplating such a move, the *Star* recommended that they stop and consider how any form of intervention would moderate the intense bitterness with which so many "less thoughtful" Unionists regarded Britain. It was an animosity which concerned some Englishmen, irritated many, but of which few were any longer ignorant. Rumour had it that the shopkeepers of Boston were putting signs in their windows—"No British merchandise sold here."[36]

In an important respect the position of the *Daily News* dovetailed perfectly with that of the *Star*, and that was in its development of the other journal's warnings about American bitterness. The basic and by no means unreasonable assumption of the *News* was that the Federals would fight rather than accept foreign intervention, which, under whatever name, mediation or recognition, promised to effectuate the independence of the Southern states. It would be madness because of the present distress to throw away in a war with the United States "a hundred times as much money" as would relieve the suffering in the cotton districts. No doubt France and Russia would encourage Britain "to rush into that bottomless pit of expense," the *News* suggested darkly, playing upon fears of these European opportunists, for they had neither an extensive colonial frontier with the Union to defend nor a large mercantile marine in American waters to protect. In short, the costs of the inescapable war would be heavy, and it would not be possible to weigh them simply in money.[37]

If in the case of the more Radical national daily newspapers distance from the misery and anxieties of Bury, Preston, and Ashton permitted the heart to grow cooler, the two most important organs of the Conservative party exhibited an unsurpassed depth of concern for the operatives. Presumably there was a measure of genuine sympathy, perhaps a sense of noblesse oblige towards the less fortunate members of society, but partisan considerations unquestionably were dominant. Although the *Morning Herald*, the official journal of the party, and the more popular, livelier, and cheaper *Standard* could offer no convincing elaboration of Tory policy, which was not surprising for the Conservatives had failed to develop one, these organs had no trouble lambasting the government and the domestic enemies of Conservatism for their responses to the crisis. They denounced newspapers supporting the Palmerston administration, as well as those of the "Americanizing Radicals," for deliberately striving to make "light of the suffering of their countrymen." Yet if the war was to continue for another six months, the *Standard* warned on May 28, there would be starvation in Lancashire. Millowners would be ruined, the manufacturing districts almost annihilated, national prosperity seriously and permanently damaged, all in the name of an "absolute neutrality" adopted "in order that a Government which has shown itself hostile to us, regardless of law, and unworthy of respect, may have the opportunity of injuring to the utmost of its power a gallant and kindred people, fighting for everything that brave men hold dear." In the opinion of the opposition press the "crime of all this ruin—ruin on our own shores, ruin on the Continent, ruin incalculable and irreparable in America, lies heavily at the door of the English Government."[38]

Before this continuous assault on the government, the repeated charges of being weak-kneed abroad and stony-hearted at home, the two major newspapers most closely identified with Palmerston began, as June opened, to give ground. Both the loyal *Morning Post* and the independent but usually dependable *Times* had, as their Tory competitors charged, played a role in the government's earlier campaign to reassure the nation that the troubles of Lancashire were well under control. *The Times* had responded promptly to Villiers's personal appeal to Delane, and had helped him to calm the excited members for the distressed districts. The *Post*, meanwhile, had manfully struggled to relieve the pressure that was building behind the calls for government action by endeavouring to break the iron link in most people's minds between the war and the suffering. In vain it reminded Englishmen that the falling demand in the United States for manufactured cotton, as a native industry developed, and the overstocking of Britain's Eastern markets because of the overproduction which had immediately preceded the outbreak of the war, had made it certain that "the depression of the Lancashire trade would now be the same, even if Liverpool had a weekly supply of the raw material more than equal to her powers of manufacture in her utmost prosperity."[39] Only three weeks later, on May 29, the *Post* was admitting that the policy of strict neutrality had been rooted in the conviction that the war could not last long and the privation in the spinning towns would therefore be brief. "That those calculations may ultimately prove incorrect we now begin to receive a terrible inkling," it conceded. Four days later the *Post* was warning the American "fanatics" that even long suffering had its limits, and that the European nations were not likely "to remain very patient spectators" of a conflict which seemed to have no other object than to kill and destroy. This was the language that so worried Charles Francis Adams, convincing him that a change in British policy was in the offing.

Once Palmerston and Russell indicated that the government was not contemplating any imminent change of course, all but the Tory press fell in behind them. Nevertheless, the *Post* and *The Times* thought it prudent to stress that the government's resistance was merely to intervention at this time. Much as Britain might desire to mediate between the rival states, this particular moment was not a good one. "The time may come, and that shortly," the *Post* concluded, "when it will become the paramount duty of the neutral states to interpose," but for the present they should continue to "stand aloof." In any event it would be far better to leave such a delicate task as that of stepping between belligerents securely in the hands of the government, permitting it "to choose such an opportunity and mode of action as it may think proper."[40] On the same day, June 14, Walter Bagehot discussed at some length in the *Economist* the circumstances under which friendly mediation might not merely be justified but also be in accordance with "the usual etiquette of nations." The principal grounds for an intervention, he observed, were that the objects of the war had become unattainable, at least in the eyes of dispassionate observers; that the two combatants, after a lengthy period, remained so evenly balanced that the conflict threatened to be interminable; that there was a danger of the struggle degenerating into "a phase of savagery deplorable to humanity and disgraceful to civilization;" that it was causing distress to unoffending and inoffensive countries greater than any neutral could be expected to bear; and finally, that the war had reached a stage where there was a real hope of bringing it to an end through negotiation. Not surprisingly, Bagehot found virtually all these conditions present in the American war. He recognized that mediation would not be an easy task, and in the face of the Americans' "unreasoning dislike" of Britain he believed like many others that the offer should be made by France. This anxiety to defer to the French, to welcome the prospect of French mediation, was shared now even by the *Spectator*.[41]

There was, then, an unmistakable air of impermanence about Britain's nonintervention. The Conservative press, unrelenting in their onslaught, contemptuously described the government's policy as one of "postponement"—postponement of mediation, postponement of recognition. But there were signs that before long the cabinet would be compelled to face the American problem. The active Confederate lobby in the Commons had not withdrawn Lindsay's motion, they were simply holding it back, waiting for the most opportune moment. While they waited the *Standard* was urging the House "to compel a cold and sluggish Government" to abandon its "heartless isolation of a withering neutrality," for conditions in Lancashire were continuing to deteriorate. By June 25 the existing stocks of cotton at Liverpool were reported to be shrinking so quickly that there was barely enough for a further ten weeks of short-time work. "How long are we to suffer," the *Herald* asked, "while the North strains its powers to the uttermost to restore a Union, which, while it existed, was the common enemy of Europe, and in a special sense the enemy of England?"[42]

The government's decision to hold its course, at least for the time being, was one of expediency not principle. How would recognition of the Confederacy, or an offer of mediation which was certain to be rejected by one of the belligerents, shorten the war? Palmerston, for one, professed his inability to see how either course would have this effect. Caution was also dictated by divisions within the cabinet, where there was a small coterie of Union sympathizers. Furthermore, the prime minister and Russell remained as suspicious as ever of Napoleon III. They believed the emperor would capitalize upon any British embarrassment in North America to reorder the affairs of Europe, and the civil war's end might well provide him with his opportunity, given the uneasy relationship between Britain and the United States. Would Canada's vulnerability tempt a vengeful Union to seek there compensation for the loss of the South and retribution for the aid the Confederacy had obtained from Englishmen? This spectre seemed real enough to some in Britain, and it convinced them that their nation's interests would best be served by a prolongation of the conflict until both sides were more nearly exhausted. One threat to the policy of inaction, whatever its inspiration, was that the suffering in Lancashire and Cheshire would force the government's hand. Hence Russell's suggestion that the Union cooperate in permitting Britain to obtain Southern cotton. Simultaneously, Villiers sought to prevent the spread of panic in the hard-hit textile districts. He was helped by the fact that the area of distress was restricted, and even within it the suffering was by no means uniform. Moreover, it was increasingly evident that the

American war was conferring economic benefits on some parts of Britain while working hardship in others. However, the absence of any compelling economic reason to intervene in the war was not an aspect of the situation everyone noted. There were signs of mounting impatience in the mill towns, and both the local press and the national organs of the opposition dwelt upon the suffering. Under these circumstances it was not at all certain that Britain was fixed in her policy of nonintervention.

FOUR

Home Intervention

JAMES MURRAY MASON thoroughly enjoyed his first few months in Britain, as he hobnobbed with both gentry and aristocracy, and occasionally even with a member of European royalty. This marked social attention and in some instances acceptance had further inflated the self-esteem of a man whose exaggerated pride in his ancestry had helped to earn him a reputation for arrogance among many of his countrymen. He carefully noted in his private memorandum book not only where he went but whom he met, especially the titled, which breakfasts, receptions, and dinner parties he attended, and whose country seats he visited. But for all his success socially, Mason had achieved little diplomatically. The British government continued to keep him at a safe distance, as if he were a political leper.

Across the Channel, although the Slidell family's social life was "very retired," the commissioner was encountering fewer difficulties in gaining access to the members of a government that had proved to be somewhat less punctilious. In mid-April Slidell's growing confidence that the Confederate question would not long remain unsettled had been bolstered by the information that "Measures have been taken to procure petitions from the Chambers of Commerce of the principal cities, asking the intervention of the Emperor to restore commercial relations with the Southern States."[1] Why would the government orchestrate such a call if it was not planning to respond? A month later he had an encouraging conversation with Auguste Billault, minister without portfolio and a government spokesman on foreign affairs in the Senate. Billault was full, perhaps a little too full, of reassurances of his personal sympathy for the Southern cause, and that of the entire Ministry of Foreign Affairs. The emperor was a fellow sympathizer, he implied. His explanation of the government's failure to act decisively sooner—the refusal of the British to cooperate—was plausible. Nevertheless, he spoke optimistically of some "decided" Southern success in the field bringing on recognition, for although France still refused to act without the British Billault thought he had detected a change of tone in London.[2]

If Mason was ostensibly at the centre of the efforts of the Confederate lobby in Britain to prod the government of that country into action, in fact James Spence was at their heart. It was Spence who had made contact with representatives of some of the unemployed operatives and who, as June opened, dissuaded them from getting up meetings prematurely. Their voices would carry much farther, he stressed, in the stillness following a Confederate military victory. It was Spence who urged William Lindsay, both directly and through Mason, to postpone his Commons motion. "It is plain that the tide of opinion is now moving favourably," he wrote to Mason on June 3, "but it is yet far too undecided I think for a move."[3] News of a Southern setback at Corinth, which arrived a week later, merely reinforced his argument. To act now and be beaten, which seemed certain, would do "terrible harm," he counselled. Yet although in his opinion the time was still not ripe to seek recognition, Spence did consider it timely "to begin active measures to that end." Leading by example, he selflessly cut up a pamphlet he had just completed, publishing it instead as a series of letters to the editor of *The Times*. This would be the most telling way both of making his case for British recognition and exciting public discussion of the topic, he believed. Meanwhile Lindsay had decided to postpone his motion, realizing that the House "was not *yet* prepared to vote." Informing the Foreign Office privately of this decision, before announcing it in the Commons on June 20, he pressed the government to take the question in hand itself. There was no real danger of British recognition causing war with the United States, he insisted, in a letter to Layard. On the contrary, the leading men of the North would thank Britain for exercising this undoubted right, and even Seward might welcome it as an opportunity to end the war. France was only waiting for Britain's lead. On the other hand, should the American crisis be settled without British recognition of the Confederacy, there could be no doubt that Northern troops would invade Canada. Finally, he claimed the support of nine-tenths of the Commons and maladroitly proposed that the cabinet sponsor recognition rather than suffer the embarrassment of having the House vote it at the prompting of a private member.[4] It was a feeble threat to make against a government led by Palmerston, whom few could rival when it came to discerning the mood of the House, and fewer still equal in the art of manipulating it.

While their supporters in Britain cautiously prepared the ground, Mason and Slidell coordinated their plans. Slidell took the initiative. What he proposed was that at the first favourable moment they present simultaneously, in Paris and London, formal requests for recognition. It was not essential that their notes be identical, simply that the reasons and arguments be compatible. Mason replied quickly and positively, and by June 3 they were in general agreement. News of an important military victory would be the signal for the presentation of the requests. The sudden talk of mediation, with Persigny's visit to London, caused them to modify their plans. After all, as Slidell pointed out, any offer to mediate "would be virtually to recognize us." But this hope quickly flickered out. Slidell soon discovered that Persigny had not crossed the Channel on a diplomatic errand, and was at most authorized to impress unofficially upon the British cabinet "the necessity of prompt action in some way or other." In their statements to Parliament Palmerston and Russell ruled out any immediate change of course and a disappointed and frustrated Slidell dallied with the foolish notion of making a formal demand simply in order to compel the British to come to a decision. Fortunately Mason, listening to his British friends and advisers, and anxious to ensure that any request would be made "as a demand of right," and not in the humiliating "posture of a supplicant," refused to gamble. The upshot was a slight revision of the commissioners' "cordial understanding." They would continue to work closely but no longer bind themselves to a simultaneous request for recognition in the two capitals. Clearly Slidell wanted to be free to take full advantage of the friendlier climate of Paris, for he had given up hope of their ever achieving much in Britain. "I think that it is now more evident than ever that England will do nothing that may offend the Lincoln Government," he wrote to Mason at the end of June, "and I shall await as patiently as I can the course of events."[5]

Less pessimistic about the chances of ultimate success in Britain, Mason was also awaiting the course of events. He looked for news of Confederate victories and for the English public's response to the war to be sharpened by the suffering in Lancashire. Nor did he have long to wait. Already the news had arrived of Jackson's march up the Shenandoah Valley. It was hailed as "the most skillful and strategical operation effected by either of the belligerents during the present campaign." And so began the Jackson cult in Britain, for the significance of his exploits was manifest even three thousand miles away. He had reestablished Southern command of this rich and fertile bread-basket, and had effectively denied McClellan reinforcements for his march up the peninsula to Richmond. By dint of "unsurpassed skill and energy" this latter-day Cromwell and his "foot cavalry" had tied down large numbers of enemy troops before Washington and removed them from any offensive operations.[6]

This was the kind of news for which Spence had been waiting, before encouraging the operatives to demonstrate for intervention. That they were ripe for action was only too evident, for their gloomy prospects were continuing to darken. Another 11,000 had been forced onto relief in June, and the existing stocks of cotton were being deplenished at an alarming pace. Supplies were trickling in but they were a mere fraction of the demand, whether for consumption or speculative exportation. "Matters are now beginning to look very serious," one millowner wrote in his diary on June 28. Stories abounded of wild speculation in cotton on the Manchester market, where sellers found themselves in so favourable a position that they scarcely knew what to ask. Watching all of this, even the level-headed Walter Bagehot appeared to be in danger of losing his composure. Nothing could mitigate the distress in Lancashire except peace in America, he wrote in the *Economist*. Without peace it "*must* augment from day to day in an ever increasing ratio."[7] Moreover, cool, wet weather was threatening the harvest and a poor crop usually meant higher prices for bread. For those ekeing out an existence on an inadequate relief payment here was one more reason to demand government action.

Meetings were called in Blackburn, Stockport, and at Bollington, just outside of Macclesfield, to demand recognition of the South or mediation of the war. Sensing that a crisis was imminent, and after conversations with Argyll and Gladstone doubly fearful that Britain was on the slippery path to intervention and thus involvement in the war, Richard Cobden frantically sought to reduce the momentum. He had visited Adams at the American legation on June 28 to impress upon him the importance of an expression of sympathy by Seward for the difficulties confronting the European nations, and to urge that the secretary do all within his power to see that they received more cotton. Personally he was convinced that a shipment of a few hundred thousand bales from New Orleans "would stave off this dangerous step." And when Cobden met with Mason on July 6, the Confederate guaranteed that if any Englishman was permitted by the Federals to go to New Orleans with a noncontraband cargo, whether it be gold, coffee, salt, clothing, or other manufactures, and after payment of duties was allowed to proceed into the interior, he would be able to exchange it for cotton. Cobden wrote to Charles Sumner urgently recommending this expedient, which was not unlike that recently proposed by Russell. He persuaded Argyll to write to the influential senator in the same sense. "I know it will be said that this is giving them means and money for a prolongation of the contest," the duke conceded. "But its effect in this way would be comparatively small, whilst it would greatly tend to dissipate the danger which is really a growing one—not only as regards England, but as regards the rest of Europe also." Finally, at Cobden's urging, Bright added his powerful voice to theirs.[8]

For John Bright the American war was fast becoming an obsession, almost driving from his mind other political questions. "Till America is disposed of," he once wrote to his wife, "I cannot feel deeply about English or European subjects." She was under orders to forward immediately to London, whenever he was there during a session, any American letters addressed to his Rochdale home. At critical moments in the war he was often unable to sleep at night, or if he did it was fitfully, dreaming of telegrams he could not read. He would visit the offices of the *Star* to read the latest bulletins arriving by telegraph, and he followed and marked the various campaigns on his own map. For him it was vital that the war continue. Only its continuance would "bring the slave question into due prominence," therefore "it must and will go on till *it* becomes the one question." To him it was inconceivable that God would have permitted such a bloody conflict to be waged "without a plan for the redemption of the four millions of his creatures whose wrongs and sorrows have hitherto appealed to man in vain." Fortified by the hope that "the deliverance of the whole negro race may come from this terrible strife," Bright saw in European intervention the danger of its premature end. Like Cobden, but for a somewhat different reason then, he was worried by the stirrings in the mill towns. "I hope the meetings in favour of recognition will not go on or have any effect," he remarked to a Manchester friend.[9]

As it happened, the impact of these demonstrations upon the rest of the nation was softened by poor organization and the failure of those demanding action to speak with one voice. While the gatherings in Stockport and Bollington were both well attended and passed resolutions calling upon the government to put an end to the American war through recognition of the South, the focus of attention was Blackburn. The meeting there had always been intended as the show-piece. Reeling from the effects of the conflict, the town was a natural choice for a rally and a good-sized crowd was assured. Indeed, some five thousand or more turned out on a Saturday afternoon, June 28, to express their support for British mediation. But the organizers, and one of those in the background may well have been Spence, bungled. Too many of them were outsiders, which irritated locals. Then again, the assembled operatives were to be asked to petition Parliament in support of a motion urging mediation which a neighbouring member intended to introduce in the Commons on Monday. It was an inept plan for the member in question was J. T. Hopwood, a notorious opponent of any enfranchisement of working people. The result was a propaganda disaster for the pro-Confederate cause. Union sympathizers mingled with the crowd, distributing slips ridiculing both the motion and the leading actors, and when Hopwood and the other principals unaccountably failed to appear the crowd's impatience and irritation were neatly vented upon them. The motion before the meeting was artfully amended. Proposed by the secretary of the Weavers' Association and seconded by an "operative mechanic," and therefore, in a symbolic sense at least, more truly representative of working-class opinion, the amendment called upon the government to do everything compatible with the maintenance of peace to settle the American difficulty, "by restoring the confidence of the planters to [sic] the policy of President Lincoln, and the reorganization and preservation of the American Union." And as if this standing of the organizers' intent upon its head was not enough, the day ended with votes of nonconfidence in them and Hopwood.[10] Two days later, in the Commons, Palmerston quickly and easily turned aside the suggestion of mediation.

Embarrassing as the reverse at Blackburn was for those seeking to force the government's hand, it was felt that the lost ground could be recovered if future meetings were carefully planned. A more serious weakness, for it lent itself to no easy correction, was their inability to channel all the anxieties and miseries of the spinning towns into a common demand for some form of intervention in the American war. Instead, the operatives' pent-up fears and resentment continued to be diverted into angry protests against the labour test. Ever conspicuous in these demonstrations was Thomas Evans, who soon earned notoriety as a pro-Union agitator. Time and again he summoned the unemployed to Stevenson Square, Manchester, to denounce the degrading and dangerous work demanded of them, whether it was grinding corn in some windowless workhouse cubicle or working in the open air on Crumpsall Farm. Used to the heat of the mills, the operatives not only disliked outdoor farm work in the damp and cold of a Manchester summer but readily believed that it was exposing them to all sorts of diseases of legs and lungs which would leave them unemployable whenever the mills reopened. So, with Evans's encouragement, they spent their energies seeking some betterment of these daily and immediate conditions, rather than in debating the distant cause of their predicament.[11]

Others, operatives as well as manufacturers, continued to respond to the promise that India would be their salvation, if only the government would help. In Manchester Henry Ashworth had been elected president of the Chamber of Commerce in January. His aim was to commit that body to stronger support for state intervention in India. At the same time he endorsed the policy of neutrality and nonintervention in the United States. Yet Ashworth was a Southern sympathizer. Many of the friends with whom he had stayed during his visit to North America in 1857 had been Southerners; the cotton firm with which he dealt had been ruined by the war; he received heart-rending letters from the South; he disliked slavery but considered the Northern attitude hypocritical; and he was alarmed by the expansionist record and aggressive posture of the Union. Both he and his brother Edmund, another millowner, considered peace and separation the desired ends in America. But Henry Ashworth made no move to throw his considerable weight behind those who were arguing that peace, separation, and therefore cotton would come quickly only as a result of mediation or recognition. The explanation for this silence seems to have been his close friendship with Cobden and Bright, his aversion to war and political interference in the affairs of other countries, and the fact that his own "strong instinct for survival was not aroused." Despite the troubles of the industry, New Eagley was still returning a handsome profit.[12]

Although substantial quantities of cotton were now arriving from India, more than 400,000 bales having been shipped from Bombay between February and June, and the Indian contribution was now rising to 90 per cent of the country's total raw cotton imports, it was not enough. A "Manchester Circular" published on July 2 pointed to the continuing shortages as evidence of the need for more assistance from the government. On July 14 a meeting was held in the Preston Mechanics Institution, and it was packed to the rafters, for in a town where one-third of the population was directly involved in the cotton industry half the looms and mules in the mills were idle. There was little attempt to disguise the tension. The fear was voiced that unless somebody did something soon the discontent of the working class would erupt into a "row." There were bitter attacks on Sir Charles Wood and calls for him to be turned out of office; there was a denunciation of the government's policy of building railroads in India for military purposes but not to promote the cultivation of cotton; and one workingman bravely stood up to remind the spinners and manufacturers present that they shared the responsibility for the industry's dependence upon a single source. Nonetheless, the meeting had aired once again the beliefs that India could provide Britain with much more cotton and that the government should be doing more to encourage its cultivation there.[13]

Two days later the Board of Directors of the Manchester Chamber entered the fray with a memorandum that had been in preparation for a week. In part, it was a reply to those who insisted that if only the manufacturers would guarantee to purchase the entire crop at a "remunerative price," all the cotton Britain might need would come from India. They refused to do this largely out of fear that peace might suddenly be concluded in the United States, leaving them in the unenviable position of meeting the competition of inexpensive American cotton. However, in their memorandum the directors assailed the proposal as "a direct renunciation of the law of supply and demand," as an "interference that would paralyse private enterprise," and as "a species of protection in its worst form," for it would amount to a "bounty from the public purse for the production of an inferior article." There remained one species of intervention that they continued to find palatable—public works. These, they hastened to explain, stood in a somewhat different position. Once executed they could not fail to be beneficial to India itself, and they did not depend for their success on the continuing failure of the American cotton supply but were of intrinsic value.[14] The self-serving nature of the Manchester men's reasoning did little to burnish their image or advance their cause. Bagehot's *Economist* gave them some support, as did the *Star*, and even the *Saturday Review*, though it was also very critical of their refusal to invest in India. But *The Times*, with its commitment to free trade, would not listen. Neither would Palmerston. Like Charles Wood he held to the doctrine that "Those who want cotton from India should themselves take the same means of obtaining it from there which they would take for obtaining any other article of commerce from any other part of the world and without any interference by the government."[15] It was a belief Argyll, speaking on behalf of the government, subsequently reaffirmed in the Lords. Enough had been done out of public funds already, the time had come for private enterprise to play its full part.[16]

This dispersal of popular agitation ought to have disconcerted Mason and his English friends. The irresistible force of public opinion was a vital ally of their cause and whatever diminished the clamour for intervention also lessened their chances of success. However, the far-reaching significance of the noisy meetings demanding an end to the labour test in Lancashire and more public works in India went unnoticed by them. Instead, they were swept along by a wave of optimism, as news of the battles in Virginia slowly rolled across the Atlantic. By July 11 it was known in Britain that Mc-Clellan's army had been in severe difficulties at the end of June. Even the *Morning Star* was ready to concede that "the men of the South have undoubtedly gained a considerable advantage over the men of the North." The *Index* moved smartly to capitalize on the news, with a leader on which Spence had left his imprint. Surely a people who numbered eight millions, inhabited a "large and distinct" country, and who had proven their determination and ability to maintain their independence, constituted a nation. As such they had a right to recognition, and if ever there was an opportune moment for the European powers to act it was now, "now that the winter and spring campaign has ended in disastrous failure, now that the North is panting for breath, and is preparing, with superadded difficulties, to begin its work anew." By a mere diplomatic act Europe had a splendid opportunity to end this terrible struggle "without becoming itself entangled in the war."[17]

The reaction elsewhere to the battle news was no less predictable. The Tory dailies took up the cry for recognition and repeated the warning that if this chance was allowed to pass it might never return. "The present moment or never, Earl Russell! The tide is rolling by," was their refrain. From the other end of the political spectrum *Reynolds's* renewed its pleas for mediation. "We therefore urge our rulers to interfere promptly and effectually, or else they must, in the sight of both God and man, be held accountable for the crime which they could, but would not prevent." No less interesting were the comments of the Palmerstonian *Post*, which voiced both a hope that the Union would finally admit the futility of the struggle and a reluctance to wait patiently for it to do so. If Lincoln decided to prolong the war, actually summoning to arms those additional 300,000 men, then it would remain for neutrals to decide whether the South had not "by its recent prowess established a claim to be considered independent."[18]

Reading all of this, it was not surprising that the Confederate lobby in Parliament was tempted to seize the initiative and bring forward at long last Lindsay's oft-postponed motion. Spence still counselled delay. He did not dispute that public opinion was "ripening fast" for recognition, what he did question was the readiness of the Commons to take this step. A meeting with a "favourably disposed" member of the cabinet merely hardened this opinion; as he explained to Mason, "no movement there is essential to us whilst defeat there would do harm, grievous harm." A delay of a fortnight might make all the difference between failure and success. It would probably see the Confederate cause strengthened by the news that McClellan had not merely been defeated but had failed utterly. With this fact established Mason could make a formal demand in London for recognition, which would in turn greatly influence the lines of the subsequent parliamentary debate.[19]

Perhaps Spence's arguments had some effect for Lindsay suddenly showed himself reluctant to bring the question before the House. However, his hand was forced by a foolish action of Lord Vane Tempest. The Duke of Newcastle's son-in-law, but a member with no real influence, Vane Tempest gave notice of a motion which contemplated nothing less than physical intervention in the American quarrel. Its defeat was certain, if debated. Clearly it was essential to link the cause of the Confederacy to a more realistic proposal. This necessity, together with the laying before Parliament of H. B. Farnall's First Report on the distress in the spinning towns, and the news that McClellan had indeed abandoned his campaign against Richmond, made Lindsay first commit himself to propose a motion on July 18 and then attempt to phrase one that was mild enough to attract general support. Thus calls for recognition or physical intervention were deleted, and in their place was inserted "the idea of *mediation* in conjunction with other powers, and that of pledging Parliament to sustain the ministry in any policy they might think proper to pursue." Once this decision had been taken, Spence threw himself behind it. In particular, he was anxious to ensure that the South's "champion in the House"—William Gregory—was in attendance and spoke.[20]

For Charles Francis Adams another period of trial had begun. McClellan's failure in Virginia and the evidence that Southern sympathizers constituted "much the greater part of the active classes" of Britain were a sobering combination. All his hopes of the war's quick end had been dashed and all his fears of European interference were revived. Old doubts of the length of his mission resurfaced, and the Yankee in him must have rued his optimism just a few months earlier in signing a three-year lease on his new official residence. Then, on July 17, Consul Morse came to see him bringing a batch of papers that had allegedly been obtained from the Austrian embassy. They indicated the existence of an Anglo-Austrian scheme to summon an international conference to settle the American question. Adams did not doubt for a moment that the European powers had been in communication, and he was sure he could identify the "main instigator" of any policy founded upon the assumption that the disruption of the United States would be a benefit for Europe—Palmerston. The delay so far had obviously been caused by the difficulty in inducing the five Great Powers to join in a common offer of mediation. But they would surely achieve unity soon. Then, if the North rejected their intervention, they could use the refusal as an excuse to recognize the Confederacy. The result would be the same, an independent South. With this disagreeable international scenario taking shape in his mind, Adams thought the time fast approaching for his nation to clarify its war aims.[21]

The minister's concern was to ensure that responsibility for the failure of foreign mediation be laid at the Southerners' door, for this would deny the British and the other European nations the excuse to extend to them full recognition. Difficulties over a boundary line and the control and navigation of the Mississippi were promising in this regard, but the Union's most formidable weapon was slavery. A settlement of the slave question should be the North's eminently reasonable prerequisite for its acceptance of Confederate independence, Adams argued. As a republic dedicated to freedom, it could not be asked to live alongside a nation founded on slavery and for that very reason animated by a bitter hatred towards it, "much less if established and upheld by the intervention of the most enlightened nations of the world." No one wished to have "a neighbor in whose house a thousand tons of gunpowder are manufactured every day of the year." The essential preliminary, therefore, was for the Union to contradict the widespread impression that the North was fighting simply to subdue the South, and the way to do this was to make explicit the "true state of the question." Once the "fuller establishment of free principles" had been embraced by the North as its principal objective, the Europeans would have great difficulty mediating on any less "honorable" basis. Of course, there was no proposal the South was less likely to accept. Here was a more subtle and diplomatic use of emancipation than Seward's dark allusions to servile insurrection, which Adams had passed along to Russell a few weeks earlier. The minister saw the freeing of slaves not as a threat with which to ward off desperately the blow of foreign intervention, but as a lead which would throw it off balance and throw onto the South all the odium for the war's prolongation. And it was a boxing metaphor Henry Adams used, when, in explaining the situation to his brother Charles, he wrote, "You see we are stripping and squaring off, to say nothing of sponging, for the next round."[22]

That an offer of mediation should be followed, if the North rejected it, by recognition of the South was the call heard in the House when the debate opened there. Initially Adams had expected little to come of Lindsay's motion. Nevertheless, one of his staff had written to Thomas Dudley in Liverpool seeking any evidence of the mover's involvement in blockade-running. Just one case would "damage him greatly both socially and as a Member of Parliament," Benjamin Moran observed. Presumably the consul was unable to turn up anything compromising and it was the legation that was suddenly thrown onto the defensive with the publication in London on the very day of the debate of the story that McClellan and his entire army had surrendered to Lee. Although a visiting American was with John Delane when the report reached Printing House Square, and he questioned its accuracy, the editor was determined to publish it in the late edition. He wanted to believe the news, thinking it would signal the end of the war, and reasoned that "something might be done for pacification" as the North went about the painful task of recovery. Of course, the report was false, possibly a ruse to influence the vote that evening. Adams spent the afternoon reassuring worried Union sympathizers who called to see him. Fortunately he had copies of recent American newspapers, including the *Tribune* of July 5, which proved the story's inaccuracy. These he gave to Forster to take with him down to the House, but now more nervous about the outcome he asked Benjamin Moran to observe the proceedings.[23]

Moran found the Commons very nearly full and the public galleries packed. His jaundiced eye detected the sartorial vulgarities of the assembled Confederates. Mason was overdressed and one of his companions undressed, having forgotten to button his trousers. As for the debate, the protagonists were as familiar as their arguments. For the South, Lindsay led off but he quickly bored the House and lost much of his audience. He was supported by William Gregory, who in Palmerston's opinion made a "strong and well argued speech," as indeed did James Whiteside. His eloquence, force, and attractive Irish voice carried even Moran away briefly, until he reminded himself that Whiteside was speaking for the motion. Less effective was Vane Tempest, who appeared to be somewhat the worse for drink. Between them they recited the entire pro-Southern litany: secession had been constitutional; slavery was not an issue in the conflict but Confederate independence would advance not retard the cause of freedom; the war was sinking into barbarism and was wreaking havoc in Lancashire; a division of the Union was in Britain's political and commercial interests; the North could never completely subdue the South; recognition could be justified with a string of precedents stretching from the Dutch revolt against Spain in the sixteenth century to the Greek rebellion against the Turks in the present one; Britain would not have to act alone but would be able to rely on the French. Finally, Gregory offered another guarantee of peaceful intervention—European mediation would encourage all those Northerners to speak out who ached for peace but until now had been cowed into silence. It was the case Benjamin was making in his correspondence with Mason, who no doubt primed Gregory, and Hotze was urging in the columns of the *Index*.[24]

The main burden of answering the Southern lobby was shouldered again by Forster, although Peter Taylor, the newly elected Radical member for Leicester, spoke up for the Union. Their basic propositions were identical: slavery had caused the war, would be ended by the war, and British intervention would result in a collision with the Union. From such a conflict few would benefit, least of all the distressed operatives whose welfare so concerned the Confederate lobby. Taylor seized upon the Blackburn meeting, citing it as proof that the sympathies of the working people were with the North. Forster pointed out that it would be less expensive to keep the unemployed in luxury than fight the United States, and he raised the bogy of a corn famine. One week earlier, Vane Tempest's announcement of his intention to introduce a motion had been immediately followed by the annual ritual of the member for Carlisle commenting on the returns of agricultural statistics. What they revealed for the preceding year was a substantial dependence on the United States for foodstuffs. Both Richard Cobden and the *Morning Star* had seen the possible implications for Anglo-American relations, and corn was soon to be enthroned alongside cotton. But King Corn was never more than a propaganda slogan and appears to have had little impact upon public opinion. Nor did Forster put much fear into the House with another bogy, the likelihood of British intervention converting the Civil War into a servile rebellion. The fact that he used it at all suggests how uneasy Adams had become at the last minute about the debate, for there was no doubt where the House's sympathies lay. Forster's short speech was listened to respectfully and even won moderate applause, but Taylor was interrupted by jeers and his mention of "honest Abraham Lincoln" brought a burst of horse-laughter and ridicule. Cobden, a little surprised at the extent as well as the depth of the pro-Southern feeling, attributed it to the belief that the Union could not be restored. Members thought that Britain, as one of the principal sufferers in this "pointless" conflict, should have a say in what happened. Palmerston was as ever alive to the mood of the House. However, what must have been just as clear and no less important to him was the indecision of the Conservative opposition on this issue. There was scant danger of their wresting leadership from the hands of the government. They showed no signs of being willing to accept the responsibility for forcing upon him a policy that might lead to war with the United States.[25]

Mason had been rubbing shoulders with a number of important Tories in the days before the debate. He had met with the Earl of Malmesbury, foreign secretary in the most recent Tory government, whose deputy in that government, Seymour Fitzgerald, was a neighbour and intimate friend of Mason. And to some Conservative strategists it seemed obvious that the party would be "*Southern*, more or less, sooner or later."[26] Their difficulty was in finding a safe way to exploit the American question. There was a disinclination to risk alienating the Manchester men at a time when the House seemed too timid anyway to lead the government, and especially over an issue on which the ministers had not committed themselves. They were free to take whatever position parliamentary need dictated. Beyond this, there were reservations about the practicality of mediation and the validity of recognizing a country which had no means of ingress or egress. Moreover, intervention would surely protract the war, or so Lord Stanley, the Conservative leader's son, argued. Hating Britain, the North would be stimulated to fresh efforts by talk of interference by her in the struggle.[27]

For Derby, an isolationist by conviction, and as a large landowner in Lancashire deeply concerned about the suffering there, fear of prolonging the conflict may well have been the decisive consideration. Certainly the question was "of so much importance and delicacy" that he summoned his senior advisers to a meeting to map a course before the debate, and this resulted in an indecisive contribution to the proceedings. Disraeli, the leader in the Commons, remained silent. Fitzgerald, under-secretary of foreign affairs in the last Derby government, spoke but briefly and then not until the debate was to all intents and purposes over. It was James Whiteside who carried the opposition's standard. He was a former office-holder, as attorney general for Ireland, and when Derby came into the lower house to listen to the Irishman's carefully prepared speech, it appeared to both Moran and Forster that the Tories "had thrown off the cloak and fixed their position." But the choice of such a minor figure as spokesman, the failure of any person "of first class position" to speak, betrayed the Conservatives' irresolution.

They wanted to establish a claim to the issue of intervention without risking too close an identification with it.[28]

The knowledge that those calling for a change in his government's policy were politically leaderless eased considerably the prime minister's task of preserving its complete freedom of action. Nevertheless, he gave a masterly performance. Despite his years he was in his seat at the Treasury bench throughout the more than seven hours of debate. Often he struck the characteristic pose, hat over the eyes, legs outstretched, apparently slumbering, but he did show conspicuous interest in the speeches of Taylor and Forster. When he finally rose to speak he shook himself, as ever, like a Newfoundland dog which had just come out of water, and having captured the full attention of the House with this performance he deftly turned aside the challenge to his policy. His audience, at first silent, was soon applauding and voicing its approval of his remarks. When he sat down there was little for Lindsay and his friends to do but withdraw the motion. The House left the government "free to determine what to do, and when, and how to act if any step towards the restoration of peace in America should appear likely to be attended with success."[29] Adams, reading it the following morning, thought Palmerston's speech cautious and wise, but fancied that "enough could be gathered from it to show that mischief to us in some shape will only be averted by the favor of Divine providence on our efforts."[30] Five days later Mason made a formal demand for recognition, having previously accepted the advice of his Conservative friends to allow the debate to take place first. They had expected that it would show unmistakably that House and country were ready for intervention.

The delay in London had suited Slidell nicely in France. He had met with Persigny on July 10 and had been assured that the imperial government was "now more anxious than ever to take prompt and decided action" in the Confederacy's favour. Six days later he was at Vichy pleading the Southern case before the emperor. Napoleon "talked freely, frankly & unreservedly, spoke in the most decided terms of his sympathy & his regret that England had not shared his views," Slidell excitedly reported to Mason. For his part, in this audience, as in his meetings and correspondence with Thouvenel during the following week, Slidell expertly baited the hook of recognition. Benjamin's promise of a cotton subsidy was passed along and the commissioner was quick to exploit the evident imperial concern about the Mexican adventure and the Union's mounting hostility towards it. Unlike the political proselytizers in the North, he remarked, the Confederate States had no other interest in Mexico than to see established there a "respectable, responsible and stable" government. In short, Slidell welcomed the French intervention and was even proffering an alliance to guarantee its success. He also strove to break the French government's iron determination to act only in cooperation with Britain. French and British interests in the American conflict were widely divergent, he stressed. This the Confederacy had recognized by offering the cotton subsidy to France alone, but the French should also ponder the consequences of a prolonged war if as a result Britain successfully established a broad and stable system of cotton production in India. Did France wish to see a British cotton monopoly created, as the American war dragged on and on? Did she wish to find herself totally dependent upon Britain for this important commodity, a nation with an ambition to achieve global commercial supremacy and a history of using whatever means came to hand to attain her ends?[31]

Slidell emerged from his long interview with the emperor in an exultant mood. He dashed off a note to Mason, informing him that things were "right" in France. "I shall ask immediately for recognition and hope that it will meet your views to do so at London," he reported from Vichy on July 16. No doubt he believed that he had made some headway with his emphasis upon the divergence of French and British interests. He was confident that if England continued to drag her feet France would speed ahead alone. He had not advised Mason of the special treatment Richmond was willing to accord France, in part because he was worried about the danger of their correspondence being intercepted by Union agents. By July 20 he was recommending to the Virginian that the demand for recognition be submitted in Paris first, so that news of it would reach the Foreign Office from the French embassy in London before Mason's note arrived.[32] Here was a ploy worthy of the vulpine Slidell, for it was not unreasonable to expect that the French ambassador would disclose at the same time his government's inclination to respond favourably. This revelation might have had a helpful effect in London. But the scheme came to naught.

Although Mason waited until Slidell had delivered his request on July 23, there was little likelihood of any sympathetic French response arriving quickly enough to influence the British. For in the end, after all the plotting, Slidell's move had been ill-timed. He acted just before Thouvenel accompanied his sick wife on a trip to Germany, and the foreign minister did not plan to return for at least ten days. He promised that in the meantime he would "fully examine" the whole matter, but it was a leisurely pace he was setting for himself. He did so safe in the knowledge, which he had extracted from Slidell, that an almost simultaneous request was being made by Mason. Opposed to any intervention in the American quarrel at this time, Thouvenel could relax at a German spa while the British decided against recognition. He was confident that their decision would hold his restless sovereign in check. Tempting as the rewards of cotton and an alliance against the Mexicans were, Napoleon knew that unless he was partnered by Britain the punishment for meddling would be a conflict with the United States.[33]

Fighting one war in the Americas already, the emperor was in no position to compound his problems there. He was all too aware of his political isolation in a Europe suspicious of his opportunism and ambitions. His dilemma was most acute in Italy, where his involvement had satisfied neither his own conservative Catholics nor liberals and revolutionaries. Indeed, it seemed impossible to devise a policy which would not alienate one of these important segments of domestic opinion. Moreover, he was not entirely convinced that Austria had abandoned all hope of regaining her influence in the peninsula. In fact, she maintained a large army because she feared Napoleon and an attack against Venetia, but its existence did not ease the emperor's mind about her intentions. Additional French difficulties across the Atlantic would provide the Austrians with an opportunity to strike. As one perceptive Austrian observer remarked, Napoleon was "in the unfortunate position of men who are capable of anything but who are also capable of nothing."[34]

In London Mason's request seems to have taken the government by surprise. Palmerston had made it perfectly clear during the debate a few days earlier that the cabinet saw no reason to depart from its present course at this time. That the great majority of the nation favoured the South and saw in the Union's division benefit for both sides was clear enough to Russell. Yet on the morning following Palmerston's little triumph in the Commons the foreign secretary could truthfully report to William Stuart, the chargé d'affaires in Washington during Lyons's absence, that there was "no pressure on the Government to recognize the South prematurely." There was within the Foreign Office a sense that the Union had not been sufficiently humbled by its recent setbacks to entertain any thought of peace. Moreover, although the Confederates had "almost" established their claim to foreign recognition, nothing but the hope of relieving the distress in the textile districts ought to lead Britain to interfere till the Northern cause was "more thoroughly degraded, and the power of doing mischief eradicated."[35] As for the distress, there was confidence that it could be borne until March or April of the following year. For the government had decided, several days before the debate on Lindsay's motion, to bring before Parliament "some precautionary measure" to meet the additional miseries likely to befall the spinning towns during the autumn and winter. It was, as *Punch* depicted it, an act of "Home Intervention." Fair Britannia, accompanied by sturdy John Bull carrying a basket of supplies, would enter the homes of the impoverished operatives and drive back though not away the spectre of famine.[36]

The need for action of some kind, as the shadow of calamity continued to lengthen across the industrial landscape of Lancashire, was widely acknowledged. One by one, or so it seemed, the spinning towns were being swallowed up in the gloom of universal pauperism. There had been a more pessimistic tone to H. B. Farnall's reports lately, Villiers advised the House on July 14. With the American war threatening to drag on, the price of cotton had shot up on speculation and as a result of its continued exportation by profiteers. This would inevitably hasten the closure of more mills and throw additional thousands of operatives out of work at a time when in many areas those on relief were already increasing at the alarming rate of a thousand each month. Furthermore, many thousands of unemployed had earlier been too proud to accept the designation of pauper, preferring to delve into their savings instead. But the deposits were nearly exhausted, the banks had reported to the Poor Law Board, which meant that these sturdy people would now have no alternative to relief.[37]

On July 22 Villiers rose in the Commons to introduce the Union Relief Aid Bill. The ground had been well prepared for him by that morning's *Times*. The newspaper had discussed the alternatives. To meet the crisis the government could either revive the traditional device of a rate in aid, empowering parishes to call upon the union for assistance, and a needy union then to obtain help from the county, or it could permit the guardians to borrow money on the rates to alleviate the distress. *The Times* endorsed the rate in aid and Villiers had left little doubt on July 14 which choice the government would make. The reasons were as much political as economic. In the rest of the nation the wealth of Lancashire excited considerable envy. It was generally believed that the profits from land rentals in that county had increased tenfold over a few years, thus enriching a nobility which had in some cases multiplied its gains by investing in canals, railroads, and coalpits. Even more conspicuous were the "hundreds of millowners" who lived in splendour a few miles from their factories. To outsiders it did not seem at all unreasonable that these plutocrats should "subsidize the parishes breaking down under their burdens." Conversely, to go on rating a parish where industry was paralysed was "like feeding a dog with a joint of its own tail."[38]

If the government expected an easy passage for the rate in aid they were mistaken. Although the session had been long and many members were keen to be off to the moors for the opening of the grouse season (a concern which did ensure a short debate), the going was heavy. The fact that the rates in the hardest-hit parishes were still below or were no higher than those borne elsewhere induced some non-Lancashire members to question the need for extraordinary measures. In reply Villiers explained that in the mill towns the rates were paid largely by the workingmen themselves. Once they lost their jobs they were unable to pay. In Stockport alone almost 50 per cent of the rate could not be collected. This threw an unbearable burden upon the remaining ratepayers, such as small shopkeepers whose businesses were already in difficulties as a result of the inability of the unemployed to pay for their goods. Without help they would soon collapse under the additional weight. However, the most insistent opposition to the government's bill came from Lancashire itself.

From some of the more radical members there came a demand for the measure Villiers had been so anxious to avoid—a national grant to aid the suffering artisans. On more than one occasion the government had suspended the Bank Charter Act for the benefit of the capitalist class, millowner Edmund Potter reminded his colleagues, "and he thought they could not do less than propose an ample grant for the support of the destitute operatives of Lancashire." He believed that £100,000 a month for the next seven months would be enough. Meanwhile, on the right, the landed interests were resisting the unpleasant precedent that in such crises all the property in the county should pay a fair quota of the cost of relief. Of course, they decked out their self-interest in more appealing garb. A union which could compel others to contribute was more likely to be careless in its expenditures. Far better, they urged, that the worst-hit unions be given the power to borrow. It was a suggestion quickly taken up by a number of other members for the county, but for less selfish reasons. Richard Cobden rallied to its support at the request of the Rochdale guardians. His concern and theirs, and it was shared by the guardians of Wigan, Stockport, Chorley, Oldham, and Blackburn, was that the unions would not be empowered to turn to the county for a rate in aid until their rate had reached five shillings. Yet they were finding a rate of two shillings a terrible burden because of the declining numbers of rate-payers. Under the government's scheme, they would be crushed long before they could demand help. What would be wrong, therefore, Cobden asked, with a bill that provided for the power to borrow as well as a rate in aid?

Initially the government resisted this proposal. A policy of postponement would solve nothing, both Villiers and Palmerston argued. Parishes confronted with capital and interest payments on a loan would find that they had not benefited. Equally, the prospect of being loaded with debts for years to come would drive people from the parish and thus place an even heavier burden upon those who remained. When the demands for this amendment continued to grow, the prime minister rounded upon the great manufacturers and landowners. A Malthusian, and for that reason more than a little suspicious of relief, Palmerston had long harboured a contemptuous dislike for manufacturers. In the past he had likened them to people who held out their dishes and prayed for plum pudding. Now, as he reminded the House, they were exporting cotton for the sake of profit rather than using it to keep their operatives in employment. Why should those who had made immense fortunes from the textile industry, and those landowners who had benefited from the prosperity of the county, escape sharing the burden of the present misery? This would be the effect of the borrowing provision, he complained. But this angry intervention was of little avail and the government was forced to give ground, though it did so grudgingly. At Palmerston's insistence the rate in aid was retained, while an effort was made to establish a parity between it and the authority to borrow which was added to the bill. A union was to be able to select either course whenever its rate reached four shillings. Once again the Lancashire coalition of landed and manufacturing interests would not be denied. They demanded and they obtained a differential, or, as Villiers termed it, a premium on borrowing. Whenever a parish rate exceeded three shillings it could call upon the union to cover the excess, and whenever a union rate topped this same level the guardians could ask the Poor Law Board for authority to borrow. As for the rate in aid, the unions could only demand county help when their rates reached five shillings.[39]

Outside of Parliament the legislation received a cautious welcome. *Reynolds's* might denounce Villiers as a "homoepathic humanitarian" administering relief in "doses of the most infinitesimal description," and the *Standard* complain that the help it had long demanded for the operatives had finally been "grudgingly accorded," but the general opinion was more favourable. Thanks to the amendments, the bill was a "neat piece" of work.[40] Nevertheless, it was only a palliative and a very impermanent one at that. The legislation was to expire in March unless renewed. So it was not surprising that Englishmen persevered with their search for the cure. As before, they recommended different remedies. Some continued to place their confidence in the full exploitation of the cotton-producing potential of India. Others still favoured a national grant for the distressed. For the Tory press and for *Reynolds's* the sole hope for a recovery remained a massive transfusion of cotton from America, and that meant intervention in the war.[41]

No doubt this persistent and vigorous advocacy of recognition encouraged in Mason the belief that he could bring the British government up to the mark, even though all the evidence pointed to a decision to intervene at home and not abroad for the time being. But he underestimated the size of the obstacles in his path. Of these one of the most formidable was Britain's respect for the North's power to do mischief, which found its clearest reflection in concern for the security of Canada and fury at the province's failure to organize a more effective system of self-defence. Understanding the connection, British partisans of the Southern cause struggled to convince their countrymen that safety for Canada lay in a political alliance with the Confederacy.[42] The measure of their failure was to be seen in the debate on colonial fortifications which took place in the upper chamber on the very day the Commons discussed Lindsay's motion. To a man, the peers who spoke expressed their angry dismay at the half-hearted if not half-baked commitment of the Canadians to their own defence, and almost to a man they predicted that "an irruption into Canada" would be the immediate result of the war's end. If they lost the South, the Federals would attack in search of compensation. If they restored the Union, they would cross the border drunk with victory. Before such an invasion the 12,000 British regulars in the colony, unsupported by a large and reasonably proficient body of Canadians, would be condemned to ignominious defeat.[43] "The Canadian Parliament shows itself strangely insensible to the great change that has taken place in the international politics of North America," the *Morning Post* observed. In *The Times* Robert Lowe, whose visit to Canada in 1856 had not enhanced his opinion of its worth, lectured the colonials on their dangers and duties. "The question is much simpler than the Canadians seem to think," he wrote in a long and acid leader. "If they are to be defended at all, they must make up their minds to bear the greater part of the burden of their own defence." Publicly as well as privately, explicitly and by implication, well-placed Englishmen now spoke of their willingness to give up a people who would not fight for themselves.[44]

Had the British washed their hands of Canada they would have been able to respond more freely to the conflict across the Atlantic. This thought may well have been in the back of John Roebuck's mind when that ardent Southern sympathizer urged the government to make the Canadians understand that "we do not care one farthing about the adherence of Canada to England."[45] But no administration headed by Palmerston was likely to abandon this part of the empire, leaving it to be annexed at their pleasure by the Americans. That the United States retained a proprietary interest in the province the prime minister did not for a moment doubt, nor did Russell or Newcastle. They had watched uneasily the recent moves in Congress to amend or annul the Reciprocity Treaty, and to obtain the construction of a new and more powerful line of fortifications along the border. It was plain, in the aftermath of the *Trent* affair, that in the Union hatred for Britain was matched only by that for Canada. The readiness with which the Canadians had supported Britain's warlike policy during that crisis had shaken some

Americans. They cited it as proof that the policy of tying the colony ever more tightly to the United States with the bonds of economic generosity had failed, and angrily described the Canadians as more British than the British themselves. Surveying the situation in July, Newcastle informed Governor Monck that he did not expect an American attack on the province during the coming winter "but such an event is assuredly by no means impossible."[46]

In Canada the Cartier-Macdonald government, defeated on a militia bill, had been replaced by one led by Sandfield Macdonald. The new premier "has no following—little influence—no ability, but is respectable," commented one highly respected colonial to his English business associates.[47] His administration was founded upon the "double majority," which Newcastle understandably characterized as a "foolish" compromise. Roughly, it was agreed that major measures would have to win the support in the House of a majority of the members from both sections of the province. The new premier had promised the governor that he would tackle quickly the pressing problem of militia organization. What emerged was an expansion of the existing volunteer force. "The specimen I have seen of that system here has not enamoured me much of it as a sole basis of national defence," the sorely disappointed Monck wrote home, "but if we can get nothing better we must put up with it, and try to do the best we can with the instruments with which we are supplied."[48] Laudably practical as this response was, the fact remained that Canada had not made adequate preparations for the contingency of a war with the Union. And the only comfort Monck could offer was his ministers' promise to bring forward a new militia bill, based upon sounder principles and a more comprehensive organization, in the next session of the legislature. This did little to assuage Newcastle. The conduct of the Canadian ministers had produced in Britain, he warned, a feeling of alienation "which two months ago had no other existence than in their imaginations and in the clever but eccentric brain of Goldwin Smith."[49]

The government promptly set about the task of disabusing the province of the notion that it could continue to rely entirely upon the British army for its defence against the "Military Democracy." Newcastle sought to do this publicly in the Lords on July 18 and privately in his correspondence with Monck. It was a warning repeated by the prime minister in the Commons a week later. Replying to an irritating speech by Disraeli, in which the Tory gleefully recalled his opposition to the despatch of more troops to Canada the summer before on the grounds that it would dissuade the colonials from making adequate military provisions themselves, Palmerston declared that Britain had done as much for Canada as she intended to do. The government did not intend either to recall the troops now in Canada or to send any additional men there.[50]

The caution instilled into the British government by the evident, infuriating, and seemingly indefinite vulnerability of Canada to American mischief, was carefully tended by Lyons. When he had called at the American legation on July 1 to pay his respects to Adams, he failed to impress Moran who found him a "dull man with a heavy intellect" given to measuring his words too much. However, in the excitement of London, as in the periods of frenzy in Washington, these were pedestrian qualities not to be sneezed at. Lyons had returned home with a pessimistic view of the war. He saw "very small chance" of his nation getting cotton from America for "a very long time to come." He had been unable to detect any sign of Union feeling in the South, and foresaw a prolonged struggle fought for "separation—or subjugation." As for his government's posture, he thought that American uncertainty about the intentions of Britain and France was not without its value. He had found the Federals more disposed to be considerate, or at least civil, when they were nagged by doubts. Nevertheless, he was resolutely opposed to British intervention in the conflict. He considered it a dangerous course, ever likely to do harm but rarely good. For this reason he was "alarmed at the feelings" in England, and he "purposely abstained" from attending the debate on July 18. Undoubtedly he made out his case during frequent visits to Russell at Pembroke Lodge, and long conversations with Palmerston and Lord Derby.[51]

Lyons was ably seconded by the younger man who was standing in for him at Washington. William Stuart was no diplomatic novice, as he soon proved. He had served as secretary of legation in Brazil, Sicily, and Greece before being posted to the American capital in 1861. The minister's return to England and the coincidental setback for McClellan on the peninsula encouraged Henri Mercier to visit the chargé d'affaires. He had broached the subject of joint mediation several times during the spring with Lyons, but his own ardour had cooled in the face of the Englishman's impassive response. On June 30 he called on Stuart in order to revive the question. The difficulty was, as he admitted, to intervene without running too great a risk of war. Were the British and French governments to act energetically now they might pull off this feat, he suggested. Stuart was dubious, and in reporting the meeting to Russell he offered the opinion that they would "be playing too great a stake at present." Far better to wait for a disaster, which would both undermine the Federals' confidence and diminish that arrogance and vindictiveness which still persuaded them they could fight all of Europe if necessary. Better, too, if they were exhausted financially and physically as well as mentally, and Stuart thought he had detected the signs of this total collapse. The sharp rise in the price of gold was a measure of the economy's weakness, he observed, while the army was having difficulty raising men. By mid-July Mercier had reached the same conclusion; namely, that nothing would be lost but much gained by waiting a little longer. By October joint mediation would have "some chance of being listened to."[52]

The advice of the men on the spot, fear for the safety of Canada, and uneasiness about the state of affairs in Eastern Europe, where Russell suspected France, Russia, Prussia, and Italy of conspiring to partition Turkey, all ensured that Mason's demand for recognition would not be met. There was a delay of a week before Russell replied, but this was not the result of any indecision. The government's formal response merited discussion by the full cabinet, which was to meet at the beginning of August. In the meantime Russell answered the note in which Seward had held before the British the gorgon of servile war. The foreign secretary refused to flee even in the face of this monster. It would be one more disaster, one more element of destruction, loss, and waste in a country lately so prosperous, he responded. As for British policy, the government saw no reason at the present time to deviate from "impartial neutrality." This qualified reaffirmation of nonintervention went out to Stuart on July 28, and Lyons, having spent the weekend at Pembroke Lodge, concluded that his government had not the least desire to interfere in the war. Yet there were dangers, as he recognized. Public opinion would not allow the government to "tolerate anything like an insult or injury" from the Union, so he was fearful of some second Captain Wilkes resorting to high-handed proceedings. Equally, there might be an irresistible pressure for intervention should the distress in Lancashire grow worse.[53]

The last day of the month found Russell preparing a reply to Mason which broadly followed the line taken by Palmerston in his speech on Lindsay's motion. Yet to a group of his cabinet colleagues, led by Gladstone, the draft "seemed to lay down the principle that recognition of the South by the United States government ought to precede its recognition by foreign powers." This was far too restrictive a self-imposed restraint upon Britain's freedom of action, and it was at variance with Russell's recent note to Seward in which he had expressly declined to commit his nation indefinitely to the continuance of nonintervention. The upshot was a note informing Mason that the British government was still determined to wait, but did not rule out the prospect of the time coming when the Confederacy would win a place among the nations of the world. There was no suggestion that the Union would first have to acknowledge this fact.[54]

The Confederates were bitterly disappointed. Once more the British government had revealed itself to be "tardy and supine," clinging tenaciously only to a policy of postponement. Still held at arm's length by Russell, who had politely rejected his request for an interview, Mason was a little bewildered by his inability to drive the cabinet to "a decided position." Henry Hotze attributed the indecision to a combination of Palmerston's extreme old age, which had chilled his blood, Russell's mind, which thought "procrastination the perfection of statesmanship," and the Conservatives' feeble American policy.[55] Yet although the Confederates in London were discouraged, and Slidell's higher hopes had even farther to fall in Paris, they were offered a morsel or two of encouragement. Russell suddenly published Seward's May 28 despatch to Adams (a copy of which the minister had forwarded for his information) and his own reply, which had stopped far short of any guarantee of nonintervention. What was unusual in this conduct was the decision to publish so soon after the answer had gone out. There was also some question as to the propriety of publishing Seward's letter to the minister. A "gross breach of faith and an act of worse manners" this may have been, but it had given added significance to the foreign secretary's answers to a number of questions from Malmesbury in the Lords several days earlier, on August 4. He had then made it clear that the government was not setting its face against participation in a joint interference by the Great Powers in the war.[56]

The idea of a collective offer of mediation was, as Adams had feared, gaining ground. One of its principal attractions was safety. "It might lead to nothing but it could not provoke war." Within the cabinet it had a powerful advocate in Gladstone. He had been much encouraged by a long conversation with Henry Hotze over dinner on July 30. The chancellor impressed the Confederate as friendly to the South but had voiced the government's fears for the safety of Canada and had spoken of the difficulty confronting any mediator when it came to determining a boundary between the Union and an independent Confederacy. Hotze had been able to persuade him that the boundary obstacle at least was not insuperable. Confidently, Gladstone began to urge that the government communicate with France and Russia concerning a joint representation to the Americans. However, if the other powers were not ready Britain should wait until they were rather than go ahead alone. The chancellor was sure that Palmerston shared his view. In fact, both the prime minister and the foreign secretary had concluded that Mercier's suggestion of a move in October had merit and might be initiated by a proposal for an armistice. "We shall see in October what is the disposition of the North," Russell informed Stuart, "but if they are then determined to go on, it will be of little use to ask them to leave off." Personally he could not imagine that the Federals still expected to succeed after their failure before Richmond.[57]

One dissenter from this proposed course of action was Argyll. He did not think Britain should interfere, even in conjunction with other powers, until there were "some symptoms of doubt and irresolution" on the part of the Union. To offer mediation before would be to invite rejection, leaving the powers with little alternative except armed interference. Anyway, he did not think that the tremendous questions involved in the conflict, and of these slavery was always in the forefront of Argyll's mind, had "been brought sufficiently near a solution to enable neutral Powers to form any sound opinion on the conditions which the one side sh[oul]d be advised to demand, and the other to concede." And if he was worried by the drift of opinion in the government, Argyll found some consolation in the fact that it had been agreed to summon a cabinet, and due notice was to be given so that all members might attend, before any step towards intervention was taken.[58] At least there was little danger of the two old men taking matters into their own hands.

Revealing as was the decision merely to continue the policy of postponement, just as significant was the comparative ease with which the Palmerston government had resisted the pressure exerted by the Confederates or organized by their sympathizers. Although James Spence worked hard, writing letters to the editor of *The Times*, contributing to the early numbers of the *Index*, counselling representatives of the distressed operatives, his efforts to advance the Southern cause through a campaign of popular agitation were ill-starred from the first. At Blackburn it was a simple case of bungling, but the inability to unite the unemployed behind one solution to their misery—interference in the Civil War—was a serious weakness. The dissonant demands of the demonstrators made it easier for the government to ignore those calling for recognition of the Confederacy or mediation of the conflict. Nor did the parliamentary advocates of action pose any more dangerous a threat to Palmerston. Here he was aided by the indecisiveness of the Conservative leadership.

Mason had established contact with a number of prominent Tories, especially their spokesmen on foreign affairs, and the party's national organs were in the vanguard of those who in the name of suffering Lancashire demanded a diplomatic initiative to bring the conflict to an end. But when it came to exploiting the issue in Parliament, the opposition was well-nigh paralysed by caution. Anxiety to avoid alienating any influential segment of opinion, such as that of Manchester, was heightened by an awareness that the government had protected its freedom of action on this question by not committing itself irrevocably to a particular course. Together with Derby's isolationism and the fear that British intervention would serve to prolong rather than shorten the war, these considerations explain the feeble support the Tories offered as a party to the Confederate lobby. None of this escaped Palmerston. He was able to relax, secure in the knowledge that the American question was unlikely to become a partisan one. So, although the situation in Lancashire continued to worsen, the government was not forced to come to a decision with respect to the American war. Instead, it introduced temporary measures designed to facilitate the relief of distress. However, Palmerston and Russell were looking no further than October. By then they expected the situation in the United States to be clearer, and the prospects of success for some joint action with France brighter.

FIVE

The Cause of Freedom

IN WASHINGTON, SEWARD WATCHED anxiously for any sign of a European move. Like many of his countrymen, he experienced growing anger as he waited. He resented as much as Adams Palmerston's "unjust and censorious homilies" on the Butler incident, and knowing this, Stuart was timorous about presenting Russell's mild complaint. The open discussion in London of proposals to mediate or to recognize the Confederacy made the secretary seethe. So did the knowledge that vessels were being sent out to the South from British ports, some of them having been built there for the Confederate Navy. "The British nation sympathizes with the insurgents," he complained to his daughter. "The British Government either sympathizes, or allows itself to seem to sympathize, with them."[1]

Seward's first duty remained the avoidance of foreign complications and to this end he masked his fury. In his meetings with Stuart he was affable and conciliatory. The complaint that British subjects had been compelled by over-zealous military commanders to take an oath of allegiance to the United States brought a prompt and satisfactory response. On the important matter of cotton supplies, Seward readily conceded that the fibre had not flowed out of the Southern ports controlled by the Union as freely as he had expected, and he reacted with surprising sympathy to Russell's suggestion, and that of Cobden, for improving the situation. However, when he took the proposals to cabinet they met stiff opposition. Lincoln, for one, opposed letting $50 million worth of cotton out of the Southern states and its value in. This way the Union "would never succeed in crippling them much in their resources," the president protested. Nor could it be denied that such a concession to the hated British would have been extremely unpopular. Thus little came of either scheme, but Seward had convinced Stuart that he was doing everything possible to facilitate the exportation of cotton and when the

Englishman finally gave up hope of obtaining it in quantity he held the Confederates largely responsible. They would have refused to forward their staple anyway, he reported home.[2]

Meanwhile dangerous incidents were multiplying on the high seas. American officers on blockade duty were exasperated at their inability to prevent the sleek, low, lead-painted runners slipping past them into Charleston and Wilmington. Every failure was a blow to their pride, their nation's cause, and their pockets, for it cost them handsome prize money. Perhaps recalling the indignities suffered by American captains at the hands of the Royal Navy in the past, the frustrated Union officers had a tendency to be cavalier and brusque when they fell in with British merchantmen. There were unnecessary shots across bows, refusals to give the names of cruisers, failures to fly the correct colours and pennant, and the use of offensive language by boarding officers. All of this was protested by the British. With the *Trent* episode still fresh in his mind, fearful where such disputes might lead, Seward thought it prudent to make concessions. On August 9 he read to Stuart instructions which, in the president's name, he had asked Secretary Welles to issue to the commanders of all Union vessels. Under no circumstances were they to seize a foreign ship within the waters of a friendly nation; they were forbidden to chase and fire at a foreign vessel without first giving her the customary preliminary notice of a desire to speak and visit; after a visit there was to be no seizure without a careful search which gave rise to a "reasonable" belief that she was "engaged in carrying contraband of war to the insurgents and to the ports or otherwise violating the blockade." Finally, there was to be no tampering with bags and parcels bearing official seals and locks once a vessel had been seized. On the contrary, they were to be handed over to the nearest consulate or legation of the nation concerned. Subsequently Seward went further, requesting the Navy Department to ensure that even properly certified public mails be returned unopened. In Gideon Welles, however, he faced another opponent of concessions to the British.[3]

The secretary of the navy was theatrical in appearance. His long white beard and "stupendous white wig" suggested that he might have been well cast as an Old Testament prophet, the Roman god of the sea, or "the heavy grandfather in a genteel comedy." As befitted any of those roles there was about his face an "air of ponderous deliberation," and he liked to pose as a calm, cautious, and contemplative man of affairs. In reality, Welles was "insecure," "highly emotional," and a "self-conscious pessimist" innately sceptical of the motives of his fellow-men.[4] A former newspaper publisher and minor politician, he had some experience of naval administration but found little opportunity during his first months in Washington to acquire self-confidence in his new role. As secretary he bore the responsibility for the navy's failure to halt blockade-running and found himself ridiculed in the press as a modern Rip Van Winkle. Painful as this was, he resented still more his treatment by Seward. Aware of the other man's contempt, the doubts of his fitness to hold such an important post, he was acutely sensitive to any meddling from that quarter in his department's affairs. Above all he was jealous, almost childishly so, of Seward's close and seemingly privileged relationship with the president.

Welles watched with jaundiced eye the growing friendship between the two men. They met daily, sometimes several times, and Welles knew that the New Yorker had the capacity to keep the melancholy Lincoln entertained with his fund of anecdotes. He saw in this intimacy an undue and unwise influence on the administration's policies. None of this disposed Welles to accept Seward's directions on naval affairs, least of all in matters of etiquette designed to appease the British. They were responsible for too many of his troubles, especially for the public mockery he was so ill-equipped to face, and no less than his officers he was angered by "the sneaking method which the Englishmen practised of stealing into Charleston in the darkness of the night." In his opinion "continued and degrading submission to aggressive insolence" would promote neither "harmony nor self-respect." Anyway, Seward was ready to concede far more than the law required. Yet Welles quickly abandoned any thought of openly fighting this question through. He backed away from a contest with the secretary of state over the strength of his influence with the president. Unable to face the prospect of defeat, he settled for the safe course. He modified the instructions somewhat, disguising as best he could the concessions. At the same time he did not relinquish his own position, and gave fair warning that his harsher definition of belligerent rights had undergone no substantial modification.[5] Moreover, there was a need, as Seward recognized, to place some effective check upon British activities embarrassing not only to Welles but to the Union cause.

Of these, the emergence of Nassau as an entrepôt of the blockade trade was one of the most conspicuous. The quantity and quality of coal required for the long transatlantic crossing discouraged blockade-running from Britain directly to the South. It was found to be "more economical to transship at an intermediate port." Approximately 600 miles from Charleston and Wilmington, the Bahamas were conveniently close to the South. A collection of islands and cays surrounded by shallow water, they afforded small blockade-runners of minimal draught countless opportunities to give the slip to ocean-going vessels of the Union navy seeking to shadow and then seize them once they left British territorial waters. The Confederates had been quick to recognize the islands' possibilities and they soon stationed an agent there, Louis Heyliger. From an obliging governor he had obtained, in December 1861, a relaxation of the regulations concerning the breaking of bulk cargoes and the transshipment of goods, which fostered a mutually beneficial expansion of the trade between colony and Confederacy. A thirty-fold increase in the value of the goods leaving Nassau brought to a spectacular conclusion for the time being the colony's long search for economic security, and enabled many of the seven thousand inhabitants to escape from poverty. Little wonder that they wholeheartedly sympathized with the South.

The United States consul had a miserable time. Ostracized socially and convinced, not without reason, that everyone in the colony was a friend of the rebels, the unhappy Samuel Whiting sought solace in drink. Once under the influence, he became fighting mad. On one occasion he physically assaulted a group of tormentors in a local hotel, and on another launched into a violent tirade against the governor. Dismayed and disgusted, he resigned before the British could request his recall. His successor met with the same hostility, as did their colleague at Bermuda, where the local bloods cut down the consul's flagstaff. The American war had brought prosperity to this colonial outpost as well. It was less popular with blockade-runners than Nassau, because the distance to the Confederate coast was longer and the journey more hazardous for the heavily laden vessels during the winter gales. Nevertheless, the Confederates did establish an agency on the island and the number of ships entering the colony increased by a full 50 per cent in the first year of the war alone. Before its end business was so brisk that there was not enough space to store the goods at the two ports of St. George and Hamilton.[6]

Much as this trade was resented by Northerners, the sense of indignation was deepened by the knowledge that many of the supplies shipped from Nassau to the South had been obtained in the Union. In this roundabout way the United States was providing Lee's army with shoes, clothing, medicines, and meats. Adding insult to the injury was the fact that the smokeless, sparkless anthracite coal which made the detection of blockade-runners by the Union navy so difficult, by day or night, also came from the North.[7] Not surprisingly, the Treasury Department had begun to impede the shipment of anthracite to the Bahamas in April 1862, and on May 20 Secretary Chase had been empowered by Congress to impose restrictions on American trade with a view to preventing supplies reaching the Confederacy. At the beginning of June the New York Customs House began to deny clearance to any vessel carrying a cargo to Nassau that might be useful to the South, unless a large bond was put up. It was retrievable with a certificate from the American consul at the port, a proof that the merchandise had not been reshipped to the Confederates. Naturally merchants protested the costs and inconvenience of this system and it led to a long and niggling correspondence between Seward and the British government.

The British denounced the Federal regulations as a violation of the terms of an 1815 treaty which had been extended to the West Indies in 1830, and they pointed out that trade with the Confederacy was not a violation of international law. The law officers concluded that "the real object and tendency" of the American measures was "to innovate upon the established principles of International Law, and to supply the deficiencies of an inadequate blockade, by domestic legislation, extended beyond the due limits, to the injury of the rights of neutrals under Commercial Treaties." Ominously, they argued that it would be impossible to look upon the activities of the New York Customs House, if they continued to receive the "deliberate sanction" of the United States government, "as having any other character than that of hostility towards a colony of Great Britain, and, therefore, towards Great Britain herself."[8]

Russell had no intention of going to "extremities" to maintain an unhindered trade between New York and Nassau. He wished to avoid a separate grievance with the United States "on which no other nation in Europe would feel the least sympathy with us."[9]

Anyway, while they considered the conduct of the Union to be illegal and continued to protest it, the British could always console themselves with the continuing profits of the trade. The regulations failed to disrupt the Bahamas' newfound prosperity. This realization soon tempted the North, already "sore" at the British, to resort to heavier handed methods when another and more serious grievance sailed over the horizon.

Thomas Dudley had arrived in Liverpool to take up his consular duties in November 1861. His commitment to Lincoln's candidacy at the Republican convention in 1860, where he had worked to ensure that the New Jersey delegation threw its support to the man from Illinois after first-ballot support of William Dayton as a favourite son, and his energetic participation in the election campaign, had assured him of preferment. Eventually he had been offered the choice of appointment as minister to Japan or consul at Liverpool. He chose the lesser position largely because he was worried about his health and was anxious always to be near good medical advice. As his gaunt face with its deepset eyes suggested, he was an intense man. Condemned to work and live in a "nest of pirates" at Liverpool, he buckled down at once to the task of frustrating the Confederates and their British friends.[10]

Not long after his arrival Dudley's attention was drawn to two vessels then under construction, and with the assistance of a small army of private detectives and informants he soon identified one of them as a man-of-war intended for delivery to the Confederacy. Adams brought her to the notice of Russell on February 18 and the Foreign Office asked the lords of the Treasury to make enquiries. The request was forwarded to the Board of Customs which in turn ordered the collector at Liverpool to supervise the investigation. Despite this long channel of communication the bureaucracy proved that it could respond quickly, for only three days after Adams had raised the case of the *Oreto (Florida)* the surveyor of customs at the port reported to the board that "She is a splendid Steamer suitable for a Despatch boat—pierced for guns but has not any on board, nor are there any gun carriages—coals and Ballast are all that the holds contain."[11] There was talk in Liverpool, he added, that she was being built for the Italians. This news Russell telegraphed to the British minister in Turin and by March 1 he had replied that the Italian government denied all knowledge of the vessel. When Adams renewed on March 25 his pleas to the British

CHAPTER FIVE

government to stop the *Oreto* leaving port, the foreign secretary asked the Treasury to ensure that she "be vigilantly watched and if any armament prohibited by the Foreign Enlistment Act is discovered the vessel may be at once detained."[12] The request came too late. Carefully registered in the name of a Liverpool owner, cleared for Palermo and Jamaica in ballast, carrying neither powder nor weapons, not even a signal gun, the *Oreto* had slipped away on March 22. Confederate agents had grown alarmed over the evident interest of the customs officers in her. On April 28 she arrived at Nassau, then moved off to a remote anchorage in the islands to complete her fitting out.[13]

Dudley had little time to brood over this initial setback, for by the beginning of April his suspicions about the second ship under construction had been fully aroused. She was being built in the Laird yards across the Mersey at Birkenhead. William Laird, a Scottish engineer, had first established an iron works there in 1824 but had rapidly progressed from the production of that metal to the construction of iron ships. In 1828 his son John had given up his career as a solicitor to join the enterprise, of which in time he became the senior partner; subsequently he had passed it on to his own sons to administer and had entered Parliament.[14]

An experienced, innovative concern, the Laird firm was painstakingly completing a vessel known in the yards by her number— 290. Although larger and better built than the *Oreto*, at first she seemed a twin and this alone excited comment and suspicion. Dudley kept Adams informed of her progress, though from the outset the minister doubted that the British would seize her. He sought to calm the impulsive and excited consul by feigning confidence in the government's good intentions, but took the precaution of summoning a Federal warship from Spanish waters to be on hand to try to intercept the 290 should she be permitted to sail from Liverpool. Meanwhile he urged Dudley to gather "depositions of her guilty intentions" and on June 23 he warned Russell that a "new and still more powerful war steamer" was nearly ready for departure from the northern port. "Our object is to put them on record as hypocrites and we shall do it," Benjamin Moran commented.[15]

More than five weeks later the 290 succeeded in stealing away from Liverpool, easily avoiding the Federal steamer seeking her, and renamed the *Alabama*, she embarked on a brilliantly successful

121

career as a commerce raider. As a result she bedevilled Anglo-American relations for years to come. This escape, despite the frantic last-minute efforts of Dudley and the representations of Adams, whose pessimism had not diminished his persistence, was greeted by Unionists as further evidence of Britain's ill will and insincere neutrality. The truth was less sinister and the responsibility for the vessel's successful escape was not entirely British. In part, it was a tribute to the skill and intelligence of James Bulloch, the Confederate officer supervising the construction of cruisers in Great Britain. Repeating the strategy that had worked so well in the case of the *Oreto*, he made sure that misleading talk was spread throughout Liverpool about the ownership of the 290. This time the Spanish government was named, and although this ruse did not deceive those watching the vessel for long it did distract them for a short time. Once again no armament, not even the customary signal gun, was taken aboard. Bulloch was as always careful not to commit any overt breach of the law, whether of the Foreign Enlistment Act or the Merchant Shipping Act, and he followed the customs regulations to the letter. Finally, when he learned from his lawyer that these precautions notwithstanding the Unionists were gathering sufficient evidence to have the ship detained, he smartly improvised an elaborate scheme to get her away safely. Yet the fact that he was able to do so owed as much to the British government's long delay in reaching a decision to seize the 290 as it did to his ingenuity. For this procrastination Thomas Dudley was in some measure to blame.[16]

Adams had instructed the consul on June 20 to prepare depositions for a possible action in the courts, but Dudley took a trip to Paris first to visit his friend Dayton. When he returned to Liverpool on July 7, and then only because he was unwell, he discovered that the minister, responding to a suggestion from Russell, had just written to his vice-consul ordering him to turn over to the local collector of customs all the evidence against the ship. This Dudley now did, but not in the legal, properly sworn form which he would have had at hand had he followed his earlier instructions. Understandably, the legal advisers of the Board of Customs rejected the evidence as inadmissible. And while the consul was incensed by this standing on technicalities, Adams admitted "that we should ask as much at home," namely, "affidavits from the consul and his witnesses."[17] He advised Dudley to employ a solicitor to ensure that the correct procedures were strictly followed. On July 21 six affidavits supporting the claim that the 290 was intended for the Confederate service were presented by the consul to the collector in Liverpool, and the following day copies were forwarded to the Foreign Office by Adams. Subsequently three others were submitted to the British authorities. But a full calendar month had elapsed since Adams first asked Dudley to prepare depositions. Seventeen days had gone by since Russell's suggestion that the evidence be laid before the Board of Customs. The vessel might yet have been seized had either the board or the Foreign Office acted with dispatch, but the board did not move because it doubted the legality of a seizure, and in all probability was doubly reluctant to act rashly against a well-established firm whose senior partner was a member of Parliament and an important figure in the Conservative party.

The lawyers offered widely divergent interpretations of the Foreign Enlistment Act, and its prohibition of the equipping, furnishing, arming, or fitting out of ships of war within British territory. Some placed a narrow construction on these words, arguing that it was only illegal to send out ships in a condition "at once to cruise or commit hostilities against an enemy at sea." Among them was the solicitor of customs, hence the board's rejection even of sworn American evidence as insufficient to warrant action. The 290 was not armed.[18] Others protested that this interpretation was contrary both to the letter and the spirit of the legislation. "In their view, any equipment, within British territory, of a ship constructed for warlike use in the service of a Foreign Belligerent Power, and with the known intent that she should be employed against its enemies with whom Britain was at peace, was within the words and policy of the Act."[19] In short, evidence that the 290 was intended for the Confederate service as a cruiser was sufficient grounds for her detention. It was to this school that Robert Collier belonged, as Adams discovered when he turned to the eminent counsel and judge advocate of the fleet for an expert opinion. "It appears difficult to make out a stronger case of infringement of the Foreign Enlistment Act," Collier wrote after reading the affidavits, "which, if not enforced on this occasion, is little better than a dead letter."[20] Adams forwarded the opinion together with copies of two additional affidavits to the Foreign Office on June 24. Dudley and his solicitor had taken them to the Board of Customs the day before. The Customs' solicitor disputed Collier's interpretation of the law but admitted that it could not be ignored. So, late in the afternoon of July 23, the board turned the question over to the Foreign Office and the law officers. That another five days were allowed to pass before the opinion of the Crown's legal advisers was obtained ultimately cost the British taxpayer dear. If any one person was to blame it was Henry Layard, that "mighty self-sufficient gent" whose conceit and discourtesy in debate so irritated those who tangled with him. Dubbed "Mr. Lie-hard" by some of his fellow members, he was more accurately depicted by *Punch* as "the Bull in the China-ware shop for he smashes everything about."[21]

With Russell's sanction Layard sent off to the law officers the documents received from the Board of Customs, and by the evening of July 23 eight affidavits and Collier's opinion ought to have been in their hands. Instead, precious time was lost owing to Layard's negligence. The under-secretary was familiar with the procedure followed when the law officers were consulted. Marked simply for them, papers were taken by a Foreign Office messenger to the chambers of Sir John Harding. The Queen's advocate was responsible for passing them on to his colleagues, the attorney general and the solicitor general. But Harding was seriously ill. He had been teetering on the brink of a mental breakdown for weeks. A physician called to attend him on June 11 had quickly diagnosed his malady and had prescribed rest and quiet. The patient was sent from London to stay with friends in Reading. It was at this time that Harding wrote, signed, and had witnessed a formal letter of resignation. Unhappily, the friend to whom he entrusted it did not consider himself authorized to forward the letter to Palmerston until August 1. By that time Harding had been formally committed as a lunatic, having returned to London under escort and restraint on June 28.[22]

Layard could not claim ignorance of the seriousness of Harding's affliction prior to that event. The under-secretary had heard in mid-June that the Queen's advocate was so unwell that he had been "obliged to give up business and go out of town for some weeks." As a result, Harding had not participated in the drafting on June 30 of the law officers' first opinion on the 290. This was the work of William Atherton and Roundell Palmer and it formed the basis of Russell's note to Adams suggesting that the Americans submit their evidence to the collector at Liverpool. Meanwhile talk in the capital of the Queen's advocate being "off his head" had been followed early in July by the preliminary skirmishing over the appointment of a successor. Clearly ignorant of the circumstances under which Harding had returned to his London house, Layard must have assumed that the Queen's advocate had recovered his health. Yet, at the very least, he ought to have ascertained whether Harding was fit enough to resume his duties. Even the appearance of Dudley's worried solicitor at the Foreign Office on the afternoon of July 23, seeking information about the law officers' opinion, failed to disturb the undersecretary. Although he promised to send for it "at once," by Friday, July 25, Layard still had not heard from the law officers. This silence was all the more puzzling since additional documents had been forwarded to them two days earlier. But the weekend had now arrived and with Russell out of town (he would have to be consulted before action was taken against the *290*) Layard appears to have decided to let matters rest for another day or two.[23]

On Monday, July 28, Layard finally awoke to the likelihood of there being a connection between the law officers' silence and the continuing talk of Harding's ill-health. He called at the London home of the Queen's advocate where he discovered that the law officer had been committed and had carried off with him to the asylum the Foreign Office bag containing the initial batch of six affidavits. It appears to have been forwarded from his chambers to his home on the very day he was officially certified as a lunatic. Lady Harding was unable to separate her demented husband from the bag because he refused to allow her to come near him. The only person he still trusted was Robert Phillimore, the custodian of his letter of resignation. Layard hastily contacted Phillimore, and he sped to the asylum, which fortunately was located in the suburb of South Kensington, and persuaded Harding to part with the papers. They were sent to Attorney General Atherton, to whom they ought to have been directed in the first place. Palmer and he met hurriedly in the earl marshal's room near the House of Lords that evening and quickly endorsed much of Collier's opinion. Acknowledging the widely divergent interpretations of the 7th section of the Foreign Enlistment Act, they argued against the narrow construction of the words "to equip, furnish, fit out or arm" because it "would fritter away the Act, and give impunity to open and flagrant violations of its provisions." They recommended that the vessel be seized, and without delay. But Russell did not return to London until the following evening, which may account for the Foreign Office's failure to transmit the necessary order to the Treasury until July 30. Already it was too late.[24]

Although the escape of the *290* on July 29 was an acute embarrassment, Russell had some reason to hope that the damage it was likely to inflict on relations with the Union would be minimized by the belated detention of the *Oreto* in the Bahamas. Convinced that she was completing her fitting out there, the American consul had several times requested the colonial authorities to investigate. The governor sent naval officers to examine her, and for a short time had a naval vessel watch her, hoping all the while that this conspicuous interest would persuade the Confederate officers to take the vessel out of his jurisdiction. He willingly authorized her departure for Havana in ballast. However, she remained and it became notorious that her furnishings and arming were being completed. Eventually, on the complaint of several of the men who had shipped in her from England that she was intended for the Confederate service, the *Oreto* was seized. The governor, acting with the support of the colony's attorney general, promptly released her. As he explained to the Colonial Office, he was unwilling to assume "a hostile air" and doubted that she could be successfully prosecuted. This did not satisfy the senior British naval officer in the islands, who repeatedly warned that she was being readied for immediate belligerent operations on leaving British waters. Reluctantly the governor rearrested the *Oreto* and sent the case to the Vice-Admiralty Court, for he was beginning to fear that a failure to take action would encourage the Federals to demand the same privileges in British waters, which if refused would lead to difficulties with the Union ships off the colony.[25]

In London it was the judgment of the Colonial Office that the governor's conduct had been "weak and vacillating," though it was recognized that the wording of the Foreign Enlistment Act made prosecution in the courts far from easy. "The difficulty w[oul]d be in proving legally the intention to employ her in the service of the Confederates."[26] When he discovered on August 1 that the gunboat was still in custody, Russell asked the Colonial Office to instruct the governor to hold her until he received fresh orders from home. By the middle of the month he was making arrangements with the Treasury for a Customs House officer to be sent out to Nassau from Liverpool to give evidence as to what had taken place there.[27]

Once again the Foreign Office was too late. Long before the order to hold the vessel reached the colony a judge in the Vice-Admiralty Court had ordered her to be released and she had made good her escape. One month later she ran the blockade and put in at Mobile. Judge Lees found that the Crown had failed to prove the three facts he considered necessary for condemnation—that she had been equipped within the court's jurisdiction, that there was an intent to employ her in the service of the Confederacy, and that she intended to commit hostile acts against the citizens of the United States. As the governor remarked in his report to the Colonial Office, "I do not think it likely that we shall ever obtain stronger proof against any vessel than was produced against the *Oreto*, of an intention to arm as a Belligerent. Therefore, we may assume that no prosecution of the same kind will be instituted, or if any be instituted that it will fail."[28] Understandable as this pessimism was, the cases of the *Oreto* and the *290* had produced a significant if subtle change in attitude at the Foreign Office. In March Russell had accepted the narrow construction of the Foreign Enlistment Act favoured by the solicitor of customs. By the end of July the broader interpretation was shaping the government's conduct. Whether the courts in Britain would uphold a seizure remained to be seen.

Even before the *Alabama*'s escape Seward's conduct suggested that the conciliatory face he continued to show Stuart was a mask in danger of slipping. The stream of blockade-runners pouring out of Nassau, and the building of Confederate commerce raiders in British shipyards, brought a threat of privateering. Of course, Union privateers would prey only upon vessels flying the Confederate colours. Using a member of the Naval Affairs Committee as his spokesman, though it was plain that the senator's heart was not in the task, Seward sought from Congress authority for the administration to issue letters of marque and reprisal. The proposal immediately ran into heavy seas. Privateering was repugnant to the spirit of the age; it would be an admission of the navy's failure; would it not amount, as had the blockade, to a recognition of Confederate belligerency? What navy or commerce did the Southerners possess to justify such an extreme measure? Few senators doubted that it was aimed at the British and none thought it wise at this time to sail so near the wind. As one of many critics asked, "if we legalize this business again, and turn loose upon the ocean a large number of privateers," will not those privateers be more likely "to get us into difficulty with foreign nations than to do any real, practical good, over and above that which can be accomplished by armed vessels of the United States?"[29] Thus in authorizing Adams to give the British notice of the Union's intention to issue letters of marque, which the minister did on July 31, Seward acted prematurely. Two weeks later, when he met with Stuart, the secretary was obliged to lift the threat for the time being.[30] Restrained by the Senate from this act of folly, Seward joined hands with his old adversary Welles in turning loose on the high seas a figure no less controversial and potentially far more dangerous than any privateer.

The belief that both the *Florida* and the *Alabama* were in the West Indies decided Welles to form a special flying squadron to hunt them down before they could wreak havoc on Union shipping and his reputation.[31] A sensible decision, it was marred by the choice of commander. He selected Charles Wilkes, and Seward supported him. Perhaps, as Welles believed, there was an understanding between the secretary of state and the hero of the *Trent* affair that he would have another important command. However, Wilkes had already been rewarded with the James River Flotilla. This new opportunity, together with promotion to the rank of acting rear-admiral, was probably motivated by the knowledge that Wilkes was detested by the British. Here was a startling way to warn them off from aiding the rebels, but it was a foolish gamble in which the element of risk was greater than any possible gain. "These helpless grave-diggers, above all, Seward, are on the way to pick a quarrel with England," commented Adam Gurowski.[32] No one could hold Wilkes in check. Welles knew him to be "troublesome" and considered him "ambitious, self-conceited and self willed." During his command of the James River Flotilla he had exhibited once again his disposition "to rashly assume authority, and do things that may involve himself and his country" in difficulty. As a matter of course, in his letters of instructions for the West Indies Squadron, Welles ordered Wilkes to observe and respect the rights of neutrals and to keep all his acts "within the recognized limitations of international law and regulations." "With these precautions, unnecessary perhaps in your case," the secretary added, with a touch of irony, "you will proceed to discharge the great trust committed to you of guarding and protecting the commerce of our countrymen, and conquering and capturing its enemies and assailants."[33]

If the capture of the *Florida* and the *Alabama* was Wilkes's publicly avowed purpose, there can be little doubt that Welles privately encouraged him to do all that he could to disrupt the blockade-running centred on Nassau and Bermuda. Almost all the arms, munitions, and ordinary supplies the Southerners received came through Nassau, the secretary believed. He may have reminded Wilkes that "Our Officers and people are treated with superciliousness and contempt by the authorities and inhabitants [of these British colonies], and scarcely a favor or courtesy is extended to them while they are showered upon the Rebels."[34] What was certain, however, was that Wilkes would stir up fresh controversy. His presence let alone misbehaviour would make it more difficult for the British government to continue to deny the merchants engaged in blockade-running the protection they loudly sought.

As Wilkes set off to prowl the West Indies, ominously resolved to make this cruise "the apex" of his long service in the navy,[35] another likely source of friction with Britain was drawing closer—emancipation. Profiting from the Union's setback at Bull Run in July 1861, that cause had been advanced by the first Confiscation Act, and it had made further strides during the following winter and spring. Organizations dedicated to freedom for the slaves proliferated and Greeley's powerful *New York Tribune* became a consistent champion of antislavery with the appointment of Sydney Howard Gay as its managing editor. An abolitionist of long standing, a former lecturer for the American Anti-Slavery Society, and editor of the *Anti-Slavery Standard* before Greeley lured him away in 1857, he took over the *Tribune*'s management in April 1862. While the newspaper's antislavery campaign was gaining fresh momentum, petitions and memorials poured into Congress and the government pushed ahead with those practical measures which convinced English friends that the war had already become a struggle for freedom. But freedom in the national capital, freedom in the territories, the offer of compensation to states willing to free their slaves, the recognition of Liberia and Haiti, the slave trade treaty with Britain, and the prohibition of the return of fugitive slaves to their Southern masters by military personnel, all this ceased to be enough by the summer of 1862. The emancipation of all of the slaves in the Confederacy, by decree, was demanded as a moral, military, and diplomatic necessity. At a stroke, its advocates claimed, four million people in the heart of the South would be secured as staunch Unionists. Consternation, fear, and distrust would enter every rebel home, forcing the withdrawal of large numbers of troops from the field to provide "domestic protection." Once they knew that every victory for Federal troops meant freedom, slaves "would find a thousand ways not easy to point out of injuring the Rebel cause, and serving our own." They were sure to escape in large numbers and seek refuge behind the Union lines, where they could be organized as labourers or soldiers, and would be particularly useful if stationed in the South during the sickly season to which they were "acclimated." What better preparation for freedom was there than for negroes to be called up, disciplined, and permitted to fight for it?[36]

The diplomatic benefits of emancipation were also paraded by its advocates. Abolitionists and the more radical Republicans saw in a proclamation declaring free the Southern slaves an impenetrable shield against foreign intervention. Only decisive victories in battle or an affirmation of the conflict's grand humanitarian purpose could keep Britain and France at bay, and after McClellan's failure on the peninsula the prospect of the former had receded. Therefore "the only certain way of averting the intervention, and saving the integrity of the Republic" was to emancipate the slaves and "enlist the moral sentiments and convictions of the civilized world on the side of the United States." Under Gay's direction the *Tribune* repeatedly returned to the argument that such a policy was essential if British sympathy was to be won and intervention avoided.[37] For its part, Congress responded to the antislavery agitation with the second Confiscation Act which declared free the slaves of those Southerners guilty of treason and empowered the president to use negroes in any way he saw fit. As the nine senators and twenty-four representatives who signed the "Address to the Loyal People of the United States" made clear, it was time to arm blacks.

Encouraged by Orville Browning and Seward, Lincoln threatened to veto the Confiscation Act. He took little exception to the emancipatory features, but did protest as unconstitutional other confiscatory provisions extending beyond the lifetime of the traitor. Although he subsequently signed a modified bill into law, as well as a measure granting freedom not only to those slaves who served with the Union forces in some capacity but to their families also, the pressure for a ringing declaration of the war's aim was unrelenting. Unable to persuade the border states to come to his assistance by implementing the scheme of compensated emancipation, despite a moving plea to a delegation of their senators and representatives at the White House on July 12, Lincoln drafted a proclamation. He had long been pondering such a step and may have mentioned the possibility to both Stanton and Vice-President Hamlin before he suddenly broached the matter with Seward and a startled Gideon Welles on July 13.[38]

On the evidence of Welles's recollections of that famous carriage ride to the funeral of Edv 'n Stanton's infant son, the president's motives seem to have been entirely domestic. Forced emancipation in the rebellious South might at last induce the border states to free their slaves voluntarily. A dramatic blow aimed at the heart of the rebellion would invigorate the Union army, Lincoln suggested, and impede the Confederacy's military exploitation of slaves. At no point did he describe his proposed action as an instrument of diplomacy, though he may have thought of it as one. Francis Cutting, a former proslavery Democrat from New York who was advocating a proclamation as a deterrent to foreign intervention, was sent to see him by Stanton. No doubt Sumner made the same case. Certainly Zebina Eastman, the Illinois free-soiler whose appointment to a consulate in England Lincoln had personally arranged because he was "just the man to reach the sympathies of the English people," was privately urging the adoption of emancipation as a means of winning to the Union's side British middle and lower-class opinion.[39] And if Carl Schurz's memory served him well, the president had remarked somewhat earlier in the year: "I cannot imagine that any European power would dare to recognize and aid the Southern Confederacy if it becomes clear that the Confederacy stands for slavery and the Union for freedom."[40] Yet it remains a fact that Lincoln did not discuss, let alone emphasize, the foreign implications. Moreover, conscious of his own ignorance of international affairs, he deferred to Seward's opinion and the secretary of state was convinced that a proclamation would do more harm than good, at home and abroad, at this time.

Having employed emancipation as a menace, as recently as July 18 when he had repeated his warning that "Intervention will end the exportation of cotton by extinguishing the slavery which produces it," Seward's opposition to a proclamation was understandable.[41] If for no other reason, he required time in order to perform a diplomatic about-face. During the cabinet discussion of Lincoln's draft on July 22 he dwelt upon the foreign dangers. The European powers would "intervene to prevent the abolition of slavery for the sake of cotton," he warned; indeed this step threatened to "break up" both American "relations with foreign nations and the production of cotton for sixty years." Together with Thurlow Weed, whom he summoned to his aid, Seward voiced the concern that instead of admiration and sympathy Lincoln's proposal would excite international scorn as an empty and ridiculous gesture by a desperate government. "Purposes can usually better be accomplished without Proclamations," he later observed flippantly to John Hay, and "failures are less signal when not preceded by high sounding promises."[42] Why expose the government's impotency by declaring free slaves it did not have the power to liberate? Would this really encourage more of them to escape behind Union lines? In some parts of the South slaves were not coming into Federal camps because they doubted the Northerners' ability to protect them, and in others military weakness had actually resulted in many who had fled being carried back into bondage. Before being encouraged to flee Confederate territory in far greater numbers, with the promise of freedom, the fugitives deserved to receive the guarantee of safety which only up-to-strength armies could provide. As Seward wrote to his wife, "Proclamations are paper, without the support of armies. It is mournful to see that a great nation shrinks from a war it has accepted, and insists on adopting proclamations, when it is asked for force."[43] In short, recruitment was the most pressing problem facing the United States, and Seward for one did not think it would be eased by a declaration of war on slavery.

July had not been a good month at the recruiting stations, and for an administration which accepted McClellan's wild exaggeration of the size of Lee's army the poor response to Lincoln's call for 300,000 volunteers was disquieting if not grave. Seward was doubly alarmed. Unless the Europeans saw the Union armies rapidly increasing in strength the temptation to intervene might prove too strong. Hopefully he looked overseas for "emigrants to supply the demand for purposes of war and tillage," hence his discreet activities to promote immigration. But this was a long-term solution for a war of attrition, it did not answer the Union's present and urgent need for men. In his anxiety Seward supported the proposal to arm blacks, yet they could not be used to fill up the ranks of existing regiments which were exclusively white. Only fresh recruits from the North could solve this immediate problem. Would conservative whites continue to enlist or to serve if Lincoln proclaimed the struggle as one to free blacks? Would the Irish riot in protest? At the very least a proclamation would widen divisions in Northern opinion at a moment when greater unity was vital.[44]

Lincoln shared many of the concerns Seward voiced, and when urged by Charles Sumner to celebrate July 4 with an edict of emancipation he had then dismissed such a document as a *"brutum fulmen"* that would cause half the officers in the army to throw down their arms in protest and the border states of Kentucky, Missouri, and Maryland to rise in resistance. Nor was he ready to resort to the weapon offered him in the Confiscation Act—black troops. Instead, on the very day the cabinet discussed the draft proclamation, and in order to obtain men "very soon," he suggested to Stanton the drafting of men from the state militias to bring the number up to the 300,000 he had called for on July 1. The order was issued on August 4.[45] Against slavery the president had decided to make no dramatic gesture for the time being.

The proclamation postponed, Seward prepared for the day when it would be issued. In his diplomatic correspondence, he drew attention to the inconsistency of European nations whose long advocacy of an end to slavery on the American continent seemingly did not inhibit a predisposition "if not in favor of the slaveholders and their cause, at least against the Union and the cause of humanity that is now for weal or woe identified with its preservation." Responding to the debate in Britain on some form of intervention, and in order to quell any British or French thoughts of taking action to preserve the South's capacity to supply them with cotton, he returned to first principles. Any failure to respect the sovereignty of the United States would see the Civil War transformed into "a war of the world." In such a conflict, whatever else survived, "the cotton trade built upon slave labor" would be "irredeemably wrecked in the abrupt cessation of human bondage" within American territory. The British would do well to consider the safety, honour, and welfare of their Empire. It was not necessary to mention Canada by name. In the event of moral rather than physical intervention, perhaps a recognition of the Confederacy accompanied by protestations of continuing neutrality, Charles Francis Adams was to suspend the exercise of his functions and assure the British that the ports which had been opened would be closed, and the war from which they suffered lengthened not shortened.[46]

To those Americans peering nervously ahead, down the ill-lit path to emancipation, colonization had long seemed an indispensable travelling companion. Black protests against it did not lessen the allure of free negro emigration for conservative antislavery whites. If they accepted that slavery was a wrong, an outrage upon the rights and dignities of manhood, and asserted the negro's claim to all the rights of a man, it was often on the understanding that he would not enjoy them in "one and the same civil and political society with white men." Thus Harriet Beecher Stowe's black spokesman in *Uncle Tom's Cabin*, having argued his race's claim to equal status in the United States, took himself and his family off to Africa. And in the departure of blacks some whites saw a hope of winning to the cause of abolition the vast numbers of slaveless fellow-whites in the South. Perhaps influenced by Hinton Rowan Helper's *Impending Crisis*, which had enjoyed an astonishing popularity before the war as abolitionist propaganda, they assumed that these people had no liking for slavery but supported the slaveholders out of fear of the "Africanization" of free American society.[47]

Whether or not he shared in this racial pessimism and hostility, Lincoln was very much alive to it and he had long been advocating gradualism and colonization as remedies. His affinity was with those gentler but no less sincere opponents of slavery who preceded the more militant abolitionists of the 1830s. In 1862 Congress offered financial help by attaching appropriations to assist colonization to the bills freeing slaves in the District of Columbia and those held by the army. Within the administration the president was able to count upon the support of Caleb Smith, the secretary of the interior, to whose staff an emigration agent had been added in May of that same year. Although the deportation of free blacks favoured by Attorney General Bates and Montgomery Blair was too extreme a policy to be accepted by Lincoln, in his enthusiasm he did endorse such hare-brained schemes as the plan to settle freedmen in the Chiriqui province of Central America, there to mine coal for the navy.[48]

Watching closely the movement towards emancipation, the British quickly saw a chance to profit from the American government's anxiety to see at least some of the freedmen leave the Union. American blacks could secure their freedom by emigrating to the West Indies, where they would add to the wealth of the British colonies and might give an impulse to the growth of tropical produce such as cotton. There was, however, a humanitarian concern also. The treatment of blacks in the Northern states had rarely been generous and some English observers feared that former slaves would be "sacrificed without scruple, if the North and the South should ever come to an understanding." Thus the suggestion that discussions be held with the North received Russell's hearty support. The Foreign Office then established a number of basic conditions, which were revealing. Any arrangement with the United States must "be conducted so as not to encourage runaway slaves in the Southern States," it had to be offered to the French as well, and all emigration was to be "quite voluntary." Russell was determined that Britons not expose themselves to the charge of "kidnapping." "Those who go to our colonies must be men already free in the United States," he insisted, "and go of their own free will to a British Colony."[49]

In Washington, Stuart moved just as cautiously. He was determined to protect his nation from "incurring the odium of having by premature action encouraged servile insurrection, and the vindictive prosecution of the war."[50] He was aided by Seward whom he discovered to be far less sanguine than the president about the freedmen's willingness to leave the country of their birth. In time the British concluded that the secretary's apparent uninterest was also of a political and military nature, springing from a disinclination to alienate those Americans who objected to any donation even of black muscle and sinew to British or French colonies and an unwillingness to lose potential black recruits for the Union Army. In any event, the result was desultory and fruitless negotiations. This came as a disappointment to the British governors of the Bahamas, British Guiana, British Honduras, and Jamaica, whose colonies had responded enthusiastically to the prospect of black immigrants. Lincoln must have been equally disappointed, for soon after the Central American states made plain their resistance to the settling of American freedmen there, the president intervened personally to revive the negotiations with the British. He even met with an agent of the British Honduras Company who came to Washington seeking emigrants for both Honduras and British Guiana. By June 1863 the negotiations seemed set for success but they finally collapsed when the military need for blacks proved stronger than the racial aversion to them.[51]

Reports of an emigration agreement between Denmark and the United States led Judah Benjamin, in August 1862, to instruct A. Dudley Mann to represent to the Danes the Confederacy's confidence that they would reject complicity "in the system of confiscation, robbery, and murder which the United States have recently adopted under the sting of defeat in their unjust attempt to subjugate a free people."[52] Had Britain been the nation involved, the response would surely have been harsher. As William Stuart surmised, and this was another reason for his reluctance to rush into negotiations, the Confederacy would have regarded any settlement as an act of British hostility. For the dormant Southern bitterness against Britain had been reawakened. There was heartening news of public sentiment in Britain, which did seem to be growing more favourable to the South, but not of diplomatic progress. From Palmerston's remarks during the debate on Lindsay's motion it was evident that his government was still neither ready to acknowledge Confederate independence nor even to proffer mediation. In short, the Palmerston ministry refused to move. It was an inertia which Southerners, like Unionists, continued to attribute to fear, fear for the security of Canada and the balance of power in Europe. No less loudly than their enemies to the North, they repeated the charge that British conduct was an act of "supreme malevolence." Behaviour interpreted by one of the belligerents as an effort to destroy democratic government was seen by the other as a plot to exhaust them both in order to establish a world monopoly in Indian cotton.[53]

Inevitably there were renewed calls in the Confederate press and Congress for the recall of the commissioners in Europe and the dismissal of the foreign consuls in the South, although as a matter of dignity and self-respect rather than of policy. At the same time there were louder and more insistent demands for an aggressive war. By the middle of August it was apparent that a combination of large bounties and the draft of militiamen was bringing Lincoln his 300,000 men, and this caused some uneasiness. The solution to the Confederacy's problems, the Rhetts' *Charleston Mercury* asserted, was a string of military victories which would drive the invader from Southern soil and culminate in an invasion of the Union. "This would remove doubts about our strength, and manifest the folly of the war of conquest. It would bring home to the people of the North the hopelessness of their undertaking, and teach them, at the same time, the terrible cost to themselves. It would show the

European trimmers in diplomacy what they are too ignorant to see without—the great power of the South subtracted from the feared United States."[54] In short, there would be no peace until the South conquered it, and following Lee's and Jackson's shattering defeat of another Union advance at the second battle of Bull Run the road north lay open. This was no time to repeat the "folly" of the year before and wait south of the Potomac while the Union gathered itself for a fresh onslaught. The "Rubicon of aggressive war" had now to be crossed. Robert E. Lee agreed.

In a series of letters to Jefferson Davis at the beginning of September the Confederate general detailed what he hoped to achieve by his invasion of Maryland, a gamble he took on his own initiative, knowing full well that the government could do little but approve it. The public pressure for this strategy was too strong for his decision to be countermanded. The presence of a Confederate army in Maryland would provide a people whose support of the Union had been equivocal with "an opportunity of throwing off the oppression" of the North. Some Marylanders might join up, swelling his ranks with sorely needed recruits, while the state beckoned his ragged men as a rich source of chronically short provisions— food, clothing, shoes, and medical stores. Lee also saw diplomatic advantages. Although he had long thought it unlikely that foreign nations would come to the Confederacy's assistance, the opportunity to score a propaganda victory was not to be scorned. If the Confederacy, with its triumphant troops on Northern soil, merely proposed that the Union recognize it, this "would show conclusively to the world that our sole object is the establishment of our independence, and the attainment of an honorable peace." Even more importantly, "The proposal of peace would enable the people of the United States to determine at their coming elections whether they will bring it [the war] to a termination which can but be productive of good to both parties without affecting the honor of either."[55]

For the visitor returning to Washington after a year's absence a sense of *déjà vu* would have been no trick of the mind. Another defeat at Bull Run had been followed by another flight by demoralized troops back to the panic-stricken capital, though this time the heavy atmosphere of crisis was thickened by the news that the Confederates were on their way north. Themselves burdened with guilt and doubt, some members of the administration, the president included, suspected McClellan of being a party to this catastrophe.

His failure to reinforce the man who had replaced him at the command of the invading Union army, the all too fallible Pope, was thought to be motivated by a desire to regain his position through his successor's defeat. If this was indeed his strategy, it succeeded. A desperate Lincoln recognized that McClellan's undisputed organizational skills and popularity with the rank and file were indispensable if the army was to be restored quickly as an effective fighting force. While "Little Mac" performed that wonder, Seward pondered how best to limit the foreign damage of this latest disaster. It was no easy task, and as he remarked to Lincoln's secretary, John Hay, "our foreign affairs are very much confused."[56]

Only three weeks earlier, with new troops at last flooding into Washington, the outlook had been so promising. A confident Seward gave Stuart the impression of still being anxious "to anticipate any cause for quarrel," but unwilling "to dole out" more satisfaction than he considered "absolutely necessary." He boasted to the Englishman that volunteers were now coming forward in such numbers that there had been no need to resort to the draft. All of this made its calculated impression upon the chargé d'affaires. "There is nothing to be done, in the presence of these enormous fresh levies," Stuart reported to London, "but to wait and see what the next two months bring forth." Then, as if visited by a premonition, he added, "If they contribute to another Bull Run, there may be some hope of more pacific tendencies, and the financial smash might then be precipitated."[57]

In the aftermath of the defeat Mercier excitedly discussed with Stuart a more active diplomatic response. He had already written to his own government to express the opinion that the time for offering mediation was approaching. What he sought from Paris was the authority to decide when to make the offer, and he urged the British to invest Lyons with a similar discretion. Indeed, by sending the minister back to his post somewhat earlier than had been expected they could do much to prepare the Northern public for European intervention. That said, he did admit that Russian participation would lessen the Union's resistance to mediation. With this, at least, Stuart agreed. "It would be a great object to get Russia to join," he advised Russell, "as so long as she holds aloof it would be hoped here to separate her from us." But the prospects of involving Russia were not good, according to her minister. She would encourage the

Americans to accept mediation, he informed Stuart, but would not join with Britain and France to offer it.[58]

As those foreign envoys who had been absent from Washington when the blows of defeat and invasion were struck hastened to return, thereby emphasizing the gravity of the crisis, Seward got wind of the talk of mediation. From Weed he received a disturbing report of the contents of Mercier's despatches home. Although he pooh-poohed the information, he understood the necessity "to be firm, calm, collected, and look all emergencies fully in the face."[59] Such was the tone of a note to Adams, in which he insisted both that the army was still in place and that recruitment continued. Beyond this, he sought to strengthen his diplomatic forces in Europe. He had a poor opinion of Dayton's abilities and urged Thurlow Weed to slip away "carelessly" to the French capital. At the same time he wanted to send Edward Everett to Britain, if he could do so "without letting the world know of it."[60] In effect, he was planning to send out more "collateral missions," hoping to repeat the success of Weed, Hughes, and McIlvaine the previous winter. However, Everett subsequently declined to go, and Seward withdrew the invitation to Weed.

Naturally Seward made no move to recommend to Lincoln a declaration of war on slavery, even though the agitation for this step had gone on without cease. Before Second Bull Run Greeley had published his "Prayer of Twenty Millions," expressing disappointment with the president's emancipation policy, which brought from Lincoln his celebrated answer: "What I do about slavery, and the colored race I do because I believe it helps to save the Union; and what I forbear, I forbear because I do *not* believe it would help to save the Union." Then, on September 13, with Confederate troops occupying the town of Frederick in Maryland, he replied to an "Emancipation Memorial presented by Chicago Christians of all Denominations." To proclaim emancipation "would secure the sympathy of Europe and the whole civilized world," they argued. "No other step would be so potent to prevent foreign intervention." Lincoln conceded that slavery was at the root of the rebellion and that emancipation would help the Union in Europe, by showing that the North was moved by something nobler than ambition. He admitted "that it would help *somewhat* at the North" in firing patriotism, though not quite as much, he thought, as the Chicago delegation fancied. Yet he also admitted to being in two minds, unsure whether these benefits outweighed the risks of exciting not only divisiveness at home but ridicule abroad of a document as effective as "the Pope's bull against the comet!"[61]

His doubts notwithstanding, Lincoln did at this time make up his mind to strike against slavery as soon as the Confederates were driven from the North. By September 19, after a bloody repulse at Antietam which dashed Lee's hopes of a far-reaching success, they had withdrawn across the Potomac. Three days later Lincoln summoned his cabinet to the meeting at which he read his proclamation. Although still far less sanguine than the more ardent advocates of this action, he had hopes that it would divide and weaken the South but strengthen the Union. In the forefront of his mind were domestic rather than foreign advantages. As he explained confidentially to Vice-President Hamlin, he was looking for an "instantaneous" effect upon the North. Hence his disappointment when, six days after the publication of the preliminary proclamation, neither a decline in stocks nor a falling off in recruitment had been halted. "The North responds to the proclamation sufficiently in breath," he remarked, "but breath alone kills no rebels."[62]

Of those members of the cabinet who along with Seward had secured the postponement exactly two months earlier, only Montgomery Blair continued to voice his opposition on September 22. Seward acquiesced, even cosigning the momentous document as secretary of state. It was a measure of the depth of abolitionist suspicion of him, however, that there were fears he had affixed his name for no other reason than to prepare the ground for a Supreme Court decision invalidating the proclamation as not purely a war measure. Surely, it was rumoured, such a measure required the signature of Stanton as secretary of war. In truth, Seward signed without enthusiasm but Lincoln's demeanour at the cabinet meeting had indicated the futility of renewed resistance. The president's mind was made up. "The general question having been decided," Seward observed drily, "nothing can be said further about that."[63] He contented himself with some minor improvements in the language. But this mild response, which surprised some of his colleagues, probably owed as much to political necessity as it did to his recognition of Lincoln's determination.

Seward's enemies had been gathering against him back home in New York, using his opposition to emancipation as their rallying cry. A deputation claiming to represent the views of the five New

England governors, and seeking his removal from the cabinet, had seen the president on September 10. They received a hearing but obtained no satisfaction. Shortly afterwards a worried Thurlow Weed arrived in Washington, concerned at the erosion of support for the ambitious secretary at his political base. The time had come for Seward to refurbish his old image as a thorough and unrelenting foe of slavery, but he could not bring himself to do it. Increasingly his natural conservatism was asserting itself. Moreover, he still saw foreign trouble in a radical antislavery policy. Thus the withdrawal of his opposition to a proclamation was not followed by a ringing international declaration of the Union's supremely moral purpose. Instead, emancipation was announced in a circular which accurately but "coldly" stressed both the military necessity and the deferred nature of the measure. Lincoln had given the Confederates until January 1, 1863, to return to their allegiance and thereby avoid the loss of their slaves by presidential fiat. Here was proof, Seward observed defensively, of "the moderation and magnanimity with which the government proceeds in a transaction of such great solemnity and importance."[64] Evidently he was still uneasy about the reaction of the powers on the other side of the Atlantic to Lincoln's action. "Are they to enter, directly or indirectly, into this conflict, which, besides being exclusively one belonging to the friendly people of a distant continent, has also, by force of circumstances, become a war between freedom and human bondage?" he asked.[65]

The Russian minister to the United States did nothing to put Seward's mind at rest. In an interview on September 24, Edouard de Stoeckl, whose nation was regarded by an increasing number of Northerners as their one European friend, deplored the proclamation as a "futile menace" which "set up a further barrier to the reconciliation of the North and South—always the hope of Russia."[66] The secretary's concern would have deepened had he been able to read the despatches of the Spanish minister, Gabriel García y Tassara. Denouncing Lincoln for "an act of vengeance and cowardliness," he reasoned that emancipation had modified Spain's position and he urged his government to join in any formal European proposal of mediation.[67] At the British legation the reception was no friendlier. The proclamation "is cold, vindictive and entirely political," Stuart charged. "It does not abolish slavery where it has power; it protects 'the institution' for friends and only abolishes it on paper for its enemies. It is merely a Confiscation Act,—or perhaps worse, for it offers direct encouragement to servile Insurrection."[68]

In this frame of mind, satisfied personally that the South had "nobly earned its recognition, and that the very fact of its being a recognized Power before the rest of the World would lead this insane People to see that they are striving for an impossibility," Stuart at last lent a hand to the service of the insidious Mercier. What the Frenchman urged was that Lyons first pay a visit to Paris, in order, presumably, to remind the watchful Unionists of the close cooperation of the two nations in American affairs, and then return to Washington empowered to join with him in proposing an armistice. A cessation of hostilities would give the belligerents the time in which to reach a settlement. Further, to ensure the effectiveness of this friendly intervention Mercier proposed that it be backed by the threat of unilateral action. Finding "much sense" in this diplomatic strategy, the British chargé d'affaires also reported home that "it might be followed with perfect safety, due latitude being given to the Representatives to choose their moment for acting upon their instructions." And what better time was there for an Anglo-French armistice proposal than at the beginning of the imminent Congressional elections?[69]

For Seward, then, the summer of 1862 proved to be a difficult period. His anxiety to persevere with a conciliatory policy was evident from his willingness to allow the British to obtain cotton from the South. But a potent mixture of foreign irritants and domestic necessities drove the Lincoln administration to adopt measures that did little to facilitate smooth relations with Britain. The goods carried into the Confederacy by British blockade-runners, and the emergence of the Bahamas and Bermuda as entrepôts of this thriving trade, angered all Americans, including Seward and especially Welles. Smarting from the abuse and criticism heaped upon him for the Navy Department's failure to halt blockade-running, Welles resisted Seward's policy of concessions. Although his opposition was overcome initially, restrictions were placed upon the flow of supplies from the Union to the British colonies. This quickly led to an irritable exchange with the British government. More serious was the construction in Britain of war vessels for the South.

First the *Florida* sailed and then the *Alabama* escaped from Liverpool. These Confederate successes were a tribute to the skill of Bulloch, but what had made them possible was the ambiguity of the Foreign Enlistment Act, which was subject to contrastingly narrow and broad interpretations. The fact that the legal advisers of the two government departments whose cooperation was necessary in order to effect the seizure of a suspected vessel disagreed over the law's meaning caused both confusion and delay. However, the responsibility for the *Alabama*'s escape was also attributable in part to Dudley's failure to follow his instructions fully and promptly, and to Layard's negligence.

Seward's response to the conduct of the British was to threaten them with a resort to privateering and to join Welles in letting Charles Wilkes loose in the Caribbean once again. Yet the secretary of state had no wish to provoke them too severely. He opposed a resort to emancipation, nor is this surprising given the line of argument he had been developing in his diplomatic correspondence; namely, that the restoration of the Union was the only way to preserve for some considerable time the institution generally considered necessary for the cultivation of cotton. Furthermore, he doubted whether the domestic advantages Lincoln saw in an Emancipation Proclamation would in fact be gained. But in September, with the president determined to act, there was no point in further opposition. Nevertheless, Seward did not believe for a moment that this measure was going to ease his task of fending off foreign intervention.

SIX

Intervention Deferred

WITH THE APPROACH OF AUTUMN the shadows lengthened over the mill towns of Lancashire and neighbouring Cheshire, and the chill winds of distress strengthened. The weekly reports from the poor law unions told a dismal tale of accelerating applications for parochial relief. From H. B. Farnall, at the end of September, came the disquieting news that the number of operatives actually dependent upon the guardians had leapt by 16,000 during the first three weeks of that month alone. In the twenty-four unions of the cotton manufacturing district there were now more than 156,000 persons in receipt of parochial relief, which was an increase of 263 per cent over the figure for the same week in 1861. Nor had the full depth of misery yet been plumbed, for the informed estimate was that recipients of all forms of relief would eventually total 400,000. Even towns which housed a broader range of industries, such as Rochdale, were being battered by the storms of short time and unemployment. October found more than 9,000 on the guardians' list there while another 10,000 were being helped by the local relief committee. In Manchester, the volunteers at the Friends' Soup Kitchen were working overtime distributing almost 15,000 quarts of soup each week. A local firm quickly established in the city centre a second large kitchen, modelled upon a successful one in Glasgow. Here the operatives were able to get good food for the cost price of one penny a meal. It offered a double advantage, for the labour was provided by young factory girls who in exchange received instruction in plain cooking.[1]

Inevitably, in the harder-hit unions the resources of the guardians were soon overtaxed and Villiers's bill did not prevent a drop in the level of assistance they provided. Thus in Ashton twenty-one of the thirty-six mills had closed by the end of October, thirteen were operating on short time, one was working full time but with a reduced workforce, and a solitary mill was in full operation. In all, only one operative in twenty was earning his normal wage. The result was an average relief payment of just over a shilling a head, considerably less than the guardians' own scale called for. But as the correspondent of *The Times* who was touring the region remarked, "In this respect, however, Ashton is but a type of the district, for I have not visited a town yet in which I have not found the performance of the Guardians frequently halting short of their professions."[2]

Although conditions were hard and prospects gloomy, the situation was not quite as bleak as it sometimes appeared. Low as the average relief payment was in areas such as Ashton, it remained just that, an average. Operatives were paid both more and less. In unions where manufacturers sat on the Boards of Guardians and on the private committees relief was often used as a wages supplement, bringing up to the local standard of perhaps two shillings a head the income of millworkers on short time. Happier still was the evidence that the suffering in the cotton towns had touched the heart as well as the mind of the nation. Groups of well-intentioned ladies journeyed up from London to inquire about the distress and distribute "to the deserving poor" monies they had collected. Donations even began to arrive from distant parts of the empire. By mid-September £10,000 had reached Britain from the Australian provinces of Victoria and New South Wales, and the Canadian mails brought news of the launching of a fund there. Clothing as well as cash was being contributed in abundance to the Mansion House Committee, organized by the lord mayor of London earlier in the year.[3]

Belatedly, relief committees had been established in Manchester and Liverpool. Another was formed in London by a group of Lancashire magnates. To this Bridgewater House Committee, as it was called, the Queen promptly paid £2,000 as the Duchess of Lancaster, and eventually more than £50,000 was collected. But it was clear that the private relief activities stood in need both of more centralized direction and closer coordination with those of the state. So, in the summer of 1862, the Manchester Committee was reorganized to serve as a conduit for most of the others. Important figures from the Bridgewater House group were added to the executive, including first Lord Ellesmere and then the Earl of Derby as its chairman. Farnall also joined, and at its weekly meetings the central executive allocated the monies forwarded by the Manchester,

Liverpool, and Bridgewater committees. There were conditions to this cooperation, the most important being the Bridgewater group's insistence that none of the funds be used to give additional relief to those persons already on the poor rates. The Mansion House Committee remained outside this alliance despite the urgings of Derby and others, and continued to distribute funds weekly according to its own rules. Nevertheless, order had been brought to the chaos of good intentions and from this the operatives derived timely benefit. Collecting committees connected with the central executive were organized in more than 1,200 locations, while a second network radiated out of the hub of the Lord Mayor's Committee.[4]

Efforts to alleviate the distress were at last accompanied by steps to mitigate the hardships of the despised labour test. When a deputation from the Operative Spinners' Association called on Villiers at the Poor Law Board at the beginning of August to object to the test, he repeated what Farnall had already told the guardians of several unions; namely, that the requirement need not be inflexibly applied but could be adapted to suit the recipient of relief. At the end of the month the Manchester Board led the way in the exercise of this discretion, recommending the employment of men, women, and children in schools. Young millwomen were enrolled in sewing and reading schools, for four-fifths of them did not know how to sew and three-quarters could not read. Despite petty tyrannies, such as the enforcement of absolute silence in some of the schools, the program was a success and before long it was extended. Guardians paid the school pence of children whose parents were receiving parochial relief, with the result that one of the ironies of the cotton famine was a substantial increase in the number of children with schooling if not education. Relief schools were opened for men as well. Here they received the traditional educational instruction and in some towns were also taught industrial skills, such as tailoring, shoemaking, clog-mending and rough carpentry.[5] All of which brought the editor of *Macmillan's* to the happy conclusion that "An unexceptionably good feature in the present management of the destitution consists in the efforts made everywhere, as by a common instinct, on the part of persons of influence, and especially of the clergy, to convert this time of compulsory idleness into a time" of instruction for the sufferers.[6]

Despite the opportunities for self-improvement, and the inevitable charges that operatives were forsaking work for the idleness of charity, relief remained a synonym for privation. Most "frauds" were desperate attempts to bolster the family income, either by claiming a nonexistent child as a dependant, on occasion borrowing one in order to deceive inspectors, or by concealing earnings from occasional or part-time employment. For life on relief meant the elimination of meat from the diet, except for that found in the soup served at the kitchens, and often it meant moving to cheaper dwellings which were usually to be found in the unhealthier parts of a town. There, crowded together, the operatives were more frequently visited by epidemics of typhus, measles, whooping cough, and scarlatina. Yet, to the surprise of observers, the mid-year report of the registrar general in 1862 did not indicate any serious deterioration in public health. Not only was the birth rate high but the death rate had been "decidedly low." Especially marked was the decline in infant mortality which local registrars and doctors attributed to the better care provided by unemployed mothers. No longer were infants left all day long with minders whose neglect of their charges resulted, not uncommonly, in female operatives losing their children one after another. Beyond this, the explanation for the stable death rate was sought in the fact that unemployed operatives were engaged on work that was "considerably more wholesome" if less remunerative than their usual labour in the mills. Another important factor was the continuing low price of food. Fortunately the cotton famine did not coincide with a failure of the domestic or foreign harvests.[7]

From its study of the returns of the registrars *The Times* concluded that "If we do our duty properly no person in the manufacturing districts should perish for want of food and, though the public health would necessarily decline under such conditions, there are, as we have said, some countervailing elements to restore the balance."[8] Or as John Bright confidently replied to Richard Cobden, who had admitted that Lancashire's troubles "haunt me in spite of myself," the population of the mill towns appeared to be "very tranquil." "The people go on with apparent ease during the summer weather," he wrote reassuringly, "and if they can get 2s[hillings] per head per week, they will not starve. There is less crime than normal, and our medical men have less work than usual." He admitted to sadness that so many frugal families had been obliged to eat up their savings, but saw no remedy for that.[9]

Evidence that the cotton famine was still not wreaking the predicted social havoc in Britain was no more startling to Englishmen than its continuing failure to disrupt the economy. From the statistics released by the Board of Trade it was "hardly discernible" that anything had gone wrong. The figures for the nine months ending September 30 astounded Bagehot among others and confirmed the rosy forecast made by Gladstone in his budget. What they revealed was that there had been no significant falling-off in the consumption of provisions and spirits, despite the virtual impoverishment of many thousands of Lancashire operatives. Distress had brought no drop either in those imports traditionally consumed by the working class, such as corn, bacon, ham, salt beef, and salt pork. Still more encouraging, exports had equalled those of the previous year, even in manufactured cotton goods. Trade with the United States had continued to show a "considerable recovery," led by that in linens and woollens, and exports to France were still booming.[10]

The extent to which Britain was benefiting from the American war was impressed upon the worried Richard Cobden during his vacation in Scotland. He encountered happy lairds whose wool was fetching prices 50 per cent above those of 1859, and he witnessed the "fabulous profits" being turned by Dundee manufacturers from their trade with the United States. The managing partner of the ironworks in the region made light of the troubles of Lancashire. The unemployed operatives would soon find alternative work, the industrialist remarked optimistically, for there was "a great scarcity of labourers" and "every other industry was prosperous." For good measure, he reminded Cobden that Manchester was not Britain. The long and the short of the matter was that the national economy was ticking over very nicely. This was not the moment to jeopardize the general well-being through an adventurous policy in America, and certainly not in the name of economic or social necessity.[11]

There was even optimism that Lancashire had seen the worst of its misery. Many of the region's difficulties originated in the high price of cotton and the depressed prices of yarns and goods, Bagehot argued in the *Economist*. However, one consequence of the war had been a steady accumulation of the raw material while the stocks of manufactured items were diminishing. Before long the economic realities would cause the price of the former to decline and of the latter to rise, thus making it profitable to reopen the mills. There remained the nagging problem of a steady supply of the fibre. Bagehot expected enough to come from areas other than the United

States to employ the operatives for four days a week, and that would put enough money in their pockets to keep them adequately supplied with food and clothing. But this meant the full exploitation of India, for the quantities of cotton obtainable from elsewhere were small and the experiments with non-cotton fibres had proved disappointing. The British Association for the Advancement of Science, which met at Cambridge in 1862, heard that a wide variety of fibrous substitutes had been investigated, from flax and hemp to the common stinging nettle. Of these, seaweed had caused a stir when a specimen of the fibre obtainable from it was exhibited, but the excitement quickly subsided. "Under no other circumstances short of the total disappearance of the cotton plant from the face of the earth can we imagine this being resorted to as a substitute," commented the author of one paper.[12]

The refocusing of attention upon India provoked the Manchester men to round again on Sir Charles Wood. The meeting of the Cotton Supply Association held in Manchester on September 23 had been marked by renewed attacks upon the Government of India for its refusal to invest large sums in public works and by fresh demands for the dismissal of Wood. During the British Association's deliberations in Cambridge two weeks later the Indian government was accused of bad faith, of failing to honour a commitment made to the Manchester Cotton Company to construct a road from Dharwar to the sea, and to improve the existing port facilities. The consequence had been substantial losses to the company. Was it any wonder therefore, one speaker asked, "that private capitalists refuse to embark in commercial enterprises in India."[13]

These persistent efforts to lift all responsibility for the half-hearted exploitation of the subcontinent from the shoulders of the textile industry continued to anger many observers. "Having done nothing themselves," the *Saturday Review* remarked of the members of the Supply Association, "they were naturally indignant that persons less interested in the matter of cotton supply had followed their example and done nothing likewise." Savage though its criticism was, the "Reviler's" claim rang true. Had Manchester really wished for cotton from India she would have found a way to obtain it for herself. Her cotton men much preferred the cleaner American staple, a pound of which gave thirteen and a half ounces of yarn while Indian provided no more than twelve. They disapproved of the shortness of the ordinary Indian staple, which meant that without expensive adjustments it simply blew off machinery set up for American. Finally, Indian cotton was baled in a "foul and adulterated state." Hence the preoccupation of the spinners with the war news from across the Atlantic. Every promise of an imminent end to the conflict and with it the freeing of cotton bottled up in the South paralysed efforts to develop and adapt to Indian supplies. It also depressed the market in the available high-priced American fibre. And as James Garnett observed on September 23, very important news was daily expected from America.[14]

If they were pleasantly surprised by the robust health of their own economy, the British were less than enthusiastic about the Union's capacity to fight on despite the terrifying costs of the conflict. Apparently the abyss of national insolvency held no fear for the North. *Punch* might depict Lincoln with his pockets empty of both money and men yet the Union showed no sign of abandoning the struggle. Consequently, as admiration for the South continued to grow, especially following the second triumph at Bull Run, so talk of intervention revived. Significantly, the sufferings of Lancashire enjoyed less prominence as a justification. Instead, intervention was urged as an act of Christian statesmanship, a means of halting a savage, bloody, and useless war.

Confident that the Union would in the light of its reverses be willing to listen to a proposal of foreign mediation, Bagehot had launched a series of articles in the *Economist* recommending this course of action well before Pope's military catastrophe at Bull Run. In the wake of that Union disaster the Tory dailies took up the call, although more stridently. "Let us do something, as we are Christian men," the *Morning Herald* implored. "It does not matter what they call it. Term it arbitration, intervention, diplomatic action, recognition of the South, remonstrance with the North, friendly interference or forcible pressure of some sort—whatever form or shape our action may assume, let us do something to stop this carnage."[15] Suggestions of physical intervention in the conflict were resolutely opposed by *The Times*. What it did not rule out (and this was also true of the other Palmerstonian organ, the *Morning Post*) was serious consideration by the government of the South's claim to recognition.[16]

For a short time it seemed possible that the decisive moment of the war had finally arrived. In mid-September the reports reaching Britain indicated that the fall of Washington and Baltimore was imminent, and if the Confederates took those cities neither Philadelphia nor New York were beyond their grasp. There was an atmosphere of expectancy in London as in Manchester, as Englishmen awaited news of Lee's invasion of Maryland. Had he overreached himself? Would the greater skill and daring of the Southern officers and men triumph over the mightier resources of the North? The answers to these questions were indecisive, although by October 1 it was known that the Confederate army had withdrawn across the Potomac following the battle of Antietam. Realistically, Englishmen accepted that this turn of events was unlikely to have convinced the Federal government of the futility of its cause.[17]

For those journals sympathetic to the Union the desperate days before Antietam had been difficult ones. Samuel Lucas of the *Star*, whose contempt for Lincoln's ability had been increasingly apparent in the newspaper's editorials, had thought it necessary to revive the slavery question. This he did, he once explained to a visiting American, whenever the pressure for intervention became especially strong.[18] The *Spectator* followed much the same line of criticism and exhortation, conceding that it required the strongest faith in principles to sympathize with the North. "Never was a cause so great defended by men so imbecile." Lincoln was chastised for his adherence to a paper constitution which events had torn to shreds, Seward for sinking out of sight, Stanton for locking up people on mere suspicion, and Chase for confining himself to the affairs of the Treasury Department. What they had to do, in order to win the sympathy of the world and seal the fate of the Confederacy, was declare war on slavery.[19]

"The inevitable has come at last," the *Star* announced joyously on October 6. "Negro emancipation is formally and definitively adopted as the policy in war and peace of the United States." Here was the "turning point" in the history of the American commonwealth, an act second only in courage and in probable results to the Declaration of Independence. Lincoln's proclamation was a "grand move," John Bright wrote to Thomas Dudley, "not too soon nor too late, in my opinion. It must have a good effect here in putting your enemies more and more in the wrong."[20] His brother-in-law voiced the same belief in the *Star*, while Harriet Martineau sought "to set things right in English eyes" with her leader in the *Daily News* on October 10. An enthusiastic John Stuart Mill labelled all critics of Lincoln's measure as "deeply-dyed" Tories. Yet even "truthful journals" admitted to some disappointment. They disliked the delay until January in the implementation of emancipation and bemoaned the president's failure to assert boldly "the principle of freedom." It was a "feeble and halting" document, the *Daily News* conceded. The "hopeful promise" of freedom was held out "as a mere incident in the war." "The principle asserted is not that a human being cannot own another," the *Spectator* observed caustically, "but that he cannot own him unless he is loyal to the United States." Both organs of the antislavery movement, although they hailed this "memorable day in the annals of the great struggle for the freedom of an oppressed and despised race," stopped short of unreserved approval. The *Advocate* offered up no hymn of praise to Lincoln who they suspected would not have issued the proclamation "if he could have helped himself." For its part, the *Reporter* betrayed some uneasiness lest "so great a social revolution" be accompanied by "calamities."[21] This response by emancipation's natural allies in Britain was merely a foretaste of the general reaction by those less ardent in their support of freedom.

As Seward had warned and Lincoln had feared, most of the British press poured scorn on the proclamation. Irrespective of political persuasion, they made much of the president's own publicly expressed doubts as to its wisdom and usefulness. Indeed, his reference to the Pope's bull against the comet set the tone for much of the British editorial comment. Why had he not taken the same opportunity to declare free the slaves of Africa, perhaps those of the entire universe? Those leader-writers with a taste for epigrams indulged it. Lincoln had decided "that in future the negroes in the slave states should be free, and that only the negroes in the free states should be slaves." In effect, he was associating his government with slavery "by making slaveholding the reward to the Planters of rejoining that old Union." Viewed as an adoption of antislavery principles, this was "the most grotesquely illogical and inconsistent decree ever issued by a Government." Far from being guided by moral considerations, the proclamation was a cry of despair, a confession that it was impossible to subdue the South by the regular forces of the Northern states. The spirit was one of vengeance. *Punch* portrayed the president playing out his hand of rouge-et-noir over a barrel of gunpowder, and casting his final card—the ace of spades. This was a last desperate effort to unite the North, terrorize the South into submission, and excite foreign sympathy.

Few British commentators disputed the likelihood of the proclamation having a profound effect upon the American struggle.
However, they thought it would be the reverse of the president's
"aims." As had some conservative Unionists in the United States,
they predicted that far from unifying Northerners it would further
divide them, arraying Democrats and moderate Republicans against
abolitionists. Only in the South would it foster unity, conceivably
driving the border states into the Confederate camp. Therefore as a
measure of political and belligerent policy it appeared "singularly
Irish and illogical." A measure "so half-hearted and inconsistent"
could never command the moral support of Europe and would
alienate what little sympathy for the Northern cause had survived
the long series of "blunders, boastings and affronts." Nonetheless, it did seem to one thoughtful observer who was no Union
sympathizer that Lincoln had at least succeeded in threatening
embarrassment to any European nation disposed to recognize the
Confederacy.[22]

The evident moral shortcomings of the proclamation fail to
explain the depth of antagonism it aroused in England. Englishmen
were not entirely ignorant of the constitutional restraints on the
president, preventing him from going much farther. How else was
he legally to deal with the slaves of loyal citizens than with proposals
of compensation, or those of the disloyal than by the confiscation of
the property of rebels? Anyway, halting though it was, this decree
did commit Union troops to conduct themselves as liberators in the
disaffected States after January 1, 1863. Moreover, never again
would they be fighting to restore the Union as it was, never again
would the Union be able to lend the weight of its arms "to rivet the
fetters of the slave under the pretence of protecting property."[23]
These were considerable gains for the cause of human freedom but
they generated precious little enthusiasm in antislavery Britain. For
the truth was that what attracted British attention and sympathy
were the horrors, slaughter, and miseries the war was inflicting, or
threatening to inflict, upon whites, especially the outnumbered
Southerners, not the benefits its prolongation would bring to
blacks.[24]

"Why is it that the nation which is at the head of Abolitionism,
not only feels no sympathy with those who are fighting against the
slaveholding conspiracy," John Stuart Mill had asked, "but actually
desires its success?" In seeking to answer this riddle, he emphasized

the weakening of antislavery feeling in Britain. The slavery issue no longer gripped a generation grown to manhood since the great victory over the institution in the West Indies. "The public of the present day thinks as their fathers did concerning slavery," he argued, "but their feelings have not been in the same degree aroused against its enormities." It had receded into the background of their minds as no more than one special evil among many. Meanwhile they had devoted their reforming energies to the amelioration of the evils of industrialization, and to such admirable causes as poor relief, suffrage reform, temperance, and peace.[25] And who better exemplified the generational gap than Charles Buxton? A member of Parliament for Maidstone, he bore an illustrious name, second only to that of Wilberforce on the roll of British antislavery heroes. He was "the hereditary leader of the anti-slavery party." Nevertheless, in a speech to his constituents, he admitted that he had no sympathy for the Union. A third of its citizens were slaveholders, he asserted incorrectly, and the North would throw over the negro in order to get the South back.[26]

The morbid if not moribund condition of the British antislavery movement during the 1850s, publicly mirrored in dwindling membership and revenues, an aging leadership, and a newspaper shrinking in size as well as subscriptions, was not simply a matter of different generations with changing priorities. The decline had been accompanied by a rising preoccupation with race which did little to enhance the postion of blacks or advance the struggle for their freedom. As man studied himself more closely, and anthropology and ethnology gained in popularity, racial distinctions increasingly posed problems and challenges for him. To argue the diversity of racial origins and beyond it the inferiority of certain races was to invite the charge of heresy, for this proposition seemed to contradict the creation of man as revealed in the Book of Genesis. This pitfall some scientists such as Louis Agassiz, the distinguished Swiss immigrant to the United States, sought to avoid by pleading the lack of clarity in Genesis. Had there been one creation or many? Ultimately Charles Darwin settled the controversy, for "he described a process which made it possible to derive all categories of life from an original one and placed the organic kingdom on a self-sustaining basis."[27]

By no means all of the members of the "American School" of anthropology relinquished their notion of diversity immediately after the publication of the *Origin of Species* in 1859. But these disputes were truly academic for the negro. Thus the president of the British Anthropological Society, in an address to his colleagues in November 1863, detailed how blacks differed from whites—their pigment, heavier bones, longer arms, elongated heels and jaws, and flattened foreheads. He did not contend that negroes were a nonhuman species, merely subhuman in their mental capacity. Having undergone a manifest improvement in their physical type as a result of their transshipment across the Atlantic as slaves, their misfortunes there stemmed in large part from "mistaken attempts to benefit them on the theoretical ground of the mental equality of the different races of men." They were more humanized when in their natural subordination to Europeans. There was no place in "scientific racism" for the "sentimental" antislavery depiction of the negro.[28]

Those who justified slavery on the physiological ground that the negro was very low on the scale did not have the field entirely to themselves. Thomas Henry Huxley was to start a lively controversy with his Hunterian Lecture in 1864. He accepted the negroes' inferiority but not some of the "scientific" explanations of it, and he attacked their enslavement. He was not moved by compassion for blacks, however. His avowed concern was with the evil slavery worked upon white men, promoting "bad political economy; bad social morality; bad internal political organization, and a bad influence upon free labour and freedom all over the world."[29]

The doctrine of racial inferiority had found intellectual support in both anthropological camps and in the rise of ethnology. Its growth may also have been promoted in Britain by the class-ridden nature of society, with its descending ranks of social inferiors. Certainly the doctrine of racial unity, the conviction that all men sprang from the same species, offered scant hope of any immediate improvement in the lot of blacks. The racial differences and inferiority which anthropologists had been documenting for years might not be permanent according to Darwin, but in his concept of time what was?[30] In this climate of opinion books on race were common and popular. Dwarfing them all in importance was Count Arthur de Gobineau's *Essai sur l'Inégalité des Races Humaines*, which was published in four volumes between 1853 and 1855.

In a work of synthesis, Gobineau blended anthropological racial studies with the historical racial ideas of a number of earlier writers.[31] He paid lip service to the unity of man's origins, out of deference to his own Catholicism, but insisted that the different families had grown absolutely separate. In fact, by "unconvincing intellectual convolutions" he arrived at the conclusion that mankind was divided into three races of unequal worth, and that all civilizations derived from the white race. In this crude and arbitrary hierarchy, black people were at the base. They were, in Gobineau's words, a "civilized nullity," characterized "by animality and severely limited intellect," though he disdained the argument that every black was stupid.[32] Although more progressive and less pessimistic scholars, such as the German, Theodor Waitz, disputed the existence of significant differences in the "native capacities of races" and argued that favourable environmental circumstances" were the true determining factor, a case some abolitionists had been making for some time, theirs was an uphill fight in the battle for popular acceptance. The theory that innate differences would prevent some peoples, particularly blacks, from ever advancing as far as others (whites) was gaining support.[33] In Britain, for example, Anthony Trollope's account of his visit to the West Indies in 1858, which he published under the title of *The West Indies and the Spanish Main*, supported the popular stereotype of the negro. Not only was he intellectually inferior to the white man, unable to reason, but he was innately lazy. Since his emancipation in the West Indies, Trollope reported, the negro had been content to do no more than was necessary to "eat to-day and be clothed tomorrow." As for anything beyond that, he was content to lie in the sun. "To recede from civilization and become again savage—as savage as the laws of the community can permit—has been to his taste. I believe that he would altogether retrograde if left to himself," Trollope warned.[34]

If the economic decline of the West Indies since the end of the transitional apprenticeship system had hardened the racial attitudes of many Englishmen, and raised doubts in their minds as to the benefits complete emancipation bestowed upon blacks, the Indian Mutiny had confirmed their racial distrust, even hostility. Indignation at this act of betrayal by the sepoys was soon overwhelmed by hatred. The ill-treatment and massacre of the British residents of Cawnpore made the name of the local Hindu ruler, Nana Sahib, who had promised them safe conduct, synonymous with treachery and terror. For the British, the Mutiny conjured up images of "cowering white ladies in fetid cellars; goggle-eyed Indians, half blood-mad, half lustful," violating women and butchering children.[35]

The call in Britain was for a racial and religious war of extermination, and the retribution exacted was bloody and savage. With the Indian horrors, real and imaginary, still fresh in their memories, fears of servile insurrection and a massacre of white women and children in the slave states undoubtedly played as large a role as "the social and psychological repressions within English society itself" in shaping and distorting the initial response of many Britons to Lincoln's proclamation. Well before its publication the analogy between a despairing act of emancipation and the Mutiny had been drawn in England. The Union's only purpose in declaring the slaves free at this late stage would be to diminish the Southern army by calling away officers and men to defend their homes, the *Morning Herald* had charged on August 7. The object would not be emancipation but servile insurrection, "not the manumission of slaves, but the subornation of atrocities such as those at Cawnpore and Meerut against the women and children of Southern families." Inferior in every respect to the Indian sepoys, "the negro race would, if once excited to rebellion, outdo them in acts of outrage as they would fall below them in military courage." And having been in the vanguard of those calling for a war of extermination a few years earlier, *The Times* was no laggard in echoing loudly the *Herald*. The intent of the Republicans who were calling for abolition was "to organize a series of Cawnpores as a legitimate device of warfare."[36] Nor did the newspapers doubt that the enraged Southern whites would seek a terrifying vengeance for a slave uprising.

While he did not share these fears of a race holocaust, Walter Bagehot questioned the wisdom of suddenly changing the entire social status of four millions of "ignorant and very helpless creatures." He was not alone. J. A. Froude, the historian and editor of *Fraser's*, made much the same point to an American abolitionist friend. Slavery must be allowed "to wear itself gradually away" as civilization advanced, he enjoined. An institution as old as mankind could not be treated as a crime to be put down by force. To attempt to do so was unjust and to make "wrong into right by treating it unfairly."[37]

Froude's commitment to gradualism may have had its origins in the philosophical historian's aversion to revolutionary or militant reform, but that of his fellow-historian W. E. H. Lecky, soon to make his name with the publication in 1864 of his *History of the Rise and Influence of the Spirit of Rationalism in Europe*, was less intellectual in its motivation. His fear of social upheaval was equalled by his alarm at the thought of economic dislocation. Britain needed cotton for her textile industry, yet it was considered tantamount to murder to make anyone except the divinely provided blacks labour in the cotton fields of the hot South. The conclusion drawn from the West Indian experience was that some form of compulsion was necessary, and although even in Lancashire this did not spur a defence of slavery, it was one reason for the self-deception that an independent South would ultimately free its slaves. Thus the president's action was dismissed as amoral, a cynical move in a military game. Never one to understate his point, James Murray Mason concluded that "Lincoln's Proclamation has had no other effect here than to arouse the indignation of many, and the contempt of all."[38]

For the Southern agents and sympathizers labouring to bring about Britain's intervention in the war there appeared to be a wealth of tools at hand. As the American translator of Gobineau, Henry Hotze was well qualified to exploit in the *Index* the racial hysteria fanned into flame by the prospect of emancipation. Scientific interest as well as hope of diplomatic advantage for the South explain his service on the Council of the Anthropological Society from the summer of 1863, and he charged his donations to the secret service account. Spence sent another "S" letter to *The Times*. By this act, he argued, Lincoln had recognized the independence of the Confederacy. "No man sets fire to a house of which he expects to become the owner by process of law."[39] Hiram Fuller, who under the pseudonym "A White Republican" was contributing a series of articles to *Fraser's*, quickly turned his fire on the proclamation. Although a native of Massachusetts, his open support for the South had obliged him to leave the North. Settling in England, he threw himself into the task of promoting Confederate independence. In his earlier articles he had dwelt upon the Americans' foolishness in founding their government upon unrestricted suffrage. This was the single most important cause of the Civil War, he had argued. Now, with the appearance of the proclamation, he devoted himself to feeding the British alarm over emancipation. With gradualists such as his editor in mind, he deplored the sudden freeing of four millions of negroes "without any preparation therefor, even *could* they be prepared." Nor did he overlook Britain's interest in the continued production "of the great staple which keeps the mills of Manchester in motion, and the poor labourers of Lancashire from starvation." Slavery not only guaranteed a steady supply of cotton, but was a kindly, paternal institution from which blacks derived both benefit and enjoyment. The black man's journey through the land of bondage must be long, Fuller concluded, "and the time of his deliverance is not yet."[40] However, it was one thing to reflect British opinion and prejudices but another entirely to harness them to the demand for intervention.

In a crude attempt to bring some additional public pressure to bear upon the prime minister, John Arthur Roebuck had used the platform they shared during Palmerston's visit to Sheffield in August to deliver a characteristically intemperate speech calling for recognition of the Confederacy. Roebuck had never had much time for the Manchester School. His Radicalism had its philosophical origins in the hatred of inherited privilege common to Benthamites. He had backed Bright's campaign for parliamentary reform in 1859, but his support for the broadening of the franchise lacked the Chartist passion of his younger years.[41] Almost as old as the century, he wanted to advance slowly and he fastened upon the American struggle as an excuse. "We ought, in my opinion to take every safe opportunity offered for enlarging the suffrage, and we ought in every way to promote the education of the people," he later wrote. "I have great faith in my countrymen; but the experience of America frightens me."[42] Moreover, he had not failed to note the lack of interest with which the cause of reform had been greeted outside the large cities.

Instead of domestic reform, Roebuck concentrated increasingly on foreign questions and here he found himself poles apart from Cobden and Bright. Contemptuous of their pacifism, he became the loudest spokesman of patriotic, bellicose Radicalism. "To be prepared for war," he once remarked, "is the best preservative of peace." Suitably enough, the high mark of his career was his motion to inquire into the mismanagement of the Crimean War, for it brought down the government of Aberdeen. Nevertheless, he remained an isolated figure, imprisoned in his unattractive personality. An orator of power, he was feared rather than respected. He exhibited the self-assertiveness and tetchiness common to many very small men and employed too readily, because he relished it too much, his capacity to wound opponents. By 1862 he was exercising his talent for vituperation upon the United States, in whose division he saw great profit for his own nation. The struggle to preserve the Union was dismissed as immoral and without a hope of success. The "insolent and overbearing" conduct of the North, evident in its treatment of British vessels on the high seas and in threats against Canada, excited him to jingoistic fury. With that region Britain could never be friendly. Then, in his favoured style, he added: "Of the South you can make friends. They are Englishmen. They are not the scum and refuse of Europe."[43]

Roebuck's foolishness in seeking both to upstage and embarrass Palmerston at Sheffield was matched by that of the founders of the Confederate States Aid Association in London. The idea of forming an association consisting "principally of Englishmen sympathizing with the Confederate States of America, as well as with the sufferings of their own countrymen," was sound enough. What ensured failure was the use to which the association's members pledged themselves to put the funds for which they appealed "in the name of suffering Lancashire, civilization, justice, peace, liberty, humanity, Christianity, and a candid world." All monies were to be "appropriated for purchasing and forwarding to the Confederate States of America, the materials which, in the judgment of the association, shall be considered the best calculated to enable them to carry on the war, and to bring their present protracted struggle to a successful issue."[44] The impropriety of Englishmen contributing directly to the Confederate war effort was too obvious to require comment. Even the partisans of that cause were expected to avow some more elevated purpose. One man who always contrived to put a more acceptable face on his sympathies was Lord Robert Cecil.

Another younger son of the aristocracy, although the death of his elder brother in 1865 was eventually to bring him his father's title and estates, Cecil had made his way into Parliament through the traditional entrance of peers' sons—an uncontested election in a family-controlled borough. There he proved to be as offensive in manner and as sarcastic in speech as Roebuck. During debate he would laugh noisily in an effort to drown out or disrupt the delivery of an adversary's best lines, and he was not a man who measured his phrases. However, his personal charm did much to counteract the animosity this behaviour excited, and he won respect as a man of intellect as well as of strong Tory opinions. Furthermore, unlike so many other aristocratic scions, who sought an easy escape from their state of limbo through patronage, Cecil worked. He wrote for the *Saturday Review*, which had been founded by his brother-in-law, Alexander Beresford-Hope, and for the leading Tory literary periodical of the day, the *Quarterly Review*. Frequently he was the author of their articles on the American war. And a conflict which he used initially as little more than a convenient whip with which to flay domestic reformers—it was proof that democracy did not work—soon awoke in him feelings as profound as those of a very different character it stirred in John Bright. Fascinated by the skill and heroism of the greatly outnumbered Confederate troops, touched by the suffering the people bore, "his sympathy with the Southern cause developed into a whole-hearted championship which eventually threw all other considerations into the background."[45]

Both sentiment and reason informed the long article which appeared in the October number of the *Quarterly Review*. Cecil carefully stated the case for recognition of the Confederacy and skilfully refuted the charge that this amounted to a British endorsement of slavery. Left to themselves, exposed to the moral influence of the world, and with the passing of time, Southerners would institute a policy of gradual emancipation, he asserted. Here was the wise and safe course, one that would bestow freedom on negroes as they advanced in culture. This said, he dismissed the question of slavery's ultimate fate as irrelevant to the determination of British policy. Britain was on terms of friendship with Spain and Brazil, he pointed out, and both nations tolerated slavery in their dominions. She had recently gone to war to protect Turkey, a state whose subjects practised white slavery. Moreover, the dispute over the institution of slavery was trivial when compared to the human carnage of continued warfare and the miseries of Lancashire. Humanity and domestic interests demanded an end to the conflict.[46]

The same points were being driven home by Frank Lawley in his reports to *The Times*. Describing the slaughter of Second Bull Run, he wrote: "He who could witness that sight and not from his heart abhor the grasping vaulting nature of those politicians who, rather than accept what has long been inevitable, would month after month subject poor human nature to such unutterable anguish, must have been cold indeed." After Antietam he asked again, for what had all the blood been shed? Peace was no closer, for a confident Confederate army was secure in Virginia. Another winter of war would not merely intensify the suffering in America but would lead in all likelihood to the destruction of four-fifths of the cotton still remaining in the Southern states.[47]

Against this background, and after learning from John Slidell that the Palmerston cabinet intended to take up the American question in October, the Confederates and their British friends attempted once again to marshal the cotton operatives behind the call for intervention. A large open-air gathering at Mossley in July had passed a resolution in favour of British recognition of the Confederacy, as had an assembly of factory workers' delegates in Ashton. A second meeting at Ashton towards the end of August had provided a timely reminder of the need to proceed with caution, for it had been successfully disrupted by Thomas Evans and a band of Northern sympathizers from Manchester. The site chosen for the new demonstration was the Cheshire mill town of Stalybridge, though it also was dangerously near to Manchester. This time a local committee to promote the policy of recognition was formed and 150 of the town's principal inhabitants signed a requisition for a meeting of the ratepayers. The mayor not only consented to call the meeting but agreed to chair it. In the meantime one of the committee's members wrote to Mason, perhaps at the suggestion of Spence, seeking from him as the "official" representative of the South a statement of the benefits recognition would confer on the textile region. Naturally Mason welcomed this opportunity to restate the Confederate case and his reply was subsequently published in *The Times*. British recognition was fully justified under international law, he argued, and would dispel lingering Northern delusions of reunion. In short, it would encourage peace and thus free the flow of cotton to the mill towns.[48]

Despite the preparations, the meeting was another disaster for the Confederates. An hour before it was due to come to order hundreds of people began to gather outside the hall, which was quickly filled once the doors were opened. Most of those who entered appeared to be working people and they proved to be opponents of recognition. By an "immense" majority they passed a resolution which blamed the Southern rebels for the operatives' suffering. It was Blackburn revisited. No doubt the meeting had been packed, and by Northern supporters, though Spence suspected it had been manipulated by the holders of yarns who saw in the prolongation of the American crisis the prospect of being able to shift their stocks at still higher prices. Whatever the explanation, the damage had been done and a shaken Spence temporarily lost his taste for organizing popular opinion. He quickly abandoned his scheme to regain the initiative lost at Stalybridge by staging a more carefully planned mass gathering in friendly Liverpool. The arrival of large supplies of the more expensive Indian cotton, and the news that another 300,000 bales were on their way, had created a strong party in the port "holding cotton and dead against recognition for that reason," he explained to Mason. The influence of this same powerful group, along with a popular "feeling of disinclination to interfere" in the war, were the reasons he gave for not pursuing a suggestion that a general meeting of the Liverpool Chamber of Commerce be summoned "to memorialize the government to concert with other powers for a common recognition of the Southern States." Eventually the Southern partisans settled for a dinner which Spence thought it judicious not to have reported by the press.[49] It was an admission of weakness, if not impotence.

Another meeting of unemployed operatives was held at Oldham in October, and it forwarded a memorial to the Foreign Office "praying" for the recognition of the Confederacy. Russell's response suggests that expressions of public opinion were not ignored. At his request the Home Office made enquiries about the meeting and the petition's signatories. Asked for a report, the mayor of Oldham skilfully minimized the affair. He suggested that the resolution had failed to attract the support of a majority of those in attendance, and he disputed the extent to which it truly represented opinion in the town. No more than one thousand people in a community of ninety thousand had been in attendance, he observed. Moreover, "a majority of the intelligent and respectable inhabitants" were opposed to any interference in the American War.[50]

"Mr. Mason has been trying to instigate popular demonstrations, but without success except in spending money," Charles Francis Adams wrote to Edward Everett at the beginning of September. These Confederate failures induced the American minister to join the ranks of those optimists who had identified the poorer classes of Britain as Union sympathizers. It was a comforting conviction, all the more so because "the present ministry sufficiently reflects the popular side to be in little danger of precipitation so long as no impulse from that quarter shall be manifested against us," Adams observed to Seward.[51] His confidence was sustained by the evidence of Britain's general prosperity, while Garibaldi's activities in Italy provided additional security against European meddling in America. During an interview with Russell, Adams lightheartedly suggested that the European powers "had quite too much to occupy their minds in the present condition of southern Europe to think of troubling themselves with matters on the other side of the Atlantic."[52]

The Union had one other stroke of international good fortune. The news of Second Bull Run, Lee's invasion of Maryland, and the Emancipation Proclamation reached Britain at "the most dead season of the year." Parliament was not in session; Queen, court, and ministry were off in the country or abroad on vacation. The shutters were up in the squares and the best streets, and often not a single cabinet minister was to be found in the capital. "Our life is placid; our amusements not exciting, and our pleasures few," Henry Adams remarked. "We drag on from day to day, writing, writing and eating." Everything was as calm as a summer's night, his father wrote on October 5 in reply to a note from Dayton, to whom Thouvenel had voiced the suspicion that the British were contemplating early recognition of the Confederacy. "I have not seen Lord Russell for a month," he went on, "but when last I did, he gave me a distinct intimation that nothing was in agitation in any part of Europe on our subject."[53]

This mood of confidence was not surprising. There had been no indication throughout the summer and autumn of any wavering in the British government's adherence to nonintervention. The speech proroguing Parliament had contained a "very explicit" reaffirmation of this policy and a confident Adams cheerfully set out on an extended tour of the West Country. Palmerston, as he made his own summer circuit, drawing renewed vigour from the popular acclaim, touched upon the American problem infrequently. When he did discuss it he did not mark out any new ground. Rather, he defended the government's decision not to seek relief for Lancashire in measures which might bring on war with the United States. Strict and rigid neutrality was "the only course which it became the country to take, and it has received, and will continue to receive, the approbation and sanction of the people of England," he had declared to great applause during his confrontation with Roebuck at Sheffield. To Henry S. Sanford it seemed obvious that the British had settled for the safe and prudent path, limiting their intermeddling in his nation's affairs to expressions of hope for an early end to an "unnecessary" war.[54]

Privately cabinet members held the same ground as that occupied by Palmerston publicly. A meeting with a group of ministers reassured Lyons that there was "great indisposition to interfere in any way in the American contest," although there remained some "apprehension that interference may be forced on them." For his own part, he continued to argue against schemes of mediation or recognition. The United States was far from ready to entertain any proposal of mediation on the basis of separation, he warned, and one founded on any other basis would be futile. As for recognition, leaving aside the danger of diplomatic difficulties with the Union, such an act would be useless unless "thrown into the balance at a moment when only a hair was wanting to tip the scale." If it failed to bring about peace at once, the North would soon discover it had done them no harm and the South no good. The only results would be a loss of European prestige and undying Union enmity. In short, recognition should at least be withheld until by extending it Europe could end the war.[55]

Within and outside the government, Argyll and Bright had warned throughout the summer of the folly of intervention. Brandishing letters from Seward and Sumner, they denied that the North was nearing exhaustion either of resources or of spirit. On the contrary, there was an unwavering resolve to employ every means to crush the rebellion. Sumner had alluded in his correspondence to the use of new weapons, such as a declaration of war on slavery. "It is evident at all events, I think," Argyll wrote in September to Palmerston, "that the time for any active interference is not yet in sight." It was pointless to intervene at a moment when both parties showed themselves to be as determined as they had been at the war's outbreak, and just as extreme in what they were demanding from each other.[56] The only safe course for the nation, Clarendon confided to the British minister in Paris, was to keep repeating to themselves the old adage: "They who in quarrels interpose are sure to get a bloody nose." And in this nonbelligerent mood he refused to heed the requests of friends to urge mediation upon the prime minister.[57]

Others were less bashful, among them William Gregory. In mid-September he willingly participated in the efforts by a group of Southern sympathizers privately to bring "very strong pressure" to bear upon the government. Approaching the prime minister indirectly, he wrote to complain that by withholding recognition of the Confederacy Britain was favouring the North and forgoing a splendid opportunity to bring the conflict to an end.[58] It was a well-timed move for both Palmerston and Russell were now rethinking their policy. A scant three weeks earlier they had still been impressed with the strength of the mutual animosity in America and Russell had informed the Queen that "There is no other course to be taken at present than to wait. For the effort tends to exhaustion and finally to peace." Once Lincoln had spent his fresh levies of troops then he and his democracy might be willing to listen to reason.[59] What caused them to change their minds in September were the latest reports from the scene of battle, which encouraged Palmerston and Russell to think that the period of waiting was at last drawing to a close.

Important as was the "complete smashing" of the Federals at Second Bull Run, the prospect of still greater Union disasters, including the loss of Washington and Baltimore, excited Palmerston more. "If this should happen would it not be time for us to consider whether in such a state of things England and France might not address the contending parties and recommend an arrangement upon the basis of separation, and whether if the Northerners should refuse to negotiate upon that footing England and France might not acknowledge the independence of the South as an established fact," he proposed to Russell. But the prime minister repeatedly stated his determination to move cautiously, to avoid premature action. He intended to wait for the outcome of Lee's invasion of Maryland. If the Union troops were "thoroughly beaten to the north of Washington, and Baltimore should declare against them, they may be brought to a more reasonable state of mind," he argued. On the other hand, if the Federals won it would be as well to delay a little longer to see what happened. Although Russell readily agreed that the time was coming for offering mediation, he placed less emphasis on the need for another heavy Union defeat. Second Bull Run had provided him with all the evidence he required that after sixteen months of war the North had made "no progress in subduing the Insurgent States." And whatever happened in Maryland, it was clear to him that the South could not be reconquered. By October the question would be "ripe for the Cabinet."[60]

This difference aside, and Russell soon fell into line with Palmerston on this point as well, the two men were of a like mind on how to proceed. The first step was to seek the cooperation of France, which both assumed would be forthcoming. Next, acting jointly, Britain and France should approach Russia and other leading European powers. As Palmerston remarked, Russia might well decline the invitation "but we should have paid her a compliment & have shewn confidence in her." Admittedly her participation might create difficulties, for "she would be too favorable to the North," but it would in all probability better dispose the Union toward acceptance. Meanwhile Britain must make Canada more secure, not by sending out more troops but by concentrating those already there in a few defensible places before the onset of winter. In addition, it would be wise to reemphasize Britain's steadfast opposition to physical intervention in the conflict by accompanying a proposal of mediation with a repeated declaration of neutrality.[61]

Acting on his own initiative Russell had instructed Cowley on September 13 to sound out Thouvenel discreetly. However, the French foreign minister, heeding advice he had received from Mercier, was disposed "to wait to see the result of the elections." The assumption was that the military success of the South would strengthen the peace faction and return to Congress men who supported a negotiated end to the war. This message was doubly discouraging. In approaching the French the impulsive Russell had been seeking the kind of positive response that would strengthen his hand at home as well as abroad. Several of his colleagues were sympathetic to the Union while others were simply reluctant to interfere, and as he admitted, "It would be very awkward to have a Cabinet upon this, unless France thought the opportunity favourable and this was previously ascertained."[62]

Frustrated in Paris, Palmerston and Russell quickly acted to bolster their position by gaining the support of Gladstone. Together they would be "a formidable phalanx" even if faced by the opposition of the entire cabinet. Confident he would join them, Palmerston wrote to the chancellor on September 24 to inform him of the steps he and Russell were contemplating. Gladstone, like them deeply impressed by the war news, offered additional reasons for initiating a proposal of mediation. He was anxious that Britain make a friendly effort to induce the North to abandon the struggle before the victorious South "fairly" demanded British recognition of its independence. Furthermore, the longer the war lasted, and the more successful the Confederacy proved to be, the more difficult would become the task of finding an acceptable boundary between the two states. He was also worried that at some time or another there would be an "outbreak" in the mill towns. Should that happen, he observed to Palmerston, "we might *then* seem to be interfering, with loss of dignity on the ground of our immediate interests, and rather in the attitude of parties than as representing the general interests of humanity and peace." But in joining forces with Palmerston and Russell on this question the chancellor imposed one condition—the participation of Russia. Britain's North American interests and France's Mexican adventure aroused suspicions about their impartiality, only the accession of Russia would stamp any effort they made to end the conflict "with the one great requisite namely moral authority."[63]

That it was not going to be easy to persuade the cabinet to alter course, even with the assistance of Gladstone, was soon apparent. Learning from both Palmerston and Russell what was in the wind, Granville quickly expressed his dissent. From Gotha, where he was in attendance on the Queen, he sent a long memorandum detailing his reservations. There were obvious difficulties confronting would-be mediators, including the possibility of the Europeans being duped by one side or the other. The consequences of extending recognition to the South in the all too probable event of the North rejecting mediation were unappealing. British efforts, such as they were, to develop alternative areas of cotton supply would be discouraged, yet recognition in itself would neither end the conflict nor bring large quantities of American cotton to Lancashire. Even worse, it might set Britain on a collision course with a people who hated her. Under the present circumstances Granville did not doubt that she would emerge triumphant from such a conflict, but only at great cost in blood and treasure. Moreover, he did not forget the bogeyman. Whether the French emperor joined with them or not, the effect would be to give him a free hand in Italy and elsewhere. Consequently, as he informed Russell, "I have come to the conclusion that it is premature to depart from the Policy which has hitherto been adopted by you and Lord Palmerston, and which notwithstanding the strong antipathy to the North, the strong sympathy with the South, and the passionate wish to have cotton, has met with such general approval from Parliament, the Press and the Public." The reaction of Sir George Cornewall Lewis, who may have been approached by Russell about the redeployment of troops in Canada, was no warmer. Satisfied that both combatants were determined to fight on to victory, he declared himself opposed to any move by Britain.[64]

The opposition of Lewis and Granville, and later reports from America, confirmed Palmerston in his caution. "These last battles in Maryland have rather set the North up again," he wrote to Russell after Antietam, "and unless Things should take a more decisive turn against them, they would probably not be prepared to accept the Principle of Separation as the Basis of negotiation." Obviously the prospect of recognizing the Confederacy in the event of a Northern rejection of mediation lost its allure the more likely it became. "The whole matter is full of difficulty," he concluded wearily, "and can only be cleared up by some more decided events between the contending parties."[65] Nor did he dismiss lightly Granville's fears of Napoleon's intentions in Italy. Palmerston doubted the emperor's sincerity when he spoke of wishing to leave Rome. If he really meant what he said, surely fear of earning the displeasure of fanatical priests, sentimental ladies, and disappointed and factious politicians would not prevent him taking "French leave" of the Pope. No, the emperor was striving to undo his own work of unification. By making a "last stand" in Rome he was hoping to disorganize Italy. Therefore it was Britain's business to thwart him, "to stand firm upon the principle of a single and united Italy; and to wait till truth and justice, and the public opinion of enlightened Europe shall have swept away the cobwebs of the Crafty Spider of the Tuileries."[66]

Russell was also getting cold feet about intervention in America, but not quite as quickly as the prime minister. "This America question must be well sifted," he admitted at the beginning of October. He was disinclined to take any action without Russia, for her "separation from our move would ensure the rejection of our proposals,"[67] and he sensed that the North was far from ready to abandon the struggle. "The flood of paper money still appears to flow, and so long as there is no ebb, public opinion will be for war —Such is my view at least," he confided to Stuart.[68] In these altered circumstances he no more wished to bind Britain to recognize the Confederacy than did Palmerston. Yet he was loath to retreat completely and make no effort to halt the war and the suffering. Hence his welcoming of Mercier's suggestion of a joint Anglo-American proposal of an armistice, for this would give the warriors time in which to negotiate a settlement. However, Palmerston was lukewarm from the first. An "armistice without some agreement as to a Basis of negotiation, and that Basis can be none other than separation, would only be like the breathing Time allowed to Boxers between Rounds of a Fight, to enable them to get fresh wind," he commented. Here was the rub—the scant likelihood of the Unionists agreeing to the principle of separation "before they have had a good deal more pummelling by the South."[69] Nevertheless, the prime minister thought Mercier's proposal worthy of consideration by the cabinet which Russell had planned to summon on October 16, but now put back to the following week.

Sceptical of his ability to win his colleagues to the support even of this inoffensive armistice proposal, fancying they might well opt for the "easy and plausible" policy of "wait," Russell turned once again to the French for help. What he sought was a confidential but sufficiently official initiative from the imperial government to lay before his colleagues. He suggested that one of Mercier's despatches be forwarded along with the emperor's observations upon it.[70] In the meantime he put the finishing touches to the memorandum on the American war which he had been preparing for a week. But his slim hopes of carrying the day had already diminished. Gladstone had stirred up public debate with a speech at Newcastle on October 7 in which he seemed to be preparing the ground for British recognition of the Confederacy.

With a promise to Palmerston to be discreet, and forswearing any intention to launch a crusade against high taxes and large defence establishments, Gladstone had set out on a triumphal progress through the Northeast. It began at Newcastle on October 7 with a speech to a "crowded and enthusiastic dinner of near 500." The chancellor was among friends, for the area had prospered during his years at the Exchequer. The French treaty, which the dinner celebrated, and his raising of the price of coals, had enabled this region to escape the difficulties afflicting some centres of trade, notably Lancashire. However, the troubles of the textile districts were seldom out of his mind. He had provided temporary employment for several "distressed Lancashire men" at Hawarden (the Gladstone estate on the Welsh border near Chester), their transportation being paid by relief committees, and "a little house" had been set up there for factory girls, who were fed and trained for domestic service. It was a scheme his wife privately urged other members of the privileged classes to adopt. Throughout the day of his Newcastle speech Gladstone reflected on what to say about the American war, which like most other Englishmen he blamed for the suffering in the mill towns. Undoubtedly his remarks were also influenced by the knowledge of the new course Palmerston and Russell had planned to chart with his help, though he was unaware of their recent steering away from recognition. So at Newcastle, and four days later at York, he decided to open the eyes of the people of England to the "facts." "We may have an opinion about slavery," he told his Newcastle audience, "we may be for or against the South; but there is no doubt that Jefferson Davis and other leaders of the South have made an army; they are making, it appears, a navy; and they have made what is more than either, they have made a nation." This statement was followed by "loud cheers and great sensation," and the excited crowd was soon cheering again. "We may anticipate with certainty," Gladstone went on, "the success of the Southern States so far as regards their separation from the North. I cannot but believe that that event is as certain as any event yet future and contingent can be." Why persist therefore with a war which, in the chancellor's opinion, was destroying the rule of law and fundamental liberties in the United States? At York he posed the question: "how is America hereafter to return to a state of things in which, at any rate, whether we prefer English views of freedom to hers or not, she did afford perfect guarantees to personal and individual liberty both as to property and life?" By way of reply he called on the North to abandon the struggle, and argued further that in the division of the Republic lay the best hope for the slaves.[71]

John Bright, fearing that Gladstone would say something foolish at Newcastle, had urged Cobden without success to advise the chancellor to speak liberally about home affairs and say not a "single word" unfriendly to the United States. This was the way "to place himself more distinctly in the eye of the public as the most likely man of official rank to be the liberal minister of the future." But the Newcastle speech disqualified Gladstone in Bright's opinion as a candidate for the highest of offices. The chancellor's mind was "too unstable for a great success as guide and leader of a party or a nation." "His moral sense did not keep him out of the Russian War," the disenchanted Radical recalled, "and now it has no light to guide him on the American question." Gladstone had been tainted by his birth into a great slaveholding family and had moved too long in aristocratic circles where the Republic was hated, Bright concluded sourly.[72]

Bitter as Bright's disappointment with Gladstone was, the advocates of intervention in the American war had little to cheer about. The public response to the speech at Newcastle suggested a widespread disinclination to extend recognition to the South at this time. Newspapers freely conceded that the chancellor, "whether the utterance was individual or ministerial," had echoed "the general sentiment of the country." But they professed their inability to see what a simple act of recognition would achieve, apart from embittering further relations with the Union and uniting the North in a determination to press on with the war? It would not end the fighting or bring cotton to Britain.[73] If this reaction merely followed the drift of Palmerston and Russell's thinking, the debate over intervention had been polarized. Britain appeared to be faced with a choice between a continuance of "strict neutrality" or recognition of the South. Certainly the furore provided Lewis with an excuse to present these as the only alternatives in a speech at Hereford on October 14, which advertised the cabinet's divisions on the American problem. "Mr. Gladstone proved what we have never doubted," the *Spectator* observed, "that there is in the Cabinet a strong element of aristocratic leaning towards the South; Sir George Lewis proved that there is still there also a strong counterbalancing element of frigid caution and reserve."[74]

Frigid caution and reserve fairly described Lewis's attitude towards the war and the Union, and his opinion carried weight. Above all others, one contemporary remarked, Lewis knew how "to conciliate theory with practice, and to play the part of the Statesman without forgetting the principles of the philosopher." Another described him as "coldblooded as a fish," "of an imperturbable temper, calm and resolute, laborious and indefatigable," and "exceedingly popular with the House of Commons, from his general good humour and civility, and the credit given him for honour, sincerity, plain dealing and good intentions."[75] "He is again one of those very trusty, tried, upright, honest, clean, fearless men who were invaluable to us," the Queen wrote. Little wonder that he was much admired as the epitome of the modern statesman, was widely touted as Palmerston's successor, and that his untimely death in 1863 was so widely mourned.[76]

Lewis had long been pessimistic about the Union's chances of

survival. In 1856 he had seen "no solution for the political differences of the United States, but the separation of the Slave and Free
States into distinct political communities."[77] Nor had the outbreak
of war excited his sympathy. Instead, he derived some satisfaction
from the fact that Northerners were finding out what it was "to be
governed by a village attorney appointed Prime Minister" for a
fixed term of four years. Were the American system of government
"a little more flexible, Lincoln, with all his clerks would speedily be
sent to the right about." It was not safe, he believed, "for a large
country with shifting interests to have a written constitution." But
Lewis was secretary of state for war as well as political philosopher,
and in this capacity he saw in the Union's mismanagement of the
war security for British North America. "The probability of a winter
invasion of Canada seems to have become infinitesimally small," he
wrote to his deputy at the War Office, De Grey. Why sacrifice this
gain by meddling in the war, thereby inviting trouble with the
United States? His public opposition to recognition was followed by
a private attack upon Russell's armistice proposal, which he thought
"would certainly do no good, and might not improbably do harm."[78]

The foreign secretary's memorandum, together with supporting
documents, was finally printed and sent off to his scattered colleagues on October 13. He developed three main arguments for
diplomatic action. First, the war had reached a bloody stalemate.
Second, the two communities were irreconcilably divided politically.
Third, and "the most important of all," the social question. Firmly
convinced that the prospect of a servile war would make the
European nations "more desirous to see an end to this desolating
and destructive conflict," Russell subjected Lincoln's slavery "decree" to close analysis and withering criticism. As had much of the
press, he warned of the consequences of making emancipation an
act of punishment and retaliation. There would be "acts of plunder,
of incendiarism, and of revenge." In these appalling circumstances
the time had come to ask "whether it is not a duty of Europe to
ask both parties, in the most friendly and conciliatory terms, to
agree to a suspension of arms for the purpose of weighing calmly
the advantages of peace against the contingent gain of further bloodshed and the protraction of so calamitous a war."[79]

The initial response to Russell's paper was far less discouraging
than he had feared it would be. Newcastle, who had been expected
to back action of some kind, did advocate the policy of "wait." "I

do not think it can be long before a large Party in the North declares itself adverse to the war," he opined. "Premature intervention by Europe would prevent any such movement, and unite the two Parties in the North in the same mad resolve to go on."[80] However, from Argyll, a Union sympathizer, there came a measure of support. Sadly he conceded that the result of the latest campaigns "almost prove that the subjugation of the South is, in a military and political view, impossible." He did contest Russell's interpretation of Lincoln's proclamation, citing it as "a signal proof" of the war's antislavery effect. "Halting, imperfect and inconsistent as the Proclamation is—interpreted strictly—it has nevertheless been hailed by the Abolitionists as a great—irrevocable step—towards their 'Platform'," he reminded the foreign secretary. Yet Argyll admitted that these remarks had little bearing on the "practical conclusion"— "that Europe, acting together, might without harm, and with possible good, advise a suspension of arms with a view to negotiation, and to Peace." He assumed that the advice would be given "in a friendly and conciliatory spirit," and nothing more would be said or done which would commit Britain "to any farther step, tending to direct interference."[81] Here was the weakness in Russell's scheme, and Lewis pounced upon it.

In a long and closely reasoned memorandum, which was also printed and circulated to cabinet members, he pointed out that to propose an armistice was tantamount to asking the Union to recognize the independence of the Confederacy. But Lincoln, Seward, and the other members of the American government were all committed to complete reunion. "Their personal honour, their credit and character, are involved in perseverance for this purpose," he added. Therefore, at this moment of "peculiar bitterness and exasperation," what likelihood was there that they would agree to a step which would virtually, "if not expressly, concede the independence of the South?" Far more probable was an angry rejection of the suggestion, leading ultimately to a disruption of diplomatic relations. This would compel Britain to send additional troops to Canada during the winter, which could only be done "at great cost and with severe privations" to the men; "and all hope of a reduction of the Army Estimates for the next session would vanish."[82] Indeed, the extensive and expensive measures that were required in order to make Canada defensible had been detailed by a commission of military and naval experts who had submitted their report little more than a month before.[83]

For the sake of argument, Lewis also speculated on the consequences of a Northern acceptance of this "philanthropic proposition." Although less perilous than those of rejection, they threatened to be unpleasant and embarrassing. Having agreed to an armistice at Britain's prodding, the North might very well throw onto her the responsibility for mediation. Could Britain propose a settlement which amounted to a guarantee of Southern slavery? Or as Palmerston put it, could "we without offence to many People here recommend to the North to sanction Slavery and to undertake to give back Runaways, and yet would not the South insist upon some such Conditions after Lincoln's Emancipation Decree?"[84] Neither widespread popular revulsion, which many ministers shared, for an act perceived as an incitement to "servile insurrection," nor the decline of the antislavery movement, had freed Britain to follow a course so at variance with her philanthropic tradition. Only if she waited until the hopelessness of the North's attempt to subdue the South was more clearly demonstrated would it be possible to intervene without fear of embarrassment on this sensitive subject. All in all, Lewis wrote, it was "Better to endure the ills we have, Than fly to others which we know not of."[85] Palmerston had already reached the same conclusion for much the same reasons, though his disinclination to make any move had been reinforced by Lord Derby, who let him know that as leader of the opposition he opposed any change in the government's policy. The "Pugilists must fight a few more Rounds before the Bystanders can decide that the State should be divided between them," the prime minister announced to Russell.[86]

His request for French assistance unanswered, for the imperial government was in the throes of a brief ministerial crisis following the dismissal of Thouvenel in mid-October, Russell did not struggle long against the policy of complete inaction. As early as October 18, still unaware of Lewis's memorandum but alive to Palmerston's growing caution, he was seeking to do no more than sound out Russia. There was to be no mention of recognition, simply an enquiry to see whether she would consider joining with Britain and France to recommend a cessation of hostilities. This "short step now may lead to a long step hereafter," he explained to the prime minister, "and at all events accustom the three Courts to ventilate the question."[87] Even this innocuous proposal was soon lost sight of, however. The reports arriving from Stuart all seemed "to point to the word wait," and this was the course favoured by a majority of the cabinet. So, at Palmerston's suggestion, the special meeting to discuss the American question was abruptly cancelled. If this irritated those members who had interrupted their vacations to travel up to London, it pleased Lyons whose return to Washington it signalled. "I am quite satisfied with the course the government mean to take with regard to American politics," he wrote to his sister, "which diminishes the annoyance of going back."[88]

After a month of activity Russell had brought the government not a step closer to what Gladstone called "an interference limited to moral means." Testily, he engaged Lewis in a brief correspondence, accusing him of having misrepresented his position. He was supported by the disappointed Gladstone. The danger of the Union taking offence at any British initiative, and thus the disagreeable prospect of a diplomatic rupture, would have been removed by the participation of Russia, the chancellor argued. Her involvement had always been an integral part of the foreign secretary's scheme. As for the other main argument for delay—the concern to avoid being tarred with the brush of proslavery—Gladstone met it unflinchingly. Was Britain to refuse to try and cure one enormous evil because she could not cure another along with it, he asked his colleagues. If she intervened, she could use "every moral influence with a view to the mitigation, or, if possible, the removal of slavery." Conversely, the longer she kept her distance, and the more successful the South became, the less favourable would be her position "for urging on the Government of the Southern Confederacy the just claims of the slave."[89] But it was too late to reverse the decision to cling to the policy of "wait." Russell himself became its advocate. Next spring, with Parliament in session and another horrifying military campaign in the offing, would be a better time to recognize the Confederacy, he declared. Also, the Democratic party might have gained the ascendancy in the Union by then. Palmerston quickly concurred. "I believe you are right in fixing next Spring for the period for the acknowledgement of the Confederate States," he commented. "Their Independence can be converted into an Established Fact by the Course of Events alone."[90]

No sooner had the British government decided to wait, at least until the following spring, than the French reopened the question.

Belatedly, they responded to Russell's request for a proposal he could bring before his colleagues. It was not the work of the new minister of foreign affairs, Drouyn de Lhuys, who had little knowledge of the American problem and was preoccupied with the affairs of Europe. Returning to an office he had held on three previous occasions, he brought with him a conviction that France's future lay in an alliance with Austria, and in pursuit of that end he was fully prepared to destroy the unity of Italy.[91] Not surprisingly, he was reluctant to make any immediate move in America, but was driven on by Napoleon. Reading the reports of his officials in the provinces, the emperor had concluded that the time had come for his government to give some evidence of its search for a solution to the growing unemployment in those industries dislocated by the American war. Recognition of the Confederacy was too dangerous, for it might provoke Union retaliation in the form of assistance to the Mexicans. Far safer was the course Mercier suggested—one which unbeknown to the emperor the British had just rejected—a joint European proposal of an armistice. Even if limited to a period of six months it would give time for the excitement in America to cool down, he explained to the British minister, and allow "more pacific counsels to prevail." However, Napoleon was also willing to have the Europeans offer their good services as mediators. Indeed, in his meeting with Cowley on October 27, he made it clear that he preferred the larger role. Questioned by the Englishmen about the likelihood of Russia joining with them, the emperor agreed that there was no chance of successful intervention without her cooperation.[92]

"You will see that a step has been taken in the direction you indicated to me some time back," Cowley reported to Russell, "and that proposals come from here for making some offer to stop the war in America."[93] Both Palmerston and Russell greeted this news coolly. Nothing had happened over the past few days to suggest that the Union would heed a call for an armistice. On the contrary, the Federal government's reported placing of an order in Europe for 20,000 tons of lead, ten times the amount ever consumed by Britain during time of war, did not "look like peaceful Prospects" to Palmerston. As for mediation, the difficulty about slavery had already excluded that from British consideration. "The French Government are more free from the shackles of Principle and of Right and Wrong on these matters, as on all others, than we are," the prime minister disdainfully observed. Yet he did not rule out entirely all thought of cooperation. Instead, he expressed the opinion that "it would be wiser to wait till the Elections in North America are over before any Proposal is made."[94] Russell agreed. "There seems no use in talking of America until the elections are over," he replied to Cowley. And when he did turn over in his mind the kind of proposal that might be made to the Americans, he was more concerned to see something drafted that "would be creditable to us in Europe" than acceptable to the belligerents.[95]

The arrival of the formal French proposal that Britain, France, and Russia jointly propose a cessation of the hostilities in America, which Russell decided to present to the cabinet at its scheduled meeting on November 11, coincided with the circulation of a second paper signed by Lewis. This new shot in the battle of the memorandums had in fact been fired by the husband of the war secretary's step-daughter. William Vernon Harcourt was recognized as a man of "great abilities, and not less ambition." Connected to the great Whig families, he "was conspicuous in London society for his commanding figure and lofty artificial manner."[96] With great force, and parading an impressive familiarity with historical precedents, Harcourt developed the argument Lewis had sketched out at Hereford —recognition of the South could not be justified under international law. Although this was not the question due to come before the cabinet, the memorandum did repeat Lewis's earlier warnings against "amicable interference." The assumption that success and security were to be found in numbers, which had been the basis of Gladstone's paper, was tested historically and found wanting. "We have seen that even the decrepit Sultan ventured to refuse to the Greeks the terms dictated by Russia, France and England," the cabinet was reminded, "and that the insignificant kingdom of Holland disobeyed the London Conference, and dared to make war upon Belgium in defiance of its command." What reason was there to believe, therefore, that the Union would not reject any European intervention and take "umbrage." If the Great Powers were not content to wait until the American conflagration had burned itself out, "they must not expect to extinguish the flames with rose water." In short, the only sure way to bring the war to an end was through armed interference and no one contemplated that.[97]

On the day Lewis circulated this "confidential" paper to his colleagues Harcourt published an abbreviated version in *The Times*.

He wrote under the pseudonym of "Historicus," but the *Spectator* immediately identified him as "a barrister in the councils of Sir George Lewis." With this remarkable letter, the *Spectator* claimed, "the whole tone of opinion on recognition and intervention" had changed.[98] Equally pertinent and more revealing were Palmerston's remarks at the Guildhall banquet on November 10. It was plain he did not contemplate any imminent change in his government's policy towards the American war. Naturally he voiced sympathy with the Lancashire operatives, but he also pointed to the thriving condition of the economy in general. The American war notwithstanding, trade and commerce had increased and the nation's finances were in good order. The farmers were not complaining, he added jocularly, for the harvest had been far better than expected. What he did not say was that all of this had placed his government in the happy position of being able to pursue an American policy free from effective popular pressure to intervene. Indeed, to the extent that it had found expression, and despite Lincoln's proclamation, public opinion seemed "almost universal" against interference at this time.[99]

Surprisingly, when the prime minister introduced the French proposal in cabinet Russell urged acceptance. In part, he was responding to the latest news from the United States. The sweeping gains by the Democrats in the Congressional elections, in which even New York seemed certain to fall to them, "afforded a most favourable opportunity for intervention," he argued. He may have been influenced by Stuart's suggestion that in the light of these results the European powers might consider appealing to the American people over the head of the Lincoln administration, by proffering their services in the interests of peace. But Russell's behaviour was also a measure of his distrust of Russia. Mercier had warned Stuart that the Russian minister in Washington was attempting to engineer a Franco-Russian mediation of the conflict with the aim of separating England from France. These suspicions found an echo in the reports of the British minister to Russia. On November 8 he had telegraphed the news that Russia's response to the French proposal was a peremptory rejection, only to report subsequently that Palmerston's remarks at the Guildhall had brought an immediate softening of the Russian refusal to have anything to do with the matter.[100] If Britain rejected the French overture, Russell warned his colleagues, "Russia would reconsider her decision, act directly with France, and thus accomplish her favourite purpose of separating France and England." None of this impressed his listeners. Although Palmerston spoke in favour of acting with the French it was clear that he did not expect the cabinet to agree and simply wished "to seem to support" the foreign secretary. Gladstone did urge acceptance of the proposal, as did Westbury, but to no avail. Others could find no sense in the proposal unless it was intended to go farther, and Russell eventually "gave way without resolutely fighting out his battle."[101]

Rumours of the government's decision were confirmed when Russell published his answer to the French proposal, and the rejection won general applause. The Tory dailies did mount a bitter assault but they did not speak for the party's leadership. As Derby informed Disraeli, "I should not be disposed to find much fault with the decision, especially if Russia held back, as she seems to have done."[102] Sir John Pakington, an influential Conservative who had earlier shown some enthusiasm for "Gladstone's dictum about the nationality of the South," had both anticipated and conceded the wisdom of the government's course. "Even the soberer Tories are clearly with the Government in the matter," the *Spectator* observed, "and England may be said to be unanimous."[103] Across the Channel the French press heaped abuse upon the British for rejecting the emperor's overture. However, Drouyn de Lhuys took the decision calmly. He had always thought Napoleon's action precipitate and Russell's reply stressed the fact that the subject was deferred not closed. The British government believed that there was no reason "at the present moment" to hope that the Union "would accept the proposal suggested," the foreign secretary had written, and a refusal from Washington at this time "would prevent any speedy renewal of the offer." It remained British policy to wait for the spring. American affairs were now "at a standstill."[104]

In summary, the British government's decision to opt for the "easy and plausible" policy of "wait" had been governed by a combination of factors. Of these, not the least important was the continuing lack of evidence of any compelling social or economic reason to meddle in the Civil War. The robust health of the economy discouraged an adventurous American policy. Why gamble with prosperity? Admittedly, the Emancipation Proclamation met with a hostile reception in a nation where the antislavery movement had been languishing for some time, where racial antipathy for blacks was strong and concern for fellow-whites in the slave states was high, but the efforts of the advocates of intervention to turn this to good account had little practical success. Their renewed campaign to organize the unemployed brought another setback so humiliating that it undermined the confidence even of Spence. Consequently, neither Palmerston nor Russell could have sensed a stiffening breeze of popular opinion favourable to, let alone requiring, a change of course. However, the prospect of decisive military developments encouraged them to enter into an alliance with Gladstone in the cabinet and seek the company of France in proceeding down the path to mediation or recognition. The failure of Lee's invasion of Maryland, the opposition of senior members of the cabinet to action, fears of Napoleon III's intentions in Italy, the embarrassment of any intervention which appeared to favour the Slave South, all persuaded Palmerston to draw back. The prime minister's disinclination to move was strengthened by the public response to Gladstone's unfortunate speech at Newcastle and Derby's private warning that he opposed a change of policy. Although Russell's commitment to a diplomatic initiative of some kind was more resolute, he steadily retreated before the threat of entanglement in the conflict. The fact that he subsequently rallied to the support of a belated proposal from France that the two nations, together with Russia, call for a temporary cessation of hostilities was a measure less of Russell's determination to intervene in the American war than of a profound distrust of the Russians, whom he believed to be scheming to alienate France from Britain.

SEVEN

The Failure of Confederate Foreign Policy

FOR LINCOLN THE WEEKS FOLLOWING ANTIETAM were another period of trial and anguish. Despite his urging and in defiance of his orders McClellan remained north of the Potomac until the last week of October. This inactivity heightened the demoralizing and politically harmful impression of military stalemate, and angered those Unionists impatient to press on to victory. Meanwhile the Emancipation Proclamation was proving a political liability in large areas of the North, infusing fresh vigour more often into the enemies than into the friends of the administration. The New England intellectual community, with Emerson in the vanguard, did shower the president with praise and many Protestant churches and most church conventions meeting at the time drafted resolutions of support. Nevertheless, there could be no ignoring of the uneasiness in the Northern states over possible negro immigration and competition for jobs. Negrophobia was growing, especially in the Midwest. The depression caused by the war's closing of the Mississippi river trade; the tariff acts which threatened to raise the price of all goods farmers had to buy; the arbitrary arrest of political opponents; the military failures, and now the proclamation provided midwestern Democrats with an arsenal of weapons for the coming Congressional elections. Depicting themselves as champions of individual liberty and defenders of the West, and in their familiar role as spokesmen of exclusively white interests, they fulminated against the "fanatics" of New England and summoned all conservatives to help them throw out Republicans.[1]

That candidates identified with the administration were in difficulty was all too apparent. From Pennsylvania the influential John Forney warned the president that emancipation and the suspension of habeas corpus had ensured an attack on all fronts by political enemies and the need for every exertion to stave off defeat. The news from Lincoln's own state was no more cheering. Knowing that any movement into Central Illinois of the negroes gathered in Cairo at its southern tip would not improve Republican chances, David Davis pressed the administration not to allow more blacks to enter the state or those already there to spread out before election day. In New York the State Central Committee asked Lincoln to send in Gen. Franz Sigel to make a few speeches, in the hope that this would attract German votes to the support of the Republican candidate for governor. It was all for naught, as Republicans went down to defeat in state after state. "It looks like a great, sweeping revolution of public sentiment," George Templeton Strong wrote in his diary after the New York gubernatorial election. "We the people are impatient, dissatisfied, disgusted, disappointed."[2] As a wave of defeatism swept across the North there was talk in the Democratic press of the Northwestern states withdrawing from the Union to form their own confederacy. The alarmed governors of Indiana, Iowa, and Illinois impressed upon the president the need for a military campaign to reopen the Mississippi in order to forestall this danger.[3]

In the election results and the public discussion of a northwestern Confederacy foreign observers thought they detected the tell-tale signs of a popular yearning for peace, even at the price of disunion. They listened to the exultant leaders of the Democratic party who predicted privately that Lincoln would seek to strengthen the moderate and conservative elements in his cabinet, would attempt to effect a reconciliation with the South, and would renounce the policy of subjugating the Southern states. Instead, he announced the dismissal of McClellan, thereby signalling his determination to prosecute the war with more energy if not greater skill. Moreover, in public the Democrats themselves thought it prudent to call for a more vigorous war effort and to accuse the administration of slackness. With similar caution the party's leaders in New York volunteered the opinion to Lord Lyons, whom they discreetly sought out as soon as he landed in the United States, that although the day of foreign mediation must eventually come, this was not the moment. For the Europeans to act now was to play into the hands of the "Radicals" in the Republican party, they warned.[4]

As he scanned the New York press following his arrival there Lyons could not have failed to mark the ever-increasing bitterness against his nation. Frustrated and bewildered by the Union's lack of military progress against the South, the major journals increasingly fastened upon the British a full measure of the responsibiilty. The hostile reception accorded Lincoln's proclamation, and Gladstone's remarks at Newcastle, were cited as fresh evidence that nearly every voice from almost every class in England had been "the voice of hatred and scorn," revealing a "base malignity and injustice" of which Americans "had hardly supposed human nature to be capable."[5] The British government's policy was portrayed as one of "giving all the aid and comfort possible to the rebellion within the limits of safety against war with the United States." English powder and ball, English rifles and cannon, had armed the rebels in every battle of the war. Not content with this, the British were also building a Confederate navy.

In American eyes the escape first of the *Florida* and then of the *Alabama* were not unrelated incidents but the work of "an extensive and dangerous combination, threatening the direst injury to the Northern cause." Embracing British shipping, manufacturing, and political interests, this conspiracy had been organized for the general purpose of ensuring the success of the rebellion and with the express aim of destroying the Union's carrying trade, thereby throwing "the great profits of American commerce into the hands of British shipowners." And a sharp drop in the number of American vessels clearing New York was cited as proof that the "British-built, British-armed and British-crewed" *Alabama* was performing her appointed task of forcing their transfer to foreign flags.[6]

There was a flight from the American flag. In 1862 more than 117,000 tons of United States shipping was bought cheaply by foreigners, which was a sevenfold increase over the sales for 1860 and almost five times the figure for 1861. Yet the role of the British-built Confederate commerce raiders in the dramatic decline of the American mercantile marine was a secondary one at best. Far more important had been the Southern-led withdrawal of Federal shipping subsidies in 1858. This dealt a "crushing blow" to those progressive American merchants and shipowners who had perceived that the future lay in iron-hulled steam ships. As a result, in 1862 the large merchant fleet engaged in foreign trade was still made up almost entirely of sailing ships. Less than 5 per cent of the total tonnage was powered by steam, and in the lucrative and prestigious North Atlantic trade the American sailing packet service was being driven from the seas by low-priced, iron-hulled British steamships. Even in those activities where sailing vessels held their own, such as the general cargo business out of American ports, United States ships were in difficulty. Rising costs of production and operation made them less competitive than Canadian and British vessels, and as their ships ceased to be profitable American owners offered them for sale at prices the British in particular could not refuse. The war certainly hastened this process, though more as a result of the disruption of the cotton trade than of the raiding activities of the *Alabama*. Undoubtedly she encouraged the panic selling by causing a sharp increase in insurance charges for vessels flying the Union flag, but that was the extent of her real influence. However, angry Northerners preferred the simple explanation of this otherwise complex problem. The "British pirate" was responsible. Britain had done "all that she has dared to do, to break down and destroy us, in the day of our agony," the *New York Times* charged. "This thing will be remembered. England will be hated for it, till the last American now on the stage goes to his grave."[7] Nor did her rejection of the French armistice proposal lessen the animosity. Her refusal had been motivated by fear of war with the Union, the press concluded, for she was a cowardly enemy.[8]

Even in their darkest moods, Unionists knew they had some friends in Britain. The belief that the sentiment of "the people" was right had been further strengthened by the events at Stalybridge. Yet these "dumb masses," with "no voice" in Parliament, were suffering cruelly as a result of the war. Hence the suggestion by the *New York Times* that the American people give "some substantial expression of the sympathy entertained for these, our only friends in England, in this their day of terrible distress." There was a danger, or so that newspaper's London correspondent reported, of the operatives' misery providing the government with an excuse to intervene in the war.[9] To send provisions to Lancashire would therefore be both humanitarian and expedient. This measure of enlightened self-interest quickly gathered support. There were collections in many New York churches during the Thanksgiving services on November 27, and the city's business community soon took the cause in hand. Assembling in the rooms of the Chamber of Commerce on December 4 they formed the International Relief Committee and launched an appeal. More than $26,000 in cash and in kind was subscribed on the spot, along with a ship to carry the provisions to England. Later contributions came from Philadelphia as well as New York, but hopes of a national response went unfulfilled. Preoccupation with the war and anger with Britain stifled generosity, while some Northerners may have thought the appeal too obvious a bid for popular support in that country. Certainly the *New York Times* was frank enough. "Now that it is settled that magnificent contributions of food will soon be sent from our shores towards the relief of the British operatives," it observed, "Englishmen can afford to make a little effort to understand the real state of American feeling toward them and their Government."[10]

From the president's annual message to Congress on December 1, 1862, it was evident that both he and Seward wished to avoid inflaming public opinion against Britain. Relations with other nations were not as "gratifying" as they had been at former periods, Lincoln conceded, but they were "more satisfactory" than the divided Union "might reasonably have apprehended." Admittedly the American struggle had been "contemplated by foreign nations with reference less to its own merits, than to its supposed, and often exaggerated effects and consequences resulting to those nations themselves." Nevertheless, complaint on the part of the United States, "even if it were just, would certainly be unwise."[11]

Gideon Welles could ill-afford to tread so warily in his report. The depredations of the *Alabama* had brought fresh demands from Chambers of Commerce for adequate naval protection of American vessels on the high seas and had excited renewed public mockery of the "old fogy" in the Navy Department. Defensively, Welles repeated the charge that she was a British ship and warned that "still other vessels of a similar character" were being fitted out in British ports. Furthermore, he blamed Britain for the navy's lack of success in hunting down the raiders. "Our own cruisers not being permitted to remain in British ports to guard against these outrages, nor to coal while cruising, nor to repair damages in their harbors when injuries are sustained," he complained, "the arrest of them [the raiders] is difficult and attended with great uncertainty." Such accusations and complaints were repeated in Congress, where it was proposed that the navy protect the vessel carrying provisions to the suffering operatives of England—protect her, that is, from the *Alabama*. More ominously, the question of issuing letters of marque was revived and referred to the Committee on Foreign Affairs for a prompt opinion.[12]

Seward had betrayed no sign of this animosity in his dealings with the British minister or in his correspondence with Adams.

Reacting to the worrisome talk of intervention in Britain, he moved to lessen the friction caused by the war. Unfortunately his efforts to return mail found on board blockade-runners, unopened and without delay, were resisted by Welles, while Edward Bates opposed stoutly his proposal that Britain and France be allowed to obtain cotton from the Confederacy. "I find a new difficulty to contend with in managing matters here," Lyons reported home soon after his return to Washington. "Mr. Seward has apparently lost very much of his influence with the President and the Cabinet. He seems to be very conciliatory, but not to be able to carry his points with other Departments."[13] Undismayed by these setbacks Seward pressed on with his efforts to avoid any confrontation with Britain. He exhibited remarkable forbearance in tackling the "abuses of neutrality daily committed by British subjects, in British ports," and on the high seas. The activities of the *Alabama* and reports from Dudley that similar vessels were under construction at Birkenhead brought queries and protests but no sabre-rattling. Could it be claimed, Seward asked, that a nation was really neutral when vessels-of-war, "without restraint and with impunity," were "built, armed, manned, equipped and sent out from its ports to make war on a peaceful and friendly nation?" Ironically, the secretary's very moderation and caution were now seized upon by his opponents as they sought a scapegoat for the administration's inept management of the war.[14]

Seward was attacked for his "Dirt-Eating Diplomacy." *Brownson's Quarterly* even questioned his personal courage, nerve, and back-bone. This "weak" man's influence in cabinet served to explain the Union's failure to subdue the rebellion. To his family the resentful Seward wearily protested the injustice of these "clamors and accusations." He had "no army or navy or control over them." Publicly he could do little, but what he did was a tribute to his integrity if not discretion. The publication of the great bulk of his diplomatic correspondence for the preceding year provided his detractors with additional ammunition. Already the despatch in which he had urged the British to withdraw their recognition of Confederate belligerency, arguing that it tended to prolong the war and thus jeopardize the survival of slavery, had been released to the press by Russell. To radical enemies here was proof that his policy all along had been "to preserve slavery, and to prevent the war from operating its ruin." Now his angry denunciation in July of the Southern advocates of slavery and the Northern abolitionists as conspirators in a plot to excite a servile rebellion appeared in print. Anger may have provoked him to publish these controversial remarks, for he held the radicals responsible for the administration's poor showing in the elections, but the decision quickly heightened the hostility towards him.[15]

Charles Sumner was in the vanguard of the movement to oust Seward, just as he had been eighteen months earlier. Returning to Washington after an exhausting campaign for re-election, he had a personal score to settle. He suspected Seward of having given tacit support to those in Massachusetts who had fought so hard to block his return to the Senate. He also blamed Seward for the Democrats' triumph in New York, and by implication for their resurgence elsewhere. It was Seward who had forced the delay in issuing the proclamation, Sumner argued, and the hesitation displayed by the government in adopting the policy of emancipation had rallied the Democrats. A more determined antislavery policy would have prevented them from showing their heads, he asserted. Seward had been unable to grasp this because he was a mere politician. Although a man of "talent and prodigious energy," his "want of seriousness" and moral shallowness explained his failure to recognize the war's true character or "the elemental forces engaged." In his diplomatic correspondence he had discouraged the antislavery forces in Britain, the Union's natural allies.[16] Furthermore, "he had subjected himself to ridicule in diplomatic circles at home and abroad"; had uttered "statements offensive to Congress and spoken of it repeatedly with disrespect in the presence of foreign ministers"; and had written "offensive despatches," such as that of July 2 which had placed the Confederate advocates of slavery and the institution's Congressional opponents on the same level. It was a sweeping bill of indictment, certain to command the support of colleagues whose dignity was easily wounded and whose confidence had been shaken by the Democrats' victories in the recent elections. Among this group was William Pitt Fessenden. Touted as a possible replacement for Seward, he grumbled that the secretary's language in his despatches had not been bold enough, that he had "diplomatized too much," and Fessenden willingly saddled Seward with the responsibility for the military defeats at home.[17] At this juncture it was yet another disaster in the field that coalesced the opposition and precipitated a brief political and constitutional crisis.

The mangling of the Union army at Fredericksburg on December

13 filled "the heart of the loyal North with sickness, disgust and fear." The "most thorough Republicans" shared the general indignation, "fast growing revolutionary." Who was to blame? Many held the secretary of war, Edwin Stanton, responsible. "Unless Stanton be speedily shelved," diarist Strong concluded, "something will burst somewhere."[18] But powerful figures in the Congressional party had already selected Seward as the sacrifice. After two caucus meetings the Republican senators appointed a delegation to call upon the president seeking Seward's removal as part of a wholesale reconstruction of the administration. Forewarned by Preston King of New York, the secretary had already tendered his resignation and that of his son and assistant Frederick when the senators called at the Executive Mansion on December 18. Indeed, Seward had withdrawn from the State Department and visitors to his residence found him packing up his books and papers for a return home to Auburn. These were the theatrical gestures of a deeply wounded man, conscious of how well he had served his nation and how shabbily he was in danger of being treated. He could not have been confident that his colleagues would stand with him to a man, for at least two of them were known to have carried complaints about his influence with the president and their irregular methods of conducting business to critics in the Senate.[19] Where Seward did have resolute support was at the other end of Pennsylvania Avenue.

"It appears to me the Almighty is against us, and I can hardly see a ray of hope," the weary and disconsolate Lincoln confessed after Fredericksburg. Low though his spirits were, he found the energy and possessed the political skill needed to defeat this challenge to his authority. He liked and valued Seward and considered the charges brought against him ridiculous. Nor could he see how anything would be gained by reconstructing his cabinet. A new one would soon be assailed as fiercely as was the existing one, so that the Union cause would not have been strengthened. Even more important were the consequences of accepting the Senate's right to interfere in the executive branch. To Lincoln it seemed obvious "the whole Government must cave in. It could not stand, could not hold water; the bottom would be out."[20] With so much at stake he had to move cautiously. He listened patiently to the senators, invited them to come back on the following evening, and then deliberately summoned all the cabinet except Seward to that meeting. Not one of his department heads dissented when he spoke of their unity and asserted that they had all acquiesced in measures when once decided. Blair spoke up in defence of Seward, as did Bates, though less forcefully. Lincoln insisted that Seward had always supported the thorough prosecution of the war and had frequently read to him his despatches before sending them off. The secretary of state had often consulted also with Chase, the president added. It was a shrewd remark, for the secretary of the treasury was the Senators' principal ally in the cabinet. When Lincoln went on to say that Seward had fully concurred in the proclamation, Chase felt obliged to add that his absent colleague had actually strengthened its wording. Evidently uncomfortable throughout the meeting, muttering that had he known he was going to be arraigned he would not have attended, for the president had successfully shown that the responsibility for the Union's predicament belonged to them all, Chase subsequently submitted his resignation.[21] With both men's resignations in his hand Lincoln resolved the crisis by declining to accept either.

Lord Lyons had watched this unfolding drama with concern. He did not wish to see Seward chased from office. The secretary had long since ceased his browbeating in favour of conciliation and the acceptance of his resignation would indicate, or so Lyons believed, that Lincoln had thrown himself completely into the hands of the "ultra Radical Party." The British minister distrusted its members. They would do anything to prevent their overthrow, he thought, even risk a foreign war. "We are much more likely to have a man less disposed to keep the peace than a man more disposed to do so," he warned Russell.[22] Nor was his mind put completely at rest by Lincoln's success in keeping Seward in the cabinet. Lyons established a regular line of communication with Admiral Milne, commander of the North American Station, "for the times are dangerous, and we cannot ever be entirely free from disquiet."[23]

A smiling Seward and a pale, tense Chase attended the cabinet meeting held on December 23. If all the old jauntiness had returned, Seward was nevertheless careful not to invite a fresh outburst. It was at this time that he asked Weed to deny publicly that he had been invited to go to Paris. "The reasons you can imagine," he added cryptically.[24] Furthermore, the secretary understood the extent to which he was dependent upon the president. Their relationship, which had begun with Seward entertaining notions of intellectual and political superiority and had then developed into the easy familiarity of equals, was now marked by his recognition of the other man's dominance. Respect as well as appreciation prompted his private eulogizing of Lincoln "without limitation." The president was "the best and wisest man" he had ever known, Seward confided to friends, and his "grade and place in history" would not be settled for another half-century.[25] In this frame of mind he struggled to relieve some of the pressure his fellow conservatives continued to exert upon the exhausted president over emancipation. For having failed to persuade Lincoln to withhold the final proclamation with their warnings of the political unrest it would excite in the North, friends and advisers like Orville Browning and David Davis pestered him at least to modify his policy. Seward shared some of their misgivings, and with an eye to the British response he had persuaded Lincoln to insert in the final version of the document an order rather than an appeal to the slaves to abstain from violence. Nevertheless, he loyally advised these persistent conservatives that foreign considerations had required the proclamation. Nor could there be any retreat. The European nations, "all of whom were urging that the slaves should be declared free," had to be made to understand that a successful war would put an end to slavery.[26]

What upset conservative Republicans and radicals alike, and inspired the attacks on emancipation, as on Seward, was the poor management of the war. A month after Fredericksburg the military situation remained desperate. The army was in "a bad way." There was a lack of central inspiration or command, reminiscent of the condition of the Prussians before Jena, or so it seemed to Sumner. Demoralized men were deserting in large numbers, while injury and disease were carrying off others. Were the military forces of the Union simply going to melt away like a "snow wreath" with the approach of spring, when the terms of many volunteers would expire? One way to offset the losses was to open armed service to blacks, and this Lincoln had done in the final proclamation. But there were doubts about their fighting capabilities and they were initially assigned to garrison and other noncombatant duties. To obtain men for the line the government would eventually be forced to turn to conscription, and on March 3 a national draft would be enacted. Yet this was in itself an admission that the "stream of enthusiasm" had run dry. Was it surprising, therefore, as volunteers failed to come forward, that in January despair was everywhere? It fostered and was fed by the strong political opposition to the administration in New York and other important Northern states. And the failure of the first campaign to take the Confederate strongpoint of Vicksburg on the Mississippi did nothing to allay worries about midwestern sectionalism. Lincoln admitted privately that he feared "the fire in the rear."[27]

The emerging spokesman for the midwestern sectionalists, Clement L. Vallandigham of Ohio, delivered a carefully prepared speech in the House of Representatives on January 14. It was his swansong, for he had been surprisingly defeated in the recent elections. The attempt to crush the South had failed, he asserted, and it could not be long continued. The time had come to settle the conflict by arbitration and compromise, or to accept the friendly mediation of a foreign nation. "As proposed by the Emperor of France, I would accept it at once," Vallandigham added.[28] A fellow enthusiast for peace and mediation was Horace Greeley, which naturally excited suspicion that the two men were in league. Perhaps they were, for Vallandigham had made a peace and compromise speech in New York while on his way back to the capital after his unsuccessful bid for re-election. However, Greeley's principal ally in a quixotic endeavour to push the Lincoln administration into accepting foreign mediation was William Cornell Jewett. A colourful adventurer, he had recently returned to the United States from Europe convinced both of Napoleon's friendship for the Union and of the need for European intervention to end the war. Greeley became a convert and through the mighty *Tribune* sought to galvanize public support. He immediately met resistance from the popular *New York Herald* and the influential *Times*. The *Herald* ridiculed Greeley's advocacy of this solution to the war as just another circulation stunt, the latest addition to a list which included a lottery of strawberry plants, the sale of gold pens, and the publishing of "poor" translations of French novels which were then sold cheaply to the *Tribune*'s subscribers. Yet there was a serious side to the activities of these "Blessed Peacemakers," as Henry Raymond noted in the *Times*. Jewett could be and was dismissed as a "lunatic," but Greeley had "great ability, and an established political position," consequently his words would be given great weight by foreign ministers. It was an ill-kept secret that both men had met with Mercier.[29]

As Lyons discovered on his return to Washington, intervention remained the uppermost thought in Mercier's mind. The Frenchman was toying with the notion that his country might offer to mediate, having first secured Britain's consent and support. In the wake of the elections he was buoyed with confidence, sure that public opinion could be rallied behind foreign mediation. That Seward would never accept such intervention, unless driven to it, was the one clear conclusion Lyons was able to draw from the secretary's published correspondence. Consequently, the Englishman kept his distance from Mercier as the latter pressed on with his schemes to prepare the Americans for French mediation, perhaps in the spring. With Jewett's help the French minister not only maintained but broadened the contacts he had somewhat indiscreetly established with Northern Democrats following their election triumphs, and he offered encouragement to those from the midwest where the peace sentiment appeared to be strongest. He left to Greeley the task of organizing public support.[30]

Seward was enraged by Greeley's conduct, especially his dealings with Mercier. Aided by Raymond and Weed, whose newspapers published accounts of the *Tribune* editor's meddling in foreign policy, he embarrassed both men. When the Frenchman called at the State Department to explain his conduct, Seward made it plain that division of the nation "was a subject that could not be discussed in his office." On the face of it, this did not ease Mercier's task when immediately afterwards he received instructions from Paris to propose that the two American belligerents send commissioners to neutral ground, there to negotiate peace. He returned to the State Department with this proposal in hand on February 3. There was as he knew little likelihood of its being accepted by Seward, but he had persuaded himself that the American government would "be very much embarrassed by the reply." It would not dare to challenge the prevailing feeling for peace in the country by peremptorily rejecting all negotiations with the rebels. The watchful Lyons, to whom Mercier confided this opinion, understood the mood of the North rather better. Tired as they undoubtedly were of the war, most Northerners were not yet ready to negotiate for separation. Neither Vallandigham in his speeches nor Greeley in his editorials had contemplated disunion. Somehow peace would lead to reunion. Indeed, in defending himself from the Seward-inspired attacks, Greeley admitted that the people of the North were not willing to purchase peace at the price of Southern separation.[31] By February

10 the *Tribune*, whose directors had made known their opposition to Greeley's course, was announcing that "This nation has no moral right to surrender to a wanton, wicked Rebellion, unless it is beaten; and it surely is not yet beaten." On the contrary, a "very nearly exhausted" Confederacy would be defeated once the Union summoned all its energies.

Outright rejection of the French proposal thus entailed few problems for Seward. What did concern him was how to turn the refusal to domestic advantage. He was dismayed by the "spirit of faction." "Everybody distrusts everybody and recklessly scatter about the Union seeds of disunion," he complained to one correspondent.[32] A forthright reply to the French was certain to be popular and by making every effort to rally the people behind it, he remarked to Raymond, "we could override the various smaller issues that are dividing the country."[33] There was no need to dwell upon the timely boost it would give to Seward's personal popularity and prestige, thereby fortifying him against his congressional enemies. So when he released his answer to the French proposal on February 13, the well-briefed *New York Times* backed him up strongly. No less full-hearted in its praise was the *Herald*. Hailing this latest masterstroke of a "sagacious patriot and enlightened statesman," it predicted that in any conservative reconstruction of the cabinet Seward would retain his post.[34] As for his radical enemies, some of them greeted the secretary's victory with ill grace. Aided by Sumner, the *Tribune* launched a vigorous assault upon his diplomacy only to be driven from the field by the *Times*, supported by the mocking laughter of the *Herald*. By the end of February Seward's hold on his position was once again secure and his popularity high.[35]

"We are perhaps a shade less unpopular," Lyons informed Milne. "This is owing to the growing ill will towards France."[36] It was an animosity the emperor had invited, both by seeking to meddle in the war and by intervening in Mexico. The publication of one of Napoleon's despatches to his commanding general there, in which he spoke of establishing a monarchy to serve as a check to the southward expansion of the United States, "caused great wroth." Who could now believe the emperor when he protested that his sole object in Mexico was to recover the debts owed to French citizens? Yet it would be foolhardy for the Union to challenge France, exciting her hostility and thereby giving fresh support to the Confederacy. "Let us all unite to put down the rebellion," Sumner urged in moving successfully to have a set of inflammatory resolutions against France tabled by the Senate. "This is enough for the present."[37]

Despite the Union's miserable failures on the battlefield, there was a fresh sense of purpose and confidence. A new commander, Joseph Hooker, had reorganized and revitalized the Army of the Potomac, while the threat of foreign intervention was fast receding. Reports from Britain of massive demonstrations of popular support for the cause of emancipation both planted and nourished this optimism. "The people of England—the millions of the middle and lower classes of society—begin to speak on the questions of the American War and American Slavery in a tone not to be mistaken," the *Tribune* crowed, with reason, for it had urged emancipation on just this basis. Moreover, the unenfranchised masses had "an unrecognized but substantial veto on foreign wars." There would be no hostile intervention by Great Britain, despite the "unfriendly declarations" in Parliament. The proclamation had secured the Union from that danger.[38] This was not an argument the *Herald* accepted. Having roundly condemned the final proclamation in January, it attributed the increasing security from foreign meddling to the Polish rebellion against Russia. Once more Europe was threatened with turmoil, either from eruptions by other revolutionary nationalists, perhaps in Italy or Hungary, or from difficulties between Russia and European powers sympathetic to the Poles. Here was the "Counter Check to French Intervention," and also to British.[39] Yet these two explanations were by no means mutually exclusive, as the moderate *Times* pointed out. Conceding the good effect the proclamation had had in Europe, it concluded that the outbreak of the Polish revolution "has opportunely cooperated with this to make it impossible for any monarch or ministry in Europe to interfere against us, in favor of Slavery, without the imminent hazard of overthrow at home."[40]

Mounting confidence encouraged a new freedom of action in the Union's response to the assistance some Britons were affording the rebellion. Earlier, extreme language had not been accompanied by extreme measures. Now the proposal empowering the president to issue letters of marque was again taken up in Congress, and this time it passed. The bill's sponsor had not sought to disguise its intent, which was to discourage blockade-running out of Nassau and the construction of Confederate warships in Britain. Reports that additional commerce raiders and two ironclads were being built there for the South had infuriated and alarmed Northerners, and the Chambers of Commerce petitioned Congress to make this drastic response. Unavailingly, Sumner opposed it in the Senate, repeating the arguments that had proved effective several months before. Nor was he any more successful with procedural devices. He failed to have it referred to an unfriendly committee and was defeated in a last-ditch effort to render it innocuous through amendment. By March 2 both Houses had approved the bill.[41]

Seward showed himself eager to employ the weapon of privateering, confident that the suspicions the British harboured of Napoleon and their concern about the political instability of Europe would check any dangerous response. Here was an opportunity to take a dramatic step in defence of American commerce and force the critics of his "Dirt-Eating Diplomacy" to swallow their words. He drafted several pages of regulations for letters of marque, which were printed and submitted to the cabinet for approval, and made enquiries in New York to find out whether merchants there would fit out privateers. Before long he was able to inform Welles that he had received applications from several responsible persons and expected many more. Seward's alacrity drove Sumner into a frantic burst of activity. Letters to Cobden, Bright, and Argyll warned of the dangerous temper of the American public and the seriousness of this crisis. "I try to tranquilize the sentiment, but I clearly see that, as events now stand, all who talk peace will be powerless," he warned his British friends. He carried his objections to privateering and his fears of a rupture with Britain to the president, who invited him to present them to the cabinet. As ever, Sumner shied away from a direct confrontation with Seward. Instead, he turned to Bates and Welles who carried the burden of opposition within the cabinet. It was an uphill struggle, for Chase strongly sided with the secretary of state and Blair and Lincoln tended to agree with them. Seward almost made a convert of the secretary of the navy. He allowed him to read the latest despatches from Adams which suggested that the British would fail to prevent the departure of vessels intended for the Confederacy. However, Welles suppressed his anger and resisted the temptation to support Seward, for he agreed with Sumner that a conflict with Britain would follow the commissioning of privateers. The upshot would be the foreign intervention that Unionists were congratulating themselves they had escaped. Anyway, perhaps the threat of privateering would be sufficient to induce a change in British policy. Meanwhile, unsure of the outcome in the cabinet, Sumner made the debate a public one. He sent an open letter to the Chambers of Commerce and inspired worried leading articles in the *Tribune*, the *New York Evening Post*, and the *National Intelligencer*. Uneasily, Northerners contemplated the possibility of war with Britain. Hence there was a sigh of relief when the news reached the Union that the British government had in fact detained one of the vessels being built for the South. As the *Tribune* observed on April 22, and the *New York Times* repeated the observation on the following day, "There is reason, therefore, to hope that the aid hitherto furnished to the rebel cause, from England, is at an end so far as a navy is concerned."[42] The need to issue letters of marque was now even more questionable, although they remained a useful threat to hold in reserve.

Sumner had recommended that agents and attorneys be sent off to Britain to institute legal proceedings and to do in and out of court what the British government ought to be doing on its own initiative. This policy was quietly implemented. Operating in great secrecy, Chase and Welles despatched a pair of agents to buy up or acquire a share of warlike vessels that might otherwise fall into Confederate hands. They were empowered to borrow £1 million from Baring Brothers in London, secured by $10 million of a new issue of American bonds. Acting independently but in consultation with them was a special Treasury agent, Robert Walker. A veteran politician and schemer, he was sent off by Chase to boost British confidence in the strength of Union finances and undermine their faith in the credit of the South. The reported success in London of a recently announced Confederate loan gave urgency to this task. William M. Evarts also journeyed to England to do all he could, in cooperation with British lawyers, "to arrest the guilty vessels." Evarts was an eminent counsel and a friend of Seward's. With Richard H. Dana Jr. he had recently represented the government before the Supreme Court in the Prize Cases, though the star of the proceedings had clearly been Dana. His was the only argument for the government the Supreme Court reporter chose to print, and it persuaded a bare majority of the justices of the legality of the president's action in proclaiming a blockade of the South before Congress recognized the existence of a state of war. It had been an extremely important decision and victory, made possible by Bates's astuteness in delaying the hearing until Lincoln had had time to appoint three Republican justices. Had the court found the blockade illegal it would have placed the Union in an impossible position before the world, Dana had observed to his friend Charles Francis Adams.[43]

There was something more than inordinate vanity, then, in Sumner's boast to a British friend at the end of April that his policy had at last prevailed. Letters of marque had not been issued, though the news from Britain of the detention of the *Alexandra* had probably been as important a factor in the withholding of them as the senator's arguments and lobbying. Instead, more collateral missions had gone off to Britain. But apart from Evarts these agents were neither appointed by Seward nor responsible to him. The implications were clear enough. With the president's support Seward had retained his office in December and had consolidated his position by skilful handling of the French proposal. However, he no longer wielded the influence he once had in the government and his grip on its foreign policy had been loosened. Not that he was powerless. To the chagrin of Welles, Bates, and Sumner, he won Lincoln's support for the release of captured foreign mail. This long-simmering issue finally came to the boil over the mailbag carried by the *Peterhoff*. She had been seized by a Federal cruiser on suspicion of carrying contraband. The mailbag was opened by a prize commissioner, but he did not tamper with the sealed packages. Fearful of trouble with Britain, Seward ordered the mail returned to the British authorities. A month later Welles was instructed to direct naval commanders to forward captured mail to their neutral destination. Clearly, unlike his Confederate counterpart, Seward was not an international nullity.[44]

Victory after victory on the battlefield had failed to bring the foreign intervention vital to the successful establishment of the Confederacy. Diplomatic defeat proved as demoralizing to the South as military reverses had to the North. "Hope after hope has gone out in darkness, and expectations we had fondly cherished have turned out to be miserable delusions," the *Charleston Daily Courier* admitted in November 1862. "Our foe is as active and determined and powerful as he ever was, and the agent that was to compel foreign nations to intervene and put an end to this wicked and infamous contest, has not been potent enough to accomplish that end."[45] The flicker of excitement produced by Gladstone's speech at Newcastle was quickly extinguished by that of Lewis. There was a suspicion that he had been "put forth to modify the statements and rectify the rather rash admissions" of the chancellor. Moreover, it was all too easy to read into Lewis's remarks at Hereford the dismal prospect of Britain withholding recognition of the South until the North had granted it. Reluctant as many Southerners were to admit that England had settled upon "so heartless a course," they found little to reassure them in her subsequent conduct. The failure of Lyons to signal any change of policy on his return to the United States, the "Historicus" letters in *The Times,* and the British government's rejection of the French armistice proposal, all tended to confirm that she planned to persist with her "strict neutrality" until "the exhaustion of one or both of the belligerents determined the result."[46] Those two "old painted mummies, Russell and Palmerston," were publicly roasted for having totalled up the pounds and pence of feeding the impoverished millions of Lancashire, and the cost of a war with the United States, thus following the path of "cold-blooded selfishness." Privately, in a letter to his friend William Gregory, the influential W. Porcher Miles reviled "that little perverse and narrow minded scion of the House of Bedford," Russell. Forgetting the assistance they did receive from the British, for which of course they paid, Confederates warned that the Palmerston government's policy was fast engendering a profound bitterness towards that nation. Next to the North, the *Richmond Whig* declared, "we have a right to hate them more than any other Government upon earth."[47]

In his message to the Confederate Congress, Jefferson Davis studiously refrained from deepening the public enmity toward Britain. He did deliver "some eloquent reproaches of England and France for the maintenance of their neutrality," repeating the familiar Confederate complaint that as defined by them it gave an unfair advantage to the Union.[48] Yet he was careful to close on a high note. He found in the published correspondence of Russia, Britain, and France concerning Napoleon's armistice proposal "a gratifying advance in the appreciation by those Governments of the true interest of mankind as involved in the war on this continent." Neither Britain nor Russia had controverted "the clear and direct intimation" in the language of the French note that the Confederacy was able to maintain its independence. Clearly the South's claim to "its just place" in the family of nations could not long be denied.[49]

Less dignified, less calm, and certainly far less optimistic were those Southerners in and out of Congress who were again demanding the expulsion of the foreign consuls and the recall of the Confederate commissioners in Europe. It was an expression of helpless fury. Realizing the Confederacy's inability to effect any change in British policy, they wanted the satisfaction of striking out in retaliation. In their rage they also rounded upon the aliens living among them, especially the British. There were proposals in Congress that they be conscripted, for the South "could not afford to feed these drones in the hive." The idea that such a decision would offend foreign nations was dismissed as "absurd." Anyway, what "considerable right" had foreign nations to say, after having submitted to the "illegal" blockade of Southern ports, that their citizens should remain within the Confederacy's limits to the injury of its cause?[50] Congress had declined to legislate aliens into the army, but this did not prevent substantial numbers of them being enrolled. Although the Confederate authorities disclaimed any intention to draft foreign nationals except those who had made it clear that they had left their native land never to return, this merely encouraged military officials, anxious not only to obtain recruits but to do something disagreeable to Britain, to lay traps for the unwary. British subjects were required "to sign papers wanted for their lawful pursuits," and were then deprived of their certificates of British nationality on this and a number of other pretexts. Impediments were also placed in the way of their obtaining such documents. Those British subjects living far from the consulates were often denied the affidavits they required from justices in order to obtain certificates by mail. When they attempted to travel in person to the nearest consular office, they were refused the necessary passes by provost marshals. Some were jailed on spurious charges and when released were not awarded any "commiseration" for their hardships. "I have lived 32 consecutive years in despotic countries (from 1826 to 1862) without having witnessed so much frightful, unmitigated, remorseless tyranny any where as what is daily enacted on this continent," one angry and powerless consul wrote to Lyons.[51]

Appeals to the Confederate War Department were rudely rejected and Benjamin declined to help. When the British consul at Richmond wrote to him in February to raise the matter of a Mississippi conscription law which embraced aliens, Benjamin brushed him aside with an ominous enquiry as to the extent of his authority. The Confederate secretary of state asked to see his consular commission, "in order that the precise nature and extent of your functions may be ascertained, before further correspondence can be held with you as Her Majesty's Consul at the Port of Richmond."[52] And when at Lyons's suggestion he obtained an interview with Benjamin, the consul derived little comfort from the meeting. On the contrary, the secretary frankly admitted that he was retaliating for the reception accorded Mason in London. In France Slidell had been received unofficially as the acknowledged representative of a belligerent power but Russell had kept Mason at arm's length.[53]

After two years of triumph and hardship the Confederacy was still in existence. Benjamin no less than most other Southerners resented Britain's refusal to recognize what they regarded as the established fact of their independence, and he sensed that the chance of her intervening was remote at best. It was a judgment he founded upon a close reading of the Northern press, for he was still labouring under the handicap of infrequent and inadequate communications with the Confederacy's representatives overseas. Eventually a reasonably secure and regular system was established. Despatches were sent by Mason and Slidell to the Confederate agent at Nassau and were forwarded by him on blockade-runners. Simultaneously Benjamin accepted in a modified form a proposal made by George N. Sanders. A notorious political adventurer who had contracted with the Navy Department for the construction of six ironclads in Britain, Sanders offered to carry despatches on fast, shallow draft vessels to and from Halifax, where they could be placed aboard the regular British transatlantic steamers. The first courier was one of Sanders's sons, both of whom he planned to employ in order to protect them from the perils of military service. The other was earmarked for the post of dispatch agent at Halifax. Furloughed from the army, Major Reid Sanders set out to run the blockade. Unaccountably, he chose to take passage on a sailing vessel instead of a waiting steamer, and then failed to destroy his despatches when she was caught by a Federal warship. They were soon published in the Northern press, much to the Confederate government's embarrassment. The disclosure of the British contract for six ironclads, including the names of the firms, caused that project to fall through. Benjamin's captured correspondence made no less interesting reading. He was sharply critical of Russell and darkly suspicious of the French emperor. He announced to Slidell the expulsion of the French consular agent at Galveston for behaviour which had given rise to the suspicion that his imperial master was scheming to detach Texas from the Confederacy. This note set Southern heads shaking in dismay and tongues wagging in criticism. Benjamin was attacked for his "imputations" against the emperor as well as for his employment of such an incompetent messenger.[54]

Opportunist that he was, Benjamin had authorized Slidell to inform the British of this "secret attempt on the part of France to obtain separate advantage of such vast magnitude" in North America. Would the knowledge "induce a change in the views" of the Palmerston government, finally convincing it that the establishment of a Confederacy strong enough to counterbalance the Union and French imperialism was in Britain's "true interests?"[55] It was a faint even forlorn hope, as Benjamin well knew. Nothing he read in the Northern press or belatedly received from his agents in Europe gave him any cause for genuine optimism regarding Britain's course. He did respond to the news of the French armistice proposal, and its rejection by Britain and Russia, with a long restatement of the commercial advantages the Europeans would obtain even from a limited cessation of hostilities. He estimated that during the first six months of peace the Confederacy would import goods to the value of $300 million and export cotton worth no less. Only the reestablishment of normal commercial relations with Europe prior to a final settlement of the conflict would prevent the United States from using its proximity to the Confederacy to monopolize this vast and profitable trade. Attractive as it sounded, Benjamin had little faith in this inducement. He feared that there was a "settled determination" among the European powers to "overlook any aggression on their rights" by the United States.[56]

Although he had long ceased to expect much from Europe, especially the British, Benjamin resisted the strong temptation to humour a public clamouring for the recall of Mason if not of Slidell. Earlier he had urged Mason to remain at his difficult post "for the purpose of correcting false opinions, disseminating favorable impressions of our Government and people, as well as for affording a common center or rallying point" for the Confederacy's British sympathizers. Benjamin did not withdraw him from London, while keeping Slidell in Paris, for fear that such a step "would probably cause serious interference with the success of the preparations now nearly completed for the purchase of the articles so much needed in the further prosecution of the war."[57] In short, the Confederacy was reluctant to antagonize the British government or to do anything at this time that might encourage it to cut off the flow of supplies and seize the ironclads nearing completion at Birkenhead. The Navy Department's agents in England had already expressed apprehension that obstacles might be placed in the way of the vessels' departure. At the request of the uneasy Mallory, Benjamin wrote to Mason and Slidell urging them to cooperate in arranging for the transfer of the ironclads to France "if such a course should become necessary."[58] So, for the time being, Mason remained in London.

Unable to make any theatrical gesture of retaliation against Britain, Benjamin struggled to break the stranglehold she had on the Confederacy's chances of international recognition. He attempted to broaden the South's diplomatic horizons. A. Dudley Mann was empowered to initiate communications with the Dutch government. Lucius Q. C. Lamar was appointed commissioner to Russia, and in January he set off on his long journey there in search of recognition. But the Russian response to the French proposal had rendered the mission futile before it was undertaken. Then in the spring Slidell was appointed special commissioner to Spain, replacing Pierre Rost who had returned to the South several months before. By offering to guarantee Spain's retention of Cuba, Davis and Benjamin hoped to coax her into taking the lead in recognizing the Confederacy. However, when he received no encouragement to visit Madrid, Slidell remained in Paris.[59] Spain had not changed her position, but would continue to follow Britain and France. Reduced to clutching at straws, among them the belief that the force of public opinion and its pressure in Parliament would compel the British government to intervene, Benjamin increased Henry Hotze's budget. Additional funds were also made available to Edwin DeLeon, who was encouraged to extend his field of operations to the press of central Europe.[60] And it was political rather than financial desperation that impelled the Confederate government to enter into an agreement with the prominent French banking house of Erlanger.

By the autumn of 1862 the Confederacy had at last begun to implement the policy initiated by Benjamin at the beginning of the year, to use cotton to establish its international credit. Cotton certificates were to be sold in Europe, specifying a price of fivepence a pound. Although not obliged to honour the certificates until peace was made, for a premium the Confederacy was willing to deliver the cotton to a port in its possession, so long as the holder agreed to pay the cost of transportation. He could then take his chances in running the blockade. Mason confidently forecast that this scheme would bring in as much as £5 million and it was at his suggestion that James Spence was appointed to supervise the sale both of cotton certificates and of cotton bonds. Certain that in this way the Confederacy's agents would be provided with sufficient funds to purchase supplies and build vessels, Benjamin responded coolly at first to Erlanger's offer to float a loan secured with cotton. As he and his colleagues quickly perceived, it was less a loan than a cotton purchase scheme and at prices which guaranteed the French banker a huge profit. Nevertheless, a deal was struck with the agents the banker sent to Richmond, though on terms somewhat less favourable to Erlanger than those he had provisionally negotiated with Slidell. The Confederate government's motive in signing the contract was frankly political. Benjamin was grasping at the lifeline Slidell had proffered when he urged acceptance of the Erlanger proposal, promising that "even in anticipation of its acceptance the very strongest influence will be enlisted in our favor."[61]

With all hope of British intervention fading if not gone, anything that might persuade the French to act alone in America could not be overlooked. But this was the faintest glimmer of light in the gloom enveloping the Confederacy. Provisions were in such short supply that there was talk in March of disbanding part of the army and Congress was obliged to enact a sweeping measure authorizing their impressment. Never had the need for foreign intervention been greater and the prospects so remote. Deeply involved in Mexico, Napoleon had been further distracted by the events in Poland and Hungary. "Neither England [n]or France will have anything to do with us," a disconsolate aide to Jefferson Davis remarked. "England is afraid of Lincoln and privateering, and France is too busy in Europe to be able to pay attention to America."[62]

As they surveyed the wreckage of the Confederacy's foreign policy, few Southerners surrendered to despair or responded to the occasional calls for peace. While it had been the assurance of foreign intervention that had helped to carry them so confidently into secession and war, the residents of the South had invested too much in the struggle simply to abandon it now that all hope of international assistance had faded. Although the disadvantages under which they fought had become far more daunting, Southerners took fresh heart from the reports of disaffection in the northwest. If it degenerated into disloyalty the South would yet emerge triumphant. "A core of diplomatists, of sharp shooters of the brain, to take up and weave into shape the tangled elements of Northwestern politics, could do more to win us bloodless victories, weaken our enemies, and lift the mist from the horizon of the Confederacy's future, than many battalions of infantry, artillery, and cavalry," was one characteristic comment.[63] Above all, Vicksburg must be held. Confederates, no less than Unionists, realized that possession of this city was crucial to the development of western sectionalism. So long as the Confederacy held Vicksburg and kept the Mississippi closed to western traffic the anger of this region's residents would continue to mount and their alienation from the Union grow.[64]

By the spring of 1863 the South had accepted defeat in its battle for foreign support. If the Union's international position was at last relatively secure, to what extent could the "wise macaw," his wings finally clipped, claim credit? Without doubt, Seward had played a vital role during the first year of war. His spirited and at times threatening conduct during the early, confused weeks of the Lincoln administration had served a purpose. It discouraged the British government from confronting the Union over the "paper blockade" of the Confederacy. Later in the year Seward's behaviour during the tense and dangerous *Trent* affair had been prudent, his advice to the president astute, and his despatch announcing the release of Mason and Slidell a model of its kind. In some respects this was the high point of his influence, popularity, and diplomatic effectiveness. The treaty to suppress the slave trade was a considerable achievement, but the British made most of the running on this important agreement. The persistence with which Seward pursued a withdrawal of European recognition of Confederate belligerency went unrewarded. The conciliatory face he showed the British throughout 1862, despite the public anger their conduct aroused, helped reduce tension but neither it nor his warnings that interference in the conflict would precipitate emancipation were central to their decision to keep their distance.

Palmerston and Russell were concerned that intervention might be seen as a repudiation of their country's antislavery tradition, but this was more a matter of appearance than of principle. Unquestionably Britain's hand was stayed also by the desire to strike only in absolute safety. Union retaliation against Canada would offer Napoleon an opportunity for fresh mischief in Europe, and as the war continued it was Americans in general rather than Seward in particular who exercised this restraining influence. By the winter of 1863 Russell could join with Lyons in welcoming the outcome of the cabinet crisis following Fredericksburg because Seward was regarded as more pacific than anyone likely to replace him. Moreover, if, as many Americans believed, the danger of foreign meddling had been removed by emancipation and the political turmoil in Europe the secretary could claim but a small measure of the credit. After all, he had been an opponent of the proclamation and he had not created the troubles that distracted the European nations. He had grasped from the very outset the importance of European affairs to the outcome of the diplomatic struggle with the Confederacy, and had acted accordingly in the spring of 1861. But the timely events of 1862–63 were simply the Union's good fortune.

EIGHT

The Friends of the North

IN THE ARMY OF ANTISLAVERY few soldiers had served with more loyalty and honour than the Evangelicals, although not without division in the ranks. When the annual meeting of the Evangelical Alliance opened at the Freemasons' Hall in London in October 1862, the secretary reported that the Paris branch was drafting an address to the American brethren, affirming its belief that the Northern states represented the cause of liberty, freedom, and Christian civilization. The ensuing discussion exposed the lack of agreement within the alliance on this vital question. For some, abhorrence of slavery was overlaid by alarm at the possible consequences of a "total and sudden" emancipation of slaves. Moreover, there was reluctance to enter into a political question which might open the door to others. As a result, the alliance responded equivocally to the call from France for action.[1] There was a similar lack of forthrightness in the position belatedly assumed by the British and Foreign Anti-Slavery Society. At the prodding of a number of visitors to its headquarters, prominent among them Peter Sinclair, a Scottish abolitionist and Union sympathizer who had recently published a book entitled *Freedom or Slavery in the United States*, the society's committee resolved in mid-November to compose an address "sustaining" Lincoln's policy. However, these sincere pacifists could not bring themselves to express approval of the North's military efforts to subdue the South, and the final version of their address "was so obscurely worded that it could be read as a plea to Lincoln to send his armies home."[2]

Seeking an unreserved endorsement of the North, and a more effective organization to counter the activities of the Confederacy's partisans, Sinclair placed "a short pungent appeal" in the *Daily News* and the *Morning Star*, and attended the meeting subsequently held at the Whittington Club.[3] Those who gathered there on November 11, 1862, decided to reorganize the London Emancipation Committee. It had been formed in 1859 by a group of Garrisonians led by F. W. Chesson—a journalist and son-in-law of Britain's famous antislavery orator, George Thompson—but had made little mark. Renamed the London Emancipation Society, it appointed an active executive committee of which William Evans, a stockbroker with extensive holdings in the United States, was elected chairman and Chesson secretary, and recruited members of a much larger general committee. There were few names of note. John Stuart Mill did lend the society some distinction, as did Thomas Hughes, the author of *Tom Brown's Schooldays*. Another prominent figure was Samuel Lucas. The editor of the *Star* had presided over the meeting at the Whittington Club and had donated the first subscription to the new society, while his newspaper guaranteed that it did not want for publicity. This commitment reflected his conviction that the American struggle was "perhaps the most momentous which has taken place in the history of the world." In the success of the Northern states were involved the interests of liberty in Britain and everywhere else, Lucas believed.[4]

As originally described, the aims of the society were "to counteract the alleged sympathy of England with the pro-slavery Confederacy," and "to encourage the Federal Government and people in the prosecution of a thoroughly free-labour policy." What its members sought was an "unequivocal expression of English feeling in favour of the Republican North," for this would sustain the friends of liberty in America and thereby hasten the "satisfactory termination" of a war that was afflicting the Old World as well as devastating the New. To organize public opinion the society resorted to those tried and true techniques of popular agitation exploited so successfully by the Anti-Corn Law League twenty years earlier— pamphlets, lectures, and public meetings. Some activists turned to American friends and the United States government for documents "to give to the press and to the leaders of the people." In the meantime 3,000 copies of a popular pamphlet by Cairnes were purchased and circulated. Eventually the society established a kind of rudimentary wire service for local newspapers in Britain, sending out each week to more than three hundred of them selections from the leading antislavery journals of the United States. But it was to the task of organizing demonstrations all over the country that the society devoted much of its attention and energies. Sinclair spoke at one of the earliest meetings of this kind, held in Hammersmith on

November 13, and "with a most favourable result." The following evening there was another gathering, this one in the London Metropolitan Institute.[5] In this campaign of agitation the most indefatigable trooper was George Thompson, the veteran abolitionist.

By 1861 Thompson had fallen on hard times, with little to exist upon except memories of distant glories. The 1850s had seen his fortunes decline even more precipitously than those of the cause he had served so well. Infirmity and indigence had made him an object of pity and charity. Now, in the winter of 1862–63, his health improved, he was given an opportunity that falls to few men—to repeat the triumphs of the past. On November 13, 1862, he went down to Maidstone to refute Charles Buxton's heresies in that member's own constituency. The meeting concluded with the passage of a resolution which proclaimed that the emancipation policy of the Lincoln administration deserved the support and sympathy of the British people. By the middle of December Thompson was happily informing his friend Garrison of this new lease on life. After a hectic tour of Staffordshire he reported that at every meeting he had encountered large and enthusiastic audiences, and although at each one he had invited Southern sympathizers to come forward "no antagonist appeared."[6]

Fortified by the evidence that the "anti-slavery sentiment" of Britain was at last being "called forth," John Bright threw himself into the fray with a speech at Birmingham in mid-December. Bright flayed the Confederate cause, accusing Southerners of seeking "the power to breed negroes, to work negroes, to lash negroes, to chain negroes, to buy and sell negroes, to deny them the commonest ties of family," or to break their hearts by splitting families. However, his principal purpose was to remind English workingmen of their ties of family, class, and political interest with the North. The two and a half millions of men, women, and children who over the past fifteen years had left the United Kingdom for the United States had made their homes in the free states, Bright declared, and there six millions of grown men were not "excluded from the Constitution of their country and their electoral franchise" as they were in Britain. "My countrymen who work for your living, remember this," he implored, "there will be one wild shriek of freedom to startle all mankind, if that American Republic should be overthrown."[7]

The need to identify the working people, especially the cotton operatives, with the Union cause did not escape the Emancipation

Society, as preparations were made for an outpouring of British support for the final Proclamation of Emancipation. Ministers of all denominations were requested to give prominence to it in services held at the beginning of the New Year, and public meetings were organized in London, Manchester, and Sheffield. The demonstration to be held in Manchester's Free Trade Hall was intended to be the centre-piece of these celebrations of the "last day of slavery."[8] The reports of the opening of the relief subscription in New York, which some observers were predicting would raise as much as $1 million, had created a favourable climate of opinion. A memorial from the "working men of Lancashire" to President Lincoln would be a propaganda triumph, a "just rebuke to the mean feeling of so great a portion of the public on this momentous subject."[9] The meeting was carefully planned by members of the Union and Emancipation Society of Manchester, which had been formed in 1861 and was soon to affiliate formally with the London group. The address and resolutions were drafted by one of its members, while two others, leaders of the local cooperative movement, were asked to move and second them in order to maintain the fiction that this was a working-class gathering. Then, in the week before the meeting, Manchester was flooded with handbills giving extracts from the indiscreet speech of the Confederate vice-president, in which he had conceded that slavery was the cornerstone of the new state. This handbill invariably appeared in those towns where demonstrations were being organized. Nor was it uncommon for the proceedings to be opened with the reading of alleged extracts from Southern newspapers advocating the reopening of the slave trade and even the establishment of white slavery. As one Union partisan informed Seward, "this has roused the labouring classes here especially to go in for the North."[10]

The Free Trade Hall was packed with six thousand people on the evening of December 31, 1862, most of them "respectable" in dress and appearance. The "fortuitous" discovery that the mayor was in the audience, "formally attired," led to his selection as chairman. One of the city's wealthiest men spoke, as did a distinguished barrister, but those who addressed the meeting were "for the most part" workingmen. In the name of "the working people and others of the city," the gathering duly expressed its fraternal sentiments for and rejoiced in the greatness of the American president, honoured the free states as the happy abode of the working millions, and voiced its "warm and earnest sympathy" for them now that they were committed to the abolition of slavery. How much good this demonstration would do the Union cause in Britain remained to be seen, Consul Henry Lord reported to Seward on the following day, "but the Free Trade Hall has its prestige and it has never yet been filled with such an audience as convened there last night, without creating an influence that made its mark on the times." Certainly this spectacular triumph of careful organization helped obscure subsequent failures in Lancashire. When George Thompson ventured into the predominantly spinning region of the county in the spring of 1863 even the power of his oratory failed to prevent the passage of resolutions sympathetic to the South.[11] That these setbacks did not prove troublesome was due to the skill with which supporters of the North distracted the public with a series of well-staged, eye-catching successes.

That same New Year's Eve had seen an assembly in Roebuck's Sheffield resolve that it was England's duty "to give her sympathy and moral influence to the northern States, to disapprove of the origin and continuance of the slave-owners' rebellion, and by all peaceable means to try to cement a closer and stronger union" between Britain and the government and people of the United States. No less satisfying and symbolic was a victory over James Spence in Liverpool, where some of the city's "best merchants" gathered "to consider what steps should be taken to bring the policy of the American Government on the slavery question fairly before the public mind." Spence attempted to head off any expression of sympathy for the Union, and failed. The meeting adopted, with only two dissentient votes, a resolution to the effect that the Federal government was entitled to "the generous sympathy" of the British people. Then, on January 29, two other large rallies were held, one in Bradford and the second in London. The crowd, much of it identified as working-class, was so large at the London meeting that it spilled out of Exeter Hall into the Strand, where members of the Emancipation Society organized "impromptu" speeches and the simultaneous passage of the resolutions being moved inside—that the purpose of the Southern revolt was not merely to maintain but to extend slavery, and that Englishmen should support the Union and its policy of emancipation. Against this background the pro-Union *Spectator* was quick to contend that "the masses of the people all over England—including especially the districts suffering most heavily from the war—are nearly as unanimous in sympathizing with the North as is the opinion of the wealthier classes in favour of the Slave States."[12] A marked change in the editorial policy of two newspapers that professed to speak for the working class—*Reynolds's* and the *Bee-Hive*—lent some credence to this sweeping claim.

With his proclamation the American president had "to a great extent redeemed the errors of the past," *Reynolds's* announced, and had ensured that his name would forever be associated "with one of the most humane and thoroughly Christian measures that had ever been decreed by the rulers of the earth, or sanctioned by the legislatures of nations." The abolition of slavery, "and the admission to the privileges of human beings of four millions of blacks," were well worth the risk of a repetition of the horrors of St. Dominique. If *Reynolds's* had a criticism of Lincoln it was that he had not gone far enough, a reservation George Thompson voiced privately.[13] The *Bee-Hive* took a little longer to change course, but change it did when a newly elected board of directors dismissed editor George Troup in January 1863. Support for the North in its struggle on behalf of human freedom, publicity for the activities of the Emancipation Society, denunciations of the South, slavery, and their "effete" aristocratic British supporters were now the order of the day.[14]

The standard of emancipation, raised by Lincoln and paraded so cleverly in Britain by the London society and its provincial allies, was one to which most Radicals and many Liberals were prepared to rally. Their earlier divisions on the American war were put aside, and in a city like Leeds, with a long evangelical and antislavery tradition, local leaders of these two political groupings were at last able to share the same public platform. Not that the alliance was always comfortable, particularly when both the more advanced Liberals and the Radicals tied freedom for the slave to the cause of political reform in Britain, as Bright had done at Birmingham and did again at Rochdale in February. Similarly Goldwin Smith, his own doubts about the American struggle swept away by emancipation, proclaimed that the Union cause was not that of the negro alone, but of civilization, Christian morality, the rights of labour, and the rights of man. Together with Mill, Bright, Hughes, and others he worked for support of the North and the extension of the franchise.[15] Writing in the *Bee-Hive*, Prof. E. S. Beesly declared that "This American war has made apparent the profound chasm between the upper and lower classes. The struggle for political rights on the part of English labourers will be worthily inaugurated by their disinterested and generous protest on behalf of the enslaved labourers of America."[16] But although this association was often made, the demonstrations in support of the Union continued to take place under the umbrella of antislavery. It alone protected the Liberals' fragile unity on the American war. "It is good generalship in politics as it is in war not to bring all your enemies upon you at once, but to divide them, and fall upon each division apart from the rest," Mill advised a member of the Manchester branch of the society.[17]

The men "who have taken hold of this matter are good agitators," Thomas Dudley remarked admiringly, "and will continue the fight." Their skill was evident not only in the number of these "manifestations of the popular feeling," but in the timing of them. Late January and early February, 1863, brought demonstration after demonstration, in Scotland and Wales as well as across the length and breadth of England. Densely crowded and "sublimely enthusiastic" assemblies were held, and resolutions passed "all but unanimously," in places as far apart and as dissimilar as grimy Salford and rural Cobham. In Lancashire, meetings ostensibly convened to express appreciation for the aid shipped on the *George Griswold* and two other vessels quickly turned into antislavery gatherings. The cities witnessed a number of monster demonstrations. There were several in and around London, of which the highlight was that at Exeter Hall. Another assembly of Liverpool's residents, much larger than the earlier one, was held. Three thousand people turned out in Leicester while four thousand attended the Bradford meeting chaired by W. E. Forster, and two of the four resolutions they adopted deprecated any British intervention, moral no less than physical, on behalf of the "slave power." Clearly the crescendo of agitation was calculated to impress members of Parliament as they prepared for the new session which opened in February. As early as December Bright had privately predicted that an "uprising of antislavery feeling" would prevent any "serious attempt at mischief when Parl[ia-men]t meets." "This anti-slavery movement is assuming gigantic proportions," George Thompson informed Garrison. Wisely and energetically conducted, it "will be of vital importance in this country." "It will teach a salutary lesson to our public men," he predicted, and "will mould the decisions of our government." Even "the most audacious Secessionists" in Parliament or the press would now fear to propose recognition of the "confederated Slave States," the *Daily News* confidently proclaimed.[18]

The significance of what was taking place in Britain was not lost upon the Union's representatives there. "Agitation helps us and injures the South," Dudley observed succinctly. Even life in Liverpool became more tolerable, for there appeared to be less bitterness towards the North and a greater disposition to "listen" to the Union's case. In Dudley's opinion the question of intervention had been settled so far as Britain was concerned. "The Government will not dare however much disposed," he concluded.[19] Although he lacked this depth of assurance and was by nature more restrained, Charles Francis Adams was nonetheless cheered and relieved by the stream of popular addresses inundating the legation. His burden of worry was at last beginning to lighten, even though there seemed to be no end to the demoralizing military news from home. "It is quite clear that the current is now setting pretty strongly with us among the body of people," he wrote in his diary. "This may be quite useful on the approach of the session of Parliament." Particularly encouraging in this regard was the decision of two cabinet ministers "to speak with a less uncertain sound."[20] Argyll attacked not only slavery but also the Southern Episcopal Church for its willingness to see a nation founded upon that institution, in his presidential address to the National Bible Society. These remarks clearly implied support for the campaign being waged across the face of Britain. Thomas Milner Gibson's comments to his Ashton constituents were even more pointed. "I don't believe that an empire having slavery as its basis can be a prosperous, happy, and enduring empire," he declared, "and therefore cannot desire to see one established in any part of the world." The cumulative effect of "this development of sentiment is to annihilate all agitation for recognition," Adams noted, "and to keep my position more quiet than ever before."[21]

Discreetly, Unionists sought to offer aid and encouragement to their British friends. Adams agreed to give the Emancipation Society £100, so long as the donation was kept secret. However, when a member of the committee blurted out the news of the gift at a public meeting it could no longer be made for fear that the society would be dismissed as a creature of the American minister. Thus all that Adams was able to do personally was to meet with the delegations bearing addresses who streamed into the legation, even though he grew a little irritated with these constant interruptions and was uneasy about the propriety of frequent identification with such activities.[22] He did send Benjamin Moran to Manchester to deliver to the mayor Lincoln's typically graceful reply to the address voted on New Year's Eve. The president deeply deplored the suffering of the Manchester workingmen, victims of the attempt to overthrow a government founded upon human rights in order to establish one raised upon human slavery. "Under these circumstances," Lincoln wrote, "I cannot but regard your decisive utterance upon the question as an instance of sublime Christian heroism which has not been surpassed in any age or in any country."[23]

The torrent of resolutions flowing from Britain prompted an effort by Lincoln to channel English opinion. He drafted a resolution which he hoped public meetings in Britain would adopt. Forwarded to Bright by Charles Sumner, it summoned Christian and civilized men everywhere to resist to the utmost, by all lawful means, any recognition of the "embryo" state whose fundamental object was to maintain, enlarge, and perpetuate human slavery. It was never used, for as one contemporary explained it would have been ridiculed as implying that the war's purpose was no more than to keep slavery within existing bounds.[24]

The limitations of Lincoln's policy had not escaped the members of the Emancipation Society, but they had deliberately glossed them over. Hence their concern when they heard that the noted American abolitionist, Wendell Phillips, who had been unsparing in his censure of the Lincoln administration, was thinking of coming to their aid. Chesson hurriedly wrote to an American associate to explain that the society had made "a generous allowance" for defects which appeared to stem from "the very nature of things," and had not "cared to afford even incidental assistance to the enemies of human liberty" who would have rejoiced at any admission that the United States "was indifferent to the cause of Emancipation." All of which the society urged Phillips to bear in mind should he decide to visit Britain. Instead, he sent Moncure Daniel Conway, who was both the son of a slaveholder and a Southern abolitionist, and thus a doubly attractive spokesman. Conway was to be disappointed by what he found in Britain—an antislavery sentiment by no means as deep as he had supposed and a widespread conviction that blacks were "hopelessly" inferior.[25] But this merely serves to re-emphasize the achievement of the Emancipation Society and its allies, many of them dissenting ministers, in getting up so many demonstrations during the winter and spring of 1863.

Another measure of the society's effectiveness was the abuse to which it was subjected by organs of the establishment. The *Morning Post* uneasily complained of the tendency "in a small but highly respectable section of our fellow countrymen to run wild on the question of American slavery." This problem needed to be put on "a right footing," for the attempts to identify the cause of abolition with the triumph of Northern arms were "not creditable to English common-sense." Why was there no discussion of the fact that Lincoln's proclamation had been a war measure, that slavery had not been abolished in the Union, and that brutal discrimination was the lot of free blacks there? The reason for the renewed activity of the antislavery movement was the inability of the North's partisans to justify its war on the South, cynics charged. The members and supporters of the society were dismissed as "Dissenting preachers and second-rate littérateurs," and denounced as Radicals, ex-Chartists, Socialists, vendors of infidel publications, religious fanatics, and irreligious fanatics. With the exceptions of Mill and Forster, they were nobodies, "self-elected representatives of anti-slavery," "the three tailors of Tooley Street," "professional spouters" indulging in a "Carnival of cant" and in the pay of the North.[26] In that case, the *Daily News* asked, after a particularly harsh attack by *The Times*, "Why should our contemporary be so indignant with the Emancipation Society if it is really so contemptible?"[27]

The most serious charge brought against this "little knot of illustrious nobodies" was that they were lending British support to "an undisguised summons to servile war." Yet even this terrible accusation no longer carried quite the same conviction or excited the same public response. Months had passed since Lincoln's preliminary proclamation and there had been no hint of a slave uprising. This was a point the North's partisans drove home during the celebration of Charles Buxton's re-entry into the fold. Appearing at a meeting of the British and Foreign Anti-Slavery Society, this "gentleman of gentile sentiments, limp liberalism and fluent philanthropy" confessed that he had been wrong to fear that Lincoln's action would excite a slave revolt. Instead, the negroes had exhibited a wonderful patience and forbearance, and had endured cruel suffering and bitter trials in order to make their way to the Federal flag of freedom. Flight not rebellion had been their response. It was impossible to look at the United States without being optimistic about the ultimate abolition of slavery, Buxton declared.[28]

The Confederates in Britain were slow to recognize the danger of the Emancipation Society's activities. For obvious reasons they were more anxious to chronicle the decline of the antislavery movement. Its enfeebled condition had long been evident, and this, together with the initial British response to Lincoln's proclamation and the failure of the North to attract the support of the movement's "shining lights," reassured them that they had little to fear in this quarter. Even when Buxton moved into the camp of the North's sympathizers, neither Shaftesbury nor Wilberforce's son accompanied him. On the contrary, privately they admitted to Southern sympathies. There was an irresistible temptation simply to repeat the jeers of such influential and representative organs as *The Times*. "All persons of social and political respectability have held aloof," Hotze assured Benjamin, and in the *Index* he reprinted the attacks by the English press on "the very small dogs who have taken possession of the old lion's den."[29]

Underestimating their opponents, buoyed by the news of the Union's defeat at Fredericksburg and the Republicans' setback at the polls, cheered by the audacity of Bright's fellow member of Parliament for Birmingham in coming out strongly for recognition of the Confederacy at a joint constituency meeting, Southerners and their British friends began to plan for the forthcoming session of Parliament. To them this seemed to be an ideal time to press for the recognition of the Confederacy. The reports of the attempt to drive Seward from the Federal cabinet convinced Mason that the Lincoln administration was "in process of disintegration." The "dykes are broken, the floods let in, and the waters of discord will do the rest," he wrote to William Gregory at the beginning of the New Year. Mason, Lord Campbell, and James Spence all urged Gregory, as the South's ablest champion in the House, to return early to London "to perfect a thorough organization & push the matter this time to a vote."[30] They had an ally in Frank Lawley, whose reports to *The Times* were intended to spur British intervention. He dwelt upon the heroism and indomitable spirit of the Confederates, and thus the futile carnage of battle. "Death, nothing but death everywhere," he wrote of Fredericksburg, "great masses of bodies tossed out of the churches as sufferers expired; layers of corpses stretched in the balconies of houses as though taking a siesta. In one yard a surgeon's block for operating was still standing, and, more appalling to look at even than the bodies of the dead, piles of arms and legs, amputated as soon as their owners had been carried off the field, were heaped in a corner." How long would Christian Britain and France stand aside and allow this to continue, he asked.[31]

From the relative warmth of Nice, which he naturally had little inclination to forsake prematurely for the cold winter fogs of London, Gregory counselled his fellow partisans of the South to pursue a policy of "wait and watch." They accepted his advice, even though they were not entirely convinced by those of his arguments which rested upon the North's "dilapidation." Western alienation and the desire for peace would spread and grow if left alone, Gregory asserted, but British intervention, even the "empty compliment" of recognition without interference, would surely reunite the North "under the cry of resistance to British insolence, domination & so on." Furthermore, the fear lingered in Parliament that the members of the Lincoln administration would welcome a pretext for war with Britain "as an excuse for their failures and a cloak for their discredit." Among the Jeremiahs was the venerable Edward Ellice, who worried about the danger to Canada in the event of British action. He urged Gregory to dissuade the South's friends from committing suicide with a motion to recognize the Confederacy. And when he returned home, Gregory found another reason for inaction. "I must not also conceal from you," he wrote to his friend William Porcher Miles, "that Bright and other agitators have had of late considerable success among the working classes in raising up the antislavery agitation." Gregory doubted the devotion of this class to the cause of the negro but not their anxiety to protect "ultra democratic institutions" from "a patent failure." As a result, for the government "to take part with the South would expose it to great risks and loss of support in the large towns." Unless provoked by some Union outrage, he went on, it would not act.[32]

Unwilling to bestir himself, Gregory was undoubtedly seeking reasons to justify his inactivity and the string of demonstrations in support of the Union provided him with a convenient excuse. Yet it was not one that had a hollow ring. While there was little evidence of a massive shift in middle and working-class opinion on the American war, the meetings had been numerous and often impressively large. The prominent roles given to workingmen had not deceived many observers, who noted the strong middle-class element among the organizers and in the audiences. Some of the former and more of the latter were enfranchised, and both were evidently of a Liberal if not Radical persuasion. In short, those who were demonstrating in support of the Union tended to be political supporters or allies of a government which was far too insecure casually to risk their alienation. Thus, as Gregory suggested, the well-attended meetings served as one more check on any ministerial desire to intervene in America.

If there was scant likelihood of Palmerston initiating a change of policy, neither was there any prospect of the Tories making "an issue with him on American affairs." Mason had accepted this a full three weeks before the opening of Parliament. The parties were so evenly balanced in the House and in the country, he explained to Benjamin, that the Tories were "very coy in measuring strength with their opponents." Once the session got under way and his prediction of a large measure of bipartisan unity on America was fulfilled, Mason conceded that both parties were "guided in this by a fixed English purpose to run no risk of a broil, even far less a war, with the United States." There was nothing to be done except "to be silent and passive."[33]

"In the House of Commons there is not a whisper about recognition or mediation in any form," Bright wrote to Charles Sumner early in March, "and so far I see no sign of any attempt to get up a discussion on the part of any friends of the South." However, a restless Lord Campbell did bring forward, after several delays, the question of recognition on March 23. He recited the familiar arguments—the North's task of reconquest was hopeless; the South had proved its independence; an alliance with the South would ensure the security of Canada; peace would bring relief to Lancashire; Southern independence would see a steady amelioration of slavery. All of which Russell brushed aside with the warning that recognition would be an act unfriendly to the Union.[34] For Southerners the conclusion was inescapable—recognition and intervention would only be proffered when they were no longer needed.[35] The hope that the British public could be aroused on these questions now faded. "The public mind has settled down into a state of quiescence on American affairs which resembles stagnation," Hotze reported to his masters in Richmond. Although the "masses of intelligence and respectability" wished well to the Confederate cause, nobody was speaking, writing, or thinking about recognition. This lack of interest he attributed in part to the widespread conviction that the ultimate victory of the South was certain. But he did not attempt to disguise the fact that after two years of fighting the war had "worn off its startling effects." Even alarm at the conflict's disruption of the British economy had subsided. Lancashire continued to suffer, but elsewhere prosperity reigned. England had discovered that she could "dispense," at least for a few years, with the American trade.[36]

What the published returns of the Board of Trade had long suggested Gladstone confirmed in his budget speech on April 16, 1863. He reported a small but healthy surplus of revenue over expenditure, and thus vindicated his forecast of the year before. The continued expansion of trade with France had more than compensated for the failure of that with the United States to recover its prewar volume. British exports to the Republic, although increasing, were still £6 million below the figure for 1859; however, in the same period trade with France had grown by more than £12 million. Together with his success in obtaining some reduction in military and naval estimates, these figures left Gladstone in the happy position of being able to propose a cut in taxation. He recommended a lowering of the general rate of the income tax, a number of minor adjustments that would benefit those on small incomes, and a substantial reduction of the duty on tea. In all, the remission of taxes totalled more than £4.5 million.[37]

There was some concern that the prosperity, cheap bread, and plentiful work elsewhere in England would cause the public to forget the misery in Lancashire. Walter Bagehot warned that people who had earlier overestimated the effect of a cotton famine were now in danger of underestimating it. Certainly the advance of distress with "gigantic strides" during November 1862 did not alarm the nation unduly. After all, donations had reportedly kept pace, largely as a result of the coordination of relief activities and the appointment of collecting committees. Nevertheless, there were fresh efforts to encourage the spirit of giving. The *Morning Post* urged all families of the middle and upper classes to save their scraps and unused food; for thickened with meal, seasoned, and then evaporated down to the point of solidification they would provide Lancashire with a food treasure—soup.[38]

In a speech at Chester at the end of 1862, Gladstone had voiced optimism that the situation was at last improving in the mill towns. Of the 400,000 operatives only one in eight was fully employed and half of them were wholly unemployed, he admitted. Nor did he minimize the cost to the national economy. He estimated that more than £12 million was being lost annually in wages and work in the cotton industry and its subsidiaries. Moreover, he put the number of those receiving relief from one source or another at half a million. But the situation was well in hand, he declared, for the Poor Law guardians and the various charity committees were spending at an average rate of two shillings a week per head, which he described as "sufficient and satisfactory." Donations continued to flow in, while the small decline in December 1862 of those in receipt of relief suggested that the high-water mark of distress had at last been reached. "It seems to be the opinion of the best informed," the chancellor went on, "that, under the operation of the Providential laws which regulate supply and demand both for materials and manufactures, there will probably exist in the month of March a state of things which will bring about a small but stable revival of trade and employment."[39]

To others the outlook seemed far less hopeful. A few mills had reopened after a fall in the price of cotton to fourteen pence a pound, Bright reported to Cobden on Christmas Eve. Unfortunately the increased purchases had promptly pushed up the price almost to the level that had "shut up nearly all the mills" three months earlier. No less disturbing was the continued decline of cotton stocks. They would last until March, Bright calculated, but without supplies from America there would be insufficient cotton to keep the operatives in employment for more than fifteen to twenty hours each week. Cobden shared this pessimistic opinion. After a three-week journey through the textile districts he had concluded that the workers were safe for the next few months, "thanks to the really noble burst of spontaneous liberality in all parts of the Kingdom." But what of the future? "The enthusiasm of giving is necessarily evanescent," he observed, "and is not to be rekindled by any appeals for the same object." It was unrealistic to expect more than £1 million to be raised by charity, and what was to be done once the donations inevitably began to fall off? The only solution, he believed, was to impose a rate in aid upon the whole kingdom.[40]

Charles Villiers rejected the proposal. As president of the Poor Law Board, he deprecated any step which amounted to a national grant to Lancashire. "I attach great importance to the Government not interfering at present, with local liability and local administration, in providing for local destitution," he wrote to Palmerston, to whom he forwarded Cobden's suggestion. There were pockets of chronic and severe distress in other parts of the nation, he pointed out, and once public money was provided it would be extremely difficult "to draw the line as to places where it shall be given." It was his opinion that the powers of the distressed unions, to levy a rate in aid on the county and to borrow, together with the voluntary subscriptions, were adequate for the crisis. As a reserve power, however, he authorized the guardians to overdraw their accounts with the treasurers of the unions—usually the district's principal bankers—until they were able under the law to borrow again. Then early in the new session he piloted through Parliament a continuance for another six months of the Union Relief Aid Act which permitted loans to be repaid over a period of fourteen years.[41]

Cobden was no more successful when he sought to persuade Bright that they should exploit the Lancashire distress to shelve that "old dodger" Palmerston, "the evil genius of our generation." Under the pressure of the distress "there will be for the first time for the last 8 or 10 years a chance for a hearing for a little common sense in the House," he argued. The moment was ripe "to score a notch or two" for people who had been denied "an 'innings' during the late prosperity." But to achieve anything they had to revert to their traditional policy of accepting aid from any quarter. Cobden was confident that Lord Derby's personal involvement in the troubles of Lancashire would cause him to lead the Tories along the path of retrenchment. If the Conservatives were willing to support a reduction of expenditures by £1 million, if they offered help to stop the "insidious fortifications scheme," their assistance should be accepted. "If too, as before, a government should be overturned by the process, and the 'liberals' find themselves on the opposition benches again, every liberal principle will gain by the change," he asserted.[42]

The obstacle in the way of this strategy was Bright's decision to make American affairs the pivot of his domestic politics. He suspected the Tories of being, "body and soul," supporters of the South. Preeminent in his mind was the thought that to help them regain office was to put them in a position where they could make matters far worse than they already were as a result of "the unfriendly neutrality of the present government."[43] Cobden struggled to overcome Bright's suspicions of the Conservatives and to curb his obsession with the American war. There was little to choose between the political parties in their response to the conflict, he observed. The *Morning Herald* was no more hostile to the Union than *The Times*, while the leading Tories—Derby, Disraeli, and Stanley—had been "far more reserved & indeed conciliatory to the North" than their counterparts—Palmerston, Russell, and Gladstone. Admittedly the rank and file had often followed the lead of Gregory, Lindsay, and Roebuck, but these three either sat or voted with the government, he reminded Bright, while the Tory backbenchers would show better discipline and follow their leaders if returned to power. In short, preference for Whig or Tory should not be governed "by appeal to foreign policy in which the two aristocratic factions" occupied the same ground. If retrenchment was to triumph in Britain it was necessary "to avoid as much as possible" the tactics of making the domestic affairs of the United States, or some other foreign nation, the topics of long debates in Parliament. "We must press every argument against intervention," Cobden conceded, but "without involving ourselves in the fate of American politics." He questioned the wisdom of too close an identification with the Federal cause. Disclaiming both moral obtuseness and any belief in the permanent success of a "horde of mandealers," affirming his conviction that slavery was the real issue in the war, Richard Cobden remained a pacifist. He deplored war even when it was freeing slaves. He would have been happy to see the negroes enslaved longer and freed peacefully. He also deplored the Unionists' "frightful incapacity." Their tariff policy revealed them as "unsound and ignorant on economical questions" of "vital importance in the affairs of nations."[44] His arguments fell on deaf ears. Bright could not be moved. Moreover, Gladstone's budget suggested that a change of government was not essential to the success of economic reform at home.

Cobden's one achievement was to provoke a public debate on the important question of how the nation should respond to a prolonged period of massive unemployment in Lancashire. Speaking at Manchester in the previous November, he had alluded to the possibility of Parliament coming to the rescue of the distressed districts. Almost immediately, the Stockport guardians boldly called for state aid and alarm bells sounded all over the country. Cobden was attacked for straying too far from the path of economic orthodoxy and Lancashire was accused of seeking to shirk its responsibilities. "Nothing can be more masterly than the game which the Lancashire Boards of Guardians seem to be playing," Charles Kingsley wrote in a letter to the editor of *The Times*. "They count correctly on John Bull's impatient generosity. They know that we cannot compel them (at least at present) to tax themselves as highly as they ought. They know that we cannot wait to see their paupers starve."[45] The old grievance of the county's abnormally low poor rate was revived. Once again complaints were heard that its wealthy residents were not doing enough. As for the lower classes, it was charged that "there were still on the 1st of September last, *three millions and three quarters of pounds sterling in the local savings banks*, and that this enormous sum represented the disposable funds of the operatives and small tradespeople."[46] Furthermore, hard as conditions were for many cotton hands, they were "not worse than that of families of the labourers on an outlying Buckinghamshire or Dorsetshire farm."[47]

Both Gladstone and Cobden spoke out in defence of the unpopular millowners. To impose additional burdens on these men, all of whom were already paying poor rates on their fixed and at present unproductive capital—their mills—was to run the risk of forcing them to liquidate their assets. If that happened the disruption of the important textile industry would be permanent, the member for Rochdale warned, so also would be unemployment among the operatives.[48] Privately the Earl of Derby admitted that as a class the millowners had contributed a great deal more to relief funds "than the wealthy bankers, merchants, brokers and other speculators," some of whom had also made fortunes from cotton. But he snared many of these laggards at the county meeting convened in Manchester at the beginning of December. The well-publicized success of this meeting in raising money for relief—Derby led the way with a donation of £5,000—did much to still temporarily the criticism of Lancashire's well-to-do.[49] What did not subside was the uneasiness about the economic and social consequences of keeping an army of unemployed on relief, private or public, for month after month. For even those who were convinced that a recovery was under way admitted that it would be slow.

One understandable concern was with the cost, which *Reynolds's* put at £3 million annually, simply to maintain the unemployed at "the present level of semi-starvation." Another was the gnawing fear that the poor might acquire a "fatal taste for money without work." Was Britain creating a class of paupers who would rather live on charity than seek employment? "There are many who are content to do nothing, and who are daily becoming more content, and, of course, less qualified," *The Times* warned.[50] Stories abounded of carpenters, painters, and other workmen collecting relief intended for the operatives. Yet prosecution on the charge of obtaining money under false pretences was costly, for local magistrates were not competent to hear such cases. What was to be done? Significantly, no one suggested intervention in America as a means of securing the abundant supplies of inexpensive cotton that would reopen the mills. Lord Derby recommended that relief payments be kept down to a level of "bare but sufficient" subsistence. There were calls for an improved and more regular system of inspection, to ensure that households receiving assistance truly required it, and demands for some more consistent effort to find "spade work" for the unemployed. The competition and waste that often resulted from rival relief committees working in the same community had to be ended. Emigration gained in popularity as a solution. Reports from Australia that Victoria had appropriated £5,000 and Queensland double that sum to pay the passages of suitable immigrants brought thousands of applicants to the doors of the Emigration Office in Manchester long before they were due to open. In Blackburn the operatives sought a grant of £5,000 from the relief committee to aid emigration, and even *The Times* gave encouragement to such requests. *Reynolds's* proposed a national scheme, and groups of workingmen applied to the government for state aid.[51] But discussion of the possible remedies for the malaise of chronic unemployment became more urgent with the outbreak of rioting in the mill towns.

In submitting his annual Police Returns to the Manchester Watch Committee on February 12, 1863, the chief constable paid handsome tribute to that city's unemployed operatives. "With so many thousands of persons thrown out of work it was scarcely to be expected," he wrote, "that the duties of the Police would not be to some extent increased, and, although this anticipation has been realized, I feel that, in justice to the great bulk of the working population of this city, I ought not to omit bearing my testimony to the admirable and patient manner in which they have borne their privations."[52] Nevertheless, there were signs that their patience was wearing thin in the face of the increasing harshness and insensitivity of the relief committees and guardians. People were refused help if they held any shares in a cooperative or building society; there were charges that persons who had in the past made themselves obnoxious to manufacturers by taking part in trades union activities were being persecuted—they received partial support only; those granted maximum assistance often had to listen to lectures on the twin evils of idleness and fraud; the old clothes being distributed were conspicuously marked "lent" or with the name of the local relief fund in order to prevent their being pawned. In some communities, such as Ashton, there were working-class electors, but those of them forced to seek aid from the guardians were struck off the parliamentary roll as paupers. Resentment and shame nourished one another and unrest began to manifest itself in open air meetings and disturbances. The successful prosecution in Blackburn of a group of unemployed men for poaching sparked an attack on the Town Hall by a mob. The Riot Act was read and a detachment of troops summoned to the town. In Glossop the immediate cause of disorder was the decision of the relief committee not to distribute a quantity of American flour it had received but to put it up for public auction and add the proceeds to the local relief funds. The possibility that the sale would be manipulated to the profit of local merchants brought out a crowd of 5,000 angry operatives who threatened to smash every barrel. They did break a few before dispersing after an affray with the police, who were promptly strengthened by the appointment of forty special constables. A week later, on March 10, it was Manchester's turn. A "Bread Riot" erupted when Union sympathizers organized a meeting in Stevenson Square to distribute 15,000 loaves, one for each of the barrels of flour carried aboard the first American relief ship. The crowd, perhaps ten thousand strong, sensitive about their dependence upon charity, stormed the bread vans when they discovered that they were expected to perform in a demeaning pro-Union pageant. But it was at Stalybridge, only a few miles from Manchester, that the most serious disturbance occurred. A "miserable-looking place at best," with a population which even in normal times had the appearance of being "ill-fed, ill-clothed and altogether of a low order," Stalybridge like other mill towns had seen the system of relief distribution tightened and the amount provided reduced.[53]

Complaints by the Central Executive Committee that the relief payments were too generous, and stories that much of the money was being frittered away in the town's public houses, induced the Stalybridge Committee to substitute shilling tickets for cash. They were redeemable at local shops in goods but merchants were not to give more than fivepence in change. On March 18, 1863, at a meeting held to protest the new system and the accompanying reduction in the rate of relief (still well above the standard of two shillings a head), the unemployed resolved not to accept tickets. During the next few days there were sporadic acts of vandalism— the smashing of windows in the adult schools, an attack on the home of the honorary secretary of the Relief Fund, and the raiding of a number of relief stores. The authorities responded by swearing in more than one hundred and fifty special constables and calling from neighbouring Ashton a detachment of cavalry and a company of infantry. Then on March 24 perhaps as many as one thousand demonstrators marched the two miles from Stalybridge to Ashton, passing through Dukinfield on the way, where they entered stores to demand food and provisions. They took whatever they wanted if it was refused. Nervous magistrates, some of them cotton spinners, appointed scores of special constables in the nearby towns, but the combined might of the military and the police was never in any danger of losing control of the situation. In a reassuring report to the Home Office on March 25, the chief constable of Cheshire did not "attach any great importance to the character of the Riots." He noted that there was an "absence of organization," that the number of actual rioters had never exceeded "some few hundreds," and that the majority of these "were youths of the lowest class of Irish." He also pointed out that with the exception of Ashton very few of the unemployed in other towns had joined the Stalybridge rioters. Large numbers had assembled out of curiosity and had occasionally taken the "plunder" proffered to them, but that was all. However, as a precaution, the Home Office instructed magistrates who had reason to fear serious disturbances to apply to the general in command of the military district for a force to aid the police.[54]

Once the excitement subsided the search for an explanation and ways to prevent further outbreaks began. The violence was laid at the door of "that floating body of vagrant, destitute, half-barbarian Irish who are the drudges and the enemies of the inhabitants of most of the larger towns of England."[55] The work of agitation was attributed to the Chartists, at least at Stalybridge, for it was a stronghold of their "vague passionate chimeras." If this association carried some memories back to the widespread unrest during the summer of 1842, the recollection should have served to emphasize the mildness of these disturbances. At Ashton "the greatest difficulty" had been the competitive activities of two relief organizations, one an agent of the Central Committee and the other of the Mansion House Fund. The Lord Mayor's Committee was roundly criticized also for its decision, during the early days of the unrest in Stalybridge, to respond to an appeal from a local clergyman for money to aid those operatives who had not taken any part in the violence but had been left destitute by their refusal to accept the tickets. This ill-timed act of generosity, critics claimed, had encouraged the rioters to persist in their demand for a return to cash payments.[56] Yet beyond these particular factors one general conclusion loomed large—the restlessness in parts of Lancashire was the result of "long idleness and long recipience of relief."

To follow Lord Derby's advice and make the life of those on relief even more unpleasant was to invite trouble, as the recent events had shown. There was renewed talk of the need to restore the self-respect of those dependent upon charity by requiring them to work. But the most insistent cry after the disturbances was for a policy of emigration. "Surely some company, some society, some association might be formed to assist in carrying out effectually so noble and patriotic an object," the *Daily News* declared.[57] In fact, 1862 had seen 50,000 hands leave the textile district. The Central Executive Committee ensured that all offers of free passage to the colonies received publicity, and emigration agents visited the principal towns in the distressed districts to interview applicants and select the most suitable. Before the Stalybridge riot the Mansion House Committee had several times rejected appeals for funds to aid emigrants, but in the aftermath of the disturbances the lord mayor of London endorsed emigration as one way of easing Lancashire's troubles. On April 20, 1863, he announced that his committee had set aside £5,000 to assist those operatives who wished to make new lives for themselves in the colonies. By the end of that month a trickle of assisted emigrants had begun to make its way to the Antipodes. Upwards of one thousand left Manchester for Birkenhead, there to take ship for New Zealand. In mid-May another three hundred from Manchester and the neighbouring mill towns sailed from Liverpool. Of these, eighty were financed by the Manchester Relief Committee and the remainder by the government of Victoria.[58] However, emigration was not a solution the British government promoted.

Early in April an inspector of factories, Robert Baker, had been sent into the cotton districts to report on conditions there. He concluded that "to emigrate the hands would be a fatal step for these districts." His report, marked "Private and Confidential" and printed for cabinet circulation, emphasized the prevalence of the belief that the worst had passed. There was confidence in Lancashire, he reported, that the industry would be able to carry on until either the American war ceased or cultivation elsewhere provided the English market with other suitable cottons. The most important manifestation of this optimism was the continuing capital investment by mill-owners. Some were taking advantage of the standstill to modify or renew their machinery, so that they would be able to use "any cotton hereafter available." Others were whitewashing their mills, extending them, or building new ones, and this was true even in Wigan where the relief fund had been in operation for sixty-five weeks and not a mill had been open for a year. Predictably, mill-owners objected strenuously to any policy which threatened to increase their labour costs and would "prevent them employing capital profitably." Cobden privately condemned assisted emigration schemes as "all *spite* against the Masters."[59] In the House of Commons it was Edmund Potter, the prominent cotton manufacturer, who took the lead in opposing those who called upon the government to assist emigration. The Duke of Newcastle had sent a circular to colonial governors seeking information on the operatives' suitability as immigrants, but Baker's report seems to have ended any thought of this solution. Villiers made the government's position clear on April 27. "When we are doing everything we can to increase the growth of cotton in various places abroad with the view of supplying the raw material to the manufacturers here and keeping up that industry in the country," the president of the Poor Law Board observed, "it would be inconsistent on our part to send the people connected with the manufacture out of the country, and thus part with their labour." Instead, the government had decided to send a member of the Local Government Office, a civil engineer who was a Lancashire native and therefore familiar with the area, to investigate the possibility of creating employment through useful public works.[60]

The proposal that operatives be employed by local governments came not merely from millowners anxious to maintain a large pool of skilled and relatively inexpensive labour. Long before they rioted the unemployed operatives in Stalybridge had met to draft a memorial in which they disclaimed any desire to be supported longer in idleness and begged for work. One passage in particular had caught the eye of the Home Office, for in it the operatives urged "most respectfully, but also most earnestly, upon her Majesty's Government, the importance of providing such work for them, whether on waste lands or otherwise, as to their wisdom shall seem fit."[61] However, after the mayor had testified that all was quiet in the town, that the vast majority of operatives were well satisfied, and that there was no likelihood of trouble, the request had been shelved. Now the disturbances revived it and the Central Executive Committee added its influential voice to those recommending that Parliament empower municipalities to raise money at low rates of interest "and thus to undertake works which would otherwise be neglected." In some areas storage reservoirs would be useful, both to towns and local mills, while in smaller communities there were a host of minor works that would be of benefit—sewerage, drainage, road-widening, street-paving, the improvement of footpaths and water supplies, and the creation of recreation grounds.[62] Such a program would have the added value of offering a measure of reassurance to those who feared that the recipients of relief were losing their taste for work.

Accompanied by Farnall, the government's investigator set out at the end of April. If Parliament passed an act enabling "money to be advanced at some fraction per cent more than will secure the country from loss," he promptly reported, work would "be found for every able-bodied distressed operative" and the districts permanently benefited. Not only would property be improved, but the "sanitary state of every locality operated upon" would be "vastly bettered." Following his advice the government announced that it intended to allow places that were distressed "to have the advantage of any public money for public works," and legislation was introduced to give to municipalities that did not possess them the powers to borrow and to carry out public works. Despite the warnings of the most fervent advocate of emigration, who calculated that the £1.5 million to be set aside would give work to no more than 27,000 adults, and thus remove only 82,000 persons from the relief rolls, the Public Works (Manufacturing Districts) Bill made its way through the Commons in June.[63] By the year's end only twenty-two loans had been issued, and most of these for very small sums. Blackburn and Preston did obtain £10,000 each and Oldham £18,000. Inevitably there were complaints about delays in responding to requests, though in many cases the delay was due to the slowness of the local authorities in submitting or returning necessary documents to the Public Works Loans Office in London. However, by this time the number of persons on relief had fallen dramatically to 203,000 from almost 500,000 in January 1863. The bill had served its purpose, which was to apply a little balm to the sore of unemployment. "Lancashire is no longer to be idle," the *Morning Star* had proclaimed. The operatives "will arm themselves with the spade and the pickaxe, to make war on undrained streets and moors."[64] Grossly exaggerated as such statements were, they did offer hope to the unemployed. No less importantly, the introduction of this measure served to confirm that Palmerston and his colleagues had no intention of meddling in the American war. Nor did the Stalybridge riot excite an outcry for a change of foreign policy. Indeed, if there was any pressure upon the government, it was being exerted by "the little knot of illustrious nobodies" who had broadened their campaign of agitation to include demands that there be no more *Alabamas*.

With the founding of the London Emancipation Society the Union's friends in Britain had created the nucleus of an effective organization. The affiliated provincial societies, such as that at Manchester, made possible a popular campaign of support for the North which was truly national in scope. Glossing over the deficiencies of Lincoln's Emancipation Proclamation and hailing its undoubted merits, they stole the initiative from the numerically larger and socially and politically more influential body of sympathizers with the Confederacy. Hard work, skilful planning, and moral fervour made a formidable combination. The prominence of "dissenting ministers" might excite the scorn of some establishment observers but their participation was important during a revival of dissenting religious feeling. The society and its allies in the provinces were particularly successful in creating an impression of widespread working-class support for the Union as the standard-bearer of human freedom in the American struggle. This in turn influenced the behaviour of some of the South's friends, such as William Gregory, and no doubt was another factor serving to restrain any impulse the Palmerston government may have felt to meddle in the Civil War. Even the outbreak of disturbances failed to revive talk let alone serious consideration of intervention as the solution to the problem of obtaining inexpensive cotton in quantities sufficient to reemploy many of the operatives who had been thrown out of work. There was precious little official sympathy either for schemes to assist the emigration of the unemployed to British colonies, despite the enormous cost of maintaining them on relief and the fear that a large class of paupers was emerging who had lost the taste for honest toil while living on charity. For obvious reasons, neither government nor millowners wished to see a significant fall in the reservoir of experienced labour available to a vital industry. So, in order to offer the unemployed some hope and to ensure that the habit of work survived, a modest public works program was sponsored by the Palmerston government.

NINE

Strict Neutrality

"I THINK MATTERS ARE GETTING more satisfactorily muddled in Europe every day," Henry S. Sanford reported to Seward in January. In this political confusion the Union's harassed diplomats, and of these Charles Francis Adams remained the first, saw a further respite from the danger of intervention in the war. Adams welcomed the increase in number and complexity of European "questions"—the Prussian, the Danish, the Eastern, and the Greek —inasmuch as they diverted public attention from America and preoccupied the British government. Palmerston uneasily watched Russian and French activities in the Balkans, convinced that they were intriguing to stir up "all the European Provinces of Turkey against the Sultan."[1] It was with these nations that Britain had also to contend following the revolution in Greece. All three had been parties to the Greek settlement thirty years before and were recognized as the protecting powers.

The news in October 1862 of a Greek insurrection, the deposing of King Otho, and a call for a constituent national assembly, came as little surprise to the British government. Popular discontent with the reactionary monarch had long been manifest. Palmerston accepted some responsibility for the crisis, having played a large role in placing the Bavarian prince on the throne. "However it was found impossible to make a silk purse out of him," he remarked to Russell.[2] Now the problem was to find a successor acceptable to the Greeks and the protecting powers. The search occupied Palmerston and Russell for months and proved appropriately byzantine.

Suspecting the French of playing a double game with them in this as in other matters, the British vetoed the candidacy of the duke of Leuchtenburg, for he was a Beauharnais with Russian connections. For their part France and Russia made plain their unwillingness to accept an English prince, even had his mother been willing to part with him, and when the Greeks themselves named Prince

Alfred the nomination was graciously declined. A more distant relative of Queen Victoria, the Duke of Coburg, was put forward despite Palmerston's reservations about the "queer fellow," but he withdrew after a brief period of indecision. And so it went on, with Palmerston growing concerned that if the Greeks did not soon have a good man proposed to them they would be driven to establish a republic, which he equated with "anarchy within and Turbulence without."[3] To hold the Greeks steady the British put up a tempting prize for this monarchical sweepstakes, from which so many runners were scratched or fell at the first hurdle. The Greeks' own choice of Prince Alfred had been inspired, the prime minister believed, by the hope that he would bring with him the Ionian Islands. The provisional government of Greece was informed, therefore, that if it undertook to uphold constitutional monarchy, refrained from all acts of aggression against Turkey, and chose a king acceptable to Britain, the islands would indeed be handed over to the new kingdom. Eventually Prince William of Denmark, whose sister married the prince of Wales in March 1863, succeeded to the Greek throne as George I.[4]

The prospect of a personal tie between the British and Danish royal families had not prevented Russell from venturing into the treacherous maze of Schleswig-Holstein, and in a direction that was far more favourable to the Germans than the Danes. His Gotha despatch in September 1862 may have been an attempt to improve relations with Prussia as part of the general strategy of restraining the adventurous French emperor. Perhaps it was a response to the influence of the pro-German Court; conceivably Russell was seeking an honourable escape for Britain from the obligations imposed upon her in the Treaty of London—once the Danes had rejected his proposals for a settlement he could wash his hands of the affair. Whatever his motives, the published despatch aroused a storm of criticism in Britain. In the words of his Tory predecessor at the Foreign Office, "This restless and impotent meddling is peculiarly ill-timed on the eve of the marriage of the Prince of Wales with a Danish Princess." The Conservative leaders determined to make foreign affairs "the chief topic" of the new session of Parliament.[5] Denmark, Greece, the proposed surrender of the Ionian Islands, Russell's scheme to solve the prolonged Italian crisis by sending the Pope to Malta, these were "all points in which Johnny has made more blunders than I had thought possible to crowd into the space of a few months," Derby wrote to Disraeli.[6]

The throne speech at the opening of Parliament on February 5, 1863, "revealed nothing, promised nothing and proposed nothing," the *Spectator* complained. In this it truly reflected the attitude of a government content to remain in office and to mark time. Palmerston fully expected Derby to be pushed by Disraeli and his more impatient followers into an effort to unseat the government, and to look to the Radicals for assistance. Villiers had therefore approached Bright, urging him not to make desperate attacks on the cabinet that might topple it from power.[7] As Cobden discovered, Bright had no intention of helping the Tories into office. Then, with the death of Cornewall Lewis, Palmerston made those fine adjustments to his administration which kept it idling quietly in both Houses. De Grey took charge of the War Department and the Marquis of Hartington was transferred from the Admiralty to serve as his deputy. Hartington "being the son of the Duke of Devonshire will tend to keep in order the Tory Colonels and Generals who keep barking at us so often to the length of their tether," the prime minister explained to Russell. The vacancy at the Admiralty was filled by James Stansfeld, the Radical who had moved a resolution calling for a reduction of expenditures the previous year. His appointment served as a "Pledge" to Cobden, Bright, and company that "due Economy" would be practised in that costly branch of the public service.[8]

"The sole prestige of the present Cabinet centres in the Premier," one Tory journal averred. "In the estimation of the country, Lord Palmerston is the Government."[9] Unquestionably his popularity protected it from any serious attempt by the Conservatives to defeat it in the House, even after their surprising victory in a by-election at Devonport. For if they detected a "Conservative reaction" in the country, there was no escaping the fact that "old Pam" appeared "as young and as popular as ever." Any doubts about his vigour and grip upon the public were dispelled by a triumphal visit to Scotland during the Easter recess, to be installed as lord rector of the University of Glasgow. He showed no signs of tiredness after his journey of 400 miles, and his voice seemed to grow in strength with every speech he made. "I have never seen so enthusiastic a reception as at the Glasgow dinner," one of his admiring companions observed.[10] From there Palmerston travelled to Edinburgh to receive the freedom of the city and an honorary degree from the university he had attended sixty years earlier. What then was the point in bringing down the government, for Palmerston would certainly go to the country and would just as certainly be returned to power? Anyway, many members of the opposition admired him and in domestic affairs had every reason to embrace him as a fellow conservative.

Although Tory attacks on Russell's handling of European problems did not threaten the government's survival, the worrying turmoil on the continent showed no sign of lessening. Instead, a new question was suddenly thrust forward—Poland. After months of unrest the Poles rose in rebellion against their Russian masters. The rebels obtained support from those regions of the unhappy country previously annexed by Prussia and Austria, and looked to Catholic France for sympathy and assistance. Initially the Russians sought to prevent the insurrection from becoming an international crisis, but their signing of the Alvensleben Convention with Prussia on February 8, providing for cooperation in frontier districts against the insurgents, defeated this purpose. Whether Bismarck coaxed the Prussian king into offering aid to the Russians because he saw this as an opportunity to drive a wedge between them and the French, or was simply responding to his own anti-Polish sentiments and to the fear that the revolt would spread to Posen, "without thinking of the international consequences," the news of the arrangement reverberated across Europe.[11]

Confronted by a public opinion overwhelmingly sympathetic to the Poles, yet anxious to preserve his entente with Russia, the French emperor sought to divert domestic anger and international attention to Prussia. On February 21 he proposed to London and Vienna that the three powers address identical notes to Berlin protesting against the convention. This implied support for rebels met with little favour in Austria, where there was natural concern for the security of her Polish province of Galicia. In Britain the proposal excited the fears of those who like Disraeli were already alarmed that, as a result of the rebellion, "The cards seem most unexpectedly to throw the Rhine into the grasp of Napoleon." Dreading a collision with Prussia, and a French army on the Rhine, which she believed to be the true aims of Napoleon's policy, the Queen turned to Granville and the cabinet for support in checking any plot Palmerston and Russell might be hatching to respond favourably.

But so great was the popular enthusiasm for the Poles, and the enmity toward Russia and Prussia, Granville warned the Queen, that the situation would be "embarrassing" if the two old men went "warmly into a course of interference." With this danger in mind he urged her "to continue to insist on every step being submitted to the Cabinet" before it was formally adopted, for he was confident that most of its members were inclined to be "extremely prudent."[12]

As it happened, the old war-horse was not champing at the bit. "These poor Poles are almost sure to be cut down and shot down, and to have their Houses and villages burnt," Palmerston wrote to Russell, yet "any representation to be useful to them must be friendly and informal to the Russian Government." Napoleon's conduct, he agreed, "was dictated by a desire to conciliate Catholic support, and probably by ulterior plans of aggrandisement."[13] He willingly fell in with his colleagues who argued that a remonstrance "might give a slight footing to French ambition, and that to make any demand which would probably be rejected would give the Emperor an important advantage." A despatch drafted by Russell, rejecting the French proposal of a joint protest in Berlin, was approved by the cabinet on February 25. Palmerston did suggest that they take one additional step and urge the tsar to give a constitution and an amnesty to the Poles, but this was "shelved for the present."[14] During the emotional debate on Poland in the Commons on February 27 the prime minister's was a voice of caution. He praised the "kind-hearted and benevolent" tsar, and expressed the belief that the Russian monarch did mean, and had meant for some time past, "to improve the conditions of his Polish subjects." Moreover, Palmerston was careful to draw a sharp distinction between Britain's rights and obligations under the terms of the Treaty of Vienna. She was under "no obligation" to interfere, he informed the House.[15]

The debate had demonstrated the depth and breadth of the sympathy for the Poles and convinced the government that it had to make some remonstrance at St. Petersburg. On March 2 Palmerston's earlier suggestion was taken off the shelf and acted upon. But as *The Times* warned that same day, "We can and shall doubtless remonstrate, as we have often done before, but it is to excite vain hopes when we speak of intervention which we cannot make, and assistance which must necessarily limit itself to well meant but fruitless protest." Britain had to be careful in resisting one despotism not to play in effect the game of another. It was no part of her policy to risk a war from which Napoleon might profit. In the hope that a joint representation of Britain, Austria, and France would induce the tsar to restore to Poland the constitutional privileges she had lost after 1831, the British did approach the two other nations. However, fear of losing Galicia continued to dissuade the Austrians from entering any such joint venture, while it was soon clear that the French intended to make threats with which the British had no wish to be associated. The result was that three very different notes were eventually addressed to Russia. By the middle of March the prospect of French military action seemed far from remote.[16]

The upheavals in Europe served the purpose Adams had foreseen. They rather than America now filled the minds of many Englishmen. Lucius Lamar, passing through London en route to Russia, discovered that Palmerston was "far more deeply engrossed with conferences, jealousies, and rivalries between the leading powers of Europe than with the fate of constitutional government in America." To thwart Napoleon in Greece and to prevent his ascendancy in European affairs were objects of far greater importance to the British "than to pursue any policy with reference to America," he observed.[17] Indeed, there was every reason for Palmerston and Russell to pursue a passive American policy while they concentrated on more pressing problems. The government's reluctance to intervene in the Civil War had been the one aspect of its conduct of foreign affairs to escape the censure of the Tory leadership in the debate on the throne speech, and the policy of nonintervention seemed to command general support in the country as well. Of no less importance was the certainty that a change of course would divide the cabinet and might well precipitate the government's collapse just as it became clear that the Tories were not seeking to topple it. Disraeli had drawn attention to the divisions in his reply to the throne speech, mocking the gulf that separated Gladstone at Newcastle from Lewis at Hereford, and contrasting the recent pro-Confederate remarks of Sir Robert Peel, chief secretary for Ireland, with those of Milner Gibson. Argyll's position was equally well known, but he reaffirmed it at the banquet celebrating Palmerston's visit to Edinburgh. "As a Government and people we must be what we have always been—absolutely neutral," he declared. "We must take no part whatever in that contest."[18]

The futility of any form of intervention at this time was the constant theme of Lyons's private correspondence with Russell. Dark as the Union's future appeared in the weeks after Fredericksburg, and dispirited as was the public mood, the minister repeatedly warned that Northerners had "not lost confidence to such an extent as to reconcile them to the loss of territory." The Democrats' failure to declare themselves for peace he attributed to prudence. They had discovered that the people were still not ready to accept disunion. For Lyons the only hope was that peace would come of itself "from the difficulty of recruiting men enough in the North to go on fighting." As for foreign mediation, he complained that the French proposals had ruined whatever slim chance there had been of acceptance. Made at "bad times," either too conciliatory or not conciliatory enough, insufficiently attractive "to enlist any amount of public opinion in their favour," the proposals had served only to lead "the government to declare itself strongly against them" and to accustom the people to the idea that it was quite safe to reject them.[19]

Not surprisingly, Russell abandoned the notion of Britain taking some initiative in America during the spring. In mid-December he had written to Lyons of the need to "lie still 'til after March," but two months later he was reemphasizing the government's disinclination "to interfere at present in any way in the civil war." Until both parties were "heartily tired and sick of the business" he saw no point in talking of good offices. Then in mid-March he instructed Lyons to inform Seward, if the American asked him about Britain's intended course, "that our opinion is that the Republican Party ought not to leave the glorious work of Peace to the Democrats, but as a Neutral Power our intention and wish is to let the war work itself out, as it is sure to do by the moral exhaustion of the war spirit." In short, Britain had "no thoughts of recognizing [the South] at present." This was the essence also of his reply to Campbell in the Lords on March 23. However, he did acknowledge at that time, albeit indirectly, the success of the Emancipation Society. Its demonstrations had lent force to Palmerston's warning that any interference which appeared to benefit the cause of slavery would give offence to many people. "If we have taken part in interventions, it has been in behalf of the independence, freedom and welfare of a great portion of mankind," Russell boasted. "I should be sorry, indeed, if there should be any intervention on the part of this country which could bear another character." The implication was clear enough—Britain's noble record of promoting the freedom of mankind demanded that she continue to pursue her policy of impartiality and neutrality, at least for the present.[20]

Russell's reassuring remarks were welcomed in the Union, yet tempers were rising dangerously in both nations. The escape of the *Alabama* and her success as a raider enraged the North, as did reports that additional vessels were being built for the Confederacy in Britain. Meanwhile the provocative behaviour of Charles Wilkes in the West Indies was arousing the fury of many Englishmen. Thus at a time when the government was most anxious for quiescent relations with the United States there was talk of war.

Adams had interpreted the British government's belated decision to detain the *Alabama* as an admission that her construction and escape had been violations of the law of neutrality. Citing the British claim for damages against the United States during the French Revolutionary War as a precedent, a claim his nation had accepted, and protesting that he had done all in his power to warn them of "the illegal enterprise in ample season for effecting its prevention," Adams wrote to Russell on November 20, 1862, "to solicit redress" for national and private injuries, "as well as a more effective prevention of any repetition of such lawless and injurious proceedings in her Majesty's ports hereafter."[21]

Russell confessed to Lyons that the activities of the *Alabama* were "enough to *rile* a more temperate nation" and that he owed "a grudge to the Liverpool people on that account."[22] That was not to say that Britain owed an account to the United States and for a legal opinion he turned to the law officers. With the resignation of Harding, Robert Phillimore had been promoted from Admiralty advocate to Queen's advocate and had thus joined Atherton and Roundell Palmer. He had been strongly recommended by his life-long friend Gladstone, who assured the prime minister that Phillimore had sound political sympathies and reminded him of the lawyer's good connections. A supporter of the government and an old and intimate friend of many of Palmerston's friends and colleagues, he was also the brother-in-law of the speaker and an "able, honourable, high minded man." But first and foremost he was in the opinion of the lord chancellor and the solicitor general the "fittest man." He alone among living British authorities had achieved international renown for his writings on international law.[23] However, in "a compilation so large and multifarious as that

242

of Dr. Phillimore it is impossible but that some errors will creep in," *The Times* hurriedly explained when Americans cited him in support of the contention that the government of a neutral state was responsible to a belligerent for preventing its subjects from selling, furnishing, or transporting contraband.[24]

Organs sympathetic to the Union had already taken the government to task for its failure to prevent the *Alabama*'s escape, while even *The Times* conceded that when the case was stated from the Federal point of view "we cannot help feeling a certain degree of sympathy with their remonstrances." Here was a ship built with British materials by British workmen and manned largely by trained gunners of the British Naval Reserve putting into British colonial ports for supplies and repairs and then sailing out to overhaul and destroy one Union merchantman after another. The exasperation of the New York Chamber of Commerce was understandable. But *The Times* steadfastly refused to admit that Britain had failed to honour her obligations as a neutral, and on this question it undoubtedly reflected the opinion of most Englishmen. Quoting chapter and verse from Chancellor Kent and President Pierce, they pointed out that her behaviour had conformed to the accepted international standard even as interpreted by the United States. Britain was doing neither more nor less than had the Union during the Crimean War. However, for a more authoritative discussion of the problems and precedents the newspaper referred Britain's "friends and allies in America" to the writings of "Historicus."[25]

Harcourt contrived to explain the complex problems of neutrality with great clarity and an impressive display of erudition. In his opinion much of the confusion stemmed from the Foreign Enlistment Act. Such statutes, he pointed out, were purely municipal enactments for the benefit and protection of the neutral and "not laws in furtherance of any international obligation due from the neutral to the respective belligerents." An infraction of the act was therefore an offence against the neutral but violated "no right inherent in the other belligerent." Similarly, it was absurd to hold the neutral government responsible for negligence in the vindication of his violated neutrality. "The other belligerent, who, though he may have sustained injury, has suffered the violation of no right, has no definite or lawful claim upon the neutral for reparation."[26] As for the duties of neutrality under international law, they lacked a precise, theoretical definition. A neutral was expected to deny use of his territory as a base for hostile expeditions, but this did not impose any obligations to prevent his subjects from trading in contraband with the belligerents. In his memoirs Roundell Palmer was to point out that "No writer of any authority before 1862 had maintained that a ship constructed for warlike use, but powerless for purposes of offence when delivered to a belligerent purchaser within neutral waters, and so continuing down to the time of leaving them, came within any rule differing from that applicable to arms and munitions of war." Only in cases when at the time of departure a ship had the means to commit an act of war, had procured those means in a neutral port, and had the intent to use them, could the port "be justly said to serve as a base or point of departure for a hostile expedition."[27]

The law officers took essentially the same position in the point by point refutation of Adams's arguments they forwarded to Russell. His citing of the conduct of the United States during the French Revolutionary War as a precedent was dismissed as invalid. Then the French had openly violated the principles of international law, outfitting privateers in American ports, sending them out to prey upon British commerce, even going through a form of prize adjudication there. These activities together with the seizure of vessels within American territorial waters had formed the basis of the demands for redress. Britain had not complained of accidental evasions of municipal law, which was what the United States was doing in the case of the *Alabama*. As for Adams's demand for compensation, that was described as "wholly unwarranted by the principles and precedents of International Law." Sarcastically, the law officers likened it to Britain demanding compensation for damage done by the *Alabama* to British property on the grounds that the Union claimed authority and jurisdiction over the Confederacy. The tone of the reply Russell addressed to Adams on December 19, 1862, was sharp. Palmerston had made extensive amendments to the draft which did nothing to blunt its edge. In particular, he emphasized the complaints Britain had against the United States. The Union had profited "by far the most" from those violations of the Queen's Proclamation of May 1861 which breached neither municipal nor international law. British merchants and manufacturers had been induced to send vast quantities of warlike supplies to Northern ports and the Union's command of the seas had enabled it to intercept much of the *matériel* being carried to the Confederacy.[28]

"Insolent," "supercilious," "savage," was how Americans at the legation described Russell's note. Unlike his father, Charles Francis Adams did not "exult in the exercise of his power in strife." Nevertheless, convinced that his was "the side of truth and justice," he persisted with the correspondence much to Russell's irritation. As their relations gradually grew less cordial Adams also sensed that he was "less useful by reason of these collisions." Despite the encouraging achievements of the Emancipation Society in organizing opinion, and the welcome turmoil in Europe, March found the minister sunk in despondency. "My representations have little or no effect," he complained to one friend. "The violations of neutrality grow more and more glaring."[29] Yet another vessel denounced by him as intended for the Confederacy, although so slightly built that she seemed better suited for the role of blockade-runner than that of raider, had sailed from Liverpool in January. Next, the door to the negotiation of a strengthened Foreign Enlistment Act, which Russell had left ajar in December, was now slammed shut. The law officers had raised no objection to the law being amended to arm the government with the power to interfere earlier against ships whose construction "might" denote that they were intended for a belligerent purpose, so long as the American law was altered in the same way at the same time. As the two laws were almost identical, the British were determined not to afford the Union more protection than it would be obliged to reciprocate as a neutral when Britain was at war. Initially Adams had insisted that the American law was already stronger, but in February he announced that his government was willing to make common changes and asked if Russell had any proposals to make. Instead, the foreign secretary replied that on the advice of the lord chancellor the cabinet had decided that the British law was perfectly adequate. "What explanation the Government was ready to give for its utter failure to execute a law confessed to be effective, did not then appear," Adams acidly observed.[30]

The American's temper was not improved nor were his spirits lifted by the success of the Confederate loan. The prospectus had been issued in London on March 18, 1863, and within a few days the loan was being quoted at a premium of 5¼ per cent. By the month's end it was still firm and Erlanger assured Mason that there was "little fear of its falling lower and none that it would touch par." This optimism was misplaced and the beginning of April saw the loan slip to 2 per cent discount. James Spence held Erlangers responsible; they had been too greedy in issuing the bonds at 90 per cent of their face value, he complained to Mason. The bankers themselves blamed Federal agents, claiming that they were making large purchases at low rates in order to discredit the loan. These "bears" might so depress the stock, they warned, that when settlement day came on April 24 investors would forfeit the 15 per cent they had already paid rather than go on with their subscriptions. Whoever was responsible, it was obvious that if the loan broke down the Confederacy would suffer the "utmost political injury." Moreover, a collapse would be "disastrous in its effects on any other mode of raising money." The only solution was for Erlangers, using some of the money already raised, to enter the market and buy bonds. This they did, taking care not to reveal that it was on the Confederacy's account. Between April 7 and April 24 bonds to the face value of slightly more than £1.5 million were bought, with the result that on settling day the loan was once again at a 2 per cent premium and there was no difficulty with subscribers.[31]

"The success of the Thieves Loan of course decreases our chance of success," John Forbes wrote to Gideon Welles. Together with William Aspinwall he had been sent to Britain to purchase vessels out of the hands of shipbuilders. Hard-headed businessmen both, they concluded that there was no chance of any offer being accepted by a builder, at least for the present. So they turned their attention to other tasks. The establishment of a more effective system for ferreting out information on Confederate ships was vital if the Union's representatives were ever going to be able to provide the British government with the legal evidence necessary for detentions. At the same time, anything that bred "further distrust of the swindling loan" would serve to shake the confidence of the builders and eventually open them to Northern offers.[32]

Before the arrival of Forbes and Aspinwall the Union had relied largely upon its seventeen consuls in Britain to gather intelligence. Their activities had been loosely coordinated by Morse and Dudley, whose ports of London and Liverpool were at the centre of Southern schemes. Occasionally they sent agents to other cities where Confederates seemed particularly active, but they had been hampered by a shortage of funds. From Forbes and Aspinwall they received encouragement and money, as well as a clearer delineation of responsibilities. Britain was divided into two zones, with Morse supervising the surveillance system in the South. In the North, Dudley soon undertook a trip around the English and Scottish yards to see for himself what vessels were being constructed and to organize a network of agents and informants. As a result of this and other surveys Forbes was able to present Adams, by the third week of April, with a general review of the British shipyards and descriptions of every suspicious vessel building in them.[33]

The related task of undermining the credit of the Confederacy was left in the capable hands of Chase's special agent, Robert Walker. He was well known and highly respected in Britain as a secretary of the treasury who had advocated free trade and as the governor of Kansas who had resisted the wretched Lecompton Constitution. In mid-April John Bigelow expressed surprise that no one had thought to collect the evidence of Jefferson Davis's defence years before of Mississippi's repudiation of her debt. If laid before the public it "would have the double effect of hitting Davis & Slidell who has tried to whitewash him," he argued. Soon after his arrival Walker was hard at work in the British Museum, thumbing through its files of the *National Intelligencer* in search of Davis's public statements on this sensitive subject. He also obtained material from Chase. Taking the polemicist's customary liberties with the truth, he sought to show that slavery, Davis, and repudiation were intimately connected if not synonymous. Could the president of the new state be trusted not to repeat his earlier performance if a victorious Confederacy's finances encouraged repudiation, he asked. Nor was there any chance of a triumphant Union honouring the South's debts, and to emphasize this fact Walker had persuaded Chase to obtain a presidential proclamation declaring the Confederate bonds null and void. A flamboyant man, who had taken up residence in a fashionable section of the British capital and rode through its streets in splendour, as a means of dramatizing the Union's wealth, Walker chose to shower London with his propaganda while riding over the city in a balloon. The spectacular drop in the value of the Confederate loan in July he modestly attributed to the Union's repulse of Lee at Gettysburg as well as to the appearance of his first pamphlet.[34]

Adams had watched with dismay the initial success of the Confederacy's financial dealings. The open negotiation of a loan of £3 million on the London market seemed certain both to aid the

Confederates' "extensive operations" in Britain and to enrage further an American public whose mood was already dangerous. This latest development, together with his apparent failure to persuade the British to act with more energy to prevent the outfitting of ships for the South, despite the disclosure of the Sanders contract for six ironclads, might even excite an irresistible popular demand in the Union for the issue of letters of marque. This was all too likely to lead in turn to maritime incidents which would strengthen the hand of those in Britain who favoured a hostile policy. It seemed evident to Adams that the two nations were drifting towards war, yet the British government gave no indication of having grasped the gravity of the situation.[35]

Hoping to bestir Russell, Adams obtained an interview with the foreign secretary on March 26. The minister brought with him and read a despatch from Seward, which while "not unfriendly in tone" complained of the injuries inflicted by vessels fitted out in British ports and manned for the most part by British seamen. This amounted to England making war on the United States while the Union was not at war with England, Seward observed, and had given rise to "strong feeling." The solution was for Britain to enforce her law. In reply Russell repeated that the authorities could only proceed "according to the regular process of law, and upon sworn testimony," though he did admit that "the cases of the Alabama & Oreto were a scandal, & in some degree a reproach" to British laws. Rather than send out privateers after these vessels, he suggested that the Union offer far higher rewards to the crews of men-of-war for their capture, perhaps doubling or even quadrupling the usual prize money. This would encourage the searchers who as members of the United States Navy were subject to effective control and "amenable to the laws which govern an honourable profession." Russell added his voice, moreover, to those who insisted that if all the weapons and munitions sent to the North were weighed against the aid the Confederacy obtained from Britain "the balance would be greatly in favour of the Federals." This Adams "totally denied," pointing to the loan as additional proof of the existence in Britain of a conspiracy "to produce a state of exasperation in America, & thus to bring on a war with Great Britain with a view to aid the Confederate cause." He warned that as hard as he had worked for peace "it had become a most difficult task." At the very least the British government should condemn the infractions of their law, for this would do something to remove the suspicion in America that they were indifferent to its violation.[36]

Adams left the Foreign Office cheered by the conversation for it seemed to him that Russell was "really inclined to go as far as he could to prevent difficulty." In his official report to Seward he emphasized the foreign secretary's friendliness and expressed the belief that the Englishman had not been "unimpressed by the earnestness" of his representations. Indeed, Russell suggested to Palmerston that the prime minister take the opportunity presented by a Commons debate on the Foreign Enlistment Act on the following evening to make the kind of reassuring statement the American minister had sought. As the fitting-out and escape of the *Alabama* and the *Florida* were clear evasions of the law there could be no problem in voicing the government's disapproval, he remarked. "A few words, in this case, may do much good." Instead, Palmerston "indulged as usual in derogatory and insulting language, rather than in conciliation."[37]

Adams had long discouraged the Union's sympathizers from raising the *Alabama* case in the House, believing that it was better to give the Foreign Office time both to reflect and to pursue the question through normal diplomatic channels. But in the face of the urgent need to persuade the British government to act with greater energy he withdrew this opposition and briefed Forster, who had put down a question on the Foreign Enlistment Act for March 27. Bright, having stayed away from the Commons for three weeks "owing to a desperate cold and cough," was determined to be present. He and Cobden had been alarmed by Sumner's letters describing the dangerous temper of the North and his long but as yet undecided battle against the commissioning of privateers. Of the additional ships reported to be outfitting in Britain, Sumner implored: "Stop them pray. Stop them." Cobden forwarded one such letter to Russell, along with a note expressing his personal opinion that "something more than mere passiveness was due to a friendly government in a case where the interests at stake were so great; that our authorities ought to exercise greater vigilance in enforcing the observance of our own law." However, on the eve of the debate he was worried that Adams had muddled "the matter by complaining of the sale of munitions of war to the Confederates."[38]

Cobden's concern was well founded. Opening the discussion, Forster dwelt upon the delay between Adams's denunciation of the

Alabama and the government's decision to act, and stressed the "curious coincidence" of the vessel stealing away even as the law officers submitted their opinion. He repeated the American accusation that she was a British ship in everything except her officers, and he contrasted unfavourably Britain's behaviour in the present instance with the conduct of the United States during the Crimean War. Warning his listeners of the dangerous precedents that were being established, and the hostility that had been aroused, he called upon the government to do its utmost to preserve neutrality. To all of this Roundell Palmer made a brilliantly effective reply. The Americans had compiled a catalogue of grievances against Britain in which the *Alabama* was but a single item, he declared, holding in his hand a copy of the diplomatic correspondence Seward had forwarded to Congress. They complained of the export of munitions to and the raising of money for the Confederacy, though no nation had been more emphatic and constant in upholding such neutral rights in the past than the United States. He drew the distinction between the Foreign Enlistment Act and the obligations of neutrality, and protested that there had been no unreasonable delay in acting upon the evidence against the *Alabama* supplied by Adams. Several weeks had been lost as a result of the Americans' failure to provide it in a legal form, he pointed out, and by taking the last date upon which depositions forwarded by Adams had reached the Foreign Office—July 26—he managed to convey the impression that the matter had been handled with all due speed given the fact that it had occurred on a weekend. Then, for good measure, he sought to show that the working of the British law had taken no longer than that of the United States under somewhat similar circumstances during the Russian war. A speech "in argument more unanswerable, in talent more unequalled, and in tone and temper more becoming to the Government he represented and the country to which he belonged, he had never listened to in that House," Seymour Fitzgerald declared from the opposition benches.[39]

Bright struggled to prevent the cause from foundering. He suggested that the law be altered to give the government greater power, in much the same way as the United States had acted when a similar measure was found inadequate to restrain those Americans sustaining the Canadian rebels a quarter of a century earlier. Critical of Britain's "cold" and "unfriendly" neutrality, he spoke of the claim the people of the United States had "upon the generous forbearance and sympathy of Englishmen," and sought from Palmerston "those genial and friendly words which none know so well how to utter." They would do much to allay the irritation on the other side of the Atlantic and give "great confidence" to the friends of peace on both, he explained. The prime minister could not bring himself to offer even the mild assurance Russell had recommended. In his eyes the Federal government had no just cause for complaint. The extent to which the United States resorted to Britain as a supplier of weapons had been documented in a short speech by Laird, who had also inflicted a damaging blow on the pro-Union cause when he announced that his firm had been approached to build vessels for the United States as well as the Confederacy. To Palmerston it seemed clear that the Americans were up to their old game of distracting an angry public from domestic failures by raising a cry against Britain, and were hoping to harry him into some dishonourable and undignified modification of her law to boot. He refused to amend it at the behest or in the interest of one of the belligerents. Angered by the remarks of Forster and Bright, he left to those who had made themselves "the mouthpieces of the North" in the House the task of explaining to their American friends that the charges against the British government were not "founded in reason or in law." Further, he suggested that they inform the North that the British government would continue to enforce the law whenever it was provided with legal evidence on which to act—a deposition upon oath—and upon facts that would stand examination before a court of law.[40]

To bring on the debate had clearly been a mistake. Adams attributed Palmerston's remarks to the advance of senility but there was no escaping the fact that the good effect of Russell's reply to Campbell four days earlier had been undone. When the reports of the prime minister's speech reached the United States, Adams foresaw, there would be mounting popular pressure for letters of marque to be issued. Anxiously, he encouraged Seward to resist any resort to "extreme measures." He was not at all sure, he warned, that some groups in Britain would not be willing to risk war in order to tip the scale against the Union. Without abandoning any "strong positions," policy should therefore be so shaped as to avoid giving the British "just causes of complaint." Only three days later he was informed of the British government's decision to detain the *Alex-*

andra. "This is so favourable a sign that my hopes revive of main-taining peace," he wrote in his diary.[41]

Dudley had been watching the vessel's progress for some time. He reported the launching on March 7, and the subsequent installation of her engines. Although he retained a local solicitor, for he was determined not to repeat the mistake of submitting inadmissible evidence, he despaired of success. "The Government gives us no aid and leaves us to make out the case in the best way that we can," he explained to Seward, "and having no process to compel persons to testify we cannot obtain one particle of evidence except such as is voluntarily given and the Government here requires us to produce legal evidence before they will move." And when he again turned to Collier for an opinion, the lawyer refused to provide it. Holding a minor legal office in the Admiralty, Collier had doubts about the propriety of his serving as counsel for Americans, and the public criticism of his opinion in the *Alabama* case had merely confirmed them. Adams gloomily predicted that no lawyer of eminence would now have the courage to repeat Collier's "experiment." Neverthe-less, on March 30 the minister was able to forward to the Foreign Office several depositions taken before the collector of customs at Liverpool and "tending to shew" that the *Alexandra* "was being fitted out for warlike purposes, and was intended for the Confeder-ates." Here, and in good time, was the legal evidence the British had always demanded. The collector concluded that the vessel was intended for the Confederate government, and ordered a watch to be kept on her until he heard from the Board of Customs.[42]

As in the case of the *Alabama* there was conflicting legal advice. Consistent in his narrow interpretation, the solicitor of the board reported his opinion that there did not appear to be any evidence to show that the *Alexandra* was equipped, fitted out, or armed "within the meaning of the Act." The law officers had on March 30 also insisted that a proved violation of the Foreign Enlistment Act was required before the government could properly interfere with the commercial dealings between British subjects and the Confederate States. But the arrival of the depositions Adams had forwarded that same day to the Foreign Office encouraged Atherton and Palmer, with the support of Phillimore, to rally to the far broader construc-tion of the act for which they had first argued in July 1862. What was prohibited under the law was fitting out with intent that the vessel be employed by a foreign prince, they asserted, but "no specific *mode* of fitting out" was pointed at. If the intent constituted "the gist of the offence," and any fitting-out with illegal intent was illegal, the question at issue was whether the evidence provided by the Americans was "enough to shew a 'fitting out,' with prohibited intent?" With no precedents to guide them here, the law officers recommended that the government test the question by trial. Furthermore, they enquired whether the character of the construction and fittings of the *Alexandra* as described in the depositions was "not within the fair meaning of the words of the Statute supposing that any particular *kind* of fitting out ought to be proved." It was clear to them that within the meaning of the act there could be a fitting out without arming, and that "each expression, 'equipment,' 'furnishing,' 'fitting out,' 'arming,' ought to be construed as capable of a distinct meaning."[43]

The law officers' opinion reached the Foreign Office at 3 p.m. on Saturday, April 4. There was to be no repetition of the *Alabama* incident. At midnight the deputy chairman of the Board of Customs received a note from Edmund Hammond ordering the seizure of the *Alexandra*. He hurried down to the Knightsbridge telegraph station, but finding both it and the Regent Street station closed returned on Sunday morning to telegraph the collector at Liverpool to detain her. Three days later Adams informed Russell of another vessel, the *Japan*, which had "just departed from the Clyde with the intent to deprecate on the commerce of the people of the United States." He suggested that she might be on her way to Alderney in the Channel Islands to complete her fitting out, and within half an hour of the arrival of this news at the Foreign Office the Home Office, in whose jurisdiction the islands lay, "had been set on the tracks of the vessel." In the event, the *Japan* did not put into Alderney and thus escaped detention.[44] Nevertheless, the British had acted with dispatch and there were other encouraging signs of a more energetic policy.

The government was no longer the passive spectator of whom Dudley complained, waiting for the Americans to produce legal evidence. Russell had announced as much to Adams on April 12, though he took care to convey the news in a long and pedestrian justification of Britain's earlier conduct as fully consistent with American interpretations of international obligations. The government, he stated, "have renewed the instructions already given to the custom-house authorities of the several British ports where ships-of-war may be constructed, and by the secretary of state for the home department to various authorities with whom he is in communication, to endeavour to discover and obtain legal evidence of any violation of the foreign enlistment act." Following the escape of the *Japan*, the lord provost of Glasgow was instructed by the Home Office to cause enquiries to be made about any other ship in the Clyde fitted for war purposes. Meanwhile, at Liverpool, two detective constables had been set to work investigating suspicious vessels. They met frequently with Vice-Consul Henry Wilding, to discuss whatever information the Americans had collected. They also sought evidence from workmen. *The Times* was soon complaining that an elaborate surveillance system had been set up in the port and that detectives were offering bribes to the employees of firms in return for information. This charge the mayor indignantly denied.[45]

The seizure of the *Alexandra* did not signal a dramatic change of course. Rather, it was the successful execution of a line of action first recommended more than eight months earlier. When he informed Palmerston of the decision, Edmund Hammond emphasized that the Foreign Office was simply following the advice of the law officers who thought it "important to ascertain the true construction of the Act." Yet in a sense this action was also a reflection of Russell's belief that while the outcry in America was "much exaggerated," the spectacle of the *Alabama* roaming the ocean "with English guns, and English sailors to burn, sink and destroy" the ships of a friendly nation was "a scandal and a reproach." Already, in March 1863, the foreign secretary foresaw the necessity of referring "the question of indemnity to an impartial arbiter." It would be dangerous either to do this now or even hold out the hope of it, he wrote to Lyons, but "When things are more advanced towards a termination I think this might be done." On their side the British might refer the case of the *Peterhoff* and other claims arising out of the blockade.[46] Obviously it would be as well to prevent the escape of another raider.

The government's greater vigour in the enforcement of the Foreign Enlistment Act was a response to a number of other concerns and pressures as well. Adams willingly gave some of the credit to the "moral sense" of Britain, which had not been dulled by the "parliamentary narcotic" administered by Palmer and Palmerston. The possibility of a war growing out of this question had prompted those "really friendly to peace" to exert themselves, he reported to Seward.[47] Bright hastened to assure Sumner that demonstrations would be held to condemn both the builders and the government. In fact, at Cobden's suggestion the great gathering of London trades unionists at St. James's Hall on March 26 had taken up this question. Although convened by the unions and ostensibly a manifestation of spontaneous working-class support for the United States in the war on slavery, it was yet another of the meetings carefully organized by the Emancipation Society. Among the invited guests on the platform sat several of the society's luminaries, including Mill, and the meeting's principal purpose was to show that even such long-standing foes as Bright and the trades unions were united in their response to the war. After a speech by Bright, in which he attacked the Confederate loan as a scheme to pay for the additional *Alabamas* under construction, thereby heightening the danger of Britain being dragged into the conflict on the side of the South and slavery, the resolutions were moved. The first, proposed by a bricklayer and seconded by two other workmen, denounced the efforts of the slaveowners to break up the Union, the politicians, capitalists, and journalists in Britain who were abetting them, and the government for negligence in permitting the *Alabama* to escape. The British government stood convicted of having failed "in its duty to a friendly power." Here was a warning to the government, or so the *Bee-Hive* believed, that any war with the United States over vessels such as the *Alabama* would not be supported by the workingman.[48]

The first of several large meetings called by the Emancipation Society specifically to protest the building and fitting out of warships for the Confederacy was held in Manchester on April 6. George Thompson was there, as was Goldwin Smith, and the Free Trade Hall was packed. Following speeches cast in the same mould as Bright's eleven days before, it was agreed to petition the Commons "to interpose its authority in order to prevent any more ships leaving England for the use of the Confederate States." *The Times* angrily condemned this attempt to urge the government "into a violent and unconstitutional course by the threat of foreign war, of the disaffection of millions of its subjects, and of their sympathy with the cause of the enemy."[49] Unrepentant, the society staged another impressive demonstration before the end of the month, this one in the heart of the Scottish shipbuilding district. Thirty-five hundred people gathered in Glasgow City Hall to express their concern at the construction of vessels for "rebel slaveholders" and to urge the government to prevent any more from leaving Britain's shore.[50] But that decision had been taken before this popular campaign was launched. Consequently, to the extent that these demonstrations had an effect, it was to support rather than to initiate the more energetic enforcement of the Foreign Enlistment Act.

Concern over the "somewhat ticklish state" of Britain's relations with the United States had certainly influenced the government's behaviour. Like the prime minister, Russell believed that the Lincoln administration was "getting up war cries" to help its declining popularity. Lyons had helped implant this belief. Initially he viewed Seward's threat to issue letters of marque as no more than "a return to the old bluster." It was the same old story, he reported. Neither Seward nor his party had "the least idea of really going to war with England," but they were willing to go to the brink in order to make political capital. There was, of course, the danger of their going too far before they realized where they were. This was a peril much increased, Lyons believed, by the confidence the anti-slavery demonstrations inspired that public opinion was "coming so completely round to the North" that the British government would be obliged "to favour the North in all ways." Lyons faithfully reported the existence of genuine public exasperation against Britain in the United States, and he forwarded Seward's pleas for news that would tend to allay it.[51]

Before the seizure of the *Alexandra* Russell gave no sign of being unduly disturbed either by the threat of privateers or talk of war. He recognized that the issuing of letters of marque would increase the chances of an angry collision between the two nations, and his mind was not put entirely at ease by Adams's reassurances that there would be no interference with neutral commerce and the law of blockade. Privateers were not intended to meddle with "nice questions of international law," the American minister insisted, merely to hunt down the *Alabama* and similar vessels. If that was truly the case the foreign secretary doubted whether the letters of marque would be issued, and he must have been heartened by Lyons's private and public despatches of March 24, which suggested that the opponents of this step appeared to be gaining the day with the president. Writing to Somerset and Lewis, at the Admiralty and the War Office, before this intelligence arrived, Russell conceded that there were "some uneasy symptoms" on the part of the United States, but he did not "apprehend any thing however unless our naval forces on the American Station and our troops in Canada are diminished." Nor was he unnerved by his discussion with Adams on March 26, though he did admit to Lyons that he would "like any thing better than being obliged to take the part of the Confederates."[52] This sentiment was strengthened by events in Europe.

The news on April 5, the day of the *Alexandra*'s detention, that Russia had placed her army on a war footing heightened the tension on the Continent. Clearly the Russians were readying themselves for a possible war with France. Palmerston's profound suspicion of Napoleon quickly surfaced again. He repeated to Russell his conviction that the humbling of England, "the traditional Rival of France and the main obstacle to French supremacy in Europe and all over the world," was the "real object" of the emperor as of every Frenchman. He "would wish to bring us upon our marrow bones in the most friendly way if we would let him do so," the prime minister added. For his part the foreign secretary did not doubt that Napoleon would grasp any opportunity to occupy the left bank of the Rhine, and so both men must have read a sinister motive into the suggestion from Paris that as Britain's relations with the United States were so uneasy she should secure the good will of the South by recognizing Confederate independence. If England was to exercise a restraining influence upon the French emperor a quiescent relationship with the United States was essential. But as Palmerston pressed on with his quest for a diplomatic solution to the Polish question, outlining to Russell a scheme to establish an independent kingdom of Poland, the foreign secretary continued to fret about the possibility of the European and American crises becoming entangled.[53]

The thought that Russia might "seek a buttress for her Polish Crown in North America" had first crossed Russell's mind at the beginning of March; now he was once again struck by the fearful possibility of Russia and the United States together making war on Britain. "We think much of Poland," he wrote to Lyons on April 11, but the *Alabama* and *Peterhoff* cases "prevent our forgetting America." What was needed, if Britain was to be able to give her full attention to the problems of Europe, was a policy which would allow her to forget the United States. Although the seizure of the *Alexandra* had not been effected for this express purpose, it should serve, together with the evidence of continuing vigilance to prevent infractions of the Foreign Enlistment Act, "to calm the American mind." The problem that remained was the mounting irritation in

England over the conduct of Charles Wilkes. No doubt it was with this public anger in mind that Russell instructed Lyons to warn Seward that any interference by "lawless Adventurers intent only on plunder" with *bona fide* British commerce would excite indignation "very difficult to restrain within due bounds."[54]

That Wilkes would become the centre of controversy had never really been in doubt. The very mention of his name was enough to rile Englishmen, especially naval officers, and his appointment to the command of the flying squadron had been greeted as "almost an offensive act." On his side, Wilkes shared the widespread Northern convictions that the British were sustaining the rebels and that Bermuda and Nassau were nests of "unprincipled rascals." Moreover, he was determined not to be hidebound by legalities and naval etiquette in his efforts to discourage blockade-running. He had reached the conclusion that the traditional form of blockade was an anachronism in the age of steam. "The breaking up of the contraband trade is more readily accomplished by intimidation and the fear of loss of vessels and cargoes from the apparent and not real difficulties that blockade runners have to encounter," he subsequently explained.[55] In short, he and the British were set on a collision course and the first clash came at Bermuda.

When Wilkes arrived off the colony on September 26, 1862, he found seven ships in St. George's, all but one of them notorious blockade-runners. Informed that a law prohibiting the transshipment and exportation of munitions from the islands had been passed and would be promulgated as soon as it received the approval of the Crown, word of which was daily expected, he made the bottling up of the vessels until the law took effect his first "great object." On September 27 he brought two of his ships into port, leaving the third to cruise outside. The visit opened on a sour note. As he entered the harbour the traditional courtesies were not extended by a negligent British officer. Next, a copy of the governor's regulations for belligerents was delivered to Wilkes by an "individual without rank or position." Masking his indignation at what he believed to be studied disrespect for the United States, Wilkes proceeded to "set at nought" the regulations requiring him to leave port within twenty-four hours. One delay followed another after he had obtained permission to coal. Surely he was not expected to include the Sabbath in his permitted time; then it rained; then he discovered that his flagship and the vessel cruising outside the port needed repairs.

Meanwhile in defiance of the British authorities he had one of his ships anchor in the fairway every evening, which prevented any of the blockade-runners slipping out under cover of darkness. To all intents and purposes British shipping had been blockaded by Wilkes in British waters, an outraged governor reported to the Colonial Office. No less offensive was the American's placing of two sentinels on British territory while he coaled. The governor summarized the admiral's behaviour in two words—"very insulting." And when he did finally sail Wilkes left alone. The two vessels that had accompanied him to the colony remained behind to cruise off its coast, successfully intimidating the blockade-runners.[56]

In London, news of what had taken place in Bermuda drew an angry warning from the colonial secretary. Wilkes had gone "as 'near the wind' as possible in his proceedings," Newcastle observed, and "a repetition of them cannot be allowed without giving him encouragement to further aggressions which will endanger the public peace."[57] The law officers submitted the opinion that the conduct of Wilkes "called for very strong remonstrances," and Lyons was instructed accordingly.[58] But this was not a question the minister was disposed to pursue with any vigour. "There was so much going backwards and forwards, and so many messages by word of mouth, that for my part I have never been able clearly to make out the right of the matter," he wrote to Milne.[59] Nor was he energetic in pressing the subsequent complaints of the Bahamians against Wilkes. The American's cruising in the New Providence channel, getting with the aid of sympathetic "coloured" pilots a "thorough knowledge of all the 'dodges' of the Blockaders'," brought an order from the governor forbidding native pilots from assisting belligerents and complaints from the colony that he was blockading Nassau. As Wilkes explained privately to Welles, his intimidating presence caused all the irritations without the reality of a blockade. Such irritations were the price the residents of the Bahamas paid, Lyons believed, for pushing "to the extreme limit" the advantages their position gave them for running the blockade. Russell agreed. The British government could not object to a "vigilant look out against vessels notoriously intending to break the blockade."[60]

On the other hand, the very fact that American efforts to discourage blockade-running were certain to give rise "to a painful and dangerous irritation" emphasized the importance of selecting carefully the Union officers. With Wilkes in command, the ever-present danger was of "the commission of unlawful and even hostile acts." His habit of steaming slowly within British waters in the Bahamas so provoked one British officer that he advised the American consul that if Wilkes anchored after being informed that this was not permitted he "would fire into him whatever his force may be." For this indiscretion he was reprimanded by Milne, but Wilkes's reputation was such that rank provided no barrier to poor judgment. Milne himself, a cautious, even-tempered, sensible man who was not disposed to scrutinize too minutely the use of outlying cays by American cruisers seeking to check the "vast contraband trade" of the Bahamas, responded unwisely to the rumour that Wilkes was planning to repeat the *Trent* affair. In the event of the American seizing the English packet sailing between St. Thomas and Halifax on the grounds that she was carrying Confederate officers, British commanders were instructed to demand her instant release and to use whatever force was necessary to recover her. This impetuous order was soon cancelled at the request of the Foreign Office, but Russell instructed Lyons to give Seward "a friendly warning" on this matter.[61]

It was Wilkes's involvement in the Union's campaign to deny use of the Mexican port of Matamoros to vessels seeking to evade the blockade that finally aroused a belligerent outcry in Britain. His ordering of the seizure of the *Peterhoff* (a known blockade-runner reported to be carrying contraband) soon after she cleared St. Thomas for Matamoros, brought to the boil a long-simmering resentment of American interference with neutral commerce. The capture of the *Pearl* while en route from St. Thomas to Nassau, of the *Springbok* bound from London to Nassau, of the *Magicienne* while on a voyage from Liverpool to Matamoros, and then the taking of the *Peterhoff* and the *Dolphin* under similar circumstances raised suspicions that officers of the United States Navy were pursuing a policy of indiscriminate seizures. They appeared to be determined to block trade between two neutral ports, content to take their chances on winning convictions in the prize courts. The owner of the *Peterhoff* called at the Foreign Office on April 10 to voice this suspicion during a long interview with Edmund Hammond, and he returned with a deputation of his associates to see Russell six days later. The cry was also taken up by the press, with *The Times* in the vanguard. "Unless a firm stand be made," it warned, "there will be no end to the indignities and losses we must endure." It was Adams's misfortune to take a rare false step which raised to a new pitch the howls of indignation.[62]

Although his despatches to Seward following the detention of the *Alexandra* were generally optimistic in tone, Adams was beset by private doubts of Britain and his country long remaining at peace. He was sure Palmerston inspired the harsh leaders in *The Times* and he mourned the untimely death of Cornewall Lewis, a restraining influence in cabinet on American affairs, as Milner Gibson had disclosed.[63] The minister's deepening anxiety was shared by John Bigelow who came over from Paris to spend a fortnight in London. "I did not see how war was to be avoided," he later wrote of his first few days in the British capital. Cobden assured him that Palmerston was not looking for a conflict, explaining that a war "would shiver this ministry to atoms in an instant," but Bigelow remained uneasy.[64] Moreover, both the member for Rochdale and that town's most distinguished resident impressed upon their American friends the extent to which Wilkes was hurting the Union's friends and aiding its enemies. Forbes and Aspinwall wrote to Welles urging him to remove this officer, for "Everything he does hits twice as hard in irritating John Bull as the same thing done by anybody else."[65] Meanwhile Adams continued to worry that some incident might force him to pack his bags and return home. Perhaps he had a premonition, for the very next day he found himself the centre of a storm which before it blew itself out saw the London clubs swept by the rumour that he had been sent packing.[66]

Earlier in the month two Americans purchasing supplies and munitions for the Mexicans had sought his help. The capture of the *Peterhoff* had discouraged the underwriters at Lloyd's from insuring vessels bound for Matamoros. From Adams these two men requested and obtained a letter attesting to their loyalty, and thus a guarantee against the seizure of their cargo by the American blockade squadron. This they presented to Lloyd's in order to obtain insurance but it was copied surreptitiously and the *Peterhoff* delegation which called at the Foreign Office on April 16 read it to Russell. The conclusion was inescapable, the group's spokesman pointed out. Not content with their "unfair and illegal" course, the Federal authorities "now seemed to consider themselves entitled to dictate what trade should and should not be carried on" by British vessels. It was a charge the press quickly and loudly repeated. Adams had blundered, for in compromising himself he played into the hands of the parliamentary advocates of a stern British response to the Union's interference with neutral commerce.[67]

Seymour Fitzgerald, the Tory spokesman on foreign affairs in the Commons, had raised the question of the *Peterhoff* on March 27. He held the Palmerston government responsible. It had been Russell's acquiescence in the Union's interference with the trade between Britain and Nassau which had led to this new invasion of neutral rights, he claimed. A firmer line of conduct earlier and "this outrage" would never have taken place. With the publication of Adams's letter the debate was revived. The ugly mood of the House was quickly exploited by Roebuck. Referring sarcastically to Adams as "the Minister for Commerce in England," this bellicose Radical announced himself and the English people prepared for war if that was necessary to uphold the nation's "honour and dignity" and to establish that its commerce would no longer "be subject to the overbearing and domineering insolence of an upstart race."[68] And while Roebuck was dismissed as "of small importance," one Englishman who had "been a good deal in railway carriages lately" recorded in his journal that such sentiments were "freely mooted, exchanged, and supported."[69] In the Commons angry Tories stopped short of endorsing a resort to extreme measures but spoke with asperity. Lord Robert Cecil, among others, complained "that while our Government are idling and thinking what they shall do, Mr. Adams is master of the field. The trade of England is carried on now by the permits of a foreigner."[70]

The government's position was not an enviable one. At the Foreign Office it was recognized that British merchants had been "very daring and unscrupulous." Then again, the opinions of the law officers were frequently hedged with reservations. Too often the government had been pressed to interfere "upon very strong *ex parte* statements of injury which subsequent investigation in the Prize Court" had proven "wholly without foundation." The government could not claim for British vessels any exemption from belligerent rights of visit and search, nor could it act on the assumption that all those vessels were lawfully employed. It was not at all unusual for blockade-runners to simulate a neutral destination, supported by deceptive papers, the law officers pointed out, and the location of the Mexican ports, especially Matamoros, made it probable that they would be claimed as such.[71] But the legal reasons for a deliberate response were dwarfed by the international.

From Washington there came a string of disturbing despatches. Writing early in April, before the news of the detention of the *Alexandra* had reached the American capital, Lyons expressed the opinion that the state of things there, so far as peace with Britain was concerned, was "more alarming than it has been since the 'Trent' affair."[72] From Paris came reports that the unpredictable emperor was complaining of insomnia induced by thoughts of the wrongs being done to Poland. This did little to lessen the war panic at St. Petersburg and Berlin. Cowley soon grew to doubt that Napoleon intended to intervene forcibly in Poland—the difficulties were too great—but he no less than Palmerston and Russell feared the emperor's opportunism. Should Britain "unfortunately become involved in hostilities with the United States, and be fully employed out there," then Napoleon would seek to enhance his reputation by grabbing the left bank of the Rhine. "But so long as we are at peace," Cowley reported reassuringly, "he will do nothing that will risk a rupture with us." Thus Russell's task was to "cool down" the "insane fury" in Britain and the United States before it was too late.[73]

It did not escape the Foreign Office that "none of the influential members" of the Tory party had endorsed "the violent language of their underlings," and with Palmerston's aid Russell confidently set out to douse the flames rising in Parliament and elsewhere. His method was straightforward enough. Britain must not be "led by passion into anything which is not founded on justice, and which cannot afterwards be justified in the face of the world." He revealed that he intended to protest two evident violations of neutral rights in the case of the *Dolphin*. The first was the use by American cruisers of a neutral port—St. Thomas—to lie in wait for British merchantmen; the second, the removal of several members of the crew and the landing of them upon neutral territory. However, he hastened to point out that in an earlier instance of the unneutral use of a neutral port the United States had made "proper reparation." The essence of his argument in the Lords, as of Palmerston's in the Commons, was that in those cases where Wilkes and other officers had infringed upon neutral rights there was no reason to assume that reparation when requested would be refused. He expressed himself as "being perfectly satisfied with the American Government, and under no sort of apprehension that Mr. Seward will deny just compensation and apology for any proved illegal acts of American vessels." As for Adams's letter, that was a "very extraordinary" and a "most unwarrantable act" which he intended to bring before the United States government.[74] This rebuke, painful as Adams found it, was necessary. It eased acceptance of the government's calm response to the actions of American naval commanders in the West Indies. In the words of *The Times,* "It shows that, while making every allowance for the difficulties of the Federal Executive, our Government will allow no invasion of our own rights to pass unredressed."[75]

The other organ closely identified with Palmerston also fell into line. The *Morning Post* emphasized the excellent spirit with which the United States had met earlier complaints, thereby implying that the government had not been derelict in guarding British rights.[76] Then, on April 30, *The Times* published another long letter from the influential "Historicus." Russell may have inspired it, for increasingly he looked to Harcourt for unofficial advice on the complex problems of international law. The foreign secretary's "calm, dignified and moderate language" was held up as a model of statesmanship. If the United States claimed the right to capture neutral vessels carrying innocent cargoes to neutral ports the American government would be called upon instantly to repudiate it, "Historicus" wrote. Fortunately the Americans had expressly disclaimed any such right. If there was any reason to suspect American prize courts of injustice or failure to do their duty to injured neutrals, the neutral government had the right to demand direct compensation from the belligerent. But these accusations had not been made. Captures made by cruisers must be presumed to be legal until a prize court pronounced them illegitimate, and the booming trade with the formerly insignificant ports of Nassau and Matamoros was scarcely above suspicion. "More than half the neutral vessels condemned in our Courts in the French wars were vessels with fabricated papers made to evidence a false destination," Harcourt added. On the important question of whether a neutral vessel could be condemned because the cargo had an "ultimately hostile consignment" he was a little less sure. Personally he thought not, but this was a problem to be faced when a United States prize court asserted the doctrine. Finally, he dwelt upon the necessity of a neutral Britain abiding by the rules which she had rigorously enforced as a belligerent. Englishmen should rejoice to see "the boasted champions of neutrality building up impregnable bulwarks and fortifying by modern examples those belligerent rights for which we so long contended against a world in arms."

Russell sought not only to calm the excitement in Britain but to persuade the Union to discontinue the practices that had caused it. "We have no positive ground of complaint of the American Government," he informed Somerset, "but I think that the addition of two or three stout ships to our American Squadron would be very useful, and might deter the Yankee from stepping over the limits of International Law."[77] Simultaneously he exerted diplomatic pressure. Lyons was instructed to inform Seward that the seizures of the *Dolphin* and *Peterhoff*, and Adams's "extraordinary letter," had created the impression that it was the intention of the United States, "by captures without cause, by delays of adjudication, by wanton imprisonment of the masters and part of the crew of captured vessels, to put a stop to the British Trade to Matamoros altogether." Yet the trade was perfectly legitimate, indeed it was carried on from New York. Russell further asserted, on the direct advice of the law officers, that some matters, such as determining which portion of a cargo was consumed in Mexico or transshipped to the South, were "beyond the scope and destination of the sea voyage." Therefore, should it appear that "from jealousy of trade, unjust suspicion of contraband," or some other motive, British trade was "deliberately and systematically made subject to vexatious capture, and arbitrary interference," Britain would have to intervene to protect her flag.[78]

Russell was willing to mix this warning with a substantial concession. On April 25 he broached the question of a claims convention to the cabinet. Here, he thought, was the instrument to smoothe Anglo-American relations. However, his colleagues were not prepared to entertain the idea of arbitrating the Union's "Alabama losses."[79] That was to admit fault in the vessel's escape. The position to which the majority held had been restated in the Commons the evening before by Roundell Palmer. "We are anxious, most anxious, to prevent such violations of neutrality and law by our own citizens," he declared, "but we are determined not to accept a responsibility on the part of the Government that does not belong to it, and not to concede that the United States have a right to treat us as wanting in our duty to neutrality if our laws fail to reach all particular cases that may occur."[80] In short, the vigorous enforcement of the Foreign Enlistment Act was as far as the British were prepared to go, and the belief that this would be sufficient to calm the Americans was soon confirmed.

The arrival on April 27 of the news that Seward had ordered the release unopened of the mail carried by the *Peterhoff* seemed to indicate a conciliatory attitude in Washington. Soon afterwards word came from Lyons of the eagerness with which Northerners had grasped at "the intelligence of the endeavours to stop the Confederate Vessels building in England, as a relief from their dread that they were really drifting into a war with us." This was followed by Seward's apology for Adams's letter and his intimation that "questionable" seizures of British vessels bound for Matamoros or in the neighbourhood of St. Thomas would cease. Then, at the beginning of June, Wilkes was recalled from the West Indies. Not only had he irritated the Danes and enraged the British but he had failed to hunt down the Confederate cruisers and had disobeyed orders from the navy department, thereby forfeiting the support of Welles. Naturally the report of his removal was welcomed in Britain.[81]

TEN

Precedents

BY THE SPRING OF 1863 there was no longer any likelihood of Britain intervening in the American war. Neither the recognition nor the mediation sought by the Confederacy and feared by the Union was in prospect. As one embittered Southerner put it, writing from London, "The policy of the British Cabinet, I am sorry to say, remains unaltered, or rather would seem to be more than ever opposed to the formal recognition of a universally admitted fact. I have less hope than ever of any action on its part tending to put a term to this desolating contest."[1] Yet many in Britain, including the prime minister, would still have welcomed the division of the Republic, while a great many more thought loss of the South a price Northerners ought willingly to pay for peace. Most Englishmen remained convinced that the Union could never be restored. The North might seize portions of the South but would never be able to subdue them or regain control of the entire region. Overlooking the changes wrought by the railroads, they thought the territory of the rebellious states too vast to be conquered. Why then were the British determined to hold aloof? The answer is to be found in the combined weight of several factors rather than in the predominance of one.

There was a large measure of truth in American accusations that Britain's neutrality was the product of fear. Few Englishmen accepted the Confederate proposition that recognition would of itself end the war. Without more vigorous measures it would do little to assist the Confederacy. On the contrary, it promised to solidify the Union behind the Lincoln administration and thus prolong not shorten the war. Even more unpleasant was the thought that this action might enlarge the conflict. Perhaps that consideration was not entirely absent from Southern minds, but Britain had no intention of embarking upon a course which would bring her into collision even with the "disUnited States." The dangers to her North

American empire, to her domestic harmony, and to her position in Europe were too grave.

Talk of war with the North always turned English eyes to Canada, and in this regard April 1863 had been no different from any other period of crisis. The province's military weakness was, in the words of one critic, "at present our chief source of anxiety." There was considerable anger at the Canadians' persistent refusal to shoulder a larger share of the burden of defence. They contributed a miserable fivepence a head to their own protection whereas Englishmen paid forty times that amount for the forces used to defend Britain and the Empire. It was time for British North Americans to do more, and in this cry the advocates of retrenchment in colonial expenditures were joined by members of the government. The Canadians had not responded, yet irritating though it was this did not afford Britain an excuse to wash her hands of them. Neither did the fact that Canada was in its domestic affairs "about as free as any country in the world." After all, the imperial government was supreme "in all those questions upon which the issues of peace and war depended." The Canadians had to be friends of Britain's friends, enemies of her enemies, "therefore the obligation of assisting them in case of war still rested on the mother country."[2]

Palmerston and Russell had, in addition, compelling domestic reasons to steer well clear of a possible conflict with the United States. The coalition nature of the ministry, and the sympathy for the Union shared by several members of the cabinet, discouraged the adoption of a hazardous policy. The situation might have been different had the American war caused the economic dislocation upon which Confederate hopes rode, or brought unbearable social misery. Instead, Britain was prospering, a point the prime minister repeatedly emphasized in his speeches to Scottish audiences during the Easter recess. The problems of Lancashire had been serious, and still were, but even there the corner to recovery appeared to have been turned. Slowly but surely the numbers on relief were declining, and the unrest in and around Stalybridge had not been followed by widespread disturbances. For the most part the operatives bore their suffering patiently, and the government's remedial measures offered them some hope. Agitation in the mill towns for recognition of the Confederacy, stirred by the belief that this step would somehow lead to the war's end and thereby free the cotton, had proved ineffective. Support had come from Tory journals, which fastened upon the plight of the operatives as a stick with which to beat the government and to demand a change of American policy, but the party's leadership showed no sign of following this line. The American war and its consequences for Britain had not become, as Russell once feared they would, partisan issues. The efforts of the Confederacy's advocates to harness the operatives to their cause had likewise met with little success. Badly managed meetings at Blackburn and Stalybridge, where either the speakers or the site had been poorly selected, ended in humiliating rebuffs.

In the spring of 1862 the battle for men's hearts, if not minds, seemed to have been won for the Confederacy by James Spence. A year later Southern sympathizers had been out-manoeuvred by a group whose popular support in the country was far less broad. Lincoln's proclamation had given substance to the claim made by Dicey, Martineau, Cairnes, and Mill that the war would destroy the institution of slavery. Many Englishmen continued to be more than a little dubious of the wisdom of any abrupt emancipation, especially of the blacks who laboured on the cotton plantations. However, the skilfully organized campaign of the Emancipation Society did lend weight to the belief that a policy which appeared to favour the slave states over the free would prove divisive in England. The prospect of Britain finding herself an ally of the "Slave Confederacy" in a war with the Union was even more odious, and no less so to Palmerston and Russell than to any Northern sympathizer.

The decisive factor, the consideration that finally deterred Palmerston and Russell from foreign and committed them to home intervention, was the turmoil in Europe. From the outset of the Civil War the British government's distrust of the French emperor had acted as a restraint. His recurrent proposals of joint intervention excited suspicions of a crafty plan to involve the two nations in difficulties with the United States from which France would then withdraw, leaving her free to further her ambitions in Europe. The upheavals on the Continent, particularly the Polish rebellion, seemed to have created fresh opportunities for Napoleonic mischief. They also destroyed whatever remained of the Anglo-French understanding. If she was to defeat the emperor's schemes, Britain needed to be both at peace and on reasonably good terms with the United States. Such a relationship would guard as well against the troubles of Europe and America becoming entangled in any other way.

One other danger which had to be faced was of Britain finding herself dragged into the conflict as a result of her sins of omission or commission. Her neutrality had won her the loathing of the South for what she had not done, and the hatred of the North for what she had. Hence the Emancipation Society's campaign to stop the building of vessels for the "rebel slaveholders." Yet in the spring of 1863 even this problem appeared to be receding as a threat to peace. John Bigelow returned to Paris at the end of April "less apprehensive" about the future, and even Adams admitted to himself that there had been a change in the popular mood which even *The Times* reflected. The chances of peace were improving, he concluded with characteristic caution.[3] As for the two powerful steam rams being built for the Confederacy at Birkenhead by Lairds, the detention of the *Alexandra* and the better public temper seemed to have sealed their fate. "The public spirit has made such rapid improvement within the past month," Forbes wrote to Welles early in May, "that I cannot but hope that the danger of an Iron Clad being permitted to sail is very small." Cobden and Bright assured Sumner that Russell was "sincerely alive to the necessity of putting an end to the equipping of ships of war" in British harbours for the Confederacy, and that no more would be allowed to go out "if any fair ground can be shown for interfering with them."[4]

That Britain had a peculiar reason to enforce the neutrality laws strictly was a point Richard Cobden hammered home in the Commons. Ever since the debate of March 27 he had been itching to knock away some of Palmer's "cobwebs" and to develop the true argument—self-interest. Britain had "the most at risk" from non-observance of the principle of neutrality among noncombatants. Disregard for neutral obligations now would result in cruisers issuing from New York and Boston to prey upon her commerce in future wars. "This is the only view likely to influence our shipowners and merchants," he reasoned.[5] His opportunity to state the case came when the Liverpool member, Thomas Horsfall, put down a question on the detention of the *Alexandra*. Cobden was well prepared when he rose to speak on April 24. He had breakfasted with Adams a few days before, seeking information on the American equivalent of the Foreign Enlistment Act, for he intended to plead the reciprocal nature of the legislation. The United States had a right to complain if Britain did not enforce the act, he believed, for they had "passed and enforced similar laws on that understanding." He implored Bright to attend the debate. The fact of his "being present with the power of reply exerts a restraining influence on Palmerston and the other speakers on the Treasury bench, and it is especially important that they should be restrained on this occasion," he wrote flatteringly. However, Bright's wife had just presented him with a son and his first duty was to remain with her in Rochdale.⁶

Despite his absence the behaviour of the occupants of the Treasury bench was sufficiently restrained during the debate. Cobden's "manner was cold and hesitating, but he spoke with great force and sense," and had little difficulty illustrating his points of reciprocity and self-interest. He reminded his listeners that the lowest estimate of British property on the high seas, and thus vulnerable to commerce raiders, was £100 million. Nor was his the only voice of warning. Robert Collier asked the House to remember that although they were then neutrals they had often been belligerents in the past and "it was impossible to say how soon they might be belligerents again. If they laid down rules applicable only to their neutral position, those rules might be used to their disadvantage when they became belligerents."⁷ Clearly, happy Northern observers concluded, the debate had assisted the government by making it comparatively easy for them "to observe the Foreign Enlistment Act in good faith." Palmerston and his colleagues were being urged in that direction also by some merchants and shipowners. Rathbone came up to London from Liverpool to place before the government privately "more rational views about the shipping interest" than those represented by Thomas Horsfall. The delight the Liverpool member and "the body of narrow minded and shabby shipowners" took in the decline of the American mercantile marine was short-sighted. Bagehot had warned in the *Economist* months before of the implications for Britain of the American claim that their shipping had been paralysed by the *Alabama*.⁸ On May 4, no doubt at Rathbone's inspiration, and perhaps at the suggestion of members of the government, the Liverpool Chamber of Commerce requested that in the event of another *Alabama* affair and evidence that the Foreign Enlistment Act was "not efficient for the accomplishment of its object in which British interests are so deeply involved, immediate steps be taken to remedy the deficiency before precedents grow up which may seriously harass this Country whenever it is unhappily engaged in war."⁹

Within the government there was considerable uneasiness about the act and the related question of precedents. Gladstone had been impressed by Cobden's charge in the House that the United States had a "strong claim" against Britain "for the vigilant execution of the law." Argyll was even more deeply troubled by his nation's course. In his letters to Sumner he defended the government's conduct in the *Alabama* case and protested that it was "against all reason to talk of her as 'British' in any sense which involved the British Government in responsibility." To his colleague Gladstone, however, he admitted that the more he thought of it the more sure he felt "that the Doctrine of 'Alabamas' being no violation of International Laws but only of Municipal Law—is a doctrine which will not stand investigation—and will certainly not be consistent with the maintenance of peace whenever other nations are strong enough to resent it." For the implication seemed to be that the act might be repealed and the building of war vessels undertaken in all British yards without giving any grounds of offence to the United States. "It is a doctrine in the highest degree dangerous to ourselves and against all reason and commonsense," he concluded. "Peace between two governments w[oul]d be perfectly compatible, on this doctrine, with systematic war between their respective subjects."[10]

When William B. Evarts arrived in London, and reported to the legation on May 1, 1863, he was pleasantly surprised to discover that the members of the British government were "more awake to the dangers of their stickling for the 'freedom of British Commerce' " than he had feared they would be.[11] Indeed, they were awake to more perils than he realized. The clearest example of the new appreciation of the dangerous precedents Britain might be establishing for herself was the about-face the government performed on the treatment of mail. Lyons had protested the opening of the mail bags carried by the *Peterhoff*, and through Seward's intercession the mail itself had been returned unopened. "This will, no doubt, create a precedent which will henceforth protect all mail bags of neutrals from being opened by belligerents," one English periodical observed. But that was not a protection the British wished to see them afforded. The mails might contain evidence pertinent to prize court proceedings and Britain's belligerent strength was her navy. Awakened to the danger by Hammond, Russell launched a discussion of the general question of the inviolability of mail carried by vessels seized by belligerents.[12]

Before taking the subject to cabinet the foreign secretary sought the opinion of the lord chancellor, the postmaster-general, and the prime minister. After reviewing the arguments and possible courses of action the lord chancellor emphasized the consideration they should always bear in mind: "What will be most [helpful] for our interest as a future belligerent." Palmerston agreed that they must keep before them the fact that they were "oftener likely to be Belligerents than neutrals," yet they should also be governed by their general interest in the maintenance of commercial communications free from unnecessary interruption. A compromise between these interests was therefore found. It was agreed that the mails carried by contract packets should be inviolable but that the ship itself was subject to visit and search by a belligerent. As for private vessels like the *Peterhoff*, the prize courts should be left to decide whether to examine the mails carried by them. In short, the rights of neutrals must not be made too stringent. The guiding consideration in this compromise was the realization that over a long period of time Britain's political interests were more likely to be connected with belligerent than with neutral rights. Lyons subsequently informed Seward of the new British position, which presumably struck the secretary as being much the same as that taken earlier by Gideon Welles.[13]

In the knowledge that their long-term interests were more likely to be advanced through acquiescence in rather than opposition to the Union's definition of belligerent rights, the British had found good reason for reducing irritations and thereby lessening tension. There was still an unanswered question, however. How would the government respond in the event that the court ruled against the Crown, and the law officers' interpretation of the Foreign Enlistment Act, in the *Alexandra* trial? "I fear it is a less distinct case" [than the *Alabama*], Argyll admitted, "and a failure will give fresh impetus to the trade."[14]

The law officers also fell prey to misgivings. They had urged in April that "some competent person" be employed to gather "the legal proofs" which would connect the vessel to the Confederate service "through persons shown, by facts, to have acted on former occasions as the Agents of the Confederate Government, and shown also to have interfered in the construction of the 'Alexandra'."[15] The Crown then drew up a catch-all indictment of ninety-eight counts, its length creating an illusion of strength, and the venue of the trial was moved from Liverpool to London. Suspicions of prejudice in the northern port were well founded, for members of the Watch Committee sympathetic to the South had compelled one of the detectives employed by Dudley to divulge the evidence he had collected and some of it was promptly published in local newspapers. Equally prejudicial to the Crown's case, or so Roundell Palmer believed, was the debate forced in Parliament on the *Alexandra*'s seizure. This had served to arouse feelings in favour of the builders, he feared. Soon afterwards a rumour that the solicitor general did not mean to go into court himself prompted Russell to intervene to ensure that he did. After all this was "no common case" and it required "the whole force" of the law officers.[16]

When the trial finally opened in the Court of Exchequer on June 22, before the chief baron and a special jury, Palmer proved no match for the brilliant counsel retained by the defendants. Comparatively inexperienced, he was given a lesson in courtroom pyrotechnics by his adversaries. They discredited his witnesses, especially Clarence Yonge who had provided information to Dudley. Yonge was revealed to have deserted his wife and child in Savannah, then travelled to Kingston, Jamaica, where he had gone through a marriage ceremony with a mulatto woman of means only to abandon her once he had pocketed her money. There were legal arguments for the judge, Palmer ruefully recalled years later, "and excursions into the region of prejudice for the jury." In his charge to the jury Chief Baron Pollock placed the narrowest construction possible upon the law. The intent was to stop the departure of armed vessels, he declared. Thus in his opinion there had been nothing unlawful about the *Alabama* at the time of her escape from Liverpool. Not surprisingly the verdict in the *Alexandra* case—an acquittal—was never in doubt. The law officers immediately entered a bill of exceptions, which tied up the case at least until November, while the public contemplated Pollock's behaviour and the implications of the verdict.[17]

In 1863 Jonathan Frederick Pollock celebrated his eighty-second year, having presided over the Court of Exchequer for very nearly two decades. His age and his Tory animus toward the Whig-Liberal government of the day were both seized upon to explain his directions to the jury. He had held to his place not merely for its emoluments, the angry *Bee-Hive* accused, "but because he does not wish to give the Whigs the appointment of his successor."[18] In fact, Pollock was a remarkably vigorous man who had fathered twenty-one children and continued to show no sign of senility. What he brought to court on June 22 was the conviction "that restrictions on trade are generally pernicious," and a partiality for the South. It was his belief that as soon as the Confederate flag had been hoisted neutrals such as Britain had been entitled to recognize it and insist that their commerce not be interrupted by a "sham blockade," nor even by a real one which did more mischief to neutrals than to the belligerent. Furthermore, he considered the government's noninterventionist stance "short-sighted in the extreme." The entire world, and Britain in particular, had an interest in preventing North America from becoming one great power capable of threatening all others. In his opinion Britain would not be violating any public law of nations, breaking any treaty, or breaching any political rule of morality, were she to assist the Confederates to "establish an independence to which they are entitled and which is most important to the general interests of mankind at large."[19]

Whatever inspired Pollock's conduct, the consequences of the jury's compliance with his directions promised to be far-reaching. While the *Morning Post* found his quotation of American authorities in support of his interpretation of the law a source of amusement, others deplored his reference to *Webster's Dictionary* for a definition of "to equip" which reduced all the activities prohibited under the Foreign Enlistment Act to synonyms for arming. As the *Spectator* sarcastically observed, the words equipping, furnishing, fitting out or arming should read "arming, arming, arming or arming." On this point the more conservative *Economist* also took issue with Pollock, while the Radical *Star* characterized the ruling "as crude and childish in the extreme" and certain "to bring British jurisprudence into contempt throughout both hemispheres." If, as Pollock argued, the act only prohibited the sailing of fully armed ships then it had been rendered "altogether nugatory." Britain would do well to ponder the kind of precedent she was now in danger of setting for herself, the *Daily News* warned.[20]

At the Foreign Office the immediate concern was the reaction of the United States government to the outcome of the trial. If Pollock was right, Hammond admitted privately, then the Foreign Enlistment Act was "a cheat and a delusion." However, on reflection he did not foresee trouble on the other side of the Atlantic. Evarts had been "kept fully informed of what was being done and saw that it was a weak case," even though every effort had been made to "bolster it up." If he reported this to Seward it should "allay any disappointment."[21] As Hammond hoped, Evarts reported that the law officers had done their best to procure a condemnation. Further, he expressed the opinion that the bill of exceptions together with the continued detention of the vessel would deter those seeking to provide the Confederacy with a navy. Equally encouraging was the fact that Pollock's interpretation of the law had not been well received by the legal profession, while its implications had not escaped commercial men. These were good omens for a more satisfactory outcome when the case was reheard. The same calming message was sent by Forbes and Aspinwall to the irascible Welles. Moreover, greatly encouraged by a talk with Cobden, they expressed the belief that the jubilation of the Confederates and their sympathizers would be short-lived if the verdict brought the government to a sense of its international responsibilities. Indeed, they soon concluded that the British government would, "whenever application is made by the Minister, upon a reasonable show of evidence," detain the two ironclad rams being built by Lairds. They were somewhat less sure that a detention would be made permanent.[22]

James Bulloch had reached much the same conclusion. Although the verdict in the Exchequer Court ought to have facilitated his operations they continued to be extremely difficult. Not only did Federal spies increase in number but there was no slackening of British vigilance. He complained that it was impossible for a vessel to clear for a British island close to the Confederacy "without inquiry, interruption and delay." Those ships under construction and resembling men-of-war drew the attention of "Yankee spies" and British officials, and were made the subject of letters to the newspapers, protests from lawyers, and petitions from the Emancipation Society. A little dispiritedly, Bulloch warned Richmond that "nothing more should be attempted in England." As for the two rams nearing completion at Birkenhead, in an artful attempt to protect them he completed a legal but sham transfer of ownership to the French firm of Messrs. Bravay and Company, of Paris, whose claim to have been commissioned by the late Viceroy of Egypt to purchase two such vessels added credence to the transaction. Bulloch also took care neither to visit the vessels nor even the Lairds' yards. He directed affairs through Bravay.[23]

Bulloch's precautions failed to deceive the Americans, and as work on the vessels hurried ahead Charles Francis Adams showed signs of losing his composure. He had responded with admirable level-headedness to the *Alexandra* decision, but the strain of his duties was beginning to take its toll. What he interpreted as the unrelenting English hostility to the Union cause was slowly wearing him down. He was able to give vent to his disgust with the British nation in his diary, yet this afforded little relief. He had no confidence in the Palmerston ministry which he judged too feeble and vacillating to counter this popular opinion or oppose those commercial interests, among them the shipbuilders, who were profiting so handsomely from the American war. But he was not a great deal more enamoured of his own government. To himself, he bemoaned the curse of an "incompetent" president and "insufficient" military leaders. He was enraged when he heard that Seward had apologized to the French government for the construction they had placed upon that unfortunate letter "cheerfully" giving aid to persons attempting to supply arms to Mexicans resisting Napoleon's armies. The secretary had degraded "himself, his country and me," the proud Adams wrote in his diary. Increasingly he resented the arrival of special agents from home. He cooperated with Evarts but had secretly welcomed his decision to return to the United States once the parliamentary session ended in late July. However, Evarts was promptly replaced by William Whiting. An intimate of Sumner's, he was described by one of Adams's friends as a "plebian sycophant" whose conversation could be "divided into two equal parts—flattery of himself, and flattery of the person he is talking with, and there is usually as much truth in the one part as there is of sincerity in the other." What was worse, Adams feared these arrivals were damaging his position in London, thus diminishing his effectiveness as well as wounding his pride. He was sure that the impression was gaining ground in the British capital that he was no more than a figurehead whose informal subordinates did the work.[24]

It was in this dark mood of pent-up bitterness and resentment that Adams approached the problem posed by the steam rams. Dudley reported the launching of one of these vessels and the fact that her turrets were ready to be placed aboard her early in July. He was pessimistic about his ability to stop her getting out, but on July 7 he made a formal application to the local collector of customs that she be detained, supporting the request with a number of affidavits. While the consulate's solicitor conducted this meeting Dudley carried copies of all the papers to London, delivering them personally to Adams. The minister's response was extreme. This was "the gravest event of the series" and had to be treated "with corresponding seriousness," he wrote in his diary. In the back of his mind he may have sensed an opportunity to demonstrate his full command of the legation, but in the forefront was a determination to impress the British with the gravity of the situation. "If the government do not exert themselves now," he concluded, "I fear then it will be regarded in America as war in disguise and lead to some measures of retaliation." Both directly and indirectly he conveyed this warning to Russell. The sailing of the rams could not fail "to endanger the peace and welfare of both countries," he informed the foreign secretary.[25]

Adams's mood remained a sombre one, despite the ignominious failure of another parliamentary campaign to push Britain into recognition of the Confederacy. He might have found further reassurance in the fact that the affairs of Europe were so threatening that the government seemed certain to act with prudence and self-restraint in order to save embroiling itself with the United States. Moreover, it had been intimated to him that the ministry would not let the rams get out. Favourable as these developments were, the evident public disappointment in England at the news of the Union triumph at Vicksburg and Lee's failure at Gettysburg continued to nourish the minister's contempt for and distrust of these people who had forfeited their reputation "for manliness and honesty." From Dudley he heard that the authorities at Liverpool accepted the word of the Lairds, who had indicated that the vessels were intended for Turkey or Egypt. Then in the Commons on July 23, Palmerston, replying to a question from Cobden, suggested that they were for the French. Cobden had gained nothing by his attempt to draw the government out before the end of the session, Adams concluded grimly, for while he was "really in earnest in his efforts" the drift had been "too much for him." As for the prime minister's remarks did they mean that the British were going to fall willingly for Bulloch's ruse? The rams would be allowed to go "and war may ensue for all the first minister with one leg in the grave cares," Adams feared.[26]

Seward was far more optimistic. "My foreign affairs, I think, are in good plight," he commented on June 25, before hearing of the latest developments in Britain. Yet the *Alexandra* decision, while a reminder of the ever-present possibilities of "foreign complications," did not undermine his confidence. In the victories at Vicksburg and Gettysburg he found hope of the Union being feared and therefore respected in Europe. With the same end in mind he packed his friend Samuel Ruggles off to the Statistical Congress in Berlin. Carrying all "the concentrated essence of America" in his baggage, the facts and figures of economic growth and strength, Ruggles was "to shew his Old World colleagues that the gas of American brag can be solidified and made palpable and is *real matter* after all."[27] Meanwhile Seward pressed the leading members of the diplomatic corps into accompanying him on a journey through New York. They would see for themselves that the nation was far from exhausted, either physically or emotionally. However, the one member of the "International Caravan" Seward had the greatest interest in impressing failed to take the point of the tour. "I do not suppose that Mr. Seward has any other political object in collecting so many of the members of the Diplomatic Body," Lyons observed, "than to make a demonstration to the public of the friendly character of his personal relations with them."[28]

The relationship with Britain remained the most demanding of the secretary's responsibilities. There had been no lessening of the popular enmity toward her, as British visitors to the Union quickly discovered. The Confederate loan, the publication of the notes exchanged by Adams and Russell before the *Alabama* escaped, Pollock's directions to the jury and its verdict in the *Alexandra* trial, all brought fresh accusations that in every way they could, or dared, the British had "sneakingly aided the Rebels." But in 1863 Seward was too intent on the suppression of the insurrection "to seek for occasions of dispute with any foreign power." Resisting any temptation to play to the gallery, he pursued his policy of reducing the sources of friction.[29]

Lyons had hoped that the removal of Wilkes from the West Indies was "a sign that other conciliatory acts, not words merely, will follow," and he was not to be disappointed. Arguing that they needed to strengthen the British government, for it had consistently upheld the blockade's validity, and if displaced would surely be succeeded by a group of ministers more unfavourable to the Union, Seward won Lincoln's decisive support in his long struggle with Welles over the instructions sent to naval officers. Unavailingly, the navy secretary objected to "derogatory concessions" to the British. Elsewhere, Seward offered to settle a long-standing dispute over the claims of the Hudson's Bay Company to land south of the forty-ninth parallel. Lyons jumped at the chance for he thought years would pass before another opportunity came for a settlement as advantageous to the company.[30] In addition, Seward hinted to Lyons that one way to revive good feeling between the people of the United States and those of Britain was for a distinguished American to reciprocate the highly successful visit paid some years before by the prince of Wales to the Republic. The minister had little doubt that Seward was thinking of making the journey himself and was motivated by a desire to keep alive his presidential hopes. The prospect horrified Palmerston. Seward "is essentially vulgar and ungentlemanlike and the more he is seen here the less he will be liked," the prime minister growled. "The only People whom he pleased when here [last] were some Editors of second Rate newspapers with whom he drank Brandy and Water." Moreover, those who urged the recognition of the Confederacy would "in some unmistakeable manner prove that there is a great deal of sympathy with the South in this Country." Any such demonstrations would be more likely to embitter than improve relations between the two peoples. Lyons was instructed to discourage the secretary if he returned to this subject.[31]

Lyons agreed that Seward seldom made a favourable initial impression for he possessed "so much more vanity, personal and national, than tact"; he conceded that it required "patience and good temper to be always cordial with him"; but the cautious and reserved Englishman had on closer acquaintance grown both to like and esteem this complex individual. He had agreed to join the "International Caravan," even though he was unwell and longed to escape to the relative coolness and peace of Canada, merely because he did not wish to wound Seward by declining the invitation. The secretary deserved some consideration from Britain, he believed, "for if we managed to keep the peace at all without him, we should not manage to avoid a succession of critical questions."[32] One more example of the truth of this observation was Seward's level-headed response to the crisis Adams reported over the Laird rams.

Ostensibly Seward supported the minister's stern position. He drew a dark picture in his instructions of the likely consequences if Pollock's interpretation of the law was upheld and the Foreign Enlistment Act thereby rendered nugatory. The navy, perhaps supported by privateers, would destroy the warships proceeding from British ports. The risks were obvious, both of confrontation and of collision, but he solemnly disclaimed all American responsibility for any general war that ensued. With respect to the rams, he endorsed Adams's warnings to Russell and in a long despatch at the end of July spoke of the misunderstandings which appeared to be carrying the two countries towards a calamitous conflict. Sombre as the tone was, Seward's comments were not quite what they seemed. He did not expect Pollock's ruling to be sustained, and if the unexpected did happen he saw a solution in the revival of an earlier British suggestion for a reciprocal amendment of the existing legislation. To Lyons he emphasized that the despatch was "friendly." The British minister then calmly reported home that "an impending quarrel with England is allowed to be put forward as a lure to Volunteers for the Army and Substitutes." And he correctly deduced that Seward never intended his strong language to be communicated to Russell, but that it would first see the light of day when Congress assembled in December. The truth was that the secretary did not expect a dangerous crisis over the rams.[33]

From Evarts and other unofficial sources in Britain Seward had received word that the rams would not be permitted to leave port while doubt surrounded their destination. It was an opinion to which Evarts held firmly, even after his return home in July. When Chase voiced his concern in cabinet, Seward "treated the matter lightly" and turned the discussion aside with an adroitness Welles grudgingly admired. He repeatedly assured the uneasy secretary of the navy that the rams would not get out of Liverpool. "The English Ministry are our friends with the exception of the chief," he explained. Less sure of this, the Navy Department prepared for the possibility of war with Britain. Ironclad monitors were ordered for the protection of United States ports while some thirty "men-of-war privateers" were earmarked for an assault on British commerce. Rather than roam the ocean they would lie in wait outside British ports, relying on their speed for safety.[34]

A government which had seized the *Alexandra* would surely stop the rams. Certainly the foreign and domestic considerations that had impelled the British to act in the one case called for action in the second. High summer found the affairs of Europe no more stable or less dangerous than they had been during the spring. The great questions of the day were still unresolved and thus the materials for "the infernal cauldron" plentiful. The Polish problem continued to simmer. At the end of May Russell had not expected war to arise out of this question, but events soon took a more ominous turn. Early in June there were reports that orders had gone out from Paris to ready all vessels for sea duty. This, together with the inflammatory tone of a French press closely regulated by the government, the gathering of 150,000 men at Chalons for an imperial review, and the emperor's need to offset the damaging blow his prestige had been dealt by the results of recent elections, excited fears that a conflict was near into which Britain would be drawn or would drift.[35] "A war in the centre of Europe, on the pretext of restoring Poland, is a general war, and a long one," Disraeli observed soberly. This period of nervous uncertainty extended well into the fall, with the stock market fluctuating wildly in response to the current mood.[36]

An additional complication was the increasingly serious dispute between Denmark and the German states over the duchies of Schleswig and Holstein. "People may not understand its origins, and have but an imperfect idea of its merits," the *Standard* declared, "but they cannot shirk its dangers."[37] Taking advantage of the Great Powers' preoccupation with Poland, the Danes had proclaimed in March their intention to incorporate Schleswig with Denmark. They were determined to counter mounting German interest in the administration of the duchy. Both Austria and Prussia remonstrated against the proposed constitutional changes, which violated the London agreements of 1851–52, and reserved their right to intervene, while the German Diet set in train the process of federal execution. Nevertheless, the Danish government refused to draw back. Instead, on September 28 it announced a new constitution for the kingdom and Schleswig.

A decisive British response to either of these crises was out of the question. Their profound distrust of the emperor continued to prevent Palmerston and Russell from seeking truly close cooperation with the French. To support France, they feared, might encourage Napoleon's ambitions on either the Rhine or the Vistula. As it was, the emperor's European schemes continued to shape the prime minister's attitude towards the Mexican adventure. What France "is doing there will not make her more dangerous to us," he explained to the foreign secretary, "but on the Contrary will have a Tendency to fetter her action in Europe by engaging her men and her money for some years to come in supporting an Austrian Prince on the other side of the Atlantic."[38] The two men were also held in check as a result of the Queen's suspicion of them. Before leaving Britain for Coburg in August she made it clear that she wanted no step taken "in foreign affairs *without* her *previous sanction* being obtained." This restraint applied specifically to the Polish and Schleswig-Holstein questions. Subsequently she obliged Russell to soften the language of his despatches and declared "her *determination not* to consent to any measures" which might involve the nation in war, and especially in the threatened conflict between Denmark and Germany. Furthermore, she insisted that all important decisions be submitted to the cabinet, where she knew she would find considerable support for her stand. Nor could there be any doubt that the Queen also reflected popular feeling, at least with respect to Poland. Neither in Parliament nor in the press was there any significant support for military assistance to the Polish rebels. As the *Economist* lamely explained, the best test of a people's fitness for freedom was their ability to establish it themselves.[39]

If an understandable anxiety not to repeat the miseries of the Crimean War helps explain this public reaction to the turmoil in Europe, there was also a natural disinclination to jeopardize national prosperity through an adventurous policy overseas. Life was too comfortable to be disturbed. Palmerston had detected this mood, as his speech to a Mansion House banquet on June 17 indicated. Britain had been severed from her principal supply of cotton without suffering the ruin and economic devastation so many had predicted, he reminded his audience. Instead, healthy revenues had enabled the government "to propose great and important reductions of taxation." But national and commercial prosperity depended greatly upon the continuance of peace, he added. As for those grave problems pending abroad, it was his belief that they could be settled by negotiation. "Everything is reduced to a purely mercantile standard," one American visitor noted contemptuously. "England will maintain what position she has so long as she can maintain the dignity of yardsticks, pint pots, and scales."[40]

Conspicuous among the nations with whom prosperity now required that Britain remain at peace was the United States. The reason was to be found in the Board of Trade returns for the first four months of 1863. They revealed that exports had continued to grow, exceeding in value not only those for the same four months of 1862 but of 1861 also, despite a slight falling off in trade with France. The explanation was the continuing recovery of the American trade. By 1863 British exports had regained all the ground they had lost with the outbreak of the Civil War, while imports of American wheat were being halved and those of cotton remained statistically insignificant. The visible trade balance had swung at last in Britain's favour, and this made no allowance for the earnings on her substantial investments in the United States. Moreover, this trade was being carried for obvious reasons in British ships. Over a period of five years, but most startlingly over the last two, the number of British vessels entering the principal American port of New York had increased by 300 per cent. Clearly British shipowners were doing an excellent legitimate business in the American war.[41]

Despite the strenuous efforts of the United States Navy to suppress the trade, even those merchants trafficking with the Confederates through Nassau continued to prosper. Although half of the eighty-two steamers and sailing vessels that cleared Nassau to run the blockade in the last six months of 1862 were captured, profits far exceeded losses. In 1863 the value of the islands' exports surpassed £3 million, an astonishing twenty-five fold increase over the figure for 1860. If the colony derived little direct revenue from the trade, for much of it was carried on under bond and therefore escaped payment of duty, its influence was far-reaching. Merchants and professional men made fortunes, the value of property in and around Nassau leapt by 400 per cent, and there was a corresponding price inflation. One of the first to complain of the sharp rise in the cost of living was Governor Bayley, whose imprudent public endorsement of the trade had earlier brought a sharp rebuke from the Colonial Office. However, a grateful legislature voted to increase his annual grant by £500.[42]

Beyond the economic remained the political factors which had long dictated peace with the United States. Russell's insistence that Britain would not be intimidated by American threats of war, and his doubts that they were serious, for "England, France, Mexico and the so-called Confederacy" would be more than the Union could manage, cannot obscure the fact that both he and Palmerston were never able to banish from their minds the disturbing possibility of a conflict. In June Russell had been visited by Cobden, who informed him with all the emphasis he could muster, and with the authority of a man who claimed "considerable knowledge" of the United States, that the foreign secretary's American policy was leading "either to a war or great humiliation." The warning was repeated publicly by the Radical press. American exasperation at the immense damage inflicted on their commerce by British-built raiders would surely boil over if the rams were permitted to get out, for they seemed capable of raising the blockade. For his part, Russell had instructed Lyons to use his summer sojourn in Canada "to ascertain how the British Provinces would hold together under the strains of war." The beginning of September found him complaining to Palmerston that the number of troops in Canada was "hardly enough." There was no doubt in either of their minds that the British forces in North America were inadequate for the province's defence in the event of war with the Union. But the prime minister and De Grey, the war secretary, realized that it was useless to reinforce them "by a thousand or two thousand men."[43] Nor was it possible to forget the European implications of an Anglo-American collision. Russell was anxious not to "endanger the situation of Seward," who in his opinion now understood that peace with Britain was necessary if the sympathy with slavery, intervention, and despotic rule which prevailed on the other side of the English Channel was to be held in check. Yet before the month was out Russell was citing the possibility of a war with the United States in a draft despatch rejecting another French proposal on Poland. However, this sentence was deleted by Palmerston. "It would not be well to tell the French that we could not carry on war in Europe as well as in America," the prime minister observed. "They might take advantage of such a hint if ever we became embroiled with the Americans."[44]

The threat of hostilities was only one of the embarrassments to which Britain found herself exposed as a result of Confederate shipbuilding in her ports. The example set by the *Alabama* was a persistent source of uneasiness. Cobden believed that fear of the Americans taking their revenge for the *Alabama* was helping to keep Britain at peace in Europe, and Granville explained to one Polish exile that if Britain went to war with Russia she faced the danger of American-built commerce raiders attacking her shipping. Similarly, deteriorating relations with Japan brought reports of Americans applying to that nation for commissions as privateers.[45]

As some American observers had foreseen, the thought that Britain was establishing precedents which would enable her enemies in future wars to fit out a navy in American ports was not one many British shipowners relished. Appropriately enough, the "better portion" of the Liverpool commercial community continued to voice their alarm. If the Foreign Enlistment Act was ineffectual then it ought to be amended to prevent the construction in British yards of ships destined for the use of belligerents, the shipowners told the government in June, as had the Chamber of Commerce a month earlier. Memorials to the same effect soon arrived at the Foreign Office from the shipowners of Belfast and those based in the Ports of Cumberland, as well as from the Hull Chamber of Commerce and Shipping. Then, early in July, "Young Rathbone" travelled down to London again to lobby personally for action. He consulted several members of Parliament, among them Cobden, Forster, and Thomas Baring, a member of the great commercial house, and he also saw Palmerston. But Rathbone and the other merchants and shipowners were by no means alone in expressing concern. The press took up the question of precedents.[46]

In his influential "Historicus" letters William Harcourt had long urged the expediency of England accepting, with an eye to her distant interests, the Americans' definition of belligerent rights. Organs as politically diverse as the *Spectator*, the *Saturday Review*, and the *Morning Post* echoed this call. Therefore it was not surprising that the long-term implications of the rams getting out excited comment. There was a biblical and prophetic tone to the *Spectator*'s caution: "With the measure we mete it shall be measured to us again."[47] The impact of its warnings, and those of the *Morning Star* and the *Daily News*, may have been lessened by their well-known sympathy for the Union cause. However, no one could seriously propose that *The Times* was actuated by Northern partisanship when it turned to this subject at the beginning of September. Whatever the state of the law there was a feeling among the public, it averred, that the sale of such vessels as the *Alabama* ought to be illegal. How would we have reacted if some neutral had furnished Russia with the means to prey upon our commerce during the Crimean War? "It is not our interest to allow such a precedent to be established for the first time, if it does not exist already, nor connive at its extension, if it has any existence."[48] Realizing this, the public would endorse the action of the government if it decided to stop the rams. Furthermore, if the Foreign Enlistment Act was not comprehensive enough it should be made so. The fact that *The Times* repeated this demand twice more within the week emphasized the urgent necessity for action.

The Palmerston government's awareness of the danger of permitting unwelcome precedents to be established had already influenced its response to the difficult question of the mails and was shaping its attitude towards the blockade. Thus a request by Admiral Milne for guidance on the right of vessels in his command to enter blockaded ports drew a significant reply from Russell. Bearing British interests in mind, it was "not desirable to establish any positive and unconditional right of entering a blockaded port by the ships of war of a Neutral Power." " 'Do unto others as you wish that others should do unto you' is a good rule among nations as well as among men," the foreign secretary later observed to one of his colleagues.[49] But in the case of the rams the path of expediency and of principle was strewn with obstacles.

The natural conservatism of the Crown's legal advisers had been strengthened or reawakened by Pollock's charge and the jury's verdict in the *Alexandra* trial. The solicitor of customs, to whom Dudley's request for the seizure of the rams, and the accompanying affidavits, had been referred by the Treasury, promptly took shelter behind that decision. While the evidence provided by the consul left little doubt in his mind that the rams had been intended originally for the Confederate service, he submitted the opinion that "there is nothing in all this which, according to the verdict in the 'Alexandra' case and the ruling of the Judge who tried that case, would justify the seizure or detention of these vessels. That decision must be held to be conclusive until reversed."[50] The solicitor had always argued for a narrow construction of the law, yet even the more liberally inclined law officers advised the government "not to detain or in any way interfere with the steam vessels in question." They were impressed by a report of the collector of customs at Liverpool, who had been informed by the French consul there that the rams were the property of a French subject. Although the report became a source of controversy, when in his remarks to the House on July 23 a confused Palmerston gave the impression that the consul had claimed they were for his government, the eventual clarification of this point did not cause the law officers to alter their opinion. There was still no evidence capable of being presented to a court that any persons in Britain intended the vessels for employment by the Confederacy against the Union. Indeed, the law officers admitted that even had such evidence been forthcoming they were by no means certain that it would have been proper to act upon the assumption that Pollock's recent interpretation of the law was correct.[51]

What of the demands that the existing law be amended? In his reply to the shipowners Russell insisted that the Foreign Enlistment Act was "effectual for all reasonable purposes, and to the full extent which International Law and comity" could require, provided proof could be obtained "of any act done with the intent of violating it." Herein lay the heart of the problem, as Russell realized. Could any law be effective, he asked his colleagues in a memorandum, so long as it was necessary to prove that a vessel was intended for belligerent purposes against a friendly power? Was it possible to dispense with such proof, perhaps by implementing a proposal of Cobden's that builders of warships be required to prove that their vessels were intended for a friendly nation "not at war with any other power friendly to the Queen"? The obvious difficulty, which he recognized, was that any new law which did not cause a "vexatious interruption of the business of ship-building" was all too likely to be just as easily evaded as the old.[52] Several of his colleagues raised other objections.

In their responses to Russell's paper, Palmerston, Westbury, and Newcastle underscored the complexity of the question. The lord chancellor was unwilling to listen to any proposal that would make the existing law more stringent. The Foreign Enlistment Act already went beyond international law, he observed, and it would be foolish to extend it further without the agreement of *all* nations. In short, there was another side to the precedent argument. It might very well be in the interests of Britain, "having regard to the future," that new rules covering the building and equipping of warships in the ports of neutrals be adopted. However, he thought it "silly to bind ourselves by a stringent rule unless it be common to all other Nations." Westbury also warned that he would "oppose most strongly any attempt to introduce new principles or rules of procedure, or of evidence, in the administration of our existing statute." It must be administered upon the same principle as all other English laws, he declared. The accuser must prove the offence rather than the accused party carry the burden of proving his innocence. Palmerston and Newcastle agreed. They were equally averse to bringing forward a measure which might be viewed as a response to American threats, and both men were convinced that it would be impossible to pilot through Parliament provisions severe enough to satisfy the North. Nor was Newcastle able to resist the temptation to deride Cobden's proposal as a "tyrannical" interference with trade which came "strangely from one of his school."[53]

Clearly a revision of the law was not going to win easy or prompt approval. The challenge facing the foreign secretary at the end of August remained the same—to stop the rams within the bounds of the present law.

ELEVEN

Seizure of the Rams

"I AM VERY UNCOMFORTABLE about those large iron-plated rams now fitting out at Liverpool," Henry Layard wrote to Russell on August 21, 1863. Left to supervise the affairs of the Foreign Office while the secretary retreated to Scotland for the summer, Layard had had an alarming conversation with "a gentleman of high character and respectability" whose extensive dealings with the Confederates and involvement in the munitions industry gave weight to his opinion that the rams were intended for the South, and that they were of "so formidable a character" that nothing would be able to stand against them and they would "in a very short time break up a blockade." Even if this was an exaggeration, the worried under-secretary observed, the vessels were clearly of the most advanced design.[1]

In his reply to Layard, Russell continued to insist that nothing could be done "without evidence." He had said the same to the Liverpool shipowners in July, and the necessity of proof was the point upon which he dwelt in his response to a deluge of petitions from Union and Emancipation Societies begging the government to prevent the building of ships for the Confederacy. Adams was likewise informed at the beginning of September that the depositions forwarded by Dudley were "in great measure mere hearsay evidence" and thus inadmissible in court, and were "not such as to show the intent or purpose necessary to make the building or fitting out of the vessels illegal under the Foreign Enlistment Act." There was certainly no "legal evidence" contradicting Bravay's claim of ownership. But this note to the American minister had been drafted several days before the date it bore—September 1—and Russell's position had already advanced well beyond its promise of continuing vigilance. By August 31 the foreign secretary had resolved to detain the rams "until further examination can be made." What he required was an excuse.[2]

Russell first proposed that if any person could be found "to declare" that he had "reason to believe" that these two ships of war were intended for the Confederacy a detention order should be issued. He suggested that the authorities at Liverpool be asked if they knew of anyone willing to make such a statement. No doubt Thomas Dudley would have happily provided a host of declarants, but he was never given the opportunity. A declaration of the kind proposed by Russell could scarcely be considered adequate legal grounds for interference in the Lairds' business arrangements. Fortunately the foreign secretary had instructed Layard to consult the law officers about the possibility of detaining, "till further enquiries can be made," the vessel nearing completion, and it may have been at the insistence of Roundell Palmer that the proper test for action was restored. Both rams were to be held "if sufficient evidence can be obtained to lead to the belief" that they were intended for the Confederacy.[3]

Yet matters were in Russell's words "getting very critical." By September 1 he had received from the Foreign Office papers which raised the possibility of the vessel on which work was well advanced slipping away unfinished. Facing another *Alabama* "scandal," he no longer thought it necessary to await the formal opinion of the law officers. The vessels ought not to be allowed out of the port until the suspicion about them was cleared up. What was required was someone who would say that he would give "evidence," or could bring forward evidence, leading to the belief that they were destined for the Confederate service. In his opinion this would be sufficient to order their detention, Russell wrote on September 2. To emphasize his sense of urgency he informed Layard that he would return to London to argue the case himself with the law officers and the Treasury if they did not consent to detain the rams. However, this dramatic confrontation never took place. Roundell Palmer provided Russell with the excuse for which he had been searching and towards which he had been instinctively moving.[4]

For some time the Foreign Office had been seeking to discover whether there was any truth to Bravay's claim that the rams were for Egypt. Then on August 31 a telegram arrived from the consul-general in Egypt announcing the viceroy's refusal to honour the "verbal" commission Bravay cunningly claimed to have received from his predecessor. The consul drew Russell's attention to an earlier despatch in which he had convincingly disputed the Frenchman's claim.[5] But the strong suspicion that Bravay was a "swindler" did not solve the problem. As Palmer pointed out, the fact that the Egyptian government was disputing the contract might be interpreted as evidence that

Bravay had ordered the rams "with a bona fide intention." Moreover, the Foreign Office had still failed to turn up any evidence admissible in court either that the vessels were intended for the Confederates or might ultimately come into their possession. In short, there was "no power whatever under the law" to stop these fearsome ships. Nevertheless the solicitor general believed they might be held as "a question of policy." Russell could direct the Custom-house officers to prevent them "from proceeding to sea until sufficient evidence was furnished as to their destination." It was the opening the foreign secretary had himself begun to perceive. "Mr. Bravay is not a State—and cannot make war on his own account—The French and Egyptian Governments disown him," he observed. Therefore it was not unreasonable to ask for whom the rams were intended.[6]

"I quite agree in the course suggested by Roundell Palmer," Russell cabled Layard on September 3. He instructed the under-secretary to write immediately to the Treasury "to desire that the vessels may be prevented from leaving the port of Liverpool till satisfactory evidence can be given as to their destination—not to stop the building or fitting the vessels but to prevent their going out for trial, or on any other pretext."[7] Layard did as he was ordered. Two days later, on September 5, he wrote again to the Treasury, amplifying Russell's instructions. Evidently the foreign secretary was concerned that a department which had consistently questioned the legality of any action would drag its feet. However, the more he thought about the matter the more certain Russell became that he had acted correctly. The case of the rams was "clear to commonsense." Unlike the *Alabama*, they were evidently vessels of war; no government claimed them; they could not be for an individual; they must be intended for the Confederates; they could not reach a Confederate port without first making war on the blockading squadron, thereby "making war from England on one of the Queen's Allies." Russell likened his behaviour to that of the magistrate who saw before him a person found by the police in the early hours of the morning near an inhabited house and carrying a burglar's tools. "He would say 'there is not enough evidence to convict, remand him for future enquiry'."[8]

Russell had acted on his own initiative and readily accepted "all the responsibility in any shape or form." Prior consultation with the prime minister had been impossible, for Palmerston had been off in Wales. However, he promptly endorsed the decision on his return to London. His only concern was the long-standing one—proof. Evidence on which to justify the rams' seizure would be harder to come by than the excuse for holding them. It was a point Palmerston instructed Stuart, who in Lyons's absence was once again acting as chargé d'affaires in Washington, to explain confidentially to Seward. The government had detained the rams on their own risk but there might be difficulty obtaining the legal proof that the vessels were intended for the South. Consequently the only promise the British could make was to do "whatever we may be advised by legal authority to be proper and justifiable for the enforcement of our municipal law."[9]

Unfortunately no one thought to inform Adams of Russell's decision and by September 5 the American was in a "fever" about the rams. A month before he had gone off to Scotland for a well-deserved and needed rest. There, far from the scene of his troubles, he had been able to relax. Increasingly he "leaned to the belief" that the rams would be stopped. When he returned to London for a few days in mid-August he sent off a despatch to Seward which reflected this newfound confidence in the British government's willingness to act "to the outside of its powers" to prevent difficulties. Rejoining his family in the Highlands, Adams visited the Argylls at Inveraray. He took the opportunity to voice his concern about the rams to the duke but was "very temperate in his language."[10] Meanwhile, during the minister's absence, the tension was mounting at the legation and in Liverpool. The launching of the second ram and the advanced state of the first, together with the official denials that they were for France and the exposure of Bravay's "pretended contract" with Egypt, had heightened considerably Dudley's anxiety and that of the staff in London.[11]

When Adams returned to the legation on September 3, to find his excited subordinates and the information they had gathered awaiting him, he quickly succumbed to the old fear. The British government had decided not to take preventive measures. "Moral feebleness" had ended in a "cowardice which acts like the greatest daring," he concluded, but it was his duty to inform the British as calmly as he could of the probable consequences. He immediately sent off a note to Russell warning of "the grave nature of the situation in which both countries must be placed in the event of an act of aggression committed against the government and people of the United States by either of these formidable vessels." The following day brought more disquieting news from Dudley. The nearly completed ram had taken on coal, got up steam, and had successfully completed a trial of her engines. With her departure seemingly imminent, Adams wrote once againt to Russell to place on record a "last solemn protest."[12] This did little to dispel the mood of foreboding which oppressed the legation. Neither did the tone of a leading article in the previous evening's *Globe*, the publication of Russell's answer to the Emancipation Society, nor his note of September 1 to the minister, which Adams did not receive until the afternoon of September 4. These developments fed the fears that the British government had "fallen on the feeblest policy" of continuing to shelter behind the demand for "positive testimony from *credible* witnesses." Yet as Dudley explained it was difficult to persuade people to volunteer evidence in Liverpool. The city's numerous Southern sympathizers ostracized or otherwise persecuted persons suspected of aiding the North. The alternative was to resort to bribery, which the consul did, but this "tainted" the evidence. "I have done the best I can," a weary Dudley wrote defensively on September 4, "and unless I should be fortunate enough to stumble upon some unexpected testimony the case will have to rest on the evidence now before the Government."[13]

For his part, Adams decided to send off one more note to Russell. To permit the Confederates to build and sail away vessels which they boasted were capable of bombarding the lightly defended port cities of the North and raising the blockade of the South was to wage war on the United States, he observed. However, his principal purpose now was to gain time. Clinging to the hope that something helpful might yet turn up, he announced that he had forwarded to Washington a copy of the foreign secretary's communication of September 1 and would await further instructions. Even as this note reached the Foreign Office Adams received a brief reply to his warning of September 3. Although Russell had drafted it himself on September 4 he curiously made no mention of his decision to detain the rams. The American was merely advised that the matter was under the "serious and anxious consideration" of the government. Not until September 8 did the minister learn that the vessels had been stopped. He hurried the news home by the Liverpool steamer, which sailed the following day, while his secretary of legation, thinking this good news might reach Seward a little sooner via Southampton, sent word that way.[14]

In the first rush of relief Adams believed his "agony" was over. Newspaper reports of a sympathetic speech Russell made at Dundee on September 9 were a pleasure to read. This was at last the true tone, he wrote cheerfully to Seward. Indeed, he was more confident now of being able to preserve friendly relations than at any moment since his arrival in England.[15] His optimism was short-lived. On September 11 the American consul at Cardiff watched from his window groups of men landing from a French brig which had brought them from Brest where the *Florida* was docked. They were to take the afternoon train for Liverpool and claimed to be crew for the rams, he reported. An obvious question which came to his mind was: Why would they be going there "if there was not some confidence felt that these rams would be allowed to go out?"[16] From Liverpool itself Dudley reported that work on them was being pushed ahead at breakneck speed. One had "all her boilers and machinery in, her masts up and rigged, her smoke stack up and both turrets in." He could see nothing to prevent her sailing at almost any time and questioned whether the authorities had ever formally informed the Lairds that the vessels had been detained. By September 14 she was completed and coaled, seemingly ready to repeat the *Alabama*'s successful escape by making a trial trip from which she would never return. Adams uneasily scanned the newspapers for some clue as to what was likely to happen. The reports he read were contradictory. The *Morning Post* announced that one of the rams had been given permission to undertake trials, whereas *The Times*, the *Daily News*, and the *Morning Star* declared that she would not be allowed to go out. Somewhat more reassuring, in a sense, was the late news from Dudley "that the vessel did try to get out but was stopped." Nevertheless, Adams was sure the controversy had not ceased when he read Russell's reply to his note of September 5.[17]

The British answer had been drafted by Palmerston. Sarcastic, ironic, and didactic by turn, he repeated the government's "earnest desire faithfully to perform the duties of neutrality" and declared that it had taken every step to enforce the Foreign Enlistment Act "which by legal authority" it had been advised was within its competence. As for the future, the government would continue to pursue the same course. Adams, although anxious "to soften in a degree the character" of his earlier remarks, could not ignore this reminder of the constraint to which British action was subjected. "I respectfully submit that the interests of two nations are of too much magnitude to be measured by the infinitesimal scale of the testimony permissible before a jury in a Common Law Court," he wrote to Russell on September 16. He quoted George Canning, who, in a parallel case many years before, had "deprecated the consequence of 'permitting the paltry, pettifogging way of fitting out ships in British harbours' to 'sneak his country into war'." The American minister also seized this opportunity to indicate his uneasiness over the unabated vigour with which preparations for the immediate departure of the rams were being pushed at Birkenhead.[18]

The unpleasant thought that the Confederates might outfox him again, and steal away with at least one of the ironclads, never left Russell. On September 8 Lairds had informed the local collector of customs that they wished to take the nearly completed ram out for a trial trip, and they gave an assurance that she would be brought back. The Treasury recommended that permission be granted, fearing that a refusal might bring actions for damages from both Lairds and Bravay, but a suspicious Russell wanted security against the vessel's escape. However, there was insufficient time to arrange a bond and no body of Custom-house officers placed aboard would be able to resist a determined effort to prevent her return to Liverpool. Thus it was with marked reluctance that Russell gave permission for the trial, obliged as he was to depend upon "the honourable engagement" of Lairds. He had some insurance in the form of the Channel Fleet, then nearing Liverpool, and with its arrival Hammond made arrangements with the Admiralty for the commander to put aboard the ram a force which would guarantee her return. The excuse for this extraordinary precaution was the arrival in Liverpool of the men from the *Florida*. Unless Lairds accepted "adequate support for carrying out their engagement," and thus protection from the danger of it being violated by desperate men, the trial was prohibited. The following day Lairds made the discovery that they did not need to leave the dock in order to test the engines.[19]

Russell's initial grudging consent to a trial had followed the receipt of another report by the law officers. On September 12 they reaffirmed their opinion that "no legal grounds" had yet been shown to exist on which the government could interfere with the rams. If this explains the foreign secretary's wariness about further irritating Lairds, without the excellent excuse the arrival in Liverpool of the *Florida*'s crew subsequently provided, the principal effect of the law officers' latest opinion was to cause the government to re-examine its position. That same day Russell drafted another memorandum, which was printed and distributed to the cabinet on September 14.

If the "moral certainty" that these two vessels of war had been built for the Confederacy was not sufficient ground for their "legal forfeiture," where would this lead? If two rams were allowed to leave Liverpool to break the blockade, why not ten or even twenty? "Can such an operation be distinguished from war?" he asked. "Is it not contrary to the whole spirit of our Foreign Enlistment Act?" In his anxiety Russell clutched at the lifeline Palmer had thrown out once before and the law officers now offered as a body. Why not extend the Customs Consolidation Act, which authorized the Crown to prohibit the export of munitions, to include vessels of war built in British ports without a license? Here was a way to circumvent the necessity under the Foreign Enlistment Act of obtaining "legal proof" of the purpose and intent with which a vessel was equipped or fitted out.[20]

Russell was assured of the support of several of his colleagues, if not for the extension of the Customs Act then for action of some kind. Milner Gibson, for example, seemed to believe that Britain was not only morally but also legally responsible if a ship built in one of her ports passed into Confederate hands and inflicted losses on the Union. Argyll had been urging the detention of the rams upon Palmerston and Russell ever since his conversation with Adams at Inveraray, and he now advocated that the construction of such vessels be prohibited unless the government for which they were intended was named. Gladstone believed that the Foreign Enlistment Act held out a promise to America which it was Britain's duty to fulfil. He thought it well-nigh impossible to solve the problem of enforcement short of a total prohibition on naval construction during a maritime war, but a unilateral provision of this nature could never be legislated, as he recognized.[21] It was left to Palmerston and George Grey to suggest a practical solution. They followed the law officers' argument that the "unavoidable inference" to be drawn from the Egyptian viceroy's refusal to accept the rams was that they had at least been offered to him bona fide. Yet there was a danger, with his refusal of them, that they would be bought by the Confederates and provoke a "diplomatic wrangle" with the Union. Alternatively, they might fall into Federal or French hands and Palmerston had no wish to see such formidable warships added to the fleets of either of those nations. Since the law officers had plainly said that they could not be legally seized, why not buy them? As Grey observed, "This w[oul]d only be an expedient applicable to the present case pending a consideration of what if any change in the law is practicable & expedient."[22]

The idea of purchase was not a new one, having first crossed Russell's mind on September 3. The law officers had earlier proposed that the government attempt to settle the *Alexandra* case in this way. But Somerset, with his budget already stretched to the limit, had refused to waste money on a vessel which would "only make an inferior gunboat."[23] He responded with greater interest, however, when Palmerston and Russell joined forces to press the rams upon him. While the prime minister emphasized the strength they would add to the Royal Navy and the importance of denying them to potential enemies, especially the United States, Russell mentioned the possibility of the Admiralty reselling them to the Turks. The rams appeared to be ideally suited for the defence of Constantinople and the bottling up of the Russians in the Black Sea. An officer was promptly sent to Liverpool to examine them and in the report that followed he raised questions about their value and design. He found the construction inferior in all respects to that of the navy's ironclads. The upper decks were so close to the waterline that they would ship seas even in moderate weather. The poops and forecastles, while offering valuable accommodation for officers and men, interfered with the firing of the guns, of which there were two in each of the twin revolving turrets. Nevertheless, Somerset conceded Palmerston's claim that they would be an effective addition to the nation's naval power, though the decisive factor in his mind may have been the opportunity they would provide, should the sale to the Turks fall through, to test the qualities of a turret ship at sea.[24]

Like Russell, Somerset also saw in an offer to purchase the vessels a means of exposing Bravay. The fact that work on them was still being pushed ahead frantically, despite the viceroy's repudiation of any bargain, excited fresh doubts as to whether the transaction had ever been genuine. Thus if the Frenchman refused to sell to the Admiralty would this not be "presumptive proof" that the ships had been bought already by the Confederates? Perhaps he saw the trap, for Bravay sought some plausible grounds on which to refuse the British offer. He claimed that the Russians and the Danes were anxious to have the rams. When both governments denied that they had approached him, he resorted to the unconvincing explanation that he was obliged to take them to Alexandria. Only when the Egyptians had refused them there, he insisted fatuously, would he be in a position to sell the rams to Britain or some other nation. As Edmund Hammond commented, having returned to supervise the daily affairs of the Foreign Office while Layard took a summer vacation and Russell remained in Scotland, "We have not done with those iron-clads, but I think there is no moral doubt that they were Confederate property and are so now, though it may be difficult to obtain legal proof. We shall certainly not let them go, until we acquire assurance that they will get into hands that will not make a bad use of them."[25]

This determination "to take the Iron Clads away from the Confederates" prompted Palmerston to give some thought to the protection of his domestic flank. No doubt his irritation with Adams's "interminable notes" matched that of Hammond, who complained that the American had "all the spirit and special pleading of a pettifogging attorney," but the prime minister's main concern was to avoid the appearance of having made a "humble submission to Yankee Bullying." The menacing tone of the American minister's recent letters to Russell, "his repeated [and] somewhat insolent Threats of war," could not be overlooked. It was time to say "in civil terms 'you be damned'," and this Palmerston did "in measured Terms."[26] But his anxiety to ensure that Russell's reply was couched in fearless language had probably been heightened by reports in the press of the tirade against Britain which Charles Sumner had delivered in New York on September 10.

Sumner's speech had its origin in the campaign much earlier in the year to drive Seward from the administration, but as he worked on it over the summer it was transformed into a swingeing attack upon British policy. Personal unhappiness, the anglophobia of those who had traditionally been "most Anglican"—the "merchants and educated" who admired English culture, his own conviction that England's course had been "bad—very bad," and his fear that unless it was reconsidered a collision was inevitable, all these factors influenced Sumner's remarks.[27] Yet his fear was less of an immediate conflict if the rams got out than of a tendency to war "just as soon as our rebellion is suppressed." Although a large number of Americans, especially businessmen, were very exercised about the rams, it was Sumner's opinion that the public generally was in a greater uproar over French policy in Mexico. Furthermore, although no "authentic" news had come from Britain before he spoke, William B. Evarts had recently visited the senator to inform him of his impression that the ironclads would not be permitted to sail, and J. M. Forbes, who also spoke with the authority of a recent visitor to England, had written on the eve of the speech to urge Sumner to treat the problem of the rams with the greatest caution. The direction in which Palmerston wished the British public mind to be turned was evident in the support *The Times* had given to a petition of the Emancipation Society, Forbes observed. This was not the moment to make threats.[28]

Had he refrained from all menace Sumner would have negated his purpose when he addressed the 3,000 people gathered in the Cooper Institute. "My hope is that England will so far reconsider her course and fraternize with us that war will be impossible. But there can be no hope of this, unless the truth is put before her plainly," he later explained to Cobden. So great was his vanity that he believed himself uniquely qualified to perform this self-appointed task. He could reach influential persons across the Atlantic and his reputation "as a lover of peace" guaranteed that his "austerity" would mean more than that of the *New York Herald*. He presented to both audiences, the near and the far, a "highly wrought enumeration of the wrongs of England." The failure to perceive or to admit that a moral issue lay at the heart of the American struggle, and "the absurdity of conceding Ocean Belligerency to rebels," had led the British astray.[29]

In Britain, of the major newspapers only the *Morning Star* responded sympathetically to Sumner's "heart-moving reproaches." Even the *Daily News* and the *Spectator* attacked his "ornate, diffuse, fanciful, acrimonious" tone, rejected his charges against Britain as "womanishly unfair," and scorned the core of his argument—that she ought to have given the Union the benefits of a virtual alliance against the slave-ridden Confederacy—as "sadly childish."[30] No one resented Sumner's "misrepresentations" more keenly than Russell. He replied to them at Blairgowrie on September 26, in a speech (Henry Hotze reported to Richmond) "made ostensibly before the tenantry of a highland estate which he has rented for the summer, and therefore obviously on an 'occasion' specially contrived." The British government would never yield British law or rights to menaces, Russell vowed. In the circumstances, he could have said nothing less. Far more significant was his explanation of the government's policy with respect to ships being built for the Confederacy. Seizures could only be made on evidence, he observed, but certain activities clearly violated the law. To build a ship, arm it, and then allow it to get out, and thus make war at once upon a foreign belligerent, was to take part in the war. Had the rams been permitted to leave Liverpool they might have waged war against the Union without ever touching at a Confederate port. This defence of his decision to detain the vessels merely served as a prelude to Russell's assurance that "Everything that the law of nations requires; everything that the Foreign Enlistment Act requires I am prepared to do, even if it should be proved to be necessary for the preservation of our neutrality that the sanction of Parliament should be asked to further measures that her Majesty's Ministers may still adopt."[31]

The speech won widespread public applause. Russell was praised for his "calm statesmanship and unanswerable reply" to Sumner, for his "fearless and candid" address which "proved in twenty ways" that British neutrality was not merely a name. No American could doubt that there was a determination on the part of the government to act fairly by the United States.[32] Although Adams's misgivings were not to be so easily dispelled, he did regard the speech as an important event. Thanks to Sumner, Russell had been drawn a little farther out of his shell. "The attack from America enables him to get on a high tone of retort which will give him popular strength to sustain his position," Adams remarked.[33]

Russell's avowal of support for whatever legislative changes were required to uphold British neutrality, and Bravay's refusal to sell the ironclads, revived the debate among his colleagues on what the government could or should do. On September 22 Bravay had given to the English naval officer sent to open negotiations for their purchase a copy of the deed by which Lairds released Bulloch from his contract for the rams when the Frenchman was brought forward as a substitute purchaser. Regarding this transfer of ownership as a "deception and meant only as a cloak," even Palmerston was willing by the beginning of October to contemplate some "alteration" of the Foreign Enlistment Act. A provision might be inserted, he remarked, "to prevent any Ship Builder or other Person from building and equipping a ship of war for any Foreign Authority without Special Permission from the Crown." And while this would not solve the problem of evasion of the law, at least "it would prevent Iron Plating, Broadside Port Holes, and Turrets." Russell was quick to flatter the prime minister that his was "the true course," even though he himself had already suggested just such a solution. Its attraction was the ease with which it could be justified. After all, it was "the law in France" and there was "something like it in America."[34]

Gladstone, who complained privately that in his speech at Blair-gowrie Russell had been "very incautious in saying so much about the ironclads,"[35] admitted that the conditions imposed by French and American law on the building of vessels might be "a practical solution." However, his was one of the most powerful voices within the cabinet urging extreme caution. He engaged in a lively discussion of the problem's complexities with Argyll, whose conviction that a change in the law was an "absolute necessity" had been reinforced by his reading of the correspondence about the rams which had been printed for circulation among members of the cabinet. The lawyers still demanded "legal proof" of destination before authorizing seizure, Argyll noted, but what possible proof could the government have more than these papers afforded? The government had obtained a copy of the deed in which Lairds stated that their original contract was with Bulloch; they had sworn affidavits that this man was a Confederate agent; they had the deed transferring Bulloch's "legal interest" in the ships to a Frenchman who lied "abominably" when he declared that the Pasha of Egypt wanted them. Was it possible that an international obligation could be evaded "by technicalities feebler than those by which any man might evade a Turnpike Act in England?" In Argyll's opinion the printed correspondence proved the "reasonableness" of requiring that vessels such as the rams be constructed only for a "government," and one entitled to use such ships. In short, that the purchaser be a state not at war with a nation at peace with Britain.[36]

Gladstone was not convinced by Argyll's argument. By October 7 he had reached the conclusion that it would be "very difficult to found a proposal to extend the Foreign Enlistment Act, with a view to meeting the case of the Ironclads at Birkenhead, upon the policy announced by England of maintaining neutrality, as neutrality is understood under the general provisions of international law."[37] He was not alone in his belief that this municipal statute was more rigorous than international law. Hence Argyll's complaint that several of their colleagues, persuaded that the municipal law alone obliged them to intervene to prevent the building of ships of war for belligerents, saw in its repeal the easiest way out of the difficulty.[38] While the chancellor did not follow this line of specious reasoning, his careful reading of the act and of the debates at the time of its passage had left him with the very strong impression that the purpose of this measure was "to facilitate as regards to ships what is much beyond and indeed at variance with the general international obligations of neutrality." Furthermore, could it be extended without driving out of Britain and into other countries the valuable industry of building ships of war? Could it be extended with any hope of persuading other nations to follow suit and thus secure Britain's immunity in war from the depredations of ships built for her enemy in neutral ports? Finally, would a stricter law not be unneutral to the extent that it restrained the supply of one particular munition of war to the peculiar disadvantage of the weaker belligerent at sea? In effect, in the name of a stricter neutrality would not Britain be deciding the outcome of a war? Gladstone paid little heed to Argyll's observation that it was "not the business of neutrals to keep up a balance between contending parties."[39]

It was against this background of continuing discussion and disagreement that Russell summoned the cabinet to meet in the second week of October to discuss the rams. The question to be decided was that of seizure. Did the government have the necessary "legal proof" of the ironclads' Confederate destination? If not, would the cabinet decide to exceed the authority the present act conferred and seek indemnifying legislation later? The resistance several of his colleagues had shown to measures which would clearly empower the government to intervene in such cases may have caused the foreign secretary to approach the meeting with some uneasiness, and therefore welcome the opportunity to present it with a *fait accompli*.

On October 6 the senior officer of the small naval force which remained in Liverpool when the fleet steamed off, Capt. E. A. Inglefield, reported that one of the ironclads was rapidly being prepared for sea. This sudden spurt of activity, for work on her had been slowed for some time; the arrival in Liverpool of a captain and a chief engineer; the presence there of the crewmen recently paid off by the *Florida*; the suspicion that Lairds intended to moor the vessel in the Mersey, which would assist anyone plotting her escape; all of these developments demanded action from a foreign secretary who had concluded that the sending of steam rams from Liverpool to raise the Union blockade of the Confederacy "would not be honest." Russell's first response was to request the Treasury to place a customs officer aboard the ironclad that had been readied for departure. He was to be armed with the authority to seize her if there was any attempt to get up steam or move her into the river. But information on October 8 of an imminent effort to take the ram led Russell to order the seizure of both ships. Subsequently Captain Inglefield was instructed to place marines "in such a position as you consider best to enable them in case of need to assist the officers of Customs in maintaining the seizure of the iron ships."[40]

Although he had cooperated fully with the Foreign Office, George Hamilton, the secretary to the Treasury, doubted the legality of the action. The Treasury solicitor, the solicitor of customs, and the commissioners of customs themselves, through whom Russell's directions were channelled, had all warned him that this step went beyond the law. Hamilton reminded his counterpart at the Foreign Office, Hammond, that he had ignored this advice without first obtaining the support of his political superiors. There had been no time to consult Palmerston, Gladstone, or even the political under-secretary. The worried civil servant was quickly assured of Russell's support in the event of trouble, but when the cabinet met it approved what had been done. Some members may have questioned Russell's failure to seek an opinion from the law officers before ordering the seizure, for the suspicion that he had decided to act first and then seek legal support was surely not confined to Argyll. The Foreign Office had a plausible explanation ready—urgency. The choice on October 8 had been to seize at once the ram ready to sail "or to stand by and see her run away with." Of course, "the fate of her consort, although not so far advanced in her construction, could hardly be separated from her own."[41] In any event, the cabinet meeting went smoothly. The lord chancellor helped by stating his belief that the seizure would come within the law, and Russell prudently refrained from raising the contentious issue of its extension. "We must see what the present Foreign Enlistment Act will do for us before proposing any alteration," he remarked to Granville.[42]

"They never would have advised you to do what you have so rightly done," Argyll wrote to Russell of the law officers. "They will find reasons why it sh[oul]d have been done—now that it is done."[43] No doubt the foreign secretary shared his confidence. On the resignation of Sir William Atherton as attorney general Palmer had been promoted to that post and Robert Collier appointed solicitor general. The change clearly strengthened the influence of the advocates of a broad construction of the act. Collier had written the opinion upon which Adams had based his demand for the stopping of the *Alabama*, and it was rumoured that as counsel to the Admiralty he had advised that the *Alexandra* be seized and the rams stopped. When Palmer returned to his Richmond constituency to deliver a speech on October 14 he strongly defended the government's action and roundly condemned those merchants who seemed to think it was "fair" for them to carry on an "unlawful" trade with a belligerent power. The British government, were it a belligerent, could not permit warlike expeditions to be fitted out in neutral ports, he declared. Whether the Foreign Enlistment Act answered its purpose or not, these were the very activities it was intended to prevent in Britain's ports when she was a neutral. Evidently the new attorney general agreed with those who interpreted the act "as one intended to *enable the government to carry into effect a clear principle of international obligation.*"[44]

On October 21 the law officers delivered their formal opinion. As Argyll had predicted, it supported Russell. The government appeared well placed to justify the seizure of the ironclads "by sufficient evidence" that they had originally been ordered for the Confederacy. The onus of proof had been shifted to Lairds and Bravay. They now had to show, the law officers asserted, that there had been "a real and *bona fide* transfer" of the contract to the Frenchman. Even if they were able to do this a further question would arise: in fitting out the rams at Birkenhead did Bravay have "a fixed intention that they should be employed in the Confederate service?"[45] This reasoning and the line of proceeding founded upon it came close to violating that hallowed principle of English law—the presumption of innocence until the accused is proven guilty.

The welcome support of the cabinet and of the law officers did not end entirely all Russell's worries about the rams. "We have and shall have much trouble with the Ironclads," he wrote to Lyons, explaining that Liverpool was a port "specially addicted to Southern proclivities, foreign slave trade and domestic bribery."[46] Indeed, Inglefield had already reported that a plot was still on foot "to carry off one or both vessels." Their preparation for sea was continuing, for the authorities had been reluctant to throw out of work the 500 men they employed. Thus the danger existed of a party of seamen being smuggled aboard by the workmen. Lairds' sudden disclaiming of all responsibility for their men if this happened, and the onset of the season of winter fogs, under cover of which escape would be all too easy, brought a tightening of precautions. Over the vehement protests of Lairds, all work on the vessels was stopped and they were removed by Inglefield to a position where he could guard them closely. At the same time a warship was stationed in the mouth of the Mersey. Four months later

Bravay finally offered to sell the rams to the navy. Somerset now considered them "not good for much," and certainly not worth the Frenchman's asking price of £300,000. However, in May 1864 the Admiralty agreed to offer Bravay £195,000 for the vessels in their present state, and an additional £25,000 on their completion. The offer was accepted and Bravay returned £188,000 to the Confederates.[47]

At the American legation word of the rams' seizure finally put to rest the fear that they might yet get out. The energetic action of the government "has produced an excellent effect in inspiring confidence in the prosecution of their declared policy," Adams informed Seward. The minister kept to himself his opinion that the policy of Britain towards the United States was, as ever, "cold, selfish and short-sighted."[48] In Washington, the detention of the ironclads and then Russell's Blairgowrie speech had produced "the best effects" long before word arrived of the seizure. In the instructions he wrote for eventual publication Seward had continued to refer to the danger of war if the rams got out, but he was at pains to stress to Adams the administration's anxiety for "amicable and even cordial" relations with Britain. He readily conceded that disloyal Americans inaugurated and instigated many of the activities which tended to embarrass the British ministry, and he paid generous tribute to its firmness and its fidelity to "just principles." In the same conciliatory mood he quietly postponed the controversial issue of American claims against Britain for the depredations of the *Alabama*, though he was careful to emphasize that they were just and would be revived.[49]

Seward had another opportunity to parade his amiability when Admiral Milne, whose tour of duty on the North American station was coming to an end, visited the American capital early in October. Milne was "most courteously received" by Lincoln and all the members of his cabinet, but Seward lavished attention upon him. As for the more celebrated naval visit at this time, that of the Russian fleet to New York, it made little impression upon the British. They took Seward at his word when he declared that he had known nothing of it until the ships arrived and that the reception accorded the Russians was entirely the affair of the New York municipal authorities. There was no "understanding" between the Russian and American governments, Stuart reported home.[50]

For Americans long preoccupied with the dangers of foreign meddling

305

or involvement in the Civil War the implications of the news from Britain were far-reaching and cheering. First, the character of Anglo-American relations was "no longer so critical and therefore of so absorbing an interest" as it had been only a year earlier. Second, "the masses of the English people" had again given "unmistakable proofs" of their ardent sympathy with the Union cause. Third, the British government, whether in response to this "bolder" popular support for the North or the conviction that the rebel cause was doomed, had determined to pursue a policy of friendship towards the United States.[51] Clearly this was too optimistic an assessment of British opinion. It was also too simple an explanation of British policy. Yet the failure to recognize the complexity of her motives had not misled American observers about the significance of Britain's conduct in the affair of the rams.

Russell had been determined to stop the vessels leaving Liverpool, and his decision to detain them had been taken well before the arrival of Adams's dire warnings of the consequences of their escape. The problem that remained was to obtain the legal proof to justify seizure. Several expedients were considered, including amendments to the law to lighten the burden of proof, and purchase. But even as his uneasy colleagues pondered the alternatives, Russell grasped the opportunity presented by the growing suspicion that a plot had been hatched to get at least one of the rams out of Liverpool to seize them both and present the cabinet with a *fait accompli*. The seizure helped to make 1863 the decisive year in Britain's response to the conflict across the Atlantic. The spring had seen the government finally turn away from all serious thought of intervention in the war; in the autumn of the same year it resolved to eliminate the risk of entanglement, at least as a result of Confederate shipbuilding. Confidently, Unionists concluded that any lingering Southern hopes of British "collusion" with the Confederacy would now be dispelled.

TWELVE

The Friends of the South

IT WAS A CONFIDENT Charles Francis Adams who took stock of his position in October 1863. Not only had the rams been stopped but his Confederate adversary, James Murray Mason, had retired from the field. Mason's withdrawal from Britain was a formal admission of the defeat of Southern diplomacy, and it terminated a prolonged period of frustration for the commissioner. Reports reaching Adams early in May of the Virginian's sullen, rude, and disorderly behaviour were undoubtedly exaggerated, but Mason had ample reason to be both disgruntled and disconsolate.[1] He found his position as an "unaccredited diplomat" far from agreeable, and there seemed little prospect that spring of formal acceptance. Slidell reported that the French believed they had done as much as they could for the Confederate cause, and would now await action by England. But the British government remained "unmoveable." An attempt by Clanricarde in the Lords, armed with information provided by Mason, to stir it into activity against the blockade was turned aside with disheartening ease. Russell blandly declared himself convinced that the United States was not intentionally disturbing British commerce, and he expressed the belief that the British people had no greater wish to meddle in the conflict than had their government.[2] Significantly, the leader of the opposition, Lord Derby, agreed with much of what the foreign secretary had said. Clearly the Conservative leadership was as inert as ever on the American question.

Before the month of May ended Mason's drooping spirits had been lifted by the news of another triumph of Confederate arms. The new Union commander, "Fighting Joe" Hooker, had failed "as egregiously, perhaps more completely, than the rest."[3] Even the South's grievous loss of "Stonewall" Jackson at Chancellorsville worked to its advantage in England. The spontaneous expressions of sorrow startled Hotze and prompted a group of sympathizers in Britain to form a committee and open a subscription for the erection of a statue of the fallen general. Over the angry protests of the *Bee-Hive*, which suggested that the only appropriate pedestal for such a monument would be the emblems of human slavery, "in whose *glorious* cause Jackson lost his life," the contributions poured in. As for fears that Jackson's loss would fatally blight Confederate hopes, Frank Lawley assured his fellow-Englishmen of the general's powers of ethereal inspiration. "He is gone," the correspondent of *The Times* wrote in a maudlin tribute, "but will not his memory be a pillar of fire, leading, kindling, vivifying, and inspiring his men, and from the tomb calling them to deeds of more than mortal valour?"[4]

The revival of Confederate military fortunes and the evidence of continuing and widespread public sympathy for the Southern cause in England brought Mason, Roebuck, and William Schaw Lindsay together at the latter's estate of Shepperton Manor just outside London. Lindsay had succeeded William Gregory (who like many of his countrymen was now more interested in European than American affairs) as "premier" of the Confederate sympathizers in the Commons. Although there was much truth in Charles Francis Adams's remark that Gregory had been the South's "best advocate," and that it "lost ground in each successive transfer," Lindsay was a man of rare ability. He had not been born into the aristocracy or the landed gentry but through hard work and with intelligence and good fortune had conquered poverty and then purchased position. His sympathy for the South came from the heart and the mind. He was emotionally committed to Confederate independence, though at the same time he saw in the Southern states supporters of free trade and may have hoped to prosper personally from their success. The Lindsay shipping line might reasonably expect to receive preferential consideration when an independent South traded directly with Europe. However, self-interest was less of a determining factor than many of Lindsay's hostile contemporaries assumed. He scrupulously refused all business offered to him by the Confederate government, but this did not silence his critics. Led by the *Morning Star*, they attributed his conduct to "pecuniary or selfish motives." In fact, his sympathies cost him dear and not only in his extensive business dealings with the North. Samuel Lucas, the editor of the *Star*, broke with him personally and read him out of the Radical section of the Liberal Party. "I cannot believe that a man who exerts himself in support of a Confederacy the object of which is to found a government of which Slavery shall be the Chief Corner Stone can have sufficient foundation for the faith he professes in regard to parliamentary and other reforms," Lucas wrote.[5] As they plotted the strategy of another parliamentary campaign for Confederate recognition, Lindsay and Roebuck warned Mason of the need to advance cautiously. To win a victory, Conservative support was vital. Roebuck spoke to Disraeli and was sufficiently encouraged by the conversation to give notice of a motion. He also threw himself into public agitation. On May 26, 1863, he persuaded a large open-air meeting at Sheffield to call for recognition of the Confederacy. The call was quickly repeated by large gatherings at Manchester, Preston, Burnley, Bury, Bolton, and Mossley. These, together with a number of successful meetings in smaller Lancashire communities, were clearly intended as a show of mass support for Roebuck's motion. With the same aim in mind, Henry Hotze went to work. He planned to have every available space in London placarded with posters showing the Union Jack and the Confederate battle flag conjoined, thinking that this would impress the "masses" with the vitality of the Southern cause. He hurried ahead with a scheme to distribute among the many thousands of large wholesalers in Britain a list showing the foreign goods a peaceful Confederacy could consume. To underline the profitability of Southern independence the specialities of each individual wholesaler were to be marked on the list he received. Hotze was promised regular articles in support of Roebuck's motion by the editors of the *Morning Herald* and the *Standard*. Indeed, the regularity with which these two Tory dailies endorsed the motion appeared to confirm Roebuck's impression that the opposition was about to throw off its torpor. "The policy of partial concession and one-sided conciliation, which ministerial special pleaders call neutrality, is a complete and ignominious failure," the *Morning Herald* declared. "It is time for a change of measures."[6]

No matter how carefully the plans were laid, there was a lingering uneasiness among some Confederates and their friends about the wisdom of proceeding. Unless Roebuck had received a "positive" promise of Tory support he would do more harm than good, Edwin DeLeon warned. The debate was certain to inflame the North, rekindling military enthusiasm. If they failed to carry Parliament with them, the advocates of recognition would find themselves in the ridiculous position of serving as recruiters for Lincoln's armies. The wise course, DeLeon informed British friends, was to muzzle Roebuck whose " 'honest bark' on this occasion, may only serve to warn the burglar, not protect the mansion."[7] Much the same advice came from James Spence, even though he helped both to organize and orchestrate the agitation in Lancashire. He cautioned against moving for recognition "until some very important event from the seat of war startles the public mind out of the dogged state it has got into." Mason shared these doubts. Only news of a decided Confederate military victory, or of another French invitation to Britain to join them in recognizing the South, could rescue Roebuck's motion, he believed.[8]

Seeking a French initiative, Lindsay and Roebuck travelled to Paris. They had been disconcerted by a rumour circulating in London that Napoleon had changed his mind and no longer thought this the time to recognize the Confederacy. Knowing that this report if true would be fatal to his motion Roebuck sought and obtained an interview with the emperor. He pressed Lindsay to accompany him, for the shipping magnate had been granted several audiences in the past, and Mason urged that they both go. Such a meeting would aid the Southern cause, he argued. Although Lindsay agreed to go along he suspected Napoleon's motives in seeing them. Roebuck had often made the personality and policies of "Napoleon the little" the target of his invective. Was the emperor merely seizing an opportunity to flatter him, to charm him into holding his savage tongue in future? Others interpreted the emperor's conduct as an effort to revenge himself on Palmerston by embarrassing the British government at a time when there were reports in France of its being in some difficulty. Whatever his motives, Napoleon's interview with Lindsay and Roebuck led to another humiliating reverse for the Confederate cause in Britain.[9]

What was actually said during the meeting subsequently became a matter of controversy, with Napoleon disputing the Englishmen's version of his remarks. However, he did inform them that he had taken steps to contradict the rumour which had brought them to France. He authorized them to explain to their parliamentary colleagues that in all important international questions he wished to act with England. With respect to recognition of the Confederacy, he disclosed that the French minister in London, Baron Gros, had been instructed to sound out the British government. More significant was Napoleon's rejection of Roebuck's suggestion that he make a formal proposal of joint action to Britain, and in the event that it was declined act alone. In short, the French emperor left the Englishmen in no doubt that he would not take the kind of initiative Mason had concluded was indispensable if Roebuck's motion was to have any chance of success in a Commons vote. Equally troubling was the evidence that Conservative support was far less certain than Roebuck had appeared to believe after his conversation with Disraeli. Hotze reported that the opposition as a party was "still on the ledge." When Russell, in reply to a question from Clanricarde on June 26, declared in the Lords that no proposal or suggestion of recognition had been received from Paris, the worried Mason quickly contacted Slidell.[10] The response was reassuring. A visit to the Ministry of Foreign Affairs filled Slidell anew with confidence. Baron Gros had been instructed to remind Palmerston of France's willingness to join Britain in recognizing the Confederacy, he replied to Mason. What was even more exciting, Napoleon had suggested to his foreign minister that Palmerston be informed that he had decided to recognize the South. "This is by far the most significant thing that the Emperor has said either to me or to others," Slidell commented, and "it renders me comparatively indifferent to what England may do or omit doing."[11] Such confidence in French determination to recognize the Confederacy was misplaced. Indeed, the emperor's alleged remark departed so radically from his comments to Lindsay and Roebuck that Slidell ought to have guessed that there had been a mistake.

Napoleon had certainly thought of making some such statement, but intending it only as a prod with which to stir the British he had planned to hedge it with conditions. "I ask myself whether Baron Gros may not be instructed to state unofficially to Lord Palmerston that I am resolved on recognizing the independence of the Southern Provinces," he wrote to Drouyn de Lhuys. "We could not be compromised by such a declaration, and it might determine the British government to take the step." More cautious than his monarch, the foreign minister had then simply telegraphed to Gros: "See Lord Palmerston and in the course of conversation give him to understand that the Emperor has no objection to recognizing the independence of the South."[12] Nevertheless, London was soon buzzzing with the rumour that Gros had privately voiced the opinion that his monarch would renew his proposal to recognize the South and in the event Britain declined would proceed alone. When the story was confirmed by Slidell's report, and word arrived of Lee's second invasion of the North, Mason cast his doubts aside and encouraged Roebuck to press on with his motion and inform the House of his conversation with the emperor. Even the behaviour of the Tories seemed more promising. Prominent figures on the opposition benches, such as Seymour Fitzgerald, took an active part in yet another debate on the American seizure of British vessels. Launched on the very eve of the Roebuck motion it was well calculated to create a favourable climate for that discussion. It offered fresh hope that the Conservatives would rally in voice and vote to Roebuck's support. At the same time the party's two national organs coordinated their calls for his success.[13]

Roebuck rose to speak in a chamber crowded and expectant, but his guns had already been spiked. Russell and Layard had earlier informed Parliament that no recent proposals had come from France. Moreover, Gros had called on the foreign secretary in the afternoon specifically to deny that he had received instructions to propose recognition. Vulnerable from the outset, Roebuck delivered a characteristically "ungenerous and studiously indiscreet" speech which did nothing to strengthen his position. He abused those who did not agree with him and repeated more of his and Lindsay's conversation with the emperor than was prudent. His imprecise account of the French overtures to Britain exposed him to a sharp riposte which Layard promptly delivered, while the manner in which he relayed the latest news from the Tuileries made him, and to a lesser extent the silent Lindsay, the target of mockery as "amateur French Minister as well as amateur English Ambassador."[14] So badly had the affair been managed, one American observer chortled, "that Roebuck contrived to make it impossible for some 150 or 200 gentlemen to vote with him who would other wise have been glad to do so." When Roebuck turned to the emperor for help, following the debate's adjournment, Napoleon declined to provide him with the ammunition to subdue his assailants. Instead, the French released a somewhat different account of the audience, for they were anxious to separate themselves from this "catastrophe."[15] Briefly resumed on July 3, and again on July 10, the debate petered out three days later. Palmerston, who had missed the opening rounds due to an attack of gout, offered to allow the two embarrassed members to retreat as gracefully as was possible. On this understanding and with the Conservative front bench silent, Roebuck agreed to withdraw his motion on July 13, though the end was not as painless as he and Lindsay had expected.[16]

Roebuck had been urged to retire gracefully by fellow Confederate sympathizers. A humiliatingly small vote for the South had been certain, once it became clear that the opposition would not support the motion as a party. Mason found the explanation for this continued inaction in the peculiar state of British politics. The Tories believed, he reported to Benjamin, that defeat of the government in the House would bring on an election in which Palmerston's immense personal popularity might very well see the Liberals returned in larger numbers. Whatever the cause, the result of this "most disastrous contretemps" escaped no one. Roebuck's motion had "spoiled the chances of any other on a different basis." "Now, all hope of parliamentary action is past," Hotze concluded. "Diplomatic means can now no longer avail, and everybody looks to Lee to conquer recognition."[17]

Benjamin had long held this belief, and the Southern press never tired of cataloguing the Confederate grievances against Britain. By closing her ports to prizes she had effectively prevented the Confederacy from employing privateers to prey upon Union shipping, yet she tolerated the North's "illegal" blockade of the South. She permitted munitions to leave her shores for the Federal states but stopped warships built for the Confederacy. She had helped scuttle the French mediation scheme and refused to extend recognition. Beleaguered Southerners railed against "the selfish and unfeeling apathy of a great Nation whose sympathies have hitherto always professedly been with a people struggling for 'Constitutional Liberty'."[18] Nor was the public fury lessened by the ineradicable conviction that there had never been a moment since the second battle of Bull Run "when simple recognition by England and France would not have ended this war."[19] The demands for retaliation grew louder, and in June Benjamin responded. First, he revoked the exequatur of the British consul at Richmond and then refused to permit the official sent by the British to Mobile to exercise the consular functions there. Next, he ordered the remaining British consuls, and their French counterparts, to cease communicating directly with their respective nations' ministers in Washington.

Public criticism of Benjamin's actions was limited to their insufficiency. Cries for the dismissal of the two remaining British consuls and the withdrawal of Mason were even more shrill following the demoralizing loss of Vicksburg and Lee's failure in Pennsylvania. With the initial newspaper reports of the debate on Roebuck's motion plainly foreshadowing the outcome, Benjamin decided to humour the popular temper. He instructed Mason to leave England. At the same time he persisted in his efforts to draw a line between Britain and France. Slidell remained at his post in Paris. Gratifying as this demonstration was it provided only a brief fillip. Public despondency and fears of military demoralization "encouraged the croakers." "Away with spiteful, unmeaning, useless regrets, harmful criminations and cowardly apprehensions," the press both exhorted and implored. Yet people on street corners were talking very much as if they thought the South had had about enough of war, one diarist recorded. There were disturbing rumours of cabinet members selling up their property and converting the money into European funds. Even the president was believed to have "a large special fund in Europe." Not surprisingly, the "terrible idea" was gaining currency that Confederate affairs were in a "desperate condition." Victims of a terrifying inflation, seeing nothing but ruin and death before them, a great portion of the people "have given themselves up to almost every species of devilish desire conceivable until lying, blasphemy, drunkenness, gambling, licentiousness and robbery have become the order of the day," one British observer reported to the Foreign Office.[20]

The lot of the "Britisher" living among these angry, bewildered, and frightened people had long since ceased to be a happy one. Now it became more difficult. Lawley, whose habit of "viewing things through Southern optics" in his letters to *The Times* had "served to curb and countervail the evil effects of the scurrility of the Southern Press against England,"[21] retained his personal popularity but the hatred publicly and incessantly expressed for Britain fostered many new acts of petty tyranny against the Queen's less distinguished subjects. Labourers were "frequently discharged from their employment and subjected to contumely for not taking up arms."[22] Often they were arrested and jailed. Their position became even more uncomfortable when, on receipt of the news of Russell's detention of the rams and of his speech at Blairgowrie, the South was swept by a tidal wave of anglophobia. Riding the crest, Benjamin quickly found an excuse to expel the two remaining British consuls.

This breaking of the few contacts the Confederacy had been able to maintain with Britain amounted to the public abandonment of all hope of her intervention. "The open declarations of the leading journals and of the public men of that country, and, above all, the course pursued towards the steel-clad rams at Birkenhead, have caused everyone to dismiss utterly that hope," the *Charleston Daily Courier* summarized.[23] The hopes that remained centred upon the military campaign in Tennessee and the political battles in the North.

But Southerners had long understood that their possession of the fortress of Vicksburg, which enabled them to block the Mississippi, was essential if Northwest disaffection toward the Union was to grow. Its loss in July should have prepared them for disappointing political results in October, among them the defeat of the most prominent Copperhead, Vallandigham, in Ohio. "If the stupid and bigoted dwellers upon the Prairies are content with the future from such a settlement so are we," one Southern newspaper ranted.[24] However, the South was ill-prepared for the shattering defeat the Army of Tennessee suffered near Chattanooga. The critical state of the Confederacy was outlined for the congressmen reassembling in the capital on December 7, 1863, by the *Richmond Whig*. Serious reverses had been suffered in the field and important military positions had been lost. The expectation that ships of war could be obtained from abroad had had to be abandoned and the last hope of foreign intervention or recognition relinquished. The public credit was sinking, the currency declining precipitously in value, the blockade tightening its grip, supplies for army and people becoming even more scarce, the territory of the Confederacy shrinking in size, and the men in the field diminishing in number. For these maladies Davis was able to prescribe few remedies in his Annual Message to the Congress, which did little to silence the growing number of "croakers." He took the foreign powers to task for their failure to extend recognition, but admitted that further acts of retaliation would not do any good.[25]

"You will doubtless have observed," Benjamin wrote to the Confederacy's one formal representative still in Britain, "Commercial Agent" Henry Hotze, "that the President's message is careful (while expressing the duplicity and bad faith of the English cabinet, and Earl Russell's course of abject servility towards the stronger party and insulting arrogance towards the weaker) to show no feelings of resentment towards the English people."[26] It was a distinction that had to be drawn, for in Britain friends of the South were striving to organize the popular sympathy for the Confederacy and shape it into an effective instrument of political pressure.

The military news from across the Atlantic had been hard enough to bear for Confederates and their sympathizers without the self-inflicted wound of Mason's withdrawal. Edwin DeLeon wrote urgently to Benjamin, deploring the attacks in the Southern press on Britain and the praise of France. While the British public gave sympathy to the South and their merchants and capitalists provided aid, the French offered only empty phrases, he reminded the secretary of state. In these circumstances to recall Mason and leave Slidell at his post would be insulting to England and cringing to France. Worse, it would be "utterly suicidal." France would wait for Britain's lead in recognition, he warned, "but so insulting a discrimination will merely make highly unlikely their indispensable cooperation."[27] However, the decision had already been taken in Richmond. In London Lindsay was one of the first persons to whom Mason read his instructions. The Englishman was dismayed. He urged the commissioner to exercise whatever discretion he possessed and remain. In conversation and then in writing he drove home a number of points. The enemies of the South would make political capital out of the withdrawal while the North would be encouraged to press on to "greater acts of wrong, desperation and madness." The South needed "a highly confidential representative" in Britain. But the Virginian had already conferred with Slidell and they were agreed that nothing had occurred to justify his remaining. "Prospects of favorable action in England appear to be hopeless," Slidell judged. So Mason retired to Europe to await further instructions, staying close enough at hand to maintain the intimate relationship with the South's friends in Britain. His departure failed to produce the "profound" sensation that Hotze for one had expected. Instead, it was generally regarded as proof of Britain's "rigorous bona fide Neutrality." "If the Confederates are offended with us for this and withdraw their agents," *The Times* commented, "we are sorry for it, but the loss is theirs, while the relief to our Government will be great, and the nation will have nothing to repent."[28]

Depressed as they had good reason to be, British friends of the South could see a glimmer of hope. In the wake of the dreadful tidings from Vicksburg, and the disappointing setback at Gettysburg, that English "barometer" of Southern fortunes, the loan, had fallen sharply. Despite "the utmost exertions of its friends," it touched 36 per cent discount in August. Subsequently there was a modest recovery but it was still being quoted at more than 30 per cent discount on the eve of the news of the Confederate military disaster in Tennessee. Yet low as the barometer had fallen, the British public seemed far from convinced that the South could not weather the storm. The *Morning Star* might declare the Confederate cause "past help, past hope," but it had always been a Northern partisan. At the *Daily News* the midsummer victories of the Federal armies had come only in the nick of time to prevent a revolution in editorial policy. The newspaper's management had received instructions to assume a more popular position, less sympathetic to the Union. By persuading him that the Union might ultimately triumph the battles of Vicksburg and Gettysburg dissuaded the owner from pressing his order to the point of forcing the resignation of the editor and the manager.[29] But few people in Britain could see an end to the fighting. There was a feeling that Union successes merely tended to prolong the conflict without altering its outcome. This was the theme of Lawley's letters to *The Times* and of the newspaper's editorials. Appraising the position of the combatants at the close of the year, Walter Bagehot pointed out in the *Economist* that the North had failed to take Charleston or Richmond. The Confederacy continued to occupy an area ten times that of Britain. This vast size, the hot climate, a topography of swamps and forests, the scanty population, all made invasion more than usually difficult and dangerous, and conquest well nigh impossible if the defenders remained true to themselves and each other.[30] In short, fighting defensively, perhaps liberating and arming their slaves, the Confederates had the capacity to struggle on and on.

The exploitation of this sentiment was the challenge confronting the Confederacy's partisans. One organization formed for that express purpose was the Society for Promoting the Cessation of Hostilities in America. Its leading light was the Reverend Francis Tremlett, rector of St. Peter's Church, Belsize Park, but the guiding spirit was Matthew Fontaine Maury. A noted nautical scientist, he had arrived from the South in November 1862 with instructions to purchase ships and to work for recognition of the Confederacy. He quickly concluded that "British admiration of Southern 'pluck', and newspaper spite at Yankee insolence," had been mistaken by others as Southern sympathy. His opinion was that in its American policy "the British government fairly represents the British people." Although he despaired of his usefulness in England, Maury nevertheless threw himself into the task of exerting pressure on that government to intervene. He cooperated discreetly with the South's friends, providing Tremlett's society, which sought support from "the great mass of the clergy and ministers of the gospel," with money and helping to draft its circulars and petitions. Essentially, these expounded the view that the American war was a calamity and a disgrace to the age, and that its further prosecution was to be deplored.[31]

Useful as these activities were, there was a rather more ambitious project afoot to promote Confederate independence and James Spence was again at its centre. He had been hard at work since the spring of 1863 establishing Southern Clubs in a number of Lancashire communities, attracting "young men of energy with a taste for agitation but little money." Carefully tended and fostered by Spence, these "germs of important work" quickly grew and flourished first in Manchester, and then in Oldham, Blackburn, and Stockport. By August there were clubs in twenty-four textile centres, and in places as far apart as Glasgow and Ipswich. They found in Joseph Barker "a capital lecturer." He had returned to England in 1860 after nine years in the United States and was already well known as a "controversialist, preacher and teacher." Barker's conduct in breaking up a number of Emancipation Society meetings indicated the extent to which the Southern Clubs were a belated response to the remarkably successful campaign of agitation being waged by the supporters of the Union. Had the field been "left clear to the other side they would have swept all before them and completely deluded public opinion so far as the issues are concerned," Spence explained. In particular, the claim that Lincoln and the Union were warring for freedom and humanity had to be demolished. So the clubs sponsored meetings at which Barker starred, and sent lecturers to Mechanics' Institutes, to denounce the insincerity of the North's emancipation policy. In the Northern states, they reminded their audiences, blacks were abused and discriminated against. Why, they asked, did the Union government show greater interest in the deportation of freedmen than faith in the coexistence of the races in America?[32]

Another Manchester-based group was the Central Association for the Recognition of the Confederate States. "The frightful and vain slaughter of myriads of human beings in battles wholly indecisive, the symptoms of a retaliatory policy in the further prosecution of the war, the evidence that it is assuming a vengeful and exterminating character, and the vouched for fact that every man and woman of the South will die rather than submit to Mr. Lincoln's domination, convinces us that the reconstruction of the Union by the sword is impossible," the association's committee announced.[33] Although the name of James Spence was not to be found among this circular's signatories, whom the *Morning Star* dismissed as "ardent Tories and equivocal Liberals," he was intimately involved. He served on the executive committee, seconded the nomination of an important local figure, Lord Wharncliffe, as honorary president, and staged the gathering at the Clarence Hotel in Spring Gardens, Manchester, on October 5, 1863, which formally amalgamated the local Southern Club and the association under the title of the Southern Independence Association. Voted into the chair by the more than one hundred gentlemen present, Wharncliffe advanced the new association's arguments. Recognition of the South would bring an early end to the war, it would deflate American Unionists puffed up with the notion of their importance, and it would begin the gradual eradication of slavery. But this emphasis upon eventual abolition if the Confederacy survived was another admission of the Emancipation Society's success in Britain. The disadvantage under which the Independence Association began its labours, Wharncliffe admitted to his audience, was the general impression that the South and those who worked on its behalf supported the institution of slavery.[34]

Having fathered and delivered it, Spence gave close and thoughtful attention to the infant organization's upbringing. If that was natural enough, his determination to ensure its success was strengthened by his awareness of the consequences of failure. For Spence did not deceive himself about the South's predicament. "The news is gloomy —very," he wrote to Mason after word arrived of the defeat in Tennessee, "& I really do not see how the war is to be worked out to success without the action of Europe." The British government remained the obstacle and the only hope of moving it was to stir up public opinion. To despairing Southerners who questioned whether anything could be achieved he replied that he had known a man "brought back to life two hours after he seemed stone dead." At first the effort had appeared hopeless, "but in a case of life or death what effort should be spared?"[35] Could the Southern Independence Association save the Confederate cause without a resort to desperate measures of revivification?

To finance the association's campaign Spence looked not only to Confederate agents but also to Englishmen who had profited handsomely from the war. He turned to Alexander Collie, who had made "a terrific sum of money" with his blockade-runners, "and told him he must come out for the cause in proportion thereto." Collie responded like a "brick," promising to contribute a percentage of the cotton brought through the blockade on his vessels. He immediately gave £500 on account. Spence's second step was to organize a string of meetings in the North of Britain. Originally the intention had been to open the campaign with a great demonstration in Manchester, but remembering the embarrassing failures of the previous year Spence preached caution. His plan called for the initial meetings to be held in those secondary towns where Southern strength was "indisputable." Even there care was taken to ensure a friendly audience. At Stockport the association scheduled its meeting to coincide with one held by the local Emancipation Society. Moreover, the petition calling on the government to join with other European powers and find a way of restoring peace to America had been sent through the mills that were working and the operatives threatened with the loss of work if they did not sign. At Glasgow, where Spence addressed a crowd of four thousand, the organizers of this public meeting restricted admission to holders of private tickets, having already set aside a large bloc of reserved seats. As a result, the hall was "crowded to excess by a promiscuous audience, including all the chief businessmen." By the beginning of December six successful demonstrations had taken place, three more were ready to come off, and agents had been sent as far afield as Derby, Cheltenham, Worcester, and Nottingham to organize new branches of the association.[36]

The third stage in Spence's master plan called for monster meetings in the larger centres on the eve of the new session of Parliament, and the establishment of a London branch of the association which was to be "an auxiliary of the first importance." Lindsay, Alexander Beresford-Hope, and James Murray Mason, who was making a "private" visit to Britain, had resolved to found an association in the capital before Spence came down to London for that purpose in November. However, it was his ability to show extensive promises of financial help which overcame Lindsay's reluctance to rush into "an expensive society." An impressive if small provisional committee was formed, composed of the Marquis of Lothian, Wharncliffe, two Cecils, Lord Campbell, and three other members of Parliament. A circular was drafted, explaining that the association had been founded to act in concert with that of Manchester and to serve as a rallying point of "all who believe that the dignity and interest of Great Britain are best consulted by speedily and cheerfully recognizing a brave people" sprung from themselves. But the founders realized that success depended upon their ability "to operate directly and efficiently in the House of Commons." They had to influence the parliamentary, journalistic, and business mind of England in favour of action. The first step was to publicize their prospectus, to put it into the national and provincial press and into the hands of members of Parliament, peers, city men, and *littérateurs*. Plans were also made to issue short tracts and handbills which would drive home a single point, such as the right of secession or the Union's insults to England. A skilled parliamentary canvasser was hired and offices opened amid the clubs of Pall Mall. Reflecting on these preparations, as the reopening of Parliament neared, Mason asked William Gregory: "Does not this look well?"[37]

One member who showed no sign of apprehension on the eve of the new session was W. E. Forster, the Union's best tactician in the Commons. A year earlier he had spoken at length on America to his Bradford constituents. With others he had then been seeking to exert a popular pressure on the government which would countervail that of the advocates of intervention. Now he saw no need to dwell upon the American question. He dismissed the activities of the pro-Southern groups, confident that the military success of the Federals would check any move in Parliament to intervene in the conflict. Adams was no less sanguine. His ability to escape from the mist, smoke, and hurly-burly of London to the bracing peace of St. Leonards-on-Sea, where nobody rang his doorbell to appeal for passage money to America or to present letters of introduction from people he had never met, helped to sustain his buoyant mood. So did the more moderate tone of *The Times*, which promised "to diminish the barking of the curs big and little at the Clubs and elsewhere." Adams fancied that the cue for this change for the better had come from Palmerston. Indeed, he was convinced that the British government and his own were at last getting to understand one another. The British seemed to have overcome their "absurd prejudices" against Seward. Russell was "more courteous than ever before" and his policy was "more rather than less conciliatory." The cause of this improvement in relations the American found on his nation's battlefields (where the Union had won several important victories) and in Europe. The death of the King of Denmark in November added another snarl to the Schleswig-Holstein crisis. The state of things all over Europe was becoming so alarming as "to render every nation careful not to multiply complications."[38]

The new Danish monarch, Christian ix, bowing to the nationalists' demands, promptly signed the controversial constitution incorporating Schleswig in Denmark and announced that it would take effect from January 1, 1864. In December German troops entered Holstein, but war was avoided when the Danes offered no resistance. However, the smaller German states were now urging Prussia and Austria, whose forces had been the instrument of the federal execution in Holstein, to invade Schleswig and place the Duchies under the control of the Augustenburg family even though their claim to them had been surrendered years before. Such an invasion, Palmerston and Russell decided, would be an act of war entitling Denmark to British military and naval support. As the prime minister recognized, this could not be declared without the concurrence of the Queen and the cabinet, but neither appeals to national honour and interest nor warnings of personal unpopularity could persuade the Queen to oppose "stupid German nationalism," while a majority of the two old men's colleagues remained unconvinced that a demonstration by Britain would be sufficient to restrain the Germans. On January 2 the cabinet insisted that the support of Russia and France be obtained before any warning was issued to the Germans. The support was not forthcoming, for both of those nations were angry with Britain. The Russians had been offended by Britain's diplomatic meddling in Poland and the French by her rejection of Napoleon's latest proposal for a European Congress to settle the affairs of the Continent.[39]

Britain's evident diplomatic isolation and the Queen's energetic lobbying served to keep Palmerston and Russell effectively in check. When on January 27 the foreign secretary made one more effort to rally his colleagues behind a forceful policy, urging them to sanction army and naval preparations, he failed again. Five days later German forces crossed into Schleswig and the impotence of British diplomacy was exposed. Facing troubles enough in Europe, suspecting that the French emperor had played the characteristically machiavellian game of "encouraging Denmark and Germany by turns to bring on a war by which France may profit," Palmerston and Russell had as Adams grasped every reason to keep matters quiet behind the back Britain presented to the Atlantic.[40]

Speaking at the Lord Mayor's Day Banquet in November Palmerston had reaffirmed his government's determination not to intervene in the Civil War and "to maintain a strict and impartial neutrality." Meanwhile Russell was confiding to Lyons: "I am more and more persuaded that amongst the Powers with whose Ministers I pass my time there is none with whom our relations ought to be so frank and cordial as the United States."[41] And the reports reaching the Foreign Office from the minister in Washington encouraged the belief that it would be possible to keep relations running smoothly, at least for the time being. Russell's speech at Blairgowrie and the detention of the rams had led Seward to express his willingness to manufacture an excuse "to say something handsome as to the satisfactory relations at present existing between the Governments." Clearly there was "a better feeling towards England" and no desire by the government of the United States to pick a quarrel with her.[42] However, difficulties were lurking over the horizon.

Russell fully expected the demands of a presidential election campaign "to impose on Lincoln and Seward the necessity for a great deal of buncombe." He hoped that electoral need would not require much more abuse of England than the British had borne already. Another source of uneasiness was the course of the United States once the Civil War ended. But in the winter of 1864 this worry was more remote than that of the election. Russell, like most of his countrymen, could not see any cessation of hostilities in the offing. His immediate task, while he concentrated on European problems, was to mitigate those unavoidable questions "which touch the gall of the two nations." He wrote to Somerset to ensure that the new admiral on the North American station was "very strongly cautioned not to take any important steps without referring home." All of Milne's "forbearance and discretion" had been required, he reminded the Admiralty, "to keep us in good tho' not very friendly terms even at the best with the Yankees." Admiral Sir James Hope was subsequently instructed to be careful always to maintain a perfect neutrality, to make sure that his subordinates did not give "countenance" to blockade-runners, to protect legitimate British trade but to exercise forbearance, and to refer home serious difficulties.[43]

Russell also strove to head off fresh trouble with the United States over the Foreign Enlistment Act. When the government was denied a new trial in the *Alexandra* case on a technicality it immediately appealed, which purchased time. A vessel being built for the Confederacy on the Clyde, the *Canton*, was seized in December, and the foreign secretary acted quickly to lessen the embarrassment caused by the escape of the *Victor*. An old Royal Navy despatch boat condemned by the Admiralty as "rotten and unserviceable," she had been sold with the consent of the Foreign Office to a person who had often bought such hulks. As a precaution, however, and at Russell's suggestion, her masts and sails had been withheld. Nevertheless, understanding she was intended for the opium trade, the dockyard authorities had permitted some fitting out at Sheerness. Her owner, who was secretly acting for Matthew Maury, managed to persuade the proud captain of a naval vessel equipped with a new derrick for masting gunboats to test it upon the *Victor*. Then, when Maury heard that Adams had got wind of the vessel's true ownership, she sailed unfinished across the Channel to Calais, stopping midway to pick up a small party of Southern officers and be commissioned as the Confederate ship of war *Rappahannock*.[44]

Furious at being gulled again, Russell wanted to take strong measures. He was quite willing to contemplate the seizure of the *Rappahannock*, either in the Channel when she left Calais or in any British port she entered. Alternatively, she might be denied entrance to every British port. The law officers advised against both steps. They suggested he content himself with a warning to the Confederacy not to repeat this offence to British neutrality on pain of the navy pursuing and capturing such vessels. Russell had also turned to the Admiralty for help. To Somerset he proposed that the navy stop selling old ships of war so long as the American conflict continued. The duke refused. His department could not afford to bear the financial burden of maintaining all these useless vessels. It would take twelve years, his experts estimated, simply to break them up. What he did propose was that harmless sailing-ships be sold but additional precautions be adopted before obsolete steamships be put up for sale. None of this was revealed to the Americans, yet some of the steps which were publicly taken could be expected to diminish their irritation. Russell informed Adams that all the dockyard workmen who had aided the *Rappahannock* to escape had been dismissed from the service and that the inspector of machinery at Sheerness was to be prosecuted under the Foreign Enlistment Act. Although Inspector Rumble was later acquitted by a jury, the judge in his charge gave "a just construction" of the act, and the Admiralty punished Rumble by putting him on half pay. Thus the affair did not shake Adams's confidence in the foreign secretary's "honest intention to do all within his sphere as a public man to remove any just causes of complaint on our side."[45]

The government's desire to avoid American complications at this time of crisis in Europe precluded any mention of the Civil War in the throne speech opening Parliament on February 4, 1864, but there was never any hope of members remaining mute on this subject. Not only were the pro-Southern groups planning one final effort on behalf of the Confederacy but the Tories soon showed that they intended to harass the government over its American policy.

The tottering Liberal ministry seemed about to fall. The Conservative leaders had long resisted the temptation to try and overthrow Palmerston. His domestic conservatism was much to their taste and his personal popularity was such that any election following a dissolution promised to leave the Tories with a fragile majority at best in the Commons. However, time's devouring hand at last appeared to be tightening its grip on the prime minister. Increasingly, he was incapacitated by gout or fell victim to colds, and his once remarkable memory now occasionally failed him. The fact that he had been cited in a divorce action scarcely enhanced his position, at least initially. Few doubted that he was the prey of conspirators hoping to extort money, but many ridiculed the aged Prince Cupid. Watching this, Adams feared that the government would be driven from office. He did not welcome the prospect of a change at the Foreign Office, but as the new session opened Derby and his senior advisers were privately discussing who should be the foreign secretary in their government.[46]

Replying to the speech from the throne, Derby struck the government hard where it was vulnerable. He castigated Russell for his foreign policy of "meddle and muddle." With respect to the United States, he seemed to be almost ready to draw a line between the parties. He spoke of "the so-styled United States," of Russell "rightly or wrongly" opposing Napoleon's proposals for recognition of the Confederacy, and criticized the foreign secretary's "one-sided" neutrality. Making full use of the extensive diplomatic correspondence once again sent to Congress by Seward and published in the United States, the Tory leader portrayed Russell as a weak-kneed victim of Yankee bullying. It was a charge Derby and his followers repeated during debates on the seizure of the Laird rams and Union captures of British merchantmen suspected of running the blockade.[47]

The same accusation of "one-sided" neutrality was levelled at the Foreign Office by those parliamentary friends of the South who fuelled the controversy over Federal enlistments in Ireland. By 1864 several thousand young, able-bodied Irishmen were embarking every month from Cork alone, and it was alleged that their passages were paid in "greenbacks" or with sterling cheques signed by officials of the United States government. In all, 53,000 single men left Ireland for the United States in 1863 and the number rose to 64,000 in the following year. The total number of emigrants from all parts of the British Isles was 146,000 in 1863, and the suspicion that many of them were destined for military service was not ill-founded. Seward had long seen immigration as a means to replenish the Union armies, and through his circulars to consuls he consistently but discreetly endeavoured to encourage it. He sought from Congress an appropriation to help pay the passage of those unable to bear the expense themselves. "It is not unlikely that one hundred thousand men capable of bearing arms and willing to enlist in our service would have come if their passages could have been paid," he wrote to the chairman of a congressional committee at the end of 1863. However, Seward was not exclusively interested in recruits. He met with the board of directors of the American Emigrant Company and made several suggestions which induced them to enlarge its activities. The company's principal purpose was to attract skilled labour to American industry.[48]

The military advantage the North gained from immigration had not escaped Judah Benjamin, and he had turned to the task of cutting off the foreign supply of Federal troops in April 1863. Through Mason he had hoped to bring the question before the British government, which could be expected to be peculiarly sensitive on this matter. In 1855 Britain had suffered the indignity of her minister to the United States being dismissed, along with three consuls, for attempting to enlist British subjects living in the Republic for service in the Crimea. But Mason had difficulty unearthing evidence. The men did not carry arms and were able to produce labour contracts with railroads. "Against such peaceful emigration, supported by such proofs, the Irish Viceroy and his government were powerless," DeLeon recalled years later when writing of his efforts to persuade the lord-lieutenant to halt the traffic.[49]

Benjamin had resorted to direct action even before the failure of diplomacy was clear. He decided to send two or three Irish-born Confederates to their homeland to inform their countrymen of "the folly and wickedness" of aiding the Union in its savage war. Although hampered by a shortage of funds, these agents waged an energetic and intelligent campaign. They approached influential figures, such as newspaper editors, and were rewarded with leaders warning of the perils of emigration. Of course, in a country as impoverished as Ireland a newspaper subscription was a luxury many potential emigrants did without. However, in a country as Catholic as Ireland the clergy remained the most effective disseminators of information, and the Confederate agents successfully cooperated with many of them. Copies of letters from disillusioned earlier emigrants, written either to their families or to Catholic newspapers in the United States, were circulated to every priest. Extracts from the letters were also used on the posters pasted up outside churches and in the boardinghouses of port cities, while thousands of handbills and pamphlets were distributed to likely emigrants.[50]

The effectiveness of the Confederate effort did not match its thoroughness. A succession of crop failures in Ireland and the eviction of tenants by landlords had created a tide of emigration which could not be stemmed. The image of the United States as a land of hope and opportunity was fixed in Irish minds. As Bishop Fitzpatrick of Boston observed, "the Irish who are starving at home will be deaf to all the representations of Southerners so long as plenty and fair play await them in the Northern States." If their general task was hopeless, the Confederate agents did have one success. In November they discovered that men had been enlisted for service when the *Kearsarge*, a Union warship, put in to Queenstown for repairs. Moreover, they took care to place the evidence in the hands not only of the authorities but also of the opposition. Copies were sent to the Tory member for the University of Dublin, James Whiteside.[51]

Russell had often complained of Federal enlistment of British emigrants to the United States, many of them, in the prime minister's words, "recently landed and still preserving in every sense of the Term the character of British subjects." Here was "a set off" to Adams's repeated protests against British sailors entering the Confederate service. Charges that Union consuls in England were offering $400 to men who would cross the Atlantic and join the Federal army had been investigated but not substantiated. Now came the *Kearsarge* affair. Russell wrote to Adams accusing the consul at Queenstown and the vessel's captain of enlisting men.[52] The minister denied their involvement, arguing that the men had stowed away with the connivance of some members of the crew, and he was able to draw the foreign secretary's attention to the "existence of a regular office in the port of Liverpool for the enlistment and payment of British subjects, for the purpose of carrying on war against the government and people of the United States."[53] This information led to several convictions for violation of the Foreign Enlistment Act, and the men who had joined the *Kearsarge*, having been returned to Cork by the captain, were also prosecuted. However, the denial and disavowal by the ship's officers of any involvement in their crime, and the fact that the men had been returned, brought from the law officers an opinion that they did "not see any necessity for further remonstrance with the United States government."[54]

This was how the situation stood when the new session of Parliament opened in February. Led by Clanricarde, some of the South's friends on the government benches soon echoed the Tory cry against a craven, one-sided neutrality. Federal enlistments in Ireland in general and the *Kearsarge* incident in particular served to reemphasize the government's partiality, they claimed. Had the Confederates done one-tenth of what the Federals had done their activities would have been quickly halted. What other explanation was there except fear of the North for the government's conduct in this matter and that of the Laird rams? Why had Russell accepted the excuses of an American captain but not the assurances of respected British merchants when they pledged their honour not to send a vessel to sea without first giving a week's notice? Under this onslaught Russell did reopen the case and at Palmerston's suggestion sought the dismissal of at least one of the *Kearsarge's* junior officers. The Emigration Board was instructed to issue a circular putting emigrants on their guard against the dangers awaiting them in the United States. Meanwhile Seward instructed Adams to assure Russell that the American government "neither authorizes, nor approves, nor even knows of any proceeding" for recruiting in Ireland. This profession of innocence was accompanied by instructions designed to enhance its credibility. Adams wrote to the consuls in Ireland directing them to refrain from, and to caution other Federal agents there against countenancing, any violation of the enlistment law.[55]

The almost nightly badgering of the government over its American policy may have prompted the weary Palmerston's observation to a visiting Frenchman that the time had come to recognize the Confederacy. Not that he was contemplating action himself. He seems to have expected an initiative by the French emperor, who had called Frank Lawley (then on leave in Britain) to Paris for a long interview. These rumours of movement notwithstanding, the Tories' conduct did not long mislead either Confederate or Union observers. Derby had belatedly taken the field—he twice intervened briefly in the enlistment debates to imply his support for those harassing Russell— but he had not come as an ally of the South. It was the skill and temper of the pilot not the direction of the ship that he was attacking, Hotze soon realized. America was no more than the opposition's battering ram, and when they made their attack in earnest they would look elsewhere for weaponry.[56] Where they would find it was equally obvious. On February 18, having overrun Schleswig, Prussia and Austria launched an invasion of Denmark itself. The Channel Fleet was ordered home and Palmerston and Russell recommended that a squadron be sent to the Baltic, as soon as the season allowed, to help defend Copenhagen from any attack. Once again they were frustrated by the Queen and their colleagues. So Britain stood inert and isolated, and the conviction grew that the government was too feeble and vacillating to deserve to survive. Its prestige was further tarnished by a series of by-election defeats and a scandal involving a junior minister. By the end of March the ministry appeared to be stumbling along without adequate support in either House. The opposition, on the other hand, showed every sign of having patched up its internal differences and being hungry for power. "Parliament is dragging to its end," Adams concluded.[57]

Palmerston was not finished yet. The prospect of an all-out attack by the opposition saw him put his "ship in good fighting order." The junior minister's resignation was accepted as was that of the failing Newcastle. The prime minister was anxious to deny his opponents the advantage to be gained in charging that he allowed an important office to be held by someone whose infirmities prevented him from performing its duties. Edward Cardwell was brought into the cabinet as colonial secretary, thus bolstering the ministry's defences in the Commons, while Clarendon, a former foreign secretary, was coaxed into accepting "the cushion of the Cabinet" as chancellor of the duchy of Lancaster. He was promptly sent off to Paris on a forlorn quest— to secure French cooperation with Britain when the international conference Russell had convened in London to try to resolve the Schleswig-Holstein problem met at the end of April. Domestically, the conference and a truce in the war staved off the expected Tory assault. By June 21 it was certain that the conference would break up in failure and the war resume, but four days later the cabinet abandoned all thought of intervention. The arguments against war were too numerous and too strong.[58]

Britain simply did not have the men to fight in Europe. Never large, her army was scattered across the Empire. At most she could put 30,000 troops into the European field. She could not trust France. War would certainly disrupt the domestic prosperity Gladstone had described in his budget speech on April 7 and which permitted him to recommend further reductions in taxation. Drawing attention to the "astonishing sum" of British trade, which had exceeded £444 million in 1863, he concluded that these figures meant that England must "be the champion of peace and justice throughout the world; and to take part, with no view to narrow and inferior interests, but only with a view to the great object of the welfare of humanity at large, in every question that may arise in whatever quarter of the globe."[59] It was a statement that had a Cobden-like ring. Not surprisingly, the chancellor "took the decided peace line" in the cabinet. Another prominent dove was Milner Gibson, the president of the Board of Trade, in whose ear Cobden had been whispering a single name—*Alabama*. That vast wealth of trade would be exposed "to reprisals from Yankee Lairds" if Britain went to war. At the Admiralty, Somerset knew that Britannia's rule of the waves was limited. War with Germany would see hordes of *Alabamas* despatched from American ports to prey upon British commerce, he had warned Palmerston and Russell.[60]

The government had received a number of reminders of the vulnerable position in which Britain had placed herself. In April the law lords upheld the decision of the lower court with respect to the *Alexandra*, thus reviving discussion of the adequacy of the Foreign Enlistment Act. "Although the insolent assumptions of the northern Americans may make Parliament unwilling to pass new measures at a time when the presumed concession may be misinterpreted," *The Times* remarked, "yet, after all, we ought not to shrink from doing that which is not only just to others, but advantageous to ourselves." It would be suicidal for Britain to accumulate against herself "a mass of precedents capable of disastrous application."[61] The government's dilemma was how to avert this disaster without inviting another? In other words, how to escape trouble in the future without admitting to errors in the past? It was paralysed, Adams concluded, by the "dread of making any concession which might even remotely imply responsibility" for the acts of the *Alabama*. Replying to demands in the House for more effective measures, and to warnings that the Germans had grasped the significance of the precedents England had established in the matter of the Confederate cruisers, Palmer and Collier revealed the government's overriding concern. Britain must always guard against "those extraordinary and extravagant" demands made upon her "to pay the value of all the ships taken on the high seas by the *Alabama* and similar vessels."[62] This fateful pronouncement had been brought about by the *Tuscaloosa* affair.

CHAPTER TWELVE

In 1863 the *Alabama*'s captain decided to cruise off the Cape of Good Hope. On his way there Raphael Semmes captured six Union merchantmen. Aboard one of them, renamed the *Tuscaloosa*, he placed a small crew and some light guns. On August 8, claiming to be the *Alabama*'s tender, she was admitted to Simons Bay in Britain's Cape Colony. Yet there was strong suspicion that her claim to the status of a war vessel was fraudulent. As the American consul was quick to point out to the authorities there, she had never been condemned in a prize court and still carried her original cargo of wool, itself a prize. Reassured by the colony's attorney-general that the *Tuscaloosa* was in law a ship of war, the governor permitted her to make repairs and take on provisions. However, when Adams raised the case in London and the Foreign Office referred it to the law officers for an opinion they criticized the conduct of the officials at the Cape. The law officers attacked the local attorney-general's opinion that the vessel had ceased to have the character of a prize merely because at the time she entered British waters she was armed and carried a Confederate crew. The correct course, they advised, would have been to investigate the American consul's charge that she was an uncondemned prize and therefore had entered the port in violation of British neutrality. Semmes should have been asked to produce the *Tuscaloosa*'s papers, and if as a result of these enquiries the consul's claim had been proven she should have been seized and held until reclaimed by her original owners.[63]

Newcastle incorporated the opinion in a despatch to the governor of Cape Colony, who interpreted the letter as an instruction to seize the *Tuscaloosa* if she returned, which she did at the end of the year. When Newcastle forwarded the report of the seizure to the law officers they responded with a recommendation that the vessel be released. She had been accepted as a war vessel on her previous visit and had not been given notice that she would be treated differently this time, they explained. "The authorities at the Cape have it seems twice done wrong as to the *Tuscaloosa*," Somerset summarized. "They let her go, when they should have detained her; and now they have detained her, when they should have let her go!"[64]

When Russell wrote to Lyons on February 27, 1864, to explain the decision to release the *Tuscaloosa*, he referred to the case of the *Alabama*. He conceded that she had been "not only to a certain extent, equipped in, but, in a great measure, manned" from Britain, and further admitted that he had long hoped to have this "creature of fraud and deception" excluded from British ports. Acting on a suggestion of the law officers, he drew a distinction between the prizes of the *Alabama* and other notorious evaders of the Foreign Enlistment Act and those of regular ships of war. If any of the former entered British ports they would be seized, he informed Lyons, whereas the latter would merely be asked to leave.[65]

The despatch alarmed several of Russell's colleagues. Somerset urged the foreign secretary to consult the lord chancellor before sending it off, only to be informed that it had already gone. The admissions it contained "will be of great use in laying the foundation of a claim for damage done by the Alabama," Somerset feared. No doubt he took little comfort from Russell's confident assertion that he would know how to deal with the Americans when they demanded compensation. Westbury agreed with Somerset. He summoned Palmer and Collier in order to give them a wigging. The opinion they had sent to the foreign secretary went beyond law to meddle in policy, he charged.[66] He also expressed himself forcibly to Russell. Only two conclusions seemed to be clear, the lord chancellor observed. First, "That in the present state of Judicial decision on the Foreign Enlistment Act, whatever may be the existing evidence as to the *Alabama*, no one can say with confidence that a breach of the Statute was committed." Second, that even if the government was satisfied that the law had been violated in this case, it would be foolish to strengthen the American claim for compensation by volunteering an admission that the *Alabama* was equipped, manned, and armed in British ports. With the full support of Palmerston, the cabinet forced Russell to withdraw this despatch and replace it with a more innocuous account of the *Tuscaloosa* episode.[67] Fortunately the contents of the first one had not been communicated to Seward by Lyons.

One colleague who came to Russell's support was Argyll. "I hope you will not let them *hustle* you out of the course you have most wisely taken in conformity with the Law Officers' opinion," he had written before the despatch was withdrawn. The fear of Britain compromising herself was "childish," he believed. In letters to Somerset and Palmerston, and then in a cabinet circular, he argued this point, citing the "well-known precedents of 1793," when French privateers had been fitted out in American ports. President Washington had then admitted a violation of neutrality but not liability for the depredations that resulted. Therefore Britain should not be afraid to seize and restore to their owners any prizes the *Alabama* brought within her jurisdiction. "In the first war in which we are engaged 'Alabamas' will certainly be fitted out against us from neutral ports," Argyll asserted. "It will be found important to be able to say that we did our best to protest against the legitimacy of such proceedings."[68] But the majority of the cabinet was afflicted with myopia, as the withdrawal of Russell's despatch and Palmerston's subsequent behaviour confirmed. The prime minister took care to warn Collier, just before a debate in the Commons on the *Tuscaloosa*, "to avoid arguing upon the ground that the *Alabama* had broken our law because by doing so he would give the Federals a ground for their Demands."[69] In holding to this course the British government was fully aware that it was charting the way for others.

A year after the event Russell admitted that fear of Prussia fitting out cruisers in American ports "had contributed materially to cool his ardour for war" on behalf of Denmark.[70] Even the Union's cornering of the *Alabama*, and her destruction off Cherbourg on June 19, 1864, did not relieve British anxiety. Although a well-armed gunboat, the *Kearsarge*, had finished the corsair's career, and the Royal Navy had many such vessels, the hunting down of Prussian or Austrian *Alabamas* would also take time. Firmly convinced that the Confederate vessel's destructive career had been decisive in keeping Britain out of the Danish war, an ironic Cobden hailed Laird "as the greatest contributor to the success of non-intervention principles."[71]

Russell's statement of policy in the Lords on June 27, which one leading Tory interpreted as an admission "that the Government were for peace at any price, and meant to desert the Danes," precipitated the long expected opposition attack. Early in July censure was moved in both Houses, though Derby was too unwell to lead in the Lords. The motion was narrowly carried in the upper House, but the ministry survived by a slightly larger margin in the Commons, skilfully taking refuge in an amendment which gave "the go-by" to the motion. But Palmerston had thought it necessary to court the Southern lobby.[72]

The spring had failed to bring that revival of Confederate fortunes in Europe so carefully plotted during the winter. In France, Napoleon's flattery of Slidell, his showing of "numerous little personal attentions" to the Confederate and his family, could no longer disguise his refusal to offer the Southern cause any substantial assistance. "With the fairest professions, even sedulously made, I look now for no movement of any kind in that quarter of value to us," Mason concluded in April. In Britain, while the Tories could no longer be described as inert their pro-Southern policy had proven "tentative" at best. Even more disappointingly, the Southern Independence Associations had made little impact. They were in a state of suspended animation, Hotze reported to Benjamin on April 23. "The Danish question shields them with a decent excuse, but the cause is natural impotence."[73]

James Spence was still active in the north of England, organizing branches and staging meetings, but the London association, which had been formed to exploit this agitation and bring the issue of recognition before Parliament once again, remained "dormant." It was so lifeless that Lindsay wished to resign, but he maintained his membership when Beresford-Hope threatened to follow him out. Meetings were poorly attended and divided, with some members recommending action and others urging postponement. Nevertheless, Lindsay eventually resolved to go ahead. He obtained an interview with Palmerston at the end of May to seek government support. The prime minister referred to the South in very friendly terms and expressed his willingness to meet privately with Mason whenever the Confederate was in England. On the subject of a motion, he not only avoided committing himself but persuaded Lindsay of the merits of one which, were it to be introduced and passed, would not embarrass the government unduly. Palmerston suggested that the government be requested "to avail itself of the earliest opportunity of mediating in conjunction with the other powers of Europe to bring about a cessation of hostilities." Fearing that neither Mason nor Slidell would look kindly upon such an innocuous proposal, Lindsay hastily explained to them that "it would raise a debate favourable to the cause of the South, and the fact of our Government accepting it would have a good moral effect." Moreover, if the European powers could bring about a cessation of hostilities it was unlikely that the war would ever be resumed, and thus peace would establish the independence of the Confederacy.[74] This was the foundation, of course, upon which Tremlett's society had been built.

By June 1864 the Society for Promoting the Cessation of Hostilities had made "capital headway." Mason and Maury had provided it with money, while the Confederate agents in Ireland circulated its petitions there. In England it numbered more than 5,000 members, had drawn them from every county, and boldly claimed to represent the sentiments of twenty millions. Its founder had a ready explanation for this popular success and the apparent failure of the Independence Associations. The country "feels no interest in the question of recognition," Tremlett judged, but was keen to see the end of a war which had driven up the price of cotton goods. Peace would remit the tax of £50 million which, according to the society's calculations, the conflict had imposed upon clothing in Britain. Here was something all Englishmen could understand. Yet Tremlett deplored the fact that the London Independence Association had " 'ratted' from its principles" and stolen his. He drew attention to the ambiguity of Lindsay's proposed motion, with its request that the government avail itself of the earliest opportunity of mediating a halt to the fighting. "This is just leaving the government where they have been all along," Tremlett complained to Mason. "They have always professed to take 'the earliest opportunity' but of which they are to be judges." Although he had already sent an appeal for action to every member of Parliament, Tremlett did what the London Association had been formed to do—he entered the lobby and canvassed individual members. In addition, he began to organize a deputation to call on Palmerston and "represent to him that he must do something *now*" to bring the senseless slaughter in America to an end.[75]

Meanwhile Lindsay kept postponing his motion. It took several days to persuade Mason to come to London without a more personal invitation from Palmerston. There were fruitless efforts to obtain from the government a firm commitment of support for the motion. During a second meeting with Lindsay, Palmerston explained that Russell "if not altogether against it, was not yet in favour of it." Lindsay persuaded Layard to speak to the foreign secretary and then met with Russell himself. It was one of those interviews at which the lordly Whig greeted him with a three-fingered handshake but offered only two on parting. This was generally considered a sign that he had not been convinced, yet it kept open the possibility of a change of mind. Lindsay also delayed at the urging of such Southern stalwarts as Lord Campbell and William Gregory. "The uncertainty of the Virginia campaign, the fear of war in Europe, the reluctance to risk the slightest hazard in America, the disposition to forget it [the American war] in the face of nearer exigencies, the fact that the French Government no longer urge as they did last year" intervention, these were all serious impediments to action, they warned.[76]

The tantalizing possibility of winning the Palmerston government's support for Lindsay's motion may have been in the minds of some of those who voted on the Conservatives' censure motion. Perhaps it helped to persuade such members as Roebuck and Horsman to rally behind a government they had criticized severely in the debate. The fact that the ministry had not committed itself to the Southern sympathizers, whereas the Tories had conducted a sustained assault upon Russell's "one-sided" neutrality, may have played a part in deciding Cobden, who not long since had been anxious to get rid of the "old dodger," to follow the same contradictory course. Once the government had survived, Palmerston saw first Mason and then a delegation from Tremlett's society, indicating to them that he had finally concluded that this was not the time to move. "Those who in quarrels interpose," the prime minister reminded his visitors, "Will often wipe a bloody nose."[77]

Without government backing Lindsay knew that there was no hope of securing a majority for his motion, and he withdrew it. He did ask Palmerston in the Commons on July 25 whether it was the government's intention, "in concert with the other powers of Europe, to use their endeavours to bring about a suspension of hostilities?" The prime minister had thought of sweetening his answer with the "hint" of good offices at some later date, but Russell urged him to be careful. "All sorts of unfounded inferences may be drawn from the suggestion," the foreign secretary cautioned. So Palmerston merely replied that "in the present state of things" there was no advantage to be gained "by entering into concert with any other Powers for the purpose of proposing or offering mediation, or of negotiating with the Government of the United States or of the Confederate States to bring about a termination of this unhappy war."[78] This hint of a hint went unnoticed.

"Thus has terminated an operation which has cost much labor and money to somebody or other," Adams reported to Seward with considerable satisfaction at the end of July 1864. The "very elaborate effort" to organize British public opinion behind some form of intervention had failed.[79] The conclusion was inescapable, Mowbrey Morris wrote to Lawley, "This Government will not be moved from its policy of non-intervention in America, and it is not likely that its Danish experiences will give Earl Russell a taste for further meddling."[80] One man who was still unwilling to concede the final defeat of the Confederate cause in the House was the energetic Lindsay, but shortly after a speech to his Sunderland constituents in August he was felled by a disabling stroke. Lindsay's subsequent resignation of his

Commons seat meant that the South had lost its last effective parliamentary champion.

As the American war dragged on into the summer of 1864, with Grant's terrifyingly costly march on Richmond stalled at Petersburg, and Sherman's thrust through Georgia halted at Atlanta, Englishmen expected the Northern states to weary of the struggle. Military stalemate promised to make the arguments of the advocates of peace, who seemed to be in control of the Democratic party, "irresistible" in the approaching presidential election. Speaking to his Tiverton constituents, Palmerston drew attention to the "favourable symptoms" of peace in America. In Manchester, the possibility of the North abandoning the fight to restore the Union threw the cotton market into confusion. No one wished to be caught holding stocks of the fibre purchased when the price of it had been high. "Cotton completely floored today," one millowner wrote in his diary on September 14, "going down, down, down." Nine days later he was unable to find customers for yarn and cloth because buyers dared not speculate in the falling market.[81] But the Northern war-weariness which paralysed the cotton trade in Manchester also breathed life into some of the South's friends there.

The Confederate cause had clearly lost much of its attraction even in Lancashire's mill towns by 1864. The futility of passing resolutions calling on the government to intervene in America, and a vigorous counterattack by the Union and Emancipation societies, had resulted in sparse attendance at meetings addressed by Southern sympathizers. The despairing Spence forsook agitation, though he attributed the "present stolid and hopeless state" of the public mind to the disasters which had overtaken the Confederacy in 1863. He began to question whether the Manchester Southern Independence Association worked "any practical good," and claimed that it was "kept up only to suit the views of Kershaw." T. B. Kershaw was a man of "much energy and some ability," Spence conceded, "but little judgement—very little. The talent he does possess he overestimates enormously."[82] Whatever his deficiencies, Kershaw had loyally soldiered on for the Confederacy. He had continued to carry the message of the justice of the Southern cause to such groups as Burnley's Church of England Literary Institution, and it was Kershaw who conceived the idea of getting up a Peace Address from the people of Britain to those of the United States. Maury helped him to draft it and Hotze donated £150 to cover some of the costs of collecting signatures. In London, walls were covered with large posters urging people to sign and men went from house to house, while others stationed themselves in busy thoroughfares, to solicit support. By the end of September more than 300,000 Britons had placed their names on a document which described the war for the Union as hopeless, deplored the violations of American civil liberties it had occasioned, and endorsed the validity of the South's claim to self-determination.[83]

The startling success of the Peace Petition, which was forwarded to a prominent Democrat, Governor Horatio Seymour of New York, worried such stalwart friends of the Union as the *Morning Star* and the *Daily News*. However, they realized that an improvement in the North's military fortunes would undo the work of Kershaw in Britain and the "Peace Party" in America. The political significance of Sherman's capture of Atlanta was in fact not lost upon the British, and the subsequent news that the Democratic party's presidential candidate, Gen. George McClellan, had cast aside the peace provisions of the platform upon which he had been nominated to run, was received as confirmation of the Northern people's unwillingness to admit "the necessity of putting an end to this most cruel and wicked war."[84] Given this popular mood of obduracy Kershaw's petition suddenly appeared to be absurd as well as improper. That at least was the opinion of Spence, who occupied himself organizing a bazaar in Liverpool to raise money for the relief of Confederate prisoners of war. Although a social and financial triumph, for many of the stalls were sponsored and tended by aristocratic ladies, it could not be turned to political advantage. When Wharncliffe sought permission from the Union to send an accredited agent to visit its prisons "and minister to the comfort" of those for whom £17,000 had been raised, Seward delivered a scorching reply. In refusing, he contemptuously dismissed the money as a mere fraction of the profits the contributors had made from the supply of weapons to the South in exchange "for the coveted productions of immoral and enervating slave labor."[85]

Slavery was a millstone the South's English friends had long urged it to shed. In *The American Union* Spence had gently called upon Southerners to prepare their slaves for eventual freedom. The prospectus of the Southern Independence Association, which he helped to compose, "kindly" advised the Southern states that European recognition would necessarily lead to the gradual extinction of the institution. William Gregory had recommended in 1862 that the

South take the initiative on emancipation. Could not some scheme be devised, he had asked Ambrose Dudley Mann, "whereby the intelligent and industrious negro might be able to elevate and educate himself, and eventually, if he has the good fortune to accumulate money, be able to purchase his freedom?" Such a program would have been greeted sympathetically by Englishmen whose view of emancipation was coloured by racial prejudice and fears of social disorder. Gregory's proposal was too bold for Southerners to contemplate in 1862, while Spence's heretical ideas became something of a domestic political embarrassment to the Confederate government. But the certainty of Lincoln's re-election and the deteriorating military position in Tennessee and Georgia obliged the South, as Spence guessed it would, to compromise with the harsh realities of survival.[86]

Proposals to arm slaves, offering freedom in return, had been made publicly in the South in 1863 and privately even earlier. Slave soldiers would help fill up the ranks and the promise of emancipation might remove the "insurmountable" barrier to foreign recognition. Then, in November 1864, Davis suggested to the Confederate Congress that 40,000 slaves be employed in noncombatant military roles and be liberated on their discharge. In the following month an envoy was sent off to Europe to scout the possibility of bartering emancipation for recognition. He met with Mason and Slidell in Paris and accompanied the Virginian to London in March. It was a fruitless mission. Mason's interview with Palmerston confirmed what *The Times* had already announced—British policy would not be influenced by a Southern commitment to abolish slavery. As Spence feared, the time for this concession had passed. Word of the passage through the United States Congress of the Thirteenth Amendment to the Constitution, abolishing slavery, reached London long before Mason arrived. Furthermore, British confidence in the South's capacity to prolong the struggle almost indefinitely had been eroded.[87]

To elect Lincoln again, John Bright had informed Charles Sumner in September, was to tell Europe that the war would be prosecuted until the Union was restored and slavery destroyed. But English Liberals and Radicals were quick to find another message in the president's political victory. Democracy had trounced aristocracy. Lincoln was held up to British workingmen as one of their class. Here was a man who had raised himself, "by his force of character and unaided efforts, from the position of a day labourer to the chief magistrate of the great American Republic." This was a tribute not merely to his own ability but to a political system founded upon the "legitimate and uncontrolled suffrage" of the people, for it made possible such careers. And the fact that the Tories had gleefully exploited the disruption of the Union as ammunition in their battle with Radicals like Bright inevitably identified the cause of reform with the Union's survival. In her final triumph America would "overthrow more than her enemies."[88]

"I think the reform question only waits old Palmerston's fall, and the success of the Washington Government, to rise again and to march on to success," Bright had written in December 1863.[89] A few months later the prime minister's days, personal no less than political, seemed to be numbered. Herein lay the explanation, Tories argued, for Gladstone's dramatic emergence as an advocate of a virtually universal manhood suffrage. Speaking in the debate on a bill to broaden the borough franchise, the chancellor stunned the House with the declaration that every man who was not "incapacitated by personal unfitness, or whose admission would not be attended by political danger," was "morally entitled to come within the pale of the constitution." The workingman had shown, especially in Lancashire, that he could be entrusted with the vote. He had demonstrated all the required attributes of an elector—"self-command, self-control, respect for order, patience under suffering, confidence in the law, regard for superiors."[90]

No doubt Gladstone's earlier more conservative views on popular government had been modified by the conduct of the operatives in England and the events in America. Long before Lincoln's re-election, the chancellor had admitted to being impressed with the power and resolution of the Union government. Evidently democracy did not condemn a state to weakness or threaten national life. However, his proclamation of "a new political programme" at a time when Palmerston's health was failing convinced observers that Gladstone was staking a claim to the leadership of the party. "The speech is absolutely right in principle, and will give Mr. Gladstone a firmer hold over the Liberals," the *Spectator* declared. Indeed, despite having been written off by Bright and Cobden as a potential leader of reformers, following his Newcastle speech in 1862, Gladstone managed to establish close ties with both men early in 1864, when he consulted them on matters of finance and reform. Palmerston's rule was coming to an end "without having associated his name with any one measure by which the people are indebted to him for an increase of prosperity or freedom," Cobden observed in one letter. As a result, the government would soon expire from "the apathy and distrust" of true Liberals. If Gladstone allowed this to happen without making a personal protest he would present a "great triumph" to his political opponents and produce an "equally great discouragement" among his friends.[91]

Gladstone took care not to discourage his friends. He promptly published his reform speech as a pamphlet, explaining to an angry prime minister that this was necessary in order "to get rid of the strange misconstructions of which it has been the subject." But in expressing the hope, which he did in an introduction, that exaggerated expectations had not been raised, he did not alter the general conclusions readers were certain to draw. Gladstone was opposed to the present limitations on the franchise, the *Morning Star* reminded fellow Radicals, and was seeking a more liberal and equitable political system. The chancellor also shared the Radicals' passion for retrenchment, and he carefully protected his reputation as a determined foe of enormous military and naval expenditures. In his budget speech he had made explicit his support for a foreign policy of nonintervention. His reward came soon enough. At a Rochdale Reform Association meeting in November Cobden praised him as "the best Chancellor of the Exchequer that England has ever had," while a demonstration at Bradford in favour of Parliamentary Reform, which was held in December, hailed him as the Liberal man of the future. "Reformers throughout the country, do your duty, and you will not be forsaken by Mr. Gladstone," W. E. Forster promised.[92]

The reformers were already organizing. In preparing for a renewal of agitation they were undoubtedly encouraged by the achievements of the Union and Emancipation societies. Many of them had participated in the campaign to prevent British intervention in the American war, justly connecting the issue of that struggle with the chances of "progress" in their own land. It was a connection Bright rarely failed to make in his speeches, while the link was implied by Milner Gibson in an address to his constituents in January 1864. Two months later, when the National Reform Union was founded, George Wilson, a friend of Cobden and of Bright, and a vice-president of the Manchester Union and Emancipation Society, was selected as chairman. He had first made his mark by chairing the Council of the Anti-Corn Law League almost a generation earlier. The reformers' demands were for a redistribution of seats and a broader franchise, and the meeting at Bradford was soon followed by one at Birmingham addressed by Bright. The time to agitate had come, for 1865 was likely to bring a general election as well as the final triumph of democracy in America. "Assert your Rights! Be United," the *Bee-Hive* commanded workingmen. "These were the watchwords of victory in America. Shall they not make us victorious in England?"[93]

The American war gave another important fillip to the reform cause in Britain by bringing together Radicals and a number of University Liberals, and their alliance was symbolized if not sealed by Bright's brief visit to Oxford in May 1864. Drawn together by a common sympathy for the United States, the academics happily accepted the myth of working-class support for the Union which the Radicals had invented. The people's conduct had been governed by the realization that at the root of the conflict lay a struggle between freedom and slavery, or so the story went. This moral sense was proof that enfranchised workingmen would be guided by loftier interests than those of their own class. The academics' budding faith in democracy was nourished by the visits some of them paid to the Republic. Dicey had gone there in 1862, Leslie Stephen in 1863, and in 1864 Goldwin Smith made a triumphal tour. To their delight they found men much like themselves, a discovery which disproved the worrying charge that democracy was incompatible with civilized and cultivated society.[94]

In the lectures he delivered and the articles he wrote during his three months in the United States Smith dwelt upon the natural fraternity of the two peoples. "From England you are sprung," he reminded his audiences, "and it is because you are Englishmen that English freedom, not French and Spanish despotism, is the law of this continent." Some Englishmen had withheld sympathy from the Union cause, he admitted, but they had come from the privileged class whose defeat would be signalled by the North's victory. "Show by your example, by your moderation and self-control through this war and after its close," Smith implored, "that it is possible for communities, duly educated, to govern themselves without the control of an hereditary order." This was the road to revenge for Britain's conduct during the Civil War. To force a war upon her would only strengthen the "worst part of the English aristocracy" in the worst way.[95]

The years 1863 and 1864 found the South's friends still struggling to find the key which would unlock the door to British intervention in the American conflict. Despite the misgivings of several of the participants, an attempt was made to prod Parliament into action following the Confederacy's successes in the field during the spring of 1863. Those plotting this political strategy thought they had a willing accomplice in Napoleon III, but confusion over what the emperor was prepared to do, false expectations of Tory support, and the folly of permitting John Arthur Roebuck to take the leading role, all doomed the scheme. Instead of playing out the high international drama they had envisaged the principal actors found themselves performing in a French farce. This sorry episode, Russell's Blairgowrie speech, and the seizure of the rams forced the Confederacy to acknowledge that virtually all hope of British intervention had gone. Nevertheless, in Britain some sympathizers continued to strive to mobilize public opinion behind a demand for a change in the Palmerston government's policy. Aided by Mason and Maury, Francis Tremlett exploited the widespread British conviction that the Confederacy had the capacity to maintain the bloody struggle for years. Another active figure was James Spence. Through the Southern Independence Association he helped to found, and the Southern clubs he did so much to form, Spence fought to expose the "insincerity" of the Union's emancipation policy and thus counter the activities of the Union and Emancipation societies. The association and the clubs were intended to provide the organizational heart of a campaign of popular agitation which would be climaxed by the reopening of Parliament in 1864. Spence not only threw himself into this work but helped to launch the London branch of the association, which was expected to exert the popular pressure directly upon the government.

The South's friends achieved little. Why? One reason was the division within their own ranks; another, a lack of energy in some of those involved. Men such as Spence, Tremlett, and Lindsay worked hard enough, but too many of the leading lights were persons unused to the politics of popular agitation and with little taste for it. They lacked the experience and the fervour of the old abolitionists, the dissenters, and the Radicals in the North's camp. However, even if they had possessed a greater appetite for agitation they could never have succeeded in their essential purpose. In 1862 the result might have been different, but in 1864 intervention was unthinkable. Continental affairs had raised insurmountable barriers to British action in America. The Schleswig-Holstein crisis and Britain's all too evident diplomatic isolation and impotence created problems enough for Palmerston and Russell without their risking entanglement with the Union. Their prime concern was to keep relations with the United States running as smoothly and as quietly as possible. Significantly, although the Tories seized upon the government's handling of foreign affairs in a serious attempt to drive it from office they did not demand a change in American policy, and their irresolute response to the American war may have cost them a few vital votes in the crucial Commons division. Attacks on the government's conduct towards the United States probably helped Cobden and others to resist the temptation to defeat the "old dodger," while the persistent failure of the Conservative leadership to enunciate a clear policy with respect to America allowed Palmerston to dangle the bait of a reappraisal of the government's position before several members of the Confederate lobby.

Another formidable obstacle to any British intervention helpful to the Confederacy was slavery. Had the South hearkened to the advice some of its British friends offered in 1862 later embarrassment might have been avoided. But the activities of the Southern clubs no less than Wharncliffe's speech at the founding meeting of the Independence Association were an admission of the success the Union and Emancipation societies had enjoyed. By the time the Confederacy steeled itself to tamper with the "peculiar institution" the prospect of winning diplomatic advantage had disappeared.

Finally, the course of the war worked to the double disadvantage of Southern sympathizers seeking to effect a change of British policy. During the summer of 1864, with Grant's advance on Richmond checked and apparently stalemated, many Englishmen clung to the belief that the Union would eventually tire of the fighting and killing and accept peace on terms which acknowledged Confederate independence. Thus British intervention was unnecessary. Then in the fall the Union advance suddenly recovered its momentum with the capture of Atlanta. Lincoln's subsequent triumph in the presidential election could only be interpreted as proof of the Union's determination to press on to victory, while Sherman's march to the sea caused not a few Englishmen to change their minds about the South's ability to protract the struggle almost indefinitely.

344

THIRTEEN

The Perils of Peace

UNEASY RELATIONS WITH THE UNITED STATES always turned the eyes of worried Englishmen to Canada, and as the Civil War continued a rash of troubles between the Republic and the provinces intensified the traditional concern. Northerners had regarded Sandfield Macdonald's ramshackle government as friendly, for it had proved extraordinarily cooperative. Although the premier's wife came from a prominent Southern family—her brother had served in the Confederate army until taken prisoner in 1862—and the two Canadian newspapers closely identified with Sandfield Macdonald tended to be Southern in their sympathies, he exhibited no such partiality. On the contrary, he knew Seward well and cultivated the relationship. When the ubiquitous George N. Sanders passed through Quebec in August 1862, carrying important despatches to the Confederate commissioners in Europe, and discussed their contents with Macdonald, the premier immediately forwarded the information to the American consul. Several of his ministers were avowed admirers of the Republic and the organ of one of his French-Canadian allies boldly proclaimed its Union sympathies. Little wonder that Consul Ogden at Quebec happily boasted of unparalleled opportunities for "private intercourse" with the men in power. The government "is with us almost unanimously in our present struggle," he reported to Seward.[1]

Unfortunately the popularity of Sandfield Macdonald's ministry in the United States failed to protect Canada from unpleasant difficulties with her neighbour. The American practice of exacting prohibitive bonds on shipments of merchandise from New York to several of Britain's West Indian possessions, in order to discourage reshipment to the Confederacy, was extended to trade with North America, while the export of livestock and anthracite coal to Canada was prohibited entirely. Complaints that the "numerous iron foundries and other factories" in the western part of the province faced ruin, because of their dependence upon American anthracite, left Seward unmoved.

The ban was not relaxed until the Canadian government forbade the exportation of coal.[2]

A more serious colonial grievance arose out of the activities of Federal recruiters. Young men were carried across the border drunk and insensible, or duped into entering the United States with promises of employment, and then "induced to enlist." The Canadian government sent agents to the border regions to investigate and detectives to assist the local police, and their presence did discourage the traffic. In addition, the bishops of Quebec and St. Hyacinthe were persuaded to send a circular letter to the curés of their dioceses instructing them to warn their flocks. However, the difficulty of securing evidence upon which to base prosecutions, and the fact that some of those who crossed the frontier did find well-paid jobs awaiting them, limited the effectiveness of countermeasures. Nor did the Canadians obtain the assistance they sought from the United States. All their efforts to suppress crimping would fail, they realized, so long as the Union continued to pay "bringing money."[3]

Canadian anger was occasionally directed towards the unpopular American consul general, Joshua Giddings. John A. Macdonald's old organ in Canada East, the *Quebec Morning Chronicle*, implied that Giddings was in some way involved in the nefarious enlistment practices. Fortunately the newspaper did not discover that he strongly supported the American ban on coal exports to Canada. Giddings had reported to the State Department that ships were being loaded with Pennsylvania anthracite at Montreal for Nassau. Nevertheless, the *Chronicle* portrayed him as a latter-day Fouché controlling a vast network of Federal spies in the province, and those Canadians who viewed the American with a jaundiced eye must have enjoyed the spectacle of his being hauled before the courts in November 1863, for alleged complicity in the kidnapping and false arrest of a British subject. The consul general was arrested and detained briefly, being saved from prolonged detention by his health—he suffered from "atrophy of the heart"—and by two Canadian friends who entered bail for $30,000. Although Giddings had clumsily stumbled into a Confederate snare, and the case against him was later dropped, he blamed Canadians for his embarrassment and plotted revenge.[4]

Giddings was a foe of the Reciprocity Treaty, believing that it had "proven beneficial only to exporters of Canadian produce and to smugglers of dutiable goods." In the summer of 1863 he had pressed Seward to give the earliest possible notice of its termination, explaining later that the end of reciprocity and a withdrawal of the warehouse and bonding privileges extended to Canadians importing or exporting goods through the United States would strengthen the hand of those in the province who wished to sever the link to Britain. Hence, when he heard that members of the Canadian Parliament had turned up in Washington to lobby for the treaty's renewal Giddings rushed there himself. His opposition now had all the intensity of a personal grievance. He was determined "to arouse our government to such a sense of its dignity as will teach our Canadian neighbors that while England sends out her ships under secession flags to prey upon our Commerce, and Canada sends her blockade runners to feed and clothe the rebels and her presses are constantly slandering our President and officers and [she is] imprisoning our Consuls General at the instance of skedadlers from our States, I think it most extraordinary for them to call on us to continue to hold our markets open for their produce free of duty."[5]

The treaty had been under attack in Congress for several years, but charges that it was a poor bargain for the United States grew in number with the outbreak of the Civil War. Where was the reciprocity, opponents asked, in an arrangement which permitted most of the Canadian goods imported into the Union to enter duty-free while American manufactures exported to the province were subject to a tariff? Furthermore, as a result of this exchange the Federal government had been denied an important source of revenue at a time when it desperately needed money to wage the war. Thus when Justin Morrill introduced a motion on the first day of the new session of Congress in December 1863, calling for the treaty's abrogation, Lyons hoped that this was nothing more than another manifestation of the congressman's "protection mania." Unfortunately the assault was soon taken up by several other members of Congress and was broadened to include a call for the end of the Transit Trade Bill. When the worried Lyons discussed the situation with Seward, the secretary attributed this "ebullition" of irritation to the resentment many Republican congressmen felt at the treatment of Giddings in Canada. But the enemies of reciprocity had also sought to gather support from colleagues embittered by the general conduct of Britain and Canada. "The colonies on our border, who are directly benefited by this treaty, have displayed the same feeling of hostility toward us that pervades the mother country," cried one advocate of abrogation. Clearly the treaty had failed in its fundamental objective of cultivating a strong and intimate friendship for the United States in Canada.[6]

Canadians knew that reciprocity was far more profitable for the Republic than its enemies there alleged. The overall balance of trade was still tipped heavily in the Americans' favour, though the annual figures were now moving the scales in Canada's direction. Yet the treaty's profitability for the Union did not prevent it from being identified in the minds of Canadians with their own commercial prosperity, which explains the deepening anxiety in the province during the winter of 1864. As one of the Quebec organs of the Sandfield Macdonald government summarized, "il est très important pour nous que cette source de prosperité matérielle ne soit pas fermée, mais qu'au contraire, elle soit élargie, s'il est possible de le faire sans troubler d'autres exigences." An end to reciprocity would be "disastrous," the government's English-language mouthpiece had warned.[7] Responding to the widespread concern, and recognizing the political necessity to guard against opposition charges of neglecting Canadian interests, Sandfield Macdonald and his colleagues decided to send an "extra official" agent to Washington. Their first choice was George Brown, whose Union sympathies would have assured him of a friendly reception, but he begged off. So they turned to John Young, an "able and prudent man" who had had extensive business dealings with the United States.[8]

Initially Lyons refused to have a Canadian "supposed to be peculiarly" in his confidence lobbying in Washington. Repeating the advice he had given earlier, he suggested that the residents of the province maintain a discreet silence. "The more they agitate, the more they convince people here that the Treaty is a good bargain for Canada and a bad bargain for the United States," he warned Monck. In his opinion the only hope of success was to make the question an imperial one. However, when Seward informed the British minister that he thought visits by influential Canadians to conciliate senators and representatives would be helpful (having implanted the idea in Sandfield Macdonald's mind in the first place), Lyons fell into line. He promised to do all he could "in a quiet way to help and be civil to men coming under the conditions mentioned by Mr. Seward," provided they did not appear to compromise either him or the imperial government, and there was no chance of establishing an "inconvenient precedent with regard to independent Canadian Diplomacy." Happily, Young played his part "very judiciously" and did "all the good that could be done." He met with Lyons, Seward, and many members of both houses of Congress. He agreed to equip reciprocity's supporters with helpful documents and statistics, but was pessimistic concerning their chances of defeating the motion calling for abrogation of the treaty. Opponents drew their strength less from the conviction that the present arrangement was unfair to the United States, he explained to the Canadian government, than "from the views entertained of a prevalent feeling in Canada hostile to the North."[9]

Perhaps influenced by Lyons, John Young recommended to the provincial government that it respond to the very real likelihood of Congress voting to terminate the treaty by seeking the establishment of a joint Anglo-American commission to investigate possible changes. Beyond this, he sought to allay some of the anxiety within the government by attempting to show that the irretrievable loss of reciprocity would not be "very disastrous to Canadian interests." The United States would still have to import Canadian lumber, barley, and oats, he pointed out. Furthermore, the province's revenue could be raised from tolls on canals, a direct tax on property, and a tax on incomes, which would be not only "the most equitable and the most economical mode" of proceeding but would permit the abolition of every custom-house. Here was the alternative road to commercial prosperity, he argued. "Imports from Europe, from the United States and other Countries, would, by being admitted free of duty, flow to the St. Lawrence and a vast trade would thus centre in Canada, which the United States could not prevent, unless they too adopted a similar policy."[10]

Less confident than Young of Canada's ability to prosper without reciprocity, the Sandfield Macdonald government followed his advice in urging Britain to initiate negotiations for a modified treaty before the old one could be terminated. Finance Minister Luther Holton's dread was that notice of abrogation would be given and negotiations for a renewal so protracted by opponents "that the Treaty in its present form would fall through before any substitute for it should have been provided." Monck even proposed the appointment of Cobden as one of the British commissioners, thinking that his presence would allay those feelings of hostility to England which were believed to be at the root of the abrogation movement. But negotiations were not opened. The fall of Sandfield Macdonald's government in March 1864, and its replacement by Conservative ministers who were "likely to be less free trade," brought matters to a standstill while the latter clarified their position. Lyons continued to advocate delay, in the hope of "scraping" through the congressional session without a vote against the treaty, and the imperial government supported him. It seemed a sound decision, for the House of Representatives decided to postpone the question until December. And when Lyons visited the province a few weeks later he impressed on the Canadians the wisdom of continuing to leave the treaty alone for the time being. The next session of Congress would be a short one, he observed, and the Lincoln administration had shown no disposition to encourage the attacks on reciprocity. Thus the probability was that Congress would not pass any motion calling for abrogation, and if the treaty survived this brief winter session it would be safe for another two years. The minister could not foresee the complications that were soon to arise out of Confederate activities in Canada.[11]

On September 14, 1863, the British consul at Baltimore had been informed that a scheme was afoot to use Canada as a base for Confederate raids across the border. The information was quickly relayed to Quebec, for it was assumed that the principal object of such attacks would be to embroil Britain with the United States. Although he doubted the accuracy of the information Monck made sure that it was investigated. He realized that the popular hostility to the North in the province placed an added responsibility on his government to see that nothing was done that "could give just cause of offence" to the American authorities. The investigation failed to turn up any evidence of a Southern plot, but less than two months later an employee of the provincial government whose family ties with the South enhanced his credibility revealed that one did indeed exist. According to this Canadian informant, a group of Confederate refugees in Canada planned to board one or more of the Lake Erie steamers as passengers, overpower the crews, seize the vessels and make for Johnson's Island in Sandusky Bay. Then, having freed the Confederates imprisoned on the island, they intended to attack Buffalo or some other city on the American side of the lake.[12]

It was Monck's opinion that the project held very little promise of success, but both he and his ministers (still led at this time by Sandfield Macdonald) hastened to impress upon their American neighbours Canada's anxiety to cooperate with them in frustrating raids. Steps were taken to guard against any gathering of Confederates along the Canadian lakeshore. The premier travelled to Buffalo to confer personally with the mayor, while his colleagues assured American consular officials of the government's diligence. "The acts of this Government in relation to the recent 'Plot' are satisfactory proofs of their friendly feelings, and their desire to preserve the neutrality of these Provinces," the consular agent at Toronto reported to the State Department.[13] Seward agreed.

Monck had immediately sent word of the plot to Lyons, who passed it on to Seward. The secretary responded by despatching Preston King to Canada as a special agent. His mission was "to secure a perfect understanding between the Governor General and the Agents of the United States."[14] Privately Monck deplored King's arrival. Eyeing the large body of Southern sympathizers in the province, he did not wish to appear to be on terms of "extraordinary intimacy" with the Union government. Any appearance of partisanship for the North might stir these sympathizers "into action in connection with some scheme such as that about which we are corresponding at present," he explained to Lyons. Naturally Monck concealed these misgivings from King whose visit he skilfully turned to advantage. So friendly was the unofficial reception given to Seward's agent that he failed to notice how quickly if politely he had been sent packing. What he did mark and report, however, was the governor general's "frank and decided" commitment to maintain the laws and preserve the public peace.[15]

The affair had helped rather than hindered relations with the Union, Lyons concluded. Thanks to Monck, the Confederates' plan to do mischief and embroil Britain with the United States had backfired. Good will not ill will towards British North America had been produced in the Northern states. Newspapers praised the provincial authorities for reciprocating President Van Buren's efforts a quarter of a century earlier to prevent similar raids in the opposite direction, while the Canadian minister who had been delegated to carry the first information of the plot to Washington attended the dedication of the Gettysburg Cemetery as Seward's special guest.[16] But this American cordiality did not survive the strains to which further Confederate mischief soon subjected it.

In December 1863 a small group of men boarded an American steamer, the *Chesapeake*, at New York. They had tickets for Portland, but once the vessel was on the high seas they seized control of her in the name of the Confederacy and headed for Saint John, New Brunswick, intending to take on the coal needed to run south to Wilmington. Off the coast of the Maritimes their plans went awry, and they abandoned the ship. She was retaken in British waters by pursuing Federals. Also taken, from a British ship within the territorial limit, was a British subject involved in the affair, and he was being held in chains aboard one of the two Union vessels which entered Halifax with the *Chesapeake* on December 17.[17]

For Gen. Charles Doyle, the administrator of Nova Scotia, the incident posed problems of some delicacy. How was he to uphold the dignity of Britain and not wound the pride of the Americans? In response to an application from American officials a warrant had already been issued for the arrest of the ringleader of the Confederate "pirates." However, the "flagrant violation of neutral rights committed by the United States Men of War," and their "outrage upon British authority," necessitated the "unconditional surrender" both of the *Chesapeake* and the prisoner. The American officers bowed to these demands, but when the prisoner was put ashore he made good an escape with the help of some local citizens before a warrant issued under the Extradition Treaty could be served upon him. As an embarrassed Doyle explained to the Colonial Office, it had been necessary to free the man from his improper detention in order to arrest him properly.[18]

In Washington, Lyons's first thought was to avoid exciting irritation at a time when the Reciprocity Treaty was being debated in Congress. Yet, once familiar with all the details of the episode, he realized that Britain could not overlook the conduct of the American officers, and Seward eventually wrote out a statement which the British accepted as a "full apology." Like Doyle and Lyons the American wished to prevent the *Chesapeake* affair "becoming a serious one," and in this they were successful. What they could not prevent was a souring of American opinion. The Southern sympathies of the people of Halifax, who had not only freed one prisoner but had stopped police officers from arresting the leader of the "pirates" when they ran him to ground; the belief that the principals were British subjects; the decision of the colonial authorities to put the *Chesapeake* into the Vice-Admiralty Court instead of restoring her immediately to her owners; the dismissal of the extradition proceedings against the few men who had been arrested elsewhere, all combined to reawaken and confirm American suspicions of British North American hostility to the Union. Nor was any exception made for the Province of Canada, even though she had not been involved in the affair.[19]

When the United States drew attention in January 1864 to reports of a gathering of Confederates in Windsor the Canadian government again responded promptly. In addition to an investigator, a company of troops was sent to the town. A pleased Seward asked for this information to be communicated to him officially, in writing, thinking to use it to check the growth of ill feeling towards the British provinces. Monck refused, and for a familiar reason. "At present there is in Canada an absence of prejudice against the United States, which leaves my hands free to take any needful steps for the maintenance of our neutrality," he informed Lyons, but if the impression was created that he favoured the North and was interfering with the freedom of action of Southern refugees the result might well be a public reaction troublesome to him personally and seriously damaging to his efforts to prevent raids.[20]

Any flickering hope that angry Americans would distinguish between Canada and the Maritimes was extinguished by the fall of Sandfield Macdonald's friendly government in March 1864. The other Macdonald and his fellow Conservatives, now returning to office, were the same men whose "rabid hate of the Union and idolatrous love of the Pro-Slavery Rebellion" had been noted three years before. Those members of the Canadian Parliament who had stood and cheered the news of Fredericksburg had been their supporters. D'Arcy McGee had joined forces with them, and he had become the *bête noire* of many Northerners. Once an admirer of the United States he had undergone a radical change of heart. Dropped from the Sandfield Macdonald government in 1863, McGee had quickly moved closer to the Macdonald-Cartier camp. In letters and speeches he warned of the perils facing Canada whenever peace returned to the United States. He drew attention to an "immense new fortress" at Rouse's Point, allegedly capable of holding the supplies for an army of 100,000 men and of housing a permanent garrison of 5,000. These preparations lent added significance, he suggested, to Seward's remark in 1862 that in the event of war with Britain the Union would not repeat the mistakes of 1812. Evidently the Americans planned to push north to Montreal in overwhelming numbers and sever Canada East from the West. "Either Canada must be defended or it must be Americanized," McGee declared. And when his former colleagues attacked him for scaremongering John A. Macdonald quickly came to his defence. In March 1864 this strident foe of American influence entered the Taché-Macdonald government as minister of agriculture, immigration and statistics.[21]

The animosity revived by the *Chesapeake* incident and the change of government in Canada was deepened by the conspiracies and raids set on foot from the British provinces by a trio of Confederate commissioners. First to arrive, late in March 1864, was J. P. Holcombe, a professor of law as well as a politician. Holcombe's mission was twofold. First, he was to protect the men who had seized the *Chesapeake* from extradition to the United States and to claim the vessel for the Confederacy. However, on reaching Halifax he discovered a number of embarrassing details about the escapade. The vessel had been seized in the name of the South by men without any "public authority" to undertake belligerent operations. Moreover, all the participants bar one seemed to be British subjects. They could not have been defended on the legal principle that citizens of one belligerent may, even without a commission, capture the enemy's property at sea. Fortunately the men arrested had already been released, so Holcombe decided to maintain a "diplomatic reticence" on the subject of the *Chesapeake* and to concentrate on the secondary duties assigned to him. He established a network of agents across the province whose task was to facilitate the return to the South of the men who had escaped to Canada from Federal prisons. But the response of the refugees was disappointing and Holcombe found the work of supervising this system "troublesome and tedious." Far more exciting was his association with the two commissioners who had followed him to British North America in May.[22]

Jacob Thompson and Clement C. Clay were political heavyweights. National figures before the Civil War, their connections, experience, and skills apparently equipped them ideally for the task of "aiding the disruption between the Eastern and Western States in the approaching election at the North."[23] Perhaps Davis and Benjamin genuinely believed that the Southern cause might yet be rescued by disaffection in the North, for they convinced Thompson and Clay of the vital importance of their mission. Together with Holcombe, the newly arrived commissioners willingly fell in with a scheme to embarrass Lincoln and the Republicans by initiating peace discussions. It appears to have been the brainchild of George N. Sanders, who was staying in Canada and soon attached himself to the Confederate party. Although the Niagara Falls peace meeting (with Horace Greeley speaking for the Union) proved to be a fiasco, and was recognized within the Lincoln administration for what it was—an election raid, it did draw from the president a statement reaffirming reunion and abolition of slavery as the Union's war aims. The Confederates flattered themselves that this exchange had been doubly profitable. First, it would convince their "own weak brothers" in North Carolina and Georgia, who had been clamouring for Davis to make peace proposals, that "peace with Lincoln means degradation." Second, it seemed certain to strengthen the hand both of peace and war Democrats in the forthcoming elections in the North by convincing all but "fanatical abolitionists" that there could be no peace while Lincoln presided over the United States government. Significantly, even the chairman of his party's National Executive Committee pressed the president to abandon abolition as a prerequisite for peace.[24] Lincoln refused. As he well understood, his chances of electoral success did not hinge on concessions over slavery but on victory in the field.

Jacob Thompson, sharing the opinion that coercion rather than negotiation could alone bring the war to an end, was soon plotting to detach the Northwest from the Union by force. In an armed uprising he saw the defeat of Lincoln, the demoralization of the Union, and a victorious peace for the Confederacy. His instrument of subversion was to be a secret Democratic society, the Sons of Liberty, but they sadly disappointed him. They proved to be neither as numerous as they had boasted nor as fierce in their defence of "States Rights" and "Civil Liberties" as he had hoped. Thompson's grandiose plans all came to nought. "A large sum of money has been expended in fostering and furthering these operations and now seems to have been to little profit," he admitted at the end of the year.[25] Growing sceptical of revolution erupting in the Northwest, or anywhere else in the Union, the Confederate commissioners sponsored ever more wild and sinister activities. They found ample justification for a campaign of terror against the citizens of the North in that waged by Federal troops on those of the South. Papers allegedly found on the body of the commander of a Union raid on Richmond early in 1864 indicated that the intent was to kill Davis and fire the city. Richmond newspapers carried reports of atrocities by Grant's troops in Virginia and demanded retaliation. Then, later in the year, Sheridan devastated the Shenandoah Valley and Sherman set off on his destructive march through Georgia to the sea. Against this background civilized men sanctioned attempts to set Northern cities ablaze, including New

York, and financed schemes to start epidemics of disease.[26] However, it was the launching of two military raids from Canada that inevitably led to international complications.

On arrival in British North America, Holcombe had informed Lord Monck that he had been instructed "to avoid most scrupulously any infringement of municipal or public law, and in this connection, particularly the laws for the preservation of Her Majesty's neutrality."[27] The instructions given to Thompson and Clay before their departure for Canada appear to have been somewhat less explicit, and while Thompson frequently betrayed uneasiness about possible violations of British neutrality such scruples were a luxury with which he, his colleagues, the refugees in Canada, and the Confederate government eventually dispensed. The widespread sympathy for their cause in the provinces inevitably tempted Southerners, as the Confederacy's position deteriorated, to cross the boundary of permissible behaviour. Moreover, desperation did not dispose them to honour a neutrality they despised. The European nations, and Britain in particular, bore the "moral" responsibility for the suffering caused by the unnecessarily prolonged war, Davis reminded the Confederate Congress in November.[28]

In supporting the revival of the earlier, abortive scheme to seize a lake steamer and free the Confederates imprisoned on Johnson's Island, Thompson did instruct the leading participants to "abstain from violating any laws or regulations of Canada or British authorities in relation to neutrality." "The combinations necessary to effect your purposes must be made by Confederate soldiers," he explained.[29] But this time the enterprise was even more ambitious and Thompson must have realized that its success would cause both the British and Canadian governments acute embarrassment. The plan called for the capture of the most formidable vessel on the Great Lakes, the Federal gunboat *Michigan*. In Southern hands she would guarantee the liberation of the prisoners, would throw Union shipping on the lakes into panic and chaos, and could be used to bombard the Northern cities and towns strung along the shoreline. With so much at stake the Confederates showed a surprising lack of sophistication when they plotted the vessel's seizure. Everything turned upon one of their number, who had ingratiated himself with the *Michigan*'s officers and men, plying the crew with drugged wine. While the Federals slept a group of Confederates were to come alongside in a captured lake steamer and take control of the gunboat. But the pivotal agent was betrayed by an informer and arrested on September 19. Meanwhile the main body of men had seized a lake steamer, the *Philo Parsons*. When, after some indecision, they put into Middle Bass for fuel, another vessel, the *Island Queen*, made fast alongside. Unaware of what had happened she was promptly captured and later scuttled. By this time, however, the men aboard the *Philo Parsons* were losing heart. With the *Michigan* still sitting in Sandusky Bay under Federal command they refused to run into the bay, as their leader proposed, and attempt to capture the gunboat and release the prisoners on the island. Instead, they set course for the Canadian town of Malden, where most of them had originally boarded the *Philo Parsons* in the guise of passengers. Finally docking at Sandwich, a few miles from Malden, they landed some plunder and before dispersing tried to sink the steamer. Although no more successful in this than in the entire enterprise, they had clearly abused if not infringed British neutrality. Furthermore, Thompson's presence in Sandwich on the eve of the ill-fated venture pointed to his involvement with this "piratical expedition" against the United States.

Exactly one month later, before the excitement of the Lake Erie affair had subsided, Confederates from Canada raided the small Vermont town of St. Albans. The foray was led by Lieut. Bennett Young, who had personally secured the approval of the Confederate secretary of war, James Seddon, for a campaign of retaliation against the North. It was financed by Clement Clay who had recommended both Young and his plan to Seddon. Although Clay repeatedly advised the young officer to "Burn and destroy, but don't rob for this will demoralize your command," he did concede that if after firing St. Albans Young "could seize and carry off money, or treasury or bank notes, he might do so, upon condition that they were delivered to the proper authorities of the Confederate States."[30] However, when the score of Confederates struck St. Albans on October 19, having quietly infiltrated the town over the previous two days, they reversed the agreed procedure. They began by robbing banks and citizens of $200,000, taking care to identify themselves as Confederate troops sent north to plunder and rob in retaliation for the behaviour of Grant's men in Virginia. Only as they fled the town, pursued by some of its enraged residents, did the Confederates attempt to set it afire. They failed, but did make good their escape to Canada.

For Seward, Confederate activities in Canada were an opportunity as well as an irritant. The public ill will created by the *Chesapeake* incident did not brighten the future of the Reciprocity Treaty, he remarked several times to Lyons in December 1863. If the treaty was to be saved a friendlier opinion of British North America was essential, and the only way to foster this was through a more strictly enforced neutrality. But the principal if not insuperable obstacle to good Anglo-American relations was Britain's "fatal recognition" of Confederate belligerency. Thus by making the most of the "inconveniences" in Canada Seward hoped to achieve the central aim of his diplomacy—the withdrawal of British recognition of that belligerency.[31] Their belligerent rights revoked, Southerners would encounter even greater difficulty obtaining the supplies and weapons necessary to wage war. More importantly, their spirit might at last break.

In London, Charles Francis Adams brought characteristic tact to the task of convincing the British to retrace their steps. He toned down Seward's menacing references to the Reciprocity Treaty. If you do not behave better, he understood the secretary to be saying to the British, "we will cut off your sugar plums." Adams did point out to Russell "the danger of the complications to which even a casual and temporary success" by Confederates might lead.[32] Meanwhile there was a whiff of menace in Seward's continuing discussions with Lyons. He informed the British minister that the administration was thinking of taking up the extraordinary powers granted to it by Congress in July 1861, to proclaim the Southern ports closed under municipal not international law. The Union's progress in suppressing the rebellion, Seward argued, fully warranted the recognition by foreign nations of its jurisdiction over the territory in insurrection. And he reminded the British how important it was that Anglo-American relations be placed on a friendly footing before the war came to an end.[33]

"Circumstances favor a good understanding now with the Cabinet in London," Seward observed in February 1864. The conflict over Schleswig-Holstein and the likelihood of Britain becoming embroiled in it were the source of his confidence that he could draw or drag from her a revocation of Confederate belligerent rights. "The situation of the Ministry, in face of the new European complications, is manifestly an embarrassing one," he observed.[34] But the Tory attacks upon the Palmerston government's foreign policy soon revealed how domestically embarrassed it already was and how feeble was its grip on power. Like Adams, Seward had no wish to see ministers who had "exhibited much wisdom and discretion in difficult trial" displaced, and for this reason all American diplomatic pressure on the British government was relaxed. "At the present conjuncture I am especially desirous to avoid writing or doing any thing that might tend to embarrass the Ministry of Lord Palmerston," he informed William Evarts in April.[35] His attitude towards foreign affairs during the summer of 1864 was governed by the hope that the Union would "have quiet."[36] Thus he acted quickly to head off the danger of trouble with France over Mexico. Fiery congressional attacks on imperial policy in Mexico were followed by Seward's reassuring explanations to the French government, while Sumner buried all resolutions in his committee.

Seward responded quietly to the *Philo Parsons* affair in September, seemingly content to calm the excited Edwin Stanton and the population along the border by agreeing to the charter of two additional steamers to patrol the Great Lakes. This was merely a temporary measure "made necessary by an emergency," he assured the British, and ought not to be regarded as "contrary to the spirit" of the Convention of 1817 (the Rush-Bagot agreement) governing armaments on the lakes. However, the raid on St. Albans found him preparing a lengthy despatch on the subject of Confederate activities in the provinces. It signalled his decision to renew the pressure on Britain to withdraw her recognition of Confederate belligerency. After all, there was no longer any need to handle gently a government which had survived the opposition's attack and would not have to face Parliament again until February. So Seward invited "the serious attention of her Majesty's government to the instances, which unfortunately seem to be multiplying, in which the British possessions in our neighbourhood, both continental and insular, have been made bases for hostile proceedings of the insurgents against this country."[37]

In extending the invitation Seward took care to underline the consequences of declining it. He instructed Adams to give the required six months' notice of the abrogation of the 1817 agreement. He warned Lyons that it would be impossible to resist the demands for abrogation of the Reciprocity Treaty also, if incursions from Canada continued. He alluded to the danger of raids in the opposite direction, for the British were watching apprehensively the activities of militant Irish-Americans. Enrolled in the Fenian Brotherhood, they were determined to see Ireland freed from British rule. Meanwhile Seward made no immediate move, despite British protests, to have a controversial order of General Dix, the commander of the Department of the East, countermanded. Dix had instructed troops who were in "hot pursuit" of the St. Albans "marauders" to follow them into Canada.[38] Thus the order served a purpose by illustrating the dangers of international incidents.

The probable consequences of the "insufficiency" of British neutrality served as the preamble to Seward's recommendations. Under similar circumstances in 1838 the United States had enacted a temporary but more stringent law. Now that the situation was reversed Britain might do well to reciprocate, he suggested. However, Seward was seeking more than this. There was no remedy "adequate to the present exigency," he declared, "but the recognition by her Majesty's government of the just and exclusive sovereignty of the United States in all the waters and territories legally subject to the jurisdiction of this government."[39] The secretary of state's essential purpose was plain, but matters took a dramatic turn in mid-December.

In Canada, Lord Monck had investigated every American report of Confederate conspiracies. His diligence, the defeat of the Conservative government, and the formation of a coalition of Tories and Reformers which included several friends of the Union (Brown, McDougall, and Mowat) promised to conciliate Northern opinion. John Potter, who had succeeded Giddings as consul general in July 1864, quickly concluded that the new provincial government was "anxious to detect and prevent any movement within its borders of a hostile character to our Government."[40] Although it failed to detect and prevent the Lake Erie and St. Albans forays, the Canadian government did manage to convince the United States of its good faith. Canadian officials at Windsor were instructed to cooperate with the American in an effort to discover and arrest the perpetrators of the Lake Erie raid, and a detachment of troops was sent to the town. As for the St. Albans raiders, a Montreal police magistrate, C. J. Coursol, was despatched to the border along with a body of policemen. His instructions were to give "all assistance in men or otherwise in your power to American Authorities for arresting guilty parties." Also ordered to give all possible aid was the commander of the British troops in Canada. This energetic response and the capture of Young and thirteen of his men, all of whom were ordered to be detained until a demand for their extradition could be investigated, quickly stifled the immediate outburst of American anger with Canada for permitting the raid.[41]

If American confidence in the provincial government rested upon the evidence of its determination "to put a stop to these violations of Canadian hospitality," no less important was the underlying assumption that the prisoners would be extradited. Cartier and McGee called at the consul general's office to emphasize the government's "earnest desire effectually to put in force all the requirements of the law" and "to render up" the prisoners. They revealed that senior and experienced counsel had been retained to conduct the case in order to prevent any "technical inaccuracy."[42] American observers were doubly reassured by the appointment of Coursol to preside over the preliminary proceedings.

Coursol had become something of a favourite at the consulate. His zeal in rounding up the raiders was duly appreciated, as was his service as an intermediary between the American authorities and a mercenary informer. Information passed on by "the highest criminal judge" in the city of Montreal "was certain to be worthwhile." Indeed, David Thurston, the acting consul general (Potter had returned to his home in Portland where his youngest child was seriously ill), was so sure of Coursol's reliability that he sought his appointment as presiding magistrate at the preliminary hearing. He approached his "old and intimate friend" William McDougall, one of the Reformers in the governing coalition, and requested "that the prisoners may be brought before Judge Coursol of Montreal." Thurston's confidence soon began to waver. The gifted defence counsel retained for Young and his men by the Confederate agents in Canada contended that the court should make a separate inquiry into each of the five extraditable offences with which the prisoners were all charged, and that witnesses should be examined on the single offence under investigation even when it was known that they had knowledge of more than one. The purpose was to defeat justice, the chief counsel for the United States reported to Thurston. Coursol's acceptance of the defence counsel's argument raised suspicions that he shared the hope that during protracted proceedings the prosecution would fall into irregularities which would eventually prove fatal. By the beginning of December Thurston had come to suspect Coursol of intending to discharge the prisoners at the preliminary hearing. Nor did the magistrate's decision to recess the hearing until December 13, in order that Young might seek documents from Richmond verifying his commission, ease Thurston's mind. It was the contention of the defence that the raiders were soldiers who had acted under orders from the Confederate government and therefore did not come within the terms of the Extradition Treaty.[43]

By December 13 no word had come from Richmond. A request by the defence lawyers that the Union grant safe conduct to a special messenger had been rejected by Lincoln, while an appeal that the Canadian government send an agent to the Confederate capital had been peremptorily refused by Monck. This at least reassured Thurston of the province's continuing good faith. The Canadian government was still investigating all suspicious proceedings, he reported to Seward; it had sent more detectives to the border, and in the event of the prisoners being discharged by Coursol would rearrest them and see them punished for violating British neutrality. Unfortunately Coursol's decision came with a suddenness that took everyone by surprise. When the hearing resumed the defence challenged his jurisdiction in the case. The repeal some years before of the colonial act concerning extradition had brought back into force the original imperial measure, the counsel for the Confederates argued, even thought the province had subsequently re-enacted its measure in a modified form. Under the imperial act it was the governor general who issued warrants for the arrest of persons accused of extraditable offences, but Coursol was hearing the case under a warrant issued by the attorney general according to the provisions of the revised colonial statute. After a recess to ponder the argument, Coursol delivered his opinion. To loud cheers from a throng of Confederate sympathizers, he announced that he had concluded that he did not possess any jurisdiction in the matter. Over the protests of the prosecution he discharged the prisoners. To add injury to injury, the chief of police immediately turned over to a financial agent of the Confederacy the $90,000 found on the raiders when they were detained.

The Canadian government desperately strove to limit the harm these two actions were certain to do to relations with the United States. Cartier admitted that Coursol's decision was "erroneous and most unfortunate," and fresh warrants were immediately issued for the rearrest of the raiders. Thurston forwarded this information to Seward, along with the news that the Canadians had instituted a stipendiary magistracy. A special police force was placed under the command of the magistrate. Further, a reward of $200 was offered for information leading to the capture of any of the raiders, and a handful including Young were quickly taken into custody. Even more eye-catching was the calling out of several thousand volunteers for duty along the border. In short, the provincial government was doing everything in its power "to remedy the evils arising from Coursol's decision." Nevertheless, although Thurston took care to inform Seward that public opinion did not support the magistrate's action, the Union was in no mood to be easily placated.[44]

Tension along the border was heightened by the publication of another "hot pursuit" order by General Dix on December 14. He instructed all military commanders on the frontier, "in case farther acts of depredation and murder are attempted," to shoot down the marauders while in the commission of their crimes, but in the event of their escape to Canada to pursue them there and under "no circumstances" to surrender captives to the British authorities.[45] The prospect of dangerous confrontations was not one Lincoln relished and Dix's order was soon modified. Yet, as Seward was quick to point out for the benefit of the British, the order had not been countermanded. The secretary listed the complications to which the deficiencies of the "so-called neutrality" of the provinces had given rise. On the same day that Dix had issued his sensational order Congress had voted an appropriation of $1 million for the construction of half-a-dozen lightly armed steam cutters to patrol the Great Lakes. Seward also drew the attention of the British to the rapid progress of the movement to abrogate the Reciprocity Treaty. The question had been taken up on the first day of the new session, December 13, and the joint resolution authorizing the president to give the required notice for the treaty's termination sailed through the House. When reports of Coursol's decision appeared in Washington newspapers on the following day, the vengeful and venomous mood of the Senate doomed reciprocity. The joint resolution was not delayed in Sumner's committee, but an appeal by John Hale of New Hampshire for an opportunity to address the Senate resulted in postponement of the debate until January 1865. Meanwhile Seward exerted additional pressure on the British by requiring persons entering the United States from Canada to obtain a passport.[46]

The honour of representing Britain in the American capital and the task of dealing with Seward had fallen to J. Hume Burnley, for Lord Lyons had finally escaped from the United States one week before this new flurry of activity. Many years later Henry Layard wrote of Lyons: "He was the type of what the modern English diplomatist must be—without initiative or views of his own, unwilling to accept any responsibility and merely a superior clerk united by a wire to Downing Street and taking his orders from them and strictly obeying them." Allowing for the bitterness that infected Layard, who had abandoned politics for diplomacy but had continued to be dogged by controversy, there was a good measure of truth in this assessment. But there had been no wire linking Lyons in Washington to his superiors in London during the Civil War, and consequently the minister had been obliged to exercise more initiative than was necessary later in his career. What was more, the qualities of caution, discretion, good temper, good sense, and steadiness were displayed by Lyons to an uncommon degree during the tense and difficult years of his tenure in Washington. By 1864 the stress and the strains of his position were beginning to tell. He had never enjoyed his residence in the United States but now his unhappiness deepened. One reason was loneliness. Mercier, an "agreeable" and "very good colleague," had returned to France. Stuart had joyfully gone home to England, and the junior members of the legation, men in whose company the shy Lyons felt at ease and was able to relax, had followed him one by one. The discovery that Stuart's replacement was married and would be bringing his wife to Washington unnerved this confirmed bachelor. A woman would involve them all in incessant quarrels, he gloomily predicted to his sister. The turnover in legation staff, the fact that men left before replacements arrived, increased the heavy burden of work. Much of it Lyons carried himself, for he took a painstaking approach to his duties. Although he complained of "troublesome, wearing, uninteresting work for the most part," the fear that something might go wrong drove him to give it his "constant and minute care." Exhausted and depressed, Lyons fell victim again to migraine. Nor were his headaches eased by anxiety about his future in the diplomatic service. If he resigned his post in the United States would this blight his career? To be without a place altogether would be inconvenient "in a pecuniary point of view," he informed Russell. Eventually Lyons found a solution to his predicament. He proposed that he be given leave of absence and thus continue technically to fill the position of minister. This would enable him to draw his salary while recuperating in England. The foreign secretary consented to this arrangement and Lyons sailed for home early in December.[47]

Deeply regretted as Lyons's sudden departure was by Seward, and by Lord Monck, his loss was not a serious one in December 1864. The minister had long since ceased to attend to the business of the legation, for as a result of his headaches "he seemed to be averse to anything which required application." The day to day affairs had been supervised by Burnley, who had come up from Baltimore to run the legation during Lyons's summer sojourn in Canada, and was now reappointed as chargé d'affaires. The Foreign Office thought he would prove agreeable to a republican government, for he was the nephew of Joseph Hume. Even more to the point, he had impressed his superiors as a calm and steady man. Calmly, he appraised Seward's response to the Coursol decision. The passport regulations "may be looked upon as a sort of retaliation," he observed, and then reminded Russell that the American's "peculiar monomania" was Britain's recognition of Confederate belligerency.[48]

Russell had already rejected Seward's "demand" that Great Britain "cease to acknowledge the belligerent character of the Southern States, and treat the Southern citizens as felons and pirates." To allow belligerent rights to the United States and to refuse them to the other party in the war, who had possession of an extensive territory, had all the forms of a regular government, and wielded large regular armies, would "be as contrary to the practice of civilized nations as it would be to the rules of justice and of international law."[49] If considerations of pride and honour no less than justice and that proverbial concern for "fair play" explain this British determination not to be bullied into a premature withdrawal of recognition of Confederate belligerency, it was not expediency alone which demanded some appeasement of the United States. Russell admitted to "feeling outraged and humiliated" by the Confederacy's violations of British neutrality, while no one disputed Lord Monck's opinion that the United States had a "right" to expect "some substantial reassurance" in British conduct.

After a brief delay, while the three law officers debated Coursol's decision (Palmer agreeing with the magistrate's interpretation), the apparent loophole in the Extradition Treaty was plugged. An order in council was issued to remove all doubts respecting the suspension in Canada of the imperial act. Then, after a number of false starts, the government addressed a remonstrance to the Confederacy. Russell had long wished to protest against the conscription of British subjects and the use of British ports to fit out ships of war, but had been frustrated by difficulties of delivery. The raids launched from Canada, which showed "a gross disregard of Her Majesty's character as a neutral power, and a desire to involve Her Majesty in hostilities with a conterminous power," now spurred him into more resolute activity.

One copy of the demand that the Confederacy cease "practices so offensive and unwarrantable" was forwarded to the Confederate commissioners in Paris for transmission to their government. At the suggestion of the lord chancellor, a second copy was given to Adams along with a request that Seward communicate it at once to Richmond. Belatedly, the Queen objected to this procedure as unbecoming the British lion. Russell replied loftily: "To bring on this country the calamities of a war not because we have a good cause, but because we do not like to be thought afraid would be a course hardly becoming the dignity, the power, or the humanity of this country."[50]

The main thrust of the British effort to mollify the United States was directed through Canada, however. Monck had suggested in the spring of 1864 that small armed vessels be placed upon the lakes to discourage Confederate raids, and their presence might well have prevented the Lake Erie incident. The imperial government had rejected the proposal then, and did so again even after the seizure of the *Philo Parsons* and the *Island Queen*, because it feared that the United States would respond by creating a similar squadron of its own. But with this exception the home government both initiated and supported proposals to arm Monck with extraordinary powers, and both agreed that it would be "more prudent to pass Colonial acts than to go to the Imperial Parliament for an act which would be essentially local in its operation and which might provoke opposition there which it would not meet with" in Canada.[51]

Cardwell had written to Monck in mid-November to suggest that he consult his law officers "as to the propriety of obtaining additional Statutory powers for the prevention of Confederate aggressions on the Territory of the United States." Both in London and in Quebec there was a recognition that Seward's reference to the American model of 1838 was an appropriate one. Similar legislation would empower Monck to seize suspected vessels on the lakes and other munitions of war, including the incendiary materials used by rebels attempting to fire American cities. Further, in the event that the courts decided that the raiders were belligerents and not liable to extradition, the imperial authorities recommended that they be retained in custody and put on trial "on a charge of misprision and violation of the Royal Prerogative by levying war from Her Majesty's Dominions against a friendly power." Finally, Monck's suggestion that he be equipped with the power to expel aliens suspected of conspiring to compromise British neutrality was endorsed.[52]

With an eye to the diplomatic and political ramifications, Russell urged Cardwell to convey the imperial government's directions to Monck in a despatch "which can be produced." When he met with Adams on February 14, 1865—he had gone to some lengths during the winter to cultivate the American, even to the extent of expressing the opinion that the Federal passport regulations and the threats to end reciprocity would have a beneficial effect if they checked Canadian sympathy for the South—Russell voiced the hope that the instructions sent to Monck, the governor general's actions, and those of the Canadian legislature, would convince the Union that everything had been done, and would continue to be done, to prevent the carrying out of hostilities against the United States from British territory.[53] It was at this same meeting that Russell presented Adams with a copy of his remonstrance to the Confederacy.

The calling out of another fifteen hundred militia, the suspension of Coursol pending an investigation of his conduct, the resignation of the Montreal chief of police, the introduction into the Provincial Parliament of a bill to indemnify the St. Albans banks for the money so hastily turned over to the Confederates, the decision to extradite to the United States the one Lake Erie raider who had been arrested, and the passage of the legislative measures conferring extraordinary powers on Monck, eventually worked their desired effect. They did not dissuade the American Senate from voting to abrogate the Reciprocity Treaty, but, as Sumner emphasized during the debate, a full year would elapse between the notice of abrogation, which could not formally be given until March, and the termination of the arrangement. This interval would provide ample time for a renegotiation of the terms. What the actions of the Canadian government, and Russell's remonstrance to the Confederacy, did help to achieve was the rescinding of the passport regulations. Americans as well as Canadians had protested their useless inconvenience, and Thurlow Weed advised Seward that the province was offering compensation to the Vermont banks on the understanding that its citizens would be "relieved from the Passport embarrassment." In addition, Seward withdrew the notice of the termination of the Lakes Convention and indicated that he would be "perfectly willing" as time went by to enter into negotiations for the remodelling of the Reciprocity Treaty.[54]

The end of the passport system and Seward's announcement that the Union would not put more armed vessels on the lakes were welcome developments which helped to still although they did not entirely silence fears of an Anglo-American rupture. The British had developed an *idée fixe* which one member of Monck's family expressed succinctly if indirectly when she wrote in her journal: "As long as the Americans fight together, they will leave England alone."[55] The suspicion that the United States was preparing for a foreign war with Britain once the domestic one was over had prompted the Palmerston government to despatch three officers to the Republic early in 1864 to report on the military and naval establishments. It was not a secret mission, though the avowed purpose to collect information "interesting in a scientific or professional point of view" was the lesser part of the officers' task. Their reports were far from reassuring. The Americans, confident of military and naval superiority, expected to be able to throw an overwhelming force into Canada and strike against the island colonies of Bermuda and the Bahamas. They were building sleek, fast cruisers, evidently intended as commerce raiders. Nor had they overlooked the need to protect themselves from a counterattack. The British had traditionally taken comfort from their navy's might, and believed that its capacity to blockade the American coast and attack the Union's principal ports discouraged Yankee belligerence. But the officers who visited the United States discovered that in the North fortifications and a fleet of ironclads and turreted ships had been constructed, sufficient to defend the larger ports and break up any blockade which might be established.[56]

Lyons had accepted the reports as confirmation of his impression that the Americans, three-fourths of whom, he estimated, longed for a safe opportunity to strike against Britain, were "very seriously preparing for a foreign war." He urged in April 1864 that a naval officer be formally attached to the legation, a step he had earlier opposed. In March 1865 the aptly named Captain Bythesea was appointed naval attaché.[57] More urgent was the need to ready Canada for the possibility of an invasion by an American force of perhaps 150,000 men. "To do them justice they act fairly and above Board, and they give us due warning of their future hostility whenever their civil war shall be over, and they shall be free to quarrel with us," Palmerston observed of the Americans. "It is our Business to profit by the warning and to employ the interval in due Preparations for Defence."[58]

The defensive works recommended by the commission which reported to the War Office in September 1862 were so extensive and costly, and the available forces of British regulars and Canadian militia so inadequate, that Britain's ability to defend the province against a serious American attack was called into question within the cabinet. Palmerston countered with his traditional warning that the loss of the North American colonies "would lower us greatly, and if Reputation is strength, would weaken us much," but he was unable to win over those of his colleagues who objected to proposing expensive outlays to Parliament before the Canadians improved and enlarged their militia. The tone of the subsequent debate in the Commons on colonial defences reinforced their position.[59]

The defence question severely strained relations between Newcastle and the Sandfield Macdonald government. Anger in London over the fall of the Conservatives in the spring of 1862 after the defeat of a Militia Bill was mixed with distrust of the men who succeeded them. Reports that Sandfield Macdonald had "expressed an opinion that England wished for a favourable opportunity of getting rid of the Colony" did nothing to lessen it. The stinging rebuke the provincial government delivered to Newcastle, when it responded to some ill-considered proposals of his for avoiding annual votes of money for an enlarged militia, enraged the colonial secretary. "How men can talk so nonsensically and so unfairly as to represent me as seeking to curtail the rights of the People and the legislature passes my comprehension," Newcastle wrote privately to Monck, "and they may be sure that to raise the old cry of 'Downing Street' is a dangerous game when all rational men know that there is no longer any wish to *interfere* with, though there is an abundant desire to help them."[60]

Monck conceded that his ministers were a "wretched lot." Not one of them "is capable of rising above the level of a parish politician and they are led away by all the small jealousies and suspicions to which minds of that class are prone," he reported.[61] Yet they had come into office preaching retrenchment and they intended to practise it. Moreover, there was greater public support for their resistance to extravagant measures of defence than the colonial secretary believed. George Brown's powerful Toronto *Globe*, for instance, had rallied to the standard. Similarly, resistance to imperial intrusions into local affairs won a sympathetic popular response. The traditional complaint of Canadians that war with the United States would never result from any act of theirs was repeated with conviction by the Sandfield Macdonald government.[62] It had reversed the Tories' policy of hostility to the Union, seeking security not in costly defensive preparations but in the North's good will.

Although the colonial government had a case to make, the manner in which it rejected Newcastle's suggestions for improving the militia had been unnecessarily provocative. Nor was its reputation both in England and in British North America enhanced by the conduct of the delegates who represented Canada at the meetings in London to complete the arrangements for construction of the Intercolonial Railroad. When the Canadians derailed the scheme there were bitter accusations of duplicity. During the debate on a motion of confidence which it lost in May 1863, John A. Macdonald made much of the government's unpopularity in Britain and in the Maritimes.[63]

Newcastle had foreseen the possibility of Sandfield Macdonald's defeat in the legislature and had strongly hinted to Monck that the premier be denied a dissolution. But the governor general felt constitutionally bound to honour the request when it came, though his uneasiness about the reaction at home induced him to write an explanatory letter to Delane of *The Times*. Frustrated already, Newcastle's temper was not improved by the reports reaching London of the campaign speeches of some of Sandfield Macdonald's associates. Boasts that the Intercolonial was dead, and claims that the best defence for Canada was no defence at all, evoked an angry response. "The tone of the Ministry on all occasions and still more its acts are so strongly anti-Imperial that a strong feeling is growing here, and with reason," Newcastle informed Monck privately, "that they are secretly and corruptly American and that nothing but a change of Government will prevent Canada being handed over against its will to the Yankees." Nor was the colonial secretary above making threats. The buying out of the Hudson's Bay Company by a group of capitalists left unresolved the dispute between the old company and the colony over part of the territory. Unless the Canadians honoured their promises to the Maritimers concerning the railroad and kept faith with the mother country on defence Newcastle intended to insist "upon extreme rights belonging to England and the new Company in the West."[64]

Returned to office, but with a fragile majority, Sandfield Macdonald began to mend his imperial fences. Perhaps Newcastle's threat had some effect, for the new ministry depended upon Brown's Reformers for survival, and they looked to the West. Certainly an uneasiness about American intentions once the Civil War ended, and in July 1863 that prospect suddenly seemed somewhat less remote, prompted the government to improve the militia and thereby convince "English statesmen that the attachment of the Canadians to the British connection is not affected by party feeling." Provision was made for a volunteer force of 35,000 men, "fully armed and equipped and tolerably well drilled," and for a fully organized, partially drilled and competently officered militia whose number was fixed at 88,000 men. To ensure that officers received "a thorough education in military duty," schools of military instruction were established. The province paid for the services of the British regulars who staffed them.[65]

The Canadian measures were warmly supported by the imperial government and well received by the British press. Monck had again taken the precaution of writing privately to Delane, to request that *The Times* say "something favourable."[66] It was in this improved climate of opinion that Lieut.-Col. W. F. D. Jervois, a War Office expert on fortifications, was sent out to North America to conduct another investigation of colonial defence. The report he submitted in February 1864 was welcomed by De Grey at the War Office and by Newcastle's successor at the Colonial, Edward Cardwell, for the proposals it contained were "moderate and reasonable." Jervois recommended the fortification of Quebec and Montreal, and the concentration there of the British regulars. He estimated that the works at Quebec would cost £200,000 and those at Montreal £443,000. Behind them that small and otherwise vulnerable British force could shelter and thus keep open the vital line of communication to England until reinforcements arrived.[67]

De Grey and Cardwell immediately saw the possibility of reaching an agreement with the province. The imperial government might offer to fortify Quebec in return for a colonial undertaking to complete the works at Montreal. But there was opposition in cabinet to a specific proposal being made at this time. Gladstone still questioned whether it was possible to defend Canada, and while this drew from Palmerston another summons in the name of duty there was general acceptance of Somerset's suggestion that their first step be the small one of asking the provincial government for its opinion on the report. Jervois was soon on his way back to Canada carrying instructions to meet with Monck and his ministers "and to give them all the advice and assistance in his power in the consideration of questions connected with the defence of the Colony."[68]

The actual withdrawal of some British troops from North America in the spring, and reports that those remaining were under orders to concentrate at Quebec and Montreal, had already excited the opposition of Monck and his ministers and stirred public protests by residents of Canada West. However, the members of the coalition ministry which had been formed in June decided to wait for Jervois before replying to the imperial enquiry. They met with him in October and received his report early in the following month. This one made provision for the defence of the western half of the province. He recommended additional fortifications at Kingston, regarded as the best site for a naval station on Lake Ontario (he proposed that six ironclad gunboats be built and held ready to be sent there in the event of war), and less impressive works at Toronto and Hamilton to serve as a centre of refuge and action for the colonial field force of 50,000 men needed to defend Canada West. Jervois accepted that with these additional measures, and with further improvements in militia organization, it would be possible to hold the vital points in the western half of the province which an invader had to take during those few months when large-scale operations were possible in Canada.[69]

When the colonial government finally replied to the imperial enquiry on November 16, 1864, the response was shaped not only by Jervois's latest report but by the underlying purpose of the coalition. The Canadian ministers were seeking a solution to their province's chronic political problems through a union with the colonies to the east. Nor had their enthusiasm for some form of British North American federation been weakened by the tense relations with their giant neighbour. Speaking at a dinner in Halifax in September, Cartier had estimated that the united colonies would be able to call out a militia of 200,000 men and another 60,000 sailors. When this force was supported by the British army and navy, "what power would be crazy enough to attack us?" he had asked. Now, in November, having negotiated at Quebec terms of Confederation, the Canadians suggested that a settlement of the relative responsibilities of the mother country and the province in matters of defence be postponed "until it shall have been ascertained whether the negotiation is to be ultimately carried on with the Ministers of United British North America or with those of Canada alone." In the meantime, while the several colonies considered the Quebec scheme, the Canadian ministers offered to bring before the next session of the Provincial Parliament a proposal for erecting at colonial expense the works at Montreal, on the understanding that Britain would undertake the fortifications at Quebec and provide the armaments for both strong points. Further, they would "propose a vote of one million of dollars to be applied to the training of the Militia Force."[70]

In forwarding these proposals to London, Monck emphasized their advantages. This was the first instance in which a colony had offered to finance permanent defensive works, he observed, and it might serve as a useful precedent for the imperial government. He provided a political explanation for Canada's anxiety to resort to a loan in raising her share of the costs, and to obtain an imperial guarantee which would reduce the expense of borrowing. To propose a vote for a sum sufficient to construct the works recommended by Jervois might provide the opponents of Confederation in the Maritimes with ammunition. Even to seek a smaller sum was to invite a debate in the Canadian Parliament during which the government might be obliged to give a pledge to implement the plans for the defence of Canada West. Yet the willingness of the Canadians to defend themselves, and a vote of $1 million for the militia, would at least disabuse Americans of the dangerous notion that there was a strong annexationist party in the province. The notion was dangerous, Monck reasoned, because it encouraged Americans to believe that in a war they would be able to detach Canada easily from Britain. But the governor general was quietly confident that if the Yankees attempted to seize the province, they would find it a harder nut to crack than many people in the North and in Britain appeared to expect.[71]

There was support in London for a colonial union of some kind, though the legislative union of the Maritimes and the completion of the railroad had been regarded as essential preliminaries. However, for an imperial government increasingly preoccupied with the defence of the province from possible American attack the attractions of federation were obvious. Newcastle had proposed "a union for defence" in August 1862, and it was he who implanted the idea of a coalition ministry in the governor general's mind.[72] "It seems to me that the time is come for the amalgamation of the best men on both sides under some new and honourable man (if indeed such can be found)," he wrote in September 1863.[73] Neither Newcastle then nor Monck later (the governor first prescribed this remedy for Canada's chronic political ills on the fall of Sandfield Macdonald's administration in March 1864) had in mind the radical remedial measure of federation. The initial attempt to form a coalition failed, but Monck had found an honourable if not entirely new man in Sir Etienne-

373

Pascal Taché. This distinguished French Canadian led (with John A. Macdonald as his Upper Canadian partner) the Conservative ministry which took office in March, and he was accepted by both sides as leader of the coalition which succeeded it in June.

Within the imperial government, Russell was a strong supporter of "some federal tie uniting the whole of British America in a semi-independent connection with Great Britain." He had written to Newcastle in June 1862 to urge that Canada, New Brunswick, and Nova Scotia be encouraged to form a federal union. The advantages to Britain were obvious. A federal defence force, composed of regulars and militia, might be formed and then financed out of federal revenues. In such a union the representatives of French Canada would find themselves a permanent minority, always outvoted by colonists of British descent. However, Russell thought it would be wise to permit each of the old colonies to retain an assembly for local matters. The imperial government might enter into an agreement with the federal authority limiting the duty imposed upon British goods entering the union. This would quieten the indignant British complaint against the high tariff Canada had imposed upon the products of the mother country. In this way, Russell concluded, "The Federal Province might be constituted in such a manner as to form a loyal constitutional State subject always to the British Crown."[74]

Of the several advantages of North American union the military one loomed largest in the British cabinet. The questions of union, of Canadian acquisition of the territory of the Hudson's Bay Company, and of defence were regarded as interconnected. A strong Canada would be able to shoulder a larger share of the burden of defence. There was a double attraction here for men like Gladstone and Cardwell. Not only would the withdrawal of the 10,000 British regulars from North America cut the expenses of the imperial government but it would lessen the likelihood of American aggression, they reasoned. That small, scattered, and vulnerable British force was a standing temptation to a vengeful United States anxious to inflict a humiliating reverse on the hated British.

One fear was that the colonies would opt for federation not union, for the "policy of Jefferson as against that of Washington and Hamilton," and "run British North America upon the rock" on which the United States had "gone to pieces." To avoid this hazard Cardwell was inclined initially to exert "a good deal" of pressure, believing that it would be "the selfish interests of the men in the smaller Provinces" which would lead the Canadian union off-course. Yet he also recognized that it signified little what name was employed. "What we wish is a Central and strong government," he wrote to an opponent of the Quebec scheme, Arthur Gordon, "as distinguished from a number of small states united by a feeble bond."[75]

Monck provided Cardwell and his colleagues with much of the reassurance they needed. Confederation did not accurately describe the Quebec scheme, he wrote home. Although it provided for local assemblies with specific powers, the scheme "secures to the central government—in the extent of the powers conferred upon it—in the means of enforcing the execution of those powers—and in the complete subordination of the local bodies to the central authority the elements of strength and stability." Moreover, he reported, the great obstacle to full legislative union had not been the smaller colonies but "the extreme" and in his opinion "unfounded jealousy of the French population of Lower Canada lest their peculiar rights and institutions might be interfered with by the general government." Cardwell appreciated, no doubt, that any effort to exert imperial pressure here was likely to increase not lessen this "jealousy." In short, Monck claimed that the central government described in the Quebec Resolutions possessed all the powers necessary for effective government.[76]

Believing Confederation to be as great a benefit to Britain as to the colonies, the imperial government announced its "general approval" of the scheme in December 1864. And as Cardwell pointed out to Lieutenant-Governor Gordon of New Brunswick, in a vain attempt to stem his torrent of criticism, this warm support was shared by the public.[77] The British press, irrespective of political leanings, and for much the same reasons as those which occupied the minds of cabinet ministers, welcomed the advance towards Canadian Confederation. Nor was this surprising, for imperialists and Little Englanders could both take heart from the events in North America. Union would reduce the burden of defence which fell upon Britain, an embarrassment even to those proud of the Empire and a grievance of those who wished to be rid of it. A Canadian Confederacy would lessen the danger of collision with the United States and would help establish a balance of power on the American continent. It would give a fresh impulse to immigration and the growth of population would create a larger market for British goods. No doubt Canada's "hostile tariff" would become "a thing of the past." Better men would be drawn into public life, attracted by the larger national political stage. As it was, provincial legislatures had sunk "to the level of a Marylebone vestry." News of the proposed federation "falls yet more welcome on our ears as the harbinger of future and complete independence of British North America," the *Edinburgh Review* declared. Although Little Englanders and Radicals could be expected to voice this sentiment, it was not exclusively theirs. Confederation was seen as a means of softening the shock of that inevitable day when a great nation, able to manage its own affairs, would no longer wish to be ruled by an island three thousand miles away.[78]

The widespread belief that British America was on the high road to independence alarmed George Brown when he arrived in London at the beginning of December to promote the Confederation scheme and to discuss the questions of defence and Canadian acquisition of the Northwest. His suspicion that some Englishmen were actuated by a desire to sever the connection, and thus be rid of their obligations to those territories most vulnerable to American attack, may not have been laid entirely to rest by a meeting with Gladstone. The chancellor informed him that Britain would not like to double her national debt for the benefit of the province, and then "faintly glanced at the possibility of its neutralization." Brown bristled at that suggestion.[79] Happily, his interviews with Palmerston, Russell, and Cardwell were more encouraging and he returned home in January "enchanted with his visit." Confederation had restored Canada's reputation in Britain, he reported. Little progress had been made on the two related questions, those of defence and the Northwest. In acceding to the Canadian request for a postponement of a general settlement of defence responsibilities until the colonies had given a decision on federation, the imperial government had also put to one side the request for a guarantee of the loan to be raised to finance the works the province would undertake. Nevertheless, it was soon clear that Britain had no intention of abandoning the British North Americans.[80]

Within the cabinet Somerset fought against any reduction of naval strength, particularly on the North American and West Indian station. Not the least of his considerations was the bad effect the news would have in Canada. Russell and Palmerston were in no doubt that they were "bound" to go on with the plan for the defence of the province. "The best security for peace lies in defensive strength," the prime minister continued to believe, "and the cost of defensive work and arrangements is nothing as compared with the expenses of the most quickly successful war."[81] When Jervois, who had crossed the Atlantic as a fellow passenger of Brown's, submitted a second report which called for additional imperial fortifications in the Maritimes and at Bermuda it was favourably received. Over Gladstone's objections, the cabinet decided to include in the Army Estimates an appropriation of £50,000 to cover the cost of the work it would be possible to complete at Quebec during the coming year. It was understood that the Canadians would spend some £450,000 in fortifying Montreal. The chancellor then called for a reduction of 5,000 men in the Navy. Once again his economic arguments were overridden by colleagues who feared trouble with the United States. They did "let him down easy" from his "uncompromising declarations" that he would be "no party to proposing the vote for the number of men" recommended by Somerset. They agreed to the formation of a cabinet committee to re-examine the estimates to see whether reductions might "safely be made in any of the other heads of the Naval service."[82] When Gladstone reopened the question in mid-February, circulating letters he had received from Cobden criticizing any commitment to defend territories that were indefensible, and warning against placing reliance upon a navy that was obsolete, Palmerston and Somerset heaped scorn on the Radical's "Inconsistencies, Contradictions and Forgetfulness of Facts." Yet even those who conceded the accuracy of much of what Cobden had written saw no alternative to the course they had decided to follow. Impossible as it would be to hold Canada, Britain must fight for the colony. "I apprehend all men are now getting anxious that Canada sh[oul]d stand by itself," Argyll wrote to Gladstone. "But it don't seem that Canada takes the same view—Are we to kick them off? Would Cobden recommend Cardwell to go down to Parl[iamen]t and introduce this policy and write out ditto to Monck?"[83]

Argyll reflected a broad segment of public and political opinion. Public anxiety grew as the end of the Civil War neared. The beginning of March found some apprehensive merchants declining to enter into prospective commercial arrangements with Americans. Canadian securities plummeted. At Printing House Square, Delane was convinced that the United States was preparing to make "unfounded demands" on Britain for the damages inflicted by the *Alabama*, which she would naturally refuse. Did the notices of abrogation of the Lakes Convention and Reciprocity Treaty portend the Union's seizure of the British colonies as guarantee of payment? "Nobody in this country wants, we suppose, to fight for Canada *qua* Canada, to suspend commerce and interrupt industry and mortgage the future, in order to retain titular authority over a vast region whose inhabitants will not even give us a low tariff upon our produce," Bagehot declared in the *Economist*. But it was a question of imperial duty, and one that could not be shirked. To abandon the province would be fatal to national self-respect.[84]

The mood of Parliament was much the same. Although Palmerston, Russell, and several of their colleagues spoke calmly and reassuringly of relations with the United States, pointing out that the Lakes Convention had not yet been abrogated nor had any formal notice of the intention to terminate reciprocity yet been given, the debate they sought to discourage could no longer be avoided once the Jervois report was laid before Parliament. There were calls in the Commons for the total abandonment of Canada, but they were isolated and unrepresentative of the feeling in either House. Robert Lowe did urge in debate and through his leaders in *The Times* that the British regulars be withdrawn, but he coupled this with the admission that it was the duty of the English "to make it known that those who go to war with Canada go to war with us." Cardwell had already given that assurance, and Palmerston wound up the debate with the announcement that there would be no withdrawal of British troops. Honour and duty bound the mother country to defend Canada if she was attacked. Indeed, the loudest criticism of the government came from those members of the opposition who deplored its failure to do more. The initial appropriation of £50,000 was dismissed as a paltry sum. Moreover, when those who were willing to desert Canada rallied to the support of a motion opposing the grant for the Quebec fortifications the mover refused to vote for it himself. By an overwhelming vote of 275 to 40 the Commons endorsed the grants for works at Quebec, Bermuda, and in the Maritimes. As the *Spectator* observed, a debate nominally on the grants had in reality been about the propriety of defending Canada.[85]

Forster and Bright had both intervened in the debate to counsel "goodwill and peace" between Britain and the United States, and to dispute the notion that the Union was planning aggression. Reporting on the proceedings to the Queen, Palmerston was uncharacteristically complimentary about Bright's speech. Perhaps, like *The Times*, he hoped that those who spoke so eloquently of American moderation and peacefulness would "inculcate among their clients the gentle qualities they claim for them." Certainly, it was with the Americans that the future now rested.[86]

The conciliatory attitude of the Sandfield Macdonald government, in matters touching upon relations with the United States, failed to prevent new difficulties arising between the province and the Union. Although many of these problems were minor they did tend to erode further the confidence of people on one side of the border in the good faith of their neighbours on the other. American suspicions that Canadians no less than Britons wished to see the Union fail were seemingly confirmed by the activities of Confederates in British North America, culminating in the Lake Erie and St. Albans raids. Quick to exploit the hostility towards Canada were the opponents of the Reciprocity Treaty. Nor was Seward a laggard in attempting to turn it to diplomatic advantage. He remounted a favourite hobby-horse, pressing for the withdrawal of the recognition of Confederate belligerency. This was a step the British declined to retrace, but Coursol's discharge of the St. Albans raiders and the behaviour of the chief of police in returning to them the money they had stolen during the raid drove the imperial government to sanction and the colonial to implement a series of extraordinary measures in an effort to placate the furious Americans.

Canadians grew increasingly concerned about their future as the American war dragged towards its end. Convinced that reciprocity was essential to prosperity they watched with alarm the campaign being waged against the treaty by protectionists in the United States. Their hopes of dissuading the Americans from giving notice of its abrogation were dashed by the sensational incidents of the fall and winter of 1864. There remained the possibility of renegotiating the arrangement before the expiry of the twelve months' notice, but reciprocity was a hostage in Anglo-American relations and Britain's refusal to settle the *Alabama* claims was to seal its doom.

Overlaying uneasiness about the provinces economic prospects was anxiety for its security. Some Canadians believed the two issues to be related, that the abrogation of reciprocity was a victory for annexationism. More widespread was the fear that once the Civil War was over the Union would turn on Britain, and therefore on Canada. In Britain, the danger of a collision with the United States focused attention upon the defence of the North American territories. The failure of the Canadians to make adequate provision for their own defence had been a constant source of friction between the imperial authorities and the government of Sandfield Macdonald, which, wedded to a policy of retrenchment, had sought a less expensive measure of security through a friendlier relationship with the United States. The change of government in Canada brought an improvement in imperial relations, and the *raison d'être* of the coalition ministry formed in 1864 was a union of the provinces which would go far to ease its political, economic, and security troubles. The British supported Confederation warmly, for a united North America would not only be stronger but was expected to shoulder the lion's share of the burdens of defence. It was soon clear, however, that the American war would be over long before any Confederation was formed. Equally, it was evident that Canada would be impossible to defend against an American attack. Nevertheless, the debate in Parliament in March 1865 demonstrated that Britain would not give up the provinces without a fight. Imperial duty no less than international prestige would demand that the effort be made.

FOURTEEN

Peace

"THUS IT IS THAT CONSCIENCE WORKS," Charles Francis Adams commented on the alarm in Britain over relations with the United States. His satisfaction was short-lived. The suspicion, not entirely unfounded, that the Confederacy's friends planned to exploit Canada's peril in a last desperate attempt to secure the intervention which alone could rescue the Southern cause, and the conviction that the aristocracy would grasp any opportunity to prevent the final triumph of the democratic Republic, led the American minister to preach caution to Seward. Echoing Goldwin Smith's recent remarks in the Northern states, he stressed the need to pursue a policy which would assist the Reformers in the approaching general election. Their success would be the victory "of all that portion of the people in England which sympathizes with us," he explained. With the reopening of Parliament, moreover, it was important not to embarrass a ministry which, "though failing in the elements of courage," had "for the most part aimed to be friendly." So, while admitting the justice of his nation's complaints against Britain, Adams warned that "to press it here at this moment would be only playing into the hands of the mischief makers and disarming our own friends."[1]

The American minister did his best to disabuse Englishmen of the notion that his government contemplated the conquest of British territories. In the case of Canada, as in that of Mexico, any annexation would be the result of a peaceful policy of patience and conciliation, he averred. And when he received instructions from Seward which gave colour to the idea that the United States was spoiling for a fight Adams either softened or withheld them. Not until early April, and only after a flurry of instructions, did the minister reluctantly renew the remonstrances against Britain's continued recognition of Confederate belligerency and revive the claims for indemnity for the depredations of vessels fitted out in British ports. But by that time the fear of war had subsided in Britain.[2]

Tension had eased with the arrival of the news that Seward had withdrawn the notice of abrogation of the Lakes Convention, but the chief source of the newfound public confidence was a more careful assessment of the problems confronting the Union. Speaking in the debate on Jervois's report, Disraeli had dwelt upon the factors which he believed would ensure peaceful relations with the United States even after the collapse of the Confederacy. Emotionally if not physically and financially exhausted by one war, was it likely that the North would rush into another? The Federal government would find itself fully employed dealing with a discontented population of newly emancipated blacks, he predicted, discontented because "the superior race" would deny them the rights and privileges of freemen. Walter Bagehot had already drawn attention in the *Economist* to other travails of postwar adjustment, not the least of which was going to be the occupation of the defeated states. "Why do we expect that all these objects will be laid aside in order to enjoy the luxury of punishing England for allowing two or three steamers to reach the Confederates, or conquering Canada, and so adding to a vast and disaffected territory at the South another vast and disaffected territory at the North?" he asked. Others soon repeated the question and "the absurd panic" passed.[3]

Russell also began to relax. Adams's friendly and conciliatory conduct had its effect, and the foreign secretary accepted calmly the formal notice on March 17, 1865, of the Union's intention to terminate reciprocity. At the beginning of April he surprised Palmerston by doing an about-face on the income tax, now supporting its abolition. Replying to the prime minister's query, Russell cited the substantial budget surplus and the improved foreign outlook. "I have become sanguine of maintaining peace both with France and America," he explained. Of course, he was not "without some anxiety" but his mind inclined "to hope rather than fear."[4] What was required of Britain was "a great deal of prudence and a great spirit of conciliation together with calmness." The "sad intelligence" of Lincoln's assassination served to strengthen Russell's optimism. The cry of vengeance against the South which Lincoln had kept low would almost certainly become loud and menacing. Thus the end of the military contest would see the beginning of prolonged civil discord. "There are I should think many months if not years of trouble ahead for the United States," Russell observed dispassionately. "Punishment as well as murder in a civil war leads to vengeance and blood feuds." Moreover, there was hope that the spontaneous out-burst of public shock and dismay in Britain at the president's death would check the popular ill will toward her in the United States. With this thought in mind the cabinet prevailed upon the Queen to write a personal note of condolence to Mrs. Lincoln.[5]

Like Disraeli, Russell saw in the contentious problem of the freed-man's role in American society additional security for Britain. Per-sonally he thought Lincoln's successor "in the right" in his dispute with the "Abolitionists" over the negro. "There seems a better chance of bringing the negroes within the pale of civilization if they are first taught to work and to read and write than if they are made first to vote then to govern and lastly to learn what voting and governing are," the foreign secretary commented. However, the certainty that the question would be a "fearful" one, and the possibility Russell foresaw of the new president turning to his political enemies, the Democrats and ex-Confederates, for assistance against members of the party he now nominally led, suggested that this was not the proverbial ill wind. It might bring Britain peace, Russell coolly noted, "and that will be no small good." Confronted by the "tre-mendous task" of "reconstituting the society" of many of their states, the American people knew that they would do well to avoid a foreign war.[6]

Of course, there had been initial doubts about the international course President Andrew Johnson would steer. Weakened by illness and a little unnerved by the occasion, Johnson had taken at least one tot too many before his inauguration as vice-president in March. His behaviour at the ceremony had made him a laughing-stock, both at home and abroad, but this "unscrupulous savage whose thirst for popularity" was "as great as for strong drinks" now headed the American government. And while Russell did not expect Johnson "to do anything to change the foreign policy of his predecessor," the uncertainty could not have lessened the foreign secretary's receptive-ness to a proposal of the French foreign minister that their two nations continue to act in "close concert" on America. If the "concert" had long since ceased to be a reality, the illusion nevertheless offered some benefit. The United States would be less likely to engage either nation in a contest (and the French were as worried about Mexico as the British had been about Canada) if they appeared to be collaborating. Thus Russell was careful to seek the emperor's support for Britain's resistance of American pressure to settle the *Alabama* claims. Then, early in June, the British and French governments, acting in concert, effectively withdrew recognition of Confederate belligerency even though the Union had not yet discontinued all belligerent activities.[7]

Formal recognition of the reestablishment of peace throughout the territory of the United States had been urged upon the government by the new British minister in Washington. In February the cabinet had "expressed very decidedly" the opinion that "the grave affairs now pending" between the two nations should be taken out of the hands of a chargé d'affaires. Russell had already made up his mind to recommend Sir Frederick Bruce for the position, which Lyons at once formally resigned. A younger brother of Lord Elgin, Bruce was an experienced diplomat. He had been attached to the Ashburton commission in 1842, had served at lieutenant-governor of Newfoundland, had held posts in South America and Egypt, and had accompanied his brother to China in 1857 in the capacity of principal secretary. Soon elevated to envoy extraordinary and minister plenipotentiary, in 1860 he had added to his titles that of superintendent of British trade, and in Russell's words displayed "much sense, moderation and temper in China." Establishing an excellent relationship with his American counterpart, he gained the Union's respect by refusing to grant British registers to Confederate vessels in Asian waters. This denied rebels the protection of the British flag. His selection as Lyons's successor was evidently a conciliatory gesture and the Americans accepted it as such.[8]

Impressed with the importance of his mission, persuaded that he might be of use in "preserving friendly relations with the United States, and avoiding the great calamity of a rupture," Bruce had readily abandoned his initial intention to spend the summer in Europe's temperate climate. When he stepped ashore at New York on April 7—appropriately enough from the steamer *China*—Bruce bore instructions over which Russell had laboured long. They reflected the government's nervousness in mid-March about relations with the Union. The two nations "ought to be united by a family compact of the most intimate and exclusive nature," Russell affirmed. More specifically, the British wished to renew the reciprocity arrangement which had proven so mutually advantageous to the Union and Canada and were willing to modify the terms in order to make it even more beneficial. As for the *Alabama* and the other vessels "partly fitted out" in Britain but armed and commissioned in the ports of other neutrals, Russell did not reject the American demands for indemnity. In several carefully crafted sentences, in which Palmerston had made a number of changes no less conciliatory in tone but somewhat less sugary, Russell instructed Bruce to refer home any discussions of the *Alabama* claims. However, he was to reassure Seward that the British government would be ready to reply to any despatch sent to London and was to express its conviction that "calm and dispassionate discussion will bring the two governments to just and equitable conclusions."[9]

Bruce arrived in Washington to discover that Seward was confined to his bed, having been seriously injured in a carriage accident. Lincoln postponed the presentation of the minister's letters of credence, hoping that Seward would be able to draw up the reply, but on April 14 he decided to proceed with the ceremony on the following day. That evening the president paid his fateful visit to Ford's Theatre. The simultaneous attempt to murder the secretary of state failed but it did retard his recovery. Bruce feared that Lincoln's death and Seward's condition would have "an unfavourable effect" on negotiations with the United States. Although Andrew Johnson spoke reassuringly to the Englishman of his desire "to cultivate friendship" with Britain, it was obvious that the new president lacked the prestige and thus the influence of his predecessor. So Bruce waited for Seward's return to the State Department. Cannily, he kept his distance from Sumner despite an invitation to enter into "confidential communications." He distrusted the Massachusetts senator. "There is a want of frankness in him, which coupled with the language he has held on the 'Alabama' and the 'Reciprocity Treaty,' makes me suspect, that his object in making these advances, is to increase his own political influence by becoming the exponent of my views, rather than to forward them," Bruce reported to Russell. Nor did the minister intend to be dragged into Sumner's long struggle to wrest control of foreign affairs from Seward's grasp. Bruce fully understood the necessity of establishing cordial relations with Seward, who showed no inclination to retire from office. But the Englishman believed his nation's best security was the Union's great internal difficulties, rather than in the good will of any statesman.[10]

During the virtual diplomatic standstill in Washington, for it was June before Bruce saw Seward for the first time and July before the secretary resumed his full duties, the minister's observations on American affairs made comforting reading in London. He did call for caution and repeatedly urged, as another conciliatory gesture to

American opinion, the withdrawal of belligerent rights from the Con-federates. With many troops being sent to their home states to be discharged, "any fresh excitement against England would facilitate the views of Irish and other adventurers who would rather use their swords against Canada than turn them into reaping hooks."[11] Never-theless, he remained of the opinion that the United States would be fully occupied with the domestic problems of reconstruction. More-over, the minister was assured that Southerners were "heartily sick of war," that they were "grateful for the sympathy of foreign nations, and that their bitterness towards the Yankees would indispose them to join them in a foreign war." Subsequently Bruce saw in the speedy reconstruction of the Union the answer to the *Alabama* question. It was hardly to be supposed, he wrote to Russell, that Southern mem-bers of Congress would support "violent proceedings against England founded on her recognition of them as belligerents and on the doings of their vessels of war."[12]

Russell had summarized Britain's predicament over the *Alabama* in a note to Palmerston early in April. The foreign secretary had at one time thought impartial arbitration an appropriate means of settling the American claims for indemnity, and the lord chancellor had several times voiced the opinion in cabinet that if the question could be reduced to one of law Britain might submit to the arbitration of a friendly power. But the position of the United States did not admit of such a solution. First, there was the "almost insuperable" difficulty of finding a power "really friendly" to Britain and accept-able to the United States. Even had that been overcome there remained a second and greater problem. The American demands called into question both the British government's sincerity in putting the law into force and the law's adequacy for the fulfilment of Britain's international obligations. "I do not see how we could allow any foreign power to decide that we had not been sincere in our application of the law, or that our Parl[iamen]t had not given us the power to maintain our neutral obligations," Russell concluded. In short, to yield would be humiliating.[13] There was also the fear that it might be dangerous. Lyons, when consulted, warned that to give ground on the *Alabama* claims would see "no limit to the concessions demanded" by the Union. The Americans must not be allowed to suppose that they could squeeze millions out of Britain by pressure for that "would be fatal to future peace." The British were further encouraged to resist by the knowledge that their conduct had been consistent with precedents established by the United States. Writing in *Macmillan's*, even Goldwin Smith, that ardent partisan of the Union, conceded that the Americans "seem completely estopped" from securing compensation for the ravages of the *Alabama*. "There is nothing clearer than our case for a refusal of the claims for the Alabama captures," Russell remarked to Palmerston in June, as he prepared a despatch "making it clear we shall not yield."[14]

Although honeyed words were no longer necessary, and the minister was now instructed to use language which emphasized the cabinet's adamant stand, he was cautioned not to speak officially about the *Alabama* until formal instructions arrived. They were delayed by the general election in Britain, which saw Palmerston's hold on power confirmed. This was excellent news, Bruce quickly wrote home, for it was very important that the government dealing with the Union "should be strong and should be liberal." Satisfied that everything "tends to shew that the United States have paused in their passion ag[ain]st us," Russell seized the opportunity "to complete" his defence of Britain's neutral conduct. Yet there was every indication that the Republic would not abandon the *Alabama* claims, however firm the British refusal to negotiate and however solid a legal position founded upon American precedents. Arguments supported by international law were not going to discourage a population convinced that the nation had suffered grievous injury, Bruce observed after only a few weeks in Washington. And not long after his return to the State Department Seward began advertising for *Alabama* claims. The truth was, Bruce reported, that even the "most moderate persons here take the ground that the 'Alabama' claims cannot be settled without being referred to arbitration."[15]

The wisdom of flatly rejecting arbitration, as Russell did in August, was subsequently questioned by at least two of the foreign secretary's colleagues. Gladstone and Argyll both attacked the decision as precipitate. While admitting that the American demand was "unreasonable in a high degree, and even that we have some reason to complain of its having been made," Gladstone reasoned that the proper course was not to say "No," but "to lead the Americans to bring out the whole of their pleas and arguments, that we might have them fully before us previously to coming to a decision of great delicacy and moment." In his reply Russell revealed that this remained for him a matter of honour, national and personal. What questions would be referred to an arbitrator, he asked. "Was Lord Russell diligent or negligent in the execution of the duties of his office?" "Was Sir Roundell Palmer versed in the laws of England, or was he ignorant or partial in giving his opinion to the Government?" "Ought the Government and Parliament of England to have provided fresh laws to prevent merchant ships leaving their ports until it was proved they had no belligerent purposes?" Britain would be "disgraced for ever if such questions were left to the arbitration of a foreign Government," he affirmed. Indeed, he thought "that paying twenty millions down would be far preferable to submitting the case to arbitration."[16]

The confidence which permitted the British government to make explicit its refusal to negotiate the *Alabama* claims was not without effect on imperial relations. Canada's stock in London had fallen dramatically within three weeks of the decisive vote in the Commons on the Quebec fortifications. The defeat of the forces of Confederation in New Brunswick; the disdain with which the vote of £50,000 for the Quebec works had been greeted in Canada; reports that the $1 million voted by the provincial legislature would only be raised upon the strength of an imperial guarantee, which Englishmen dismissed as a "mere euphemism for a loan without interest"; the decision of a second Canadian judge to release those St. Albans raiders who had been rearrested, which threatened to fan the flames of American hostility; the revival of the old cry in Canada that it was the imperial connection which placed the province in danger, and the reappearance of annexationist sentiment there, all these developments had influenced British opinion recently emancipated from the threat of war with the United States. A debate initiated by that indefatigable campaigner against colonial expenses, Arthur Mills, on April 28, was marked by far less tender sentiments towards the provinces. Some imperialists had lost patience and Little Englanders took heart. "The loyalty of the Canadians, for instance, is of so ethereal and poetical a character," the *Saturday Review* observed sardonically, "that it disdains to express itself in any solid and material form." *The Times* had already issued the warning that if ever they wished Britain to defend their whole soil the British North Americans "must combine in a general organization and in mutual assistance."[17]

The coalition ministry in Canada had brought Confederation before the legislature early in February. The emphasis Taché, McGee, Cartier, and John A. Macdonald placed upon the American danger was predictable, but George Brown joined them. Confederation would better enable the British in North America to defend themselves, he declared. Disclaiming any belief that the Americans intended to attack, he recommended preparation as the best way to ward off danger. "The Americans are now a warlike people. They have large armies, a powerful navy, an unlimited supply of warlike munitions," he noted; therefore, unless Canadians were willing to live at the mercy of their neighbours, they must put their country "in a state of efficient preparation." This self-same concern, and the desire to minimize the disappointment in England, prompted the government's bold decision to respond to the news from New Brunswick by carrying Confederation in the Canadian legislature.[18]

A correspondent of John A. Macdonald's expressed another concern. Writing in May, when Macdonald was in London, together with Brown, Galt, and Cartier, to negotiate with the imperial government, he reported that "the country is depressed beyond example—and men talk of annexation, who a few months ago would have resented as an insult any imputation of the sentiments they now profess." If the delegation succeeded Confederation would go on, the Reciprocity Treaty would be renewed, and Canadians would settle down to work out their destiny within the Empire, he declared. If Macdonald and his colleagues failed, however, and the farmers once again found themselves far less favourably placed than those in the United States, then Canadians would soon be republicans. Bruce had reached much the same conclusion. He was impressed by the remarks of one friendly American who believed that Confederation was essential if the political resistance to reciprocity was to be overcome. Once Canadians showed themselves "resolved and capable of founding an Empire" they would earn the respect of their neighbours, the minister wrote home, and friendly relations beneficial to both would not "be difficult of adjustment." Not surprisingly, before long Bruce learned that Cardwell and Monck were anxious for him to communicate to the governments of New Brunswick and Nova Scotia his opinion "that the Union of the provinces as one body would greatly facilitate the negotiation for a Reciprocity Treaty." But the conviction that the provinces must be united if their connection with Britain was to be preserved explains Russell's continuing readiness to resort to coercion as well as to employ persuasion.[19]

Bruce shared the belief that Confederation would prevent the growth of annexation sentiment within Canada. There was suspicion in some quarters that the treaty's abrogation had been the work not merely of protectionists in Congress but also of annexationists. One wing of the Republican party was "supposed to think" that Canada might be peacefully annexed through measures which underscored the province's economic dependence upon the Union. In annexation these Republicans reportedly saw the means to ensure the "perpetuity and preponderance" of their party even after the return of Southern Democrats. Canadians, after all, held "nearly identical views" with New Englanders. Seward was identified as the chief of this wing, and Bruce warned that "peaceable annexation" was a game the secretary and other politicians from the Eastern States "would gladly play." All that can be said for certain about Seward's role was that he did favour the peaceful annexation of British North America; that he was assured by the consul general in Canada that many of the province's residents, especially businessmen, believed that there could be no permanent prosperity there except in "close and intimate union" with the United States; and that Henry Raymond, one of his political intimates, welcomed in the *New York Times* the defeat of Confederation in New Brunswick and drew attention to the growth of the sentiment that "it would *pay* the people of Upper Canada" to enter the American Union.[20]

Whether or not Seward's behaviour was guided by hopes of annexation, his refusal to enter into serious negotiations for the renewal of reciprocity, and his failure to exert himself upon its behalf (Canadians who came to discuss it unofficially were directed to the protectionists in Congress), were surely not unrelated to the British rejection of the *Alabama* claims. One was a hostage for the other, and Chairman Sumner of the Foreign Relations Committee had said as much during Seward's illness. Reciprocity was not a question the American government considered on its merits, Bruce reported. Instead, the Americans were "holding back, and treating it as a political question, and as a means of obtaining satisfaction from us on matters with which it is unconnected."[21]

At the meetings in London between the Canadian delegation and members of the cabinet, reciprocity was discussed but the principal question was that of defence. The extent to which the events in British North America and the confidence that there would not be a war with the United States had altered circumstances was soon apparent. Inadvertently aided by the Canadians, who with the backing of the Defence Committee sketched out a vast and expensive plan to defend the entire province, Gladstone began to make headway in cabinet with his calls for caution. Colleagues rallied to his suggestion that they demand as a condition of British assistance "unequivocal proof" that it was "the desire and intention of the Canadian people, the case arising, to fight for the separate existence, and for the connection with England, in the same spirit in which the South has fought."[22] Reacting to the shift in opinion, Palmerston wanted to confine the discussion to limited measures which could be started immediately, such as the imperial works at Quebec and the colonial at Montreal, and to the request for a guarantee of the loan. Russell agreed and suggested that the Canadians also be informed that the imperial government would do all in its power "to promote the plan of Confederation— (even to compulsion if necessary)" and would send as large a reinforcement of troops as could be spared in the event of war with the United States. As Clarendon put it, "These men however must not be sent home quite empty handed, i.e. as regards promises, or the discontent of the Canadians will increase and the Yankees will be encouraged to hostilize them by our supposed desertion."[23]

Gladstone balked at doing what Palmerston and Russell proposed. The works at Quebec should be prosecuted "with all despatch," he granted, but the imperial government should not press anything upon Canada for the coming year. Instead, it would be better employed using every means at hand to forward Confederation. He proposed that the cabinet "adhere to the ground taken by Canada in the December Memorandum, which postponed the consideration of all wider plans of defence until after the Union should have been formed." Hard though the Canadians argued for the comprehensive plan of defence, and Palmerston struggled to rescue more limited measures, Gladstone prevailed. "After many turns and twists in the communications," he informed Argyll, "the Canadian Ministers have at length been led to place Confederation in the foreground of the whole affair, which is very much what I had wished." Apart from the works at Quebec, the defence of British North America was "to stand over to a future period, while we push to the best of our power the formation of the Confederation."[24]

Palmerston was still giving thought to Canada's defence in October, shortly before his death. However, his anxiety was caused less by the conduct of the United States government than by the activities of Irish-American nationalists. He feared that the Fenians would "try and obtain in our North American Provinces compensation for their defeat in Ireland." He was relieved to hear from De Grey that there were sufficient rifles and ammunition in Canada to throw back any

Fenian invasion. As it turned out, the menace of Fenianism soon served to strengthen the hand of the supporters of Confederation in New Brunswick and elsewhere.[25]

Conclusion

IF THE MINDS OF PALMERSTON and his colleagues were rarely free of worry over the security of Canada, historians of the Anglo-American relationship have in general regarded this concern as a secondary consideration in the shaping of British policy. For the fundamental explanation of Britain's decision not to intervene in the Civil War they have looked elsewhere. There have been several attempts to reduce everything, in the words of Charles Dickens, to a "mere question of figures, a case of simple arithmetic." The notion that King Cotton was held in check by King Corn enjoyed a brief hey-day, but the most impressive economic interpretation was that offered by Frank Lawrence Owsley. His *King Cotton Diplomacy* was published in 1931, at a time of growing national disillusionment over the reasons for and the results of American intervention in the First World War. One vocal group argued that the United States had entered that conflict for no nobler purpose than to protect the war profits of Wall Street bankers and munitions manufacturers, and Owsley suggested that the same motives had convinced the British of the wisdom of staying out of the Civil War a half century earlier. "Those who are at all familiar with the war profits in the more recent wars," he declared, "ought not to have any great difficulty in grasping the rôle England played of war profiteer, and the powerful influence upon government of her war profiteers, especially when all, even the small operatives, were prosperous as a result of the war."[1] The opportunity presented to merchants and manufacturers to make a princely profit selling off the vast stockpiles of inexpensive raw cotton and goods accumulated during the late 1850s, the prosperity the American war brought to so many other British industries, and the destruction of the American merchant marine by British-built Confederate cruisers largely determined Britain's conduct, Owsley concluded. The "political motive" for intervention (the weakening of "a military and national rival") was "outweighed" by the economic advantages of remaining neutral. After all, Owsley remarked, resorting to an unforgettable metaphor, "England never doubted until it was too late that the South would win its independence and the roast pigeon would thus fly into the open mouth of the British lion without any other effort than the opening of his jaws."[2]

Writing a few years before Owsley, and at a time when there was still some bloom left on the Anglo-American war effort against Germany, E. D. Adams in his classic study argued that "there were those in Great Britain who rejoiced at the rupture between North and South, but they were not in office and had no control of British policy."[3] When fighting broke out in the United States the government's first thought was "to keep clear of it," Adams asserted. Admittedly, as the conflict dragged on and domestic pressure increased the ministry did hesitantly advance towards mediation, but even then its "desire was first of all for the restoration of world peace, nor can any other motive be discovered in Russell's manoeuvres." By midsummer of 1863, recognizing the North's determination to fight on to victory, the government's attitude "was distinctly favourable to a restored Union." This was "no special sympathy," Adams found, "but merely a cool calculation of benefits to Great Britain" in maintaining "that policy of friendship determined upon in the 'fifties'." Moreover, emancipation provided the Palmerston ministry with a guarantee against being overthrown for failing to intervene in America. It "gave to an enthusiastic and vociferous section of the British public just ground for strong support of Lincoln and his cause, and in some degree it affected governmental attitude."[4] This was a conclusion Donaldson Jordan and Edwin J. Pratt endorsed in their *Europe and the American Civil War* which was published in the same year as Owsley's study.

During the past three decades aspects of these interpretations inevitably have come under attack. The significance of "war profits" and of emancipation has been challenged. The neutrality Adams interpreted as first "cold" and later "friendly" has also been labelled "indifferent" and malleable. Frank J. Merli has drawn attention to the influence of national advantage, the absence of any precise definition of neutrality, and the fear of establishing unfortunate precedents with respect to interference in the domestic affairs of first-class powers and the maritime rights of neutrals, in his explanation of the Palmerston cabinet's "stopgap measures subject to misunderstanding, pregnant with mischief." Here is the "key factor," he contends, "in Anglo-American Civil War diplomacy."[5] Others have found it in the turmoil in Europe, on which a good many Unionists had relied to keep Britain and France out of the war. More conjectural is D. P. Crook's recent suggestion that Palmerston and his colleagues may simply have concluded "that British interests better flourished in a stable atmosphere based upon United States power."[6]

One well-placed and interested contemporary who sat down at the war's end to examine the course Britain had followed was George

Eustis, Slidell's secretary. She had refused to recognize the Confederacy but had extended recognition to the Empire of Mexico, he observed, even though the former had had the substance and the latter merely "the shadow of *viabilité*," one having been a government of the people and the other a foreign creation imposed by bayonets.[7] Of course, the conviction that the British government had behaved unjustly if not cravenly was shared by some Englishmen as well as embittered Confederates. "We have been false to our principles, and neglected an opportunity," a shamefaced *Morning Herald* declared. "We have been guilty of a crime as well as a blunder, and assuredly we or our children will have to pay for both."[8] The opportunity had been that of completing the division of a nation many Britons, and by no means all of them Tories, disliked, distrusted, and now increasingly feared. As for the principle, that was the support Britain had traditionally extended to a "subject" people struggling for their independence.

The Confederate cause excited in Britain widespread sympathy which knew no barriers of class. Had not Southerners as much "right" to leave the Union as their forebears had had to withdraw from the British Empire? And the persistence no less than the pervasiveness of Southern sentiment was startling. Matthew Arnold reported to his sister (W. E. Forster's wife) early in January 1865, that of the students in Training Colleges who had been set a composition which touched upon the American crisis almost every one had taken "the strongest possible side" with the Confederacy.[9] These were not members of the aristocracy but a new generation of the middle classes. Indeed, it was the unexpected hostility of the important centre of British society which "turned me into a life-long enemy of everything English," Henry Adams recalled in later life.[10] Similarly, the recent harsh criticism of Walter Bagehot for his lack of sympathy for the Union has gone hand in hand with the acknowledgement that he was both a Palmerstonian and "in some respects a typical member of the Victorian middle class: some of its meanness of spirit tainted his natural warmth."[11] Yet a government led by the man to whom so many of these people looked for leadership, and who shared the dislike and distrust of the "Democratic Republic" and was usually quick to catch the breeze of public opinion, held its noninterventionist course. Why?

Palmerston's policy had been weak in all the great crises of the day, the Polish, the Danish, and the American, Eustis charged, because it consisted of doing "everything in his power to avoid meeting questions & to avoid adopting some decided and positive course." Abroad as at home, this disappointed Southerner judged, the prime minister's principal object appeared to be the postponement of difficult, disagreeable, and annoying subjects, for he evidently had not long to live and wished to die in harness. By and large the Tories were willing to allow him to do so because they were generally satisfied with his conservatism and more than a little afraid of his immense personal popularity. Although there is an element of truth in this contemptuous appraisal of Palmerston's final years he did exhibit from time to time flashes of the old spirit. Queen, cabinet, and the everlasting suspicion of France had been required to rein in the desire of Palmerston and Russell to make a demonstration of support for the Danes following the Austro-Prussian invasion of Denmark. Victoria's emotional and several of her ministers' realistic objections to any action which might confront Britain with the unattractive alternatives of complete diplomatic humiliation or joining a war she was ill-equipped to fight carried the day. The American war had presented a similar dilemma.

There were indications in the spring of 1861 that the Palmerston ministry was preparing the way for a denunciation of the Union blockade of the Confederate States. But this crucial step was never taken. Part of the credit belonged to Sir John Harding, the Queen's advocate and a Northern sympathizer. He argued strongly for a cautious and evidential approach to the problems caused by the Union's action. William Seward did much to convince the British government of the wisdom of the law officer's advice. Seward's carefully cultivated reputation as an anglophobe, his public references to the inevitable annexation of Canada, his threatening talk of going to war to resist British interference, all these excited uneasiness. Although Palmerston and his colleagues doubted Seward's determination to challenge Britain at this time of profound trial for his own nation, the secretary of state did succeed in his essential purpose which was to impress them with the need to err on the side of caution in their response to the Civil War. His lasting success was to convince them that retribution would be exacted for any meddling in the conflict beyond the initial and bitterly resented recognition of Confederate belligerency. Those in the British government who contemplated some form of intervention, in order to complete the division of the Republic as well as to halt the bloodshed, wished to undertake it only in absolute safety.

A demonstration on behalf of the Confederacy, whether in the form of recognition or of an offer of mediation, would not necessarily have ended the struggle immediately but it would most certainly have subjected Anglo-American relations to a severe if not intolerable strain. In the words of the British minister to France, writing at the end of the American war, had Britain recognized Confederate independence "we should have had to look about us."[12] Few Englishmen ever considered pressing their Southern sympathies to the point of a rupture with the North, and their nervousness in March 1865 served to underscore this fact. After all, a great many of them were prospering. The suffering in the mill towns, which was generally attributed to the shortage of Southern cotton, was held within acceptable limits while the profits of neutrality and the continuing rewards of the French treaty provided compensation. Consequently there were as many economic arguments against involvement in America as there were against intervention in Europe. Why jeopardize prosperity and expose the vast wealth of trade on the high seas to attack by *Alabamas*? In short, why risk a conflict which might well precipitate the very economic catastrophe if not social disaster Britain had so far escaped? But the ledger did not dictate policy. Rather, material interests were one aspect of the background against which decisions were taken. They were certainly another reason for the government to move cautiously, but they also served as justification for inaction compelled by other considerations.

There were political constraints on those members of the government who occasionally showed a willingness to have Britain play a more active role in the American and European crises. The coalition upon which the ministry relied for survival in Parliament, composed of Whigs, Liberals, and Radicals, was not one which encouraged a bold foreign policy, and the same could be said of the cabinet. Some of its disparate members worked with the Queen to frustrate a Palmerstonian demonstration in Europe, and they rarely if ever spoke with but a single voice on the troubles of the United States. Moreover, Palmerston and Russell never forgot the vulnerability of Canada to an American attack, nor did they ever conquer their suspicions of the "crafty spider" who spun his webs from France. Napoleon's opportunities for mischief obviously increased with the turmoil on the Continent, and Russell even began to fear that the American and the European problems would become entangled. Herein lies the explanation for that tightening of British neutrality in 1863 which

397

worked to the profound disadvantage of the South. It was not a matter of the government suddenly realizing that the Union might well be restored and therefore determining to revive the "policy of friendship" initiated in the 1850s. In fact, this attitude more "distinctly" favourable to the Union predated the victories at Vicksburg and Gettysburg, and belief in the Confederacy's survival persisted long after the summer of 1863. Moreover, too much has been made of the prewar "policy of friendship." Nor does it appear that the government acted out of the conviction that Britain's interests would best be served by the maintenance of a powerful Union. Instead, a "strict neutrality" which "owing to circumstances" (to use Russell's own words) benefited the North was dictated by the need to keep relations with America quiescent in order to strengthen Britain's diplomatic position in Europe. She did what was necessary to smooth relations with the United States, for difficulties across the Atlantic might tempt opportunists across the Channel to take advantage of her embarrassment or at the very least ignore her when she spoke. Of secondary importance, yet by no means trivial, was the genuine indignation of Russell at the personal and national ramifications of the Confederates' circumvention of the Foreign Enlistment Act. By 1863 there was a growing awareness of the dangerous precedents Britain might be establishing for herself in future wars.

There was also a profoundly moral reason for the British to control their American sympathies by 1863. Admiration for the courage and ability with which the Southern cause was upheld had obscured the fact that it was a bad one, Russell eventually admitted.[13] George Eustis insisted that Britain had been unable to recognize the Confederacy because it bore the stigma of slavery, and there is some truth in the assertion. In 1861 Englishmen had readily convinced themselves that the conflict had little to do with the peculiar institution. There was then scant reason to believe that the war was being fought by the North to free blacks held in bondage. In 1862, however, it became increasingly difficult to ignore the extent to which the struggle was advancing the cause of human freedom. The legislation enacted by Congress, the "practical measures" implemented by the administration, and the president's proclamation thrust the issue of slavery into the foreground. Yet, if it cannot be ignored, the international significance of this factor in 1862 is all too easily exaggerated.[14] Although Palmerston expressed reluctance during the mediation crisis to involve himself and his nation in the erection of a new republic having slavery as its cornerstone, his concern was more with appearances than morality, more with expediency than principle. Besides, second thoughts on the wisdom of taking the diplomatic initiative at this time prompted him to seek excuses for inaction. Significantly, in the cabinet memorandum through which he sought to spur movement of some kind, Russell cited Lincoln's slavery "decree" and the horrifying prospect of "servile war" as the "most important" considerations. Nor did the president's proclamation discourage Gladstone from advocating action. It was not until the fears of a slave uprising against fellow whites proved groundless, and the torrent of public criticism and ridicule of Lincoln's measure slowed, that the members of the London Emancipation Society and its provincial affiliates came into their own. Their skilful agitation achieved its essential purpose of throwing the advocates of any form of intervention further onto the defensive, chiefly by heightening the fears of those who worried that any step to assist the establishment of "Slaveownia" would prove divisive in Britain. Once again the need for the government to proceed with extreme caution had been underlined. As for the South's British friends, although more numerous than those of the Union they all too often lacked their energy, commitment, and organizational skill. Overconfidence and incompetence undermined their efforts to exert pressure on the government in 1862, when it might have told. By the autumn of the following year, when the Southern Independence Association was formed, the battle was already lost. European questions had long since preoccupied the British government and nation, while the Confederate cause was becoming irrevocably identified with that of slavery. "If the slavery of the negro race terminates with these Federal successes," Russell observed in April 1865, "I shall rejoice at the result."[15]

For a generation of Americans weaned on distrust of Britain, her policy and her people's attitude during the Civil War were accepted as conclusive proof of British perfidy. A nation "contending for order against anarchy, for civilization against barbarism, for freedom against oppression," one enraged Unionist remarked in 1862, had the right to expect that "the friends of order, of civilization, and of liberty" would at least cheer it on in its struggle and praise its sacrifices.[16] This was to be an oft-repeated indictment in the years that followed. The fact that there had been precious little good will in Anglo-American relations before the war was conveniently forgotten by those charging Britain with apostasy. Americans had not been in the habit of hailing the English as the friends of order, civilization, and liberty, or of proclaiming that by "the closest ties of descent, language, and commerce, by traditional regard for the authority of constitutions and by the inborn love of human rights, as well as by treaties of amity, they were allied to our Government." On the contrary, they had reciprocated in full measure British disdain for their society and institutions and had made no secret of their resentment of the efforts made by successive British governments to thwart their nation's international ambitions and "destiny." Is it reasonable, given the history of the relationship, to attack the British for missing this "great opportunity" of riveting the American Republic to them "by the strongest of bonds?"[17] "It is all very well preaching about honour and good faith towards the United States," wrote Frank Lawley after several years' residence in the Union but before his appointment as correspondent of *The Times*. "Can it be pretended that we have ever met with honourable and ingenuous conduct at their hands," he asked, "and is anybody mad enough to hope that they will not hit us between the eyes, directly it suits their convenience to do so, in spite of all the justice, moderation, self-denial and temperance of England's course towards them?"[18] These were not the terms any American would have employed in a description of Britain's conduct. Yet there is some truth in Russell's remark, after the Confederacy's collapse, that the real complaint of the Union was that "we have not taken any part in the war."[19] By that he meant that nothing short of a British neutrality so benevolent as to amount to assistance would have satisfied the North. "But tho' I have been always ready to give them the benefits of the laws of neutrality which operated much more for them than against them, owing to circumstances," he went on, "I w[oul]d not allow the Law of Nations to be set aside by the newspaper scurrility of the North American Press." What cannot be denied, however, is that Americans emerged from the Civil War with a list of grievances against Britain, and an enmity toward her, that required both compensation and time in order to be erased. Happily, the legend of British working-class support for the Union, based upon the identification of the North with freedom and democracy, provided the material for an intellectual and popular reconciliation of the English-speaking peoples once their political interests pointed firmly in that direction.

NOTES

INTRODUCTION

1. Henry B. Smith, "British Sympathy with America," *American Presby-* *terian Review* (1862), p. 497.

ONE   The Belligerents

1. *Richmond Dispatch*, April 24, 1862; Emory M. Thomas, *Confederate State of Richmond: A Biography of the Capital* (Austin, 1971), p. 78.
2. A. R. Childs, ed., *The Private Journal of Henry William Ravenel 1859–1887* (Columbia, 1947), p. 136; T. C. DeLeon, *Four Years in Rebel Capitals: An Inside View of Life in the Southern Confederacy from Birth* (reprint ed., New York, 1962), p. 179.
3. *Southern Historical Society Papers* (hereafter cited as *SHSP*), XLIV, 32ff.
4. Gamaliel Bradford, *Confederate Portraits* (reprint ed., New York, 1968), p. 125; Bell I. Wiley, *Confederate Women* (Westport, 1975), p. 7.
5. Cobb to M. Cobb, March 20, 1862, Howell Cobb Papers, University of Georgia Library; Edward Pollard, *Southern History of the War*, 2 vols. (reprint ed., New York, 1969), I, 234; quoted in Thomas, *Confederate Richmond*, p. 86; *Charleston Daily Courier,* May 22, 1862; (Atlanta) *Southern Confederacy*, May 26 and 22, 1862.
6. Pollard, *Southern History*, II, 26; Stephen Mallory, Diary, May 15, 1862, Southern Historical Collec-

tion, University of North Carolina Library; *Southern Literary Messenger*, XXXIV (1862), 265.
7. *Richmond Whig*, June 14, 1862; *Richmond Dispatch*, May 5, 28, and 30, 1862; *Wilmington Daily Journal*, May 2, 1862.
8. *Richmond Dispatch*, May 28, 1862.
9. *Richmond Whig*, May 27, 1862; see also *Wilmington Daily Journal*, May 7, 1862; *Charleston Daily Courier*, May 22, 1862.
10. Richard Todd, *Confederate Finance* (Athens, Ga., 1954), p. 128; *SHSP*, XLIV, 59–61; Frank Lawrence Owsley, *King Cotton Diplomacy: Foreign Relations of the Confederate States of America*, rev. ed. (Chicago, 1959), p. 304.
11. *SHSP*, XLIV, 147–49, 163–65.
12. Ibid., pp. 163–65; see also William Kauffman Scarborough, *The Diary of Edmund Ruffin*, 2 vols. (Baton Rouge, 1976), II, 265.
13. Mallory, Diary, June 24, 1862.
14. Thomas Bragg, Diary, March 19, 1862, Southern Historical Collection; Todd, *Confederate Finance*, pp. 25–34, 174.
15. Memminger to Pickens, April 15, 1862, C. C. Memminger Papers, Southern Historical Collection; Bragg, Diary, March 19, 1862.

16. *Harper's Monthly*, XXVI (1863), 675.
17. DeLeon, *Four Years in Rebel Capitals*, p. 190.
18. *Harper's Monthly*, XXVI, 675.
19. Henry S. Foote, *Casket of Reminiscences* (reprint ed., New York, 1968), p. 237.
20. Quoted in Bradford, *Confederate Portraits*, pp. 144–45.
21. Varina Howell Davis, *Jefferson Davis Ex-President of the Confederate States of America: A Memoir by his Wife*, 2 vols. (New York, 1890), II, 206–7; Rollen Osterweis, *Judah P. Benjamin: Statesman of the Lost Cause* (New York, 1933); Rembert W. Patrick, *Jefferson Davis and his Cabinet* (Baton Rouge, 1944), pp. 155ff.; Burton J. Hendrick, *Statesmen of the Lost Cause: Jefferson Davis and His Cabinet* (New York, 1939), pp. 153ff.; Robert D. Meade, *Judah P. Benjamin: Confederate Statesman* (New York, 1943); see also his article, "The Relations between Judah P. Benjamin and Jefferson Davis," *Journal of Southern History*, V (1939), 468–78.
22. William Howard Russell, *My Diary North and South* (New York, 1863), p. 176; Bunch to Russell, March 19, 1862, FO 5/843.
23. Bunch to Russell, March 19, 1862, FO 5/843; Cridland to Russell, June 9, 1862, FO 5/846; Molyneux to Russell, May 10, 1862, FO 5/849.
24. Molyneux to Russell, May 10, 1862, FO 5/849; Bunch to Russell, May 29, 1862, FO 5/843.
25. Benjamin to Mason, April 8, 1862, *Official Records of the Union and Confederate Navies in the War of Rebellion* (hereafter cited as *ORN*), 31 vols. (Washington, 1894–1927), 2nd ser., III, 381.
26. Ibid., April 12, pp. 385–86.
27. Benjamin to Slidell, April 8, 1862, James D. Richardson, *A Compilation of the Messages and Papers of Jefferson Davis and the Confederacy*, 2 vols. (Nashville, 1905), II, 216–24.
28. Ibid., pp. 227–33, April 12; Lynn M. Case and Warren F. Spencer, *The United States and France: Civil War Diplomacy* (Philadelphia, 1970), p. 381.
29. Hotze to Hunter, February 28, 1862, *ORN*, 2nd ser., III, 352–54.
30. Bunch to Russell, March 19, 1862, FO 5/843; *Mobile Advertiser and Register*, April 18, 1862.
31. Slidell to Hunter, March 26, 1862, *Messages and Papers of Confederacy*, II, 207–8; ibid., pp. 202–6, Rost to Hunter, March 21, 1862.
32. Slidell to Benjamin, April 14, 1862, Pickett Papers, Library of Congress; *Charleston Daily Courier*, July 11, 19, and 21, 1862; *Southern Confederacy*, July 15, 1862; *Richmond Daily Enquirer*, June 20, 1862; see also *Richmond Dispatch*, June 30, 1862; *Richmond Whig*, July 11, 1862.
33. Dunbar Rowland, *Jefferson Davis Constitutionalist*, 10 vols. (Jackson, 1923), V, 290–91.
34. Benjamin to Slidell, April 12, 1862, *Messages and Papers of Confederacy*, II, 228–33; ibid., pp. 224–25, Benjamin to Mason; Benjamin to DeLeon, April 14, 1862, Pickett Papers; ibid., Browne to Hotze; ibid., Benjamin, Diary, April 12–16, 1862; Charles P. Cullop, *Confederate*

Propaganda in Europe, 1861–1865 (Coral Gables, Fla., 1969), pp. 67ff.; Benjamin to Slidell, July 19, 1862, *Messages and Papers of Confederacy*, II, 267–68.

35. Benjamin Thomas and Harold M. Hyman, *Stanton: The Life and Times of Lincoln's Secretary of War* (New York, 1962), p. 201; *New York Times*, April 12, 1862.

36. Bray Hammond, *Sovereignty and an Empty Purse: Banks and Politics in the Civil War* (Princeton, 1970), p. 246; Frederick W. Seward, *Seward at Washington as Senator and Secretary of State*, 3 vols. (New York, 1891), III, 95ff.

37. Seward to Weed, April 25, 1862, Weed Papers, University of Rochester Library; quoted in David Lindsay, *"Sunset" Cox: Irrepressible Democrat* (Detroit, 1959), pp. 76–77.

38. W. C. Ford, ed., *A Cycle of Adams Letters*, 2 vols. (Boston, 1920), I, 139; *New York Tribune*, May 20 and 22, June 25, 1862.

39. *New York Herald*, July 24, 1862.

40. Thurlow Weed Barnes, *Memoir of Thurlow Weed*, reprint ed. (New York, 1970), pp. 413–19; Weed to Seward, May 8, 1862, Seward Papers, University of Rochester Library.

41. Potter to Seward, May 6, 1862, Seward Papers; DuPont to Wife, June 30, 1862, John D. Hayes, ed., *Samuel Francis DuPont: A Selection from his Civil War Letters*, 3 vols. (Ithaca, 1969), II, 139–41; Fox to DuPont, April 3, 1862, Robert M. Thompson and Richard Wainwright, eds., *The Confidential Correspondence of Gustavus Vasa Fox: Assistant Secretary of the Navy 1861–1865*, 2 vols. (New York, 1920), I, 115.

42. *New York Tribune*, May 22, 1862; *Quebec Morning Chronicle*, July 3, 1862.

43. Adams to Seward, May 23, 1862, Adams Papers, reel 167, Massachusetts Historical Society; John Bigelow, *Retrospections of an Active Life*, 3 vols. (New York, 1909), I, 487; Weed to Seward, April 4, 1862, Seward Papers; ibid., April 8; ibid., April 11; ibid., Sanford to Seward, April 15; ibid., Grinnell to Seward, May 23; ibid., Belmont to Seward, May 15.

44. Seward to Adams, April 1, 1862, NA/M77/77.

45. For the significance of the treaty, a little overstated, see Conway W. Henderson, "The Anglo-American Treaty of 1862 in Civil War Diplomacy," *Civil War History*, XV (1969), 308–19; Seward to Adams, April 4, 1862, NA/M77/77; ibid., June 2.

46. Seward to Weed, April 25, 1862, Weed Papers.

47. Seward to Adams, April 14, 1862, NA/M77/77; ibid., April 2.

48. Sanford to Seward, April 10, 1862, Seward Papers; ibid., Weed to Seward, April 11.

49. Ibid., Seward to Chase on Sanford to Seward, April 10, 1862.

50. Ibid., Weed to Seward, April 15, 1862; Case and Spencer, *United States and France*, pp. 286–94; Weed to Seward, April 18, 1862, Seward Papers; ibid., April 21; ibid., Sanford to Seward, April 22; ibid., Bigelow to Seward, April 28.

51. *New York Times,* April 29, 1862; Lyons to Russell, May 1, 1862, FO5/829.

52. Bigelow, *Retrospections,* I, 489; Lyons to Russell, May 6, 1862, FO5/829.

53. Seward to Dayton, May 5, 1862, *Papers Relating to Foreign Affairs,* 1862 (Washington, 1862), p. 377; see also ibid., p. 88, Seward to Adams, May 12.

54. Frederic Bancroft, *The Life of William H. Seward,* 2 vols. (reprint ed., Worcester, 1967), II, 328–29; Adam Gurowski, *Diary,* 1862 (Boston, 1863), pp. 218–19; Seward to Adams, May 28, 1862, NA/M77/77; see also Kinley J. Brauer, "The Slavery Problem in the Diplomacy of the American Civil War," *Pacific Historical Review,* XLVI (1977), 439–69.

55. Seward to Adams, June 9, 1862, Adams Papers, reel 559; *New York Times,* June 11, 1862.

56. Lyons to Minna (sister), May 6, 1862, Lyons Papers, Arundel Castle, Sussex; ibid., May 16; ibid., June 6; ibid., June 9; ibid., Lyons to Russell, June 13.

57. Ibid., Lyons to Milne, June 8, 1862; Frederick W. Seward, *Reminiscences of a War-Time Statesman and Diplomat 1830–1915* (New York, 1916), pp. 206–8; *Seward at Washington,* III, 100; Gurowski, *Diary,* 1862, pp. 233–34.

58. Allan Nevins, ed., *Diary of the Civil War, 1860–1865, George Templeton Strong* (New York, 1962), pp. 237–38.

59. *Seward at Washington,* III, 114; Seward to Weed, July 9, 1862, Weed Papers.

60. *Seward at Washington,* III, 111, 104–110; Seward, *Reminiscences,* pp. 206–8; Seward to Dayton, August 23, 1862, NA/M77/56.

61. *Seward at Washington,* III, 115–16; Seward to Adams, July 5, 1862, NA/M77/77.

TWO   The Neutral

1. Dudley to Seward, May 10, 1862, NA/M141/20.

2. *Adams Letters,* I, 140.

3. Donaldson Jordan and Edwin J. Pratt, *Europe and the American Civil War* (New York, 1931), pp. 76ff.; James Pope-Hennessy, *Monckton Milnes: The Flight of Youth 1851–1885* (New York, 1951), pp. 165–68; Charles E. Shain, "The English Novelists and the American Civil War," *American Quarterly,* XIV (1962), 399–421; Moncure Daniel Conway, *Autobiography: Memories and Experiences,* 2 vols. (reprint ed., New York, 1970), I, 407.

4. *Macmillan's Magazine,* VI (1862), 97–107; R. K. Webb, *Harriet Martineau: A Radical Victorian* (New York, 1960), pp. 327ff.

5. *Macmillan's Magazine,* VI, 408–20.

6. Ibid., p. 420.

7. Jordan and Pratt, *Europe and the American Civil War,* p. 75; Spence to Mason, April 28, 1862, *ORN,* 2nd ser., III, 402–4.

8. Quoted in Shain, "English Novelists," p. 399.

9. Conway, *Autobiography*, II, 15.
10. Francis E. Mineka and Dwight N. Lindley, eds., *Later Letters of John Stuart Mill 1849–1873* (Toronto, 1972), vol. XV of *Collected Works of John Stuart Mill*, 17 vols. (Toronto, 1965–72), 783, Mill to Cairnes, June 15, 1862; ibid., p. 784, June 24; ibid., p. 787, Mill to Fawcett, July 21; ibid., pp. 788–89, Mill to Chapman, August 10; *Daily News*, June 11, 14, 17, 1862.
11. *Westminster Review*, n. s., XXII (1862), 489–510.
12. Adelaide Weinberg, *John Elliot Cairnes and the American Civil War: A Study in Anglo-American Relations* (London, 1970), p. 39; ibid., pp. 133–36, Cairnes to Sarah Blake Shaw, July 15, 1862; Chesson to Garrison, January 9, 1863, Clare Taylor, ed., *British and American Abolitionists: An Episode in Transatlantic Understanding* (Edinburgh, 1974), pp. 493–94.
13. Joseph Hatton, *Journalists London* (London, 1882), p. 53; see also Frederick M. Thomas, ed., *Fifty Years of Fleet Street: Being the Life and Recollections of Sir John R. Robinson* (London, 1904), pp. 139–41; Thomas J. McCormack, *Memoirs of Gustave Koerner 1809–1896*, 2 vols. (Cedar Rapids, 1909), II, 233.
14. Taylor, *British and American Abolitionists*, pp. 471, 476; *Anti-Slavery Advocate*, May 1, 1862; *Anti-Slavery Reporter*, April 1, May 1, 1862.
15. Joseph M. Hernon Jr., "British Sympathies in the American Civil War: A Reconsideration," *Journal of Southern History*, XXXIII (1967), 365; Smith, "British Sympathy with America," *American Presbyterian Review* (1862), p. 509; Kevin J. Logan, "The *Bee-Hive* Newspaper and British Working Class Attitudes toward the American Civil War," *Civil War History*, XXII (1976), 347; Spence to Mason, April 28, 1862, J. M. Mason Papers, Library of Congress.
16. *Bee-Hive*, October 11, November 8, 1862; *Illustrated London News*, June 14, 1862; Hotze to Hunter, March 11, 1862, *ORN*, 2nd ser., III, 360–63; D. G. Wright, "Leeds Politics and the American Civil War," *Northern History*, IX (1974), 96–122; idem., "Bradford and the American Civil War," *Journal of British Studies*, XIII (1969), 64–85; C. Collyer, "Gladstone and the American Civil War," *Leeds Philosophical and Literary Society, Proceedings*, VI (1951), 583–94; Robert L. Reid, ed., "William E. Gladstone's 'Insincere Neutrality' during the Civil War," *Civil War History*, XV (1969), 293–307; Arnold Whitridge, "British Liberals and the American Civil War," *History Today*, XII (1962), 688–95; Hernon, "British Sympathies in the American Civil War," pp. 356–67; Pope-Hennessy, *Flight of Youth*, p. 168; *Spectator*, April 26, 1862.
17. Hotze to Hunter, March 11, 1862, *ORN*, 2nd ser., III, 360–63; ibid., pp. 399–401, Hotze to Benjamin, April 25.
18. Stephen B. Oates, "Henry Hotze: Confederate Agent Abroad," *Historian*, XXVII (1965), 131–45; see also Cullop, *Confederate Propaganda*.
19. Hotze to Hunter, March 18, 1862, *ORN*, 2nd ser., III, 363;

ibid., pp. 399–401, Hotze to Benjamin, April 25; ibid., p. 371, Hotze to Hunter, March 24; Hotze to Mason, December 12, 1862, Pickett Papers.

20. Hotze to Benjamin, May 15, 1862, *ORN*, 2nd ser., III, 423–24; *Saturday Review*, August 2, 1862.

21. *Index*, May 15 and 8, July 3, 1862.

22. Ibid., May 22.

23. Harold Herd, *The March of Journalism: The Story of the British Press from 1622 to the Present Day* (London, 1952), p. 167; Hugh Brogan, ed., *The Times Reports the American Civil War: Extracts from The Times 1860–1865* (London, 1975), xix; Adams to Seward, January 12, 1865, Adams Papers, reel 172.

24. James H. Winter, *Robert Lowe* (Toronto, 1976), p. 129.

25. November 10, 1862.

26. *Morning Star*, May 16, 1863; Brogan, *Times Reports the Civil War*, xviii; George S. Wykoff, "Charles Mackay: England's Forgotten Civil War Correspondent," *South Atlantic Quarterly*, XXVI (1927), 50–62.

27. Morris to Mackay, April 8, 1862, Mowbrey Morris Papers, New Printing House Square, London; ibid., April 17.

28. Brogan, *Times Reports the Civil War*, xviii; *New York Times*, August 19, 1863; Morris to Mackay, April 25, 1865, Morris Papers.

29. Charles C. F. Greville, *The Greville Memoirs*, 3rd pt., 2 vols. (London, 1887), II, 172; see also Brian Jenkins, "Frank Lawley and the Confederacy," *Civil War History*, XXIII (1977), 144–60;

Morris to Lawley, July 26, 1862, Morris Papers.

30. Lawley to Gregory, December 12, 1857, Gregory Papers; ibid., October 23, 1861; ibid., January 21, 1862; ibid., January 23.

31. Ibid., Mason to Gregory, November 8; ibid., December 18.

32. Adams, Diary, March 3, 1864, Adams Papers, reel 77; Morris to Lawley, October 10, 1862, Morris Papers; ibid., September 24, 1863; ibid., Morris to Mackay, March 19.

33. Conway, *Autobiography*, I, 375; Benjamin F. Butler, *Butler's Book: Autobiography and Personal Reminiscences* (Boston, 1892), p. 426; Robert S. Holzman, "Ben Butler in the Civil War," *New England Quarterly*, XXX (1957), 334.

34. *Private and Official Correspondence of General Benjamin F. Butler during the Period of the Civil War*, 5 vols. (Norwood, Mass., 1917), I, 450–52, 469–71; Daniel B. Carroll, *Henri Mercier and the American Civil War* (Princeton, 1971), pp. 186–89; Robert S. Holzman, *Stormy Ben Butler* (reprint ed., New York, 1961), pp. 79–90; Gordon Wright, "Economic conditions in the Confederacy as seen by the French Consuls," *Journal of Southern History*, VII (1941), 195–214; Clifford L. Egan, "Friction in New Orleans: General Butler versus the Spanish Consul," *Louisiana History*, IX (1968), 43–52; Gerald M. Capers, "Confederates and Yankees in Occupied New Orleans, 1862–1865," *Journal of Southern History*, XXX (1964), 405–26; Lyons to Russell, May

30, 1862, FO 5/830; ibid., June 3, FO 5/831.

35. Lyons to Russell, June 3, 1862, FO 5/831; Butler, *Butler's Book*, p. 426.

36. *Private and Official Correspondence of Butler*, I, 490.

37. Quoted in Capers, "Confederates and Yankees," p. 414.

38. Butler, *Butler's Book*, p. 415; Holzman, *Stormy Ben Butler*, p. 92.

39. Bright to Sumner, February 27, 1862, "Bright-Sumner Letters," *Massachusetts Historical Society, Proceedings* (hereafter cited as *MHSP*), XLVI (1912–13), 104; *Spectator*, May 17, 1862; *Manchester Guardian*, May 13 and 27, 1862; *Spectator*, June 14, 1862.

40. *Macmillan's Magazine*, VII (1863), 234–35; Norman St. John Stevas, *Collected Works of Walter Bagehot*, 9 vols. (London, 1968), IV, 363–64; Whitridge, "British Liberals," pp. 688–95.

41. Jasper Ridley, *Lord Palmerston* (London, 1970), p. 477; see also Patricia Thompson, *The Victorian Heroine: A Changing Ideal 1837–1873* (London, 1956); J. A. and Olive Banks, *Feminism and Family Planning in Victorian England* (New York, 1964); *Saturday Review*, June 14, 1862.

42. *Parl. Debates*, 3rd ser., CLXVII, 533; Owsley, *King Cotton*, pp. 296–97; Holzman, *Stormy Ben Butler*, p. 95.

43. Gregory to Miles, April 9, 1863, William Porcher Miles Papers, Southern Historical Collection; Brian Jenkins, "William Gregory Champion of the Confederacy,"

History Today, XXVIII (1978), 322–30; Shain, "The English Novelists," p. 407.

44. Gregory to his mother, October 29, 1859, Gregory Papers; ibid., November 26; ibid., December 14; ibid., December 25.

45. Ibid., December 14; Albert A. Woldman, *Lincoln and the Russians* (reprint ed., New York, 1961), p. 99.

46. *Parl. Debates*, 3rd ser., CLXVII, 616, 535.

47. Adams, Diary, July 8, 1864, Adams Papers, reel 78.

48. Palmerston to Adams, June 11, 1862, Broadlands Mss., Historical Manuscripts Commission, London.

49. Adams to Palfrey, June 13, 1862, Adams Papers, reel 559; ibid., reel 77, Adams, Diary, May 26, 1862.

50. *Illustrated London News*, May 17, 1862.

51. Adams, Diary, May 3, 1862, Adams Papers, reel 77; ibid., reel 167, Adams to Everett, May 2; ibid., reel 77, Adams, Diary, May 10; ibid., May 3.

52. Ibid., reel 167, Adams to Seward, June 12; ibid., June 13; Sarah Agnes Wallace and Frances Elma Gillespie, *The Journal of Benjamin Moran*, 2 vols. (Chicago, 1949), II, 1029 (hereafter cited as *Moran Journal*).

53. Palmerston to Adams, June 15, 1862, Broadlands Mss.; ibid., Russell to Palmerston, June 13; ibid., Adams to Palmerston, June 16.

54. Ibid., Adams to Palmerston, June 20.

THREE   A Policy of Postponement

1. Cobden to Wilson, July 12, 1862, George Wilson Papers, Manchester Central Reference Library.

2. A. Tilney Bassett, ed., *Gladstone to his Wife* (London, 1936), p. 170; Palmerston to Russell, June 14, 1862, PRO 30/22/14C; Russell to Palmerston, June 18, 1862, Broadlands Mss.; Evelyn Ashley, *The Life and Correspondence of Henry John Temple, Viscount Palmerston*, 2 vols. (London, 1879), II, 224–25.

3. Russell to Queen, April 1, 1862, *Letters of Queen Victoria*, 2nd ser., I, 28; ibid., p. 31, June 1.

4. Cowley to Russell, May 13, 1862, PRO 30/22/57; Cowley to Layard, June 20, 1862, BM Add Ms. 39103.

5. Clarendon to Cowley, May 17, 1862, FO 519/178; Palmerston to Somerset, June 1, 1862, Somerset Papers, Buckinghamshire Record Office, Aylesbury; Russell to Palmerston, March 31, 1862, Broadlands Mss.

6. Brian Jenkins, *Britain and the War for the Union*, 2 vols. (Montreal, 1974–80), I, 97; Russell to Palmerston, March 31, 1862, Broadlands Mss.; Clarendon to Cowley, May 17, 1862, FO 519/178; Clarendon to Hammond, April 28, 1862, FO 391/4.

7. Argyll to Gladstone, April 29, 1862, BM Add. Ms. 44099; ibid., May 13; ibid., May 15, Gladstone to Argyll.

8. Quoted in Wilbur D. Jones, "Blyden, Gladstone and the Civil War," *Journal of Negro History*, XLIX (1964), 57.

9. Russell to Lyons, May 1, 1862, FO 5/819.

10. Palmerston to Russell, April 25, 1862, PRO 30/22/14C; Douglas Lorimer, "The Role of Anti-Slavery Sentiment in the English Reaction to the American Civil War," *Historical Journal*, XIX (1976), 407–8.

11. Russell to Lyons, May 17, 1862, Lyons Papers; Mann to Gregory, September 12, 1862, Gregory Papers; ibid., November 11; Clarendon to Cowley, May 17, 1862, FO 519/178; Palmerston to Russell, June 13, 1862, PRO 30/22/22.

12. Palmerston memorandum, June 19, 1862, BM Add. Ms. 38988.

13. Gladstone address, April 23, 1862, BM Add. Ms. 44690; Wood to Palmerston, May 13, 1862, Broadlands Mss.

14. Russell to Lyons, May 23, 1862, FO 5/819; Board of Trade to FO, June 6, 1862, FO 5/924.

15. Russell to Lyons, May 31, 1862, Lyons Papers; ibid., FO/819.

16. W. O. Henderson, "Charles Pelham Villiers," *History*, XXXVII (1952), 34–39.

17. Villiers to Delane, May, 1862. Delane Papers, New Printing House Square, London; *Parl. Debates*, 3rd ser. CLXVI, 1490–1521.

18. June 21, 1862; *Parl. Debates*, 3rd ser., CLXVII, 754–93.

19. Peter Harnetty, *Imperialism and Free Trade: Lancashire and India in the Mid-Nineteenth Century* (Vancouver, 1972), p. 43; Hammond to Layard, July 6, 1862, BM Add. Ms. 38951.

20. May 7, 1862; *Manchester Guardian*, April 30, 1862; *Spectator*, April 19, 1862.

21. May 6, 1862.

22. Derek Hudson, ed., *Munby: A Man of Two Worlds: The Life and Diaries of Arthur J. Munby 1828–1910*, paper ed. (London, 1974), p. 129; Michael Anderson, *Family Structure in Nineteenth-Century Lancashire* (Cambridge, 1971), pp. 22ff.

23. Anderson, *Family Structure*, pp. 137ff.

24. *Cornhill Magazine*, VI (1862), 44; *Parl. Debates*, 3rd ser., CLXVI, 1494; Henderson, "Villiers," p. 35; *Cornhill*, VI, 51.

25. *British Parliamentary Papers: Report from the Select Committee on Poor Relief and Poor Removal 1862–1879* (Shannon, 1970), *Poor Law*, XXVI, 159.

26. *Times*, June 2, 1862.

27. Rhodes Boyson, *The Ashworth Cotton Enterprise* (Oxford, 1970), pp. 66ff.; Diary of James Garnett, May 27, 1862, Manchester Central Reference Library.

28. Boyson, *Ashworth Enterprise*, p. 80; Mary Ellison, *Support for Secession: Lancashire and the American Civil War* (London, 1973), p. 86; W. O. Henderson, *The Lancashire Cotton Famine 1861–1865*, rev. ed. (Manchester, 1969), p. 14.

29. Quoted in Eric M. Sigsworth, *Black Dyke Mills: A History* (Liverpool, 1958), pp. 73–74, 202.

30. Francis E. Hyde, *Liverpool and the Mersey: An Economic History of a Port 1700–1870* (Newton Abbot, 1971), pp. 48–49, 98–99; Sheila Marriner, *Rathbones of Liverpool 1845–1873* (Liverpool, 1961), pp. 22, 77–78, 15–17.

31. Marriner, *Rathbones of Liverpool*, pp. 15–17; Peter Payne and Frank J. Merli, eds., "A Blockade-Running Charter: Spring, 1862," *American Neptune*, XXVI (1966), 134–37; Russell to Adams, May 18, 1862, FO/851; Hammond to Layard, June 12, 1862, BM Add. Ms. 38951; Horsfall to Russell, July 2, 1862, FO 5/862; ibid., Russell to Horsfall, July 5.

32. Henderson, *Cotton Famine*, p. 8; D. A. Farnie, *The English Cotton Industry and the World Market 1815–1896* (Oxford, 1979), p. 148; Earle to Disraeli, October 24, 1862, B/XX/E/263, Disraeli Papers, Hughenden Manor, Bucks.

33. *Parl. Debates*, 3rd ser., CLXVI, 446–92, 637–57.

34. Ellison, *Support for Secession*, pp. 135, 138–39, 116; *Reynolds's Newspaper*, June 1, 1862.

35. Henderson, *Cotton Famine*, p. 2; *Manchester Guardian*, June 13, 1862.

36. *Morning Star*, May 27 and 28, June 13, 1862; Garnett, Diary, July 16, 1862.

37. *Daily News*, June 13, 1862.

38. *Standard*, May 8, 1862; see also *Morning Herald*, May 7, 1862; *Standard*, May 28, June 11, 1862.

39. *Morning Post*, May 12, 1862.

40. Ibid., June 14; *Times*, June 14, 1862.

41. *Spectator*, June 14, 1862.

42. *Morning Herald*, June 17, 1862; *Standard*, June 17, 1862; *Morning Herald*, June 25 and 27, 1862.

FOUR   Home Intervention

1. A. Corbin to Corbin, March 17, 1862, F. P. Corbin Papers, Duke University; Slidell to Benjamin, April 18, 1862, J. P. Benjamin Papers, Museum of the Confederacy, Richmond.
2. Slidell to Benjamin, June 1, 1862, *Messages and Papers of Confederacy*, II, 254–56.
3. Spence to Mason, June 3, 1862, Mason Papers.
4. Ibid., June 11; ibid., June 13; ibid., June 18, Lindsay to Mason; Lindsay to Layard, June 18, 1862, BM Add. Ms. 38988.
5. Slidell to Mason, June 29, 1862, Mason Papers; ibid., May 27; ibid., June 1; ibid., June 6; ibid., June 14; ibid., June 17; Mason to Benjamin, June 23, 1862, *Messages and Papers of Confederacy*, II, 256–59.
6. *Morning Post*, June 30, 1862.
7. John Watts, *Facts of the Cotton Famine* (reprint ed., London, 1968), p. 116; Garnett, Diary, June 28, July 4, 1862; *Economist*, July 5, 1862.
8. Adams, Diary, June 29, 1862, Adams Papers, reel 77; Cobden to Bright, July 12, 1862, BM Add. Ms. 43652; Cobden to Sumner, July 11, 1862, "Letters of Richard Cobden to Charles Sumner," *American Historical Review*, II (1897), 306–7; Argyll to Sumner, July 12, 1862, "Sumner-Argyll Letters," *MHSP*, XLVII (1913), 99; Bright to Sumner, July 14, 1862, ibid., XLVI (1912), 107.
9. Bright to Elizabeth Bright, June 21, 1862, Bright Papers, University College, London; ibid., June 23; ibid., July 20; ibid., July 21;

ibid., February 2, 1863; ibid., July 19; ibid., July 22; ibid., March 4, 1865; ibid., July 27, 1862; Bright to Sumner, July 14, 1862, *MHSP*, XLVI, 107; Bright to Wilson, June 27, 1862, Wilson Papers.
10. *Reynolds's Newspaper*, July 6, 1862; *Manchester Guardian*, July 5, 1862; *Morning Star*, July 2, 1862; *Manchester Guardian*, June 30, 1862.
11. Ellison, *Support for Secession*, p. 118; Watts, *Cotton Famine*, pp. 130–31; *Manchester Guardian*, August 6 and 13, 1862.
12. Boyson, *Ashworth Enterprise*, pp. 233–35.
13. Garnett, Diary, July 11, 1862; Frenise A. Logan, "India—Britain's Substitute for American Cotton," *Journal of Southern History*, XXIV (1958), 476; *Times*, July 17, 1862.
14. *Edinburgh Review*, CXIV (1862), 478–509; *Times*, July 3 and 17, 1862; "Minutes and Proceedings of the Manchester Chamber of Commerce," Board of Directors, July 16, 1862, Local History Library, Manchester Central Reference Library.
15. Palmerston memorandum, July 13, 1862, Broadlands Mss.
16. *Parl. Debates*, 3rd ser., CLXVII, 1073.
17. *Index*, July 10 and 17, 1862.
18. *Morning Herald*, July 16, 1862; *Reynolds's Newspaper*, July 20 and 27, 1862; *Morning Post*, July 15, 1862.
19. Spence to Mason, July 11, 1862, Mason Papers.
20. Adams to Seward, July 17, 1862, *Papers Relating to Foreign*

Affairs, 1862, pp. 137; Ephraim Douglass Adams, *Great Britain and the American Civil War* (reprint ed., New York, 1958), II, 20; Spence to Gregory, July 14, 1862, Gregory Papers.

21. Adams to Seward, July 11, 1862, *Papers Relating to Foreign Affairs*, 1862, p. 133; Adams, Diary, July 14, 1862, Adams Papers, reel 77; ibid., July 17; *Adams Letters*, I, 167–69.

22. Adams to Weed, July 18, 1862, Adams Papers, reel 168; Adams to Seward, July 17, 1862, *Papers Relating to Foreign Affairs*, 1862, pp. 139–40; *Adams Letters*, I, 167–69.

23. Moran to Dudley, June 17, 1862, Thomas H. Dudley Papers, Huntington Library; Thayer to Seward, July 19, 1862, Seward Papers; Adams, Diary, July 18, 1862, Adams Papers, reel 77.

24. *Moran Journal*, II, 1040–44; *Parl. Debates*, 3rd ser., CLXVIII, 511–78; Brian Connell, *Regina v Palmerston* (London, 1962), p. 329.

25. *Parl. Debates*, 3rd ser., CLXVIII, 522–27, 534–38; Cobden to Wilson, July 12, 1862, Wilson Papers; *Morning Star*, July 14, 1862; *Moran Journal*, II, 1041–42; Cobden to Hargreaves, July 19, 1862, BM Add. Ms. 43655; Adams to Seward, July 19, 1862, Adams Papers, reel 168.

26. Virginia Mason, *The Public Life and Diplomatic Correspondence of James M. Mason* (Roanoke, 1903), p. 342; Earle to Disraeli, July 31, 1862, B/XX/E/254, Disraeli Papers.

27. Wilbur D. Jones, "The British Conservatives and the American Civil War," *American Historical Review*, LXVIII (1952–53),

522–23.

28. Derby to Disraeli, n.d., B/XX/5/305, Disraeli Papers; *Moran Journal*, II, 1043.

29. *Moran Journal*, II, 1044; biographical sketch of Palmerston in W. S. Lindsay Papers; Palmerston to Queen, July 19, 1862, *Regina v Palmerston*, p. 329.

30. Adams, Diary, July 19, 1862, Adams Papers, reel 77.

31. Slidell to Mason, July 11, 1862, Mason Papers; ibid., July 20; Slidell to Thouvenel, July 21, 1862, *Messages and Papers of Confederacy*, II, 272–89; ibid., George Eustis Papers, Library of Congress; see also Owsley, *King Cotton*, pp. 310–13; Case and Spencer, *United States and France*, pp. 300–6.

32. Slidell to Mason, July 16, 1862, Mason Papers; ibid., July 20.

33. Ibid., July 23; Slidell to Benjamin, July 25, 1862, *Messages and Papers of Confederacy*, II, 268–72; Case and Spencer, *United States and France*, pp. 306–9.

34. Quoted in Charles W. Hallberg, *Franz Joseph and Napoleon 1852–1864: A Study of Austro-French Relations* (reprint ed., New York, 1973), pp. 275, 269–274.

35. Russell to Stuart, July 19, 1862, PRO 30/22/96; Hammond to Layard, July 18, 1862, BM Add. Ms. 38951.

36. Russell to Stuart, July 19, 1862, PRO 30/22/96; Palmerston to Queen, July 14, 1862, *Regina v Palmerston*, p. 328; *Punch*, August 2, 1862.

37. *Parl. Debates*, 3rd ser., CLXVIII, 285–90.

38. *Times*, July 23, 1862.

39. *Parl. Debates*, 3rd ser., CLXVIII, 682–700, 739–78, 931–64, 1000–

35, 1039–55, 1079–83, 1159–74; see also Villiers, memorandum on Union Relief Bill, PRO 30/22/25; Villiers to Palmerston, July, 1862, Broadlands Mss.; Ridley, *Palmerston*, p. 5.

40. *Reynolds's Newspaper*, July 27, 1862; *Standard*, July 31, 1862; *Spectator*, August 2, 1862.

41. *Morning Post*, July 25, 1862; Hargreaves to Cobden, August 4, 1862, Cobden Papers, vol. 7, West Sussex Record Office, Chichester; *Morning Herald*, July 23 and 29, 1862; *Standard*, July 29 and 30, 1862; *Reynolds's Newspaper*, August 10, 1862.

42. *Morning Herald*, June 14 and 27, 1862.

43. *Parl. Debates*, 3rd ser., CLXVIII, 479–97.

44. *Morning Post*, July 14, 1862; *Times*, June 6, 1862; *Morning Herald*, July 14, 1862; Diary of William Howard Russell, June 20, 1862, Russell Papers, New Printing House Square, London; *Parl. Debates*, 3rd ser., CLXVIII, 853.

45. *Parl. Debates*, 3rd ser., CLXVIII, 853.

46. Russell to Lyons, January 18, 1862, FO 5/1089A; Lyons to Russell, May 8, 1862, FO 5/829; R. F. Sams, "The Congressional Attitude towards Canada during the 1860s" (M.A. thesis, Queen's University, 1947), pp. 21–28; Newcastle to Monck, July 26, 1862, Newcastle Papers, University of Nottingham Library.

47. Rose to Ellice, May 23, 1862, Edward Ellice Papers, A/12, microfilm, Public Archives of Canada (hereafter cited as PAC).

48. Monck to Newcastle, May 30, 1862, Newcastle Papers, A/308, microfilm, PAC; Newcastle to Monck, June 14, 1862, Newcastle Papers, Nottingham.

49. Monck to Newcastle, June 13, 1862, A/308, PAC; ibid., June 27; Newcastle to Monck, July 26, 1862, Newcastle Papers, Nottingham.

50. *Parl. Debates*, 3rd ser., CLXVIII, 486–93; Newcastle to Monck, July 26, 1862, Newcastle Papers, Nottingham; *Parl. Debates*, 3rd ser., CLXVIII, 875.

51. *Moran Journal*, II, 1031; Lyons to Russell, June 9, 1862, PRO 30/22/36; ibid., May 16; Lyons to Stuart, July 12, 1862, Lyons Papers; ibid., July 19; ibid., Lyons to Minna; ibid., July 21; ibid., Lyons to Stuart, July 25.

52. Stuart to Lyons, June 30, 1862, Lyons Papers; ibid., July 21; Stuart to Russell, July 1, 1862, PRO 30/22/36; ibid., July 4; ibid., July 15; ibid., July 21.

53. Adams, *Great Britain and the American Civil War*, II, 97; Russell to Palmerston, July 24, 1862, Broadlands Mss.; Lyons to Stuart, July 29, 1862, Lyons Papers.

54. Russell memorandum, July 31, 1862, Broadlands Mss.; Argyll to Gladstone, August 6, 1862, BM Add. Ms. 44099; Russell to Mason, August 2, 1862, *Messages and Papers of Confederacy*, II, 307–9.

55. Mason, *Life of Mason*, p. 280; Mason to Benjamin, August 4, 1862, *Messages and Papers of Confederacy*, II, 295–96; Hotze to Benjamin, August 4, 1862, *ORN*, 2nd ser., III, 505–6.

56. *Moran Journal*, II, 1055; *Parl. Debates*, 3rd ser., CLXVIII, 1184–85.

57. Cobden to Bright, August 7, 1862, BM Add. Ms. 43652; Glad-

stone memorandum, July 31, 1862, Philip Guedalla, *Gladstone and Palmerston* (London, 1928), pp. 230–31; Hotze to Gregory, August 1, 1862, Gregory Papers; Hotze to Benjamin, August 4, 1862, *ORN*, 2nd ser., III, 506; Gladstone to Argyll, August 3, 1862, George Douglas, Eighth Earl of Argyll, *Autobiography and Memoirs*, 2 vols. (London, 1906), II, 191; Donald Southgate, '*The Most English Minister* . . .': *The Policies and Politics of Palmerston* (London, 1966), p. 495; H. F. C. Bell, *Lord Palmerston*, 2 vols. (London, 1936), II, 327; Adams, *Great Britain and the American Civil War*, II, 32; Russell to Stuart, August 8, 1862, PRO 30/22/96; Hotze to Gregory, August 1, 1862, Gregory Papers.

58. Argyll to Gladstone, August 6, 1862, BM Add. Ms. 44099.

FIVE   The Cause of Freedom

1. *Seward at Washington*, III, 123.
2. T. C. Pease and J. G. Randall, eds., *Diary of Orville Hickman Browning*, 2 vols. (Springfield, Ill., 1927–33), I, 563–64; Seward to Adams, July 18, 1862, NA/ M77/77; Stuart to Russell, July 28, 1862, FO 5/834; ibid., October 6, FO 5/837.
3. *Seward at Washington*, III, 123; Stuart to Russell, August 12, 1862, Adm 1/5799; ibid., Seward to Welles, October 31; J. P. Baxter 3rd, "Some British Opinions as to Neutral Rights 1861–1865," *American Journal of International Law*, XXIII (1929), 517.
4. Herbert Mitgang, *Spectator in America* (Chicago, 1971), p. 100; John Niven, *Gideon Welles: Lincoln's Secretary of the Navy* (New York, 1973), pp. 318–19.
5. Howard K. Beale, *Diary of Gideon Welles*, 3 vols. (New York, 1960), I, 79–80, 131–39, 154–55; Niven, *Gideon Welles*, pp. 452–54.
6. Caleb Huse to Slidell, February 19, 1863, Eustis Papers; J.

Thomas Scharf, *History of the Confederate States Navy*, 2 vols. (reprint ed., New York, 1969), II, 473; Richard Drysdale, "Blockade Running from Nassau," *History Today*, XXVII (1977), 332–37; Frank E. Vandiver, ed., *The Civil War Diary of General Josiah Gorgas* (University, Ala., 1947), p. 86; Bayley to Newcastle, October 23, 1862, FO 5/867; Ord to Newcastle, April 21, 1863, CO 37/18; ibid., June 14, 1864.

7. *Cornhill Magazine*, VI, 474; Drysdale, "Blockade Running," pp. 334–35.
8. Law Officers (LO) to Russell, September 25, 1863, FO 83/2219; ibid., August 6, 1862, FO 83/2214.
9. Russell memorandum, September 16, 1862, FO 83/2214.
10. Brainerd Dyer, "Thomas H. Dudley," *Civil War History*, I (1955), 401–13; William W. Wade, "The Man who Stopped the Rams," *American Heritage*, XIV (1963), 18–22, 78–81.

11. Morgan to Board of Customs, February 21, 1862, FO 5/1313.
12. Ibid., Russell memorandum, March 26.
13. Ibid., Liverpool Collector to Board of Customs, April 4; Bayley to Newcastle, June 21, 1862, CO 23/169; see also Douglas H. Maynard, "The Escape of the *Florida*," *Pennsylvania Magazine of History and Biography*, LXXVII (1953), 181–97.
14. Hyde, *Liverpool and the Mersey*, pp. 52–53.
15. *Moran Journal*, II, 1023–24.
16. *New York Times*, September 16, 1862; Douglas H. Maynard, "Plotting the escape of the *Alabama*," *Journal of Southern History*, XX (1954), 197–209; James D. Bulloch, *The Secret Service of the Confederate States in Europe* (reprint ed., New York, 1959), pp. 227–39; see also Rupert C. Jarvis, "The *Alabama* and the Law," *Transactions of the Historical Society of Lancashire and Cheshire*, CXI (1959), 181–98.
17. Adams to Dudley, July 12, 1862, Dudley Papers; *Moran Journal*, II, 1023.
18. Roundell Palmer, Earl of Selborne, *Memorials Family and Personal 1766–1865*, 2 vols. (London, 1896), II, 411; Frank J. Merli, *Great Britain and the Confederate Navy 1861–1865* (Bloomington, 1970), p. 91.
19. Palmer, *Memorials*, II, 411.
20. See Collier's opinion, July 23, 1862, *Papers Relating to Foreign Affairs*, 1862, p. 152.
21. Gordon Waterfield, *Layard of Nineveh* (London, 1963), pp. 228–30; Arnold C. Brackman, *The Luck of Nineveh* (New York, 1978), p. 275.

22. Blandford to James, March 29, 1893, Selborne Papers, 2499, Lambeth Palace Library, London; Phillimore to Palmerston, August 1, 1862, Broadlands Mss.
23. Hammond to Layard, June 12, 1862, BM Add. Ms. 38951; Walter to Selborne, March 24, 1893, Selborne Papers, 2499; Hammond to Layard, July 10, 1862, BM Add. Ms. 38951; Squarry to Adams, July 23, 1862, *Papers Relating to Foreign Affairs*, 1862, p. 153.
24. Layard to Selborne, March 31, 1893, Selborne Papers, 2499; Douglas H. Maynard, "Efforts to Prevent the Escape of the *Alabama*," *Mississippi Valley Historical Review*, XLI (1954–55), 54, n. 52; Palmer, *Memorials*, II, 420–25; LO to Russell, July 29, 1862, FO 83/2214; Russell to Layard, July 30, 1862, BM Add. Ms. 38988.
25. Russell to Stuart, August 2, 1862, FO 5/1313; Bayley to Newcastle, June 21, 1862, CO 23/169.
26. Notation by F. Rogers on Bayley to Newcastle, CO 23/169.
27. Russell to Layard, August 1, 1862, BM Add. Ms. 38988; FO to CO, August 14, 1862, FO 5/1313.
28. Bayley to Newcastle, August 11, 1862, FO 5/1313; Merli, *Britain and Confederate Navy*, pp. 71–72.
29. *Congressional Globe*, 37th Cong., 2nd sess., pt. 4, 3325, 3335–37; Gurowski, *Diary*, 1862, p. 287; E. L. Pierce, *Memoir and Letters of Charles Sumner*, 4 vols. (London, 1893), IV, 120.
30. Stuart to Russell, August 16, 1862, FO 5/835.
31. Fox to Porter, September 6,

1862, *Confidential Correspondence of Fox*, I, 135; ibid., p. 373, Fox to Lardner, September 9.

32. *Welles Diary*, I, 73–74; Geoffrey Smith, "Charles Wilkes and the Growth of American Naval Diplomacy," in Frank J. Merli and Theodore A. Wilson, eds., *Makers of American Diplomacy: From Benjamin Franklin to Henry Kissinger* (New York, 1974), p. 155; Gurowski, *Diary*, 1862, p. 269.

33. *Welles Diary*, I, 73–74, 86–87; Welles to Wilkes, September 8, 1862, *ORN*, 1st ser., I, 470–71.

34. *ORN*, 1st ser., II, 54–56, Wilkes to Welles, January 23, 1863; *Welles Diary*, I, 74.

35. Wilkes, Diary, 1862, vol. 10, Library of Congress.

36. James M. McPherson, *The Struggle for Equality: Abolitionists and the Negro in the Civil War and Reconstruction* (Princeton, 1964), pp. 52ff.; Louis M. Starr, *Reporting the Civil War* (reprint ed., New York, 1962), pp. 8off.; *Brownson's Quarterly Review*, XXIV (1862), 373–93.

37. *Brownson's Quarterly Review*, XXIV (1862), 395; *New York Tribune*, July 12 and 22, August 1, 5, and 11, 1862.

38. *Diary of Browning*, I, 558; Hans L. Trefousse, *The Radical Republicans: Lincoln's Vanguard for Racial Justice* (Baton Rouge, 1968), pp. 224, 223; Thomas and Hyman, *Stanton*, p. 237.

39. *Welles Diary*, I, 70–71; Albert Mordell, ed., *Civil War and Reconstruction: Selected Essays by Gideon Welles* (New York, 1959), pp. 237ff.; Roy P. Basler, ed., *Collected Works of Abraham Lincoln*, 8 vols. (New Brunswick,

1953), IV, 494; McPherson, *Struggle for Equality*, p. 64.

40. Carl Schurz, *Reminiscences of Carl Schurz*, 3 vols. (New York, 1909), II, 310.

41. Seward to Adams, July 18, 1862, *Papers Relating to Foreign Affairs*, 1862, p. 144.

42. Stanton memorandum, July 22, 1862, Edwin L. Stanton Papers, vol. 8, Library of Congress; *Letters of John Hay and Extracts from Diary*, 3 vols. (reprint ed., New York, 1969), I, 127.

43. Bigelow, *Retrospections*, I, 542; *Seward at Washington*, III, 118.

44. Bigelow, *Retrospections*, I, 506, 547; Gurowski, *Diary*, 1862, p. 245; see also Seward's revealing response to the draft riots, Glyndon Van Deusen, *William Henry Seward* (New York, 1967), p. 334.

45. Sumner to Bright, August 5, 1862, BM Add. Ms. 43390; Starr, *Reporting the Civil War*, p. 102; see Dudley Taylor Cornish, *The Sable Arm: Negro Troops in the Union Army 1861–1865* (reprint ed., New York, 1966), pp. 29–53; Basler, *Works of Lincoln*, V, 339.

46. Seward to Adams, July 28, 1862, NA/M77/77; ibid., August 2.

47. *Brownson's Quarterly Review*, XXIV (1862), 234, 226; for a brief discussion of Stowe's racial conservatism see Louis B. Filler, *The Crusade Against Slavery 1830–1860*, paper ed. (New York, 1960), pp. 207ff.

48. Albert Mordell, ed., *Selected Essays by Gideon Welles* (New York, 1960), pp. 307ff.

49. Lyons to Russell, June 19, 1863, PRO 30/22/37; Rogers to Hammond, August 12, 1862, FO 5/934; ibid., Layard to Rogers,

August 19; Russell to Stuart, October 4, 1862, PRO 30/22/96.

50. Stuart to Russell, September 28, 1862, FO 5/934.

51. Ibid., Lyons to Russell, January 27, 1863; ibid., June 19; ibid., July 20.

52. Benjamin to Mann, August 14, 1862, *ORN*, 2nd ser., III, 513–14.

53. Stuart to Russell, October 21, 1862, PRO 30/22/36; Bragg, Diary, August 5 and 13, 1862; *Wilmington Daily Journal*, September 24, 1862.

54. *Charleston Mercury*, August 11, 1862; see also *Charleston Daily Courier*, August 21, 1862; *Mobile Advertiser and Register*, August 19, 23, and 27, 1862.

55. Clifford Dowdey, ed., *The Wartime Papers of R. E. Lee* (Boston, 1961), pp. 292–301.

56. Tyler Dennett, ed., *Lincoln and the Civil War in the Diaries and Letters of John Hay* (New York, 1939), p. 49.

57. Stuart to Russell, August 12, 1862, PRO 30/22/36; ibid., August 26.

58. Ibid., September 9.

59. *Seward at Washington*, III, 128.

60. Seward to Adams, September 8, 1862, NA/M77/77; *Seward at Washington*, III, 128; Stuart to Russell, August 26, 1862, PRO 30/22/36.

61. Basler, *Works of Lincoln*, V, 388–89, 419–25.

62. Ibid., p. 444.

63. Conway, *Autobiography*, I, 382; David Donald, ed., *Inside Lincoln's Cabinet: The Civil War Diaries of Salmon P. Chase* (New York, 1954), pp. 149–51.

64. Donald, ed., *Inside Lincoln's Cabinet*, pp. 128–30; Seward to Adams, September 22, 1862, *Papers Relating to Foreign Affairs*, 1862, p. 195.

65. Seward to Dayton, October 20, 1862, *Papers Relating to Foreign Affairs*, 1862, p. 398.

66. Woldman, *Lincoln and the Russians*, p. 173.

67. Kinley J. Brauer, "Gabriel Garcia y Tassara and the American Civil War: A Spanish Perspective," *Civil War History*, XXI (1975), 20–21.

68. Stuart to Russell, September 26, 1862, PRO 30/22/36.

69. Ibid., September 23; Stuart to Lyons, September 23, 1862, Lyons Papers.

SIX Intervention Deferred

1. *Times*, September 30, 1862; R. Arthur Arnold, *The History of the Cotton Famine* (London, 1864), p. 223; *Manchester Guardian*, August 20, October 17, 1862.

2. *Times*, November 1, 1862.

3. Barnard Ellinger, "The Cotton Famine of 1861–1864," *Economic History*, III (1934), 159; *Times*, September 29, 1862;

Manchester Guardian, September 15 and 18, 1862.

4. Derby to Granville, September 5, 1862, PRO 30/29/18/8; Watts, *Facts of Cotton Famine*, p. 234; Henderson, *Cotton Famine*, pp. 70–80.

5. Arnold, *Cotton Famine*, pp. 197–99, 200, 219; *Macmillan's*, VII, 158.

6. *Macmillan's,* VII, 160.
7. Arnold, *Cotton Famine,* p. 363; Margaret Hewitt, *Wives and Mothers in Victorian Industry* (London, 1958), pp. 116–17; Henderson, *Cotton Famine,* p. 165; Hewitt, *Wives and Mothers,* pp. 151–52; *Times,* August 19, 1862; Farnie, *English Cotton Industry,* p. 157.
8. *Times,* August 19, 1862.
9. Cobden to Bright, August 28, 1862. BM Add. Ms. 43652; Bright to Cobden, August 30, 1862, BM Add. Ms. 43384.
10. *Economist,* November 1, 1862.
11. Cobden to Bright, October 6, 1862, BM Add. Ms. 43652; *Economist,* November 1, 1862.
12. *Economist,* November 15, 1862; *Times,* November 3, October 9, 1862.
13. *Times,* October 9, 1862.
14. *Saturday Review,* September 27, 1862; *Cornhill Magazine,* VI, 654–62; Garnett, *Diary,* September 23, 1862.
15. *Economist,* August 23 and 30, September 6, 1862; see also Michael Churchman, "Bagehot and the American Civil War," in Stevas, *Collected Works of Bagehot,* IV, 179–94; *Morning Herald,* September 16, 1862.
16. *Times,* September 16, 1862; *Morning Post,* September 16, 1862.
17. Morris to Lawley, September 15, 1862, Morris Papers; *Morning Post,* October 2, 1862; *Manchester Guardian,* October 1, 1862; *Reynolds's Newspaper,* October 5, 1862.
18. *Moran Journal,* II, 1075; *Morning Star,* September 15, 1, and 9, 1862; Thayer to Seward, July 19, 1862, Seward Papers.
19. *Spectator,* September 20 and 6, 1862.
20. Bright to Dudley, October, 1862, Thomas H. Dudley Papers.
21. Mill to Motley, October 31, 1862, *Collected Works of Mill,* XV, 801; Cairnes to Shaw, October 16, 1862, Weinberg, *Cairnes,* pp. 144–47; *Morning Star,* October 7, 1862; Webb, *Martineau,* p. 330; *Daily News,* October 7, 1862; *Spectator,* October 11, 1862; *Anti-Slavery Advocate,* November 1, 1862; *Anti-Slavery Reporter,* November 1, 1862.
22. *Edinburgh Review,* CXVI, 549–94; *North British Review,* XXXVII (1862), 468–504; *Blackwood's Magazine,* XCII (1862), 636–45; *Economist,* October 11, 1862; *Punch,* October 18, 1862; *Illustrated London News,* October 11, 1862; *Standard,* October 7, 9, and 16, 1862; *Morning Post,* October 6, 8, and 15, 1862; *Manchester Guardian,* October 7, 1862; *Bee-Hive,* October 11, 1862; *Saturday Review,* October 11, 1862; *Times,* October 6 and 7, 1862; for a brief but useful survey of the provincial press see Richard Allen Heckman, "British Press Reaction to the Emancipation Proclamation," *Lincoln Herald,* LXXXI (1969), 150–53.
23. *Morning Star,* October 16, 1862; *Spectator,* October 11, 1862.
24. Joseph Parkes to Weed, October 7, 1862, Weed Papers.
25. *Westminster Review,* XXII (1862), 503–4.
26. *Morning Star,* November 7, 1862.
27. Harold Temperley, *British anti-slavery 1833–1870* (Columbia, 1972), pp. 228–29; William Stanton, *The Leopard's Spots: Scientific Attitudes towards Race*

in America 1815–1859 (Chicago, 1960), p. 186.

28. *Morning Post*, November 20, 1863; Christine Bolt, *Victorian Attitudes to Race* (London, 1971), pp. 14–27; Douglas A. Lorimer, *Colour, Class and the Victorians: English attitudes to the Negro in the mid-nineteenth century* (Leicester, 1978), pp. 131–61.

29. Leonard Huxley, *Life and Letters of Thomas Henry Huxley*, 2 vols. (London, 1900), I, 251–52, n. 1.

30. Stanton, *Leopard's Spots*, p. 186; for a recent discussion which emphasizes the importance of class distinctions in the growth of racism in Britain see Lorimer, *Colour, Class and the Victorians.*

31. Michael Biddiss, *Father of Racist Ideology: The Social and Political Thought of Count Gobineau* (London, 1970), p. 109.

32. Ibid., pp. 118–19; Michael Banton, *The Idea of Race* (London, 1977), p. 43.

33. Forrest G. Wood, *Black Scare: The Racist Response to Emancipation and Reconstruction* (Berkeley, 1968), p. 8; Banton, *Idea of Race*, pp. 63–64.

34. Quoted in Iva G. Jones, "Trollope, Carlyle and Mill on the Negro: An Episode in the History of Ideas," *Journal of Negro History*, LII (1967), 195.

35. James Morris, *Pax Britannica: The Climax of Empire* (London, 1968), p. 136; Ridley, *Palmerston*, pp. 474–75; Christopher Hibbert, "Nana Sahib at Cawnpore, 1857," *History Today*, XXVII (1977), 557–65.

36. Lorimer, *Colour, Class and the Victorians*, p. 174; *Times*, September 19, 1862; *Morning Herald*, August 13, 1862; *Blackwood's*, XCII, 636.

37. *Economist*, September 6, 1862; Conway, *Autobiography*, II, 204.

38. H. Montgomery Hyde, ed., *A Victorian Historian: Private Letters of W. E. H. Lecky 1859–1878* (London, 1947), p. 52; Ellison, *Support for Secession*, pp. 56, 58; Mason to Mann, October 19, 1862, Mason Papers.

39. *Index*, October 9, 1862; Lorimer, *Colour, Class and the Victorians*, p. 149; *Times*, October 9, 1862.

40. *Fraser's Magazine* (November 1862), p. 662; ibid. (February 1863), p. 199; see also Waldo Hilary Dunn, *James Anthony Froude: A Biography*, 2 vols. (Oxford, 1963), II, 334.

41. Asa Briggs, *Victorian People: A Reassessment of Persons and Themes 1851–67* (reprint ed., London, 1967), pp. 74, 229.

42. R. E. Leader, ed., *Life and Letters of John Arthur Roebuck* (London, 1897), pp. 299–300.

43. Briggs, *Victorian People*, p. 74; *Index*, August 14, 1862.

44. Confederate States Aid Association, FO 5/867; Jordan and Pratt, *Europe and the American Civil War*, p. 171.

45. Gwendolen Cecil, *Life of Robert Marquis of Salisbury*, 4 vols. (London, 1921–32), I, 169; Thomas, *Fifty Years of Fleet Street*, p. 84.

46. *Quarterly Review*, CXII (1862), 535–70.

47. *Times*, September 20, October 7, 1862.

48. Slidell to Mason, September 12, 1862, Mason Papers; Ellison, *Support for Secession*, pp. 117–18; William Boon to Mason, September 17, 1862, Mason Papers; ibid., Mason to Boon, September 19.

49. *Bee-Hive*, October 4, 1862; Spence to Mason, October 3, 1862, Mason Papers; ibid., October 2; ibid., October 15; see also Adams to Seward, October 3, 1862, *Papers Relating to Foreign Affairs*, 1862, pp. 205–6.

50. FO to HO, November 3, 1862, FO 5/866; Mayor of Oldham to HO, November 7, 1862, HO 45/7261/27.

51. Adams to Everett, September 5, 1862, Adams Papers, reel 168; Adams to Seward, October 3, 1862, *Papers Relating to Foreign Affairs*, 1862, pp. 205–6.

52. Adams to Seward, September 4, 1862, *Papers Relating to Foreign Affairs*, 1862, p. 184; ibid., pp. 182–83, August 29; ibid., pp. 189–91, September 12.

53. *Adams Letters*, I, 190–92; Parkes to Weed, October 7, 1862, Weed Papers; H. Adams to C. F. Adams Jr., October 10, 1862, Adams Papers, reel 561; ibid., reel 168, Adams to Dayton, October 5; ibid., reel 561, Dayton to Adams, October 3.

54. Holland to Weed, August 8, 1862, Weed Papers; Adams, Diary, August 7, 1862, Adams Papers, reel 77; *Daily News*, August 11, 1862; Sanford to Seward, August 13, 1862, Seward Papers.

55. Lyons to Stuart, August 15, 1862, Lyons Papers; ibid., August 22.

56. Argyll to Palmerston, September 2, 1862, Broadlands Mss.

57. Clarendon to Cowley, September 2, 1862, FO 519/178; ibid., September 15.

58. Gregory to Mason, September 16, 1862, Mason Papers.

59. Russell to Queen, August 24, 1862, *Letters of Queen Victoria*, 2nd ser., I, 42; Russell to Palmers-

ton, August 24, 1862, Broadlands Mss.

60. Palmerston to Russell, September 14, 1862, PRO 30/22/14D; ibid., September 22; ibid., September 23; Russell to Palmerston, September 14, 1862, Broadlands Mss.; ibid., September 17; Russell to Cowley, September 26, 1862, PRO 30/22/105.

61. Palmerston to Russell, September 23, 1862, PRO 30/22/14D; Russell to Palmerston, September 19, 1862, Broadlands Mss.

62. Russell to Cowley, September 13, 1862, PRO 30/22/105; ibid., September 26; Cowley to Russell, September 18, 1862, PRO 30/22/14D; Russell to Gladstone, September 26, 1862, BM Add. Ms. 44292.

63. Quoted in C. F. Adams Jr., "A Crisis in Downing Street," *MHSP*, XLVI (1914), 386; Guedalla, *Palmerston and Gladstone*, pp. 233–35.

64. Granville to Russell, September 29, 1862, Broadlands Mss.; ibid., Russell to Palmerston, October 2, 1862; Palmerston to Russell, October 3, 1862, PRO 30/22/14D.

65. Palmerston to Russell, October 3, 1862, PRO 30/22/14D; ibid., October 2, G. P. Gooch, ed., *The Later Correspondence of Lord John Russell 1840–1878*, 2 vols. (London, 1925), II, 326–27.

66. Palmerston to Russell, October 5, 1862, PRO 30/22/14D; ibid., October 23, *Later Correspondence of Russell*, II, 282.

67. Russell to Palmerston, October 2, 1862, Broadlands Mss.

68. Russell to Stuart, October 10, 1862, PRO 30/22/96.

69. Russell to Palmerston, October 6, 1862, Broadlands Mss.; Pal-

merston to Russell, October 8, 1862, PRO 30/22/14D.

70. Russell to Stuart, October 10, 1862, PRO 30/22/96; Russell to Cowley, October 11, 1862, PRO 30/22/105.

71. C. Gladstone to Wharncliffe, November 5, 1862, Wharncliffe Papers, Sheffield Public Library; Morley, *Gladstone*, II, 79–80; Collyer, "Gladstone and American Civil War," *Leeds Philosophical and Literary Society, Proceedings*, VI, 590; *Manchester Guardian*, October 9 and 13, 1862; *Morning Star*, October 13, 1862.

72. Bright to Cobden, September 6, 1862, BM Add. Ms. 43384; Cobden to Bright, September 19, 1862, BM Add. Ms. 43652; Bright to Cobden, October 8, 1862, BM Add. Ms. 43384; Bright to Dudley, October, 1862, Dudley Papers.

73. *Economist*, October 18, 1862; *Saturday Review*, October 11, 1862; *Manchester Guardian*, October 10, 1862; *Morning Star*, October 9, 1862.

74. *Spectator*, October 18, 1862.

75. Quoted in Winter, *Robert Lowe*, p. 64; A. G. Gardiner, *The Life of Sir William Harcourt*, 2 vols. (London, 1923), I, 117, 111.

76. Roger Fulford, ed., *Dearest Mama: Letters between Queen Victoria and the Crown Princess of Prussia* (London, 1968), p. 196.

77. G. F. Lewis, *The Letters of Sir George Cornewall Lewis* (London, 1870). p. 315.

78. Lewis to De Grey, September 16, 1862, BM Add. Ms. 43533; ibid., September 18; ibid., October 8.

79. Russell to Stuart, August 7, 1862, FO 5/820; Russell memorandum,

October 13, 1862, Broadlands Mss.; see also Edward W. Ellsworth, "Anglo-American Affairs in October of 1862," *Lincoln Herald*, LXVI (1964), 89–96; Kinley J. Brauer, "British Mediation and the American Civil War: A Reconsideration," *Journal of Southern History*, XXXVIII (1972), 49–64.

80. Newcastle to Russell, October 14, 1862, PRO 30/22/25.

81. Ibid., Argyll to Russell, October 15; see also ibid., October 11.

82. Lewis to Russell, October 17, 1862, Broadlands Mss.

83. Defences of Canada, Report, September 1, 1862, WO 33/11/185.

84. Palmerston to Russell, October 20, 1862, PRO 30/22/14D.

85. Grey to Russell, October 27, 1862, PRO 30/22/25; Lewis to Russell, October 17, 1862.

86. Clarendon to Palmerston, October 16, 1862, Broadlands Mss.; Palmerston to Russell, October 17, 1862, PRO 30/22/14D; ibid., October 20; ibid., October 22; ibid., October 23.

87. Russell to Palmerston, October 18, 1862, Broadlands Mss.

88. Ibid., October 20; Lyons to Minna, October 24, 1862, Lyons Papers.

89. Gladstone memorandum, October 24, 1862, Broadlands Mss.

90. Russell to Lewis, October 26, 1862, PRO 30/22/14D; Russell to Grey, October 28, 1862, *Later Correspondence of Russell*, II, 332; Palmerston to Russell, October 26, 1862, PRO 30/22/14D.

91. Nancy Nichols Barker, *Distaff Diplomacy: The Empress Eugénie and the Foreign Policy of the Second Empire* (Austin, 1967), p. 103.

92. Case and Spencer, *United States and France*, pp. 353–59; Cowley to Russell, October 27, 1862, PRO 30/22/14D.

93. Cowley to Russell, October 31, 1862, PRO 30/22/58.

94. Palmerston to Russell, November 7, 1862, PRO 30/22/14D; ibid., November 2.

95. Russell to Cowley, November 1, 1862, PRO 30/22/105; Russell to Palmerston, November 3, 1862, Broadlands Mss.

96. Palmer, *Memorials*, II, 460–61.

97. Lewis memorandum, November 7, 1862, WO 33/12.

98. *Spectator*, November 8 and 15, 1862.

99. *Morning Post*, November 11, 1862; Hammond to Lyons, November 15, 1862, Lyons Papers.

100. Maxwell, *Clarendon*, II, 268–69; Stuart to Russell, October 26, 1862, PRO 30/22/36; Napier to Russell, November 12, 1862, PRO 30/22/83.

101. Maxwell, *Clarendon*, II, 268; M. Gibson to Bright, November 14, 1862, BM Add. Ms. 43388; Bassett, *Gladstone to his Wife*, p. 140.

102. *Morning Herald*, November 12, 13, 14, and 15, 1862; *Standard*, November 15, 1862; Derby to Disraeli, November 22, 1862, B/XX/S/303, Disraeli Papers.

103. *Spectator*, November 15, 1862.

104. *Times*, November 15, 1862; Russell to Palmerston, November 14, 1862, Broadlands Mss.

SEVEN   The Failure of Confederate Foreign Policy

1. *Atlantic Monthly*, X (1862), 638–42; George M. Frederickson, *The Inner Civil War: Northern Intellectuals and the Crisis of the Union* (New York, 1965), pp. 113–15; Lorraine A. Williams, "Northern Intellectuals' Reaction to the Policy of Emancipation," *Journal of Negro History*, XLVI (1961), 174–88; Roland C. McConnell, "From Preliminary to Final Emancipation Proclamation: The First Hundred Days," ibid., XLVIII (1963), 260–76; Frank L. Klement, "Mid-Western Opposition to Lincoln's Emancipation Policy," ibid., XLIV (1964), 169–83; see also his *The Copperheads of the Middle West* (Chicago, 1960), pp. 1–38.

2. Forney to Lincoln, September 26, 1862, Lincoln Papers, reel 42; ibid., Davis to Lincoln, October 14; ibid., Field to Lincoln, October 20; Nevins, *Strong Diary*, pp. 271–72.

3. Robert S. Harper, *Lincoln and the Press* (New York, 1951), pp. 187–88, 223–24; Morton to Lincoln, October 27, 1862, Edwin M. Stanton Papers, Library of Congress; Allan Nevins, *The War for the Union*, III (New York, 1971), 55.

4. Stuart to Russell, November 7, 1862, FO 5/838; ibid., Lyons to Russell, November 17.

5. *New York Times*, November 8, October 10, November 10, 1862; *New York Herald*, October 19, November 3, 1862.

6. *Frank Leslie's Illustrated Newspaper*, October 11, December 27, 1862; *New York Herald*, November 7, December 2, 1862; *New York Tribune*, November 20, 1862; *Frank Leslie's Illustrated Newspaper*, November 15, 1862;

Harper's Weekly, November 29, 1862.

7. *New York Times*, November 21, 1862; for brief accounts of the state of American shipping see Winthrop L. Marvin, *The American Merchant Marine: Its History and Romance from 1620 to 1902* (London, 1902), pp. 320–39; John G. B. Hutchins, *The American Maritime Industries and Public Policy 1789–1914* (Cambridge, Mass., 1941), pp. 302–24; also George W. Dalzell, *The Flight from the Flag: The Continuing Effect of the Civil War upon the American Carrying Trade* (Chapel Hill, 1940).

8. *New York Herald*, November 28, 1862; *New York Times*, November 27, 1862; *New York Tribune*, December 2, 1862.

9. *Frank Leslie's Illustrated Newspaper*, November 1, 1862; *New York Times*, November 8 and 10, 1862.

10. *New York Times*, December 5, 1862; *New York Herald*, December 6, 1862; *New York Tribune*, December 8, 1862; Douglas H. Maynard, "Civil War 'Care': The Mission of the *George Griswold*," *New England Quarterly*, XXXIV (1961), 291–99; *New York Times*, December 9, 1862.

11. Basler, *Works of Lincoln*, V, 519.

12. Report of Secretary of Navy, December 1, 1862, *Cong. Globe*, 37th Cong. 3rd sess., App., 16; ibid., pt. 1, 73; ibid., pp. 92–96; ibid., p. 126.

13. *Welles Diary*, I, 180–81; *Bates Diary*, pp. 264–66; Lyons to Russell, November 21, 1862, Lyons Papers; ibid., December 16; ibid., November 14, PRO 30/22/36.

14. *Seward at Washington*, III, 136; Seward to Adams, October 20, 1862, NA/M77/77; ibid., November 3.

15. *Frank Leslie's Illustrated Newspaper*, December 6, 1862; *Brownson's Quarterly*, XXIV, 509, 517; *Seward at Washington*, III, 138.

16. Donald, *Sumner and the Rights of Man*, pp. 88, 90; Sumner to Bright, October 28, 1862, BM Add. Ms. 43390; ibid., November 18.

17. Francis Fessenden, *Life and Public Services of William Pitt Fessenden*, 2 vols. (reprint ed., New York, 1970), I, 242, 263, 268.

18. *Harper's Weekly*, December 27, 1862; Nevins, *Strong Diary*, p. 281.

19. *Seward at Washington*, III, 146; *Welles Diary*, I, 193, 203.

20. *Browning Diary*, I, 600–604; *Welles Diary*, I, 196–203.

21. *Bates Diary*, p. 268–70.

22. Lyons to Russell, December 22, 1862, PRO 30/22/36; ibid., December 19.

23. Lyons to Milne, December 27, 1862, Lyons Papers.

24. *Welles Diary*, I, 205; Seward to Weed, December 25, 1862, Weed Papers.

25. Nevins, *Strong Diary*, p. 292.

26. *Browning Diary*, I, 618–19, 606–7, 613, 616; *Welles Diary*, I, 210–11.

27. *Memoir and Letters of Sumner*, IV, 114; Lyons to Milne, January 14, 1862, Lyons Papers; *Browning Diary*, I, 618–19.

28. *Cong. Globe*, 37th Cong. 3rd sess., App., 54–55; see also Frank L. Klement, *The Limits of Dissent: Clement L. Vallandigham*

and the Civil War (Lexington, 1970).

29. "Extracts from the Journal of Henry J. Raymond," Scribner's Monthly, XIX (1880), 705; New York Herald, January 12 and 16, 1863; New York Times, January 29 and 10, 1863; for a full account of the episode see Warren F. Spencer, "The Jewett-Greeley Affair: A Private Scheme for French Mediation in the American Civil War," New York History, LI (1970), 238–68.

30. Lyons to Russell, November 14, 1862, PRO 30/22/36; ibid., November 24; ibid., December 12; Gurowski, Diary, 1862, p. 20; New York History, LI, 259–60.

31. Lyons to Russell, February 10, 1863, Lyons Papers; ibid., February 15; New York Tribune, January 30, 1863.

32. Seward to Van Sackett, February 9, 1863, Seward Papers.

33. Scribner's Monthly, XIX, 708.

34. New York Herald, February 13 and 14, 1863.

35. Donald, Sumner and the Rights of Man, pp. 103–5.

36. Lyons to Milne, February 15, 1863, Lyons Papers.

37. Ibid.; Cong. Globe, 37th Cong. 3rd sess., pt. 1, 695.

38. New York Tribune, January 15, February 13, 16, and 17, March 6, 1863.

39. New York Herald, January 3, February 23, March 14, 16, and 22, 1863.

40. New York Times, March 25 and 1, 1863.

41. Cong. Globe, 37th Cong. 3rd sess., pt. 1, 220–21; ibid., pt. 2, 960–61; ibid., pp. 1019–20; ibid., pp. 1175–77.

42. Van Deusen, Seward, p. 354; Donald, Sumner and the Rights of Man, pp. 109–11; Memoir and Letters of Sumner, IV, 120–21; Welles Diary, I, 246–60; Bates Diary, pp. 284–85; New York Tribune, April 22, 1863; New York Times, April 23, 1863.

43. Dana to Adams, March 9, 1863, Adams Papers, reel 168; Samuel Shapiro, Richard Henry Dana Jr. 1815–1882 (East Lansing, 1961), pp. 117–21; Stuart L. Bernath, Squall across the Atlantic: American Civil War Prize Cases and Diplomacy (Berkeley, 1970), pp. 18–33.

44. Stuart L. Bernath, "Squall across the Atlantic: The Peterhoff Episode," Journal of Southern History, XXXIV (1968), 389–91.

45. Charleston Daily Courier, November 13, 1862.

46. Southern Confederacy, November 22, 1862; Mobile Advertiser and Register, November 13, 1862; Richmond Daily Enquirer, November 18, 1862.

47. Richmond Whig, December 29, 1862, January 6, 1863; W. P. Miles to Gregory, September 16, 1863, Gregory Papers.

48. Jones, Rebel War Clerk's Diary, p. 151.

49. Rowland, Letters and Speeches of Davis, V, 398–411.

50. SHSP, L, 122–24.

51. Moore to Lyons, March 5, 1863, FO 5/879; Bunch to Russell, November 20, 1862, FO 5/849; Moore to Lyons, April 28, 1863, FO 5/883; Bunch to Russell, December 22, 1862, FO 5/844; Moore to Lyons, January 16, 1863, Lyons Papers.

52. Benjamin to Moore, February 20, 1863, FO 5/879.

53. Moore to Lyons, March 21, 1863, FO 5/881.

54. Heyliger to Benjamin, December

12, 1862, *ORN*, 2nd ser., III, 625–27; ibid., pp. 579–80, Benjamin to Sanders, October 28; ibid., p. 614, Sanders to Benjamin, December 8; ibid., pp. 686–7, Benjamin to Mason, February 7, 1863; Mallory to Mason, October 30, 1862, *Papers Relating to Foreign Affairs, 1863–64* (Washington, 1864), I, 89; Jones, *Rebel War Clerk's Diary*, pp. 155–57.

55. Benjamin to Slidell, October 17, 1862, *Messages and Papers of Confederacy*, II, 334–37.

56. Ibid., pp. 369–77, Benjamin to Mason, December 11; Benjamin to Mason, February 6, 1863, *ORN*, 2nd ser., III, 678.

57. Benjamin to Mason, September 26, 1862, *Messages and Papers of Confederacy*, II, 323–24; ibid., p. 407, Benjamin to Slidell, January 15, 1863.

58. Ibid., pp. 466–67, Benjamin to Mason, March 27, 1863; ibid., pp. 459–61, Benjamin to Slidell, March 24; ibid., p. 463.

59. Ibid., pp. 313–14, Benjamin to Mann, August 14, 1862; ibid., 364–68, Benjamin to Lamar, November 19; Edward Mayes, *Lucius Q. C. Lamar: His Life, Times and Speeches 1825–1893* (Nashville, 1896), p. 106; Callahan, *Diplomatic History of the Confederacy*, p. 168.

60. *Mobile Advertiser and Register*, December 6, 1862; Benjamin to Hotze, January 16, 1863, *Messages and Papers of Confederacy*, II, 411–12; Benjamin to DeLeon, January 16, 1863, *ORN*, 2nd ser., III, 657; ibid., December 13, 1862, *Papers Relating to Foreign Affairs, 1863–64*, I, 80.

61. Memminger to Mason, October 24, 1862, *Papers Relating to Foreign Affairs, 1863–64*, I, 82–84; Benjamin to Slidell, January 15, 1863, *Messages and Papers of Confederacy*, II, 405–7; ibid., pp. 398–401, Benjamin to Mason; ibid., pp. 339–40, Slidell to Benjamin, October 28, 1862. For a discussion of Confederate finances abroad and the Erlanger Loan see Owsley, *King Cotton Diplomacy*, pp. 360–93; and Judith Fenner Gentry, "A Confederate Success in Europe: The Erlanger Loan," *Journal of Southern History*, XXX (1970), 157–88.

62. Browne to Cobb, May 19, 1863, Howell Cobb Papers; Clay to V. Clay, March 12, 1863, C. C. Clay Papers, Duke University.

63. *Mobile Advertiser and Register*, February 17, 1863.

64. *Charleston Daily Courier*, February 21, 1863.

EIGHT   The Friends of the North

1. *Times*, October 24, 1862.

2. Temperley, *British antislavery*, p. 257; *Historical Journal*, XIX, 414; Jordan and Pratt, *Europe and the American Civil War*, pp. 126–41.

3. Sinclair to Seward, November 14, 1862, Seward Papers.

4. Taylor, *British and American Abolitionists*, p. 10; Temperley, *British antislavery*, p. 254; obituary of Samuel Lucas, *Morning*

Star, April 22, 1865; Lucas to Lindsay, November 10, 1863, Lindsay Papers.

5. *Anti-Slavery Reporter*, December 1. 1862; *Bee-Hive*, November 29, 1862; *Anti-Slavery Advocate*, February 2, 1863; Jordan and Pratt, *Europe and the American Civil War*, p. 142; Sinclair to Seward, November 14, 1862.

6. Taylor, *British and American Abolitionists*, pp. 10, 490; Temperley, *British antislavery*, p. 239; *Morning Star*, November 17, 1862.

7. *John Bright and the American Question*, pp. 69–128; Bright to Sumner, December 6, 1862, *MHSP*, XLVI, 110; Roman J. Zorn, "John Bright and the British Attitude to the American Civil War," *Mid-America*, XXXVIII (1956), 137–39.

8. *Morning Star*, December 12, 1862; ibid., January 2, 1863.

9. Mill to Cairnes, December 16, 1862, *Collected Works of Mill*, XV, 810–11; ibid., 812–13, Mill to Kyllman, December 24.

10. Probyn to Seward, April 7, 1863, Seward Papers; Ellison, *Support for Secession*, p. 79; Bright to Cobden, December 24, 1862, BM Add. Ms. 43384.

11. Lord to Seward, January 1, 1863, NA/T219/2; Ellison, *Support for Secession*, pp. 81, 59.

12. *Spectator*, January 24, 1863; *Daily News*, January 19, 1863; *Morning Star*, January 30, 1863.

13. *Reynolds's Newspaper*, October 19, 1862, January 18, 1863; Taylor, *British and American Abolitionists*, p. 490.

14. *Civil War History*, XX, 343; *Bee-Hive*, January 24, 1863.

15. *Northern History*, IX, 118–21; *Morning Star*, January 10, 1863;

Elisabeth Wallace, *Goldwin Smith, Victorian Liberal* (Toronto, 1957), pp. 29–30.

16. *Bee-Hive*, February 7, 1863.

17. Mill to Kyllman, February 15, 1863, *Collected Works of Mill*, XV, 839.

18. Dudley to Seward, February 20, 1863, Dudley Papers; the resolutions of many of the meetings are to be found in *Papers Relating to Foreign Affairs*, 1863–64, I; Bright to Cobden, December 24, 1862, BM Add. Ms. 43384; Lord to Seward, February 25, 1863, NA/T219/2; Thompson to Garrison, February 5, 1863, Taylor, *British and American Abolitionists*, pp. 498–99; *Daily News*, February 3, 1863.

19. Dudley to Seward, January 14, 1863, Dudley Papers; ibid., January 17; ibid., January 23; ibid., February 20.

20. Adams, Diary, January 17, 1863, Adams Papers, reel 77; ibid., reel 168, Adams to Everett, January 23.

21. *Daily News*, January 23, 1863; *Times*, January 23, 1863; Adams, Diary, February 26, 1863, Adams Papers, reel 77.

22. Adams, Diary, February 27, 1863, Adams Papers, reel 77.

23. Basler, *Works of Lincoln*, VI, 64.

24. Ibid., pp. 176–77; Conway, *Autobiography*, I, 411.

25. Taylor, *British and American Abolitionists*, p. 503; Conway, *Autobiography*, I, 388–89; II, 1–2.

26. *Manchester Guardian*, November 21, 1862; *Times*, January 15 and 31, February 6, 1863; *Morning Post*, January 21 and 31, 1863; *Standard*, January 22 and 31, April 10, 1863; *Morning Herald*, January 15, February 19, April

8, 1863; *Saturday Review*, January 24 and 31, February 7 and 21, 1863.
27. *Daily News*, January 20, 1863.
28. *Morning Star*, May 23, 1863.
29. Hotze to Benjamin, January 17, 1863, *ORN*, 2nd ser., III, 661–64; ibid., February 14, *Messages and Papers of Confederacy*, II, 434; *Index*, January 8 and 22, February 5 and 19, 1863.
30. Campbell to Gregory, January 3, 1863, Gregory Papers; ibid., Spence to Gregory, January 4; ibid., Mason to Gregory.
31. *Times*, January 23, 1863; see also ibid., December 1 and 27, 1862, January 1 and 12, 1863.
32. Gregory to Mason, December 1, 1862, Mason Papers; Spence to Gregory, January 15, 1863, Gregory Papers; ibid., Ellice to Gregory, February 9; Gregory to Miles, April 7, 1863, W. P. Miles Papers.
33. Mason to Benjamin, January 15, 1863, *ORN*, 2nd ser., III, 654; ibid., February 9, *Messages and Papers of Confederacy*, II, 429–30.
34. Bright to Motley, March 9, 1863, Curtis, *Motley Correspondence*, II, 120–21; *Index*, March 26, 1863.
35. DeLeon to Benjamin, March 31, 1863, Pickett Papers.
36. Hotze to Benjamin, May 9, 1863, *ORN*, 2nd ser., III, 760.
37. *Parl. Debates*, 3rd ser., CLXX, 200–47.
38. *Spectator*, April 11, 1863; *Economist*, January 3, 1863; *Morning Post*, November 29, 1862; *Times*, December 17, 1862.
39. Chester Address, December 27, 1862, BM Add. Ms. 44690.
40. Bright to Cobden, December 24, 1862, BM Add. Ms. 43384; Cob-

den to Bright, December 7, 1863, BM Add. Ms. 43652.
41. Villiers to Palmerston, November 23, 1862, Broadlands Mss.
42. Cobden to Bright, December 29, 1862, BM Add. Ms. 43652; Cobden to Richard, December 5, 1862, BM Add. Ms. 43659.
43. Bright to Cobden, December 24, 1862, BM Add. Ms. 43384.
44. Cobden to Bright, December 29, 1862, BM Add. Ms. 43652; Cobden to Paulton, January 18, 1863, BM Add. Ms. 43662.
45. *Times*, November 11 and 16, 1862; *Spectator*, November 15 and 29, 1862; *Edinburgh Review*, CXVII (1863), 285.
46. *Edinburgh Review*, CXVII, 284.
47. *Saturday Review*, November 22, 1862.
48. *Morning Post*, November 18, December 17, 1862.
49. Earl of Malmesbury, *Memoirs of an Ex-Minister*, 2 vols. (London, 1884), II, 288; *Times*, December 6, 1862.
50. *Reynolds's Newspaper*, February 1, 1863; *Times*, February 26, 1863.
51. Holgate to Turner, February 19, 1863, HO 45/7484; *Saturday Review*, December 6, 1862, January 31, 1863; *Daily News*, February 26, 1863; *Reynolds's Newspaper*, February 1, 1863; Unemployed Operatives Emigration Society of Pendleton to Massey, n.d., HO 45 OS 7523/3, 4.
52. Palin to Watch Committee, February 12, 1863, Manchester Police Returns, Manchester Central Reference Library.
53. *Bee-Hive*, October 18, 1862, February 28, 1863; *Spectator*, March 21, 1863; Garnett, Diary, November 7, 1862; Glossop Dis-

turbances, March 3, 1863, HO 45 OS 7523A/1; *Reynolds's Newspaper*, March 15, 1863; Arnold, *Cotton Famine*, p. 391; *Fraser's Magazine*, LXVIII (1862), 318.

54. For the correspondence concerning the Stalybridge riot see HO 45 OS 7523A/4–20.

55. *Saturday Review*, March 28, 1863; *Morning Star*, March 24, 1863.

56. *Daily News*, March 23, 1863; *Saturday Review*, March 28, 1863; *Parl. Debates*, 3rd ser., CLXX, 12–19; *Morning Star*, March 24, 1863; *Daily News*, March 23, 1863.

57. *Daily News*, March 23, 1863; see also *Morning Post*, March 25, 1863; *Saturday Review*, March 28, 1863.

58. Farnie, *English Cotton Industry*, p. 157; *Times*, March 31, 1863; *Standard*, April 1 and 30, May 20, 1863.

59. Baker to Grey, April 22, 1863, HO 45 OS 7523/5; Cobden to Slagg, April 5, 1863, BM Add. Ms. 43676.

60. Newcastle circular, April 11, 1863, CO 37/187; *Parl. Debates*, 3rd ser., CLXX, 815.

61. Stalybridge petition, February 2, 1863, HO 45 OS 7523/1.

62. Hopwood to Farnall, February 23, 1863, HO 45 OS 7523/2; ibid., Lumley to Waddington, March 6; Central Executive Committee to Home Office, HO 45 OS 7523/12; *Parl. Debates*, 3rd ser., CLXX, 805.

63. *Parl. Debates*, 3rd ser., CLXX, 1050–90, 1490–93, 1517–21, 1619–32.

64. Derby to Grey, November 30, 1863, HO 45 OS 7523/14; Public Works Office memorandum, HO 45 OS 7523/15; for statistics on the decline in unemployment see HO 45 OS 7523/22; *Morning Star*, May 8, 1863.

NINE   Strict Neutrality

1. Sanford to Seward, January 20, 1863, Seward Papers; Adams to Seward, October 28, 1862, *Papers Relating to Foreign Affairs*, 1862, p. 225; ibid., 1863–64, I, 13–14, December 4; Palmerston to Russell, October 22, 1862, PRO 30/22/14D; ibid., December 29; ibid., January 2, 1863, PRO 30/22/14E.

2. Palmerston to Russell, October 26, 1862, PRO 30/22/14D.

3. Ibid., December 28.

4. Palmerston to Queen, November 14, 1862, *Regina v Palmerston*, p. 332.

5. Keith A. P. Sandiford, *Great Britain and the Schleswig-Holstein Question 1848–1864: A Study in Diplomacy, Politics and Public Opinion* (Toronto, 1975), pp. 53–54; Malmesbury, *Memoirs*, II, 286.

6. Derby to Disraeli, January 29, 1863, B/XX/S/311, Disraeli Papers.

7. *Spectator*, February 7, 1863; Bell, *Palmerston*, II, 340; Bright to Cobden, December 24, 1862, BM Add. Ms. 43384.

8. Palmerston to Russell, April 20, 1863, PRO 30/22/14F.

9. *Blackwood's Magazine*, XCIII, 252.

10. Ibid., p. 384; Derby to Disraeli, January 29, 1863, B/XX/S/311; Argyll to Russell, April 10, 1863, PRO 30/22/26.

11. A. J. P. Taylor, *The Struggle for Mastery in Europe 1848–1918*, paper ed. (New York, 1973), pp. 134–35.

12. Hallberg, *Franz Joseph and Napoleon III*, pp. 315–16; Barker, *Distaff Diplomacy*, p. 107; W. F. Monypenny and G. E. Buckle, *The Life of Benjamin Disraeli: Earl of Beaconsfield*, IV (London, 1916), 335; Queen to Granville, February 23, 1863, *Letters of Queen Victoria*, 2nd ser., I, 66–67; ibid., 67–68, Granville to Queen, February 24.

13. Palmerston to Russell, February 23, 1863, PRO 30/22/14E.

14. Granville to Queen, February 25, 1863, *Letters of Queen Victoria*, 2nd ser., I, 69–70.

15. *Parl. Debates*, 3rd ser., CLXIX, 933–37.

16. W. E. Mosse, "England and the Polish Insurrection of 1863," *English Historical Review*, LXXI (1956), 33–36; John F. Kutolowski, "Mid-Victorian Public Opinion, Polish Propaganda, and the Uprising of 1863," *Journal of British Studies*, VIII (1969), 91; *Times*, March 2, 1863.

17. Shaftesbury Diary, February 28, 1863, Broadlands Mss.; Lamar to Benjamin, March 20, 1863, *Messages and Papers of Confederacy*, II, 454–55.

18. *American Historical Review*, LVIII, 535; Argyll, *Autobiography*, II, 195–97; Monypenny and Buckle, *Disraeli*, IV, 332–33.

19. Lyons to Russell, January 2, 1863, PRO 30/22/37; ibid., January 9; ibid., January 23; ibid., February 2; ibid., February 16;

ibid., March 2.

20. Russell to Lyons, December 13, 1862, Lyons Papers; ibid., February 14, 1863; ibid., FO 5/868; ibid., March 14, Lyons Papers; *Times*, March 24, 1863.

21. Adams to Russell, November 20, 1862, *Papers Relating to Foreign Affairs*, 1863–64, I, 5–7.

22. Russell to Lyons, December 20, 1862, Lyons Papers.

23. Gladstone to Palmerston, August 6, 1862, Broadlands Mss.

24. *Times*, December 23, 1862.

25. *Morning Star*, November 3, 1862; *Daily News*, November 3 and 6, December 24, 1862, January 6, March 14, 1863; *Times*, January 16, 1863, November 3 and 21, December 17 and 23, 1862.

26. *Times*, December 23, 1862, January 9, 1863.

27. Palmer, *Memorials*, II, 412–13; Montague Bernard, *A Historical Account of the Neutrality of Great Britain during the American Civil War* (London, 1870), pp. 390–400.

28. LO to Russell, December 8, 1862, FO 83/2215; Russell to Adams, December 19, 1862, FO 5/1318.

29. *Moran Journal*, II, 1100; *Adams Letters*, I, 221; Adams, Diary, December 29, 1862, Adams Papers, reel 77; ibid., January 26, 1863; ibid., reel 169, Adams to Everett, March 20.

30. Adams to Russell, January 16, 1863, *Papers Relating to Foreign Affairs*, 1863–64, I, 96–97; ibid., 106–7, January 26; ibid., 104–6, Russell to Adams, January 24; FO to HO, January 17, 1863, HO 45/7261; LO to Russell, December 8, 1862, FO 83/2215; LO to Russell, January 12, 1863,

FO 83/2216; Adams to Seward, February 13, 1863, Adams Papers, reel 168.

31. Hotze to Benjamin, March 21, 1863, *ORN*, 2nd ser., III, 719; ibid., 730–31, Mason to Benjamin, March 30; ibid., 735–37, April 9; Spence to Mason, April 3, 1863, Mason Papers; ibid., April 4; ibid., Slidell to Mason, April 5; *Journal of Southern History*, XXXVI, 161–62.

32. Forbes to Welles, April 10, 1863, Gideon Welles Papers, Library of Congress; Aspinwall and Forbes to Welles, April 25, 1863, Sarah F. Hughes, ed., *Letters and Recollections of John Murray Forbes*, 2 vols. (Boston, 1899), II, 44–45; Aspinwall to Welles, April 8, 1863, Welles Papers; ibid., Forbes to Welles, April 4.

33. For a thorough discussion of the consular system of surveillance see Neill Fred Sanders, "Lincoln's consuls in the British Isles, 1861–1865" (Ph.D. thesis, University of Missouri, 1971); Douglas H. Maynard, "The Forbes-Aspinwall Mission," *Mississippi Valley Historical Review*, XLV (1958–59), 75; Adams, Diary, April 23, 1863, Adams Papers, reel 77.

34. H. Donaldson Jordan, "A Politician of Expansion: Robert J. Walker," *Mississippi Valley Historical Review*, XIX (1932), 379–80; Bigelow to Seward, April 17, 1863, Seward Papers; Forbes to Welles, April 22, 1863, Welles Papers; James P. Shenton, *Robert John Walker: A Politician from Jackson to Lincoln* (New York, 1961), pp. 186–98; Amos E. Taylor, "Walker's Financial Mission to London on behalf of the North, 1863–1864," *Journal of*

Economic and Business History, III (1930–31), 296–320; Vagn K. Hansen, "Jefferson Davis and the Repudiation of Mississippi Bonds: The Development of a Political Myth," *Journal of Mississippi History*, XXXIII (1971), 105–32.

35. Adams to Everett, March 20, 1863, Adams Papers, reel 169; ibid., reel 77, Adams, Diary, March 22; H. Adams to F. Seward, March 20, 1863, Seward Papers.

36. Russell memorandum, March 27, 1863, FO 5/869.

37. Adams, Diary, March 26, 1863, Adams Papers, reel 77; Adams to Seward, March 27, 1863, *Papers Relating to Foreign Affairs*, 1863–64, I, 180–83; Russell to Palmerston, March 27, 1863, Broadlands Mss.

38. R. A. J. Walling, ed., *The Diaries of John Bright* (London, 1930), pp. 263–64; H. Adams to F. Seward, March 20, 1863, Seward Papers; Bright to Dudley, March 25, 1863, Dudley Papers; Sumner to Cobden, March 10, 1863, Cobden Papers, vol. 13, Chichester; ibid., March 24; Sumner to Cobden, March 16, 1863, *Memoir and Letters of Sumner*, IV, 129; Cobden to Bright, March 26, 1863, BM Add. Ms. 43652.

39. *Parl. Debates*, 3rd ser., CLXX, 33–59, 72.

40. Ibid., pp. 61–71, 90–94; *Moran Journal*, II, 1138–39.

41. Adams, Diary, March 28, 1863, Adams Papers, reel 77; ibid., reel 169, Adams to Seward; ibid., April 2; ibid., reel 77, Adams, Diary, April 5.

42. Dudley to Adams, March 7, 1863, Dudley Papers; ibid., Dud-

ley to Seward, March 11; ibid.,
March 13; ibid., March 20;
Adams, Diary, March 18, 1863,
Adams Papers, reel 77; Collier
to Layard, March 25, 1863, BM
Add. Ms. 39105; FO memo-
randum on 'Case of the Alexandria,' April 24, 1863, PRO
30/22/14F; see also Frank J.
Merli, "Crown versus Cruiser:
The Curious Affair of the *Alexandra*," *Civil War History*, IX
(1963), 167-78.

43. LO to Russell, March 30, 1863,
FO 83/2216; ibid., April 4, FO
83/2217.

44. Gardner to Hamilton, April 6,
1863, FO 5/1048; Adams to
Russell, April 8, 1863, *Papers
Relating to Foreign Affairs*,
1863-64, I, 232; ibid., Hammond
to Adams; Hammond to Layard,
April 8, 1863, BM Add. Ms.
38952.

45. Russell to Adams, April 2, 1863,
*Papers Relating to Foreign Af-
fairs*, 1863-64, I, 239; Waddington to Lord Provost of Glasgow,
April 16, 1863, FO 5/920; ibid.,
Preston to Waddington, April 2;
ibid., Greig to Mayor of Liverpool, April 13; Mayor of Liverpool to Waddington, April 13,
1863, FO 5/921.

46. Hammond to Palmerston, April
5, 1863, Broadlands Mss.; Russell
to Lyons, March 28, 1863, PRO
30/22/97.

47. Adams to Seward, April 3, 1863,
*Papers Relating to Foreign Af-
fairs*, 1863-64, I, 220.

48. Bright to Sumner, April 4, 1863,
MHSP, XLVI, 114-15; Cobden
to Bright, March 26, 1863, BM
Add. Ms. 43652; *John Bright
and the American Question*, pp.
170-90; Charles I. Glicksberg,
"Henry Adams Reports on a

Trades-Union Meeting," *New
England Quarterly*, XV (1942),
724-28; *Bee-Hive*, April 4, 1863.

49. *Morning Star*, April 8, 1863;
Daily News, April 10, 1863;
Times, April 9, 1863.

50. Glasgow memorial, April 28,
1863, FO 5/924.

51. Russell to Lyons, March 28,
1863, Lyons Papers; Lyons to
Russell, February 24, 1863, PRO
30/22/37; ibid., March 10; ibid.,
FO 5/879; ibid., March 13, PRO
30/22/37.

52. Russell to Lyons, March 7, 1863,
Lyons Papers; ibid., March 14;
ibid., March 21; Russell to Lewis,
March 24, 1863, PRO 30/22/
14E; Russell to Somerset, March
24, 1863, Somerset Papers; Russell to Lyons, March 28, 1863,
Lyons Papers.

53. *English Historical Review*, L, 39;
Palmerston to Russell, April 7,
1863, PRO 30/22/14E; Russell
to Cowley, April 1, 1863, PRO
30/22/105; Cowley to Russell,
April 10, 1863, PRO 30/22/59;
Palmerston to Russell, April 5,
1863, PRO 30/22/14E.

54. Russell to Lyons, March 7, 1863,
Lyons Papers; Russell to Cowley,
April 11, 1863, PRO 30/22/105;
Russell to Lyons, April 11, 1863,
Lyons Papers; Russell to Lyons,
April 7, 1863, FO 5/869.

55. *Times*, October 28, 1862; Wilkes
to Welles, February 2, 1863,
ORN, 1st ser., II, 71; Merli and
Wilson, *Makers of American
Diplomacy*, p. 155; Wilkes to
Welles, January 23, 1863, *ORN*,
1st ser., II, 54-56.

56. Wilkes to Welles, September 29,
1862, *ORN*, 1st ser., I, 483, 483-
85; Ord to Newcastle, October
3, 1862, FO 5/865; ibid., October 4; ibid., Munro to Ord,

October 3; ibid., Ord to New-castle, October 6; S. W. Jack-man, "Admiral Wilkes Visits Bermuda during the Civil War," *American Neptune*, XXIV (1964), 208–11.

57. Newcastle memorandum, October 29, 1862, CO 37/183.

58. LO to Russell, October 31, 1862, FO 83/2215; Lyons to Seward, November 24, 1862, *Papers Relating to Foreign Affairs*, 1863–64, I, 462–63.

59. Lyons to Milne, January 14, 1863, Lyons Papers.

60. Wilkes to Welles, November 4, 1862, Welles Papers; Bayley to Newcastle, December 11, 1862, FO 5/916; ibid., May 6, 1863, FO 5/924; Lyons to Russell, December 30, 1862, PRO 30/22/36; Russell to Lyons, January 16, 1863, FO 5/868.

61. Lyons to Bayley, January 31, 1863, Lyons Papers; Malcolm to Milne, November 24, 1862, FO 5/875; Milne to Romaine, December 24, 1862, FO 5/916; Russell to Lyons, January 31, 1863, Lyons Papers; ibid., February 4; ibid., February 7; ibid., FO 5/868.

62. Bernath, *Squall across the Atlantic*, pp. 67–69; Phillimore to Russell, March 3, 1863, FO 83/2216; ibid., LO to Russell, March 13; ibid, April 1, FO 83/2217; ibid., April 22; Hammond memorandum, April 10, 1863, FO 5/820; *Times*, April 18 and 16, 1863; *Morning Herald*, April 21, 1863; *Saturday Review*, April 18 and 25, 1863.

63. Adams to Seward, April 7, 1863, *Papers Relating to Foreign Affairs*, 1863–64, I, 228–29; ibid., p. 256, April 23; Adams, Diary, April 8, 1863, Adams Papers,

reel 77; ibid., April 9; ibid., April 10; ibid., April 14; ibid., reel 564, Adams to C. F. Adams Jr., April 17.

64. Bigelow to Seward, April 17, 1863, Seward Papers; Bigelow to Bright, April 30, 1863, BM Add. Ms. 43390.

65. Quoted in Maynard, "The Forbes-Aspinwall Mission," p. 73; Bright to Sumner, April 24, 1863, *MHSP*, XLVI, 115–16; Bright to Dudley, April 22, 1863, Dudley Papers; Aspinwall and Forbes to Welles, April 25, 1863, *Forbes Letters*, II, 44–45; Forbes to Welles, April 22, 1863, Welles Papers.

66. Adams, Diary, April 15, 1863, Adams Papers, reel 77; *Moran Journal*, II, 1150.

67. *Adams Letters*, I, 274–75; *Moran Journal*, II, 1147–48; *Times*, April 18 and 21, 1863; *Standard*, April 22, 1863.

68. *Parl. Debates*, 3rd ser., CLXX, 72–83, 578.

69. Bright to Sumner, April 24, 1863, *MHSP*, XLVI, 116; S. M. Ellis, ed., *A Mid-Victorian Pepys: The Letters and Memoirs of Sir William Hardman* (New York, 1913), p. 305.

70. *Parl. Debates*, 3rd ser., CLXX, 598.

71. Hammond to Cowley, April 25, 1863, FO 519/191; LO to Russell, March 21, 1863, FO 83/2216; ibid., April 1, FO 83/2217.

72. Lyons to Russell, April 7, 1863, PRO 30/22/37; ibid., April 13.

73. Cowley to Russell, April 14, 1863, PRO 30/22/59; Russell to Cowley, April 29, 1863, FO 519/200; Cowley to Russell, April 29, 1863, PRO 30/22/59; Russell to Lyons, April 25, 1863, Lyons Papers.

74. Hammond to Lyons, April 25, 1863, Lyons Papers; *Parl. Debates*, 3rd ser., CLXX, 560–66, 759; Morris to Mackay, April 27, 1863, Morris Papers.
75. *Times*, April 24, 1863.
76. *Morning Post*, April 24, 1863.
77. Russell to Somerset, April 21, 1863, Somerset Papers.
78. Russell to Lyons, April 24, 1863, FO 5/870.

79. Russell to Lyons, April 25, 1863, Lyons Papers.
80. *Parl. Debates*, 3rd ser., CLXX, 753–54.
81. Hammond memorandum, April 27, 1863, Broadlands Mss.; Lyons to Russell, April 24, 1863, PRO 30/22/37; Lyons to Russell, May 8, 1863, FO 5/935; Lyons to Russell, May 11, 1863, FO 5/883; Bernath, *Squall across the Atlantic*, pp. 111–12.

TEN   Precedents

1. Macfarland to Mann, May 4, 1863, Mason Papers.
2. *Parl. Debates*, 3rd ser., CLXX, 876–98.
3. Bigelow to Bright, April 30, 1863, BM Add. Ms. 43390; Adams, Diary, May 5, 1863, Adams Papers, reel 77.
4. Forbes to Welles, May 5, 1863, Welles Papers; Cobden to Sumner, May 2, 1863, *American Historical Review*, II, 310–11; Bright to Sumner, May 2, 1863, *MHSP*, XLVI, 118.
5. Cobden to Bright, April 8, 1863, BM Add. Ms. 43652.
6. Adams, Diary, April 21, 1863, Adams Papers, reel 77; Cobden to Bright, April 18, 1863, BM Add. Ms. 43652; ibid., April 22.
7. *Parl. Debates*, 3rd ser., CLXX, 713–17, 723–36.
8. Bigelow to Seward, April 25, 1863, Seward Papers; *Moran Journal*, II, 1152; Cobden to Bright, April 24, 1863, BM Add. Ms. 43652; *Economist*, January 17, 1863.
9. Chamber of Commerce to Russell, May 4, 1863, FO 5/922.
10. Gladstone to Russell, April 27,

1863, PRO 30/22/23; Argyll to Sumner, April 24, 1863, *MHSP*, XLVII, 74–75; Argyll to Gladstone, April 7, 1863, BM Add. Ms. 44099; ibid., April 27.
11. Bigelow, *Retrospections*, I, 638; Evarts to Seward, May 2, 1863, Seward Papers.
12. *Saturday Review*, May 2, 1863; Hammond memorandum, May 31, 1863, FO 5/921.
13. Memoranda by Westbury, Stanley of Alderley, Palmerston, Newcastle and Russell, June 2–4, 1863, FO 5/921; Bernath, *Squall across the Atlantic*, pp. 72–73.
14. Argyll to Russell, April 10, 1863, PRO 30/22/26.
15. LO to Russell, April 4, 1863, FO 83/2217.
16. Merli, "Crown versus Cruiser," *Civil War History*, IX, 167–78; Dudley to Seward, May 8, 1863, Dudley Papers; James D. Bulloch, *The Secret Service of the Confederate States in Europe* (reprint ed., New York, 1959), pp. 331–36; Russell to Grey, June 13, 1863, PRO 30/22/31.
17. Palmer, *Memorials*, II, 440–47; Merli, *Britain and Confederate*

Navy, pp. 160–77; Wilbur Devereaux Jones, *The Confederate Rams at Birkenhead: A Chapter in Anglo-American Relations* (Tuscaloosa, Ala., 1961), pp. 47–48.

18. *Bee-Hive*, November 14, 1863; Bright to Sumner, November 20, 1863, *MHSP*, XLVI, 126.

19. Pollock to Lindsay, October 11, 1864, Lindsay Papers. Lindsay also left an incisive biographical note on Pollock, as on many of his prominent contemporaries.

20. *Morning Post*, June 25, 1863; *Spectator*, June 27, 1863; *Economist*, July 18, 1863; *Morning Star*, June 25, 1863; *Saturday Review*, June 27, 1863; *Daily News*, June 25, 1863.

21. Hammond to Cowley, June 28, 1863, FO 519/191.

22. Evarts to Seward, June 26, 1863, Seward Papers; ibid., June 29; Forbes and Aspinwall to Welles, June 27, 1863, *Forbes Letters*, II, 46–48; Forbes to Welles, June 25, 1863, Hotze Papers; Maynard, "The Forbes-Aspinwall Mission," *Mississippi Valley Historical Review*, XLV, 86–87.

23. Bulloch, *Secret Service*, pp. 353–54, 383–402.

24. Adams to Seward, June 26, 1863, *Papers Relating to Foreign Affairs*, 1863–64, I, 319–21; Adams, Diary, June 8, 1863, Adams Papers, reel 77; ibid., July 9; ibid., August 21; ibid., reel 169, Adams to Dana, June 12, 1863; ibid., reel 565, Dana to Adams, July 21, 1863.

25. Ibid., reel 77, Adams, Diary, July 10; Adams to Russell, July 11, 1863, *Papers Relating to Foreign Affairs*, 1863–64, I, 361–62; ibid., p. 367, Adams to Seward, July 24.

26. Adams to Seward, July 31, 1863, Adams Papers, reel 169; ibid., reel 77, Adams, Diary, July 22; ibid., July 27; ibid., July 23; ibid., July 24.

27. *Seward at Washington*, III, 171; Nevins, *Strong Diary*, pp. 348–50.

28. *Seward at Washington*, III, 185; F. Seward, *Reminiscences*, pp. 236–37; Lyons to Russell, August 16, 1863, FO 5/892.

29. Christopher Chancellor, ed., *An Englishman in the American Civil War: the diaries of Henry Yates Thompson* (London, 1971), pp. 61–62, 82–83; *New York Herald*, April 27, 1863; *New York Tribune*, June 9, August 1, 1863; *Brownson's Quarterly*, XXV (1863), 420; *Welles Diary*, I, 384–85; Bigelow, *Retrospections*, II, 47.

30. Lyons to Russell, May 11, 1863, PRO 30/22/37; *Welles Diary*, I, 409–10, 451–53; Lyons to Russell, July 26, 1863, FO 5/891; *Seward at Washington*, III, 178–79; Lyons to Russell, June 26, 1863, PRO 30/22/37.

31. Lyons to Russell, September 2, 1863, PRO 30/22/37; Palmerston to Russell, September 19, 1863, PRO 30/22/22; Russell to Lyons, October 2, 1863, PRO 30/22/97.

32. Lyons to Russell, September 2, 1863, PRO 30/22/37; ibid., August 14.

33. Seward to Adams, July 11, 1863, *Papers Relating to Foreign Affairs*, 1863–64, I, 354–57; ibid., pp. 372–76, July 30; Lyons to Russell, August 7, 1863, PRO 30/22/37.

34. Evarts to Seward, May 30, 1863, Seward Papers; ibid., July 28; ibid., Blatchford to Seward, June

20; *Welles Diary*, I, 428–29, 435–38; *Confidential Correspondence of Fox*, II, 196.

35. Bigelow to Bright, June 12, 1863, BM. Add. Ms. 43390.
36. Monypenny and Buckle, *Disraeli*, IV, 339; *Adams Letters*, II, 41.
37. *Standard*, October 5, 1863.
38. Russell to Palmerston, May 29, 1863, Broadlands Mss.; Hammond to Layard, June 27, 1863, BM Add. Ms. 38952; Palmerston to Russell, September 2, 1863, PRO 30/22/14F; ibid., September 26, PRO 30/22/22.
39. Queen to Palmerston, August 11, 1863, *Letters of Queen Victoria*, 2nd ser., I, 102; ibid., p. 111, Queen to Russell, October 4; Grey to Granville, June 1, 1863, PRO 30/29/18/8; W. E. Mosse, "Queen Victoria and her Ministers in the Schleswig-Holstein Crisis 1863–1864," *English Historical Review*, LXXVIII (1963), 263–66; *Economist*, July 25, 1863.
40. *Daily News*, June 18, 1863; Bayly Ellen Marks and Mark Norton Schatz, eds., *Between North and South: A Maryland Journalist Views the Civil War: The Narrative of William Wilkins Glen 1861–1869* (Cranbury, N.J., 1976), p. 110.
41. *Economist*, June 6, 1863; George Hamilton memorandum, July, 1864, BM Add. Ms. 44192; *Statistical History of the United States*, p. 556; Archibald to Russell, June 30, 1863, FO 5/901.
42. Newcastle to Bayley, April 11, 1863, CO 23/171; Bayley to Newcastle, October 15, 1863, CO 23/172; Bayley to Newcastle, May 2, 1864, CO 23/174; Nesbitt to Cardwell, October 7,

1864, CO 23/176.
43. Russell to Lyons, June 20, 1863, PRO 30/22/97; Russell to Layard, September 1, 1863, BM Add. Ms. 38989; Cobden to Bright, October 26, 1863, BM Add. Ms. 43652; *Morning Star*, September 5, 1863; *Reynolds's Newspaper*, September 6, 1863; Russell to Lyons, July 4, 1863, PRO 30/22/97; Palmerston to Russell, September 7, 1863, PRO 30/22/14F; De Grey to Palmerston, September 9, 1863, Broadlands Mss.
44. Russell to Lyons, September 18, 1863, PRO 30/22/97; Palmerston to Russell, September 30, 1863, PRO 30/22/22.
45. Cobden to Fitzmayer, July 27, 1863, BM Add. Ms. 43665; John Kutolowski, "The Effect of the Polish Insurrection of 1863 on American Civil War Diplomacy," *The Historian*, XXVII (1965), 571; Jones, *Confederate Rams*, p. 53; Baxter, *American Historical Review*, XXXIV, 28.
46. The memorials are to be found in FO 5/924; *Daily News*, July 13, 1863; Rathbone to Hughes, December 16, 1898, *Forbes Letters*, II, 93–94.
47. *Spectator*, September 5, May 9, 1863; *Saturday Review*, July 4, 1863; *Morning Post*, June 17, 1863; *Morning Star*, August 29, 1863.
48. *Times*, September 1, 3, and 7, 1863.
49. FO to Admiralty, August 31, 1863, FO 5/928; Russell to Grey, September 19, 1863, *Later Correspondence of Russell*, II, 335.
50. Report from Solicitor of Customs, July 9, 1863, FO 5/1000.
51. LO to Russell, July 24, 1863, FO 83/2218; ibid., August 20.

52. Russell to Liverpool Shipowners, July 6, 1863, FO 5/926; Memorandum, "Alabama & ships equipped for war ag[ain]st U.S. of America," August 21, 1863, PRO 30/22/27.

53. Westbury memorandum, PRO 30/22/27; ibid., Newcastle memorandum, August 26, 1863; ibid., Palmerston memorandum, August 23; Palmerston to Russell, August 23, 1863, PRO 30/22/22.

ELEVEN   Seizure of the Rams

1. Layard to Russell, August 21, 1863, BM Add. Ms. 38989.

2. Russell to Executive of Emancipation Society, August 31, 1863, FO 5/1000; Russell to Adams, September 1, 1863, FO 83/2218; Russell to Layard, August 31, 1863, BM Add. Ms. 38989; David F. Krein, "Russell's Decision to Detain the Laird Rams," *Civil War History*, XXII (1976), 158–63.

3. Russell memorandum, August 31, 1863, FO 5/929; Russell to Layard, September 1, 1863, BM Add. Ms. 38989; FO to Treasury, September 1, 1863, FO 5/1000; ibid., Home Office.

4. Russell to Layard, August 31, 1863, BM Add. Ms. 38989; ibid., Russell memorandum, September 2; ibid., Russell to Layard.

5. Layard to LO, August 31, 1863, FO 83/2218; Colquhoun to Russell, February 26, 1863, FO 5/1000.

6. Layard to Russell, September 2, 1863, BM Add. Ms. 38989; ibid., Russell memorandum, September 3.

7. Ibid., Russell to Layard, September 3.

8. Layard to Treasury, September 5, 1863, FO 5/1000; Russell to Layard (telegram), September 4, 1863, PRO 30/22/97; Russell memorandum, September 5, 1863, BM Add. Ms. 38989; Russell to Grey, September 19, 1863, *Later Correspondence of Russell*, II, 335.

9. Russell to Palmerston, September 3, 1863, Broadlands Mss.; ibid., September 4, PRO 30/22/30; Palmerston to Russell, September 4, 1863, PRO 30/22/22; Palmerston to Layard, September 5, 1863, BM Add. Ms. 38989.

10. Adams to Forbes, September 7, 1863, *Forbes Letters*, II, 56–57; Adams to Seward, September 3, 1863, *Papers Relating to Foreign Affairs*, 1863–64, I, 407; ibid., p. 396, August 20; Argyll to Gladstone, September 4, 1863, BM Add. Ms. 44099.

11. Dudley to Seward, August 24, 1863, Dudley Papers; ibid., Dudley to Adams, August 26; ibid., August 29; *Moran Journal*, II, 1200–1202.

12. Adams, Diary, September 3, 1863, Adams Papers, reel 77; Adams to Russell, September 3, 1863, *Papers Relating to Foreign Affairs*, 1863–64, I, 407; ibid., p. 412, September 4; Dudley to Seward, September 4, 1863, Dudley Papers.

13. Adams to Seward, September 4, 1863, *Papers Relating to Foreign Affairs*, 1863–64, I, 412; Dudley to Seward, September 4, 1863, Dudley Papers.

14. Adams to Russell, September 5, 1863, *Papers Relating to Foreign Affairs*, 1863–64, I, 418–19; Adams, Diary, September 5, 1863, Adams Papers, reel 77; Russell minute, September 4, 1863, BM Add. Ms. 38989; Adams to Seward, September 8, 1863, *Papers Relating to Foreign Affairs*, 1863–64, I, 417–18; Wilson to Seward, September 8, 1863, Seward Papers.

15. Adams to Dana, September 7, 1863, Adams Papers, reel 170; Adams to Seward, September 10, 1863, *Papers Relating to Foreign Affairs*, 1863–64, I, 421.

16. Cleveland to Seward, September 11, 1863, Seward Papers.

17. Dudley to Adams, September 11, 1863, Dudley Papers; ibid., to Seward; *Moran Journal*, II, 1209–10; Adams, Diary, September 14, 1863, Adams Papers, reel 77; ibid., September 15.

18. Palmerston to Layard, September 7, 1863, BM Add. Ms. 38989; Layard to Russell, September 7, 1863, BM Add. Ms. 38990; ibid., Russell to Layard; Russell to Adams, September 11, 1863, FO 5/1000; ibid., Adams to Russell, September 16.

19. Edwards to Commissioners of Customs, September 9, 1863, FO 5/1000; ibid., Hamilton to Hammond, September 10; ibid., Hammond to Hamilton, September 11; Commissioners of Customs to Treasury, September 12, 1863, FO 83/2219; ibid., Hammond to Hamilton, September 13; Hamilton to Hammond, September 15, FO 5/1001; ibid., Hammond to Romaine, September 18; ibid., Romaine to Hammond, September 19; ibid., Hammond to Hamilton, September 19; ibid.,

Romaine to Hammond, September 19; Somerset to Palmerston, September 19, 1863, Broadlands Mss.

20. LO to Russell, September 12, 1863, FO 83/2219; Russell memorandum, September 14, 1863, FO 5/1000.

21. Biographical sketch of Gibson in Lindsay Papers; Argyll to Palmerston, September 1, 1863, BM Add. Ms. 38989; Argyll to Russell, September 5, 1863, PRO 30/22/35; ibid., September 9, PRO 30/22/26; Argyll memorandum, October 2, 1863, FO 5/930; Gladstone to Russell, September 25, 1863, BM Add. Ms. 44292.

22. Palmerston to Russell, September 13, 1863, PRO 30/22/22; Grey to Russell, September 16, 1863, PRO 30/22/26.

23. Russell memorandum, September 3, 1863, BM Add. Ms. 38989; LO to Russell, July 21, 1863, FO 83/2218; Somerset to Russell, August 3, 1863, PRO 30/22/26.

24. Palmerston to Somerset, September 13, 1863, Somerset Papers; ibid., September 16; ibid., September 19; Russell to Palmerston, September 14, 1863, Broadlands Mss.; Russell to Somerset, September 14, 1863, PRO 30/22/31; Somerset to Russell, September 15, 1863, PRO 30/22/26; Somerset to Palmerston, September 15, 1863, Broadlands Mss.; ibid., September 18.

25. Hore to Grey, September 22, 1863, FO 5/1000; ibid., October 2; Hammond to Layard, October 3, 1863, BM Add. Ms. 38952.

26. Palmerston to Russell, September 24, 1863, PRO 30/22/22; Hammond to Lyons, September 19,

1863, Lyons Papers; Russell to Adams, September 25, 1863, FO 5/1000.

27. Donald, *Sumner and the Rights of Man*, pp. 122–25; Sumner to Cobden, April 21, 1863, Cobden Papers, vol. 13, Chichester; Argyll to Motley, July 24, 1863, Argyll, *Autobiography*, II, 203; Sumner to Bright, August 4, 1863, BM Add. Ms. 43390; ibid., September 22; Sumner to Duchess of Argyll, June 8, 1863, *Memoir and Letters of Sumner*, IV, 140.

28. Morgan to Seward, September 7, 1863, Seward Papers; Sumner to Cobden, November 6, 1863, *Memoir and Letters of Sumner*, IV, 167; ibid., p. 144, September 4; Forbes to Sumner, September 8, 1863, *Forbes Letters*, II, 58–59.

29. Sumner to Cobden, November 6, 1863, Cobden Papers, vol. 13, Chichester; Sumner to Lieber, September 15, 1863, *Memoir and Letters of Sumner*, IV, 166; Forbes to Rathbone, October 31, 1863, *Forbes Letters*, II, 60–64; Everett to Adams, September 28, 1863, Adams Papers, reel 566; Sumner to Cobden, September 4, 1863, Cobden Papers, vol. 13, Chichester; Donald, *Sumner and the Rights of Man*, pp. 127–29.

30. *Morning Star*, September 25, 1863; *Daily News*, September 29, 1863; *Spectator*, October 3, 1863.

31. Hotze to Benjamin, October 3, 1863, *ORN*, 2nd ser., III, 921; *Morning Post*, September 28, 1863.

32. *Economist*, October 3, 1863; *Saturday Review*, October 3, 1863; *Spectator*, October 3, 1863; *Morning Star*, September 29, 1863.

33. Adams to Everett, October 1, 1863, Adams Papers, reel 170; ibid., reel 77, Adams, Diary, September 29; Adams to Seward, October 1, 1863, *Papers Relating to Foreign Affairs*, 1863–64, I, 434–35.

34. Hore to Grey, September 22, 1863, FO 5/1000; Palmerston to Russell, October 2, 1863, PRO 30/22/14G; Russell to Palmerston, October 5, 1863, Broadlands Mss.

35. Bassett, *Gladstone to his Wife*, p. 150.

36. Argyll to Gladstone, September 28, 1863, BM Add. Ms. 44099; ibid., Gladstone to Argyll, September 30; ibid., Argyll to Gladstone, October 3; ibid., October 5.

37. Gladstone memorandum, October 7, 1863, BM Add. Ms. 44752.

38. Argyll to Gladstone, October 3, 1863, BM Add. Ms. 44099.

39. Gladstone memorandum, October 7, 1863, BM Add. Ms. 44752; Gladstone to Layard, October 8, 1863, BM Add. Ms. 38989; Palmerston to Gladstone, October 9, 1863, BM Add. Ms. 44272; Argyll to Gladstone, October 3, 1863, BM Add. Ms. 44099.

40. Inglefield to Ryder, October 6, 1863, FO 5/1000; ibid., Hammond to Hamilton, October 7, 1863; ibid., Romaine to Hammond, October 8; ibid., Hammond to Hamilton; ibid., Inglefield to Romaine, October 11, 1863.

41. Hamilton to Hammond, October 10, 1863, FO 5/1001; ibid., Hammond to Hamilton, October 10; Argyll to Russell, October 17, 1863, PRO 30/22/26.

42. Grey to Gladstone, October 15, 1863, BM Add. Ms. 44162; ibid., Gladstone to Grey, October 18; Grey to Palmerston, October 16, 1863, Broadlands Mss.; Hammond to Layard, October 17, 1863, BM Add. Ms. 38952; Russell to Granville, October 31, 1863, PRO 30/29/18/8.

43. Argyll to Russell, October 17, 1863, PRO 30/22/26.

44. *Spectator*, October 3 and 17, 1863; *Times*, October 17, 1863; *Morning Star*, October 16, 1863; Argyll to Gladstone, October 20, 1863, BM Add. Ms. 44099.

45. LO to Russell, October 21, 1863, FO 83/2219.

46. Russell to Lyons, October 24, 1863, Lyons Papers.

47. Inglefield to Grey, October 23, 1863, FO 5/1000; ibid., October 25; Hammond to Hamilton, October 26, 1863, FO 83/2219; ibid., Hammond to Romaine; Laird Brothers to Treasury, October 29, 1863, FO 5/1000; ibid., Russell; ibid., Admiralty; Somerset to Russell, February 18, 1864, PRO 30/22/26; ibid., March 23; ibid., March 24; Somerset to

Gladstone, June 13, 1864, BM Add. Ms. 44304.

48. Adams to Evarts, October 14, 1863, Adams Papers, reel 170; ibid., Adams to Seward, October 16; ibid., reel 77, Adams, Diary, October 28.

49. Lyons to Russell, October 16, 1863, PRO 30/22/37; Seward to Adams, September 2, 1863, NA/M77/77; Seward to Adams, September 5, 1863, *Papers Relating to Foreign Affairs*, 1863–64, I, 416–17; ibid., p. 434, September 28; ibid., p. 444, October 5; ibid., pp. 445–47, October 6; ibid., October 24, NA/M77/78.

50. Lyons to Russell, October 12, 1863, PRO 30/22/37; Milne to Grey, October 11, 1863, Milne Papers, 107, National Maritime Museum, Greenwich; Milne to Romaine, October 13, 1863, Adm 1/5280; Stuart to Russell, September 28, 1863, PRO 30/22/37; ibid., October 6; Palmerston to Russell, October 19, 1863, PRO 30/22/22.

51. *New York Times*, October 10 and 13, November 4, 1863; *New York Tribune*, October 14, November 4 and 17, 1863.

TWELVE   The Friends of the South

1. Adams to C. F. Adams Jr., October 9, 1863, Adams Papers, reel 566; ibid., reel 77, Adams, Diary, May 12, 1863.

2. Mason, *Life of Mason*, pp. 407–10; Slidell to Benjamin, May 3, 1863, Pickett Papers; Clanricarde to Mason, May 17, 1863, Mason Papers; *Parl. Debates*, 3rd ser., CLXX, 1818–34; ibid., CLXXI, 874–85.

3. *Standard*, May 25, 1863.

4. Charles P. Cullop, "English Reaction to Stonewall Jackson's Death," *West Virginia History*, XXIX (1967), 1–5; *Bee-Hive*, July 4, 1863; *Times*, June 11 and 17, 1863.

5. Adams to Everett, June 5, 1863, Adams Papers, reel 169; Lucas to Lindsay, November 10, 1863, Lindsay Papers.

6. Mason to Benjamin, June 4, 1863, *ORN*, 2nd ser., III, 782–

83; *Spectator*, May 30, 1863; Adams to Seward, July 2, 1863, *Papers Relating to Foreign Affairs*, 1863–64, I, 348; Ellison, *Support for Secession*, pp. 110–22; Hotze to Benjamin, May 14, 1863, *ORN*, 2nd ser., III, 767–69; ibid., 783–86, June 6; *Morning Herald*, June 2, 8, 10, and 26, 1863; *Standard*, June 6 and 9, 1863.

7. DeLeon to McHenry, June 22, 1863, Pickett Papers.

8. Spence to Mason, June 16, 1863, Mason Papers; Mason to Benjamin, June 20, 1863, *Messages and Papers of Confederacy*, II, 510–12.

9. Account of Roebuck episode in Lindsay Papers; Bigelow, *Retrospections*, II, 26.

10. Mason, *Life of Mason*, pp. 419–25; Cowley memorandum, July 10, 1863, BM Add. Ms. 39106; Hotze to Benjamin, June 26, 1863, Pickett Papers; *Parl. Debates*, 3rd ser., CLXXI, 1506.

11. Slidell to Mason, June 29, 1863, Mason Papers.

12. Cowley memorandum, July 10, 1863, BM Add. Ms. 39106; Cowley to Russell, July 14, 1863, PRO 30/22/59.

13. Adams to Seward, June 26, 1863, Adams Papers, reel 169; *Parl. Debates*, 3rd ser., CLXXI, 1633–62; *Morning Herald*, June 29 and 30, 1863; *Standard*, June 29 and 30, 1863.

14. *Parl. Debates*, 3rd ser., CLXXI, 1771–1841.

15. Bancroft Davis to Welles, July 3, 1863, Welles Papers; Roebuck to Slidell, July 1, 1863, Pickett Papers.

16. Lindsay account in Lindsay Papers.

17. Spence to Mason, July 4, 1863,

Mason Papers; Mason to Davis, October 2, 1863, Pickett Papers; ibid., Hotze to Benjamin, July 11.

18. W. P. Miles to Gregory, September 16, 1863, Gregory Papers.

19. Ibid., Lawley to Gregory.

20. *Charleston Daily Courier*, July 23, 1863; *Wilmington Daily Journal*, July 18, 1863; Kean, *Inside Confederate Government*, p. 89; Jones, *Rebel War Clerk's Diary*, pp. 299, 291; Cridland to Russell, November 16, 1863, FO 5/908.

21. Moore to Lyons, June 6, 1863, Lyons Papers.

22. Walker to Russell, August 21, 1863, FO 5/907.

23. *Charleston Daily Courier*, November 4, 1863.

24. *Mobile Daily Advertiser and Register*, October 20, 1863; Lawley to Gregory, September 16, 1863, Gregory Papers.

25. Rowland, *Letters and Speeches of Davis*, VI, 96–107.

26. Benjamin to Hotze, January 9, 1864, in Bigelow, *Retrospections*, II, 125–26.

27. DeLeon to Benjamin, August 3, 1863, Pickett Papers.

28. Mason to Lindsay, September 20, 1863, Lindsay Papers; Mason to Davis, December 24, 1863, Jefferson Davis Papers, Duke University; Slidell to Mason, September 16, 1863, Mason Papers; Hotze to Benjamin, September 26, 1863, *ORN*, 2nd ser., III, 914; Morris to Mackay, September 24, 1863, Morris Papers; *Times*, September 23, 1863.

29. *Morning Star*, August 6, 1863; Thomas, *Fifty Years of Fleet Street*, pp. 140–41.

30. *Economist*, December 26, 1863.

31. Frances Leigh Williams, *Mat-

thew Fontaine Maury Scientist of the Sea (New Brunswick, N.J., 1963), pp. 397ff.; Maury to Franklin Minor, January 21, 1863, Maury Papers, Library of Congress; ibid., January 20; ibid., Maury to Tremlett, November 12, 1863; ibid., December 9; ibid., December 19; ibid., Maury to his wife, December 16; Cullop, *Confederate Propaganda*, p. 94.

32. Spence to Mason, May 4, 1863, Mason Papers; ibid., June 16; *Anti-Slavery Reporter*, September 1, 1863; Michael Brook, "Confederate Sympathies in North-East Lancashire 1862–1864," *Transactions of the Lancashire and Cheshire Antiquarian Society*, CXXV–CXXVI (1965–66), 211–17; Spence to Wharncliffe, November 24, 1863, Wharncliffe Papers, Sheffield Public Library; Ellison, *Support for Secession*, pp. 74–86.

33. Circular of the Central Association, Seward Papers.

34. *Morning Star*, August 24, 1863; Staley to Wharncliffe, September 16, 1863, Wharncliffe Papers; *Morning Post*, October 7, 1863.

35. Spence to Wharncliffe, October 6, 1863, Wharncliffe Papers; Spence to Mason, December 7, 1863, Mason Papers; ibid., December 17.

36. Spence to Mason, December 17, 1863, Mason Papers; protests against the packing of the public meetings are to be found in FO 5/931; Staley to Wharncliffe, November 3, 1863, Wharncliffe Papers; *Morning Star*, November 27, 1863; Spence to Wharncliffe, November 27, 1863, Wharncliffe Papers; ibid., December 1; ibid., December 21; ibid., November 6.

37. Spence to Wharncliffe, October 23, 1863, Wharncliffe Papers; ibid., November 9; ibid., November 19; Wharncliffe to Maury, November 14, 1863, Maury Papers; Association circular, November 7, 1863, BM Add. Ms. 43390; ibid., December 2; Mason to Lindsay, November 2, 1863, Lindsay Papers; ibid., Lindsay to Slidell, November 6; ibid., Beresford-Hope to Lindsay, December 6; Kintrea to Beresford-Hope, December 16, 1863, Wharncliffe Papers; ibid., Beresford-Hope to Wharncliffe, December 19; Mason to Gregory, January 14, 1864, Gregory Papers.

38. *Morning Star*, January 11, 1864; Adams to Everett, October 13, 1863, Adams Papers, reel 170; ibid., reel 567, Adams to C. F. Adams Jr., October 22, 1863; ibid., January 1, 1864; ibid., reel 170, Adams to Everett, December 17, 1863; ibid., Adams to Palfrey, November 10, 1863; ibid., reel 77, Adams, Diary, November 22, 1863; *Moran Journal*, II, 1244; Adams to Dana, January 27, 1864, Adams Papers, reel 170; ibid., Adams to Seward, November 19, 1863.

39. Palmerston to Russell, December 26, 1863, PRO 30/22/14G; Russell to Somerset, December 28, 1863, Somerset Papers; Mitford, *Stanleys of Alderley*, pp. 342–43; Argyll to Gladstone, January 15, 1864, BM Add. Ms. 44099.

40. Russell to Queen, January 15, 1864, *Later Correspondence of Russell*, II, 306.

41. *Annual Register*, 1863, p. 176; Russell to Lyons, November 21, 1863, Lyons Papers.

42. Lyons to Russell, October 26, 1863, PRO 30/22/37; ibid., No-

vember 6; ibid., November 3, Lyons Papers.

43. Russell to Lyons, January 30, 1864, PRO 30/22/97; ibid., February 6; see Russell's note on Hammond memorandum, October 3, 1863, Broadlands Mss.; Russell to Somerset, January 7, 1864, Somerset Papers; ibid., January 24; Stuart W. Bernath, "British Neutrality and the Civil War Prize Cases," *Civil War History*, XV (1969), 329–30.

44. LO to Russell, November 13, 1863, FO 83/2219; Williams, *Maury*, pp. 410–11; Russell memorandum, October 24, 1863, FO 5/1052; ibid., Russell to Lyons, November 28.

45. Hammond to Cowley, December 12, 1863, FO 519/191; LO to Russell, December 10, 1863, FO 83/2219; Somerset to Russell, December 9, 1863, PRO 30/22/26; Adams to Seward, January 28, 1864, *Papers Relating to Foreign Affairs*, 1864–65 (Washington, 1865), I, 117; ibid., p. 642, April 28; Adams to Seward, December 10, 1863, Adams Papers, reel 170.

46. Adams, Diary, November 22, 1863, Adams Papers, reel 77; W. D. Jones, *Lord Derby and Victorian Conservatism* (London, 1956), p. 279.

47. *Parl. Debates*, 3rd ser., CLXXIII, 22–40, 86–101, 112–18, 190–94, 427–41, 498, 547–49, 955–1021; ibid., CLXXIV, 1862–1913; ibid., CLXXIII, 501–18, 713–15, 618–34; Adams to Seward, March 18, 1864, Adams Papers, reel 171.

48. *Parl. Debates*, 3rd ser., CLXXVI, 2161–82, 1453–54; Emigration Returns, FO 5/980; Bigelow, *Retrospections*, I, 563–64; Seward to Sherman, December 23, 1863,

Seward Papers; ibid., Lyman to Seward, July 8, 1864; Maldwyn A. Jones, "The Background to Emigration from Great Britain in the Nineteenth Century," *Perspectives in American History*, VII (1973), 49–50.

49. Charles P. Cullop, "An Unequal Duel: Union Recruiting in Ireland, 1863–1864," *Civil War History*, XIII (1967), 101–13; Mason to Benjamin, June 12, 1863, *ORN*, 2nd ser., III, 804; Mason, *Life of Mason*, pp. 412–13; E. DeLeon, *Thirty Years*, pp. 38–41.

50. Benjamin to Capston, July 3, 1863, *ORN*, 2nd ser., III, 828–29; ibid., pp. 893–94, Benjamin to Bannon, September 4; Hotze to Capston, October 2, 1863, Pickett Papers; Capston to Benjamin, September 30, 1863, Capston Papers, Museum of the Confederacy; ibid., November 9; ibid., November 1, 1864; Bannon to Benjamin, November 17, 1863, Pickett Papers; ibid., December 15; ibid., March 9, 1864; ibid., May 28.

51. Bannon to Benjamin, November 22, 1863, Pickett Papers; Fitzpatrick to Sanford, February 18, 1864, Seward Papers; Dowling to Benjamin, November 25, 1863, Pickett Papers; ibid., January 28, 1864; Capston to Benjamin, December 3, 1863, Capston Papers; ibid., December 25; ibid., June 7, 1864; ibid., June 18.

52. Russell to Adams, April 20, 1863, *Papers Relating to Foreign Affairs*, 1863–64, I, 267; ibid., pp. 286–87, May 1; Palmerston to Hammond, October, 1863, FO 391/7; Cranford to Secretary of War, July 15, 1863, FO 5/927; ibid., FO to HO, July 18; ibid.,

Mayor of Newcastle to HO, July 25; *Moran Journal*, II, 1241, 1242, 1248.

53. Adams to Russell, December 7, 1863, *Papers Relating to Foreign Affairs*, 1864–65, I, 21.

54. LO to Russell, December 12, 1863, FO 83/2219.

55. *Parl. Debates*, 3rd ser., CLXXIII, 1916–30, 1317–33; ibid., CLXXIV, 295–99, 448–50; ibid., CLXXV, 1439–51; Adams, Diary, April 2, 1864, Adams Papers, reel 77; ibid., April 10; Palmerston memorandum, April 4, 1864, FO 5/977; *Moran Journal*, II, 1282; *Morning Star*, August 9, 1864; Seward to Adams, March 21, 1864, NA/M77/78; Adams to Consuls in Ireland, April 5, 1864, Adams Papers, reel 171.

56. Marks and Schatz, *Between North and South*, pp. 124, 147; Hotze to Benjamin, February 13, 1864, Pickett Papers; ibid., February 27; Adams to Seward, February 18, 1864, *Papers Relating to Foreign Affairs*, 1864–65, I, 172–73; ibid., p. 203, February 25.

57. Adams, Diary, March 10, 1864, Adams Papers, reel 77; Torrens to Sanford, March 24, 1864, Seward Papers; Adams to Forbes, March 31, 1864, Adams Papers, reel 171.

58. Palmerston to Russell, March 26, 1864, PRO 30/22/23; Palmerston to Granville, March 21, 1864, PRO 30/29/18/8; Hotze to Benjamin, April 16, 1864, Pickett Papers; George Villiers, *A Vanished Victorian: Being the Life of George Villiers Earl of Clarendon 1800–1870* (London, 1938), pp. 320–24; Palmerston to Russell, June 21, 1864, PRO 30/22/15C; Mosse, *English His-*

torical Review, LXXVIII, 280–81.

59. Sandiford, *Britain and Schleswig-Holstein*, pp. 100ff.; *Parl. Debates*, 3rd ser., CLXXIV, 549.

60. Wood to Grey, June 24, 1864, *Letters of Queen Victoria*, 2nd ser., I, 228–29; Cobden to Bright, January 28, 1864, BM Add. Ms. 43652; Cobden to Richard, February 2, 1864, BM Add. Ms. 43659; Milner Gibson to Cobden, February 1, 1864, BM Add. Ms. 43662; Somerset to Palmerston, February 22, 1864, Broadlands Mss.

61. *Times*, April 7, May 14, 1864.

62. Adams to George Bemis, September 3, 1864, Adams Papers, reel 171; *Parl. Debates*, 3rd ser., CLXXIII, 1490–95; ibid., CLXXIV, 1787–99; ibid., CLXXV, 467–514.

63. Alan R. Booth, "Alabama *at the Cape, 1863*," *American Neptune*, XXVI (1966), 96–108; LO to Russell, October 19, 1863, FO 83/2219.

64. Somerset to Russell, February 23, 1864, PRO 30/22/26.

65. Russell to Lyons, February 27, 1864, Adm 1/5901; Russell to Somerset, February 29, 1864, Somerset Papers.

66. Somerset to Russell, February 29, 1864, PRO 30/22/26; ibid., Russell to Somerset, Somerset Papers; Palmer, *Memorials*, II, 380.

67. Westbury to Russell, n.d., PRO 30/22/26; Westbury to Palmerston, n.d., Broadlands Mss.; Palmerston memorandum, March 6, 1864, PRO 30/22/27; ibid., Somerset memorandum; ibid., Newcastle memorandum; Russell to Lyons, March 5, 1864, Lyons Papers; ibid., April 2.

68. Argyll to Russell, March 4, 1864, PRO 30/22/26; Argyll to Somerset, March 1, 1864, Somerset Papers; Argyll to Palmerston, March 7, 1864, Broadlands Mss.; Argyll memorandum, dated February 18, 1864, with postscript March 8, 1864, printed and circulated March 14, 1864, PRO 30/22/26.

69. Palmerston to Russell, April 29, 1864, PRO 30/22/15B.

70. Adams, Diary, February 14, 1865, Adams Papers, reel 78.

71. J. A. Hobson, *Richard Cobden: The International Man* (London, 1918), p. 330.

72. Malmesbury, *Memoirs*, II, 326–28.

73. Slidell to Benjamin, September 22, 1862, Pickett Papers; ibid., Mason to Benjamin, April 12, 1864; Lawley to Disraeli, February 19, 1864, B/XX1/L/83, Disraeli Papers; Hotze to Benjamin, March 12, 1864, Pickett Papers; ibid., April 23.

74. Spence to Wharncliffe, June 23, 1864, Wharncliffe Papers; Lindsay to Mason, May 10, 1864, Mason Papers; ibid., May 27.

75. Maury to Tremlett, June 2, 1864, Maury Papers; Tremlett to Lindsay, June 4, 1864, Lindsay Papers; Capston to Benjamin, April 5, 1864, Capston Papers; Tremlett to Mason, June 2, 1864, Mason Papers.

76. Lindsay to Mason, May 30, 1864, Mason Papers; Lindsay to Russell, June 2, 1864, Lindsay Papers; ibid., Campbell to Lindsay, June 29.

77. *Morning Herald*, July 18, 1864.

78. Lindsay's recollections, Lindsay Papers; Russell to Palmerston, July 25, 1864, Broadlands Mss.; *Parl. Debates*, 3rd ser., CLXXVI, 2018–19.

79. Adams to Seward, July 28, 1864, *Papers Relating to Foreign Affairs*, 1864–65, II, 229; ibid., pp. 222–23, July 21.

80. Morris to Lawley, July 18, 1864, Morris Papers.

81. *Morning Herald*, August 31, 1864; *Economist*, September 7, 1864; *Morning Star*, August 24, 1864; *Morning Post*, September 14, 1864; *Daily News*, September 30, 1864; Garnett, Diary, September 14, 1864; ibid., September 23.

82. Brook, *Transactions of Lancashire and Cheshire Antiquarian Society*, CXXV–CXXVI, 215; Spence to Wharncliffe, December 12, 1864, Wharncliffe Papers.

83. Kershaw to Wharncliffe, August 23, 1864, Wharncliffe Papers; Hotze to Benjamin, September 17, 1864, Pickett Papers; *Moran Journal*, II, 1329; Adams to Seward, September 22, 1864, *Papers Relating to Foreign Affairs*, 1864–65, II, 307–8; Dudley to Seward, September 24, 1864, Dudley Papers; *Daily News*, October 8, 1864.

84. *Morning Star*, August 31, September 10, 1864; *Daily News*, September 13, October 8, 1864; *Morning Herald*, September 27, 1864; *Morning Post*, September 19, October 1, 1864.

85. Spence to Wharncliffe, November 2, 1864, Wharncliffe Papers; ibid., Wharncliffe to Adams, November 9; ibid., Adams to Wharncliffe, November 18; ibid., Wharncliffe to Adams, December 22; Seward to Adams, December 5, 1864, NA/M77/78.

86. Jenkins, "William Gregory," *History Today*, XXVIII, 329; Meade, *Benjamin*, pp. 265–66;

Spence to Wharncliffe, January 16, 1865, Wharncliffe Papers.

87. The fullest discussion of the Southern debate on freeing slaves is Robert F. Durden, *The Gray and the Black: The Confederate Debate on Emancipation* (Baton Rouge, 1972); Patrick, *Jefferson Davis and his Cabinet*, pp. 188–89.

88. Bright to Sumner, September 2, 1864, *MHSP*, XLVI, 131; *Bee-Hive*, November 5, 1864; Logan, "The *Bee-Hive* Newspaper," *Civil War History*, XXII, 344–45; *Spectator*, November 26, 1864; Adams to Seward, December 31, 1863, Adams Papers, reel 170.

89. Bright to Wilson, December 28, 1863, Wilson Papers.

90. *Blackwood's*, XCV (1864), 768–74; Guedalla, *Gladstone and Palmerston*, p. 282.

91. Collyer, *Leeds Philosophical Society Proceedings*, VI, 592; *Spectator*, May 14, 1864; Torrens to Sanford, May 18, 1864, Seward Papers; John Vincent, *The For-*

mation of the British Liberal Party 1857–1868, paper ed. (London, 1972), p. 237; Gladstone to Cobden, December 22, 1863, BM Add. Ms. 44136; ibid., Cobden to Gladstone, January 1, 1864.

92. Philip Magnus, *Gladstone: A Biography*, paper ed. (London, 1963), p. 162; Guedalla, *Gladstone and Palmerston*, p. 286; *Morning Star*, May 31, 1864; *Times*, November 24, December 10, 1864.

93. Adams, Diary, December 1, 1864, Adams Papers, reel 78; Ellison, *Support for Secession*, pp. 45–46; *John Bright on America*, pp. 256ff.; *Times*, January 19, 1865; *Bee-Hive*, April 22, 1865.

94. Christopher Harvie, *The Lights of Liberalism: University Liberals and the Challenge of Democracy 1860–1886* (London, 1976), pp. 97ff.

95. Wallace, *Goldwin Smith*, pp. 34–38; *Atlantic Monthly*, XIV (1864), 749–69.

THIRTEEN   Perils of Peace

1. J. C. Kendall, "Blueprint Defiance of Manifest Destiny" (Ph.D. thesis, McGill University, 1969), pp. 183, 443; see also Bruce Willard Hodgins, "The Political Career of John Sandfield Macdonald to the Fall of his Administration in March, 1864: A Study in Canadian Politics" (Ph.D. thesis, Duke University, 1964), pp. 281, 335; *Quebec Mercury*, July 26, November 8, 1862; J. S. Macdonald to Iselin, July 14, 1862, J. S.

Macdonald Papers, PAC; *Le Pays*, July 29, 1862; Ogden to F. Seward, August 14, 1862, NA/T482/1; ibid., Ogden to Seward, August 26; ibid., September 1.

2. Monck to Lyons, May 4, 1864, Lyons Papers; ibid., May 6; Seward to Lyons, July 30, 1864, *Papers Relating to Foreign Affairs*, 1864–65, II, 666.

3. Brooks to Dorion, December 17, 1863, FO 5/980; ibid., Phillips to Coursol, December 19; ibid., December 31; ibid., Dorion to

Bishop of Quebec, January 11, 1864; ibid., Monck to Newcastle, January 27; Monck to Cardwell, September 23, 1864, FO 5/989.

4. *Quebec Morning Chronicle*, November 25, December 30, 1863; Giddings to Seward, July 27, 1863, NA/T222/4; ibid., August 4; ibid., Giddings to F. Seward, October 7; Giddings to Seward, November 26, 1863, NA/T222/5; ibid., January 14; Monck to Lyons, February 22, 1864, Lyons Papers; Monck to Newcastle, April 9, 1864, FO 5/984.

5. Giddings to Seward, November 20, 1862, NA/T222/4; ibid., September 30, 1863; ibid., October 13; William D. Overman, "Some Letters of Joshua R. Giddings on Reciprocity," *Canadian Historical Review*, XVI (1935), 289–95.

6. *Cong. Globe*, 38th Con., 1st sess., pt. 1, 19, 377–82; ibid., App., p. 119; Lyons to Russell, December 15, 1863, PRO 30/22/37; Lyons to Monck, February 11, 1864, Lyons Papers; *New York Times*, December 19, 1863.

7. Hay to Newcastle, November 6, 1862, FO 5/1089A; *Le Pays*, January 19, 1864; *Quebec Mercury*, May 14, 1863.

8. Monck to Lyons, January 25, 1864, Lyons Papers; J. S. Macdonald to Brown, January 21, 1864, J. S. Macdonald Papers; Monck to Lyons, February 3, 1864, Lyons Papers; ibid., February 11; ibid., February 13.

9. Lyons to Monck, January 28, 1864, Lyons Papers; ibid., February 6; ibid., February 8; ibid., March 1; Young to Holton, March 8, 1864, FO 5/1089B.

10. Young to Holton, March 8, 1864, FO 5/1089B.

11. Monck to Newcastle, March 15, 1863, FO 5/983; Monck to Lyons, February 20, 1864, Lyons Papers; ibid., March 10; ibid., March 24; ibid., April 26; ibid., May 27; ibid., Lyons to Monck, March 18; ibid., March 21; Lyons to Russell, September 16, 1864, PRO 30/22/38.

12. Bernal to Stuart, September 14, 1863, PRO 30/22/37; ibid., Stuart to Russell, September 18; ibid., Monck to Stuart, September 26; Monck to Lyons, November 12, 1863, Lyons Papers.

13. Monck to Lyons, November 12, 1863, Lyons Papers; Giddings to Seward, November 13, 1863, NA/T222/4; Donohoe to Lyons, November 16, 1863, FO 5/897; Ogden to Seward, November 28, 1863, NA/T482/1; Thurston to Abbott, November 27, 1863, NA/T222/4.

14. Henry Merritt Wriston, *Executive Agents in American Foreign Relations* (reprint ed., Gloucester, Mass., 1967), p. 570.

15. Monck to Lyons, November 13, 1863, Lyons Papers; ibid., November 18; King to Seward, November 18, 1863, Seward Papers.

16. Lyons to Milne, December 23, 1863, Lyons Papers; Donohoe to Lyons, November 16, 1863, FO 5/897; *New York Tribune*, November 13, 1863.

17. For a full discussion of the *Chesapeake* episode see Robin W. Winks, *Canada and the United States: The Civil War Years*, paper ed. (Montreal, 1971), pp. 244–63.

18. Doyle to Newcastle, December 23, 1863, FO 5/998; ibid., December 24, Newcastle Papers, A/309.

19. Lyons to Gordon, December 17,

1863, Lyons Papers; Lyons to Russell, December 21, 1863, PRO 30/22/37; ibid., December 29; Lyons to Russell, January 12, 1864, FO 5/998; Lyons to Milne, January 10, 1864, Lyons Papers; Seward to Lyons, March 21, 1864, *Papers Relating to Foreign Affairs*, 1864–65, II, 562–63.

20. Monck to Lyons, January 14, 1864, Lyons Papers; ibid., January 26; ibid., Lyons to Monck., January 28.

21. Ogden to Seward, August 14, 1863, NA/T482/1; ibid., September 16; *Canadian News*, August 13, September 3, 1863; "Scrapbook Debates," September 10, 1863, PAC.

22. Benjamin to Holcombe, February 15, 1864, Pickett Papers; ibid., February 24; ibid., Holcombe to Benjamin, April 1, 1864; ibid., June 16; ibid., August 11.

23. Benjamin to Slidell, April 30, 1864, *ORN*, 2nd ser., III, 1105–6.

24. Holcombe to Benjamin, November 16, 1864, Pickett Papers; Clay to Davis, July 25, 1864, Clay Papers; ibid., Mallory to V. Clay, August 1, 1864; William F. Zornow, *Lincoln and the Party Divided* (Norman, 1954), p. 113.

25. Thompson to Benjamin, July 7, 1864, Cameron Notes, Museum of Confederacy; ibid., December 3, Pickett Papers; Confederate operations in Canada are adequately covered by Winks, and less reliably by Oscar A. Kinchen, *Confederate Operations in Canada and the North* (North Quincy, 1970); two accounts by participants are useful: J. B. Castleman, *Active Service* (Louisville, 1917) and J. W. Headley, *Confederate Operations*

in Canada and in New York (New York, 1906).

26. Clay to Benjamin, September 12, 1864, Clay Papers; ibid., Clay to Holcombe, September 14; ibid., Clay to Pendleton, September 16; *Richmond Whig*, March 4, June 11 and 14, October 15, 1864; K. J. Stewart to Davis, December 12, 1864, C. C. Clay Papers, Record Group 109, National Archives, Washington.

27. Holcombe to Monck, May 9, 1864, FO 5/950.

28. Holcombe to Benjamin, April 26, 1864, Pickett Papers; ibid., Dewson to Benjamin, August 26; ibid., October 27; ibid., Benjamin to Hotze, December 19; Walker to Russell, November 11, 1864, FO 5/969.

29. Charles E. Frohman, *Rebels on Lake Erie: The Piracy The Conspiracy Prison Life* (Columbus, Ohio, 1975), pp. 73ff.; Edward T. Downer, "Johnson's Island," *Civil War History*, VIII (1962), 202–17; *Memoir of John Yeats Beall: His Life, Trial, Correspondence, Diary* (Montreal, 1865); Headley, *Confederate Operations*, pp. 231–55.

30. Clay to Benjamin, November 1, 1864, FO 5/1056; Tucker to Clay, December 9, 1864, Clay Papers; Winks, *Canada and United States*, pp. 295–300.

31. Lyons to Russell, December 24, 1863, FO 5/900; ibid., January 12, 1864, PRO 30/22/38; ibid., February 9.

32. Adams, Diary, January 22, 1864, Adams Papers, reel 77; ibid., reel 170, Adams to Russell, February 12; ibid., February 22, *Papers Relating to Foreign Affairs*, 1864–65, I, 202.

33. Lyons to Russell, February 12,

1864, FO 5/944; Seward to Adams, February 13, 1864, NA/ M77/78; ibid., February 25, *Papers Relating to Foreign Affairs*, 1864–65, I, 201.

34. Seward to Evarts, February 22, 1864, Seward Papers; Seward to Adams, February 24, 1864, *Papers Relating to Foreign Affairs*, 1864–65, I, 200.

35. Seward to Adams, March 21, 1864, NA/M77/78; ibid., March 26; ibid., April 8; Adams to Seward, March 4, 1864, Adams Papers, reel 170; Seward to Evarts, April 22, 1864, Seward Papers.

36. *Seward at Washington*, III, 222.

37. *Welles Diary*, II, 151–53; Seward to Adams, October 24, 1864, *Papers Relating to Foreign Affairs*, 1864–65, II, 338–42.

38. Morgan Dix, *Memoirs of John Adams Dix*, 2 vols. (New York, 1883), II, 109–10.

39. Seward to Adams, October 24, 1864, *Papers Relating to Foreign Affairs*, 1864–65, II, 3.

40. Monck to Lyons, March 26, 1864, Lyons Papers; ibid., June 8, RG7 G6/12, PAC; Thurston to Seward, June 22, 1864, NA/ T222/5; ibid., Potter to Seward, August 19.

41. Monck to Burnley, September 26, 1864, FO 5/961; ibid., Burnley to Monck, October 1; Cartier to Coursol, October 20, 1864, NA/ T222/5; ibid., Thurston to Seward.

42. Ibid., October 22; ibid., November 10, NA/T222/6.

43. Ibid., October 20, NA/T222/5; ibid., October 21; ibid., November 10, NA/T222/6; ibid., November 16; ibid., Devlin to Thurston, November 4; ibid., November 17; ibid., Thurston to Seward, De-

cember 5.

44. Ibid., Cartier to Carter, December 13; ibid., December 14; ibid., December 15; ibid., Thurston to Seward, December 24.

45. Dix, *Memoirs of Dix*, II, 112–14.

46. Seward to Adams, December 19, 1864, NA/M77/78; *Cong. Globe*, 38th Cong., 2nd sess., pt. 1, 31–34, 45–47, 71, 95–96; Wilmer C. Harris, *Public Life of Zachariah Chandler 1851–1875* (Lansing, 1917), pp. 82–84.

47. Layard to Gregory, December 4, 1887, BM Add. Ms. 38950; Lyons to Russell, December 24, 1863, PRO 30/22/37; Lyons to Minna, December 26, 1863, Lyons Papers; ibid., March 11, 1864; ibid., May 23; ibid., June 6; ibid., July 4; ibid., July 15; ibid., October 18; ibid., October 21; ibid., Lyons to Elliott, April 5; Sir Edward Malet, *Shifting Scenes: Or Memories of Many Men in Many Lands* (London, 1901), pp. 21–26; Lyons to Russell, August 15, 1864, PRO 30/22/38; ibid., August 23; ibid., August 30; ibid., September 16; ibid., November 1; ibid., December 5.

48. Burnley to Russell, December 27, 1864, PRO 30/22/38; Russell to Lyons, July 16, 1864, Lyons Papers; Hammond to Layard, November 24, 1864, BM Add. Ms. 38953; Burnley to Russell, January 16, 1865, PRO 30/22/ 38.

49. Russell to Lyons, November 26, 1864, FO 5/1099.

50. LO to Russell, January 12, 1865, FO 83/2223; ibid., January 31; Cardwell to Monck, February 17, 1865, FO 5/1057B; Russell to Cowley, August 6, 1864; PRO 30/22/106; LO to Russell, January 26, 1865, FO 83/2223;

Russell to Mason, Slidell and Mann, February 13, 1865, *Messages and Papers of Confederacy*, II, 705–7; Russell to Queen, February 24, 1865, PRO 30/22/15D.

51. Monck to Cardwell, September 26, 1864, RG7 G10/2, PAC; Russell to Cardwell, November 22, 1864, FO 5/1056; LO to Russell, November 25, 1864, FO 83/2222; Monck to Cardwell, December 15, 1864, FO 5/991.

52. Monck to Cardwell, December 15, 1864, FO 5/991; LO to Russell, December 13, 1864, FO 83/2222; Cardwell to Monck, December 16, 1864, FO 5/1056; ibid., Russell memorandum, December 31; LO to Russell, January 6, 1865, FO 83/2223.

53. Russell to Cardwell, January 7, 1865, PRO 30/22/31; Adams, Diary, January 28, 1865, Adams Papers, reel 78; ibid., reel 172, Adams to Seward, December 30, 1864; ibid., January 5, 1865; ibid., January 12; Russell to Burnley, February 15, 1865, FO 5/1009.

54. *Cong. Globe*, 38th Cong., 2nd. sess., pt. 1, 206; Rose to Seward, January 12, 1865, Seward Papers; ibid., Weed to Seward, March 4; Burnley to Russell, March 9, 1865, FO 5/1090.

55. W. L. Morton, ed., *Monck Letters and Journals 1863–1868: Canada from Government House at Confederation*, paper ed. (Toronto, 1970), p. 248.

56. Russell to Lyons, November 14, 1863, Lyons Papers; ibid., November 20, FO 5/873; J. St. George to Alderson, January 25, 1864, FO 5/979; "Report upon the Military Affairs of the United States of America," August 2,

1864, WO 33/14/229; Goodenough to Lyons, April 9, 1864, FO 5/948; Gallwey to Lyons, May 27, 1864, Adm 1/5902.

57. Lyons to Russell, April 19, 1864, PRO 30/22/38; ibid., April 25, FO 5/948; Somerset to Russell, February 27, 1865, PRO 30/22/26.

58. Palmerston memorandum, n.d., PRO 30/22/14G; Palmerston to Russell, December 14, 1864, PRO 30/22/15C.

59. "Report of the Commission on the Defences of Canada," September 1, 1862, WO 33/11/185; De Grey memorandum, November 28, 1862, Harpton Court Collection, 2994, National Library of Wales; ibid., 2938, Somerset memorandum, December 1; ibid., 2939, Gladstone memorandum; ibid., 2937, Palmerston memorandum, December 2; *Parl. Debates*, 3rd ser., CLXX, 876–98.

60. Watkin to Macdonald, June 28, 1862, J. S. Macdonald Papers; Newcastle to Monck, July 26, 1862, Newcastle Papers, Nottingham; ibid., November 20.

61. Monck to Newcastle, August 11, 1862, Newcastle Papers, A/308, PAC.

62. Sir Richard Cartwright, *Reminiscences* (Toronto, 1912), p. 12; Andrew Robb, "The Toronto *Globe* and the Defence of Canada, 1861–1866," *Ontario History*, LXIV (1972), 65–77; *Quebec Morning Chronicle*, August 11, 1862; *Quebec Mercury*, October 16, 1862; Canadian Executive Council Report, October 28, 1862, CO 42/635.

63. Newcastle to Monck, January 8, 1863, Newcastle Papers, Nottingham; Gordon to Newcastle, Jan-

uary 17, 1863, Newcastle Papers, A/309; ibid., Tilley to Gordon, February 2; Bruce W. Hodgins, "John Sandfield Macdonald and the Crisis of 1863," Canadian Historical Association, *Historical Papers* (1965), pp. 30–45.

64. Newcastle to Monck, January 23, 1863, Newcastle Papers, Nottingham; ibid., May 29; ibid., June 20; Monck to Delane, August 20, 1863, Delane Papers; Elaine Allan Mitchell, "Edward Watkin and the Buying-Out of the Hudson's Bay Company," *Canadian Historical Review*, XXXIV (1953), 219–44.

65. *Quebec Mercury*, July 28, September 11, October 16, 1863; Monck to Lyons, October 22, 1863, Lyons Papers; C. F. Hamilton, "The Canadian Militia: From 1861 to Confederation," *Canadian Defence Quarterly*, VI (1929), 199–211.

66. Newcastle to Monck, December 3, 1863, Newcastle Papers, Nottingham; Monck to Delane, September 12, 1863, Delane Papers; *Saturday Review*, October 3, 1863; *Spectator*, October 3, 1863; *Daily News*, October 3, 1863; *Economist*, October 10, 1863.

67. De Grey to Palmerston, April 14, 1864, Broadlands Mss.; De Grey to Cardwell, April 14, 1864, BM Add. Ms. 43551; ibid., Cardwell to De Grey, April 19.

68. Cardwell to Gladstone, July 27, 1864, BM Add. Ms. 44118; ibid., Gladstone to Cardwell, December 21; Argyll to Gladstone, July 28, 1864, BM Add. Ms. 44099; De Grey to Cardwell, August 20, 1864, BM Add. Ms. 43551.

69. Stacey, *Canada and the British Army*, pp. 154–66; Memorandum by Defence Committee on "Re-

port of Lt.-Col. Jervois on the Defence of Canada," WO 33/15/265.

70. Monck memorandum, August 20, 1864, RG7 G10/2, PAC; ibid., Monck to Cardwell, November 16.

71. Monck to Cardwell. November 16, 1864, RG7 G10/2, PAC; Monck to Gregory, March 3, 1865, Gregory Papers.

72. Chester Martin, "British Policy in Canadian Confederation," *Canadian Historical Review*, XIII (1932), 3–19; James A. Gibson, "The Colonial Office view of Canadian Federation, 1856–1868," ibid., XXXV (1954), 279–309; see also his article, "The Duke of Newcastle and British North American Affairs, 1859–1864," ibid., XLIV (1963), 142–56; C. P. Stacey, "Britain's Withdrawal from North America, 1864–1871," ibid., XXXVI (1955), 185–98; G. P. Browne, ed., *Documents on the Confederation of British North America*, paper ed. (Toronto, 1969), p. 32.

73. Newcastle to Monck, September 18, 1863, Newcastle Papers, Nottingham.

74. Russell to Lyons, July 4, 1863, PRO 30/22/97; ibid., July 23, 1864, Lyons Papers; ibid., October 20, PRO 30/22/97; Russell to Newcastle, June 12, 1862, PRO 30/22/31.

75. Cardwell to Palmerston, September 24, 1864, Broadlands Mss.; Cardwell to Gladstone, October 27, 1864, BM Add. Ms. 44118; Cardwell to Gordon, November 12, 1864, PRO 30/48/6/39.

76. Monck to Cardwell, November 7, 1864, RG7 G10/2, PAC.

77. Argyll to Gladstone, November 25, 1864, BM Add. Ms. 44099;

Browne, *Documents on Confederation*, pp. 168–71; Cardwell
to Gordon, November 26, 1864,
PRO 30/48/6/39; ibid., December 10; ibid., January 7, 1865;
ibid., March 4; ibid., Gordon to
Cardwell, December 19, 1864;
ibid., January 15, 1865; ibid.,
January 30; Gordon to Gladstone, February 27, 1865, BM
Add. Ms. 44320; J. K. Chapman,
"Arthur Gordon and Confederation," *Canadian Historical Review*, XXXVII (1956), 141–57.
78. *Blackwood's Magazine*, XCII
(1862), 696–713; *Times*, September 15, October 15 and 22,
November 10, 23, and 24, 1864,
January 9, 1865; *Saturday Review*, December 17, 1864, February 11, 1865; *Morning Star*,
July 12, November 25, December
21, 1864; *Daily News*, July 20,
October 25, 1864, February 14,
1865; *Economist*, July 16, August
27, November 19, 1864, January
7, 1865; *Spectator*, July 16, August 20, November 26, 1864,
January 7, 1865; *Canadian News*,
November 24, 1864; *Morning
Herald*, October 28, 1864; *Morning Post*, November 17 and 26,
1864, January 13, 1865; *Illustrated London News*, August 2,
1862; *Westminster Review*, n.s.,
XXV (1865), 533–60; *Edinburgh
Review*, CXXI (1865), 199.
79. Gladstone to Cobden, February
22, 1865, BM Add. Ms. 44136.
80. Morton, *Monck Letters*, pp. 208–
9; Stacey, *Canada and the British
Army*, pp. 168–69; J. M. S.

Careless, *Brown of the Globe*,
vol. 1, *Statesman of Confederation
1860–1880* (Toronto, 1963), 176–
80.
81. Somerset to Palmerston, November 14, 1864, Broadlands Mss.;
ibid., December 1; ibid., Russell
to Palmerston, December 15;
Palmerston to Somerset, January
15, 1865, Somerset Papers.
82. Palmerston to Queen, January
20, 1865, *Letters of Queen Victoria*, 2nd ser., I, 248–49.
83. Cobden to Gladstone, February
14, 1865, BM Add. Ms. 44136;
ibid., February 20; Palmerston to
Gladstone, March 12, 1865, BM
Add. Ms. 44273; Somerset to
Gladstone, n.d., BM Add. Ms.
44304; Queen's Journal, February
12, 1865, *Letters of Queen Victoria*, 2nd ser., I, 250; Argyll to
Gladstone, February 24, 1865,
BM Add. Ms. 44100.
84. Adams to Seward, March 2,
1865, Adams Papers, reel 172;
Canadian News, March 16,
1865; Bigelow, *Retrospections*, II,
435–38; *Times*, February 8,
March 7, 1865; *Morning Herald*,
February 15, 1865; *Economist*,
February 25, 1865; *Spectator*,
February 25, 1865.
85. *Parl. Debates*, 3rd ser.,
CLXXVII, 3–38, 141–50, 415–
49, 1539–1636; *Spectator*, March
25, 1865.
86. Palmerston to Queen, March 13,
1865, *Letters of Queen Victoria*,
2nd ser., I, 262–63; *Times*,
March 14, 1865.

FOURTEEN Peace

1. Adams, Diary, February 7, 1865,
Adams Papers, reel 78; Spence to

Wharncliffe, February 13, 1865,
Wharncliffe Papers; ibid., Feb-

ruary 28; Adams to Seward, January 26, 1865, Adams Papers, reel 172; ibid., February 2; ibid., February 10; ibid., February 16; ibid., March 9.

2. Adams to Seward, March 16, 1865, Adams Papers, reel 172; Seward to Adams, February 21, 1865, NA/M77/79: ibid., March 1; ibid., March 14; *Moran Journal*, II, 1401; Adams, Diary, March 15, 1865, Adams Papers, reel 78; ibid., reel 172, Adams to Seward, March 30; ibid., April 7, Adams to Russell.

3. *Parl. Debates*, 3rd ser., CLXXVII, 1572–74; *Economist*, March 11, 1865.

4. Russell to Palmerston, April 6, 1865, PRO 30/22/30; see also ibid., February 23, Broadlands Mss.; ibid., March 17; Russell to Cowley, March 25, 1865, PRO 30/22/106.

5. Russell to Bruce, April 15, 1865, PRO 30/22/97; ibid., April 29; ibid., May 6; Russell to Queen, April 27, 1865, *Letters of Queen Victoria*, 2nd ser., I, 265.

6. Russell to Bruce, July 8, 1865, PRO 30/22/97; ibid., August 5; see also ibid., June 17; ibid., June 24.

7. Clarendon to Cowley, May 3, 1865, FO 519/179; Hammond to Cowley, April 26, 1865, FO 519/192; Russell to Cowley, April 29, 1865, PRO 30/22/106; ibid., April 26, FO 519/200; Cowley to Russell, April 27, 1865, FO 519/13; Russell to Bruce, June 3, 1865, PRO 30/22/97; Russell to Cowley, July 8, 1865, FO 519/200.

8. Russell to Lyons, February 25, 1865, Lyons Papers; Russell to Queen, February 27, 1865, PRO 30/22/15D; *Times*, February 28,

1865; Torrens to Sanford, March 27, 1865, Seward Papers; *New York Times*, March 14, 1865.

9. Bruce to Russell, February 27, 1865, PRO 30/22/38; Russell to Bruce, March 24, 1865, FO/1009.

10. Bruce to Russell, April 14, 1865, PRO 30/22/38; ibid., April 18; ibid., April 20; ibid., July 11.

11. Ibid., May 22.

12. Bruce to Russell, May 2, 1865, PRO 30/22/15D; ibid., June 18, PRO 30/22/38; ibid., October 31, FO 5/1335.

13. Russell to Palmerston, April 6, 1865, PRO 30/22/30.

14. Ibid., April 23, Broadlands Mss.; Russell to Bruce, May 27, 1865, PRO 30/22/97; Harcourt to Russell, April 24, 1865, PRO 30/22/15D; ibid., April 25; *Macmillan's*, XI, 422–23; Russell to Palmerston, June 25, 1865, Broadlands Mss.

15. Russell to Bruce, July 8, 1865, PRO 30/22/97; Bruce to Russell, August 8, 1865, PRO 30/22/38; Russell to Bruce, July 29, 1865, PRO 30/22/97; Bruce to Russell, May 30, 1865, PRO 30/22/15D; ibid., June 13, PRO 30/22/38; ibid., August 14, PRO 30/22/15D.

16. Gladstone to Russell, September 2, 1865, BM Add. Ms. 44292; Russell to Gladstone, September 17, 1865, PRO 30/22/31; Russell to Bruce, October 14, 1865, PRO 30/22/97; see also Adrian Cook, *The Alabama Claims: American Politics and Anglo-American Relations 1865–1872* (Ithaca, 1975), pp. 29–34.

17. *Saturday Review*, May 2, 1865; *Times*, April 13, 1865.

18. P. B. Waite, ed., *The Confederation Debates in the Province of Canada, 1865*, paper ed. (To-

ronto, 1963), pp. 19–22, 39–82, 130–31.

19. Joseph Pope, ed., *Correspondence of Sir John Macdonald* (Toronto, 1921), p. 26; Bruce to Russell, July 27, 1865, PRO 30/22/38; ibid., August 8; Russell to Bruce, September 4, 1865, PRO 30/22/97; ibid., Russell to Cardwell, PRO 30/22/31.

20. Balch to Cobden, January 13, 1865, Cobden Papers, vol. 7, Chichester; Bruce to Russell, July 17, 1865, PRO 30/22/38; ibid., August 8; Potter to Seward, January 6, 1865, NA/T222/6; ibid., March 15; *New York Times*, March 13 and 25, 1865.

21. Donald G. Creighton, *The Road to Confederation: The Emergence of Canada 1863–1867* (Toronto, 1964), pp. 343–44; Bruce to Russell, April 18, 1865, PRO 30/22/38; Sumner to Bright,

April 18, 1865, BM Add. Ms. 43390.

22. Cardwell to Palmerston, April 27, 1865, Broadlands Mss.; Gladstone minute, May 10, 1865, BM Add. Ms. 43551; Gladstone to Argyll, May 20, 1865, BM Add. Ms. 44100.

23. Palmerston to Cardwell, May 21, 1865, Broadlands Mss.; ibid., Russell to Palmerston, May 22; Clarendon to Cowley, May 24, 1865, FO 519/179.

24. Gladstone to Cardwell, May 23, 1865, BM Add. Ms. 44118; Gladstone to Argyll, May 27, 1865, BM Add. Ms. 44100; ibid., June 2.

25. Cardwell to Russell, July 15, 1865, PRO 30/22/26; ibid., August 15; Palmerston to De Grey, September 27, 1865, BM Add. Ms. 48583; ibid., October 4.

CONCLUSION

1. Owsley, *King Cotton Diplomacy*, p. 549.
2. Ibid., p. 558.
3. Adams, *Great Britain and the American Civil War*, II, 270–71.
4. Ibid., p. 272.
5. See Hernon, "British Sympathies in the American Civil War," *Journal of Southern History*, XXXIII, 356–67; Merli, *Great Britain and Confederate Navy*, pp. 255–57.
6. D. P. Crook, *The North, the South and the Powers 1861–1865* (New York, 1974), p. 374.
7. Eustis memorandum, n.d., Eustis Papers.
8. *Morning Herald*, April 24, 1865.
9. George W. E. Russell, ed., *Letters*

of *Matthew Arnold 1848–1888*, 2 vols. (London, 1895), I, 245.

10. William Dusinberre, "Henry Adams in England," *Journal of American Studies*, XI (1977), 163–86.
11. Hugh Brogan, "America and Walter Bagehot," *Journal of American Studies*, XI (1977), 335–56.
12. Cowley to Russell, April 16, 1865, PRO 30/22/61.
13. Russell to Bruce, April 15, 1865, PRO 30/22/97; ibid., April 22.
14. Brauer, "The Slavery Problem," *Pacific Historical Review*, XLVI, 465–66.
15. Russell to Bruce, April 15, 1865, PRO 30/22/97.

16. Smith, "British Sympathy with America," *American Presbyterian Review* (1862), p. 488.

17. Ibid., pp. 493–94, 503.

18. Lawley to Gregory, January 21, 1862, Gregory Papers.

19. Russell to Bruce, June 17, 1865, PRO 30/22/97.

INDEX